The Guides Casebook

THIRD EDITION

CHRISTOPHER R. BRIGHAM, MD, MMS
San Diego, California

Contributing Editors

Craig Uejo, MD, MPH
San Diego, California

Marjorie Eskay-Auerbach, MD, JD
Tucson, Arizona

Cases to Accompany

Guides to the Evaluation of
Permanent Impairment, Sixth Edition

American Medical Association

Executive Vice President, Chief Executive Officer: Michael D. Maves, MD, MBA
Chief Operating Officer: Bernard L. Hengesbaugh
Senior Vice President, Publishing and Business Services: Robert A, Musacchio, PhD
Vice President and General Manager, Publishing: Frank J. Krause
Vice President, Business Operations: Vanessa Hayden
Publisher, AMA Publications and Clinical Solutions: Mary Lou White
Director, Development and Production: Jean Roberts
Director, Business Marketing and Communication: Pam Palmersheim
Director, Sales and Strategic Partnerships: J. D. Kinney
Senior Acquisitions Editor: Barry Bowlus
Manager, Developmental Editing: Nancy Baker
Production Manager: Rosalyn Carlton
Senior Print Production Specialist: Ronnie Summers
Marketing Manager: Lauren Brody

Additional copies of this book may be ordered by calling 800 621-8335 or from the secure AMA web site at www.amabookstore.com.

Internet address: www.ama-assn.org

Refer to product number: OP210007

ISBN 978-1-57947-890-2
BQ78OP210007:12/08

Library of Congress Cataloging-in-Publication Data
The guides casebook : cases to accompany Guides to the evaluation of permanent impairment, sixth edition / [edited by] Christopher R. Brigham, Craig Uejo, Margorie Eskay-Auerbach.—3rd ed.
p. ; cm.
Includes index.
Summary: "Case studies in impariment evaluation and medical disability assessment"—Provided by publisher.
ISBN 978-1-57497-890-2
1. Disability evaluation—Case studies. I. Brigham, Christopher R., M.D. II. Uejo, Craig. III. Eskay-Auerbach, Marjorie. IV. American Medical Association. V. Guides to the evaluation of permanent impairment.
[DNLM: 1. Disability Evaluation—Case Reports. 2. Occupational Diseases—diagnosis—Case Reports. W 925 G945 2009]

RA1055.5.G85 2008 Suppl.
61607'5—dc22

2008044324

Foreword

Impairment evaluation requires knowledge, skills, and judgment. While the AMA *Guides to the Evaluation of Permanent Impairment* (the AMA *Guides*) provides the information required to assess impairment, it is not always intuitive about how to apply this information. As a result, books, courses, Web-based learning experiences, the *Guides Casebook*, and other educational media have been developed to ensure the correct application of the *Guides* principles. Teaching by example is an effective and proven method. In this book, the Sixth Edition of the AMA *Guides* is applied to clinical examples, reflecting the most common situations in which impairment evaluations are required. The result is a collection of essays, each discussing a clinical impairment problem. The book takes the reader through the thought process of impairment evaluation as well as the mechanics necessary to arrive at the correct impairment percentage by Fourth, Fifth, and Sixth Edition guidelines. The book cannot be used without the *Guides* and cannot replace the *Guides*, but it is a very valuable complement. For those new to the process, this book provides excellent instruction; for those experienced, it provides an opportunity to relate their understanding of the use of the *Guides* to those of others, all experts in the field of impairment evaluation. This is particularly important with the extensive change reflected in the Sixth Edition. The editors have devoted years to this process and have assembled a highly experienced group of contributors and reviewers. The result is a book unlike any other in the field. For those concerned with the fairness of the impairment evaluation process, it is required reading. Enjoy!

Gunnar B. Andersson, MD, PhD
The William A. Hark, MD–Suzanne G. Swift
Professor and Chairman, Department of Orthopedic Surgery
Rush-Presbyterian-St Luke's Medical Center
Chicago, Illinois

Acknowledgments

This book is a reflection of the talents and dedication of many participants. We express our gratitude to each of these individuals. We thank our spouses, Cathy Brigham, Nicole Uejo, and Marc Auerbach for their never-ending encouragement, patience, and love.

We are also grateful to the many contributors and reviewers and to Leon H. Ensalada, MD, and James B. Talmage, MD, who were co-editors of earlier editions. We appreciate the kindness of Gunnar Andersson, MD, PhD, in writing the Foreword.

We are indebted to Barry Bowlus, Senior Acquisitions Editor, whose vision, mentoring, and friendship have made this revision of the book possible. The production and marketing of this book would not have occurred without the talents and dedication of Nancy C. Baker, Manager, Developmental Editing and Lauren Brody, Marketing Manager. This book represents the efforts of a talented team of individuals dedicated to excellence.

Reviewers and Contributors

Third Edition

Reviewers and Contributors

Robert J. Barth, PhD, FNAN
Chattanooga, Tennessee

Bernard Blais, MD
Clifton Park, New York

Christopher R. Brigham, MD
San Diego, California

August Colenbrander, MD
Novato, California

Stephen Demeter, MD, MPH
Honolulu, Hawaii

Leslie Dilbeck, CIR
San Diego, California

Lorne Direnfeld, MD, FRCP(C)
Kahului, Hawaii

Theresa Elliott, MD
Santa Fe, New Mexico

Lee Ensalada, MD, MPH
Waitsfield, Vermont

Marjorie Eskay-Auerbach, MD, JD
Tucson, Arizona

Stuart J. Glassman, MD
Concord, New Hampshire

Mark H. Hyman, MD, FACP
Los Angeles, California

Norma J. Leclair, PhD, RN
Gray, Maine

Steven Leclair, PhD
Gray, Maine

J. Mark Melhorn, MD
Wichita, Kansas

Steven Rogers, MD, JD
Wilmington, Delaware

Barrie W. Ross, MD
Albuquerque, New Mexico

Robert Sataloff, MD
Philadelphia, Pennsylvania

Kenneth P. Subin, MD, MPH
Ithaca, New York

Aimee Topping, WCCP, CIR
San Diego, California

Craig Uejo, MD, MPH
San Diego, California

Prior Editions

Harvey Alpern, MD
Gunnar Andersson, MD, PhD
Peter V. Bieri, MD
Bernard Blais, MD
Margit L. Bleecker, MD, PhD
Richard Blonsky, MD
William Boucher, MD
Charles N. Brooks, MD
Susan Cassidy, MD, JD
Susan Simpson Crowley, MD
Lorne Direnfeld, MD
Karyn Rae Doddy, MD
Anthony J. Dorto, MD
Dwight K. Dowda, MB
Leon H. Ensalada, MD, MPH
Christopher Fevurly, MD

Prior Editions

Leslie Friedman, MD
David Gaw, MD
H. Stephen Goldberg, MD
Bart Goldman, MD
Bruce Goodman, MD
Robert Haralson, MD
Pamela Harston, MD
Frank Jones, MD
Patrick Joyce, MD
Richard T. Katz, MD
Charles Kennedy, MD
Paula Lantsberger, MD
James Z. Luck, MD
Anne MacGuire, MD
Alvin Markovitz, MD
John Meyer, MD
Sam Moon, MD
Kathryn Mueller, MD
Ross Myerson, MD
Mohammed I. Ranavaya, MS, MD
Stephen J. Rodgers, MD
Henry J. Roth, MD
Joseph Sataloff, MD
William Shaw, MD
Henry L. Stockbridge, MD
James B. Talmage, MD
Marc Taylor, MD
Margaret Tilton, MD
Kenneth A. Vatz, MD
Debra Walter, MD
Laura Welch, MD

Table of Contents

The Guides Casebook: Cases to Accompany *Guides to the Evaluation of Permanent Impairment*, Sixth Edition

Impairment assessment is a consensus-based process of defining the medical impact of an injury or illness on activities of daily living. It is a critical component in most workers' compensation, personal injury, and automobile casualty systems; therefore accurate impairment ratings are required. The Sixth Edition of the *Guides to the Evaluation of Permanent Impairment* is based on an innovative, carefully designed approach to evaluating impairment. Case exercises are a very effective approach to learning how to use this new standard in accurately assessing impairment.

The standardized methodology of the Sixth Edition of the *Guides* enhances the relevancy of impairment ratings, improves internal consistency, and promotes ease of application of the rating process. This ordered method enables physicians to become proficient in ratings for multiple organ systems and to anticipate how each chapter is organized and assimilates information. The Sixth Edition of the *Guides* applies terminology from, and an analytical framework based on, the International Classification of Functioning, Disability and Health, to generate five impairment classes that permit rating of patients from *no impairment* to *most severe impairment*. A diagnosis-based grid has been developed for each organ system. The grid arranges commonly used *International Classification of Diseases*, Ninth Revision, diagnoses within the five classes of impairment severity, according to the consensus-based dominant criterion. Functionally based histories, physical findings, and broadly accepted objective clinical test results are integrated, where applicable, to help physicians determine the grade within the impairment class.

Few physicians learn the skills of impairment evaluation during medical school and residency; therefore, many physicians first encounter the use of the AMA *Guides* only after they have entered practice. Without training in the appropriate application of the *Guides*, many physicians feel ill prepared to perform an impairment evaluation, and evaluations performed by inexperienced physicians often are erroneous. These erroneous evaluations cause significant difficulties and unnecessary controversy.

The *Casebook* addresses the need to have case examples that demonstrate the appropriate use of the *Guides*. It was developed out of our experiences in performing and critiquing several thousand evaluations and teaching the process of impairment assessment. This book reflects the knowledge and skills of some of the world's most experienced evaluators. These cases provide an excellent learning experience that will result in higher-quality impairment evaluations. This book is also a valuable resource for claims professionals, attorneys, and fact finders who read impairment reports; it provides a perspective on how ratings should be performed.

Impairment Evaluation

An impairment evaluation must be performed according to the specific steps defined in the *Guides*. Chapter 1 of the *Guides* explains the conceptual foundations and philosophy of the *Guides,* and Chapter 2 discusses the practical applications. Chapters 3 through 17 describe the specific steps involved in assessing impairment for specific problems. Users of the *Guides* must clearly understand the principles and rules described in Chapters 1 and 2 prior to using the other chapters. The final result is a report that must be clear, accurate, and complete. The report presents the results of the clinical evaluation and explains how the impairment rating was calculated.

About This Book

We chose 71 cases that exemplify the types of clinical problems encountered in evaluating impairment. Musculoskeletal disorders are the most common; therefore, the majority of the cases deal with upper extremity, lower extremity, and spinal problems. Examples of applications of the *Guides* to other systems are also included, with at least one case from each of Chapters 3 through 17. The chapters in the *Casebook* correspond with chapters in the Sixth Edition of the *Guides*. Cases from the previous edition of the *Casebook* have been rewritten and reassessed, and new cases have been added to provide a comprehensive learning experience.

Each case has a name descriptive of the clinical problem. A summary of the case is provided, presenting the information necessary to assess impairment. Irrelevant information is not included; therefore, the cases do not provide the detail one would expect in a typical impairment evaluation report. The case presentation is followed by a discussion pertinent to the specific case for the Fourth, Fifth, and Sixth Editions of the *Guides*. By reviewing solutions for each of the three editions, the reader can appreciate the significant differences. Comments explaining key teaching points are also provided. A summary table presents the relevant criteria (sections, tables, and figures) and a summary of the evaluation process for all editions. Summary information is provided in the following format:

SUMMARY

Diagnosis	Diagnosis
Fourth Edition References	Reference to applicable sections, tables, and figures in the *Guides*, Fourth Edition, including page numbers that are referenced for the particular case
Fourth Edition Summary	Summary of the essential elements of the medical evaluation and impairment evaluation process according to the Fourth Edition
Fourth Edition Impairment	Whole person permanent impairment according to the Fourth Edition
Fifth Edition References	Reference to applicable sections, tables, and figures in the *Guides,* Fifth Edition, including page numbers that are referenced for the particular case
Fifth Edition Summary	Summary of the essential elements of the medical evaluation and impairment evaluation process according to the Fifth Edition
Fifth Edition Impairment	Whole person permanent impairment according to the Fifth Edition
Sixth Edition References	Reference to applicable sections, tables, and figures in the *Guides,* Sixth Edition, including page numbers that are referenced for the particular case

Sixth Edition Summary	Summary of the essential elements of the medical evaluation and impairment evaluation process according to the Sixth Edition
Sixth Edition Impairment	Whole person permanent impairment according to the Sixth Edition

We recommend that you read the case and independently analyze the situation and the reference criteria in the *Guides* and determine your own rating, expressing this as a whole person permanent impairment percentage. You can then compare your results to those provided by the contributing author. You may not always agree with our assessment; however, you should understand that we sometimes disagree with each other about the impairment evaluation process. We ask that you seriously consider our approach and compare it to your own.

Learning Objectives

Upon completion of the case exercises, the reader will be able to:

- Explain the role of the AMA *Guides to the Evaluation of Permanent Impairment*
- Describe the process of performing impairment evaluations
- Explain the use of the diagnosis-based impairment approach
- Discuss what is required in any adequate medical evaluation for permanent impairment assessment
- Explain how findings are analyzed according to the *Guides*
- Demonstrate how to compare the results of analysis with the impairment criteria (tables and figures) to determine correctly the extent of whole person impairment, with emphasis on musculoskeletal assessments
- Discuss critical issues relevant to the appropriate use of the *Guides*, including issues of pain and causation assessment

Use of This Book

The cases in the *Casebook* can be used for a variety of purposes. They will be of value to all physicians in use of the *Guides*. For physicians new to impairment evaluation, they provide a demonstration of how the *Guides* are applied. For experienced evaluators, they offer an opportunity to refine skills and compare approaches. Readers can read this book at one time or go through the case exercises over a period of weeks as a self-directed learning experience. They may begin with the first case and read straight through or select the cases that are most pertinent to their applications.

The cases also show how to approach the assessment of a specific case (eg, identify a case similar to the one being assessed and determine how the assessment is done). Other professionals who review impairment evaluation reports, such as attorneys, claims adjusters, case managers, nurses, and fact finders (judges and hearing officers), will also find these cases instructive. These cases should also prove useful to professionals studying for examinations in the domain of impairment and disability assessment. It is our hope that the *Casebook* will contribute to more accurate assessments of impairment.

Chapter 3

Pain-Related Impairment

CASE 3-1

Fibromyalgia

Subject: Ms Gregory, a 26-year-old woman.

History: Ms Gregory was involved in a motor vehicle accident when the Ford F-150 pickup truck she was driving was stopped at a red light and was struck from behind by a Honda Civic traveling at 5 miles per hour. She was wearing a seat belt and shoulder restraint; the driver's side air bag did not deploy. Ms Gregory did not strike her head or any other part of her body on the steering wheel or any other component of the cab. She did not lose consciousness.

During evaluation at an emergency department, Ms Gregory described neck and low back pain; she denied radicular symptoms; her examination showed no signs of either neurologic or musculoskeletal impairment; and cervical spine and lumbar spine flexion and extension plain films were normal.

Two days after this episode, Ms Gregory began treatment with her family physician for symptoms and complaints of neck and low back pain. Ms Gregory's initial treatment included nonsteroidal anti-inflammatory medication, hydrocodone, prescribed work absence, and a general admonition to avoid any activity associated with pain. She reported no improvement in conjunction with this treatment regimen but rather reported pain of increasing intensity over increasingly larger portions of her body. Ms Gregory was treated by an orthopedist, a neurologist, and a neurologic surgeon, but her objective examination remained normal. Testing, including magnetic resonance imaging, myelography, computed tomographic scanning, electro-diagnostics, and screening for rheumatic diseases, was unremarkable.

Ten months after the motor vehicle accident, Ms Gregory had not returned to work, and consultation with a rheumatologist led to a diagnosis of fibromyalgia.

Current Symptoms: Ms Gregory reports diffuse aching; morning stiffness; swelling about her small joints; tenderness about her neck, shoulders, and low back; intermittent numbness of her hands and feet; decreased energy; easy fatigability; bitemporal aching; anxiety; and increased stool frequency. She associates exacerbation of these symptoms with stress and gloomy, damp, and cold days.

Functional Assessment: Ms Gregory's Pain Disability Questionnaire (PDQ) score was 68.

Physical Examination: Normal examination, with the exception of reported tenderness at 12 tender points associated with fibromyalgia.

Clinical Studies: Normal studies, as referenced earlier.

Discussion of Fibromyalgia

Fourth Edition Rating

The *Guides'* approach to the evaluation of impairment due to musculoskeletal disorders is found in Chapter 3, The Musculoskeletal System (4th ed, pp 13-94), which describes and recommends methods and techniques for determining impairments due to amputation, restriction of motion or ankylosis, sensory or motor deficits, peripheral nerve disorders, and peripheral vascular diseases. The *Guides'* philosophy for assessing musculoskeletal system impairment is based primarily on anatomic aspects of impairment assessed by examination.

Ms Gregory had normal musculoskeletal and neurologic examinations; thus, she has no impairment based on anatomic aspects of impairment assessed by examination. The *Guides* also provides diagnosis-based impairment estimates for some musculoskeletal conditions, because "some impairment estimates are assigned more appropriately on the basis of a diagnosis than on the basis of findings on physical examination" (4th ed, p 84). The *Guides* does not provide a diagnosis-based impairment estimate for fibromyalgia; that is, no specific *Guides* section or table provides an impairment estimate on the basis of the diagnosis of fibromyalgia.

Impairment: 0% whole person impairment per the Fourth Edition.

Fifth Edition Rating

The Fifth Edition states in Section 1.5, Incorporating Science With Clinical Judgment, that "subjective concerns, including fatigue, difficulty in concentrating, and pain, when not accompanied by demonstrable clinical signs or other independent, measurable abnormalities, are generally not given separate impairment ratings" (5th ed, p 10).

In Chapter 18, Pain, Section 18.3b, When This Chapter Should Not Be Used to Rate Pain-Related Impairment, advises that "the pain of individuals with ambiguous or controversial pain syndromes is considered unratable" (5th ed, p 571). The examining physician is to identify ambiguous or controversial syndromes by asking three questions:

1. Do the individual's symptoms and/or physical findings match any known medical condition?
2. Is the individual's presentation typical of the diagnosed condition?
3. Is the diagnosed condition one that is widely accepted by physicians as having a well-defined pathophysiologic basis? (5th ed, p 572)

If the answer to any one of these questions is no, the disorder is unratable. Since fibromyalgia does not have a well-defined pathophysiologic basis, the answer to question 3 is no, and this syndrome is unratable.

The *Guides* states that, "for example, the diagnosis of fibromyalgia is based on individuals' reports of widespread pain and their reports of tenderness during physical examination. Despite extensive research, no specific underlying biological abnormality has been discovered to explain the reports of these people" (5th ed, p 568). Thus, the *Guides* uses fibromyalgia as an example of a condition in which there is no "well-defined pathophysiologic basis," and so Ms Gregory's pain is clearly not ratable by pain chapter criteria.

Chapter 18 also notes that, "while the concept of sensitization is extremely important to a conceptual understanding of chronic pain, there is currently no systematic way to incorporate it into impairment ratings" (5th ed, p 568).

It is inappropriate to rate fibromyalgia as a spinal impairment, since it is not a spinal condition, nor does it reflect an injury or illness of the spine.

Impairment: 0% whole person impairment per the Fifth Edition.

Sixth Edition Rating

Chapter 3, Pain-Related Impairment, discusses the process of evaluating pain, and Section 3.3c, Rating Impairment When Pain Is Not Accompanied by Objective Findings (6th ed, pp 39-40), explains the use of the PDQ. In this case, it was administered, and the score was 68. Section 3.3d, Steps of Assessment (6th ed, p 40), defines eligibility criteria as follows:

1. Pain is determined to have a reasonable medical basis, that is, it can be described by generally acknowledged medical syndromes.
2. Pain has been identified by the patient as a major problem.
3. The patient's condition cannot be rated according to principles described in Chapters 4 through 17.
4. The pain-related impairment (PRI) rating is not specifically excluded by relevant jurisdiction.

Assuming these criteria are met, then the rating is performed. According to Table 3-1, Pain-Related Impairment and Whole Person Impairment Based on Pain Disability Questionnaire, a score between 1 and 70 is considered mild and results in 0% whole person permanent impairment.

Impairment: 0% whole person impairment per the Sixth Edition.

Comment on Fibromyalgia

The concept of a pathologic process in fibrous muscle tissue causing widespread musculoskeletal pain has been challenged since the term *fibrositis* was coined in 1904. Because fibrositis implies inflammation, which has never been demonstrated, the term was abandoned in conjunction with the development of the American College of Rheumatology (ACR) diagnostic criteria published in 1990.[1] The new term, *fibromyalgia,* abandoned the implication of inflammation in favor of pain alone. The ACR criteria define fibromyalgia as widespread pain in the four body quadrants lasting 3 or more months with the finding of at least 11 of 18 fibromyalgia tender points on digital palpation. Hence, to be labeled with the diagnosis of fibromyalgia, a person must be hurting and have special spots in the region of the pectoral and pelvic girdles and knee and elbow that are tender when probed by the examiner; these tender spots are called *tender points*. Although tender points have a long history, no convincing anatomic, biochemical, or electro-physiologic abnormality is demonstrable at these tender points. Persons with fibromyalgia have chronic, diffuse pain that cannot be explained by other systemic disorders. Physical examination is significant for a normal neurologic examination and no objective muscle weakness despite subjective reports of weakness. Joint examination is normal. Laboratory diagnostic evaluation is unremarkable.

Fibromyalgia is a diagnosis of exclusion. The etiology of fibromyalgia is unknown but is thought to be multifactorial.

Fibromyalgia is a controversial diagnosis.[2] Hadler describes the essential elements of this controversy:

> There is no debate that there are many individuals whose pervasive illness can be described in terms of fibrositis. The debate rages as to whether the illness is a consequence of an underlying organ system dysfunction or is a form of illness behavior magnified by the medical model for care.[3]

Fibromyalgia sometimes is reported to occur after minor trauma; however, this apparent temporal relationship does not establish causation. To conclude that fibromyalgia is caused by a minor trauma because the minor trauma preceded the onset of fibromyalgia is to engage in the fallacy of association being causal. Logicians call this fallacy in Latin *post hoc ergo propter hoc,* which means “after this, therefore because of this.”

SUMMARY

Diagnosis	Fibromyalgia
Fourth Edition References	Chapter 3 (4th ed, pp 13-94)
Fourth Edition Summary	Musculoskeletal examination and neurologic assessment. Verify whether the American College of Rheumatology diagnostic criteria are met. The *Guides'* approach for assessing musculoskeletal impairment is based primarily on anatomic aspects of impairment assessed by examination. The *Guides* does not provide impairment estimates for fibromyalgia.
Fourth Edition Impairment	0% whole person impairment
Fifth Edition References	Section 18.3b (5th ed, p 571)
Fifth Edition Summary	Musculoskeletal examination and neurologic assessment. Verify whether the American College of Rheumatology diagnostic criteria are met. The pain of individuals with ambiguous or controversial pain syndromes, such as fibromyalgia, is considered unratable.
Fifth Edition Impairment	0% whole person impairment
Sixth Edition References	Section 3.3 (6th ed, pp 37-40), Table 3-1 (6th ed, p 40)
Sixth Edition Summary	History and physical examination. Pain Disability Questionnaire (PDQ) administered and scored. Rating based on PDQ score can be up to 3% whole person impairment if the patient is judged reliable and credible.
Sixth Edition Impairment	0% whole person impairment

References

1. Wolfe F, Smythe HA, Yunus MB, et al. The American College of Rheumatology criteria for the classification of fibromyalgia. *Arthritis Rheum.* 1990;33:160-172.
2. Brigham CR, LeClair N. Fibromyalgia syndrome: impairment and disability issues. *Guides Newsletter*. July/August 2001:8-10, 12.
3. Hadler NM. *Occupational Musculoskeletal Disorders*. New York: Raven Press; 1993.

CASE 3-2

Posttraumatic (Alleged) Headache

Subject: Mr Peters, a 38-year-old man.

History: Mr Peters related a 1-year history of headache. His symptoms began after an episode that occurred while he was working as an over-the-road truck driver: his vehicle encountered a bump, and he was "thrown" off his seat. He reported striking his head on the ceiling of the cab. Mr Peters did not lose consciousness, nor did he experience any alteration in his mental status. He reported the immediate onset of a constant, severe, global headache but sought no medical attention until he was seen in an emergency department 5 days later, explaining, "I thought it would go away." The emergency department physicians found no abnormalities. Mr Peters denied any history of headaches; however, he had had a number of other work-related disabling injuries, each of which resolved after settlement.

In the interim, Mr Peters was evaluated and treated by a family physician, a neurologist, a neurosurgeon, and a pain specialist. His diagnostic studies, including a computed tomographic scan of the head, magnetic resonance imaging of the brain, and electroencephalography, were all normal, as were his physical and neurologic examinations. The emergency department physicians had provided Mr Peters with a prescription for work absence, pending follow-up with the neurologist. Mr Peters never returned to work and reported that he could not perform any work, stating "my headache won't let me." Mr Peters continued to be treated by a pain specialist and was currently prescribed OxyContin, Tylenol #4 (for "breakthrough" pain), Elavil, and Neurontin. On several occasions he had "lost" his prescriptions, and he was currently facing charges for drug trafficking.

Current Symptoms: At the time of the evaluation, Mr Peters complained bitterly about his headache and even more bitterly about the injustices of the workers' compensation system, his unsympathetic employer, and his vicious claims adjuster.

Functional Assessment: Mr Peters' PDQ score was 140.

Physical Examination: Mr Peters demonstrated marked pain behavior at times, grabbing his head with both hands and screaming, although at other times he appeared quite comfortable. There were no focal findings on his neurologic examination.

Clinical Studies: Normal, as referenced earlier

Discussion of Posttraumatic (Alleged) Headache

Fourth Edition Rating

The Fourth Edition does not provide a numeric value for impairment due to headache, and it notes that, "the vast majority of patients with headache will not have permanent impairments" (4th ed, p 312). In this case, there is evidence of marked illness behavior that raises serious questions about Mr Peters' credibility. There is no objective basis to provide any ratable impairment.

Impairment: 0% whole person impairment per the Fourth Edition.

Fifth Edition Rating

Chapter 18, Pain, Section 18.3b, When This Chapter Should Not Be Used to Rate Pain-Related Impairment, advises that a pain-related impairment rating is not performed when individuals have low credibility, and, therefore, the evaluation of pain-related impairment would be invalid. In this case, there is no basis to provide any ratable impairment.

Impairment: 0% whole person impairment per the Fifth Edition.

Sixth Edition Rating

Chapter 3, Pain-Related Impairment, discusses the process of evaluating pain, and Section 3.3c, Rating Impairment When Pain Is Not Accompanied by Objective Findings (6th ed, pp 39-40), explains the use of the PDQ. In this case, it was administered, and the score was 140, a very elevated score. Section 3.3d, Steps of Assessment (6th ed, p 40) defines eligibility criteria as follows:

1. Pain is determined to have a reasonable medical basis, that is, it can be described by generally acknowledged medical syndromes.
2. Pain has been identified by the patient as a major problem.
3. The patient's condition cannot be rated according to principles described in Chapters 4 through 17.
4. The PRI rating is not specifically excluded by relevant jurisdiction.

Assuming these criteria are met, then the rating is performed. According to Table 3-1, Pain-Related Impairment and Whole Person Impairment Based on Pain Disability Questionnaire, a score of 140 is considered extreme and results in 3% whole person permanent impairment. However, the *Guides* advise evaluators to "make a clinical judgment about the reliability and credibility of the patient's presentation and modify the presumptive award accordingly, within the range available for PRI (0% to 3% WPI)" (6th ed, p 40). In this case, there is substantial documentation of marked illness behavior that raises serious questions about Mr Peters' credibility. Further, some of his responses on the PDQ, such as "cannot sit/stand at all" and "cannot walk/run at all" were clearly inconsistent with direct observations. Based on the lack of credibility, inappropriate illness behavior, and serious questions about the reliability of the patient's subjective complaints, he was assigned no ratable impairment.

Impairment: 0% whole person impairment per the Sixth Edition.

Comment on Posttraumatic (Alleged) Headache

In this case, the diagnosis of *posttraumatic* headache in itself is highly suspect. Mr Peters demonstrates marked illness behavior, and it is likely that he has an underlying personality disorder.

SUMMARY

Diagnosis	Posttraumatic headache
Fourth Edition References	Chapter 15 (4th ed, pp 303-314)
Fourth Edition Summary	No percentage of impairment is provided for posttraumatic headache.
Fourth Edition Impairment	0% whole person impairment
Fifth Edition References	Chapter 18, (5th ed, pp 565-591)
Fifth Edition Summary	Pain impairment rating is not performed for individuals who lack credibility.
Fifth Edition Impairment	0% whole person impairment
Sixth Edition References	Section 3.3 (6th ed, pp 37-40), Table 3-1 (6th ed, p 40)
Sixth Edition Summary	History and physical examination. Pain Disability Questionnaire (PDQ) administered and scored. Rating based on PDQ score can be up to 3% whole person impairment if the patient is judged reliable and credible.
Sixth Edition Impairment	0% whole person impairment

Chapter 4

The Cardiovascular System

CASE 4-1

Ischemic Chest Pain and Hypertension

Subject: Dr Davidson, a 60-year-old man.

History: Dr Davidson is an orthopedist with a history of smoking two packs of cigarettes daily for 25 years. He stopped smoking 2 years ago. Other risk factors include hyperlipidemia controlled with medication and a family history of coronary heart disease. Both of his parents died of heart attacks in their 60s. He is not hypertensive and exercises regularly at a gym.

Dr Davidson became angry after reading a letter from an insurance company that denied his request to do a surgical procedure. His medical assistant observed him to become red in the face and to perspire heavily. Shortly thereafter, Dr Davidson had chest pain and became pale. His assistant called paramedics, and Dr Davidson was taken to the hospital. An electrocardiogram showed ST-segment elevation in the anterior leads. The chest pain resolved rapidly with thrombolytic therapy. Approximately 6 hours later, Dr Davidson experienced a recurrence of chest pain. He underwent emergency cardiac catheterization, which revealed a high-grade proximal blockage of the left anterior descending artery (LAD). No significant blockages were present in the other coronary arteries. He underwent percutaneous transluminal coronary angioplasty with stent placement. Cardiac enzyme testing documented that a mild myocardial infarction had occurred.
Dr Davidson was discharged on his usual medication for hyperlipidemia plus aspirin and a beta-blocker.

Current Symptoms: Dr Davidson denies any symptoms.

Physical Examination: Height, 180 cm; weight, 99 kg; body mass index, 30 kg/m^2; BP 134/86; pulse 82 and regular. Lungs clear to auscultation. No peripheral edema. Neck veins flat. Cardiac examination normal except for an S_4 gallop. Eye examination disclosed no vascular abnormalities.

Clinical Studies: A stress echocardiogram done 6 weeks after discharge from the hospital demonstrated exercise tolerance to 10 metabolic equivalents (METs) and no symptoms. The echocardiogram was normal, except for slight hypokinesis of the anterior wall at rest that did not change with exercise (normal diastolic filling and ejection fraction, no significant valvular regurgitation).

Discussion of Ischemic Chest Pain

Fourth Edition Rating

Permanent impairment evaluation was based on Section 6.2, Coronary Heart Disease (4th ed, pp 177-180). According to Table 6, Impairment Classification for Coronary Heart Disease (4th ed, p 178), Dr Davidson would be in class 2 because he had a myocardial infarction, was on medication, had recovered from a procedure, and was asymptomatic at a level of 10 METs. The range for class 2 is 10% to 29% whole person impairment. On the basis of clinical judgment and the specifics of the case, the evaluator chose to select an impairment of 15% whole person impairment.

Dr Davidson's "pre-hypertension" was not rated, as it did not rise to the level of ratable impairment according to the Fourth Edition.

Impairment: 15% impairment of the whole person per the Fourth Edition.

Fifth Edition Rating

Permanent impairment evaluation was based on Section 3.3, Coronary Heart Disease (5th ed, pp 35-41). According to Table 3-6a, Criteria for Rating Permanent Impairment Due to Coronary Heart Disease (5th ed, p 36), Dr Davidson would be in class 2 because he had a myocardial infarction, was on medication, had recovered from a procedure, and was asymptomatic at a level of 10 METs. The impairment range for class 2 is 10% to 29% whole person impairment. On the basis of clinical judgment and the specifics of the case, the evaluator chose an impairment of 15% whole person impairment.

Dr Davidson's "pre-hypertension" was not rated, as it was considered normal according to the Fifth Edition (Table 4-1, p 66).

Impairment: 15% whole person impairment per the Fifth Edition.

Sixth Edition Rating

Permanent impairment evaluation was based on Section 4.3, Coronary Artery Disease (6th ed, pp 54-57). According to Table 4-6, Criteria for Rating Permanent Impairment due to Coronary Artery Disease (6th ed, p 55). The key factor used when rating impairment due to coronary artery disease, as with all the cardiovascular cases, is the result of objective testing. In this case, Dr Davidson had an acute myocardial infarction (documented by enzyme tests), had a stent inserted, and underwent a stress test after recovery. He has recovered from the percutaneous coronary intervention and continues treatment. He also has prehypertension without other findings to suggest further vascular disease. He has no symptoms.

The objective tests are the stress test and the results of the angiogram (a high-grade proximal blockage of the LAD without significant blockages in the other arteries; treated with a stent). The high-grade blockage of the proximal LAD would place him into class 3 or 4. However, this lesion was amenable to treatment, and pages 54 and 56 state that the "impairment rating should be determined after these procedures have been completed and the patient is at maximum medical improvement (MMI), generally 3 to 6 months later." Thus, the LAD lesion is not rated in this case (and would not be rated unless, for some reason, it were not amenable to treatment or the amount of blockage following treatment remained significant after the patient had attained MMI). The objective test in this case is the stress echocardiogram done when Dr Davidson had attained MMI. Based on his ability to exercise to a level of 10 METs, the impairment is class 2, with an impairment range of 11% to 23%. The default value is grade C with 17% whole person impairment. The recovery from the angioplasty and stent placement, with the need to take aspirin and a beta-blocker, would also place this individual in class 2.

The history and physical examination findings are then reviewed to determine the grade severity within class 2. The lack of symptoms (New York Heart Association, class 1) would suggest class 0 or 1, but the history of a documented myocardial infarction would suggest class 2. Rule 12 on page 20 states that "if the *Guides* provides more than one method to rate a particular impairment or condition, the method producing the higher rating must be used." Accordingly, the patient history places Dr Davidson in class 2. The normal physical examination, from a coronary artery perspective, places him in classes 0 to 2, so class 2 is chosen, as it represents the higher level.

Because all values fall in class 2, the default value is for class 2, grade C, with 17% whole person impairment chosen as the final impairment rating for the coronary artery portion of this case.

Next, Dr Davidson's blood pressure was assessed for a possible impairment rating. Using Section 4.7, Hypertensive Cardiovascular Disease (6th ed, pp 65-68) and Tables 4-10, Classification of Blood Pressure for Adults (6th ed, p 66), and 4-11, Criteria for Rating Impairment due to Hypertensive Cardiovascular Disease (6th ed, p 67), the BP values of 134/86 are classified as prehypertension and can be rated. Table 4-10 provides values of less than 120/80 as normal blood pressures and values of 120 to 139 over 80 to 89 as prehypertension. Table 4-11 uses the results of the objective tests as the key factor. These tests include laboratory values (blood urea nitrogen/creatinine, urinalysis, and creatinine clearance), echocardiography, and electrocardiography. The tests also include the presence of end-organ damage (not otherwise specified) and hypertensive cerebrovascular damage.

In this case, the echocardiogram taken at MMI during the stress test showed "slight hypokinesis of the anterior wall at rest that did not change with exercise (normal diastolic filling and ejection fraction, no significant valvular regurgitation)." Although this abnormality could be considered end-organ damage, this finding was the result of the myocardial infarction and already accounted for within the ischemic heart disease rating noted earlier. There were no other hypertensive findings, which can include left ventricular hypertrophy and abnormalities of systolic and/or diastolic function. To use the hypokinesis again here would be an example of "double dipping." We are told that the retinal vessels were normal and that there is no evidence for cerebrovascular disease. Thus, based on Table 4-11, there is no impairment rating for the prehypertension. In summary, there is 17% whole person impairment for coronary artery disease and 0% whole person impairment for the prehypertension per the Sixth Edition.

Impairment: 17% whole person impairment per the Sixth Edition.

Comment on Ischemic Chest Pain

The rating was based on the fact that, after the myocardial infarction, there was no angina with exertion, no evidence of heart failure, and, on stress echocardiography, no evidence of further ischemia. The slight hypokinesis indicates that there was some muscle damage caused by the myocardial infarction. The procedures of thrombolysis and angioplasty limited the impairment and damage to the patient's heart. The myocardial infarction was precipitated by a stressful event, which was emotional in this example.

In the Fourth and Fifth Editions, a broad range of impairment values is given for each class. Judgment is required in selecting which impairment rating within this range should be provided. The Sixth Edition is no different, except that there are now five classes of impairment ranges, and the highest value is 65% whole person impairment versus the 100% whole person impairment provided in the previous editions.

If Dr Davidson had continued to smoke after his myocardial infarction, examiners may have been perplexed by the *Guides*. Both the Fourth and Fifth Editions contain sentences that seem to preclude rating impairment until after smoking cessation has occurred, for example, "Impairment due to coronary heart disease can be reduced but not eliminated by diet, exercise training programs, cessation of cigarette smoking, use of medications, and surgical procedures. Sufficient time must be allowed for these measures to have an effect before an estimate of permanent impairment is made" (4th ed, p 177). A similar statement occurs in the Fifth and Sixth Editions (5th ed, p 35; 6th ed, p 54). Many times individuals continue to smoke after myocardial infarction, despite repeated physician warnings. In these cases, the examiner should rate the impairment, even though the individual may not technically be at maximum medical improvement, keeping in mind the general instruction that an individual may decline treatment of an impairment, and that does not change the impairment (4th ed, p 9; 5th ed, p 20). The Sixth Edition addresses this issue as well and recommends on page 24 that the rater provide the impairment rating with:

> a written comment in his or her report addressing the suitability of the therapeutic approach and the basis of the individual's refusal. The physician should also indicate that the individual is at MMI without treatment due to declining treatment or treatment noncompliance. Additionally, the physician should estimate the impairment rating that would be likely if the patient had cooperated with the treatment recommendations (if the estimated rating is different from the one determined at the time of the examination).

SUMMARY

Diagnosis	Myocardial infarction
Fourth Edition References	Section 6.2 (4th ed, pp 177-180), Table 6 (4th ed, p 178)
Fourth Edition Summary	History of onset of chest pain with a precipitating stressful event in an individual with multiple risk factors. Rapid intervention was done, which limited impairment. Treadmill exercise study with either nuclear testing or echocardiography allows for not only evaluation of exercise tolerance but also estimation of myocardial ischemia.
Fourth Edition Impairment	15% whole person impairment
Fifth Edition References	Section 3.3 (5th ed, pp 35-41), Table 3-6a (5th ed, p 36); Section 4.1 (5th ed, pp 66-69), Table 4-2 (5th ed, p 66)
Fifth Edition Summary	History of onset of chest pain with a precipitating stressful event in an individual with multiple risk factors. Rapid intervention was done, which limited impairment. Treadmill exercise study with either nuclear testing or echocardiography allows for not only evaluation of exercise tolerance but also estimation of myocardial ischemia.
Fifth Edition Impairment	15% whole person impairment
Sixth Edition References	Section 4.3 (6th ed, pp 54-57), Table 4-6 (6th ed, p 55); Section 4.7 (6th ed, pp 65-68), Table 4-11 (6th ed, p 67)
Sixth Edition Summary	Same as above with the key factor being the history of recovery from stent insertion or the results of the stress test. The other elements used in the impairment rating were the lack of current symptoms/signs of heart failure and the history of the acute myocardial infarction, documented by blood tests. No rating for the prehypertension, as the objective test results were negative.
Sixth Edition Impairment	17% whole person impairment

CASE 4-2

Blunt Trauma Chest Injury

Subject: Mr Smith, a 42-year-old man.

History: Mr Smith worked as a driver for a delivery company. His vehicle was an older model without an airbag, and he was not wearing his seat belt. He was involved in an automobile accident that caused his chest to forcibly strike the steering wheel. He was hospitalized and during the first few days was observed to have frequent ventricular ectopic beats. These ventricular ectopic beats gradually diminished in frequency and disappeared. There was no evidence of cardiac muscle damage on the basis of cardiospecific enzymes.

While in the hospital, Mr Smith became short of breath with minor activity and was found to have a large pericardial effusion on echocardiogram. This fluid had not been present on an echocardiogram performed at the time of admission. A pericardiocentesis was done, and bloody fluid was removed. There was no recurrence of pericardial effusion on subsequent echocardiograms. However, Mr Smith did have episodes of positional chest pain while sitting up, associated with minor ST-segment elevations in anterior leads on electrocardiograms. Nonsteroidal anti-inflammatory medications were useful in diminishing the chest pain.

At discharge, a stress echocardiogram was normal at a level of 8 METs. One week after his discharge, Mr Smith had recurrence of anterior chest pain that was worse with changes in position. Treatment with nonsteroidal anti-inflammatory medications resulted in marked diminution of his symptoms. Two years later, he was evaluated by an independent medical examiner.

Current Symptoms: Mr Smith is now asymptomatic. He carries a bottle of nonsteroidal anti-inflammatory medications to use should there be a recurrence of his anterior chest pain (not used since 4 months after discharge from the hospital). He has no current cardiac complaints.

Physical Examination: Results of his cardiac examination were normal.

Clinical Studies: A repeat exercise study was done at the time of the independent medical examiner evaluation and found to be normal with an increased exercise tolerance to 9 METs. A 24-hour Holter monitor showed no significant arrhythmia. Laboratory tests showed a minimally elevated erythrocyte sedimentation rate (ESR) of 28% and elevated *B*-type natriuretic peptide (BPN) level at MMI. A repeat echocardiogram showed mild pericardial thickening but no restriction in ventricular filling.

Discussion of Blunt Trauma Chest Injury

Fourth Edition Rating

Permanent impairment evaluation was based on Chapter 6, The Cardiovascular System. Table 12, Impairment Classification for Cardiac Arrhythmias (4th ed, p 195), specifies under class 1 that there should be a cardiac arrhythmia documented. Because there was no evidence of persisting arrhythmia, there would be no rating for cardiac arrhythmia.

Cardiac contusion could be rated on the basis of Table 10, Impairment Classification for Cardiomyopathies (4th ed, p 189). In this case, there is no permanent impairment from the cardiac contusion, as the patient is asymptomatic at MMI with no evidence of impaired left ventricular function or heart failure on examination; therefore, there would be no rating.

On the basis of Table 11, Impairment Classification for Pericardial Disease (4th ed, p 192), the permanent impairment would be under class 1 because there had been evidence of pericarditis that resulted in permanent pericardial thickening, and continuous treatment was not required. The patient was not having episodes of pain, and pain is not usually a basis for a permanent impairment rating in pericardial disease or injury (4th ed, p 191). The rating for class 1 is between 0% and 9% whole person impairment. On the basis of the nature and extent of Mr Smith's injuries, 3% whole person impairment is reasonable.

Impairment: 3% whole person impairment per the Fourth Edition.

Fifth Edition Rating

Permanent impairment evaluation was based on Chapter 3, The Cardiovascular System: Heart and Aorta. Table 3-11, Criteria for Rating Permanent Impairment Due to Arrhythmias (5th ed, p 56), specifies under class 1 that there should be a cardiac arrhythmia documented by electrocardiogram or that the individual has had an isolated syncopal episode. The most recent Holter monitor disclosed no significant arrhythmia. Therefore, in this case, there would be no rating for cardiac arrhythmia.

Cardiac contusion could be rated on the basis of Section 3.5, Cardiomyopathies (5th ed, pp 47-51), and Table 3-9, Criteria for Rating Permanent Impairment

Due to Cardiomyopathies (5th ed, p 47). In this case, there was no permanent impairment from the cardiac contusion because the individual was asymptomatic, there were no echocardiographic abnormalities of the heart, per se, and there was no evidence of congestive heart failure.

Mr Smith's pericardial disease is rated according to Section 3.6, Pericardial Heart Disease (5th ed, pp 52-55). On the basis of Table 3-10, Criteria for Rating Permanent Impairment Due to Pericardial Heart Disease (5th ed, p 52), the permanent impairment would be under class 1 because there had been evidence of pericarditis that resulted in permanent pericardial thickening, a mildly elevated erythrocyte sedimentation rate that could be associated with the pericardial inflammation, and continuous treatment was not required. The patient was not having episodes of pain, and pain is not usually a basis for a permanent impairment rating in pericardial disease or injury (5th ed, p 52). The rating for class 1 is between 0% and 9% whole person impairment. On the basis of the nature and extent of Mr Smith's injuries, 3% whole person impairment is reasonable.

Impairment: 3% whole person impairment per the Fifth Edition.

Sixth Edition Rating

Permanent impairment evaluation was based on Chapter 4, The Cardiovascular System. The history of the arrhythmia was rated using Section 4.6, Dysrhythmias (6th ed, pp 63-65); the cardiac contusion using Section 4.4, Cardiomyopathies (6th ed, pp 57-60); and the pericardial abnormality using Section 4.5, Pericardial Heart Disease (6th ed, pp 60-63).

Using Table 4-9, Criteria for Rating Impairment due to Dysrhthmias (6th ed, p 64), the normal Holter monitor results and the normal echocardiographic evaluation of the heart, per se, placed Mr Smith in class 0, based on the key factor. The pericardial thickening is not rated here as it is not a common cause for an arrhythmia. Further, it is rated separately in the pericardial disease portion of this report; to have used this abnormality to rate the arrhythmia would have represented "double dipping." For a person to meet the criteria for class 0 based on an arrhythmia, the individual would need to have a normal electrocardiogram and/or occasional premature atrial contractions or premature ventricular contractions with a normal echocardiogram. Mr Smith's echocardiogram was abnormal, but the abnormality had none of the features found in classes 2 through 4, which are associated with dysrhythmias; as such, the results of this test were discounted for the arrhythmia impairment analysis. Therefore, there was no impairment.

Addressing the cardiomyopathy, using Table 4-7, Criteria for Rating Impairment due to Cardiomyopathies (6th ed, p 59), this patient did not meet the criteria for class 0, as the echocardiogram was abnormal (mild pericardial thickening but no restriction in ventricular filling). However, this type of pericardial abnormality is not identified in the descriptors for the echocardiographic abnormalities associated with cardiomyopathies as described in classes 1 through 4. Therefore, no impairment was sustained on the basis of the cardiomyopathy as a class 0 condition.

According to Table 4-8, Criteria for Rating Permanent Impairment due to Pericardial Heart Disease (6th ed, p 61), the key factor could be the echocardiogram, the ESR, the BNP level, the results of an exercise stress test, or a history of surgical intervention. Mr Smith did not have a surgical pericardial window placed, nor did he have a pericardiectomy. His only intervention was a pericardiocentesis. Accordingly, the results of echocardiography or the mildly elevated ESR to 28 could be used for choosing the class in which his case best fits. He had mild, persistent, pericardial thickening but no effusion nor evidence of pericarditis or constriction. He clearly does not qualify for class 0, as his echocardiogram is not normal. However, he also does not qualify for class 1, based on the lack of pericardial effusion or evidence of pericarditis; laboratory values in the form of ESR are consistent with pericardial inflammation; however, there is nothing in the history to suggest ongoing pericarditis. Lastly, his exercise tolerance (at MMI he demonstrated an exercise capacity to 9 METs; 1 MET is considered to be 3.5 mL [kg/min]; 9 × 3.5 = 31.5 mL [kg/min]).

Even though the echocardiographic abnormalities, by themselves, did not meet the definitional requirements of class 1, the mildly elevated ESR could be consistent with mild, persistent, pericardial inflammation (ESR is a nonspecific finding of inflammation that needs to be correlated with clinical history), which satisfies the class 1 criteria associated with a default rating of 6% impairment. The lack of symptoms without medication and the lack of signs or symptoms of heart failure would decrease the default value by two grades, resulting in a final class 1, grade A rating of 2% whole person impairment.

Impairment: 2% whole person impairment per the Sixth Edition.

SUMMARY

Diagnosis	Cardiac contusion and posttraumatic pericarditis
Fourth Edition References	Chapter 6 (4th ed, pp 189, 191-195), Table 11 (4th ed, p 192)
Fourth Edition Summary	History: Verify absence of arrhythmia by 24-hour Holter monitoring and verify absence of cardiac damage by stress echocardiography. Echocardiography to verify absence of pericardial effusion
Fourth Edition Impairment	3% whole person impairment
Fifth Edition References	Chapter 3 (5th ed, pp 47-55), Table 3-10 (5th ed, p 52)
Fifth Edition Summary	History: Verify absence of arrhythmia by 24-hour Holter monitoring and verify absence of cardiac damage by stress echocardiography. Echocardiography to verify absence of pericardial effusion
Fifth Edition Impairment	3% whole person impairment
Sixth Edition References	Section 4.5 (6th ed, pp 60-63), Table 4-8 (6th ed, p 61)
Sixth Edition Summary	History: Verify absence of arrhythmia by 24-hour Holter monitoring and verify absence of cardiac damage by stress echocardiography. Echocardiography to verify absence of pericardial effusion and/or constriction. Verify absence of heart failure on history and physical examination.
Sixth Edition Impairment	2% whole person impairment

CASE 4-3

Peripheral Venous Disease

Subject: Mr Peabody, a 42-year-old man.

History: Within days of a surgical repair of a fractured femur 3 years ago, Mr Peabody developed right lower extremity deep venous thrombosis. Since then, he has experienced difficulty in controlling the edema and has a recurrent venous stasis ulcer of his right ankle. The depth of his stasis ulcer has varied from month to month, from healed (with significant scarring) to moderate. Despite using a full-length, fitted elastic stocking, Mr Peabody has recurrent edema of the right lower extremity that was associated with dietary indiscretions and irregular adherence to a medication regime.

He is maintained on oral anticoagulant therapy (warfarin) to prevent further venous thrombosis. Mr Peabody's physician requires a blood test every month to assess the efficacy of the anticoagulation treatment, a regimen to which Mr Peabody is faithful. However, he has problems taking his medication, and he forgets the occasional dose of warfarin. Additionally, he requires daily treatment of his stasis ulcer, when present, consisting of twice daily applications of bandages and salves. He requires a daily diuretic to control the edema, as well as a very low salt diet.

Current Symptoms: Mr Peabody complains of occasional discomfort in the leg and constant itching in the area of the stasis ulcer. He has discomfort in the right lower extremity, especially when the edema is less well controlled. He has some, but not consistent or severe, difficulties with ambulation, especially during episodes of marked swelling.

Physical Examination: The cardiac examination was normal. There was 1+ pitting edema of the right lower extremity below the knee. There were chronic venous stasis changes of the right leg from the mid-calf region, down, with brawny induration. An almost completely healed skin lesion was present over the lateral malleolus.

Clinical Studies: Ankle-brachial indices, 0.92. Venous duplex ultrasound documented mild, chronic, deep venous insufficiency in the right leg below the knee.

Discussion of Peripheral Vascular Disease

Fourth Edition Rating

Permanent impairment evaluation of Mr Peabody's chronic postthrombotic deep venous insufficiency was based on Chapter 6, The Cardiovascular System, Section 6.8, Vascular Diseases Affecting the Extremities (4th ed, p 196). According to Table 14, Impairment of the Lower Extremity Due to Peripheral Vascular Disease (4th ed, p 198), he would be rated as class 3 or class 4 on the basis of his marked edema and venous stasis ulceration. Class 3 vascular disease would be manifest as "marked edema that is only partially controlled by elastic supports" and "superficial ulceration." Class 4 vascular disease would be manifest as "marked edema that cannot be controlled by elastic supports" and "persistent widespread or deep ulceration involving one extremity." No definitions are provided as to what constitutes *superficial* as opposed to *widespread* or *deep* ulceration or as to what constitutes control of the edema. Because Mr Peabody's disorder has some features consistent with a class 3 rating and some features consistent with a class 4 rating, it is reasonable to rate his disorder as class 3, but at the higher end of the 40% to 69% range of impairment of the lower extremity associated with this class. Consequently, Mr Peabody will retain a 60% impairment of the lower extremity, which equates to a 24% whole person impairment.

Mr Peabody is now being treated appropriately with warfarin for anticoagulation. Section 7.7, Inherited Thrombotic Disorders, could be considered for rating the acquired coagulopathy, although this section is titled *inherited*, so one could consider any rating based on this section to be congenital or genetic and not work related. However, that same section (4th ed, p 207) states, "Lifelong warfarin sodium prophylaxis may be needed and would constitute a slight impairment of 5% to 10%." This is because the long-term risks of warfarin therapy are significant and not because the drug produces any daily symptoms as side effects. As such, a 10% whole person impairment is considered appropriate and reasonable based on the acquired coagulopathy from chronic warfarin use.

Combining the 24% whole person impairment for vascular disease with the 10% impairment for warfarin therapy yields a final whole person impairment of 32%.

Impairment: 32% whole person impairment per the Fourth Edition.

Fifth Edition Rating

Permanent impairment evaluation of Mr Peabody's chronic, postthrombotic, deep venous insufficiency was based on Chapter 4, The Cardiovascular System: Systemic and Pulmonary Arteries, Section 4.3, Vascular Diseases

Affecting the Extremities (5th ed, p 73). According to Table 4-5, Criteria for Rating Impairment of the Lower Extremity Due to Peripheral Vascular Disease (5th ed, p 76), he would be rated as class 3 on the basis of his edema and venous stasis ulceration. Because his edema is partially responsive to therapeutic interventions, a middle rating of 55% could be justified (remembering that Mr Peabody's not being completely compliant with his medications does not impact the impairment rating because, "a patient may decline surgical, pharmacologic, or therapeutic treatment of an impairment. If a patient declines therapy for a permanent impairment, that decision neither decreases nor increases the estimated percentage of the individual's impairment" (5th ed, p 20). Consequently, Mr Peabody has 55% impairment of the lower extremity, which equates to a 22% whole person impairment (55% × 0.4 = 22%).

Mr Peabody is now being treated appropriately with warfarin for anticoagulation. Section 9.5, Hemorrhagic and Platelet Disorders (5th ed, p 203), would be used to rate any diagnosed coagulopathy. Section 9.6b, Acquired Thrombotic Disorders, and Section 9.6c, Criteria for Rating Permanent Impairment Due to Thrombotic Disorders (6th ed, p 206), also state that "long-term anticoagulation with warfarin or low-molecular-weight heparin increases bleeding risk and constitutes impairment in the 10% range." Based on this condition and risk, 10% whole person impairment is considered appropriate.

Combining the 22% whole person impairment for vascular disease with the 10% impairment for warfarin therapy yields a final whole person impairment of 30%.

Impairment: 30% whole person impairment per the Fifth Edition.

Sixth Edition Rating

Permanent impairment evaluation was based on Section 4.8, Vascular Diseases Affecting the Extremities (6th ed, pp 68-71). According to Table 4-12, Criteria for Rating Permanent Impairment due to Peripheral Vascular Disease—Lower Extremity (6th ed, p 69), Mr Peabody would most closely meet class 0 or 1 criteria, as his test of arterial abnormalities was normal. The key factor is the objective testing results. In this case, there is venous disease and not arterial disease, as supported by the abnormal venous duplex study. The first mention of venous disease findings noted on venous duplex ultrasound is under a class 2 rating for mild venous disease findings. Based on the mild venous insufficiency noted on testing, a class 2 rating is chosen. The default rating would be grade C with 17% whole person impairment. Similar to other chapter ratings, the grade is to be adjusted based on the non-key factors. In this case, these are the history and physical examination findings.

The history would suggest class 2, based on the intermittent edema and the recurrent stasis ulcer. As stated in the Fifth Edition rating discussion earlier, it should be noted in the report that this individual's edema could be under better control with better compliance to treatment recommendations; however, as noted on page 24 of the Sixth Edition, an individual need not comply with treatment recommendations to attain MMI. (Section 2.3c, p 24, provides a more complete discussion of the report in these circumstances; it states, for example, that the rater should provide a separate rating *as if* the examinee were compliant with treatment.) The physical examination would also suggest class 2, based on the ulcer. Both issues do not impact the impairment rating default grade C in class 2. The final vascular impairment would be class 2, grade C, 17% whole person impairment.

The bleeding disorder, caused by the use of warfarin, is rated using Section 9.5, Hemorrhagic and Platelet Disorders (6th ed, pp 201-206). Subsection 9.5b is used for rating bleeding disorders, and Table 9-11, Criteria for Rating Impairment due to Other Bleeding Disorders (6th ed, p 205), is used to determine the impairment rating. Using this table, the frequency of hemorrhagic events is the key factor used to determine the class of impairment. Based on the descriptors in this row, there is no impairment.

Within Section 9.6, Thrombotic Disorders, there is a statement similar to one in prior editions providing impairment for the use of chronic anticoagulation therapy. Under Section 9.6c, Criteria for Rating Permanent Impairment Due to Thrombotic Disorders (6th ed, p 207), there is a statement that provides 5% whole person impairment for this. It states that "if the individual is receiving long-term anticoagulant therapy for thrombotic disorder with warfarin, low-molecular-weight heparin, or heparin, 5% is added to the impairment rating."

When the 17% impairment for the chronic venous stasis problem is combined with the 5% impairment for the use of warfarin, there is a resultant 21% whole person impairment.

Impairment: 21% whole person impairment per the Sixth Edition.

Comment on Peripheral Venous Disease

The method for rating permanent impairment of the lower extremity due to peripheral vascular disease is the same in the Fourth and Fifth Editions of the *Guides*. The Sixth Edition method is similar; however, any extremity-related rating is now found only in Chapter 4, The Cardiovascular System, and not in the respective extremity chapters. Before evaluating impairment, the examiner must establish a specific diagnosis of vascular disease. The Sixth

Edition also places key rating importance on objective test results for arterial or venous disease. For all three editions, the impairment estimate depends on the extent, severity, and impact of the lesions rather than on the specific diagnosis. Physical signs of vascular damage must be present and are the primary determinants in placing the individual into one of the five classes of impairment. Because no definitions are stated in the *Guides*, examiners must use their own judgment as to what constitutes control of edema and what makes an ulcer superficial or deep. The rating for venous disorders (and lymphangitic disorders) in the Sixth Edition is covered less well than the rating for arterial disorders. In this edition, venous disorders are not rated unless there is documentation of mild, moderate, or severe abnormalities on venous duplex testing. It is assumed that venograms would also be accepted. Lymphatic abnormalities are also discussed in the Sixth Edition.

SUMMARY

Diagnosis	Peripheral venous disease
Fourth Edition References	Section 6.8 (4th ed, pp 196-198), Table 14 (4th ed, p 198)
Fourth Edition Summary	Establish a specific diagnosis of vascular disease. The impairment estimate depends on the extent, severity, and impact of the lesions rather than the specific diagnosis. Physical signs of vascular damage must be present and are the primary determinants in placing the individual into one of the five classes of impairment.
Fourth Edition Impairment	32% whole person impairment
Fifth Edition References	Section 4.3 (5th ed, pp 73-78), Table 4-4 (5th ed, p 74); Section 9.5 (5th ed, pp 203-206), Table 9-4 (5th ed, p 203)
Fifth Edition Summary	Establish a specific diagnosis of vascular disease. The impairment estimate depends on the extent, severity, and impact of the lesions rather than the specific diagnosis. Physical signs of vascular damage must be present and are the primary determinants in placing the individual into one of the five classes of impairment.

Fifth Edition Impairment	30% whole person impairment
Sixth Edition References	Section 4.8 (6th ed, pp 68-71); Section 9.5, (6th ed, pp 201-206); Section 9.6 (6th ed, pp 206-208); Section 9.6c (6th ed, p 207), Table 4-12 (6th ed, p 69), Table 9-11 (6th ed, p 205)
Sixth Edition Summary	Establish a specific diagnosis of vascular disease. The impairment class depends on the ankle-brachial artery pressure ratio or the results of either an ultrasound or dye study of the venous or arterial system.
Sixth Edition Impairment	21% whole person impairment

Chapter 5

The Pulmonary System

CASE 5-1

Occupational Asthma in an Automobile Painter

Subject: Mr Jones, a 54-year-old man.

History: Mr Jones was an automotive painter who had been exposed to enamels, epoxy resins, and polyurethane paints while employed at a car dealership for 15 years. He painted with "mostly straight enamel" for about 5 years and then used "acrylic enamel with hardener" for 9 years. When he began having symptoms, he was painting with polyurethane paints. He stated that he "had to go outside to breathe, because it hurt to breathe the air." A pulmonary specialist diagnosed asthma and, on the basis of a blood test, determined that the asthma was due to isocyanate-based polyurethane paints that contained toluene diisocyanate (TDI). Mr Jones' treatment included removal from exposure and medication management. Two years after removal from exposure, Mr Jones was evaluated for permanent impairment.

Current Symptoms: Mr Jones reported intermittent episodes of wheezing that he associated with fumes, dust, or smoke. He was maintained on beclomethasone, two puffs twice daily; albuterol, two puffs four times daily; ipratropium bromide, two puffs daily; and for his hypertension, amlodipine besylate, 5 mg twice daily.

Physical Examination: Mr Jones' examination revealed a few scattered rhonchi and wheezes, but the remainder of his examination was unremarkable. He is 164 cm tall.

Clinical Studies: Pulmonary function tests revealed a maximum postbronchodilator forced expiratory volume in 1 second (FEV1) of 74%, a 9% improvement compared with his prebronchodilator FEV1.

Discussion of Occupational Asthma in an Automobile Painter

Fourth Edition Rating

Permanent impairment evaluation was based on AMA *Guides*, Chapter 5 (4th ed, pp 153-166), and the *Guides Newsletter*, May/June 1997. Regarding cases of occupational asthma, Table 10, Impairments Not Directly Related to Lung Functions (4th ed, p 164), of the *Guides* states that, "persons whose asthma appears to be related to a class of chemicals or to a specific substance, such as toluene diisocyanate, may need to be evaluated for employability or the presence of an employment-related disability." The *Guides* further states, "The physician's thorough documentation of the nature of the asthmatic condition and the compilation of the nonmedical evidence, such as that relating to occupation activities, specific chemicals that may be involved, and other circumstances of work, are crucial to the determination of work-related disability" (4th ed, p 164). The *Guides* also states, "It is important to recognize that such conditions as asthma . . . may require that the individual refrain from working in a specific occupational setting where he or she is exposed to the offending agent. This does not necessarily indicate that the individual has permanent pulmonary impairment in occupational settings other than those causing the abnormality" (4th ed, p 164).

Table 10, Impairments Not Directly Related to Lung Functions (4th ed, p 164), states, "Asthma presents a difficult problem in impairment evaluation because results of pulmonary function studies may be normal or near normal between attacks. Despite the intermittent nature of the disease, severe impairment may be diagnosed when the individual is receiving optimum medical therapy and has physiologic test results in the severely impaired range on three successive tests performed at least 1 week apart." For documentation of the presence of asthma, the *Guides* does not require physiologic testing on three occasions.

In addition to physiologic measures of pulmonary impairment, the *Guides* also suggests the use of clinical parameters to estimate the impairment from asthma. In Table 10 (4th ed, p 164), the *Guides* states, "The frequency of attacks also should be taken into consideration when deciding on the level of impairment."

The *Guides Newsletter*, May/June 1997, in an attempt to mitigate the difficulties of rating asthma by means of *Guides* Fourth Edition criteria, published a rating system that used pulmonary function test results and clinical parameters. The following table summarizes this system:

Parameters	Class 1 0%-9%	Class 2 10%-25%	Class 3 26%-50%	Class 4 51%-100%
Max postbronchodilator FEV_1 (% predicted)	≥70%	60%-69%	41%-59%	≤40%
Percentage of FEV_1 change*	<10%	10%-19%	20%-29%	≥30%
PC_{20} mg/mL or equivalent†	>5	>0.5-5	0.125-0.5	<0.125
Clinical parameters (minimum medication need, frequency of attacks, etc)	Occasional bronchodilator use, or cromolyn	Daily low-dose inhaled steroid and/or bronchodilator, or cromolyn	Daily high-dose‡ inhaled steroid and/or short periods of systemic steroids, and regular use of bronchodilators	Daily systemic steroids, and maximal bronchodilator use. Asthma not controlled despite maximal treatment

* The degree of FEV_1 reversibility, which is calculated by subtracting the prebronchodilator FEV_1 from the postbronchodilator FEV_1, and dividing by the prebronchodilator FEV_1.

† PC_{20} refers to the concentration of methacholine or other challenge agent that provokes a fall in the FEV_1 by ≥20%.

‡ High-dose inhaled steroids indicates ≥800 μg of beclomethasone/day (≥40 puffs of Vanceril, or doses of equal potency of other brand names, daily).

Mr Jones' maximum postbronchodilator FEV_1 was greater than 70% of predicted, a class 1 impairment; his percentage of change in FEV_1 from prebronchodilator to postbronchodilator tests was 9%, which is class 1 impairment; his minimum medication requirements and frequency of attacks are class 2 impairment. Consequently, Mr Jones has class 2 respiratory impairment for which he retains a 10% whole person impairment.

Impairment: 10% whole person impairment per the Fourth Edition and *Guides Newsletter.*

Fifth Edition Rating

Many of the difficulties inherent in the *Guides* Fourth Edition method for rating asthma were addressed in the Fifth Edition. The *Guides* Fifth Edition method for rating asthma is found in Chapter 5, The Respiratory System, Section 5.5, Asthma (5th ed, pp 102-104), including Table 5-9, Impairment Classification for Asthma Severity (5th ed, p 104), and Table 5-10, Impairment Rating for Asthma (5th ed, p 104).

Table 5-9 Impairment Classification for Asthma Severity*

Score	Postbronchodilator FEV_1	% of FEV_1 Change (Reversibility) *or*	PC_{20} mg/mL or Equivalent (Degree of Airway Hyperresponsiveness)†	Minimum Medication‡
0	≥ lower limit of normal	< 10%	> 8 mg/mL	No medication
1	≥ 70% of predicted	10%-19%	8 mg/mL to > 0.6 mg/mL	Occasional but not daily bronchodilator and/or occasional but not daily cromolyn
2	60%-69% of predicted	20%-29%	0.6 mg/mL to > 0.125 mg/mL	Daily bronchodilator and/or daily cromolyn and/or daily low-dose inhaled corticosteroid (≤800 µg of beclomethasone or equivalent)
3	50%-59% of predicted	≥30%	≤0.125 mg/mL	Bronchodilator on demand and daily high-dose inhaled corticosteroid (> 800 µg of beclomethasone or equivalent) or occasional course (one to three courses a year) of systemic corticosteroid
4	< 50% of predicted	. . .	. . .	Bronchodilator on demand and daily high-dose inhaled corticosteroid (> 1000 µg of beclomethasone or equivalent) and daily or every other day systemic corticosteroid

* FEV_1 indicates forced expiratory volume in the first second; PC_{20} is the provocative concentration that causes a 20% fall in FEV_1. Add the scores for postbronchodilator FEV_1, reversibility of FEV_1 (or PC_{20}), and medication use to obtain a summary severity score for rating respiratory impairment.

† When FEV_1 is greater than the lower limit of normal, PC_{20} should be determined and used for rating of impairment; when FEV_1 is less than 70% of the predicted, the degree of reversibility should be used; and when FEV_1 is between 70% of the predicted and the lower limit of normal, either reversibility or PC_{20} can be used. The score for minimum medication use is added to the appropriate measurement criteria outlined above.

‡ Need for minimum medication should be demonstrated by the treating physician, for example, through previous records of exacerbation when medications have been reduced. Adapted from ATS guidelines.

Asthma-related impairment is calculated in two steps. First, the asthma severity score is calculated using the criteria in Table 5-9, which is reproduced on page 38.

The correct use of Table 5-9 requires determining whether the individual's FEV_1 is above or below the lower limit of normal. If the person's prebronchodilator FEV_1 is below the lower limit of normal, the degree of reversibility is assessed with inhaled bronchodilators (Table 5-9, column 2). If the person's prebronchodilator FEV_1 is above the lower limit of normal, a methacholine challenge is used to assess airway responsiveness (Table 5-9, column 3). Thus, calculating the asthma severity score requires either a score for percentage of change in FEV_1 (Table 5-9, column 2) or a score for PC_{20} mg/mL (Table 5-9, column 3) but not both. Second, the calculated asthma severity score is used to determine the percent impairment class and impairment of the whole person by means of Table 5-10, which is reproduced below.

Table 5-10 Impairment Rating for Asthma*

Total Asthma Score	% Impairment Class	Impairment of the Whole Person
0	1	0%
1-5	2	10%-25%
6-9	3	26%-50%
10-11 or asthma not controlled despite maximal treatment, ie, FEV_1 remaining <50% of predicted despite use of >20 mg/day of prednisone	4	51%-100%

*The impairment rating is calculated as the sum of the individual's scores from Table 5-9. FEV_1 indicates forced expiratory volume in the first second.

Mr Jones' asthma severity score is calculated by means of Table 5-9 as follows: His postbronchodilator FEV_1 was lower than the lower limit of normal, but greater than 70% of predicted, which yields a score of 1. His percentage of FEV_1 change was less than 10%, which yields a score of 0. Mr Jones' prebronchodilator FEV_1 was lower than the lower limit of normal; hence, a methacholine challenge was not used to assess airway responsiveness. His minimum medication requirements yield a score of 2. His total asthma severity score is 3. A total asthma severity score of 3, using Table 5-10, yields class 2 impairment, which is associated with a 10% to 25% impairment of the whole person. On the basis of the specifics of Mr Jones' case, namely the use of three medications for his asthma and the intermittent episodes of wheezing, a rating of 20%

whole person impairment could be justified. (It might be argued that this individual has yet to attain maximum medical improvement, as he is on low doses of inhaled steroids, is not on several other asthma-controlling medications, and he continues to wheeze. Additionally, he has not attained the definitional requirement of "minimum amount of medication to maintain control or the best overall results" [5th ed, p 103]).

Impairment: 20% whole person impairment per the Fifth Edition.

Sixth Edition Rating

Permanent impairment evaluation was based on Section 5.6, Asthma and Other Hyperreactive Airway Diseases (6th ed, pp 87-91). According to Table 5-5, Criteria for Rating Permanent Impairment due to Asthma (6th ed, p 90), the key factors in rating impairment from asthma are both the degree of hyperresponsiveness, as determined either by the postbronchodilator FEV_1 or the methacholine challenge test. Based on the maximum postbronchodilator FEV_1 at 74% of predicted, class 1 was chosen for the impairment class. (A methacholine challenge test was not performed.) The range of impairment is between 2% and 10% whole person impairment. The minimum medication needed was used to modify the default position of 6% WPI. Based on the dosage of 40 mcg per puff of beclomethasone, this individual receives 160 mcg per day. This qualifies for class 2, as class 3 medication usage requires 500 to 1000 mcg per day. Thus, the default grade C position of 6% WPI is adjusted up one grade, to grade D, which is 8% whole person permanent impairment.

Impairment: 8% whole person impairment per the Sixth Edition.

Comment on Occupational Asthma in an Automobile Painter

Many of the difficulties inherent in the *Guides* Fourth Edition method for rating asthma were addressed in the Fifth Edition. However, challenges persist in the rating of impairment due to asthma, including:

1. The issue of beclomethasone "equivalent" was not addressed in the Fifth Edition, creating difficulties for the rater when an inhaled steroid, other than beclomethasone, is used.
2. The current therapeutic armamentarium available to physicians in the treatment of asthma is not limited to inhaled and/or systemic steroids or a short- or long-acting bronchodilator. Physicians may also prescribe a leukotriene inhibitor/modifier, anticholinergic preparation (short- or

long-acting), inhaled cromolyn, oral theophyllines, and/or anti-IgE preparations.

3. Table 5-9 of the Fifth Edition used three parameters to assess asthma impairment (minimum medication need, maximum postbronchodilator FEV_1, and degree of hyperresponsiveness as determined by the improvement in the FEV_1 *or* the worsening following use of a bronchoconstrictor as reflected in the PC_{20}). The Sixth Edition also uses three parameters, including response to bronchodilators, the histamine/methacholine challenge test, and the minimum medication requirement.
4. The use of a bronchodilator is limited in that "a total of 400 mcg of albuterol should be inhaled by the patient, one deep inhalation at a time, with 30 to 60 seconds between each of the four puffs. A volume spacer should be used between the metered dose inhaler and the person." Other protocols and other medications yield similar results to this protocol.

SUMMARY

Diagnosis	Occupational asthma due to exposure to isocyanate-based polyurethane paints
Fourth Edition References	Chapter 5, Table 8 (4th ed, p 162), Table 10 (4th ed, p 10), *Guides Newsletter,* May/June 1997, Table 2
Fourth Edition Summary	Medication requirement is the parameter suggesting the greatest impairment. With the advances in asthma treatment since 1993, when the Fourth Edition was published, the amount of treatment required probably reflects the disease severity better than the frequency of attacks does.
Fourth Edition Impairment	10% whole person impairment
Fifth Edition References	Section 5.5 (5th ed, pp 102-104), Table 5-9 (5th ed, p 104), Table 5-10 (5th ed, p 104)

Fifth Edition Summary Asthma-related impairment is calculated in two steps. First, the asthma severity score is calculated using the criteria in Table 5-9. Second, the calculated asthma severity score is used to determine the percent impairment class and impairment of the whole person by means of Table 5-10.

Fifth Edition Impairment 20% whole person impairment

Sixth Edition References Section 5.6 (6th ed, pp 87-91), Table 5-5 (6th ed, p 90)

Sixth Edition Summary Simplified rating method over the Fifth Edition, using only one rather than two tables. Rating based on the same three parameters as used in the Fifth Edition, although the degree of responsiveness using a bronchodilator was eliminated.

Sixth Edition Impairment 6% whole person impairment

CASE 5-2

Occupational Asthma in a Delivery Driver

Subject: Mr Thomas, a 40-year-old man.

History: Mr Thomas, a delivery driver, developed asthma after 3 years on his job. His asthma was usually worse on weekends. Every Friday he delivered materials to a foam rubber manufacturing plant, and his asthmatic symptoms always seemed to develop on Friday, persisting over the weekend. His physician did not recognize this association and treated Mr Thomas for asthma with inhaled steroids and inhaled bronchodilators, which were predominantly used on the weekends. Mr Thomas had to take occasional "bursts" of oral steroids. His pulmonary function tests were initially normal, but after a year the FEV_1 was between 65% and 70% of predicted when tested. A pulmonary specialist determined that the asthma was related to toluene diisocyanate exposure that occurred on Fridays during delivery of products containing this substance. Mr Thomas was immediately removed from further exposure. Two years later he was reevaluated.

Current Symptoms: Mr Thomas was still using inhaled medications (salmeterol, two puffs twice a day and fluticasone 44 mcg, two puffs twice a day) because he felt better using them and because he was afraid that he would develop recurrent problems without these medications. He last took oral steroids 19 months ago.

Physical Examination: His lungs were clear.

Clinical Studies: The FEV_1 was 98% of predicted. A methacholine study yielded a PC_{20} of 5 mg/mL (PC_{20} represents the concentration of methacholine or other agent that provokes a fall in the FEV_1 by ≥20%). The post-bronchodilator FEV_1 was 104% of predicted.

Discussion of Occupational Asthma in a Delivery Driver

Fourth Edition Rating

Permanent impairment evaluation was based on AMA *Guides*, Chapter 5 (4th ed, pp 153-166), and the *Guides Newsletter*, May/June 1997. In cases of occupational asthma, Table 10, Impairments Not Directly Related to Lung Function (4th ed, p 164), of the *Guides* states that, "persons whose asthma appears to be related to a class of chemicals or to a specific substance, such as toluene diisocyanate, may need to be evaluated for employability or the presence of an employment-related disability." The *Guides* further states, "The physician's thorough documentation of the nature of the asthmatic condition and the compilation of the nonmedical evidence, such as that relating to occupation activities, specific chemicals that may be involved, and other circumstances of work, are crucial to the determination of work-related disability" (4th ed, p 164). The *Guides* also states, "It is important to recognize that such conditions as asthma . . . may require that the individual refrain from working in a specific occupational setting where he or she is exposed to the offending agent. This does not necessarily indicate that the individual has permanent pulmonary impairment in occupational settings other than those causing the abnormality" (4th ed, p 164).

Table 10, Impairment Not Directly Related to Lung Function (4th ed, p 164), states, "Asthma presents a difficult problem in impairment evaluation because results of pulmonary function studies may be normal or near normal between attacks. Despite the intermittent nature of the disease, severe impairment may be diagnosed when the individual is receiving optimum medical therapy and has physiologic test results in the severely impaired range on three successive tests performed at least 1 week apart." For documentation of the presence of asthma, the *Guides* does not require physiologic testing on three occasions.

In addition to physiologic measures of pulmonary impairment, the *Guides* also suggests the use of clinical parameters to estimate the impairment from asthma. In Table 10 (4th ed, p 164), the *Guides* states, "The frequency of attacks also should be taken into consideration when deciding on the level of impairment." In 1993, when the Fourth Edition was published, this was accepted. Now, however, with advances in the treatment of asthma, frequent attacks may reflect undertreatment, rather than severe disease.

The *Guides Newsletter*, May/June 1997, in an attempt to mitigate the difficulties of rating asthma by means of *Guides* Fourth Edition criteria, published a rating system that used pulmonary function test results and clinical parameters. The following table summarizes this system:

Parameters	Class 1 0%-9%	Class 2 10%-25%	Class 3 26%-50%	Class 4 51%-100%
Max postbronchodilator FEV_1 (% predicted)	≥70%	60%-69%	41%-59%	≤40%
Percentage of FEV_1 change*	<10%	10%-19%	20%-29%	≥30%
PC_{20} mg/mL or equivalent†	>5	>0.5-5	0.125-0.5	<0.125
Clinical parameters (minimum medication need, frequency of attacks, etc)	Occasional bronchodilator use, or cromolyn	Daily low-dose inhaled steroid and/or bronchodilator, or cromolyn	Daily high-dose‡ inhaled steroid and/or short periods of systemic steroids, and regular use of bronchodilators	Daily systemic steroids, and maximal bronchodilator use. Asthma not controlled despite maximal treatment

*The degree of FEV_1 reversibility, which is calculated by subtracting the prebronchodilator FEV_1 from the postbronchodilator FEV_1 and dividing by the prebronchodilator FEV_1.

†PC_{20} refers to the concentration of methacholine or other challenge agent that provokes a fall in the FEV_1 by ≥20%.

‡High-dose inhaled steroids indicates ≥800 µg of beclomethasone/day (≥40 puffs of Vanceril or doses of equal potency of other brand names, daily).

Mr Thomas' maximum postbronchodilator FEV_1 was greater than 70% of predicted, a class 1 impairment; his PC_{20} was 5 mg/mL, class 2 impairment; and his minimum medication requirements and frequency of attacks are class 2 impairment. Consequently, Mr Thomas has a class 2 respiratory impairment for which he retains 10% whole person impairment.

Impairment: 10% whole person impairment per the Fourth Edition and *Guides Newsletter.*

Fifth Edition Rating

Many of the difficulties inherent in the *Guides* Fourth Edition method for rating asthma were addressed in the Fifth Edition. The *Guides* Fifth Edition method for rating asthma is found in Chapter 5, The Respiratory System, Section 5.5, Asthma (5th ed, pp 102-104), including Table 5-9, Impairment Classification for Asthma Severity (5th ed, p 104), and Table 5-10, Impairment Rating for Asthma (5th ed, p 104).

Asthma-related impairment is calculated in two steps. First, the asthma severity score is calculated using the criteria in Table 5-9, which is reproduced on page 46.

The correct use of Table 5-9 requires performing a baseline spirometry to determine whether the individual's prebronchodilator FEV_1 is above or below the lower limit of normal. If the person's prebronchodilator FEV_1

Table 5-9 Impairment Classification for Asthma Severity*

Score	Postbronchodilator FEV_1	% of FEV_1 Change (Reversibility) *or*	PC_{20} mg/mL or Equivalent (Degree of Airway Hyperresponsiveness)†	Minimum Medication‡
0	≥ lower limit of normal	< 10%	> 8 mg/mL	No medication
1	≥ 70% of predicted	10%-19%	8 mg/mL to > 0.6 mg/mL	Occasional but not daily bronchodilator and/or occasional but not daily cromolyn
2	60%-69% of predicted	20%-29%	0.6 mg/mL to > 0.125 mg/mL	Daily bronchodilator and/or daily cromolyn and/or daily low-dose inhaled corticosteroid (≤800 μg of beclomethasone or equivalent)
3	50%-59% of predicted	≥30%	≤0.125 mg/mL	Bronchodilator on demand and daily high-dose inhaled corticosteroid (> 800 μg of beclomethasone or equivalent) or occasional course (one to three courses a year) of systemic corticosteroid
4	< 50% of predicted	. . .	. . .	Bronchodilator on demand and daily high-dose inhaled corticosteroid (> 1000 μg of beclomethasone or equivalent) and daily or every other day systemic corticosteroid

* FEV_1 indicates forced expiratory volume in the first second; PC_{20} is the provocative concentration that causes a 20% fall in FEV_1. Add the scores for postbronchodilator FEV_1, reversibility of FEV_1 (or PC_{20}), and medication use to obtain a summary severity score for rating respiratory impairment.

†When FEV_1 is greater than the lower limit of normal, PC_{20} should be determined and used for rating of impairment; when FEV_1 is less than 70% of the predicted, the degree of reversibility should be used; and when FEV_1 is between 70% of the predicted and the lower limit of normal, either reversibility or PC_{20} can be used. The score for minimum medication use is added to the appropriate measurement criteria outlined above.

‡Need for minimum medication should be demonstrated by the treating physician, for example, through previous records of exacerbation when medications have been reduced. Adapted from ATS guidelines.

is below the lower limit of normal, the degree of reversibility is assessed with inhaled bronchodilators (Table 5-9, column 2). If the person's prebronchodilator FEV_1 is above the lower limit of normal, a methacholine challenge is used to assess airway responsiveness (Table 5-9, column 3). Thus, calculating the asthma severity score requires either a score for percentage of FEV_1 change (Table 5-9, column 2) or a score for PC_{20} mg/mL (Table 5-9, column 3) but not both. Then, either the maximum postbronchodilator FEV_1 is used, or, if a methacholine challenge test was performed, a bronchodilator is administered, and the FEV_1 is again measured. Then the rater reviews the patient's medications. After the above assessment has been performed, the rater then calculates the asthma severity score to determine the percent impairment class and impairment of the whole person, using Table 5-10, which is reproduced below.

Table 5-10 Impairment Rating for Asthma*

Total Asthma Score	% Impairment Class	Impairment of the Whole Person
0	1	0%
1-5	2	10%-25%
6-9	3	26%-50%
10-11 or asthma not controlled despite maximal treatment, ie, FEV_1 remaining <50% of predicted despite use of >20 mg/day of prednisone	4	51%-100%

*The impairment rating is calculated as the sum of the individual's scores from Table 5-9. FEV_1 indicates forced expiratory volume in the first second.

Mr Thomas' asthma severity score was calculated by means of Table 5-9 as follows: His postbronchodilator FEV_1 was greater than the lower limit of normal, which yields a score of 0. His prebronchodilator FEV_1 was greater than the lower limit of normal; hence, a methacholine challenge was used to assess airway responsiveness. His PC_{20} was 5 mg/mL, which yields a score of 1. His minimum medication requirement yields a score of 3, as the fluticasone, 44 mcg, taken at four puffs per day, is the beclomethasone equivalent of approximately 1000 mcg. His total asthma severity score is 4 (0 + 1 + 3 = 4). A total asthma severity score of 4, by means of Table 5-10, yields class 2 impairment, which is associated with a 10% to 25% impairment of the whole person. For a class 2 impairment and interpolating numerically the total asthma score of 1 to 5 and the impairment range of 10% to 25%, this would suggest 22% whole person permanent impairment. Section 2.5d, Interpolating, Measuring, and Rounding Off (5th ed, p 20), states, "In deciding where to place an individual's impairment rating within a range, the physician needs to consider all the criteria applicable to the condition, which includes performing activities of daily living, and estimate the degree to which the medical impairment interferes with these activities." Using activities of daily living, this would suggest assignment of impairment at the lower range, and this was used as the basis of impairment rating.

Impairment: 10% whole person impairment per the Fifth Edition.

Sixth Edition Rating

Permanent impairment evaluation was based on Section 5.6, Asthma and Other Hyperreactive Airway Diseases (6th ed, pp 87-91). According to Table 5-5, Criteria for Rating Permanent Impairment due to Asthma (6th ed, p 90), the key factor in rating impairment from asthma is the degree of hyperresponsiveness, as determined either by the postbronchodilator FEV_1 or the methacholine challenge test. As this person's baseline spirometry was normal (FEV_1 of 98% of predicted), a methacholine challenge test was performed. Based on the PC_{20} of 5, the impairment class was 1. Based on the minimum medication need of 1000 mcg of beclomethasone equivalent, class 3 is appropriate. Thus, the default value of impairment is moved up two grades. The final impairment is class 1, grade E, 10% whole person impairment.

Impairment: 10% whole person impairment per the Sixth Edition.

Comment on Occupational Asthma in a Delivery Driver

Many of the issues that could be discussed here were discussed in Case 5-1. The problems surrounding the use of the term *beclomethasone equivalents* can be seen in this example. The only other issue to discuss is a clinical issue. Mr Thomas utilizes inhaled medications consisting of an inhaled steroid and a long-acting bronchodilator. However, he is doing well clinically and has had no recent exacerbations of his asthma. He has been away from the inciting/offending agent for 2 years. His pulmonary function tests are normal. It is unknown if the dosages of medications that he is currently taking are the "minimum medication that obtains the best overall outcome" (6th ed, p 89). As page 91 suggests, there can be recovery in cases of occupational asthma if the offending agent is removed from the individual's environment.

SUMMARY

Diagnosis	Occupational asthma due to exposure to isocyanates
Fourth Edition References	Chapter 5, Table 8 (4th ed, p 162), Table 10 (4th ed, p 10), *Guides Newsletter,* May/June 1997, Table 2
Fourth Edition Summary	Medication requirement is the parameter suggesting the greatest impairment. With the advances in asthma treatment since 1993, when the Fourth Edition was published, the amount of treatment required probably reflects the disease severity better than the frequency of attacks does.
Fourth Edition Impairment	10% whole person impairment
Fifth Edition References	Section 5.5 (5th ed, pp 102-104), Table 5-9 (5th ed, p 104), Table 5-10 (5th ed, p 104)
Fifth Edition Summary	Asthma-related impairment is calculated in two steps. First, the asthma severity score is calculated using the criteria in Table 5-9. Second, the calculated asthma severity score is used to determine the percent impairment class and impairment of the whole person by means of Table 5-10.
Fifth Edition Impairment	10% whole person impairment
Sixth Edition References	Section 5.6 (6th ed, pp 87-91), Table 5-5 (6th ed, p 90)
Sixth Edition Summary	Simplified rating method over the Fifth edition, using only one rather than two tables. Rating based on the same three parameters as used in the Fifth Edition, although the degree of responsiveness using a bronchodilator was eliminated.
Sixth Edition Impairment	10% whole person impairment

CASE 5-3

Pneumoconiosis

Subject: Mr Smith, a 60-year-old male.

History: Mr Smith has had shortness of breath with exertion for the past 6 years. He stated that he had been occupationally exposed to coal and rock dust for 30 years as a coal miner. He also reported being exposed to asbestos for about 4 years, approximately 30 years ago, although he could not estimate the frequency or intensity of exposure. He stated that his job duties included working as a mechanic and a welder in the preparation plant. He further reported being the plant superintendent. He denied ever using respiratory protection while working. He stated that he smoked 1 pack of cigarettes per day for 23 years, quitting 15 years ago.

Current Symptoms: Mr Smith stated that he could walk about a fourth of a mile on level ground before stopping due to shortness of breath. He could walk up a gentle incline for about 50 feet and could climb about 12 steps before stopping due to shortness of breath. Mr Smith also reported difficulties performing chores around the home, stating that he would "run out of breath" and needed to take frequent rest breaks. He denied chest tightness, wheeze, chest pains, night sweats, weight loss, fever, or any other systemic symptoms.

Physical Examination: Height, 188 cm; weight, 93 kg. He was afebrile, with a regular respiratory rate of 16/min. Examination of the chest on inspection, palpation, and percussion was unremarkable. Auscultation of the lungs revealed end-inspiratory rales at both bases that did not clear with coughing. The heart had a regular rate and rhythm without murmur, gallop, or rub.

Clinical Studies: International Labour Office (ILO) classification of the chest X ray by a National Institute for Occupational Safety and Health (NIOSH)–certified B-reader (ie, a physician who demonstrates proficiency in the interpretation of chest X rays for pneumoconioses using the ILO Classification System) revealed parenchymal abnormalities consistent with pneumoconiosis (classified as "small opacities p/s, all zones, profusion 1/1"). The forced vital capacity (FVC) was 72% of predicted, the FEV_1 was 66% of predicted, and the FEV_1/FVC ratio was 89%. Postbronchodilator studies did not show any significant change. The diffusing capacity was 65% of predicted.

Discussion of Pneumoconiosis

Fourth Edition Rating

Permanent impairment evaluation was based on Chapter 5, The Respiratory System, Section 5.2, Physiologic Tests of Pulmonary Function: Techniques, Use, and Interpretation (4th ed, pp 159-163), and Section 5.3, Criteria for Evaluating Permanent Impairment (4th ed, pp 163-164). Table 8, Classes of Respiratory Impairment (4th ed, p 162), describes four classes of respiratory impairment determined by a person's FVC, FEV_1, FEV_1/FVC (%), and diffusing capacity of carbon monoxide (DCO) or maximum oxygen consumption (VO_2max).

Although physiologic testing of pulmonary function is the quantitative basis on which the evaluation of respiratory system impairment rests (4th ed, p 159), some pulmonary impairments may not be directly related to lung function (Table 10, Impairments Not Directly Related to Lung Functions). Specifically, pneumoconiosis may cause no physiologic impairment; however, pneumoconiosis requires the individual's removal from exposure to the dust causing the condition. Mr Smith's pneumoconiosis was associated with physiologic impairment, namely, a mild restrictive ventilatory defect; hence, his impairment is determined by using Table 2, Predicted Normal FVC Values for Men (4th ed, p 156), Table 4, Predicted Normal FEV_1 Values for Men (4th ed, p 158), Table 6, Predicted Normal Single-Breath DCO Values for Men (4th ed, p 160), and Table 8, Classes of Respiratory Impairment (4th ed, p 162).

Study	Measured	Predicted	Measured/Predicted (%)
FVC	3.85	5.35	72%
FEV_1	2.73	4.13	66%
FEV_1/FVC (%)	70%	77%	
DCO	24.83	38.2	65%

Mr Smith's permanent impairment due to his pneumoconiosis disorder is class 2 (4th ed, Table 8, p 162), consistent with a 10% to 25% whole person impairment. On the basis of Mr Smith's circumstances (his dyspnea on exertion and interference with his activities of daily living), it is reasonable to rate him in the higher portion of this range. Based on extrapolations of the measured/predicted % values, it also would be appropriate to rate him at the higher level. Only one of the pulmonary function test abnormalities need be in the class for the entire impairment to fall into that class (4th ed, Section 5.3, p 163). However, no value exceeds that required for class 2.

The greatest abnormality is found in the Dco. The range of values in class 2 for the DCO are <69% and >60% of the predicted value. The measured DCO is 65%. Thus, the spread is 60 to 69, or 9 percentage points. The impairment range is 10% to 25%, or 15 percentage points. Thus, each DCO abnormality percentage point conveys 1.5 impairment percentage points. Mr Smith's rating is 6 DCO abnormality percentage points from the bottom of the category; 6 × 1.5 = 9. Thus, his impairment rating, using extrapolation, is 25% minus 9% equals 16% whole person impairment.

Impairment: 16% whole person impairment per the Fourth Edition.

Fifth Edition Rating

Permanent impairment evaluation was based on Chapter 5, The Respiratory System, Section 5.4d, Examinations, Clinical Studies, and Other Tests for Evaluating Respiratory Disease (5th ed, pp 91-102); Section 5.8, Pneumoconiosis (5th ed, p 106); and Section 5.10, Permanent Impairment Due to Respiratory Disorders (5th ed, pp 107-111). Table 5-12, Impairment Classification for Respiratory Disorders, Using Pulmonary Function and Exercise Test Results (5th ed, p 107), describes four classes of respiratory impairment determined by a person's FVC, FEV_1, FEV_1/FVC (%), and DCO or by using the VO_2max.

Mr Smith's pneumoconiosis-related impairment is determined by means of pulmonary function measures. Using Tables 5-2a and b (5th ed, p 97), 5-4a and b (5th ed, p 97), and 5-6a and b (5th ed, p 99), Mr Smith's pulmonary function test results can be summarized in the following table:

Study	Measured	Predicted Lower Limit of Normal	Predicted Normal	Measured/ Predicted (%)
FVC	3.85	4.235	5.35	72%
FEV_1	2.73	3.288	4.13	66%
FEV_1/FVC (%)	70%		77%	
DCO	24.83	30.0	38.2	65%

Mr Smith's permanent impairment due to his pneumoconiosis disorder is class 2 (5th ed, Table 5-12, p 107), consistent with a 10% to 25% impairment of the whole person. On the basis of Mr Smith's circumstances (his dyspnea on exertion and the interference with his activities of daily living), it is reasonable to rate him in the higher portion of this range. Based on extrapolations of the measured/predicted percentage values, it would also be appropriate to rate him at the higher level. Only one of the pulmonary function test abnormalities need be in the class for the entire impairment to fall into that class (5th ed, p 107). However, all the values in this case fall in class 2. The greatest abnormality is found in the DCO. The range of values in class 2 for the DCO are less than the lower limit of normal and >60%. The measured DCO is 65%. The lower limit of normal ratio is 78% (30.0/38.2). Thus, the spread is 60 to 78, or 19 percentage points. The impairment range is 10% to 25%, or 15 percentage points. Thus, each DCO abnormality percentage point conveys 0.78 impairment percentage points. Mr Smith's rating is 6 DCO abnormality percentage points from the bottom of the category; 6 × 0.78 = 4.68, or 5. Thus, his impairment rating, using extrapolation, is 25% minus 5% equals 20% whole person impairment.

Impairment: 20% whole person impairment per the Fifth Edition.

Sixth Edition Rating

Permanent impairment evaluation was based on Section 5.5, Methodology for Determining the Grade in an Impairment Class (6th ed, pp 86-87) and Section 5.8, Pneumoconiosis (6th ed, pp 91-92). According to Table 5-4, Criteria for Rating Permanent Impairment due to Pulmonary Dysfunction (6th ed, p 88), Mr Smith's pulmonary function test results can be summarized in the following table:

Study	Measured	Predicted Lower Limit of Normal	Predicted Normal	Measured/ Predicted (%)
FVC	3.85	4.235	5.35	72%
FEV_1	2.73	3.288	4.13	66%
FEV_1/FVC (%)	70%		77%	
DCO	24.83	30.0	38.2	65%

As noted on page 87, "at least one of the criteria must be fulfilled" in order to place a person in an impairment class. In this case, however, all the values used (FVC, FEV_1, and DCO) place this individual in class 1. Using the Sixth Edition, extrapolation of values is no longer performed as in previous editions. Rather, a default grade C value is chosen (6% whole person impairment in this example) and modified by the remaining elements such as the history and physical examination findings. The history would suggest at least moderate dyspnea (class 3). The physical examination findings of rales, based on a diagnosis of an interstitial fibrotic disorder, will never clear. The concept of mild, moderate, and severe abnormalities, based on the presence of rales, is not applicable. Thus, class 3 is chosen, based on the spectrum of rales without signs of heart failure. Both elements increase the impairment rating by two units, for a final adjustment factor of four in the upward direction. Thus, the final rating will be class 1, grade E, 10% whole person impairment.

Impairment: 10% whole person impairment per the Sixth Edition.

Comment on Pneumoconiosis

The impairment classification for respiratory disorders is similar in the Fourth, Fifth, and Sixth Editions, with the exception of incorporating the lower limits of normal for the FVC, FEV_1, and DCO in the latter two editions. As this case exemplifies, and as pointed out in all three editions, the use of an exercise stress in a case such as this, where the static tests of pulmonary function did not properly address the severity of the patient's symptoms, would be beneficial.

SUMMARY

Diagnosis	Pneumoconiosis
Fourth Edition References	Table 2 (4th ed, p 156), Table 4 (4th ed, p 158), Table 6 (4th ed, p 160), Table 8 (4th ed, p 162)
Fourth Edition Summary	History, physical examination, chest radiograph, and physiologic tests of pulmonary function
Fourth Edition Impairment	16% whole person impairment
Fifth Edition References	Section 5.4d (5th ed, pp 91-102); Section 5.8 (5th ed, p 106); Section 5.10 (5th ed, pp 107-111), Table 5-12 (5th ed, p 107)
Fifth Edition Summary	History, physical examination, chest radiograph, and physiologic tests of pulmonary function. The lower limits of normal are used to distinguish between class 1 and class 2 respiratory impairment in Table 5-12.
Fifth Edition Impairment	20% whole person impairment
Sixth Edition References	Section 5.5 (6th ed, pp 86-87), Table 5-4 (6th ed, p 88)

Sixth Edition Summary	History, physical examination, chest radiograph, and physiologic tests of pulmonary function. The lower limits of normal are used to distinguish between class 1 and class 2 respiratory impairment in Table 5-4.
Sixth Edition Impairment	10% whole person impairment

Chapter 6

The Digestive System

CASE 6-1

Inguinal Hernia

Subject: Mr Daniels, a 32-year-old man.

History: Mr Daniels is a laborer who for several years did heavy lifting without difficulty. One day, however, he lifted a bag of concrete and shortly thereafter was aware of discomfort and some swelling in his right inguinal area. He was not aware of any previous problems in that region. The problem persisted, and after a week he was seen by his family physician, who diagnosed an inguinal hernia. Although his doctor recommended having it repaired, Mr Daniels repeatedly declined surgery, preferring to live with it rather than risk having an operation.

Current Symptoms: One year after the injury, Mr Daniels reported that he was still having difficulties. He was aware of a slightly painful protrusion that occurred when he strained; it occurred from time to time, but not frequently. This resulted in occasional mild discomfort. He was careful of lifting but continued with his regular work.

Physical Examination: Slight protrusion in the right inguinal canal, palpable on Valsalva maneuver and easily reducible.

Discussion of Inguinal Hernia

Fourth Edition Rating

Permanent impairment evaluation was based on Section 10.9, Hernias of the Abdominal Wall (4th ed, p 247). Mr Daniels' description is consistent with class 1 impairment as defined in Table 7, Classes of Hernia-Related Impairment (4th ed, p 247), that is, "palpable defect in supporting structures of abdominal wall; and slight protrusion at site of defect with increased abdominal pressure; readily reducible; or occasional mild discomfort at site of defect, but not precluding normal activity." This corresponds with a 0% to 9% whole person impairment, and a midrange value of 5% is selected.

Impairment: 5% whole person impairment per the Fourth Edition.

Fifth Edition Rating

Permanent impairment evaluation was based on Section 6.6, Hernias (5th ed, p 136). The individual's description is consistent with class 1 impairment as defined in Table 6-9, Classes of Hernia-Related Impairment (5th ed, p 136), that is, "palpable defect in supporting structures of abdominal wall; and slight protrusion at site of defect with increased abdominal pressure; readily reducible; or occasional mild discomfort at site of defect, but not precluding normal activity." This corresponds with a 0% to 9% whole person impairment, and a midrange value of 5% is selected.

Impairment: 5% whole person impairment per the Fifth Edition.

Sixth Edition Rating

Permanent impairment evaluation was based on Section 6.6, Hernias (6th ed, pp 121-123). The rating was performed using Table 6-10, Criteria for Rating Permanent Impairment due to Herniation (6th ed, p 122). The key factor is physical findings and is consistent with a palpable defect in the supporting structures of the abdominal wall and/or slight protrusion at the site of the defect with increased abdominal pressure (easily reducible), which results in class 1 impairment. The patient's history is also consistent with class 1, that is, occasional mild discomfort at the site of the defect that does not preclude most activities of daily living. His rating remains at the default value of 3% whole person permanent impairment.

Impairment: 3% impairment of the whole person per the Sixth Edition

Comment on Inguinal Hernia

In the Fourth and Fifth Editions, there are three classes of impairment due to hernias, resulting in up to 30% impairment of the whole person. Common to each of the three classes is having a hernia, that is, a palpable defect in the supporting structures of the abdominal wall. In the Fifth Edition, although Table 6-9, Criteria for Rating Permanent Impairment Due to Herniation, describes a palpable defect as necessary for each class of impairment, Section 6.1b, Description of Clinical Studies (5th ed, p 119), states that "absent a palpable defect, imaging studies can document the presence of a hernia consistent with a class 1 impairment."

In the Sixth Edition there are four classes of impairment, also resulting in up to 30% whole person impairment. In the Sixth Edition the key factor is physical findings. If there are no physical findings, the class is 0, and there is 0% whole person permanent impairment. To have ratable impairment there must be a palpable defect and/or a protrusion at the site of the defect. A typical successful hernia repair will usually result in a 0% impairment rating.

In this case, the patient declined surgery; therefore, he is rated based on the current findings; however, it is noted in all three editions that if the hernia was repaired, it is probable there would be no ratable impairment.

SUMMARY

Diagnosis	Inguinal hernia
Fourth Edition References	Section 10.9 (4th ed, p 247), Table 7 (4th ed, p 247)
Fourth Edition Summary	Determine if hernia is present (palpable defect), note how frequently the protrusion is present and whether it is reducible, assess whether it interferes with activities of daily living.
Fourth Edition Impairment	5% whole person impairment
Fifth Edition References	Section 6.6 (5th ed, p 136), Table 6-9 (5th ed, p 136)
Fifth Edition Summary	Determine if hernia is present (palpable defect), note how frequently the protrusion is present and whether it is reducible, assess whether it interferes with activities of daily living.
Fifth Edition Impairment	5% whole person impairment
Sixth Edition References	Determine if there is a palpable defect or protrusion and assess interference with activities of daily living.
Sixth Edition Summary	Section 6.6 (6th ed, pp 121-123), Table 6-10 (6th ed, p 122)
Sixth Edition Impairment	3% whole person impairment

Chapter 7

The Urinary and Reproductive Systems

CASE 7-1

Sexual Dysfunction

Subject: Mr Jones, a 66-year-old man.

History: Mr Jones had a lifting injury at work 2 years previously, resulting in low back pain. His back pain essentially resolved, but he reported impotence that he attributed to the injury. His history was remarkable for diabetes (adult onset, diagnosed 10 years before examination and treated with oral agents) and a 30-pack-year smoking history. He underwent extensive evaluation of his impotence. Although serum hormone values were normal, duplex Doppler ultrasound findings demonstrated significantly impaired blood flow in both central corporal arteries, and the erectile response to intracavernous injection was only mildly tumescent. Biothesiometric study of the penile shaft and glans showed normal sensory thresholds. Nocturnal penile tumescence was not evaluated.

Although, with the addition of these objective vascular and neurologic studies, Mr Jones' physicians attributed most of the patient's sexual dysfunction to a vascular (not neurogenic or traumatic) cause, by decree his impotence was attributed to his workplace injury. The Workers' Compensation Commission required a rating for his sexual dysfunction.

Current Symptoms: At the time of examination, Mr Jones reported that sexual function was possible but erection was difficult. Ejaculation was preserved, but sensation was diminished. A friend gave him sildenafil citrate (Viagra), which he tried once; it appeared to help; however, it gave him a headache, so he did not pursue this treatment.

Physical Examination: Results of physical examination were normal. Genitourinary examination was unremarkable.

Discussion of Sexual Dysfunction

Fourth Edition Rating

Section 11.5a, Penis (4th ed, pp 256-257), describes the process of rating impairment of the penis for sexual functions of erection and ejaculation. The *Guides* classifies these levels of impairment in men into classes 1 to 3, depending on their severity, and accounts not only for erectile function but also for ejaculatory, orgasmic, and sensory function.

Mr Jones' impairment would be classified as class 1 (0% to 10% whole person impairment). This describes the clinical scenario of mild to moderate sexual dysfunction when sexual function is possible, but there are varying degrees of difficulty of erection, ejaculation, or sensation. The patient's condition approaches a class 2 impairment (11% to 19% whole person impairment). Class 2 implies that sexual function is possible and there is sufficient erection, but ejaculation and sensation are impaired. Therefore, he is rated at the upper limit of class 1, that is, at 10% whole person impairment. Percentage impairment decreases by 50% for men older than 65; therefore, his impairment is 5% whole person permanent impairment.

Impairment: 5% whole person impairment per the Fourth Edition.

Fifth Edition Rating

Section 7.7, Male Reproductive Organs (5th ed, pp 156-157), describes the process of rating impairment of male reproductive organs. Sexual functions of erection and ejaculation are presented in Section 7.7a, Penis, and impairment values are provided in Table 7-5, Criteria for Rating Permanent Impairment Due to Penile Disease (5th ed, p 156). The *Guides* classifies these levels of impairment in men into classes 1 to 3, depending on their severity, and accounts not only for erectile function but also for ejaculatory, orgasmic, and sensory function.

Mr Jones' impairment would be classified as class 1 (0% to 10% whole person impairment). This describes the clinical scenario in which sexual function is possible, but there are varying degrees of difficulty of erection, ejaculation, or sensation. The patient's condition approaches a class 2 impairment (11% to 19% whole person impairment). Class 2 indicates a progression of symptoms while the individual retains occasional ability to achieve and maintain erection. With class 2, impaired ejaculation and sensation are present. Therefore, the patient is rated at the upper limit of class 1, that is, at 10% whole person impairment. Percentage impairment decreases by 50% for men older than 65; therefore, his impairment is 5% whole person permanent impairment.

Impairment: 5% whole person impairment per the Fifth Edition

Sixth Edition Rating

Section 7.7, Male Reproductive Organs (6th ed, pp 143-149), describes the process of rating impairment of male reproductive organs. Sexual functions of erection and ejaculation are presented in Section 7.7a, Penis (6th ed, p 143), and impairment values are provided in Table 7-6, Criteria for Rating Permanent Impairment due to Penile Disease (6th ed, p 144). The *Guides* classifies these levels of impairment in men into classes 1 to 3, with the key factor being history.

Mr Jones' impairment would be classified as class 1. This describes the clinical scenario in which sexual function is possible with varying degrees of difficulty with erection or sensation that are responsive to medical treatment. His physical examination was normal, and nocturnal penile tumescence was not evaluated. However, the patient had abnormal duplex Doppler ultrasound findings, and erectile response to intracavernous injection was only mildly tumescent. Based on these findings "physical findings or nocturnal penile tumescence" was interpreted as "mild physical or testing abnormalities." History and physical examinations were therefore both consistent with class 1, so the patient remains at the grade B rating of 3% whole person permanent impairment. On page 143, under Section 7.7, Male Reproductive Organs, the age-related adjustment is discussed. In this case, the patient is 66 years old; therefore, his rating is adjusted downward by 10%, resulting in 3% minus 0.1(3%) equals 2.7% equals 3% whole person permanent impairment.

Impairment: 3% whole person impairment per the Sixth Edition

Comment on Sexual Dysfunction

Although medical logic would support the conclusion that Mr Jones' impotence is not related to his injury and therefore should not be ratable, there was a legal decision defining this as causally related, and a rating was required. Physicians may differ on causation; however, in the workers' compensation arena, a problem or diagnosis may have been determined legally to be attributable to an event.

Sexual dysfunction in both men and women is a disorder that significantly affects quality of life. It may also be a source of impairment and disability in men and women after injury. A range of sexual dysfunction exists, depending on the extent of injury and preexisting medical comorbidities, and may cause psychological sequelae, which should be evaluated separately. The ratings for male sexual function are for physical objective loss of function. Loss of libido, interest, or orgasm would be evaluated as a mental and behavioral disorder. Inaccurate subjective reports of erectile dysfunction may be encountered in cases involved in litigation; therefore, it is important to objectify the diagnosis before providing a rating.

Because male sexual dysfunction (MSD) and female sexual dysfunction may be of multifactorial etiology, a methodical plan of diagnosis is essential in order to identify specific causes and plan specific therapy. In broad terms, MSD is of organic, psychogenic, mixed, or indeterminate cause. This disorder is also referred to as *male erectile dysfunction.* The majority of men with MSD have an organic basis for the problem; younger men show a higher proportion of psychogenically based MSD. Organic MSD may originate from cardiovascular, diabetic, iatrogenic (radiation or surgical), pharmacogenic, neurogenic, hormonal, or local (Peyronie disease) causes.[1]

The specific cause of MSD can be identified through a sexual and medical history, physical examination, and tailored laboratory testing. A detailed sexual history documents the onset of MSD and describes whether it appeared suddenly or progressed gradually. The sudden appearance of MSD in association with trauma, the initiation of medical therapy, or the onset of newly diagnosed disease may suggest an organic basis. When the sudden appearance of MSD is associated with a life change event or stress, psychogenic MSD should be considered. The sexual history can be conveniently quantitated by using the International Index of Erectile Function, which documents the quality of sexual functions such as libido, ejaculation, orgasm, and genital sensation.[2] The presence of cardiovascular disease and its risk factors, such as smoking, hypertension, obesity, and dyslipidemia, point to a vascular basis for MSD, as is probable in this case. A careful and detailed history of all prescribed and nonprescribed medications should be documented. Medications with adrenergic activity, antiandrogen properties, beta-blockers, diuretics, and selective serotonin reuptake inhibitors are among the common drugs that inhibit erection and orgasm. The severity of MSD should be quantified in terms of the individual's perception, and a distinction should be made as to whether he has an inability to achieve or maintain erection or both.

Routine laboratory studies include complete blood cell count, serum chemistry, lipid profile, and serum free/total testosterone and prolactin levels. In routine evaluation of the impotent male, consensus maintains that, after the history, physical examination, and laboratory studies, more than 80% of individuals can be differentially diagnosed as having either organic or psychogenic MSD. When the cause still is unclear, optional specialized testing may further clarify it. Objective testing includes nocturnal penile tumescence, duplex Doppler ultrasound, and neurosensory testing.

SUMMARY

Diagnosis	Sexual dysfunction
Fourth Edition References	Section 11.5a (4th ed, pp 256-257)
Fourth Edition Summary	History assessing degree of difficulties with erection, ejaculation, and/or sensation; physical examination; and, as appropriate, laboratory and diagnostic studies
Fourth Edition Impairment	5% whole person impairment
Fifth Edition References	Section 7.7 (5th ed, pp 156-157), Table 7-5 (5th ed, p 156)
Fifth Edition Summary	History assessing degree of difficulties with erection, ejaculation, and/or sensation; physical examination; and, as appropriate, laboratory and diagnostic studies
Fifth Edition Impairment	5% whole person impairment
Sixth Edition References	Section 7.7 (5th ed, pp 143-149), Table 7-6 (6th ed, p 144)
Sixth Edition Summary	History assessing degree of difficulties with erection, ejaculation, and/or sensation; physical examination; and, as appropriate, laboratory and diagnostic studies
Sixth Edition Impairment	3% whole person impairment

References

1. Miller TA. Diagnostic evaluation of erectile dysfunction. *Am Fam Phys*. 2000;61:95-104, 109-110.
2. Rosen RC, Riley A, Wagner G, Osterloh IH, Kirkpatrick J, Mishra A. The international index of erectile dysfunction (IIEF): a multidimensional scale for assessment of erectile dysfunction. *Urology*. 1997;49:822-830.

Chapter 8

The Skin

CASE 8-1

Latex Allergy

Subject: Ms Ross, a 53-year-old woman.

History: Ms Ross is a nurse who presented to her physician because of an allergic reaction on her hands. She described a macular-papular, blister-type reaction after having used latex gloves for approximately 9 years. She also complained of urticaria on her face with swelling of her face and lips. She had not developed any pulmonary problems. She had a history of allergic rhinitis with seasonal allergies, food allergy to avocado and bananas, and cat allergy, even though she did have a cat. She had an occasional history of urticarial skin reactions on her face with gum chewing and when blowing up toy balloons.

Ms Ross' primary care physician referred her to an allergist. The allergist completed a latex skin-prick test to two different extracts, and the result was negative. Ms Ross wore latex gloves for 30 minutes and developed a few small macular lesions on her hands but no definitive urticaria. She had a positive allergen-specific IgE for latex sensitivity. Results of pulmonary function studies were normal. A second skin test for latex with a higher-level antigen was moderately positive. Because of her history of food allergies, seasonal allergic rhinitis, and skin and facial lesions after the use of latex gloves, the allergist felt the individual may have had a type I hypersensitivity reaction to latex, with facial angioedema, localized erythroderma, and hand urticaria upon exposure to latex gloves. Ms Ross was removed from her exposure to latex.

Current Symptoms: With no further exposure to latex, the patient was asymptomatic.

Physical Examination: Middle-aged woman with no facial edema, no angioedema, and no lesions of any type on her face. Her facial skin was clear, hair was intact, nasal and oral mucosa was clear, and there was no evidence of angioedema. The neck, upper chest, and entire skin were carefully examined for other reactive areas, such as where elastic in underwear would contact the skin. Her dermatologic examination was normal.

Discussion of Latex Allergy

Fourth Edition Rating

Methods of evaluating skin impairment are discussed in Section 13.2, Methods of Evaluating Impairment (4th ed, pp 278-279), and patch testing is reviewed in Section 13.6, Patch Testing—Performance, Interpretation, and Relevance (4th ed, p 280). Criteria for evaluating permanent impairment of the skin are presented in Section 13.7, Criteria for Evaluating Permanent Impairment of the Skin (4th ed, pp 280-289). Table 2, Impairment Classes and Percents for Skin Disorders (4th ed, p 280), specifies five classes of impairment. The *Guides* lists multiple examples to assist the examiner in placing the individual at the most appropriate impairment level. These are based largely on the impact of the skin disorder on activities of daily living. A list of activities of daily living is provided in the glossary on page 317.

Ms Ross falls into class 1, as "signs and symptoms of skin disorder are present or only intermittently present and there is no limitation or limitation in the performance of *few* activities of daily living, although exposure to certain chemical or physical agents might increase limitation temporarily, and *no* treatment or intermittent treatment is required" (4th ed, Table 2, p 280). Class 1 impairment is associated with 0% to 9% impairment. A 5% impairment is appropriate, because this individual has demonstrated a true allergic contact dermatitis caused by a substance that might, with further exposure, lead to more serious problems, such as pulmonary and/or anaphylactic reactions. The problem is intermittent and prevented by complete avoidance of latex. She does not belong in class 2, as this requires signs or symptoms of a skin disorder to be present or intermittently present, and limitation in the performance of some of the activities of daily living, and the need for intermittent to constant treatment.

Ms Ross has no restricted joint motion or behavioral, respiratory, cardiovascular, endocrine, or gastrointestinal problem because of her latex allergy. If she did have one or more of these problems, Section 13.5, Scars and Skin Grafts, states that those impairments should be rated, and the whole person ratings should then be combined (4th ed, p 280). The text states, "If other chapters also were used to estimate the impairment from a patient's skin disorder, the skin disorder evaluation would *exclude* consideration of the components evaluated with those chapters" (4th ed, p 280).

Thus, for example, if a skin scar caused limited elbow extension, the impact of that scar on activities of daily living, if already rated from the upper extremity chapter, would not be rated from the skin chapter.

Impairment: 5% whole person impairment per the Fourth Edition.

Fifth Edition Rating

A brief overview of latex allergy is provided in Section 8.5, Natural Rubber Latex Allergy (5th ed, p 177). Methods of evaluating skin impairment are discussed in Section 8.1, Principles of Assessment (5th ed, p 174). Criteria for evaluating permanent impairment of the skin are presented in Section 8.7, Criteria for Evaluating Permanent Impairment Due to Skin Disorders (5th ed, p 178). Table 8-2, Criteria for Rating Permanent Impairment Due to Skin Disorders (5th ed, p 178), specifies five classes of impairment. These classes are based largely on the impact of the skin condition on activities of daily living. A list of activities of daily living is provided in Table 1-2 (5th ed, p 4).

Ms Ross falls into class 1, as "skin disorder signs and symptoms present or intermittently present and no or few limitations in the performance of activities of daily living; exposure to certain chemical or physical agents might temporarily increase limitation, and requires no treatment or intermittent treatment." Class 1 impairment is associated with 0% to 9% impairment. A 5% impairment is appropriate because the patient has demonstrated a true allergic contact dermatitis caused by a substance that might, with further exposure, lead to more serious problems, such as pulmonary and/or anaphylactic reactions. The problem is intermittent and prevented by complete avoidance of latex. She does not belong in class 2, as this requires "skin disorder signs and symptoms present or intermittently present, and limited performance of some activities of daily living, and may require intermittent to constant treatment "(5th ed, Table 8-2, p 178).

Ms Ross has no restricted joint motion or behavioral, respiratory, cardiovascular, endocrine, or gastrointestinal problem because of her latex allergy. If she did have one or more of these problems, Section 8.1, Principles of Assessment, states that those impairments should be rated, and the whole person ratings should then be combined (5th ed, p 174).

Impairment: 5% whole person impairment per the Fifth Edition.

Sixth Edition Rating

A brief overview of latex allergy is provided in Section 8.5, Natural Rubber Latex Allergy (6th ed, p 164). Methods of evaluating skin impairment are discussed in Section 8.1, Principles of Assessment (6th ed, pp 160-162). Criteria for evaluating permanent impairment of the skin are presented in Section 8.7, Criteria for Rating Permanent Impairment due to Skin Disorders (6th ed, p 164). Table 8-2, Criteria for Rating Permanent Impairment due to Skin Disorders (6th ed, p 166), specifies five classes of impairment. These classes are based largely on the impact of the skin condition on activities of daily living. A list of activities of daily living is provided in Table 1-1 (6th ed, p 7).

Ms Ross falls into class 0, as "skin disorder signs have been present in the past but are currently present <1% of the time, and no medication is necessary, and there is essentially no interference with activities of daily living (ADLs)"(6th ed, Table 8-2, p 166). Class 0 impairment is associated with 0% impairment.

Impairment: 0% whole person impairment per the Sixth Edition.

Comment on Latex Allergy

The criteria for assignment of impairment for a skin disorder in the Sixth Edition are different from those of prior editions. The Sixth Edition has a class 0 disorder, which equates to 0% whole person impairment. The Fifth Edition skin disorder classification begins with class 1, which has an impairment range of 0% to 9% whole person impairment.

To meet the criteria beyond a class 0 disorder in the Sixth Edition, the condition must be present at least 1% of the time, the individual must require intermittent treatment, and there must be at least a minimal interference with activities of daily living. In the absence of these criteria, no greater than a class 0 disorder can be assigned. In past editions, these criteria were included in the class 1 disorder with an impairment range of 0% to 9% whole person impairment.

SUMMARY

Diagnosis	Latex allergic reaction
Fourth Edition References	Chapter 13 (4th ed, p 278), Table 2 (4th ed, p 281)
Fourth Edition Summary	History of exposure to latex products and any associated reactions, history of atopic dermatitis or other allergic manifestations, evaluation by a qualified allergist (with radioallergosorbent testing [RAST], patch testing, and possible skin-prick testing and pulmonary evaluation including spirometry, as appropriate), and dermatologic examination
Fourth Edition Impairment	5% whole person impairment
Fifth Edition References	Section 8.5 (5th ed, p 177); Section 8.1 (5th ed, p 174); Section 8.7 (5th ed, p 178), Table 8-2 (5th ed, p 178)
Fifth Edition Summary	History of exposure to latex products and any associated reactions, history of atopic dermatitis or other allergic manifestations, evaluation by a qualified allergist (with RAST, patch testing, and possible skin-prick testing), pulmonary evaluation (including spirometry), and dermatologic examination
Fifth Edition Impairment	5% whole person impairment
Sixth Edition References	Section 8.5 (6th ed, p 164); Section 8.1 (6th ed, pp 160-162); Section 8.7 (6th ed, p 164), Table 8-2 (6th ed, p 166), Table 1-1 (6th ed, p 7)
Sixth Edition Summary	History of exposure to latex products and any associated reactions, history of atopic dermatitis or other allergic manifestations, evaluation by a qualified allergist (with RAST, patch testing, and possible skin-prick testing), pulmonary evaluation (including spirometry), and dermatologic examination. Present clinical examination findings demonstrate no dermatologic findings.
Sixth Edition Impairment	0% whole person impairment

Chapter 9

The Hematopoietic System

CASE 9-1

Acquired Immunodeficiency Syndrome

Subject: Dr McPhee, a 32-year-old woman.

History: Dr McPhee was diagnosed with human immunodeficiency virus (HIV) infection at 22 years of age after a needle-stick injury when she was a medical student on her emergency medicine rotation. Despite receiving multiple combinations of antiretroviral treatment during the subsequent 5 years, Dr McPhee experienced weight loss, anorexia, diarrhea, nausea, fatigue, and vaginal thrush. Eight years after infection, Dr McPhee was treated for *Toxoplasma gondii* encephalitis, after which she reported difficulty with balance, memory, and concentration.

Current Symptoms: One year after encephalitis treatment, Dr McPhee's cognitive function had not returned to normal, and she developed peripheral neuropathy in her lower extremities with loss of sensation, dysesthetic pain, and problems with walking long distances. Her equilibrium was normal. Dr McPhee also had intermittent problems with diarrhea, anorexia, and generalized fatigue.

Dr McPhee's family indicated that she was able to function independently, but they had to "keep an eye on her." Dr McPhee was able to dress, bathe, and take care of her personal hygiene independently. She could no longer go to a store without a written list, as she would consistently forget several items. Her spouse had taken over most of the home bookkeeping activities, such as paying bills and balancing the checkbook, as Dr McPhee consistently made errors when she attempted those activities. She had problems with keeping her schedule as well.

Physical Examination: Examination revealed a thin woman (20% loss of normal body weight). She had generalized lymphadenopathy, vaginal thrush, and diminished pinprick and vibratory sensation in the lower extremities up to midtibia. Dysesthetic pain was also persistent despite neurogenic pain medications. Abnormalities on neurological examination, however, were related to memory and cognitive function. Mental status examination showed that she was oriented, but she did have significant difficulties with recent memory. She was able to recall only two of three objects after 3 minutes, and she made one error with serial sevens subtractions.

There did not appear to be any significant behavioral problems. Both Dr McPhee and her husband mentioned that perhaps she was somewhat depressed, but overall, her moods were normal, and there were no limitations in activities of daily living in reference to her emotional status. By Diagnostic and Statistical Manual of Mental Disorders, Fourth Edition[1] criteria, she was not depressed. There was no evidence of episodic alteration of consciousness (nothing to suggest seizures), and overall, her sleep patterns seemed normal.

Clinical Studies: The patient had a CD4 count of 30/mm^3 and an HIV RNA count of 1,400,000 copies/mL of plasma. Colonoscopy findings included scattered sigmoid diverticula and punctuate friable mucosa. No ulcerations were noted.

Discussion of Acquired Immunodeficiency Syndrome

Fourth Edition Rating

Permanent impairment evaluation was based on Chapter 7, The Hematopoietic System, Section 7.5, Criteria for Evaluating Permanent Impairment of the White Blood Cell Systems (4th ed, pp 205-206). Four classes of impairment are provided on the basis of symptoms and signs, nature of the treatment required, and difficulty in performing activities of daily living. Dr McPhee's acquired immunodeficiency syndrome (AIDS) is consistent with class 4, for which she will retain a 90% whole person impairment (WPI). Rather than performing a separate impairment evaluation for each of her other affected organ systems, given her severe disease and multiple system involvement, her class 4 impairment is adjusted upward to 95% whole person impairment.

Impairment: 95% whole person impairment per the Fourth Edition.

Fifth Edition Rating

Permanent impairment evaluation was based on Chapter 9, The Hematopoietic System, Section 9.4, White Blood Cell Diseases or Abnormalities (5th ed, pp 197-202). Four classes of impairment are provided on the basis of symptoms and signs, nature of the treatment required, and difficulty in performing activities of daily living. Dr McPhee's AIDS is consistent with class 4, for which she will retain a 90% whole person impairment. Rather than performing a separate impairment evaluation for each of her other affected organ systems, given her severe disease and multiple system involvement, her class 4 impairment is adjusted upward to 95% whole person impairment.

Impairment: 95% whole person impairment per the Fifth Edition.

Sixth Edition Rating

Hematopoietic System

Permanent impairment evaluation was based on Chapter 9, The Hematopoietic System, Section 9.4, White Blood Cell Diseases or Abnormalities (6th ed, pp 193-201) and Table 9-8, Criteria for Rating Permanent Impairment due to HIV Disease (6th ed, pp 199).

Impairment for HIV disease is frequently associated with multiple organ system involvement besides the primary HIV infection with immunologic dysfunction. Toxicity related to the multiple HIV medications is also common. The authors involved in this chapter understood the multiplicity of impairments that can be present so placed a maximum value of 80% whole person impairment even for a class 4 rating. The final rating is intended to increase, depending on the other various impairments from the other organ systems. In this case, Dr McPhee's AIDS condition is consistent with class 4, for which she will be rated at 80% whole person impairment.

Central Nervous System

The first step in rating a central nervous system impairment is to identify the primary or most severe cerebral impairment from the following four categories (Sections 13.2 and 13.3, pp 326-333):

1. State of consciousness and level of awareness
2. Mental status evaluation and integrative functioning
3. Use and understanding of language
4. Influence of behavior and mood

After the primary impairment category is chosen, any other impairments (Table 13-3, p 326) related to the cranial nerves, upper and lower extremities, bowel and bladder dysfunction, sexual function, neurologic respiratory impairment, and peripheral nervous system are evaluated. These impairments are combined with the primary impairment value identified initially.

Table 13-8 (6th ed, p 331), Criteria for Rating Neurologic Impairment due to Alteration in Mental Status, Cognition, and Highest Integrative Function (MSCHIF) provided the basis for rating Dr McPhee's impairments.

Dr McPhee's mental status examination is noteworthy for significant difficulties with recent memory. She was able to recall only two of three objects after 3 minutes. She had difficulty recalling some topics that had been discussed with her just a few minutes earlier. Dr McPhee was noted to have consistently made errors in balancing a checkbook and keeping her schedule straight.

Based on the results of the clinical mental status examination, Dr McPhee would likely be viewed as having moderate abnormalities and would therefore be rated under class 2. Ratings under this class range between 10% and 20% whole person impairment. Patients rated under this class have alterations in mental status, cognition, and highest integrative function (MSCHIF), such that it interferes with their ability to assume some normal roles or perform ADLs.

Based on the impact of the injury on significant areas of mental functioning, Dr McPhee would qualify for rating at the middle range of this class, or 15% whole person impairment.

Table 13-9 (6th ed, p 332), Criteria for Rating Impairment due to Aphasia or Dysphasia, is used for rating this impairment. Dr McPhee does not have any difficulty with speech, naming, or repetition.

Dr McPhee does not have a disturbance in the level of consciousness or awareness, nor are there any significant behavioral problems in Dr McPhee's case.

The most severe cerebral impairment is that related to alteration in mental status, cognition, and highest integrative function, at 15% whole person impairment.

Digestive System

Inflammatory large bowel disease was noted in the colon, causing chronic diarrhea and weight loss along with anorexia. Impairment for this condition is discussed in Section 6.3a, Criteria for Rating Permanent Impairment due to Colonic or Rectal Disease (6th ed, pp 113-116). Table 6-5, Criteria for Rating Permanent Impairment due to Colonic and Rectal Disorders (6th ed, p 114), was used for this rating. Based on the key historical factor of chronic diarrhea, coupled with at least a 20% weight loss by history, the most applicable rating is class 4 with a mid-range rating of 50% whole person impairment.

Peripheral Neuropathy
Impairment for the drug-induced peripheral neuropathy is rated under Section 13.9, Criteria for Rating Peripheral Neuropathy, Neuromuscular Junction Disorders, and Myopathies (6th ed, pp 339-341). Table 13-17 (6th ed, p 339), Criteria for Rating Dysesthetic Pain Secondary to Peripheral Neuropathy or Spinal Cord Injury, is used for this rating, whereas Tables 13-11 and 13-12 (6th ed, pp 335-336) are used to rate peripheral neuropathy in the upper and lower extremities. In this case, there is no upper extremity involvement. The patient is rated under Station and Gait Impairment from Table 13-12 as a class 2 rating with a mid-range 15% whole person impairment.

Impairment: The final impairment is the combined ratings for all involved conditions rated previously. The 80% WPI HIV is first combined with the 50% WPI digestive tract rating for a total of 90% WPI. This is then combined with the central nervous system rating of 15% WPI for a total of 92% WPI. The 92% WPI is then combined with the peripheral neuropathy rating of 15% WPI for a total of 93% WPI. The final rating in this case is 93% whole person impairment per the Sixth Edition.

Comment on Acquired Immunodeficiency Syndrome

HIV disease is rated as a primary hematologic disorder. Functional impairment in HIV infection is often due to the complications of HIV infection (eg, *Toxoplasma gondii* encephalitis, cytomegalovirus retinitis). Hence, the *Guides* Sixth Edition recommends determining total impairment only after assessment of each of the affected organ systems, rating each affected organ system separately and then combining these impairments with the impairment due to HIV infection (ie, with the impairment due to the white blood cell disorder). In the Fourth and Fifth Editions, this step was not necessary, given the range of impairment provided in the classes of impairment related to white blood cell disorders.

SUMMARY

Diagnosis	Acquired immunodeficiency syndrome
Fourth Edition References	Section 7.5 (4th ed, pp 205-206)
Fourth Edition Summary	Determine impairment due to the white blood cell disorder and then determine if there is any additional impairment due to the complications of the HIV infection.

Fourth Edition Impairment	95% whole person impairment
Fifth Edition References	Section 9.4 (5th ed, pp 197-202)
Fifth Edition Summary	Determine impairment due to the white blood cell disorder and then determine if there is any additional impairment due to the complications of the HIV infection.
Fifth Edition Impairment	95% whole person impairment
Sixth Edition References	Section 9.4 (6th ed, pp 193-202), Table 9-8 (6th ed, p 199); Sections 13.2 and 13.3 (6th ed, pp 326-327), Table 13-3 (6th ed, p 326), Table 13-8 (6th ed, p 331), Table 13-9 (6th ed, p 332); Section 6.3a (6th ed, pp 113-116), Table 6-5 (6th ed, p 114); Section 13.9 (6th ed, pp 339-341), Table 13-17 (6th ed, p 339), Tables 13-11 and 13-12 (6th ed, pp 335-336)
Sixth Edition Summary	History, examination, and clinical studies document support for impairment within multiple organ systems.
Sixth Edition Impairment	93% whole person impairment

CASE 9-2

Chronic Myelocytic Leukemia

Subject: Mr Jones, a 45-year-old man.

History: Mr Jones is a chemical engineer with a history of benzene exposure during his employment between the ages of 25 and 35 years. He had felt well until 3 years ago, when he developed fatigue, fever, and left upper abdominal pain. Physical examination at that time showed mild pallor, adenopathy, and an enlarged spleen. Pertinent laboratory tests showed a hemoglobin level of 10.2 g/dL, white blood cell count of 92,000/mm^3 with predominantly immature granulocytes, and platelet count of 90,000/mm^3. A bone marrow biopsy specimen was consistent with chronic myelocytic leukemia, Philadelphia chromosome testing was positive, and the leukocyte alkaline phosphatase level was low.

Mr Jones was treated with myelosuppressive agents, but within 2 years the spleen enlarged to 12 cm, the white blood cell count dropped to 2400/mm^3, the Philadelphia chromosome disappeared, and the leukocyte alkaline phosphatase level became elevated. Mr Jones required transfusion of 2 units of packed red blood cells every 6 weeks to maintain a hemoglobin level of at least 7.5 g/dL.

Current Symptoms: Mr Jones' primary symptom was fatigue. He did not have recurring episodes of hemorrhage from the low platelet count, but he did have recurring episodes of infection. He was hospitalized twice in the 12 months before the impairment examination with bacterial infections, despite low white count dietary restrictions, daily antibiotic prophylaxis, and restrictions on social contact with individuals with infections. His ECOG-PSS score was class 0.

Physical Examination: Lymphadenopathy and enlarged spleen.

Clinical Studies: The absolute neutrophil count was fairly stable at 450/mm^3. The hemoglobin level was stable between 7 and 7.5 g/dL with blood transfusions every 6 weeks. The white blood cell count was low but stable. Bone marrow aspiration was dry, but a bone biopsy specimen showed myelofibrosis.

Discussion of Chronic Myelocytic Leukemia

Fourth Edition Rating

Permanent impairment was based on the anemia (including the transfusion requirements), the infection consequences of the low white blood cell count, and the low platelet count. According to Section 7.1, Permanent Impairment Related to Anemia (4th ed, p 202), and Table 1, Criteria for Evaluating Permanent Impairment Related to Anemia (4th ed, p 202), hemoglobin levels of 5 to 8 g/dL reflect a moderate impairment. Mr Jones' hemoglobin level was maintained at between 7 and 7.5 g/dL by transfusions, suggesting a moderate impairment. Table 1 further indicates that a transfusion requirement of between 2 and 3 units every 4 to 6 weeks reflects a moderate impairment. Mr Jones was receiving about 2 units every 6 weeks. According to Table 1, the impairment percentage for anemia and transfusion requirement with moderate to marked symptoms is 30% to 69% whole person impairment. The anemia and the transfusion requirement fall toward the lesser side of the criteria in Table 1; therefore, 40% whole person impairment was chosen.

Permanent impairment related to white blood cell diseases or abnormalities is discussed in Section 7.3, Permanent Impairment Related to White Blood Cell Diseases or Abnormalities (4th ed, p 205). The individual's condition is rated as class 3 (4th ed, p 205) because continuous treatment is required (antibiotic prophylaxis) and there is interference with the performance of daily activities that requires occasional assistance from others (cooperation with social restrictions). Class 3 yields 30% to 55% whole person impairment. Mr Jones' condition is rated on the low side of class 3 because he could perform most activities of daily living, the infections were infrequent, permitting continued employment, and he did not require substantial assistance from others. White blood cell disease impairment, therefore, was 30% whole person impairment.

Mr Jones' platelet count was low at 90,000/mm^3. Hemorrhagic and platelet disorders are discussed in Section 7.6, Hemorrhagic Disorders and Platelets (4th ed, p 206). There was no bleeding and no requirement for platelet transfusion, and the patient had no symptoms of the reduced platelet count (bleeding). Thus, there was no impairment for a platelet disorder. Therefore, with the 40% whole person impairment for the anemia and the 30% whole person impairment for the white blood cell count, by means of the Combined Values Chart (4th ed, p 322), there was 58% whole person impairment.

Impairment: 58% whole person impairment per the Fourth Edition.

Fifth Edition Rating

Mr Jones' anemia was rated by means of Section 9.2, Anemia (5th ed, p 192). According to Table 9-2, Criteria for Rating Permanent Impairment Due to Anemia, Mr Jones' condition is consistent with a class 3 impairment because he has moderate to marked symptoms and a hemoglobin level of 7 to 7.5 g/dL and requires a transfusion of 2 units of packed red blood cells every 6 weeks. Class 3 provides a range of impairment from 31% to 70% whole person impairment. Mr Jones' anemia and transfusion requirements are consistent with a permanent impairment at the low end of the range. Consequently, Mr Jones will retain 40% whole person impairment as a consequence of his anemia.

Mr Jones' white blood cell disorder is rated by means of Section 9.4, White Blood Cell Diseases or Abnormalities (5th ed, p 197). According to Table 9-3, Criteria for Rating Permanent Impairment Due to White Blood Cell Disease, Mr Jones' condition is consistent with a class 3 impairment because he requires continuous treatment with antibiotics and because his social restrictions require assistance from others. Class 3 provides a range of impairment from 31% to 55% whole person impairment. Mr Jones' white blood cell condition is rated at the low end of this range because he is able to perform most activities of daily living, he is able to continue working, and he does not require substantial assistance from others. Thus, Mr Jones will retain 31% whole person impairment as a consequence of his white blood cell disorder.

Mr Jones' platelet disorder is rated by means of Section 9.5, Hemorrhagic and Platelet Disorders (5th ed, p 203). According to Table 9-4, Criteria for Rating Permanent Impairment Due to Hemorrhagic and Platelet Disorders, Mr Jones' condition is consistent with a class 1 impairment. Class 1 provides a range of impairment from 0% to 15% whole person impairment. Mr Jones' platelet disorder is rated at the low end of this range because it is not associated with bleeding, and he requires no platelet transfusions. Thus, Mr Jones will retain a 0% whole person impairment as a consequence of his platelet disorder. Combining the 40% whole person impairment due to anemia with the 31% whole person impairment for the white blood cell disorder yields a 59% whole person impairment.

Impairment: 59% whole person impairment per the Fifth Edition.

Sixth Edition Rating

Permanent impairment evaluation was based on Chapter 9, The Hematopoietic System, Section 9.2a, Criteria for Rating Permanent Impairment due to Anemia (6th ed, pp 188-191); Section 9.4a, Granulocytes (6th ed, pp 193-195); Section 9.4c Impairment from Leukemias (6th ed, pp 195-198); and Section 9.5a, Criteria for Rating Permanent Impairment due to Platelet Disorders (6th ed, pp 202-203).

According to Table 9-5, Criteria for Rating Permanent Impairment due to Anemia (6th ed, p 189), Mr Jones' condition is consistent with a class 3 impairment because he has moderate to marked symptoms and a hemoglobin level of 7 to 7.5 g/dL. Class 3 provides a range of impairment from 25% to 45% whole person impairment. Mr Jones' anemia and transfusion requirements are consistent with a permanent impairment at the low end of the range. Consequently, Mr Jones will retain a 30% whole person impairment as a consequence of his anemia.

According to Table 9-6, Criteria for Rating Permanent Impairment due to Neutropenia (6th ed, p 194), Mr. Jones' condition is consistent with a class 4 impairment because he requires continuous treatment with antibiotics and was hospitalized twice in the 12 months prior to the impairment evaluation. It should be noted that his absolute neutrophil count of 450/mm^3 would place him within a class 3 rating; however, footnote (a) within Table 9-6 documents that if both criteria are present, the higher rating should be used. Class 4 provides a range of impairment from 40% to 50% whole person impairment. Mr Jones' white blood cell condition is rated at the low end of this range because of his absolute neutrophil count (ANC) level and the fact that he is able to perform most activities of daily living, he is able to continue working, and he does not require substantial assistance from others. Thus, Mr Jones will retain 40% whole person impairment as a consequence of his white blood cell disorder.

According to Table 9-7, Criteria for Rating Permanent Impairment due to Leukemias (6th ed, p 196), Mr Jones' condition is consistent with a class 1 impairment with no ongoing chemotherapy treatment necessary. Class 1 ratings for leukemias are rated within a range of impairment from 3% to 15% whole person impairment. As noted earlier, because he is able to perform most activities of daily living, he is able to continue working, and he does not require substantial assistance from others, a low-mid-level range of 7% whole person impairment is chosen.

According to Table 9-9, Criteria for Rating Impairment due to Platelet Disorders (6th ed, p 202), Mr Jones' condition is consistent with a class 1 impairment. Class 1 provides a range of impairment from 1% to 5% whole person impairment. Mr Jones' platelet disorder is rated at the low end of this range because it is not associated with bleeding and he requires no platelet transfusions. Thus, Mr Jones will retain a 1% whole person impairment as a consequence of his platelet disorder.

Combining the 40% whole person impairment for the neutropenia with the 30% WPI due to his anemia yields a 58% WPI. This is then combined with the 7% WPI due to the leukemia which equals 60% WPI. The 1% WPI related to the platelet disorder can be combined at the end of the calculation, but does not increase the rating. The final impairment rating is 60% whole person impairment.

Impairment: 60% whole person impairment per the Sixth Edition.

Comment on Chronic Myelocytic Leukemia

There are some differences between the Fourth, Fifth, and Sixth Editions in rating leukemia cases. First, the Sixth Edition has a separate section for rating leukemia. Prior editions rated white blood cell disease based on a more generalized rating for conditions including leukemias, lymphomas, and HIV infections. The Sixth Edition's classes correspond to more specific information such as the absolute neutrophil count for the neutropenia. Because of the separate ratings, which have to be considered for this case, including anemia, neutropenia, thrombocytopenia, and leukemia, the rating may be slightly greater, based on the criteria outlined in the Sixth Edition.

SUMMARY

Diagnosis	Chronic myelocytic leukemia with transformation to myelofibrosis
Fourth Edition References	Chapter 7 (4th ed, p 202), Table 1 (4th ed, p 202)
Fourth Edition Summary	Impairment is based on the residual anemia with the level of hemoglobin and the transfusion requirements. White blood cell impairment is based on the presence of dysfunction, need for continuing therapy, recurring infections, and interference in activities of daily living. Platelet impairment is decided on the fact that there is no bleeding, need for treatment, or interference in activities of daily living. This is in comparison to the outline in Chapter 7, The Hematopoietic System.
Fourth Edition Impairment	58% whole person impairment

Fifth Edition References	Section 9.2 (5th ed, p 192), Table 9-2 (5th ed, p 193); Section 9.4 (5th ed, p 197), Table 9-3 (5th ed, p 200); Section 9.5 (5th ed, p 203), Table 9-4 (5th ed, p 203)
Fifth Edition Summary	Chronic myelocytic leukemia is rated on the basis of white blood cell diseases, anemia, and platelet disorders.
Fifth Edition Impairment	59% whole person impairment
Sixth Edition References	Section 9-2a (6th ed, pp 188-191); Section 9.4a (6th ed, pp 193-195); Section 9-4c (6th ed, pp 195-198); Section 9-5a, (6th ed, pp 202-203), Table 9-5 (6th ed, p 189), Table 9-6 (6th ed, p 194), Table 9-7 (6th ed, p 196), Table 9-9 (6th ed, p 202).
Sixth Edition Summary	Chronic myelocytic leukemia is rated on the basis of leukemia, neutropenia, anemia, and platelet disorders.
Sixth Edition Impairment	60% whole person impairment

Reference

1. American Psychiatric Association. *Diagnostic and Statistical Manual of Mental Disorders*, 4th ed. Washington, DC, American Psychiatric Association;1994.

Chapter 10

The Endocrine System

CASE 10-1

Diabetes Mellitus

Subject: Ms Phillips, a 42-year-old woman.

History: Ms Phillips has had type 1 diabetes mellitus for the past 26 years. Plasma glucose levels were controlled by a combination of regular and isophane (NPH) insulin, twice daily, 18 U before breakfast and 10 U before dinner. A history of occasional urinary tract infections along with an elevated serum creatinine of 2.8 mg/dL prompted a renal evaluation, which revealed a creatinine clearance of 70 L/24 h. The patient generally checked her glucose levels twice a day but rarely needed to supplement her insulin during the day. Her home glucose testing diary showed no episodes of hypoglycemia, and her usual fasting glucose level was in the range of 100 to 140 mg/dL. A recent hemoglobin A_{1c} measurement was 6.7%. She reported moderate dietary difficulties, such as the need for scheduled meals, the need to be discrete regarding her diet, and her caloric requirements.

Current Symptoms: None.

Physical Examination: At the time of her impairment evaluation, Ms Phillips was asymptomatic, her physical examination was unremarkable, and her laboratory evaluation (with the exception of her mildly increased serum creatinine and her decreased creatinine clearance) was unremarkable. She had a recent examination by an ophthalmologist, and no retinopathy was present.

Discussion of Diabetes Mellitus

Fourth Edition Rating

Permanent impairment evaluation was based on Chapter 12, The Endocrine System, Section 12.6, Pancreas (Islets of Langerhans) (4th ed, p 270), and Chapter 11, The Urinary and Reproductive Systems, Section 11.1, Upper Urinary Tract (4th ed, p 249).

Ms Phillips had type 1 diabetes mellitus complicated by nephropathy-related diminished renal function. First, her type 1 diabetes mellitus was rated as class 3 or class 4 (4th ed, p 272). Class 1 and class 2 impairments are for individuals with type 2 diabetes. Because Ms Phillips does not have frequent hyperglycemia or hypoglycemia, her condition is rated as class 3, which yields 10% to 20% whole person impairment (WPI). It is tempting to rate her diabetes at the higher end of the spectrum based on the presence of diabetic nephropathy. However, because her nephropathy is a ratable condition, this would represent an example of "double dipping." Based on the degree of control of her diabetes and her lack of symptoms, the 10% whole person impairment rating is all that can be justified.

Second, Ms Phillips' diabetes mellitus–related nephropathy is rated by means of Table 11-1 (4th ed, p 251). On the basis of her creatinine clearance, her nephropathy rated a class 2 impairment, for which a range of 15% to 34% whole person impairment is provided. As the range of creatinine clearances in this class is 60 to 75 L/min, Ms Phillips' impairment rating should fall at the low end of the range. Extrapolating values yields a value of 22% whole person impairment. (The range of creatinine clearances is 60 to 75 L/min, or 15 units; the range in the impairment is 20%; each decrease in the creatinine clearance by 1 L/24 h is associated with 1.3 percentage points [20/15 = 1.3]; this assumes, of course, a linear progression of impairment with the decline in renal function; in actuality, a logarithmic curve would better depict the relationship; unfortunately, no formula exists to determine the exact impairment value at each level of the creatinine clearance; hence the approximation by extrapolation.) Based on this extrapolation, for a 5 L/24 h drop in the creatinine clearance, there is 5 × 1.3, or 6.5% (rounded to 7%), whole person impairment over the low value in the range, which in this example is 15%. Thus, Ms Phillips has 22% whole person impairment based on her diabetes mellitus–related nephropathy.

With the Combined Values Chart (4th ed, pp 322-324), Ms Phillips' combined whole person impairment due to her type 1 diabetes mellitus complicated by nephropathy is 30% whole person impairment.

Impairment: 30% whole person impairment per the Fourth Edition.

Fifth Edition Rating

Permanent impairment evaluation was based on Chapter 10, The Endocrine System, Section 10.7, Pancreas (Islets of Langerhans) (5th ed, p 230), and Chapter 7, The Urinary and Reproductive Systems, Section 7.3, Upper Urinary Tract (5th ed, p 145).

Ms Phillips has type 1 diabetes mellitus complicated by nephropathy-related diminished renal function. First, her type 1 diabetes mellitus is rated by means of Table 10-8 (5th ed, p 231). Type 1 diabetes mellitus is rated in either class 3 or class 4. Because Ms Phillips does not have frequent hyperglycemia or hypoglycemia, her condition is rated as class 3, which yields an 11% to 20% whole person impairment. As in the discussion earlier regarding the rating using the Fourth Edition, a rating of 11% whole person impairment is chosen. Second, Ms Phillips' diabetes mellitus–related nephropathy is rated by means of Table 7-1 (5th ed, p 146). On the basis of her creatinine clearance, her nephropathy has caused a class 2 impairment, for which a 15% to 34% whole person impairment range is provided. Based on the creatinine clearance of 70 L/24 h, Ms Phillips will reasonably retain 22% whole person impairment due to her diabetes mellitus–related nephropathy.

With the Combined Values Chart (5th ed, p 604), Ms Phillips' combined whole person impairment due to her type 1 diabetes mellitus complicated by nephropathy is 31% whole person impairment.

Impairment: 31% whole person impairment per the Fifth Edition.

Sixth Edition Rating

The *Guides'* approach to the evaluation of impairment due to diabetes mellitus is based on Section 10.7, Pancreas (Islets of Langerhans) (6th ed, p 232). In Table 10-10, Criteria for Rating Impairment due to Diabetes Mellitus (6th ed, p 234), the history is the key factor. Based on the use of insulin, Ms Phillips qualifies for class 2, 3, or 4 impairment. Based on her degree of control and the use of insulin only twice a day, class 2 is chosen. The other two factors are used to modify the default rating of 8% whole person impairment. A normal Hb A_{1c} level is found in classes 1, 2, and 3. To this is added the burden of treatment compliance points (BOTC), an impairment value justified on the basis of the interference in a person's activities of daily living created by the need to be careful with diet and monitor glucose levels and the inconvenience of taking an injection twice a day. According to Section 10.1f, Rules for use of Burden of Treatment Compliance in this chapter (6th ed, p 217), and using Tables 10-2A, 10-2B, 10-3, and 10-4, Ms Phillips has 11 BOTC points (4 points for injectable medication taken twice a day, 5 points for moderate dietary modifications, and 2 points for glucose monitoring performed twice a day). This value is found in class 3 for a diabetic. Thus, the default value is chosen based on the key factor (8% whole person impairment) and the two adjustment factors, one in the same class and the other in a higher class, increases her rating by 1 grade above the default. The final rating is based on a class 2, grade D severity of 9% whole person impairment based on her diabetes.

Section 7.3, Upper Urinary Tract (6th ed, p 132) is used to rate the renal impairment caused by her diabetes. Table 7-2, Criteria for Rating Impairment due to Upper Urinary Tract Disease (6th ed, p 134) identifies the key factor as the history. The historical elements to be considered in identifying the proper class of impairment are discussed on page 131 and delineated in Table 7-2. Ms Phillips has a history of occasional urinary tract infections along with the mildly elevated serum creatinine level, which places her in a class 1 rating for these findings. The physical examination and static test findings would not be rated as class 1. The clinical finding of decreased creatinine clearance of 70 L/24 h would satisfy the criteria for a class 2 rating. Accordingly, the default value can then be adjusted up one grade, as the examination/static test findings is rated in the same class, but the decreased creatinine clearance satisfies one class higher. The final rating is adjusted to a class 1, grade D rating of 10% whole person impairment.

With the Combined Values Chart (6th ed, p 604), Ms Phillips' combined whole person impairment due to her type 1 diabetes mellitus (9% whole person impairment) complicated by nephropathy (10% whole person impairment) is 18% impairment of the whole person.

Impairment: 18% whole person impairment per the Sixth Edition.

Comment on Diabetes Mellitus

The method for rating diabetes mellitus and diabetes mellitus–related complications is similar in the *Guides* Fourth and Fifth Editions, although there is a minor difference. The *Guides* Sixth Edition provides a rating table for diabetes mellitus similar to the Fifth edition, although inclusion criteria are more detailed, including emphasis on interference in a person's daily life created by the need to take medications, the inconvenience of injectable medication over oral preparations, dietary constraints, and glucose monitoring. Five classes of impairment are used in the Sixth Edition rather than the four classes found in the Fifth Edition's Table 10-8 (5th ed, p 231). In addition, the key factor to be utilized to identify a particular impairment class in the Sixth Edition is the history, as outlined in Section 10.1d, Specific Methodology for Impairment Rating in Endocrine Disorders (6th ed, p 216).

When rating diabetes mellitus–related impairment, the evaluator must always consider any impairment caused by diabetes mellitus–related damage to other organs or systems. These problems should be assessed using the chapters dealing with the abnormality and the resulting impairments combined for a final rating caused by an individual's diabetes and its complications.

SUMMARY

Diagnosis	Diabetes mellitus
Fourth Edition References	Section 12.6 (4th ed, p 270); Section 11.1 (4th ed, p 249)
Fourth Edition Summary	First, the diabetes mellitus is rated using Section 12.6 (4th ed, pp 270-274). Second, any impairment caused by diabetes mellitus–related damage to other organs or systems is rated by using the appropriate chapters for the organs and systems involved, then those ratings are combined with the rating for the diabetes mellitus.
Fourth Edition Impairment	30% whole person impairment
Fifth Edition References	Section 10.7 (5th ed, p 230); Section 7.3 (5th ed, p 145), Table 10-8 (5th ed, p 231)
Fifth Edition Summary	First, the diabetes mellitus is rated using Table 10-8 (5th ed, p 231). Second, any impairment caused by diabetes mellitus–related damage to other organs or systems is rated by using the appropriate chapters for the organs and systems involved, then those ratings are combined with the rating for the diabetes mellitus.
Fifth Edition Impairment	31% whole person impairment
Sixth Edition References	Section 10.7 (6th ed, p 232); Table 10-10 (6th ed, p 234); Tables 10-2A, 10-2B, 10-3, and 10-4 (6th ed, pp 217-218); Section 7.3 (6th ed, p 132), Table 7-2 (6th ed, p 134)

Sixth Edition Summary	New paradigm for rating diabetes with emphasis placed on factors such as the interference in a person's daily life created by the need to take medications, the inconvenience of injectable medication over oral preparations, dietary constraints, and glucose monitoring
Sixth Edition Impairment	18% whole person impairment

Chapter 11

Ear, Nose, Throat, and Related Structures

CASE 11-1

Tinnitus

Subject: Mr Bradford, a 42-year-old man.

History: Mr Bradford was injured when a truck tire he was changing exploded, sending a portion of the steel rim into the left temporal region of his head. He was noted to be "dazed," but never unconscious, and immediately complained of pain, loss of hearing, and then intense "roaring" in his head. Bleeding was noted from his left external auditory canal.

He was admitted to a hospital, where physical examination revealed a central left traumatic tympanic membrane perforation and no perceptible hearing on the left side. A computed tomography scan showed an undisplaced horizontal basilar skull fracture, through the petrous ridge. Medical management was conservative, with spontaneous closure of the tympanic membrane perforation.

Mr Bradford's medical history was negative for any preexisting ear disease or hearing loss or any element of tinnitus.

Current Symptoms: Mr Bradford continued to complain of intense roaring in his left ear, which persisted after healing of the tympanic membrane perforation. Attempts to use a hearing aid have been unsuccessful, with persistent complaints of complete left ear hearing loss and constant tinnitus.

Physical Examination: No abnormalities.

Clinical Studies: Serial audiograms demonstrated a profound left sensorineural hearing loss, with poor discrimination. His most recent audiogram was typical of his other postinjury audiograms and showed hearing levels of 90 dB at 500 Hz, 100 dB at 1000 Hz, 100 dB at 2000 Hz, and 105 dB at 3000 Hz. Postinjury audiometric examinations revealed essentially normal hearing in the right ear, with persistence of the left profound sensorineural loss.

Discussion of Tinnitus

Fourth Edition Rating

Permanent impairment evaluation was based on Section 9.1a, Hearing (4th ed, pp 224-228). Mr Bradford's case meets the criteria for permanent impairment on the basis of unilateral hearing loss as well as tinnitus. Hearing impairment is determined by the procedures found on pages 224 to 228. The effects of tinnitus are discussed in Section 4.2b, The Pons-Cerebellum Segment (4th ed, p 146), and Section 9.1, Ear (4th ed, p 224). Tinnitus, in and of itself, is not measurable, but tinnitus in the presence of unilateral hearing loss may impair speech discrimination and adversely influence the ability to carry out daily activities. Therefore, up to 5% may be added to the binaural impairment because of tinnitus to an impairment estimate for unilateral hearing loss.

The calculation of impairment due to hearing loss is discussed specifically on pages 224 to 228 and is based on the individual's binaural hearing. Hearing levels are determined audiometrically for both ears. Hearing levels are measured at 500, 1000, 2000, and 3000 Hz. The four decibel hearing levels for each ear are totaled separately. This results in the DSHL, the decibel sum of the hearing threshold levels. A DSHL of 100 or less is associated with no impairment. DSHL is converted to monaural hearing loss by means of Table 1, Monaural Hearing Loss and Impairment (4th ed, p 225). A DSHL of 368 or greater is associated with 100% monaural hearing loss impairment. In this particular instance, the better-hearing ear had a 0% monaural impairment (DSHL of 100), whereas the worse ear registered almost complete loss, a DSHL of 395. The computation for binaural impairment is then based on Table 2, Computation of Binaural Hearing Impairment (4th ed, pp 226-227); the better (100) and worse (≥368) ear values are combined using the table for a percentage of binaural hearing impairment. Mr Bradford demonstrated a binaural hearing impairment of 16.8%. Because Mr Bradford clearly meets the criteria for unilateral hearing loss, his subjective complaint of tinnitus may be appropriately considered.

According to pages 146 and 224, an impairment percentage of up to 5% may be added to the impairment for unilateral hearing loss. This results in a hearing impairment of 21.8% and translates, with reference to Table 3, Relationship of Binaural Hearing Impairment to Impairment of the Whole Person (4th ed, p 228), to 8% whole person impairment.

Impairment: 8% whole person impairment per the Fourth Edition.

Fifth Edition Rating

Permanent impairment evaluation was based on Section 11.2a, Criteria for Rating Impairment Due to Hearing Loss (5th ed, pp 246-251). Mr Bradford's case meets the criteria for permanent impairment on the basis of unilateral hearing loss as well as tinnitus. Hearing impairment is determined by the procedures found on pages 246 to 251. Tinnitus is discussed in Section 11.2a, Criteria for Rating Impairment Due to Hearing Loss (5th ed, p 246). Tinnitus in the presence of unilateral or bilateral hearing loss may impair speech discrimination and adversely influence the ability to carry out daily activities. Therefore, up to 5% may be added to the binaural impairment because of tinnitus to an impairment estimate for unilateral hearing loss.

The calculation of impairment due to hearing loss is discussed specifically on pages 246 to 251 and is based on the individual's binaural hearing. Hearing levels are determined audiometrically for both ears. Hearing levels are measured at 500, 1000, 2000, and 3000 Hz. The four decibel hearing levels for each ear are totaled separately to produce the DSHL. A DSHL of 100 or less is associated with no impairment. DSHL is converted to monaural hearing loss by means of Table 11-1, Monaural Hearing Loss and Impairment (5th ed, p 247). A DSHL of 368 or greater is associated with 100% monaural hearing loss impairment. In this instance, the better-hearing ear had a 0% monaural impairment (DSHL of 100), whereas the worse ear registered almost complete loss, that is, a DSHL of 395. The computation for binaural impairment is then based on Table 11-2, Computation of Binaural Hearing Impairment (5th ed, pp 248-249); the better (100) and worse (≥370) ear values are combined using the table, for a percentage of binaural hearing impairment. Mr Bradford demonstrated a binaural hearing impairment of 16.7%. Because Mr Bradford clearly meets the criteria for unilateral hearing loss, his subjective complaint of tinnitus may be appropriately considered. According to page 246, an impairment percentage of up to 5% may be added to the impairment for unilateral hearing loss. This results in a hearing impairment of 21.8%. This translates, with reference to Table 11-3, Relationship of Binaural Hearing Impairment to Impairment of the Whole Person (5th ed, p 254), to 8% whole person impairment.

Impairment: 8% impairment of the whole person per the Fifth Edition.

Sixth Edition Rating

Permanent impairment evaluation was based on Section 11.2, Hearing and Tinnitus (6th ed, pp 248-260). Mr Bradford's case meets the criteria for permanent impairment on the basis of unilateral hearing loss as well as tinnitus. Hearing impairment is determined by the procedures found in Section 11.2a, Evaluation of Hearing Impairment (6th ed, pp 248-249), and Section 11.2c, Criteria for Rating Impairment due to Hearing Loss (6th ed, pp 249-250). Tinnitus is discussed in Section 11.2b, Tinnitus (6th ed, p 249). Tinnitus in the presence of unilateral or bilateral hearing loss may impair speech discrimination and adversely influence the ability to carry out daily activities. Therefore, up to 5% may be added to a measurable binaural hearing impairment for tinnitus.

Hearing levels are determined audiometrically for both ears, as described in Section 11.2d Audiometric Measurements to Determine Hearing Impairment (6th ed, p 250). Hearing levels are measured at 500, 1000, 2000, and 3000 Hz. The four decibel hearing levels for each ear are totaled separately to produce the DSHL. A DSHL of 100 or less is associated with no impairment. DSHL is converted to monaural hearing loss by means of Table 11-1, Monaural Hearing Loss and Impairment (6th ed, p 250). A DSHL of 355 or greater is associated with 100% monaural hearing loss impairment. In this instance, the better-hearing ear had a 0% monaural impairment (DSHL of 100), whereas the worse ear registered almost complete loss. The computation for binaural impairment is then based on Table 11-2, Computation of Binaural Hearing Impairment (6th ed, pp 252-253); the better (100) and worse (≥370) ear values are combined using the table, for a percentage of binaural hearing impairment. Mr Bradford demonstrated a binaural hearing impairment of 16.8%. An impairment percentage of up to 5% for tinnitus may be added to the impairment for unilateral hearing loss. Giving the patient the benefit of the doubt, the maximum is assigned. This results in a hearing impairment of 21.8%.

This translates, with reference to Table 11-3, Relationship of Binaural Hearing Impairment to Impairment of the Whole Person (6th ed, p 254), to 8% whole person impairment.

Impairment: 8% whole person impairment per the Sixth Edition.

Comment on Tinnitus

This patient clearly had a documented case of injury that involved the hearing mechanism, with appropriate physical findings of the ear itself. This was supported by radiographic confirmation of a basilar skull fracture through the auditory mechanism. These findings serve to confirm the anatomic site of injury, and subsequent audiometric testing is considered objective evidence of true loss. Tinnitus is well recognized as the logical and subsequent result of acoustic trauma and sensorineural hearing loss. In this instance, the history, physical findings, and objective testing are all considered reasonable and appropriate to the additional maximum percentage impairment due to tinnitus.

The method for rating impairment due to tinnitus is the same in the *Guides* Fourth, Fifth, and Sixth Editions.

SUMMARY

Diagnosis	Unilateral sensorineural hearing loss and tinnitus secondary to acoustic trauma and basilar skull fracture
Fourth Edition References	Table 1 (4th ed, p 225), Table 2 (4th ed, pp 226-227), Table 3 (4th ed, p 228)
Fourth Edition Summary	History, physical findings compatible with injury, confirming radiographic and audiometric findings. Consistent anatomic site of injury, radiographic findings, serial audiometric findings for permanence.
Fourth Edition Impairment	8% whole person impairment
Fifth Edition References	Section 11.2a (5th ed, pp 246-251), Table 11-1 (5th ed, p 247), Table 11-2 (5th ed, p 248), Table 11-3 (5th ed, p 250)
Fifth Edition Summary	History, physical findings compatible with injury, confirming radiographic and audiometric findings. Consistent anatomic site of injury, radiographic findings, serial audiometric findings for permanence.
Fifth Edition Impairment	8% whole person impairment
Sixth Edition References	Section 11.2 (6th ed, pp 248-260), Table 11-1 (6th ed, p 250), Table 11-2 (6th ed, pp 252-253), Table 11-3 (6th ed, p 254)
Sixth Edition Summary	History, physical findings compatible with injury, confirming radiographic and audiometric findings. Consistent anatomic site of injury, radiographic findings, serial audiometric findings for permanence.
Sixth Edition Impairment	8% whole person impairment

CASE 11-2

Occupational Hearing Loss

Subject: Mr Thomas, a 64-year-old man.

History: Mr Thomas was a machine operator in a noisy ammunition plant. He had started employment in 1984, and an audiogram had been performed at that time. Previously, he had worked for many years in a noisy steel company making gaskets. He admitted he noted some hearing loss at times in the past; however, he was vague in describing these difficulties. He had also been exposed to rifle and machine gun firing during 4 years of service in the Marines. He was in good health and denied having diabetes, peripheral vascular disease, any family history of hearing loss, ear infections, or other common causes of hearing loss. He claimed his hearing had gotten worse between 1984 and 1997 even though he used hearing protectors regularly.

Audiometry results were indicative of a noise-induced hearing loss affecting chiefly the outer cochlear hair cells. The effective use of hearing protectors should have prevented additional hearing loss during Mr Thomas' present job, but records showed that the hearing protector program was not monitored and enforced adequately. It was possible that presbyacusis contributed to the progression of his hearing loss, but the compensation judge ruled that Mr Thomas' loss was work related. Although the Occupational Safety and Health Administration (OSHA) permits correcting the measured hearing loss for aging, for this case it was assumed that the Workers' Compensation system requested his current impairment rating "as is."

Current Symptoms: Mr Thomas complained that he had developed more hearing trouble during the past 6 years and had communication difficulty at home, in restaurants, when driving a car, and in noisy environments. These complaints were consistent with his substantial high-frequency hearing loss that had progressively worsened during the past 13 years.

Physical Examination: Unremarkable.

Clinical Studies: Noise measurements showed that he had been exposed to a time-weighted average of more than 96 dBA, which was much louder than the 90 dBA considered safe by OSHA noise amendment of 1973. Mr Thomas' audiologic tests showed a speech reception of 20 dB and a discrimination score of 86%, which were consistent with a diagnosis of noise-induced hearing loss. His audiometric pattern of binaural high-frequency hearing loss starting in the 3000- and 4000-Hz area was also consistent with noise-induced hearing loss.

Mr Thomas denied having tinnitus or vertigo. Physical examination of the ear, nose, and throat showed no abnormalities, and the eardrums appeared normal.

The following table shows some of the audiograms performed between 1984 (preemployment) and 1997. The thresholds were consistent, and the testing appeared to be valid and reliable. The tests were done according to the requirements of the OSHA noise amendment of 1983.

	Left Ear (Thousands)							Right Ear (Thousands)						
Test Date	**0.5**	**1**	**2**	**3**	**4**	**6**	**8**	**0.5**	**1**	**2**	**3**	**4**	**6**	**8**
10-24-84	20	20	10	75	85	75	75	10	10	15	50	45	30	15
01-08-86	20	20	10	75	80	75	70	05	05	15	50	50	35	15
04-29-87	20	15	15	75	90	75	70	10	05	10	30	55	25	10
08-30-90	15	15	30	75	80	80	75	10	10	10	55	50	25	10
03-31-95	15	10	55	80	80	70	65	05	05	20	60	55	40	20
05-18-95	15	10	55	75	80	75	60	10	00	20	55	60	35	15
05-08-96	20	15	60	80	80	80	80	20	10	55	60	60	70	55
06-13-96	15	10	55	80	80	80	65	10	05	50	55	65	50	50
05-16-97	20	15	60	80	85	85	70	25	15	60	60	65	65	60

Discussion of Occupational Hearing Loss

Fourth Edition Rating

Permanent impairment evaluation is based on Section 9.1a, Hearing (4th ed, p 224), and Section 9.1b, Objective Techniques for Determining Hearing Impairments (4th ed, pp 225-228). The amount of impairment sustained in 1997 is calculated from Mr Thomas' audiogram of May 16, 1997, and is based on Table 2, Computation of Binaural Hearing Impairment (4th ed, p 226). The decibel sum of the hearing threshold levels (DSHL) is determined by adding the four decibel hearing levels at 500, 1000, 2000, and 3000 Hz for each ear separately. The DSHL for his left ear is 175 (20 + 15 + 60 + 80), and the DSHL for his right ear is 160 (25 + 15 + 60 + 60).

The computation for binaural impairment is then based on Table 2, Computation of Binaural Hearing Impairment (4th ed, pp 226-227); the

Chapter 11

better (160) and worse (175) ear values are combined using the table, for a percentage of binaural hearing impairment. Mr Thomas has a binaural hearing impairment of 23.4%. This translates, with reference to Table 3, Relationship of Binaural Hearing Impairment to Impairment of the Whole Person (4th ed, p 228), to 8% whole person impairment.

Impairment: 8% whole person impairment per the Fourth Edition.

Fifth Edition Rating

Permanent impairment evaluation is based on Section 11.2, The Ear (5th ed, p 247), and Section 11.2a, Criteria for Rating Impairment Due to Hearing Loss (5th ed, pp 246-251). The amount of impairment sustained in 1997 is calculated from the patient's audiogram of May 16, 1997, and is based on Table 11-2, Computation of Binaural Hearing Impairment (5th ed, pp 248-249). The DSHL is determined by adding the four decibel hearing levels at 500, 1000, 2000, and 3000 Hz for each ear separately. The DSHL for his left ear is 175 (20 + 15 + 60 + 80), and the DSHL for his right ear is 160 (25 + 15 + 60 + 60).

The computation for binaural impairment is then based on Table 11-2, Computation of Binaural Hearing Impairment (5th ed, pp 248-249); the better (160) and worse (175) ear values are combined using the table, for a percentage of binaural hearing impairment. Mr Thomas has a binaural hearing impairment of 23.4%. This translates, with reference to Table 11-3, Relationship of Binaural Hearing Impairment to Impairment of the Whole Person (5th ed, p 250), to 8% whole person impairment.

Impairment: 8% whole person impairment per the Fifth Edition.

Sixth Edition Rating

Permanent impairment evaluation is based on Section 11.2, Hearing and Tinnitus (6th ed, pp 248-260), Section 11.2a, Evaluation of Hearing Impairment (6th ed, pp 248-249), Section 11.2c, Criteria for Rating Impairment Due to Hearing Loss (6th ed, pp 249-250), Section 11.2d, Audiometric Measurements to Determine Hearing Impairment (6th ed, p 250), and Section 11.2f, Evaluation of Binaural Hearing Impairment (6th ed, pp 251-254).

The amount of impairment sustained in 1997 is calculated from the patient's audiogram of May 16, 1997, and is based on Table 11-2, Computation of Binaural Hearing Impairment (6th ed, pp 252-253). The DSHL is determined by adding the four decibel hearing levels at 500, 1000, 2000, and

3000 Hz for each ear separately. The DSHL for his left ear is 175 (20 + 15 + 60 + 80), and the DSHL for his right ear is 160 (25 + 15 + 60 + 60).

The computation for binaural impairment is then based on Table 11-2, Computation of Binaural Hearing Impairment (6th ed, pp 252); the better (160) and worse (175) ear values are combined using the table, for a percentage of binaural hearing impairment. Mr Thomas has a binaural hearing impairment of 23.4%. This translates, with reference to Table 11-3, Relationship of Binaural Hearing Impairment to Impairment of the Whole Person (6th ed, p 254), to 8% whole person impairment.

Impairment: 8% whole person impairment per the Sixth Edition.

Comment on Occupational Hearing Loss

The process of assessing hearing impairment is the same in the Fifth Edition as it was in the Fourth Edition.

This case exemplifies the importance of understanding the requirements of the compensation system for which the rating is performed. Specifically, because Mr Thomas was employed in Pennsylvania and had a recorded hearing loss before his current employment, the company is held legally responsible only for the amount of hearing loss acquired during his employment. In this case, this is determined by subtracting the threshold levels in 1984 from those in 1997 to obtain the amount of hearing loss for which the company is liable. When this is performed, Mr Thomas' claim entitles him to 0% hearing impairment due to occupational hearing loss acquired at the ammunition company. If impairment were apportioned, however, by the difference in the level of his whole person permanent impairment from 1984 to 1997, his incremental impairment would be 8% whole person impairment, because he had no ratable impairment in 1984. On the basis of his audiograms of October 24, 1984, he had a DSHL on the left of 125 and a DSHL on the right of 85.

SUMMARY

Diagnosis	Occupational hearing loss
Fourth Edition References	Section 9.1a (4th ed, p 224), Section 9.1b (4th ed, pp 225-228), Table 2 (4th ed, p 226), Table 3 (4th ed, p 228)
Fourth Edition Summary	History; ear, nose, and throat physical examination; audiograms; audiometric studies; noise measurements. Validity of audiometric tests is verified, and history is applied to criteria for differential diagnosis. Hearing levels at 500, 1000, 2000, and 3000 Hz are added, then corresponding impairment is determined.
Fourth Edition Impairment	8% whole person impairment
Fifth Edition References	Section 11.2 (5th ed, p 247); Section 11.2a (5th ed, pp 246-251), Table 11-2 (5th ed, pp 248-249), Table 11-3 (5th ed, p 250)
Fifth Edition Summary	History; ear, nose, and throat physical examination; audiograms; audiometric studies; noise measurements. Validity of audiometric tests is verified, and history is applied to criteria for differential diagnosis. Hearing levels at 500, 1000, 2000, and 3000 Hz are added, then corresponding impairment is determined.
Fifth Edition Impairment	8% whole person impairment
Sixth Edition References	Section 11.2 (6th ed, pp 248-260), Table 11-2 (6th ed, pp 252-253), Table 11-3 (6th ed, p 254)
Sixth Edition Summary	History; ear, nose, and throat physical examination; audiograms; audiometric studies; noise measurements. Validity of audiometric tests is verified, and history is applied to criteria for differential diagnosis. Hearing levels at 500, 1000, 2000, and 3000 Hz are added, then corresponding impairment is determined.
Sixth Edition Impairment	8% whole person impairment

Chapter 12

The Visual System

CASE 12-1

Alkali Burns to the Eyes

Subject: Mr Johnson, a 32-year-old man.

History: Mr Johnson was injured when lye (sodium hydroxide 20%) splashed on his hands and face and in his eyes. He was not wearing safety goggles. The accident occurred in a chemical laboratory where deluge showers and eye wash stations were available less than 30 m from where he was working. He was immediately disrobed by his coworkers and led to the deluge shower, where the external surface of his body was irrigated. He then tried to irrigate his eyes at the eye wash station but was unable to reach the external surface of his eyeballs and the inner surface of his eyelids because of severe blepharospasm and ocular pain.

The first responder arrived on the scene and attempted to irrigate the eyeballs, without good results. Mr Johnson was then transported to the closest emergency center, arriving approximately 15 minutes after the injury. The emergency department physician was able to irrigate the eyes after performing a partial bilateral facial nerve block. Mr Johnson was then transferred to the regional ophthalmologist, arriving at the office approximately 2 hours after the chemical injury.

Examination by the ophthalmologist disclosed that the lye had penetrated the cornea and conjunctiva into the anterior segment of both eyes, producing severe damage. According to a diagnostic classification (modified by Ballen and Roper Hall), the right eye demonstrated a grade 2 injury, where the cornea was hazy with visible iris details and ischemia of less than one-third of the limbus; the intraocular pressure was elevated to 28 mm Hg. The left eye showed a grade 4 injury, with an opaque cornea and no view of the iris or pupil; there was ischemia of more than one-half the limbus with ischemic necrosis of the proximal conjunctiva and superficial sclera. The intraocular pressure of the left eye was 35 mm Hg. Visual acuity with correction was 20/100 in the right eye and 1/1000 in the left eye.

The corneal epithelium was debrided to allow proper re-epithelialization and decrease the potential for infection. Topical corticosteroids and glaucoma medication were immediately prescribed.

Under treatment, the right eye completely re-epithelialized. However, persisting epitheliopathy required prolonged use of a lubricant.

The left eye showed no re-epithelialization. Additional topical medications were started. Since there was still no epithelialization at 21 days after the injury, surgical intervention was necessary. A limbal stem cell transplantation (limbal autograft from the right eye) resulted in some improvement, but because of the presence of a persistent corneal ulcer, a large penetrating keratoplasty (11-12 mm) was performed. The corneal transplantation had to be performed three times before a satisfactory take was obtained. The intraocular pressure returned to normal (18 mm Hg) bilaterally under medication.

Mr Johnson was seen for an examination approximately 3 years after the initial chemical injury.

Current Symptoms: He reported some difficulties with vision and frustration with the treatment regimen for his glaucoma and dry eyes; otherwise he was asymptomatic.

Physical Examination: General examination of the face, external eyelids, and hands showed an essentially normal epithelium with virtually no scarring.

Clinical Studies: The best-corrected visual acuity in the right eye was 20/30 for distance and 20/30 for near. Visual acuity in the left eye was 20/200 for distance and 20/100 for near. The best-corrected binocular visual acuity was 20/20 –2 for distance and 20/30 for near. Intraocular pressure in both eyes measured by applanation tonometry was normal (18 mm Hg) under medication.

Slit-lamp examination of the right eye showed stromal haze in the peripheral cornea and subepithelial vascularization from the 3- to 6-o'clock positions.

The right cornea was re-epithelialized with no fluorescein stain, but punctate staining was seen with rose bengal dye. A surgical scar of the limbal area of the cornea was evident from the 7- to 12-o'clock positions, where stem cells had been removed for transplantation to the left eye.

Slit-lamp examination of the left eye showed a clear corneal transplant with total re-epithelialization and peripheral subepithelial vascularization for 360°. Visual field examination with a Goldmann perimeter with a III4e stimulus was normal in each eye.

Summary: Findings relevant to the impairment rating were as follows:

- Status 3 years after chemical eye injury in both eyes and three corneal transplants in the left eye
- Best-corrected visual acuity: right eye, 20/30; left eye, 20/200; binocular, 20/25
- Visual fields: normal in both eyes
- Other findings: normal intraocular pressure under medication; no other factors affecting visual functioning

Discussion of Alkali Burns to the Eyes

This case describes a scenario that is far too common: a chemical injury resulting from failure to wear required personal safety equipment (gloves, eye and face protection, and a body apron). At the time of evaluation, the patient was left with glaucoma, controlled by topical medication (beta-blockers) in both eyes. He also had degeneration of the conjunctiva leading to dry eyes. Mr Johnson will need to use artificial tears for the rest of his life.

Fourth Edition Rating

Permanent impairment evaluation was based on Section 8.1, Central Visual Acuity (4th ed, pp 210-211).

Right Eye

The acuity values for distance and for near in the right eye are converted to impairment ratings by using Table 3, Loss (in %) of Central Vision in a Single Eye (4th ed, p 212). Since there is no aphakia, the upper numbers of each number pair apply.

Distance acuity: 20/30 Near acuity: 20/30 (14/21) → Impairment: 8%.

Since the visual field is normal, there is no adjustment for field loss.

Left Eye
The acuity values for distance and for near in the left eye are converted to impairment ratings by using Table 3, Loss (in %) of Central Vision in a Single Eye (4th ed, p 212). Since there is no aphakia, the upper numbers of each number pair apply.

Distance acuity: 20/200 Near acuity: 20/100 (14/70) → Impairment: 83%.

Section 8.2, Visual Fields (4th ed, p 211), is referenced to determine that the visual field is normal and, therefore, there is no adjustment for field loss.

Ocular Motility
Section 8.3, Abnormal Ocular Motility and Binocular Diplopia (4th ed, p 217), is referenced to determine that there is no rating for motility as there is no impaired motility.

Visual System Impairment
Section 8.4, Steps in Determining Impairment of the Visual System and of the Whole Person (4th ed, pp 217-222), explains the process for calculating impairment. Use Table 7, Visual System Impairment for Both Eyes (4th ed, pp 219-220), to combine 8% and 83% loss → visual aystem impairment: 27%

Whole Person Impairment
Table 6, Impairment of the Visual System as It Relates to Impairment of the Whole Person (4th ed, p 218), is used to convert the 27% visual system impairment to 25% whole person impairment (WPI).

Impairment: 25% whole person impairment per the Fourth Edition.

Comments
Page 209 states, "If an ocular disturbance . . . interferes with visual function and is not reflected in diminished visual acuity . . . the physician may *combine* an additional 5 to 10% impairment . . ." Since the dry eye and the glaucoma medication do not interfere with visual functioning beyond the visual acuity loss from presumed normal to 20/30, such an additional adjustment is not warranted.

The discrepancy between the 20/200 distance acuity and the 20/100 near acuity in the left eye can probably be explained by the use of a traditional chart, which has no lines between 20/100 and 20/200. In the Fifth (and Sixth) Editions, the use of an ETDRS-type chart with lines at 20/125 and 20/160 is recommended. Alternatively, the chart may be brought to 10 ft, where 20/100, 20/125, 20/160, and 20/200 can be measured as 10/50, 10/60, 10/80 and 10/100.

Changes From the Fourth to the Fifth Edition

While the principal parameters for evaluation remain visual acuity and visual field, the changes from the Fourth to the Fifth Edition were such that ratings from the Fourth Edition (or before) cannot be compared to ratings from the Fifth (or Sixth) Edition.

The Fourth Edition (and earlier ones) utilized the Visual Efficiency Scale (VES), which was based on employability estimates in 1925. Evaluation in the Fifth (and Sixth) Edition is based on the ability to perform Activities of Daily Living (ADL) and on the Functional Vision Score (FVS), which is an estimate of that ability. On the VES a visual acuity reduction to 20/200 was considered to imply an 80% reduction in employability in 1925; on the FVS, 20/200 is considered to imply a 50% reduction in ADL ability. The FVS is better aligned with ability reductions in other organ systems and with actual ADL ability.

Over various revisions the rules in the Fourth Edition had collected some internal inconsistencies; these were eliminated in the Fifth (and Sixth) Edition.

Principles of Assessment

The FVS differs from the VES in how the data from right and left eye are combined. The VES considered the two eyes as independent organs and did not consider binocular vision. The FVS emphasizes binocular vision since this is the way persons function in ADL.

Section 12.4b, Individual Adjustments (5th ed, p 297; 6th ed, pp 305-306), provides guidance on adjustments. The VES provided special scales for diplopia and aphakia, but not for any other visual conditions. The FVS has no such special scales, but allows an adjustment of up to 15 points for any well-documented factors that affect visual functioning but that are not reflected in a reduction of visual acuity or visual field.

Fifth Edition Rating

Visual Acuity

Calculation of the Visual Acuity Scores (VAS) is outlined in Section 12.2 (5th ed, pp 281-286). The acuity values for the right eye, the left eye, and binocular vision (both eyes open) are each converted to VAS as referenced in Table 12-2, Impairment of Visual Acuity (5th ed, p 284). Using Table 12-3, Calculation of the Acuity-Related Impairment Rating (5th ed, p 284), the three VAS values are then combined as a weighted average to a single Functional Acuity Score (FAS) for the person.

	Visual Acuity	VAS	Weight	Result
Right eye	20/30	90	×1	90
Left eye	20/200	50	×1	50
Both eyes	20/25	95	×3	285
FAS				425 /5 = 85

Visual Field

Determination of visual field impairment is discussed in Section 12.3, Impairment of the Visual Field (5th ed, pp 287-295). The Goldmann visual fields for each eye are reported as normal. Therefore, the Visual Field Score (VFS) for each eye and the Functional Field Score (FFS) for the person are all 100. Table 12-5, Impairment of the Visual Field, and Table 12-6, Calculation of the Field-Related Impairment Rating (5th ed, p 289), are referenced to make this determination.

Other Factors

Section 12.4b, Individual Adjustments (5th ed, p 297), is referenced to determine whether any adjustments are appropriate. Although Mr Johnson reported frustration with his glaucoma regimen, he did not report that this interfered with his overall visual functioning. Therefore, no adjustments are necessary.

Functional Vision Score

Section 12.4a, Calculating an Impairment for the Visual System (5th ed, p 296), is referenced to calculate the FVS. The FVS is calculated as (FAS × FFS)/100. In this case, (85 × 100)/100 = 85.

Visual System Impairment Rating

Section 12.4, Impairment of the Visual System (5th ed, p 296), is referenced to calculate the visual system impairment rating (VSI). It is calculated as 100 – FVS. In this case, 100 − 85 = 15.

Whole Person Impairment Rating

Section 12.4c, Impairment of the Whole Person (5th ed, p 298), and Table 12-10 (5th ed, p 298) are used to determine that the whole person impairment rating is the same as the VSI if VSI < 50. In this case it remains 15%.

Impairment: 15% whole person impairment per the Fifth Edition.

Sixth Edition Rating

The rating system for the Sixth Edition is unchanged from the Fifth Edition.

Visual Acuity

Calculation of the VAS is outlined in Section 12.2, Impairment of Visual Activty (6th ed, pp 285-293). The acuity values for the right eye, the left eye, and binocular vision (both eyes open) are each converted to a VAS as referenced in Table 12-2, Impairment of Visual Acuity (6th ed, p 288). Using Table 12-3, Calculation of the Acuity-Related Impairment Rating (6th ed, p 289), the three VAS values are then combined as a weighted average to a single FAS for the person.

	Visual Acuity	VAS	Weight	Result
Right eye	20/30	90	×1	90
Left eye	20/200	50	×1	50
Both eyes	20/25	95	×3	285
FAS				425 /5 = 85

Visual Field

Determination of visual field impairment is discussed in Section 12.3, Impairment of the Visual Field (6th ed, pp 293-303). The Goldmann visual fields for each eye are reported as normal. Therefore, the VFS for each eye and the FFS for the person are all 100. Table 12-5, Impairment of Visual Field, and Table 12-6, Calculation of the Field Radius to Field Score (6th ed, p 296), are referenced to make this determination.

Other Factors

Section 12.4b, Individual Adjustments (6th ed, pp 305-306), is referenced to determine whether any adjustments are appropriate. Although Mr Johnson reported frustration with his glaucoma regimen, he did not report that this interfered with his overall visual functioning. Therefore, no adjustments are necessary.

Functional Vision Score

Section 12.4a, Calculating an Impairment Rating for the Visual System (6th ed, pp 303-304), is referenced to calculate the FVS. The FVS is calculated as (FAS × FFS)/100. In this case, (85 × 100)/100 = 85.

Visual System Impairment Rating

Section 12.4, Impairment of the Visual System (6th ed, pp 303-309), is referenced to calculate the VSI. It is calculated as 100 – FVS. In this case, 100 – 85 = 15.

Whole Person Impairment Rating
Section 12.4c, Impairment of the Whole Person (6th ed, p 306), and Table 12-10, Classification of Impairment of the Visual System and of the Whole Person (6th ed, p 307) are used to determine that the WPI is the same as the VSI if VSI < 50. In this case it remains 15%.

Impairment: 15% whole person impairment per the Sixth Edition.

SUMMARY

Diagnosis	Alkali burns to both eyes
Fourth Edition References	Table 3 (4th ed, p 212), Table 5 (4th ed, p 214), Table 6 (4th ed, p 218), Table 7 (4th ed, pp 219-220)
Fourth Edition Summary	History, best-corrected visual acuity, visual fields, tonometry, slit-lamp examination (including use of fluorescein and rose bengal dyes to determine the integrity of the epithelium). Schirmer strip test (for determination of the volume of tears produced).
Fourth Edition Impairment	25% WPI (equivalent to 20/50 acuity in both eyes)
Fifth Edition References	Section 12.2 (5th ed, pp 281-286), Section 12.3 (5th ed, pp 287-295), Section 12.4 (5th ed, pp 296-298), Tables 12-2, 12-3, 12-4 (5th ed, pp 284, 285), Tables 12-5, 12-6 (5th ed, p 289), Table 12-10 (5th ed, p 298)
Fifth Edition Summary	History, best-corrected visual acuity, visual fields, tonometry, slit-lamp examination (including use of fluorescein and rose bengal dyes to determine the integrity of the epithelium). Schirmer strip test (for determination of the volume of tears produced).
Fifth Edition Impairment	15% WPI (equivalent to 20/40 acuity in both eyes). This is a Class 2 (10–29% WPI) impairment.

Sixth Edition References	Section 12.2 (6th ed, pp 285-293), Section 12.3 (6th ed, pp 293-303), Tables 12-2, 12-3, 12-4 (6th ed, pp 288-290), Tables 12-5, 12-6 (6th ed, p 296), Section 12.4 (pp 303-309), Table 12-10 (6th ed, p 307)
Sixth Edition Summary	History, best-corrected visual acuity, visual fields, tonometry, slit-lamp examination (including use of fluorescein and rose bengal dyes to determine the integrity of the epithelium). Schirmer strip test (for determination of the volume of tears produced).
Sixth Edition Impairment	15% WPI (equivalent to 20/40 acuity in both eyes). This is a Class 2 (10–29% WPI) impairment.

CASE 12-2

Blunt Injury to the Eye

Subject: Mr Dobson, a 43-year-old man.

History: Mr Dobson, a carpenter, sustained a blunt injury to the left eye when he was hit by the end of a 2 × 4-inch timber on a construction site. Mr Dobson was not wearing the personal protective equipment required. He immediately noted pain, a decrease in visual acuity in the left eye, and double vision, especially when looking up. Before this injury he had had no difficulties with his vision.

Mr Dobson was immediately referred to the regional ophthalmologist, who found binocular best-corrected visual acuity of 20/10 at distance; right eye, 20/10 at distance and 20/25 (14/18) at near; and left eye, 20/400 at distance and 20/200 (14/140) at near. Slit-lamp examination showed a subconjunctival hemorrhage and a hyphema. Mr Dobson experienced diplopia in up-gaze, especially when looking up and to the right. The left eye showed limited movement up and to the right. Mr Dobson was prescribed strict bedrest; the hyphema decreased and the subconjunctival hemorrhage became minimal. A computed tomographic scan (CT) and magnetic resonance imaging (MRI) disclosed the presence of a fracture of the floor of the left orbit and the roof of the left maxillary sinus. There was minimal entrapment of the inferior oblique muscle in the fracture site. Forced ductions performed on the left eye showed minimal restriction on elevation of the left eye. The intraocular tension was initially elevated in the left eye but returned to normal (18 ± 2 mm Hg) after resolution of the blood in the anterior chamber of the eye. Ophthalmoscopy showed a peripheral retinal tear at the 2-o'clock position with posterior vitreous traction. Cryotherapy of the retinal tear was performed without complications. Surgical correction of the orbital floor fracture was deemed unnecessary.

Examination: A detailed examination 1 year after the blunt injury to the left eye and orbit gave the following findings:

- Binocular, best-corrected visual acuity at distance was 20/15. Monocular visual acuity in the right eye was 20/15 at distance and 20/25 (14/18) at near; in the left eye it was 20/400 at distance and 20/60 (14/40) at near.
- The intraocular pressure was 20 mm Hg (within normal limits) in both eyes.

- Slit-lamp examination of the anterior segment, including gonioscopy, was normal, except for an increase in pigment on the posterior surface of the cornea, anterior chamber angle, and anterior surface of the lens.
- There was a minimal posterior subcapsular traumatic cataract in the left eye.
- Slit-lamp examination of the ocular fundus with a three-mirror contact lens showed a posterior vitreous detachment with traction on and scarring of the previous retinal tear site at the 2-o'clock position, but no retinal detachment.
- Visual field testing with the Goldmann perimeter with the III4e isopter white test object showed a 20° peripheral restriction in the upper right quadrant of the left eye, corresponding to the area of cryotherapy. The right eye was normal. There was still minimal diplopia with gaze upward beyond 45° with simultaneous right gaze beyond 60°.

Summary: Findings relevant to the impairment rating were as follows:

- Status 1 year after blunt injury to the left eye and repair of a retinal tear.
- Best corrected visual acuity: right eye, 20/15; left eye, 20/40; binocular, 20/15
- Visual fields: slight peripheral reduction in the left eye
- Other findings: diplopia in extreme gaze (upward, to the right). No other factors affecting visual functioning

Discussion of Blunt Injury to the Eye

Fourth Edition Rating

Permanent impairment evaluation was based on Section 8.1, Central Visual Acuity (4th ed, pp 210-211).

Right Eye

The acuity values for distance and for near in the right eye are converted to impairment ratings by using Table 3, Loss (in %) of Central Vision in a Single Eye (4th ed, p 212). Since there is no aphakia, the upper numbers of each number pair apply.

Distance acuity: 20/15 Near acuity: 20/25 (14/18) → Impairment: 0%.

Section 8.2, Visual Fields (4th ed, p 211), is referenced to determine that the visual field is normal and, therefore, there is no adjustment for field loss.

The right eye impairment is 0%

Left Eye

The acuity values for distance and for near in the left eye are converted to impairment ratings by using Table 3, Loss (in %) of Central Vision in a Single Eye (4th ed, p 212). Since there is no aphakia, the upper numbers of each number pair apply.

Distance acuity: 20/400 Near acuity: 20/60 (14/40) → Impairment: 72%.

Section 8.2, Visual Fields (4th ed, p 211), is referenced to determine that the visual field is reduced. A 20° restriction in the upper right meridian means a 4% loss.

Ocular Motility

Section 8.3, Abnormal Ocular Motility and Binocular Diplopia (4th ed, p 217), is referenced to determine that ocular motility is reduced. However, the reduction is beyond 45°, so it does not generate an impairment rating.

The left eye impairment is calculated by using the Combined Values Chart (4th ed, pp 322-324).

Acuity loss: 72% Field loss: 4% Motility loss: 0% → Combined loss: 73%

Visual System Impairment

Section 8.4, Steps in Determining Impairment of the Visual System and of the Whole Person (4th ed, pp 217-222), explains the process for calculating impairment. Use Table 7, Visual System Impairment for Both Eyes (4th ed, pp 219-220), to combine 0% and 73% loss → Visual System Impairment: 18%.

Whole Person Impairment

Table 6, Impairment of the Visual System as It Relates to Impairment of the Whole Person (4th ed, p 218), is used to convert 18% visual system impairment to 17% whole person impairment.

Impairment: 17% whole person impairment per the Fourth Edition.

Changes From the Fourth to the Fifth Edition

While the principal parameters for evaluation remain visual acuity and visual field, the changes from the Fourth to the Fifth Edition were such that ratings from the Fourth Edition (or before) cannot be compared to ratings from the Fifth (or Sixth) Edition.

The Fourth Edition (and earlier ones) utilized the VES, which was based on employability estimates in 1925. Evaluation in the Fifth and Sixth Editions is based on the ability to perform ADLs and on the FVS, which is an estimate of that ability. On the VES a visual acuity reduction to 20/200 was considered to imply an 80% reduction in employability in 1925; on the FVS, 20/200 is considered to imply a 50% reduction in ADL ability. The FVS is better aligned with ability reductions in other organ systems and with actual ADL ability.

Over various revisions the rules in the Fourth Edition had collected some internal inconsistencies; these were eliminated in the Fifth and Sixth Editions.

Principles of Assesment

The FVS differs from the VES in how the data from right and left eye are combined. The VES considered the two eyes as independent organs and did not consider binocular vision. The FVS emphasizes binocular vision since this is the way persons function in ADLs.

Section 12.4b, Individual Adjustments (5th ed, p 297; 6th ed, pp 305-306), provides guidance on adjustments. The VES provided special scales for diplopia and aphakia, but not for any other visual conditions. The FVS has no such special scales, but allows an adjustment of up to 15 points for any well-documented factors that affect visual functioning, but that are not reflected in a reduction of visual acuity or visual field.

Fifth Edition Rating

Visual Acuity

Calculation of the VAS is outlined in Section 12.2 (5th ed, pp 281-286). The acuity values for the right eye, the left eye, and binocular vision (both eyes open) are each converted to VAS as referenced in Table 12-2, Impairment of Visual Acuity (5th ed, p 284). Using Table 12-3, Calculation of the Acuity-Related Impairment Rating (5th ed, p 284), the three VAS values are then combined as a weighted average to a single FAS for the person.

	Visual Acuity	VAS	Weight	Result
Right eye	20/15	100	×1	100
Left eye	20/400	30	×1	30
Both eyes	20/15	100	×3	300
FAS				430 /5 = 86

Visual Field

Determination of visual field impairment is discussed in Section 12.3, Impairment of the Visual Field (5th ed, pp 287-295). The Goldmann visual field for the right eye is normal (VFS = 100). In the left eye, a 20° peripheral restriction is noted in the upper right quadrant. If this restriction affects both measured meridians in that quadrant, it results in a 4-point reduction in the VFS. Since the missing area in the left eye corresponds to a seeing area in the right eye, the binocular field is not restricted. The weighted average is calculated as follows:

	VFS	Weight	Result
Right eye	100	×1	100
Left eye	96	×1	96
Both eyes	100	×3	300
FAS			496 /5 = 99

Table 12-5, Impairment of the Visual Field, and Table 12-6, Calculation of the Field-Related Impairment Rating (5th ed, p 289), are referenced to make this determination.

Other Factors

Section 12.4b, Individual Adjustments (5th ed, p 297), is referenced to determine whether any adjustments are appropriate. Although Mr Dobson has some residual diplopia, this is only manifest in extreme upper right gaze and does not warrant an adjustment.

Functional Vision Score

Section 12.4a, Calculating an Impairment for the Visual System (5th ed, p 296), is referenced to calculate the FVS. The FVS is calculated as (FAS × FFS)/100. In this case, (86 × 99)/100 = 85.

Visual System Impairment Rating

Section 12.4, Impairment of the Visual System (5th ed, p 296), is referenced to calculate the VSI. The VSI is calculated as 100 – FVS. In this case, 100 – 85 = 15.

Whole Person Impairment Rating

Section 12.4c, Impairment of the Whole Person (5th ed, p 298), and Table 12-10, Classification of Impairment of the Visual System and of the Whole Person (5th ed, p 298) are used to determine that the WPI is the same as the VSI if VSI < 50. In this case it remains 15%.

Impairment: 15% whole person impairment per the Fifth Edition.

Sixth Edition Rating

Visual Acuity

Calculation of the VAS is outlined in Section 12.2 (6th ed, pp 285-293). The acuity values for the right eye, the left eye, and binocular vision (both eyes open) are each converted to a VAS as referenced in Table 12-2, Impairment of Visual Acuity (6th ed, p 288). Using Table 12-3, Calculation of the Acuity-Related Impairment Rating (6th ed, p 289), the three VAS values are then combined as a weighted average to a single FAS for the person.

	Visual Acuity	VAS	Weight	Result
Right eye	20/15	100	×1	100
Left eye	20/400	30	×1	30
Both eyes	20/15	100	×3	300
FAS				430 /5 = 86

Visual Field

Determination of visual field impairment is discussed in Section 12.3, Impairment of the Visual Field (6th ed, pp 293-303). The Goldmann visual field for the right eye is normal (VFS = 100). In the left eye, a 20° peripheral restriction is noted in the upper right quadrant. If this restriction affects both measured meridians in that quadrant, it results in a 4-point reduction of the VFS for that eye. Since the missing area in the left eye corresponds to a seeing area in the right eye, the binocular field is not restricted. The weighted average is calculated as follows:

	VFS	Weight	Result
Right eye	100	×1	100
Left eye	96	×1	96
Both eyes	100	×3	300
FAS			496 /5 = 99

Table 12-5, Impairment of Visual Field, and Table 12-6, Conversion of Field Radius to Field Score (6th ed, p 296), are referenced to make this determination.

Other Factors

Section 12.4b, Individual Adjustments (6th ed, pp 305-306), is referenced to determine whether any adjustments are appropriate. Although Mr. Dobson has some residual diplopia; this is only manifest in extreme upper right gaze and does not warrant an adjustment.

Functional Vision Score
Section 12.4a, Calculating an Impairment Rating for the Visual System (6th ed, pp 303-304), is referenced to calculate the FVS. The FVS is calculated as (FAS × FFS)/100. In this case, (86 × 99)/100 = 85.

Visual System Impairment Rating
Section 12.4, Impairment of the Visual System (6th ed, pp 303-309), is referenced to calculate the VSI. The VSI is calculated as 100 – FVS. In this case, 100 – 85 = 15.

Whole Person Impairment Rating
Section 12.4c, Impairment of the Whole Person (6th ed, p 306), and Table 12-10, Classification of Impairment of the Visual System and of the Whole Person (6th ed, p 307) are used to determine the WPI. The WPI is the same as the VSI if VSI < 50. In this case it remains 15%.

Impairment: 15% whole person impairment per the Sixth Edition.

SUMMARY

Diagnosis	Hyphema, vitreous hemorrhage, horseshoe retinal tear, posterior vitreous detachment, fracture of floor of left bony orbit; minimal entrapment of the left inferior oblique muscle at fracture site
Fourth Edition References	Table 3 (4th ed, p 212), Table 5 (4th ed, p 214), Table 6 (4th ed, p 218), Table 7 (4th ed, pp 219-220)
Fourth Edition Summary	History, best corrected visual acuity, visual fields, tonometry, slit-lamp examination, ophthalmoscopy, ocular motility assessment. CT scan/MRI
Fourth Edition Impairment	17% WPI (equivalent to 20/40 acuity in both eyes)
Fifth Edition References	Section 12.2 (5th ed, pp 281-286), Section 12.3 (5th ed, pp 287-295), Section 12.4 (5th ed, pp 296-298), Tables 12-2, 12-3, 12-4 (5th ed, pp 284, 285), Tables 12-5, 12-6 (5th ed, p 289), Table 12-10 (5th ed, p 298)

Fifth Edition Summary	History, best-corrected visual acuity, visual fields, tonometry, slit-lamp examination, ophthalmoscopy, ocular motility assessment. CT scan/MRI
Fifth Edition Impairment	15% WPI (equivalent to 20/40 acuity in both eyes). This is a Class 2 (10–29% WPI) impairment.
Sixth Edition References	Section 12.2 (6th ed, pp 285-293), Section 12.3 (6th ed, pp 293-303), Tables 12-2, 12-3, 12-4 (6th ed, pp 288-290), Tables 12-5, 12-6 (6th ed, p 296), Table 12-10 (6th ed, p 307)
Sixth Edition Summary	History, best-corrected visual acuity, visual fields, tonometry, slit-lamp examination, ophthalmoscopy, ocular motility assessment. CT scan/MRI
Sixth Edition Impairment	15% WPI (equivalent to 20/40 acuity in both eyes). This is a Class 2 (10–29% WPI) impairment.

Chapter 13

The Central and Peripheral Nervous System

CASE 13-1

Seizure Disorder

Subject: Mr Johnson, a 29-year-old man.

History: Mr Johnson was employed in a gun shop. Five years ago, while test firing a gun, he accidentally dropped the weapon. It discharged, and he sustained a gunshot wound to the left temporal region. Because the injury was to the left temporal tip, he did not have any obvious deficits beyond a slight skull defect that was cosmetically repaired with a cranioplasty.

Current Symptoms: The only residual symptoms were related to intermittent seizures.

Physical Examination: When evaluated 2 years after the incident, Mr Johnson and his spouse indicated that in the first 6 months after the gunshot wound, he experienced approximately two generalized seizures. At the time of this evaluation, he had not had a generalized seizure for a year. He was, however, experiencing episodes that sounded typical of complex partial seizures with episodic alteration of awareness, eye blinking, chewing, and automatic movements consisting of some hand gripping. During these spells, he would maintain his posture and tone, but he was clearly unaware of his immediate surroundings. The spells would last approximately 1 or 2 minutes, and he experienced minimal, if any, postictal lethargy. He had returned to routine activities, although he was not driving, and he restricted himself from working above ground level or with dangerous equipment. He was again working at the gun shop, but he was not allowed to handle loaded weapons. His current medications consisted of 500 mg of divalproex sodium

Chapter 13

(Depakote) taken three times a day, which resulted in a divalproex level of 90 mg/mL (therapeutic). His treating neurologist was also trying various second-line medications. Because gabapentin (Neurontin) had not afforded any improvement, the neurologist was considering lamotrigine (Lamictal).

Discussion of Seizure Disorder

Fourth Edition Rating

Section 4.1e, Episodic Neurologic Disorders (4th ed, p 142), discusses the process of rating seizures. Mr Johnson's rating was based on Table 5, Impairments Related to Epilepsy, Seizures, and Convulsive Disorders (4th ed, p 143). Although one may remain optimistic that his seizures could be brought under further control, it is equally reasonable to assume that Mr Johnson will continue to experience at least an occasional complex partial seizure. Fortunately, the gunshot wound involved only the anterior portion of the temporal lobe, so other than the seizure disorder, Mr Johnson had no significant deficits.

According to Table 5, his episodic seizures could place him in the first or second category. The first category is "Paroxysmal disorder with predictable characteristics and unpredictable occurrence that does not limit usual activities but is a risk to the patient or limits performance of daily activities." This is felt to be appropriate because the episodes have similar characteristics, and it is only the occurrence that is unpredictable. This first category would result in as much as a 14% whole person permanent impairment. Some evaluators may opine that his occasional seizures place him in the second category, "Paroxysmal disorder that interferes with some activities of daily living." His usual activities include driving (travel), climbing (a physical activity, eg, "restricted himself from working above ground level"), and recreational and occupational activities (eg, working with loaded guns and other dangerous equipment). Activities of daily living are discussed in Section 1.1, Impairment, Disability, Handicap (p 1), and specified in the Glossary (4th ed, p 317). This evaluator believed the first category was most appropriate; however, because Mr Johnson approached characteristics of the second category, it would be reasonable to assign a 14% whole person permanent impairment.

Impairment: 14% whole person impairment per the Fourth Edition.

Fifth Edition Rating

Section 13.3b, Episodic Neurologic Disorders (5th ed, p 311), discusses the process of rating seizures. Mr Johnson's rating is based on Table 13-3,

Criteria for Rating Impairment Due to Episodic Loss of Consciousness or Awareness (5th ed, p 312). Although one may remain optimistic that his seizures could be brought under further control, it is equally reasonable to assume that Mr Johnson will continue to experience at least an occasional complex partial seizure. Fortunately, the gunshot wound involved only the anterior portion of the temporal lobe, so other than the seizure disorder, Mr Johnson had no significant deficits or other ratable impairment.

According to Table 13-3, his episodic seizures could place him in the first or second category. The first category is "Paroxysmal disorder with predictable characteristics and unpredictable occurrence that does not limit usual activities but is a risk to the individual or limits performance of daily activities." This is felt to be appropriate because the episodes have similar characteristics, and it is only the occurrence that is unpredictable. This first category would result in as much as a 14% whole person permanent impairment. Some evaluators may opine that his occasional seizures place him in the second category, "Paroxysmal disorder that interferes with some activities of daily living." His usual activities include driving (travel), climbing (he restricted himself from working above ground level), and recreational and occupational activities (eg, working with loaded guns and other dangerous equipment). Activities of daily living are presented in Table 1-2 (5th ed, p 4). This evaluator believed the first category is most appropriate; however, because Mr Johnson's disorder almost meets the criteria for class 2, it is reasonable to rate his disorder with the highest percentage of whole person impairment (14%) from class 1.

Impairment: 14% whole person impairment per the Fifth Edition.

Sixth Edition Rating

The first step in rating a central nervous system impairment is to identify the primary or most severe cerebral impairment condition from the following four categories as explained in Section 13.2, Method for Rating Impairments due to Nervous System Disorders (6th ed, p 326) and Section 13.3, Criteria for Rating Cerebral Impairments (6th ed, pp 326-333).

1. State of consciousness and level of awareness
2. Mental status evaluation and integrative functioning
3. Use and understanding of language
4. Influence of behavior and mood

After the primary impairment category is chosen, any other impairments related to the cranial nerves, upper and lower extremities, bowel and bladder dysfunction, sexual function, neurologic respiratory impairment, and peripheral nervous system impairment are considered, as illustrated in Table 13-3, Neurologic Impairments That Are Combined With the Most Severe Cerebral Impairment (6th ed, p 326). These impairments are all combined along with the primary impairment value identified initially.

Considering Mr Johnson's clinical course, it is likely he will continue to experience occasional complex partial seizures, and Mr Johnson does not have other significant neurological deficits for which impairment rating would apply. Therefore, the impairment rating for this case came from Section 13.3b, Episodic Neurologic Impairments (6th ed, pp 327-329), which discusses the process of rating seizures. The specific rating is based on Table 13-5, Criteria for Rating Impairment due to Episodic Loss of Consciousness or Awareness (6th ed, p 328).

In reviewing Table 13-5, consideration could be given to rating Mr Johnson under class 1 or class 2. Rating under class 1 (representing between 1% and 10% whole person impairment) applies when there is a paroxysmal disorder with predictable characteristics and unpredictable occurrence that does not limit usual activities but is a risk to the individual; for example, the individual cannot drive. Rating under class 2 (which ranges between 11% and 20% whole person impairment) applies when there is a paroxysmal disorder that interferes with some daily activities.

Mr Johnson is no longer driving. He has restricted himself from working above ground level or with dangerous equipment. He is no longer allowed to handle loaded weapons in the gun shop. Based solely on the clinical description for this case, Mr Johnson would best be rated under class 2.

As Mr Johnson is minimally impacted in most ways other than those noted earlier, a rating in the middle of class 2 would apply. This would represent 15% whole person impairment.

Impairment: 15% whole person impairment per the Sixth Edition.

Comment on Seizure Disorder

As with virtually all other ratings provided in this chapter, the evaluator selects from a range. Clinical experience and careful review of the clinical findings and functional impact on activities of daily living is required and serves as a primary basis for selecting the value within each range. Each patient must be considered individually to determine where he or she may fall within the allowable range. This is particularly true in patients with seizure disorders.

SUMMARY

Diagnosis	Seizure disorder
Fourth Edition References	Section 4.1e (4th ed, p 142), Table 5 (4th ed, p 143)
Fourth Edition Summary	History. Nature of disorder is defined, and extent of interference with activities of daily living is determined.
Fourth Edition Impairment	14% whole person impairment
Fifth Edition References	Section 13.3b (5th ed, pp 311-317), Table 13-3 (5th ed, p 312)
Fifth Edition Summary	History. Nature of disorder is defined, and extent of interference with activities of daily living is determined.
Fifth Edition Impairment	14% whole person impairment
Sixth Edition References	Sections 13.2 and 13.3 (6th ed, pp 326-333), Table 13-3 (6th ed, p 326); Section 13.3b (6th ed, pp 327-329), Table 13-5 (6th ed, p 328)
Sixth Edition Summary	History. Nature of disorder is defined, and extent of interference with activities of daily living is determined.
Sixth Edition Impairment	15% whole person impairment

CASE 13-2

Head Trauma

Subject: Mr Wilson, a 42-year-old man.

History: Mr Wilson was employed as a cab driver. Four and a half years earlier, he lost control of his vehicle during an ice storm. He was wearing his seat belt, but his vehicle was an older model not equipped with an air bag. He was traveling approximately 50 mph when his vehicle hit a concrete abutment. He was unconscious at the scene, with evidence of bruises and contusions along the left side of his face as well as the left frontal parietal region. Although he had a number of other superficial cuts and bruises, his most serious injury was a closed head injury. He required intubation at the scene of the accident, according to the paramedics, and was then transported to the local emergency department. A computed tomographic scan of the brain showed evidence of right frontal contusions as well as diffuse cerebral edema. During the next few days, he was extubated, and he made a gradual but slow improvement. After 10 days he was transferred to a rehabilitation facility.

Current Symptoms/Physical Examination: Approximately 3 years later, Mr Wilson underwent an impairment evaluation. Neurologic examination showed that he was ambulating, and upper and lower extremity strength was basically normal. Reflexes were somewhat brisk throughout, and on the Babinski test he had equivocal upgoing toe signs bilaterally. He did not have any definite spasticity in terms of muscle tone, and his dexterity and gait were judged as normal.

Abnormalities on examination related to speech function. Mr Wilson had some difficulties with naming objects, and he stumbled a few times when repeating phrases. Reading aloud and for comprehension (silently) was fairly good, but he and his wife indicated that his reading ability was not as good as it had been before the accident. There was also some deterioration in his writing in that he was slow when trying to write a phrase that the examiner dictated. Mental status examination showed that he was oriented, but he did have significant difficulties with recent memory. He was able to recall only two of three objects after 3 minutes. Although Mr Wilson was a high school graduate with 2 years of trade school education, he made errors with serial sevens subtractions.

He had difficulty recalling some of the topics that the examiner had discussed with him just a few minutes earlier. His family indicated that he was able to function independently, but they had to "keep an eye on him." Mr Wilson was able to dress, bathe, and take care of his personal hygiene independently. He could no longer go to a store without a written list, as he would consistently forget several items. His wife had taken over most of the home bookkeeping activities, such as paying bills and balancing the checkbook, as Mr Wilson consistently made errors when he attempted those activities.

Further examination indicated no significant behavioral problems. Both Mr Wilson and his wife mentioned that perhaps he was somewhat depressed, but overall his moods were fine, and there were no limitations in activities of daily living in reference to his emotional status. By DSM-IV[1,2] criteria, he was not depressed. There was no evidence of episodic alteration of consciousness (nothing to suggest seizures), and his sleep patterns seemed normal.

Discussion of Head Trauma

Fourth Edition Rating

Impairment from head injury was rated using Section 4.1, The Central Nervous System—Cerebrum or Forebrain (4th ed, pp 140-144). The *Guides* indicates that one should utilize "the most severe of the first five categories shown above" (4th ed, p 140). Then, any or all impairments from the final four categories would be combined with the most severe of the first five categories. In this case, examination indicated that speech difficulty was an obvious sequela or impairment from the injury. The degree of difficulty would fit within the first category of Table 1, Impairment Related to Aphasia or Dysphasia: Minimal Disturbance in Comprehension and Production of Language Symbols of Daily Living (4th ed, p 141). This would qualify as a 0% to 9% whole person impairment.

There also was a disturbance in mental status and integrative functioning, which would fall within Table 2, Mental Status Impairments (4th ed, p 142). The impairment description appropriate in this case, relative to Table 2, would consist of the first category, "Impairment exists, but ability remains to perform satisfactorily most activities of daily living," and that would qualify as a 1% to 14% whole person impairment. Because Mr Wilson nearly approaches a moderate category, for example, "Limitation of some but not all social and interpersonal daily living functions," it is appropriate to rate him at the upper range of a mild impairment, at 14% whole person impairment.

There did not appear to be any significant limitations relative to other aspects of central nervous system function, which is apparent in reviewing Tables 3, 4, 5, and 6 (4th ed, pp 142-143).

The *Guides* indicates that one should use "the most severe of the first five categories;" hence, Mr Wilson had up to a 14% permanent partial impairment to the body as a whole, relative to his closed head injury. His difficulties were deemed severe enough to justify a 14% whole person impairment rating.

Impairment: 14% whole person impairment per the Fourth Edition.

Fifth Edition Rating

Impairment from head injury was rated using Section 13.2, Criteria for Rating Impairment Due to Central Nervous System Disorders (5th ed, p 308), and Section 13.3, Criteria for Rating Cerebral Impairments (5th ed, p 309). The *Guides* indicates that one should first determine whether a disturbance is present in the level of consciousness or awareness; this is not applicable in this case. The evaluator then assesses (2) mental status and highest integrative functioning, (3) understanding and use of language, and (4) any emotional or behavioral disturbance. The most severe cerebral impairment is identified and combined with other neurological impairments identified in Table 13-1, Neurological Impairments That Are Combined With the Most Severe Impairment (5th ed, p 308). In this case, examination indicated that speech difficulty is an obvious sequela or impairment from the injury. The process of assessing speech difficulty is explained in Section 13.3e, Communication Impairments: Dysphasia and Aphasia (5th ed, p 322). The degree of difficulty would fit within the first category of Table 13-7, Criteria for Rating Impairment Due to Aphasia or Dysphasia (5th ed, p 323), that is, "Minimal disturbance in comprehension and production of language symbols of daily living." This would qualify as a 0% to 9% whole person impairment.

Mr Wilson's disturbance in mental status and integrative functioning was evaluated using Section 13.3d, Mental Status, Cognition, and Highest Integrative Function (5th ed, p 319). Table 13-5, Clinical Dementia Rating (CDR) (5th ed, p 320), provides a basis for assessing the extent of dementia. It covers memory, orientation, judgment and problem solving, community activities, home and hobbies, and personal care. Each category is rated as 0 (no abnormality), 0.5 (questionable), 1.0 (mild), 2.0 (moderate), and 3.0 (severe). This case would support the following scores:

Area	Impairment Level	Description	Score
Memory (M)	Mild	Moderate memory loss; more marked for recent events; defect interferes with everyday activities	1
Orientation (O)	Questionable	Fully oriented except for slight difficulty with time relationships	0.5
Judgment and Problem Solving (JPS)	Questionable	Slight impairment in solving problems, similarities, and differences; social judgment usually maintained	0.5
Community Affairs (CA)	Questionable	Slight impairment in these activities	0.5
Home and Hobbies (HH)	Questionable	Life at home, hobbies, and intellectual interests slightly impaired	0.5
Personal Care (PC)	Questionable	Fully capable of self-care	0.5

Memory is considered the primary category; the other categories are secondary. The *Guides* states that "if three or more secondary categories are given a score greater or less than the memory score, CDR = the score of the majority of the secondary categories" (5th ed, p 319). All of the other categories are 0.5, whereas the memory score is 1; therefore, CDR = 0.5. Table 13-6, Criteria for Rating Impairment Related to Mental Status (5th ed, p 320), provides four classes of impairment. A CDR of 0.5 results in a class 1 impairment, which states that a "paroxysmal disorder with preimpairment exists, but [the patient] is able to perform activities of daily living." The term *preimpairment* is used because the CDR was developed as a tool to evaluate Alzheimer dementia, which is a progressive disease. Individuals who rate as having preimpairment usually would qualify for a diagnosis of mild cognitive impairment (which precedes Alzheimer disease) and would progress over time to meet the definition of Alzheimer disease and, thus, significant impairment. Because Mr Wilson approaches a class 2 impairment, that is, "impairment requires direction of some activities of daily living," it is appropriate to rate him at the upper range of a mild impairment, that is, at 14% whole person impairment.

There did not appear to be any significant limitations relative to other aspects of central nervous system function, which is apparent in reviewing Table 13-2 (5th ed, p 309), Table 13-3 (5th ed, p 312), Table 13-4 (5th ed, p 317), and Table 13-8 (5th ed, p 325). The *Guides* indicates that one should use "the most severe of the first five categories;" hence, Mr Wilson has up to a 14% permanent partial impairment to the body as a whole, relative to his closed head injury. His difficulties were deemed severe enough to justify a 14% whole person impairment rating.

Impairment: 14% whole person impairment per the Fifth Edition.

Sixth Edition Rating

Impairment from head injury was rated by means of Section 13.3, Criteria for Rating Cerebral Impairments (6th ed, p 326).

The *Guides* states that the initial step in assessing cerebral function is to determine whether disturbance is present in the level of consciousness or awareness. This may be a permanent alteration or an intermittent alteration of consciousness, awareness, or arousal.

Step two requires the evaluation of mental status and highest integrative functioning.

Step three requires the identification of any difficulty with understanding and use of language.

Step four requires the evaluation of any emotional or behavioral disturbances, such as depression, that can modify cerebral function.

Finally, step five requires identifying the most severe cerebral impairment. The most severe impairment from categories one through four would then be combined with any or multiple other distinct neurologic impairments.

In Mr Wilson's case, abnormalities on examination included difficulty with naming, repetition, arithmetic, and memory.

Table 13-8, Criteria for Rating Neurologic Impairment Due to Alteration in Mental Status, Cognition, and Highest Integrative Function (MSCHIF) (6th ed, p 331), provides the basis for rating Mr Wilson's impairments, aside from those related to language.

Mr Wilson's mental status examination was noteworthy for significant difficulties with recent memory. He was able to recall only two of three objects after 3 minutes. He made errors on serial sevens subtractions (a test of mental control). He had difficulty recalling some topics that had been discussed with him just a few minutes earlier. His spouse had taken over most of the home bookkeeping activities such as paying bills and balancing the checkbook. Mr Wilson was noted to have consistently made errors when he attempted those activities.

Based on the results of the clinical mental status examination, Mr Wilson would likely be viewed as having moderate abnormalities and would, therefore, be rated under class 2. Ratings under this class range between 10% and 20% whole person impairment. Patients rated under this class have alteration in mental status, cognition, and highest integrative function (MSCHIF) such that it interferes with their ability to assume some normal roles or perform some activities of daily living. Based on the impact of the injury on areas of mental functioning, Mr Wilson would qualify for rating at the middle of the range of this class, or 15% whole person impairment.

Table 13-9, Criteria for Rating Impairment due to Aphasia or Dysphasia (6th ed, p 332), was used. Mr Wilson was noted to have some difficulty with naming and repetition.

Using the criteria referenced in Table 13-9, Mr Wilson would qualify for impairment rating under class 1. Rating under this class applies when there is minimal disturbance in comprehension and production of language symbols for daily living. The rating may range between 1% and 10% whole person impairment. In Mr Wilson's case, a rating of 10% whole person impairment could be considered.

Mr Wilson does not have a disturbance in the level of consciousness or awareness, nor are there any significant behavioral problems in his case.

The most severe cerebral impairment is that related to alteration in mental status, cognition, and highest integrative function, at 15% whole person impairment. Therefore, this would represent Mr Wilson's final rating related to cerebral impairment.

Impairment: 15% whole person impairment per the Sixth Edition.

Comment on Head Trauma

The Sixth Edition of the *Guides* uses a significantly different approach from that of the Fifth Edition for rating impairment due to alteration in mental status, cognition, and highest integrative function (MSCHIF). Qualitatively, it is similar to that of the Fourth Edition but is more specific. The Sixth Edition explains in Section 13.3d (6th ed, pp 330-331) that "In contrast to previously held belief, the symptoms of mildly traumatic brain injury generally resolved in days or weeks, and leave the patient with no impairment. Patients with persistent postconcussive symptoms generally have noninjury related factors which complicate their clinical course. Postconcussive syndrome is a relatively rare sequelae of mild traumatic brain injury (MTBI), seen in 1-5% of all MTBI patients."

SUMMARY

Diagnosis	Head trauma
Fourth Edition References	Section 4.1 (4th ed, pp 140-144), Table 1 (4th ed, p 141), Table 2 (4th ed, p 142), Table 3 (4th ed, p 142), Table 4 (4th ed, p 142), Table 5 (4th ed, p 143), Table 6 (4th ed, p 143)
Fourth Edition Summary	History, neurological examination, detailed. Extent of impairment is determined.
Fourth Edition Impairment	14% whole person impairment
Fifth Edition References	Section 13.2 (5th ed, pp 308-309); Section 13.3 (5th ed, pp 309-327), Table 13-2 (5th ed, p 309), Table 13-3 (5th ed, p 312), Table 13-4 (5th ed, p 317), Table 13-5 (5th ed, p 320), Table 13-6 (5th ed, p 320), Table 13-7 (5th ed, p 323), Table 13-8 (5th ed, p 325)
Fifth Edition Summary	History, neurological examination, detailed. Extent of impairment is determined.
Fifth Edition Impairment	14% whole person impairment
Sixth Edition References	Section 13.3 (6th ed, p 326), Table 13-8 (6th ed, p 331), Table 13-9 (6th ed, p 332)
Sixth Edition Summary	History. Nature of disorder is defined, and extent of interference with activities of daily living is determined.
Sixth Edition Impairment	15% whole person impairment

References:

1. American Psychiatric Association. *Diagnostic and Statistical Manual of Mental Disorders.* 4th ed, Washington, DC: American Psychiatric Associaion; 1994.
2. American Psychiatric Association. *Diagnostic and Statistical Manual of Mental Disorders, Fourth Edition, Text Revision*. Washington, DC: American Psychiatric Association; 2000.

CASE 13-3

Cranial Nerve Injury

Subject: Mr Michaels, a 28-year-old man.

History: Mr Michaels worked on a loading dock for a trucking firm. His primary work activities involved loading and unloading various types of cargo from trucks. He had been employed in this capacity for 4 years. Three and a half years ago, he slipped on ice. He landed forcefully, striking the left side of his hip, shoulder, and head, his head hitting a concrete step. He was stunned and perhaps had some momentary loss of consciousness. He was aware of some aches and pains relative to his left hip and left shoulder, but he was especially aware of pain behind his left ear in the mastoid region.

Mr Michaels was taken to a local emergency department. In addition to some minor contusions of the left hip and left shoulder, it was noted that he also had a bruise about the left mastoid area. An X ray showed a linear fracture in that region. Complete left facial palsy was also noted.

Mr Michaels gradually recovered from his bruises and contusions and did not have any residual symptoms relative to his left hip and shoulder.

Current Symptoms/Physical Examination: Approximately 1 year after the incident, Mr Michaels had mild left facial weakness. When asked to raise his eyebrows, he could only partially elevate the left eyebrow. He was able to fully close his left eye, and corneal irritation from eye dryness was not a problem. When asked to smile, he could raise both corners of the mouth almost symmetrically, but when urged to give a "big smile," the left corner of the mouth lagged considerably. He had some residual pain around the left mastoid region, behind his left ear. He said that strangers no longer seemed to notice his facial weakness, and he did not alter his behavior now, although he had done so when his facial paralysis was severe. There were no psychological problems. Eating and speaking were not affected. His ability to taste had recovered to normal.

Discussion of Cranial Nerve Injury

Fourth Edition Rating

A permanent impairment rating was based on Chapter 4, The Nervous System, Section 4.1f, The Cranial Nerves (4th ed, p 144). Table 10, Impairment Criteria for Cranial Nerve VII (Facial) and Adjoining Region (4th ed, p 146), discusses impairment ratings for the seventh cranial nerve.

In view of the fact that 1 year had elapsed since the injury, one can reasonably assume that Mr Michaels' condition had reached maximal medical improvement. His impairment description falls within the mild unilateral facial weakness category. This would qualify for an impairment rating of 1% to 4%. It would be reasonable to conclude that this injured worker has a 4% permanent partial impairment to the body as a whole in reference to this injury.

Impairment: 4% whole person impairment per the Fourth Edition.

Fifth Edition Rating

A permanent impairment rating was based on Chapter 13, The Central and Peripheral Nervous System, Section 13.4e, Cranial Nerve VII—the Facial Nerve (5th ed, p 332). Table 13-12, Criteria for Rating Impairment of Cranial Nerve VII (Facial Nerve) (5th ed, p 332), provides three classes of impairment, resulting in up to 45% whole person impairment. In view of the fact that 1 year had elapsed since the injury, one can reasonably assume that Mr Michaels' condition had reached maximal medical improvement. His impairment description falls within the mild unilateral facial weakness category. This would qualify for an impairment rating of 1% to 4%. It would be reasonable to conclude that this injured worker has a 4% permanent partial impairment to the body as a whole in reference to this injury.

Impairment: 4% whole person impairment per the Fifth Edition.

Sixth Edition Rating

The Introduction of Chapter 13, The Central and Peripheral Nervous System (6th ed, p 321), states that cranial neuropathies affecting cranial nerves, including cranial nerve VII, are dealt with in Chapter 11, Ear, Nose, Throat, and Related Structures. Therefore, the rating methodology for a seventh cranial nerve injury is not specifically addressed in Chapter 13.

Section 11.3a, Criteria for Rating Impairment Due to Facial Disorders and/or Disfigurement (6th ed, pp 261-265), discusses criteria for rating impairment due to facial disorders and/or disfigurement.

Table 11-5, Criteria for Rating Impairment due to Facial Disorders and/or Disfigurement (6th ed, p 262), provides the specific criteria for rating impairment due to facial disorders and/or disfigurement.

To use Table 11-5, the examiner places the individual in the appropriate class based on the key factor, that is, the history. The middle number in that class is then selected (default value). All classes have discrete numbers and are not a range.

In Mr Michaels' case, he has a facial abnormality that does not affect activities of daily living, including breathing or eating. This places him under class 1. The middle number in this class is 3% whole person impairment.

The next step is to assess the correct class for the physical examination findings. If the class selected by physical examination is one class higher than the class selected in the first step, the examiner should move one number higher within the history-based class previously selected. If it is two grades higher, the examiner should move two grades within the history-based class. If the class from the physical examination is in a lower class than that selected from the history, the examiner would move lower within the class selected from the first step.

In Mr Michaels' case, he has mild unilateral total facial paralysis. This also falls under class 1. Therefore, this does not result in any change in the value determined by the middle number in class 1 (3%).

Finally, the examiner assesses the class of the patient's impairment using the diagnostic findings and moves higher or lower within the original class in a manner similar to that explained for the physical examination findings.

In Mr Michaels' case, there is no evidence of involvement of any bony structure or cartilage.

Based on these criteria, Mr Michaels would qualify for impairment rating under the default value of class 1, that is, 3% whole person impairment.

Impairment: 3% whole person impairment per the Sixth Edition.

Comment on Cranial Nerve Injury

The Sixth Edition of the *Guides* takes a completely different approach to the rating of cranial nerve impairment from prior editions, as almost all cranial neuropathies are rated by means of Chapter 11, Ear, Nose, Throat, and Related Structures, or Chapter 12, The Visual System.

The rating criteria in Chapter 11, Ear, Nose, Throat, and Related Structures, are somewhat different from those that might be seen in relation to cranial nerve impairments related to purely neurologic pathology. However, they nonetheless serve as a reasonable basis for the rating of cranial nerve impairment.

SUMMARY

Diagnosis	Cranial nerve injury, cranial nerve VII (facial)
Fourth Edition References	Section 4.1f (4th ed, p 144), Table 10 (4th ed, p 146)
Fourth Edition Summary	History, neurologic examination. Neurological assessment, assessing loss of anterior tongue and any facial weakness or paralysis.
Fourth Edition Impairment	4% whole person impairment
Fifth Edition References	Section 13.4e (5th ed, p 332), Table 13-12 (5th ed, p 332)
Fifth Edition Summary	History, neurologic examination. Neurological assessment, assessing loss of anterior tongue and any facial weakness or paralysis.
Fifth Edition Impairment	4% whole person impairment
Sixth Edition References	Introduction of Chapter 13 (6th ed, p 321); Section 11.3a (6th ed, p 261), Table 11-5 (6th ed, p 262)
Sixth Edition Summary	History based on the nature of the disorder and extent of interference with activities of daily living defines the appropriate class of impairment. Physical examination and clinical studies assists in determining the specific value within the chosen class.
Sixth Edition Impairment	3% whole person impairment

CASE 13-4

Headache Following Head Injury

Subject: Dr Davidson, a 62-year-old man.

History: Dr Davidson was a second-chair trumpet player for a major symphony orchestra. During a rehearsal, the two back legs of his chair slipped off the stage riser, causing Dr Davidson to fall backward and hit the back of his head against a hard plaster wall. He did not lose consciousness, and although he had some difficulty concentrating, he was able to finish the rehearsal and play several regular concerts. Two months later, he began to develop headaches along with a sense of physical disorientation. These headaches were mild but persistent, temporarily worsening every time he played the trumpet. He experienced mild bilateral tinnitus for about 2 months after the onset of the headaches. There were no other neurologic symptoms.

Current Symptoms: One year after the injury, at the time of his examination, Dr Davidson stated he still had a constant low-level generalized headache and could not play the trumpet for more than a few minutes without experiencing moderate head pain. His headaches were no longer improving; they had been of the same severity and frequency for the past 6 months.

On a scale of 0, no pain, to 10, excruciating pain, he reported his current pain as a 2, pain at the worst as an 8, and his pain on the average as a 3. In terms of his pain being aggravated by activity, on a scale of 0, activity does not aggravate pain, to 10, excruciating pain following any activity, he rated this as 5. In terms of frequency of his pain, on a scale of 0, rarely, to 10, all of the time, he stated it was a 10, because he had a constant low-level headache.

Dr Davidson completed a series of inventories reflecting interference in activities of daily living. Overall, on a scale of 0, no interference, to 10, complete interference, he averaged a 3. He was moderately anxious about his headaches overall and also that his playing made his headaches worse, rating both on a scale of 0 to 10 as a 4. He stated that, overall, his mood was extremely high and he denied depression and irritability. Despite his problems with his headaches, he appeared neither anxious nor depressed. The quality of his musical ability did not appear to be diminished.

Functional Assessment: The Pain Disability Questionnaire (PDQ) score was 80.

Physical Examination: Blood pressure 140/80, with the remainder of the general physical examination being unremarkable. He had no complaints of pain, and his pain behaviors appeared to be appropriate and tended to confirm his reports of headaches. He also appeared to be very credible. The neurologic examination was entirely normal other than Dr Davidson's sense of disorientation when looking at a rotating striped opticokinetic drum.

Clinical Studies: An infused computed tomographic brain scan (ordered by his regular physician 3 months after the injury) was normal. A brain magnetic resonance (MR) image and MR angiogram of the intracranial circulation (11 months after the injury) showed no evidence of aneurysm or other structural abnormality. An MR image of the cervical spine showed bulging disks.

Discussion of Headache Following Head Injury

Fourth Edition Rating

Permanent impairment evaluation was based on Section 15.9, Headache (4th ed, p 311), and Section 15.8, Estimating Impairment (4th ed, p 309). Figure 2, Pain Intensity-Frequency Grid (4th ed, p 310), describes the degree of impairment due to chronic pain by means of definitions provided in the Glossary (4th ed, pp 315-320). It does not provide numeric impairment ratings. In Section 15.9, under Determining Impairment on page 312, the *Guides* states, "The vast majority of patients with headache will not have permanent impairments."

On the basis of the Pain Intensity-Frequency Grid (4th ed, p 310), Dr Davidson's pain is identified on the grid as Slight Intensity-Intermittent Frequency, because he tolerates the pain, but it interferes with his capacity to carry out some specified daily activity (in this case, playing the trumpet) and occurs less than one-fourth of the time when he is awake. According to the *Guides*, there is no objective evidence of permanent impairment due to pain.

Impairment: No ratable whole person impairment per the Fourth Edition.

Fifth Edition Rating

Headaches are not discussed in Chapter 13, The Central and Peripheral Nervous System; however, they are referenced in Chapter 18.

Chapter 18, Pain, describes a process to integrate pain-related impairment into the conventional impairment rating system. Headache is listed in Table 18-1,

Illustrative List of Well-Established Syndromes Without Significant, Identifiable Organ Dysfunction to Explain the Pain (5th ed, p 571); therefore, this chapter could be used to evaluate impairment from Dr Davidson's pain related to his headache. The process of performing this rating is explained in Section 18.3d, How to Rate Pain-Related Impairment: Overview (5th ed, p 573); Section 18.3f, How to Rate Pain-Related Impairment: Practical Steps; and Section 18.5, How to Rate Pain-Related Impairment: A Sample Protocol (5th ed, p 583).

One such methodology is provided in Table 18-4, Rating Impairment Associated With Pain (5th ed, p 576), and Table 18-6, Worksheet for Calculating Total Pain-Related Impairment Score (5th ed, p 584). Table 18-6 yields a Total Pain-Related Impairment Score, which is not an impairment percentage, but rather a score to describe the apparent severity of the pain problem. The following data were obtained:

1. Pain (Self-report of Severity)

Overall, the pain severity averages 4.5 (eg, Dr Davidson's current pain was 2, at its worst it was 8, it averaged a 3, and aggravation was rated 5; the total of 18 is divided by 4), and the frequency is constant (10); therefore, the total pain severity is 14.5 (on a range from 0 to 20).

2. Activity Limitation or Interference

The overall mean for activity limitation or interference was 3. If we had completed Table 18-4, Ratings Determining Impairment Associated With Pain (5th ed, p 576), paragraph II, Activity Limitation or Interference, his total score for the 16 activity limitations would have been 48. The mean activity limitation is the total score (48) divided by 16, or in this case 3. The mean of 3 is multiplied by 3, resulting in an activity limitation score of 9 (on a range of 0 to 30).

3. Individual's Report of Effect of Pain on Mood

According to Table 18-4, paragraph III, Individual's Report of Effect of Pain on Mood, Dr Davidson reported a 4 for items A and E and a 0 for B, C, and D. The mean is 1.6, based on the total of 8 divided by 5.

4. Global Pain Behavior

Dr Davidson's pain behaviors were appropriate and tended to confirm his subjective report of headaches, and the examiner judged that on a scale of between −10 and +10, an appropriate score was +10.

5. Credibility

The examiner judged Dr Davidson as very credible and provided him a +10 for credibility.

A pain-related impairment score of 45 corresponds with "moderately severe impairment." Impairment up to 3% may be provided for pain. The examiner gave Dr Davidson the benefit of the doubt and assigned 3% whole person impairment.

Impairment: 3% whole person impairment per the Fifth Edition.

Sixth Edition Rating

There are no ratable neurological deficits per Chapter 13, The Central and Peripheral Nervous System. Section 13.11, Criteria for Rating Impairments Related to Craniocephalic Pain (6th ed, pp 341-343) provides a basis for rating migraine headaches. Page 342 states, "Note that *nonmigrainous headaches are not ratable* using the AMA *Guides*" (6th ed, p 342); however, Chapter 3, Pain-Related Impairment, does provide Section 3.3c, Rating Impairment When Pain Is Not Accompanied by Objective Findings (6th ed, pp 39-40). Dr Davidson does meet the eligibility criteria defined in Section 3.3d, Steps of Assessment (6th ed, p 40) as follows:

(a) Pain has been determined to have a reasonable medical basis, for example, can be described by generally acknowledged medical syndromes.

(b) Pain has been identified by the patient as a major problem.

(c) The patient's condition cannot be rated according to principles described in Chapters 4 to 17.

(d) The PRI is not specifically excluded by relevant jurisdiction.

Dr Davidson's PDQ score is 80, which, according to Table 3-1, Pain-Related Impairment and Whole Person Impairment Based on Pain Disability Questionnaire (6th ed, p 40), corresponds with 1% whole person permanent impairment. The examiner felt that the reliability and credibility of the patient's presentation was consistent and that this rating was appropriate within the permissible range of up to 3% whole person permanent impairment.

Impairment: 1% whole person impairment per the Sixth Edition.

Comment on Headache Following Head Injury

Subjective reports of headache may be influenced by a variety of behavioral, psychosocial, and psychological factors, and issues of secondary gain. The physician can impact the rating both by judgment of pain behaviors and by judgment of credibility. If impairment is judged not to be permanent, as in the case of most headaches, no rating should be given.

SUMMARY

Diagnosis	Exertional headaches
Fourth Edition References	Chapter 14, Figure 2 (4th ed, p 310)
Fourth Edition Summary	History, detailed neurologic examination, MR images of brain and cervical spine. Type, degree, and precipitating factors of pain are defined, establishing pathogenesis if possible. Headache is classified, and prognosis is estimated. Impact of pain on activities of daily living is assessed.
Fourth Edition Impairment	0% whole person impairment
Fifth Edition References	Chapter 18, Table 18-3 (5th ed, p 575), Table 18-4 (5th ed, pp 576-577), Table 18-6 (5th ed, p 584)
Fifth Edition Summary	History, detailed neurologic examination, MR images of brain and cervical spine. Type, degree, and precipitating factors of pain are defined, establishing pathogenesis if possible. Headache is classified, and prognosis is estimated. Reports of severity and frequency of pain, extent of activity limitations, and effect of pain on mood are obtained, and global pain behavior and credibility are assessed.
Fifth Edition Impairment	3% whole person impairment
Sixth Edition References	Section 3.3c (6th ed, pp 39-40); Section 3.3d (6th ed, p 39), Table 3-1 (6th ed, p 40)
Sixth Edition Summary	History, detailed neurologic examination, MR images of brain and cervical spine. Type, degree, and precipitating factors of pain are defined, establishing pathogenesis if possible. Headache is classified, and prognosis is estimated. Impact of pain on activities of daily living is assessed. PDQ is assessed.
Sixth Edition Impairment	1% whole person impairment

CASE 13-5

Idiopathic Seizure Disorder

Subject: Mr Andrews, a 35-year-old man.

History: Mr Andrews had a single major motor seizure nearly 2 years earlier (in 1996) while working at the local post office. Mr Andrews was told that he let out a scream, his body went rigid, and he collapsed with his entire body shaking. He did not bite his tongue or lose control of his bladder or bowels.

He was taken to an emergency facility, where he was evaluated and discharged with no medication. Two days later Mr Andrews was seen by a neurologist, who ordered several tests, including magnetic resonance (MR) imaging of the brain and electroencephalography (EEG). The EEG was said to be abnormal, showing spikes and waves. The physician notified the Department of Motor Vehicles as required by state law, and Mr Andrews' license to drive was suspended.

The neurologist started Mr Andrews on phenytoin, switching to carbamazepine 10 days later when a pruritic rash developed over the trunk and extremities. Mr Andrews also had an allergic reaction to carbamazepine, necessitating another change of medication. At the time of evaluation, he was taking 1500 mg of valproic acid per day and had been seizure-free since the first event. Mr Andrews said, however, that the medication made his hands shake and that he had gained 30 pounds during the past several months. Last month the post office gave him a poor performance rating and placed him on administrative leave because he was working too slowly.

Eight years earlier Mr Andrews had been involved in an automobile accident after apparently falling asleep at the wheel, resulting in a head injury with loss of consciousness. No definite conclusion was reached as to the cause of the accident. Although the question of a seizure had been raised at the time, no anticonvulsants had been prescribed, and no restrictions were imposed until his reported seizure in 1996.

No significant abnormalities were found on the general physical examination other than moderate obesity.

Current Symptoms: The patient was asymptomatic except for mild digital dexterity difficulties.

Physical Exam: On inspection the examiner noted a mild bradykinesia, a static tremor of the hands, and minimal loss of facial expression. Fine movements, rapid-alternating movements, and finger-to-nose testing were normal. The remainder of the neurologic examination was unremarkable.

Clinical Studies: There were no focal or lateralizing abnormalities on an EEG obtained 1 week after the seizure. Brain imaging studies were normal, as were routine blood studies. The valproic acid blood level was 70 μg/mL, which was in the therapeutic range.

Discussion of Idiopathic Seizure Disorder

Fourth Edition Rating

Permanent impairment evaluation was based on Section 4.1e, Episodic Neurologic Disorders (4th ed, pp 143-144), and the Motor Disturbances subsection of Section 4.1, The Central Nervous System—Cerebrum or Forebrain (4th ed, pp 140-141).

Table 5, Impairments Related to Epilepsy, Seizures, and Convulsive Disorders (4th ed, p 143), specifies that the maximum percentage whole person impairment for paroxysmal disorders is 70%. According to this table, Mr Andrews falls under the impairment description, "Paroxysmal disorder with predictable characteristics and unpredictable occurrence that does not limit usual activities but is a risk to the patient or limits performance of daily activities." The range of whole person impairment in this category is 0% to 14%, and the whole person impairment is judged in this case to be 10%, because the examiner believed Mr Andrews was somewhat more severely affected than most individuals in this category.

The Motor Disturbances paragraphs (4th ed, p 140) specify that impairment due to involuntary movements such as tremors and limitations of voluntary movements due to extrapyramidal disorders without paresis or weakness should be based on the effects of these disturbances on the performance of activities of daily living. Mr Andrews had mild signs of a parkinsonian state, most likely secondary to his anticonvulsant medication (valproic acid), with the tremor and bradykinesia causing interference with his activities of daily living. This was believed to represent further impairment beyond that for the seizure disorder. The *Guides* states that, "pharmacologicals themselves may lead to impairments. In such an instance, the physician should use the appropriate parts of the *Guides* to evaluate the impairment related to the pharmaceutical. If information in the *Guides* is lacking, the physician may combine an estimated impairment percent, the magnitude of which would depend on the severity of the effect, with the primary organ system impairment by means of the Combined Values Chart" (4th ed, p 9). The evaluator assessed the impairment due to the motor disturbances as 10% whole person impairment. By means of the Combined Values Chart (4th ed, pp 322-324), the whole person impairment for seizures (10%) combined with the whole person impairment for the drug-induced parkinsonian state (10%) equals 19% whole person impairment.

Impairment: 19% whole person impairment per the Fourth Edition.

Fifth Edition Rating

Permanent impairment evaluation was based on Section 13.3b, Episodic Neurologic Disorders (5th ed, pp 311-317), and Section 13.5b, Movement Disorders (5th ed, p 337). Table 13-3, Criteria for Rating Impairment Due to Episodic Loss of Consciousness or Awareness (5th ed, p 312), specifies that the maximum percentage whole person impairment for paroxysmal disorders is 70%. According to this table, Mr Andrews falls under the impairment description, "Paroxysmal disorder with predictable characteristics and unpredictable occurrence that does not limit usual activities but is a risk to the individual or limits performance of daily activities." The range of whole person impairment in this category is 0% to 14%, and the whole person impairment is judged in this case to be 10%, because the examiner believed that Mr Andrews was somewhat more severely affected than most individuals in this category. The description of the second category is, "Paroxysmal disorder that interferes with some activities of daily living."

Section 13.5b, Movement Disorders (5th ed, p 337), specifies that movement disorders resulting from cerebral dysfunction are impairments that may affect activities of daily living. Mr Andrews had mild signs of a parkinsonian state, most likely secondary to his anticonvulsant medication (valproic acid), with the tremor and bradykinesia causing interference with his activities of daily living. This was believed to represent further impairment beyond that for the seizure disorder. The Guides states that "pharmacologicals themselves may lead to impairments. In such an instance, the physician should use the appropriate parts of the *Guides* to evaluate the impairment related to pharmaceutical effects. If information in the *Guides* is lacking, the physician may combine an estimated impairment percent based on the severity of the effect, with the primary organ system impairment by means of the Combined Values Chart (p 604)" (5th ed, p 20). Mr Andrews' movement disorder is ratable by means of Table 13-17, Criteria for Rating Impairment of Two Upper Extremities (5th ed, p 340). He has class 1 impairment, based on the description, "Individual can use both upper extremities for self-care, grasping, and holding, but has difficulty with digital dexterity."

The evaluator assessed the impairment due to the movement disturbances as 10% whole person impairment. By means of the Combined Values Chart (5th ed, pp 604-606), the whole person impairment for seizures (10%) combined with the whole person impairment for the drug-induced parkinsonian state (10%) equals 19% whole person impairment.

Impairment: 19% whole person impairment per the Fifth Edition.

Sixth Edition Rating

Permanent impairment rating in Mr. Andrews' case is performed with reference to Table 13-5, Criteria for Rating Impairment Due to Episodic Loss of Consciousness or Awareness (6th ed, p 328).

Mr. Andrews has had a single generalized seizure and has been maintained on antiepileptic medication with side effects.

Mr. Andrews would qualify for rating under class 1. Rating under this class applies when there is a paroxysmal disorder with predictable characteristics and unpredictable occurrence that does not limit usual activities, but is a risk to the individual (for example, he cannot drive).

Mr. Andrews has had one definite seizure 2 years earlier and possibly one other seizure 3 years earlier. He has lost the privilege of driving.

Although Mr. Andrews' seizures have been very infrequent, their presence and their treatment have had a significant impact on him. Considering this, Mr. Andrews would be rated at the upper end of class 1, that is 10% whole person impairment.

Mr. Andrews has experienced problems with side effects on medication in the form of drug-induced parkinsonism.

Criteria for rating of movement disorders are discussed in Section 13.4b (6th ed, p 335). Movement disorders are assessed based on their interference with activities of daily living with reference to Table 13-11, Criteria for Rating Impairments of the Upper Extremities due to CNS Dysfunction (6th ed, p 335), and Table 13-12, Criteria for Rating Impairments due to Station and Gait Disorders (6th ed, p 336), for the upper and lower extremities, respectively.

Table 13-11 (6th ed, p 335) provides criteria for rating impairments in the upper extremities due to central nervous system dysfunction.

Mr. Andrews would qualify for impairment under class 1. Rating under this class applies when an individual can use the involved extremity for activities of daily living and holding but has difficulty with digital dexterity. Ratings under this class range between 1% and 5% whole person impairment for the nondominant upper extremity and between 1% and 10% whole person impairment for the dominant upper extremity.

Based on the data regarding the extent to which these side effects result in interference with activities of daily living, a rating in the midrange for the dominant and nondominant upper extremities could be considered, that is, 3% whole person impairment for the nondominant upper extremity and 5% whole person impairment for the dominant extremity. These values would be combined using the Combined Values Chart, resulting in a total of 8% impairment of the upper extremity.

Combining the impairment for the seizure disorder (10% whole person impairment) with the impairment for upper extremity dysfunction (8% whole person impairment) using the Combined Values Chart, there would be a total of 17% whole person impairment.

Impairment: 17% whole person impairment per the Sixth Edition.

Comment on Idiopathic Seizure Disorder

This case illustrates the difficulties inherent in rating impairment due to any paroxysmal alteration of consciousness or motor function, including seizure disorders and syncope, along with the inevitable side effects of the medications required to control the disorder. The history provided by the patient (or observers) and medical records is often inadequate. The evaluator may have difficulty determining whether the individual has syncope or seizures or even pseudoseizures. An individual with an idiopathic seizure disorder will have a negative or nonspecific interictal EEG in as many as 50% of cases. The seizures may be infrequent and completely unpredictable. In some cases, it may be impossible to determine whether a given event represented a true seizure, thus precluding accurate seizure frequency determination.

The principal, or most troublesome, effect of a seizure disorder on the activities of daily living is the limitation on the ability and legal right to drive a motor vehicle. Laws vary greatly by jurisdiction. It also must be attested by the patient and treating physician that the patient takes the prescribed anticonvulsants faithfully. The situation may be complicated by different standards applied to various types of driving. In an obvious example of this problem, someone with a well-controlled grand mal seizure disorder may be permitted to drive her own automobile without restriction but would never be given a license to drive a school bus.

In Mr Andrews' case, an argument could be made that he may not be stable for rating purposes, as he would benefit from trials of treatment with other antiepileptic medications, which may have a more favorable side effect profile for him.

SUMMARY

Diagnosis	Seizure disorder, convulsive, without mention of intractable epilepsy
Fourth Edition References	Section 4.1e (4th ed, pp 143-144); Section 4.1 (4th ed, pp 140-141), Table 5 (4th ed, p 143)
Fourth Edition Summary	History, detailed neurologic examination, MR imaging. Seizure type is classified, if possible. Controllability of seizures, patient's compliance in taking medication, and adverse effects of anticonvulsant medication are determined. Impact of seizure disorder and medications on activities of daily living is assessed.
Fourth Edition Impairment	19% whole person impairment
Fifth Edition References	Section 13.3b (5th ed, pp 311-317); Section 13.5b (5th ed, p 337), Table 13-3 (5th ed, p 312), Table 13-17 (5th ed, p 340)
Fifth Edition Summary	History, detailed neurologic examination, MR imaging. Seizure type is classified, if possible. Controllability of seizures, patient's compliance in taking medication, and adverse effects of anticonvulsant medication are determined. Impact of seizure disorder and medications on activities of daily living is assessed.
Fifth Edition Impairment	19% whole person impairment
Sixth Edition References	Table 13-5 (6th ed, p 328); Section 13.4b (6th ed, p 335), Table 13-11 (6th ed, p 335), Table 13-12 (6th ed, p 336)

Sixth Edition Summary	History, examination and clinical studies. Nature of disorder and extent of interference with activities of daily living are defined.
Sixth Edition Impairment	17% whole person impairment

CASE 13-6

Severe Head Injury

Subject: Mr Mitchell, a 23-year-old man.

History: Mr Mitchell was a left hand–dominant man who was struck on the right side of his head by a steel girder. Although he was wearing a hard hat, he lost consciousness. Emergency department evaluation revealed him to be oriented to person but not to time, place, or situation. He exhibited little movement of his left arm or leg. Plain films showed a right frontotemporal fracture but no cervical or thoracic spine fracture. A computed tomographic scan of the head disclosed an extracerebral mass. He underwent right frontotemporal craniotomy with evacuation of an acute subdural hematoma. Postoperatively, Mr Mitchell experienced a gradual improvement in his neurologic function.

Current Symptoms: Mr Mitchell regained his ability to speak but continued to experience difficulty with pronunciation; occasionally he could not readily identify objects or relay his thoughts. Mr Mitchell had initially lost bowel and bladder control. Although his bowel symptoms resolved, he continued to experience urinary incontinence necessitating chronic catheterization or the use of perineal padding. He was able to achieve erections and have sexual intercourse with his wife, but he had no sensation on the penis, so intercourse was not pleasurable for him. His left hemiplegia gradually improved to a hemiparesis. He was able to ambulate with the use of a long leg brace on the left and a four-footed cane for stability. He was able to grasp, hold, push, and pull with his left arm, but he was incapable of small muscle control or dexterous use of the left hand. In the immediate postoperative period, he had one generalized tonic-clonic seizure but, after being placed on anticonvulsants, had no further episodes of this type. Mr Mitchell was evaluated 2 years after his injury. He was living at home with his wife. He was able to participate in activities of daily living with some assistance. For example, his wife would help him get in and out of the bathtub and would help him fasten buttons on his shirt or buckle his pants. He was sufficiently mobile around the house and could provide himself with basic food items, but he could not use a manual can opener. He was not capable of driving a car, but he could ride comfortably. He had difficulties with his memory, more marked for recent events. His memory difficulties interfered with everyday activities.

Physical Examination: Mr Mitchell appeared approximately his stated age of 23 years and was awake, alert, and oriented to person, place, and situation. During his interview, he appeared to understand what was asked of him and was able to follow directions. Occasionally, he appeared confused. Active range of motion of the cervical spine was full. The cranial nerves were intact, with no focal abnormality. Deep tendon reflexes were increased in the left arm and leg, with an upgoing plantar response on the left but no clonus. There was generalized weakness on the left side, estimated at 30% less than the right side. Sensation was intact to pinprick and light touch on the extremities. Position sense was well maintained in the great toes bilaterally. His gait was abnormal. He had a typical hemiparetic gait on the left with inability to perform the rapid alternating movements that a normal gait requires and inability to walk without use of a four-footed cane and a long leg brace. Cerebellar examination was abnormal. There was no nystagmus. Rapid alternating movements were impaired in the left hand and arm as well as in the left leg, as much from loss of strength as from loss of control. He had past pointing on the left, negative on the right. He could not stand in the Romberg position.

Discussion of Severe Head Injury

Fourth Edition Rating

Permanent impairment evaluation was based on Section 4.1, The Central Nervous System—Cerebrum or Forebrain (4th ed, pp 140-144). The *Guides* describes nine common categories of impairment resulting from disorders of the forebrain:

1. Disturbances of consciousness and awareness
2. Aphasia or communication disturbances
3. Mental status and integrative functioning abnormalities
4. Emotional or behavioral disturbances
5. Special types of preoccupation or obsession
6. Major motor or sensory abnormalities
7. Movement disorders
8. Episodic neurologic disorders
9. Sleep and arousal disorders

The *Guides'* method for assessing impairment due to disorders of the cerebrum requires that the most severe of the first five categories be used to represent the major cerebral impairment, and any impairments in the remaining four categories may be combined with the most severe of the first five by means of the Combined Values Chart (4th ed, p 322). Hence, evaluating Mr Mitchell's impairment due to cerebral dysfunction requires two initial steps. First, his findings are compared to the specific criteria for impairment in each of the first five categories. The category from which he retains the largest percentage of impairment is used to represent his major cerebral impairment. Second, his findings are compared to the specific criteria for impairment in the remaining four categories, and any percentage of impairment from these four categories is combined with the impairment from the first five.

Three of the first five categories shown are relevant to Mr Mitchell's impairment. First, his condition is consistent with no impairment due to impairment of consciousness and awareness (Table 4, Impairment of Consciousness and Awareness, 4th ed, p 142). Second, his condition is consistent with a 9% whole person impairment due to aphasia or dysphasia (Table 1, Impairments Related to Aphasia or Dysphasia, p 141). Third, his condition is consistent with a 14% whole person impairment due to mental status impairment (Table 2, Mental Status Impairments, 4th ed, p 142). Mr Mitchell does not have an emotional or behavioral disturbance or a special type of preoccupation or obsession. Hence, his total whole person impairment from the first five categories is 14%.

One of the last four categories shown is relevant to Mr Mitchell's impairment, namely, major motor or sensory abnormalities. Although this category is named in the introduction to Section 4.1, The Central Nervous System—Cerebrum or Forebrain (4th ed, p 140), no further reference to this category is found. That is, there is no method in Section 4.1 for evaluating impairment due to major motor or sensory abnormalities as a consequence of disorders of the cerebrum. The Third Edition of the *Guides* indicates that, for motor or sensory problems due to brain injury or disease, the tables for those problems in the spinal cord injury section should be used. If this recommendation is applied to the *Guides* Fourth Edition, Mr Mitchell's impairment is evaluated vis-à-vis Section 4.3, The Spinal Cord (pp 147-149). Consequently, Mr Mitchell will retain a 30% whole person impairment due to station and gait criteria (Station and Gait Impairment Criteria, 4th ed, p 148) and a 35% whole person impairment due to one impaired upper extremity (Table 14, Criteria for One Impaired Upper Extremity, 4th ed, p 148). Mr Mitchell does not have a movement disorder, an episodic neurologic disorder, or a sleep or arousal disorder. Hence, his whole person impairment from the last four categories is 55% (30% and 35%).

In Section 4.1, the nine "more common categories of impairment resulting from disorders of the forebrain" are delineated. Sexual dysfunction and urinary bladder dysfunction, which he sustained as a result of his cerebral injury, are not discussed. Again, his impairment due to those conditions can be assessed vis-à-vis the tables for these problems in the spinal cord injury section. Consequently, Mr Mitchell will retain a 50% whole person impairment for neurologic impairment of his bladder (Table 17, Criteria for Neurologic Impairment of the Bladder, 4th ed, p 149) and a 15% whole person impairment for sexual dysfunction (Table 19, Sexual Impairment Criteria, 4th ed, p 149).

By means of the Combined Values Chart (4th ed, p 322), Mr Mitchell has an 84% whole person impairment (55% combined with 50% combined with 15% combined with 14%).

Impairment: 84% whole person impairment per the Fourth Edition.

Fifth Edition Rating

Impairment from head injury is was rated using Section 13.2, Criteria for Rating Impairment Due to Central Nervous System Disorders (5th ed, pp 308-309), and Section 13.3, Criteria for Rating Cerebral Impairments (5th ed, pp 309-327). The *Guides* indicates that one should first determine whether a disturbance is present in the level of consciousness or awareness; this is not applicable in this case. The evaluator then assesses (2) mental status and highest integrative functioning, (3) understanding and use of language, and (4) any emotional or behavioral disturbance. The most severe cerebral impairment is identified and combined with other neurologic impairments identified in Table 13-1, Neurological Impairments That Are Combined With the Most Severe Impairment (5th ed, p 308). These six other impairment categories are cranial nerve impairments; station, gait, and movement disorders; extremity disorders related to central impairment; spinal cord impairments; chronic pain; and peripheral nerve, motor, and sensory impairments.

Hence, evaluating Mr Mitchell's impairment due to cerebral dysfunction requires two initial steps. First, his findings are compared to the specific criteria for impairment in each of the first four major categories. The category from which he retains the largest percentage of impairment is used to represent his major cerebral impairment. Second, his findings are compared to the specific criteria for impairment in the remaining six categories (listed in Table 13-1, 5th ed, p 308), and any percentages of impairment from these six categories are combined with the impairment from the first four.

The process of assessing speech difficulty is explained in Section 13.3e, Communication Impairments: Dysphasia and Aphasia (5th ed, p 322). The degree of difficulty would fit within the first category of Table 13-7, Criteria for Rating Impairment Due to Aphasia or Dysphasia (5th ed, p 323), that is, "minimal disturbance in comprehension and production of language symbols of daily living." This would qualify as a 0% to 9% whole person impairment, and a rating at the upper limit of this range, that is, 9% whole person impairment, is appropriate.

Mr Mitchell's disturbance in mental status and integrative functioning is evaluated by Section 13.3d, Mental Status, Cognition, and Highest Integrative Function (5th ed, p 319). Table 13-5, Clinical Dementia Rating (CDR) (5th ed, p 320), provides a basis for assessing the extent of dementia. It covers memory, orientation, judgment and problem solving, community activities, home and hobbies, and personal care. Each category is rated as 0 (no abnormality), 0.5 (questionable), 1.0 (mild), 2.0 (moderate), or 3.0 (severe). Mr Mitchell's case would support the following scores:

Area	Impairment Level	Description	Score
Memory (M)	Mild	Moderate memory loss; more marked for recent events; defect interferes with everyday activities	1
Orientation (O)	Questionable	Fully oriented except for slight difficulty with time relationships	0.5
Judgment and Problem Solving (JPS)	Questionable	Slight impairment in solving problems, similarities, and differences; social judgment usually maintained	0.5
Community Affairs (CA)	Questionable	Slight impairment in these activities	0.5
Home and Hobbies (HH)	Mild	Mild but definite impairment of function at home; more difficult chores abandoned; more complicated hobbies and interests abandoned	1
Personal Care (PC)	Mild	Needs prompting	1

Memory is considered the primary category; the other categories are secondary. The *Guides* states that, "if three or more secondary categories are given a score greater or less than the memory score, CDR = the score of the majority of the secondary categories" (5th ed, p 319). Mr Mitchell's memory score (M) is 1.0, three of the other categories are 0.5, and two other categories are 1; therefore, CDR = 0.5. Table 13-6, Criteria for Rating Impairment Related to Mental Status (5th ed, p 320), provides four classes of impairment. A CDR of 0.5 results in a class 1 impairment, described as "paroxysmal disorder with preimpairment exists, but [the patient] is able to perform activities of daily living." Because the patient nearly approaches a class 2 impairment, that is, "impairment requires direction of some activities of daily living," it is appropriate to rate him at the upper range of a mild impairment, that is, at 14% whole person impairment.

Mr Mitchell does not have an emotional or behavioral disturbance or a special type of preoccupation or obsession. Hence, his total whole person impairment from the first four major categories is 14%.

Mr Mitchell also has impairment due to station and gait disorder, one upper extremity dysfunction, bladder dysfunction, and sexual dysfunction. These impairments will be combined with the major category impairment of 14%.

Subsection 13.5a (5th ed, p 336) provides impairments for problems with station and gait. This section is used to rate problems with dysfunction in the lower extremities secondary to central nervous system pathology, which includes pathology affecting the cerebral hemispheres, brainstem, or spinal cord. Table 13-15, Criteria for Rating Impairments Due to Station and Gait Disorders (5th ed, p 336), provides for four classes of rating of impairments due to station and gait disorders, with ratings ranging between 1% and 60% whole person impairment. Impairment ratings for station and gait disorders are determined according to their effect on ambulation. Mr Mitchell's difficulties fit the description of a class 3 impairment, that is, "rises and maintains standing position with difficulty, cannot walk without assistance," which corresponds with 20% to 39% whole person impairment. A midrange value of 30% whole person impairment is appropriate.

Section 13.6 (5th ed, pp 338-340) discusses criteria for rating of impairments of upper extremities related to central impairment. This section of the *Guides* (unlike Chapter 16, The Upper Extremities) makes a distinction between the dominant and nondominant upper extremity. This is because the basic tasks of everyday living depend on dexterous use of the dominant upper extremity. Criteria for rating impairment of one upper extremity are referenced in Table 13-16 (5th ed, p 338). Mr Mitchell meets the description of a class 3 impairment, that is, the "individual can use the involved extremity but has difficulty with self-care activities." This is associated with a range of 25% to 39% whole person impairment, and a value toward the higher range is selected, that is, 35% whole person impairment.

Sexual dysfunction and urinary bladder dysfunction, which Mr Mitchell sustained as a result of his cerebral injury, are not discussed in Section 13.2; however, Section 13.7, Criteria for Rating Spinal Cord and Related Impairments (5th ed, pp 340-342), covers "impairment resulting from spinal cord injuries and other adverse conditions including those relating to station and gait, use of the upper extremities, respiration, urinary bladder function, anorectal function, sexual function, and pain." Subsection 13.7b (5th ed, p 341) pertains to urinary system neurologic impairments. The criteria for rating neurologic impairments of the bladder are found in Table 13-19,

Criteria for Rating Neurologic Impairment of the Bladder (5th ed, p 341). Mr Mitchell has no reflex or voluntary control of his bladder and therefore has a class 4 impairment. A midrange value of 50% whole person impairment is selected.

Subsection 13.7d (5th ed, p 342) addresses sexual system neurologic impairments. The criteria for these are referenced in Table 13-21, Criteria for Rating Neurological Sexual Impairment (5th ed, p 342). He is rated in the midrange for class 2 at 15% whole person impairment, meeting the criterion, "reflex sexual function is possible, but there is no awareness." An important note in the text (5th ed, p 342) indicates that these ratings are adjusted for age according to criteria outlined in Chapter 7, The Urinary and Reproductive System. This chapter indicates (5th ed, Section 7.7, p 156) that impairment percentages for male reproductive organs are increased by 50% for men younger than 40 and decreased by 50% for men older than 65. Therefore, his rating is increased to 23% whole person impairment.

His impairment is based on the combined value of the whole person impairments for his major category rating (14%), station and gait dysfunction (30%), upper extremity dysfunction (35%), bladder dysfunction (50%), and sexual dysfunction (23%). According to the Combined Values Chart (5th ed, p 604), this results in 85% whole person impairment.

Impairment: 85% whole person impairment per the Fifth Edition.

Sixth Edition Rating

Impairment from head injury was rated using Section 13.2, Method for Rating Impairments due to Nervous System Disorders (6th ed, p 326), and Section 13.3, Criteria for Rating Cerebral Impairments (6th ed, pp 326-333). The *Guides* states that the first step in assessing central nervous system impairment is to assess the most severe category cerebral impairment rating, if any, from four categories. These are:

1. State of consciousness and level of awareness, whether permanent or episodic
2. Mental status evaluation and integrative functioning
3. Use and understanding of language
4. Influence of behavior and mood

The rater next assesses impairment, if any, of the cranial nerves, upper and lower extremities, bowel and bladder (due to neurogenic problems), sexual function, neurologic respiratory impairment, and peripheral nervous system.

These are then combined with a single most severe category of cerebral impairment.

The initial step in assessing cerebral function is to determine whether disturbance is present in the level of consciousness or awareness. This may be a permanent alteration or an intermittent alteration in consciousness, awareness, or arousal.

The second step is to evaluate mental status and highest integrative functioning.

The third step involves identifying any difficulty with understanding and use of language.

Step four involves evaluating any emotional or behavioral disturbances such as depression that can modify cerebral function.

Step five requires identifying the most severe cerebral impairment of those previously listed. This would then be combined with any or multiple other distinct neurologic impairments.

Mr Mitchell does not have a disturbance of consciousness or awareness, either permanent or intermittent. Although Mr Mitchell had one seizure in the postoperative period, he did not have a paroxysmal seizure disorder. It is common for a person to experience a seizure during the immediate postinjury period, yet not develop a chronic seizure disorder. In this circumstance, anticonvulsant maintenance therapy was discontinued 2 years after injury, so permanent drug therapy is not anticipated. He consequently retains no impairment due to paroxysmal seizure disorder, unless side effects of the anticonvulsant maintenance therapy are impairing.

Mr Mitchell has problems with cognition and highest integrative functioning.

Table 13-8, Criteria for Rating Neurologic Impairment due to Alteration in Mental Status, Cognition, and Highest Integrative Function (MSCHIF) (6th ed, p 331), was used.

Mr Mitchell was noted to appear occasionally confused. He had difficulty with memory, more marked for recent events. Memory difficulties interfered with everyday activities.

Mr Mitchell would qualify for rating under class 2 due to alteration in MSCHIF. Ratings under this class range between 11% and 20% whole person impairment. Patients who qualify for rating under this class demonstrate moderate abnormalities on mental status examination or neuropsychological testing. Alteration in MSCHIF in this class interferes with the ability to assume some normal roles or perform activities of daily living.

The possibility of rating Mr Mitchell under class 3 was considered. Mr Mitchell is unable to use tools such as a manual can opener and is not capable of driving.

Impairment ratings under class 3 range between 21% and 35% whole person impairment. Patients in this class demonstrate severe abnormalities on mental status testing and neuropsychological assessment and have alterations in MSCHIF, such that they significantly interfere with the patients' abilities to assume normal roles or perform activities of daily living.

Considering all of the data contained in the vignette, it is more likely Mr Mitchell would qualify for rating under class 2 than class 3. However, a rating at the upper end of class 2 would be considered.

In view of this, Mr Mitchell's rating under class 2 would represent 20% whole person impairment.

Table 13-9, Criteria for Rating Impairment due to Aphasia or Dysphasia (6th ed, p 332), was used. Mr Mitchell was noted to appear to understand what was asked of him. He was able to follow directions but occasionally appeared confused. Mr Mitchell would be viewed as having minimal disturbance in comprehension and production of language symbols for daily living. This would qualify Mr Mitchell for rating under class 1. Ratings under this class range between 1% and 10% whole person impairment.

Mr Mitchell does not have an emotional or behavioral disturbance related to head injury for which impairment rating would apply.

The most severe cerebral impairment in Mr Mitchell's case relates to alteration in MSCHIF (20% whole person impairment). Therefore, this represents a cerebral impairment rating component in Mr Mitchell's case.

Mr Mitchell has a left hemiparesis. He is left-hand dominant. There is generalized left-sided weakness. Rapid alternating movements were impaired with the left hand and arm related to the loss of strength and loss of control.

Per Table 13-11, Criteria for Rating Impairments of the Upper Extremities due to CNS Dysfunction (6th ed, p 335), Mr Mitchell would qualify for impairment rating under class 3; he can use his upper extremity only as a gross assistant in activities of daily living. Impairment under class 3 for lesions affecting the dominant upper extremity ranges between 21% and 40% whole person impairment. A rating of 30% whole person impairment could be considered in Mr Mitchell's case.

Per Table 13-12, Criteria for Rating Impairments due to Station and Gait Disorders (6th ed, p 336), Mr Mitchell qualifies for impairment rating under class 4. Rating under this class applies when the individual cannot stand without help, mechanical support, and/or an assistive device. Mr Mitchell has a hemiparetic gait and requires the use of a four-footed cane and a long leg brace. Ratings under this class range between 36% and 50% whole person impairment. A rating of 40% whole person impairment could be considered for this aspect of Mr Mitchell's condition.

Mr Mitchell has problems with sexual dysfunction and urinary bladder dysfunction.

Table 13-14, Criteria for Rating the Neurogenic Bladder (6th ed, p 337), was used. Mr Mitchell would qualify for impairment rating under class 4. Rating under this class applies for total incontinence. Mr Mitchell requires the use of chronic catheterization or the use of perineal padding. Ratings under this class range between 21% and 30% whole person impairment. In Mr Mitchell's case, a rating of 30% whole person impairment applies.

Table 13-15, Criteria for Rating Neurogenic Sexual Dysfunction (6th ed, p 338), was used. Mr Mitchell qualifies for impairment rating under class 2. Rating under this class applies when reflex sexual functioning is possible but there is no awareness. Ratings under this class range between 6% and 10% whole person impairment. In Mr Mitchell's case, a rating of 10% whole person impairment would apply.

Referring to Section 13.7c, Neurogenic Sexual Dysfunction (6th ed, p 336), it is noted that the individual's previous sexual functioning should be considered by the physician. Age is one of the criteria for evaluating previous sexual functioning. Adjustments for age are to be made according to the criteria outlined in Chapter 7, the Urinary and Reproductive Systems.

Section 7.7, Male Reproductive Organs (6th ed, pp 143-149) notes that evaluators can, at their discretion, adjust the ratings upward (for men younger than 40) or downward (for men older than 65) by 10% based on age and the level of premorbid sexual functioning. In Mr Mitchell's case, considering that he is 23 years old, his rating would be increased by 10%, resulting in a total of 11% whole person impairment for neurogenic sexual dysfunction.

The impairments for the most severe cerebral impairment and impairments for upper extremity, lower extremity, and bladder and sexual dysfunction, are combined using the Combined Values Chart (6th ed, pp 604-606).

The greatest impairment value is that related to Mr Mitchell's gait disorder, at 40% whole person impairment. This would then be combined with the value for Mr Mitchell's upper extremity dysfunction of 30% whole person impairment.

Using the Combined Values Chart, this results in a rating of 58% whole person impairment.

Combining this with the rating for neurogenic bladder (30%), using the Combined Values Chart, there would be a 71% whole person impairment.

Combining this with the impairment rating for alteration in MSCHIF (20%), using the Combined Values Chart, there would be a total of 77% whole person impairment.

Combining this with the impairment rating for neurogenic sexual dysfunction (11% whole person impairment), using the Combined Values Chart, there would be a total of 80% whole person impairment.

Impairment: 80% whole person impairment per the Sixth Edition.

Comment on Severe Head Injury

There are some significant differences between ratings determined with the Fifth Edition and Sixth Edition of the *Guides* for patients with severe head injury and multiple neurologic deficits. These differences include those related to the assessment of mental status, cognition, and highest integrative function. The approach in the Sixth Edition is more straightforward and, at the same time, more flexible than that of the Fifth Edition. The assessment of impairment in this category is constrained in the Fifth Edition by the use of the Clinical Dementia Rating method.

Another difference, particularly with respect to impairment rating values, concerns the rating for neurologic sexual impairment. Under the Fifth Edition criteria, ratings could range between 1% and 20% whole person impairment with upward or downward adjustments by 50%, depending on age.

In the Sixth Edition, the maximum rating for neurogenic sexual dysfunction is 15% whole person impairment. This is adjusted upward or downward by, at most, 10% at the discretion of the evaluator for criteria that may include age.

SUMMARY

Diagnosis	Closed head injury
Fourth Edition References	Section 4.1 (4th ed, pp 140-144); Section 4.3 (4th ed, pp 147-149), Table 1 (4th ed, p 141), Table 2 (4th ed, p 142), Table 4 (4th ed, p 142), Table 13 (4th ed, p 148), Table 14 (4th ed, p 148), Table 17 (4th ed, p 149), Table 19 (4th ed, p 149)
Fourth Edition Summary	History and neurologic examination. Impairment due to the nine more common categories of disorders of the forebrain is determined. The most severe of the first five categories should be used to represent the cerebral impairment; any impairments in the last four categories may be combined with the most severe of the first five categories. Additional conditions not considered in these nine categories can be assessed by means of the tables for spinal cord injury.
Fourth Edition Impairment	84% whole person impairment
Fifth Edition References	Section 13.2 (5th ed, pp 308-309); Section 13.3 (5th ed, pp 309-327), Table 13-1 (5th ed, p 308), Table 13-5 (5th ed, p 320),Table 13-7 (5th ed, p 323), Table 13-15 (5th ed, p 336), Table 13-16 (5th ed, p 338), Table 13-19 (5th ed, p 341), Table 13-21 (5th ed, p 342), Combined Values Chart (5th ed, p 604)
Fifth Edition Summary	History and neurologic examination. Disturbance in the level of consciousness or awareness is determined; mental status and highest integrative functioning, understanding and use of language, and any emotional or behavioral disturbance are assessed. The most severe cerebral impairment is identified and combined with other neurologic impairments, including cranial nerve impairments; station, gait, and movement disorders; extremity disorders related to central impairment; spinal cord impairments; chronic pain; and peripheral nerve, motor, and sensory impairments.

Fifth Edition Impairment	85% whole person impairment
Sixth Edition References	Section 13.2 (6th ed, p 326); Section 13.3 (6th ed, p 326-333), Table 13-8 (6th ed, p 331), Table 13-9 (6th ed, p 332), Table 13-11 (6th ed, p 335), Table 13-12 (6th ed, p 336), Table 13-14 (6th ed, p 337), Table 13-15 (6th ed, p 338); Section 13.7c (6th ed, p 336); Section 7.7 (6th ed, pp 143-149); Combined Values Chart (6th ed, pp 604-606)
Sixth Edition Summary	History, examination, and clinical studies. Nature of disorder and extent of interference with activities of daily living are defined.
Sixth Edition Impairment	80% whole person impairment

Chapter 14

Mental and Behavioral Disorders

CASE 14-1

Depression

Subject: Mr Krupp, a 50-year-old man.

History: Mr Krupp worked as a salesperson for a high-end stationery and writing supply company for 20 years. He was very successful in this position and won several performance awards before he experienced major depression. Mr Krupp was diagnosed with depression at 50 years of age. His depression began after a severe on-the-job back strain injury. The back strain kept him out of work for 6 months and resulted in financial and marital problems. The back pain ultimately resolved after 6 months. Mr Krupp returned to his work as a sales representative, but he has struggled to meet sales goals for a full-time position because of problems with fatigue, depressed mood, irritability, and difficulty with concentration. At the time of evaluation, he worked part-time, covering about two-thirds the number of customers he previously serviced.

At the onset of his depression, Mr Krupp reported he felt depressed nearly every day during the previous month. Normally, he was very upbeat about his work, but he found himself wanting to avoid meeting with customers because he could not pretend to be upbeat. He also described himself as withdrawn and uninterested in family events. He felt this change in his behavior contributed to increased arguments with his wife and teenage children, as he was more irritable and moody. Mr Krupp's medical records indicated he had lost 10 pounds without any attempt to diet during the first 12 months of his depression. He reported that food just did not taste the same. Although he was able to fall asleep at night, he woke early and could not get back to sleep. He reported feeling worried about his work problems and financial difficulties. He felt his sleep problems contributed to his fatigue nearly every day. He reported a reduced sexual libido. Mr Krupp described struggling with feelings of guilt, worthlessness, and hopelessness during the first 12 months of his depression. He was frustrated by his inability to make decisions and follow through on customer contacts. He found himself wondering whether life was worth living but denied any active suicidal plan, saying he would never hurt his family that way.

Mental Status Examination: The consulting psychiatrist's mental status examination documented that Mr Krupp presented as neatly groomed and meticulous in his appearance. He was dressed in casual attire, wearing pressed chinos and a golf shirt. Although he had an athletic build, he appeared somewhat thin. There was no evidence of unusual mannerisms, psychomotor retardation, or restlessness and no general signs of anxiety. He was cooperative and attentive throughout most of the evaluation. He appeared to become increasingly tired as the interview progressed and lost focus on two occasions. He also exhibited some irritability as the interview progressed.

Mr Krupp's mood was best described as consistently depressed as evidenced by his tone of voice and sad facial features. His affect, although appropriate to the content of the discussions, was restricted in range. He was occasionally tearful when discussing how difficult it was for him to engage in work activities, family events, and golf outings with friends. He demonstrated mild humor connected to self-deprecating comments. His speech patterns indicated normal speech production with no signs of disturbance in speech. He denied any perceptual disturbances such as hallucinations and illusions or depersonalization. His thought process was intact, with no evidence of vague or empty thoughts or any interruption in his train of thought. He did appear moderately preoccupied with his symptoms of depression as demonstrated by a number of comments that suggested he was worried about the change in his attitude and behavior. He also offered somatic complaints that consisted of increased incidences of headaches and stomach problems.

Mr Krupp's sensorium and cognition were assessed using the Mini-Mental State Examination.[1] He was alert and oriented to time, place, and person. His intellectual ability was judged to be above average as demonstrated by his vocabulary and the cognitive demands of his job. When asked to count backward from 100 by seven (serial sevens), he had difficulty sustaining his concentration and made a subtraction error. His immediate, recent, and long-term memory was determined to be intact. His fund of knowledge was consistent with his college level background, and he demonstrated abstract reasoning skills.

Mr Krupp did not exhibit any signs of impulsivity. He displayed social judgment during the interview and demonstrated insight about his depression and need for treatment. The information he provided about his depression and life circumstances was consistent with the signs and symptoms he displayed during the interview and with the clinical records provided by his primary care doctor and treating mental health provider. There was no evidence of any previous episode of depression or anxiety. He had a negative history for alcohol and substance abuse. He did not smoke and described himself as generally healthy. He reported a negative family history for depression or anxiety. His primary care physician had ruled out medical conditions that could account for his symptoms of depression.

Initial Mental and Behavioral Disorders Diagnosis: Mr Krupp's diagnosis of depression was derived from the *Diagnostic and Statistical Manual of Mental Disorders*, Fourth Edition (DSM-IV),[2] as follows:

Axis I: 296.22, Major depressive episode, single episode, moderate

Axis II: No diagnosis

Axis III: History of back strain injury

Axis IV: Financial difficulties related to work interruption; family discord

Axis V: Global Assessment of Functioning Scale (GAF)[2] score, 55

Treatment: The psychiatrist prescribed an antidepressant, citalopram (Celexa), initially. However, Mr Krupp experienced only a partial reduction in his symptoms of depression and found the side effects very unpleasant. Several antidepressant trials of sufficient length and appropriate dosages were tried over a 12-month period. At the time of evaluation he was taking bupropion (Wellbutrin), as this medication had been the most effective in reducing his symptoms of depression and had the fewest unpleasant side effects. His psychiatrist added lorazepam to his medication regimen to help him with the occasional sleep disturbance. Despite the problems he had with previous antidepressant therapy, Mr Krupp demonstrated compliance with the prescribed medication regimen.

Mr Krupp's primary care physician referred him to a psychologist for cognitive-behavioral psychotherapy. The psychologist administered the Symptom Checklist-90-R (SCL-90-R)[3] and the Minnesota Multiphasic Personality Inventory-2 (MMPI-2).[4] The results of the SCL-90-R, a standardized self-report instrument, were based on comparison to an outpatient psychiatric population. Mr Krupp's scores indicated moderate symptomatic distress levels. At the time of this assessment, his level of depression was moderately elevated and clinical in nature. Mr Krupp also experienced an elevated level of anxiety, although possibly not at a clinical level. The anxiety may have been secondary to Mr Krupp's experience of current life stressors. The pattern of results from the MMPI-2, a second standardized instrument, indicates a valid administration of the test. Mr Krupp's responses suggested he was moderately depressed and appeared to be tense and anxious. Other symptoms included difficulty concentrating, worry, and functioning at a low level of efficiency as a result of depressed mood. Individuals with this profile are often less able to experience pleasure.

Mr Krupp reported meeting with the psychologist once weekly for four sessions, bimonthly for 7 months, then monthly for about 5 months. The psychologist documented treatment gains, in that Mr Krupp's symptoms of moderate depression decreased to mild depression during psychotherapy. Mr Krupp agreed with this assessment and felt his symptoms improved to a point where he felt depressed, but not so intensely.

Current Symptoms: At examination 2 years after the onset of depression, Mr Krupp reported that he continued to experience mild depression with symptoms of depressed mood, continued feelings of guilt about his mental state, difficulty with fatigue and stamina, and problems with concentration. He also described feeling tense, anxious, and irritable at times. His symptoms had stabilized, and he was described by his primary care physician and the consulting psychiatrist as having reached maximum medical improvement.

Mr Krupp's wife reports that he is still not able to enjoy social activities that he once enjoyed. He tends to remain at home unless prodded to attend social activities. Both he and his spouse admitted to tension and strain in their relationship since he developed depression. Mr Krupp reported only minor interest in sexual relations. His relationship with his children is described as good. He has lost some friends during this episode of depression.

Mr Krupp continued to work at reduced hours, approximately 32 hours a week, as he had difficulty sustaining energy throughout the day. He reported napping in his car on occasion to overcome the fatigue he felt, so that he could continue with his workday. He was more likely to feel depressed and irritable when tired. His employer was willing for him to continue at that level of productivity because his pay consisted of a base rate plus commission. He maintained a smaller sales route as an accommodation for his psychiatric disorder. His difficulty with concentration continued to be an issue for Mr Krupp. His wife helped him develop an electronic checklist for each customer to compensate for his problems with concentration and focus. He had regained the 10 pounds he lost during the depression but still reported less pleasure in eating.

Discussion of Depression

Fourth Edition Rating

Permanent impairment rating was based on Chapter 14, Mental and Behavioral Disorders (4th ed, pp 291-302). The authors note, "There is no available empiric evidence to support any method for assigning a percentage of whole person impairment, but the following approach to estimating the extent of mental impairments is offered as a guide" (4th ed, p 300). The table entitled Classification of Impairments Due to Mental and Behavioral Disorders (4th ed, p 301) summarizes the approach, which provides five classes of impairment based on a person's capacity to function in four areas: activities of daily living; social functioning; concentration, persistence, and pace; and adaptation.

Mr Krupp's mental and behavioral impairment was rated with this method as follows:

Activities of Daily Living: Activities of daily living are identified as self-care, personal hygiene, communication, travel, sexual function, sleep, and social and recreational activities. According to the Fourth Edition (p 294), "Any limitation in these activities should relate to the mental disorder rather than to factors such as lack of money or transportation. In the context of the individual's overall situation, the quality of these activities is judged by their independence, appropriateness, effectiveness and sustainability." The person's ability to initiate and sustain these activities independently also should be considered in determining the impairment. Mr Krupp's current symptoms of major depression indicated no impairment in his ability to carry out self-care and personal hygiene. He was able to communicate appropriately with others, as demonstrated by his ability to work at least part-time at his sales position. He traveled independently as demonstrated by his driving to various customer locations. He continued to experience mild problems with sleep disturbance that occurred about once a week. He also reported diminished interest in sexual function. Class 1, no impairment.

Social Functioning: "Social functioning refers to an individual's capacity to interact appropriately and communicate effectively with other individuals. Social functioning includes the ability to get along with others, such as family members, friends, neighbors, grocery clerks, landlords, or bus drivers." (4th ed, p 294). Mr Krupp consistently demonstrated that he experienced problems with social functioning attributable to his symptoms of depression. His relationship with his wife was more tense and argumentative. He had withdrawn from many other social relationships. His wife confirmed that she had to urge him to engage in social activities that he once enjoyed. They rarely entertained others in their home, as Mr Krupp perceived it as too much effort. He was able to maintain social interactions in the work setting but struggled when fatigued or more depressed. Class 2, mild impairment.

Concentration, Persistence, and Pace: Concentration, persistence, and pace refers to "the ability to sustain focused attention long enough to permit the timely completion of tasks commonly found in work settings. In activities of daily living, concentration may be reflected in terms of ability to complete household tasks" (4th ed, p 294). Although Mr Krupp complained of difficulty concentrating, he was able to return to work, at least part-time (32 hours per week). He used an electronic checklist to help him organize and address his customer needs. His fatigue continued to pose problems for him, as he did not have the stamina to work 40-plus hours a week. His employer agreed to a reduced workload because he had been a valuable employee and was well liked by his customers. Class 2, mild impairment.

Adaptation: Adaptation refers to the ability of an individual to respond appropriately to changes in the work setting, including adapting to stressful circumstances. This edition of the *Guides* identifies stressors common to the work setting as "attendance, making decisions, scheduling, completing tasks, and interacting with supervisors and peers" (4th ed, p 294). Mr Krupp's persistent depressed mood and fatigue had affected his ability to carry out his full-time activities as a sales representative. He had been able to return to work with an accommodation by his employer that involved a reduced number of customers. This reduction in customers resulted in his working 32 hours per week. Mr Krupp was able to maintain this workload because he could build in break times to rest and recover his mental stamina. He was able to make decisions but became overwhelmed at times, which contributed to his mental fatigue. Class 2, mild impairment.

Impairment: Class 2, mild impairment per the Fourth Edition.

Fifth Edition Rating

Permanent impairment rating was based on Chapter 14, Mental and Behavioral Disorders (5th ed, pp 357-370). The *Guides* Fifth Edition (p 361) instructs the reader as follows:

> Percentages are not provided to estimate mental impairment in this edition of the *Guides*. Unlike cases with some organ systems, there are no precise measures of impairment in mental disorders. The use of percentages implies a certainty that does not exist. Percentages are likely to be used inflexibly by adjudicators, who then are less likely to take into account the many factors that influence mental and behavioral impairment. In addition,

the authors are unaware of data that show the reliability of the impairment percentage.

The authors of this chapter point out that no empirical evidence exists to support any method that assigns a percentage of whole person impairment for mental and behavioral disorders. Table 14-1, Classes of Impairment Due to Mental and Behavioral Disorders (5th ed, p 363) summarizes an approach using four classes of impairment based on a person's capacity to function in four areas: activities of daily living; social functioning; concentration, persistence, and pacing; and adaptation.

Mr Krupp's mental and behavioral impairment was rated with this method as follows:

Activities of Daily Living: Activities of daily living are identified as self-care, personal hygiene, communication, travel, sexual function, sleep, and social and recreational activities. According to the Fifth Edition (p 361), "Any limitation in these activities should relate to the mental disorder rather than to factors such as lack of money or transportation. In the context of the individual's overall situation, the quality of these activities is judged by their independence, appropriateness, effectiveness, and sustainability." The person's ability to initiate and sustain these activities independently should also be considered in determining the impairment. Mr Krupp's current symptoms of major depression indicated no impairment in his ability to carry out self-care and personal hygiene. He was able to communicate appropriately with others as demonstrated by his ability to work at least part-time at his sales position. He traveled independently as demonstrated by his driving to various customer locations. He continued to experience mild problems with sleep disturbance that occurred about once a week. He also reported diminished interest in sexual function. Class 1, no impairment.

Social Functioning: "Social functioning refers to an individual's capacity to interact appropriately and communicate effectively with other individuals. Social functioning includes the ability to get along with others, such as family members, friends, neighbors, grocery clerks, landlords, or bus drivers" (4th ed, p 294). Mr Krupp consistently demonstrated that he experienced problems with social functioning attributable to his symptoms of depression. His relationship with his wife was more tense and argumentative. He had withdrawn from many other social relationships. His wife confirmed that she had to urge him to engage in social activities that he once enjoyed. They rarely entertained others in their home, as Mr Krupp perceived it as too much effort. He was able to maintain social interactions in the work setting but struggled when fatigued or more depressed. Class 2, mild impairment.

Concentration, Persistence, and Pace: The *Guides* Fifth Edition states, "Concentration, persistence, and pace are needed to perform many activities of daily living, including task completion. Task completion refers to the ability to sustain focused attention long enough to permit timely completion of tasks commonly found in activities of daily living or work settings" (p 362). Although Mr Krupp complained of difficulty concentrating, he was able to return to work, at least part-time (32 hours per week). He used an electronic checklist to help him organize and address his customer needs. His fatigue continued to pose problems for him, as he did not have the mental stamina to work 40-plus hours a week. His employer agreed to a reduced workload because Mr Krupp had been a valuable employee and was well liked by his customers. Class 2, mild impairment.

Adaptation: According to the *Guides* Fifth Edition, adaptation is "deterioration or decompensation in a complex or work-like setting" (Section 14.3d, p 362). This refers to:

> an individual's repeated failure to adapt to stressful circumstances. In the face of these circumstances, the individual may withdraw from the situation or experience an exacerbation of signs and symptoms of the mental disorder; that is, he or she may decompensate or have difficulty maintaining performance of activities of daily living, continuing social relationships, or completing tasks. Stresses common to the workplace include attendance, making decisions, scheduling, completing tasks, and interacting with supervisors and peers (p 362).

Mr Krupp's persistent depressed mood and fatigue had affected his ability to carry out his full-time activities as a sales representative. He was able to return to work with an accommodation by his employer that involved a reduced number of customers. This reduction in customers resulted in his working 32 hours per week. Mr Krupp was able to maintain this workload because he could build in break times to rest and recover his mental stamina. He was able to make decisions but became overwhelmed at times, which contributed to his mental fatigue. Class 2, mild impairment.

Impairment: Class 2, mild impairment, per the Fifth Edition.

Sixth Edition Rating

Chapter 14, Mental and Behavioral Disorders (6th ed, pp 347-382) is used to determine a permanent impairment rating for psychiatric disorders. The *Guides* Sixth Edition involves the use of three scales: the Brief Psychiatric Rating Scale (BPRS),[5,6] the Global Assessment of Functioning Scale (GAF); and the Psychiatric Impairment Rating Scale (PIRS)[7]. The BPRS measures major psychotic and nonpsychotic symptoms of patients with major psychiatric illnesses. This instrument consists of a list of 24 symptoms that are judged on a scale from 1 (symptom not present) to 7 (symptom extremely severe). The GAF is used to identify psychiatric symptoms and functional limitations across psychological, social, and occupational domains. The evaluator identifies the range (eg, 61-70) consistent with the patient's symptoms and functional limitations. Table 14-5, Functional Impairment Scales for Patients with M&BD (6th ed, p 352), specifies six areas of functional impairment that are intended to provide the evaluator with a scale to rate the effect of the patient's mental and behavioral symptoms on function.

There are several points that must be taken into consideration when performing a psychiatric impairment rating according to the *Guides* Sixth Edition. These points are stated in Section 14.5d, Further Considerations (6th ed, pp 355-356). A psychiatric rating is conducted only on Axis I diagnoses that are limited to mood disorders, anxiety disorders, or psychotic disorders. Axis II diagnoses are not ratable, as these are considered preexisting conditions. The focus of this evaluation is limited to the impact psychiatric symptoms have on function. Limitations related to physical function or pain are addressed in other chapters of the *Guides*. The specific details for the method of impairment rating are addressed in Section 14.6, Method of Impairment Rating (6th ed, pp 356-360).

Using the example outlined previously, the evaluator determined that Mr Krupp's mental and behavioral disorder impairment rating was 5%. This rating was calculated according to the following four steps:

Step 1: Determine the BPRS impairment rating score.

The evaluator determined Mr Krupp's psychiatric symptoms and level of severity, as explained in Section 14.8, Appendix: Brief Psychiatric Rating Scale (Expanded Version) (6th ed, pp 369-381), rating each factor on a scale of 1 (not present) to 7 (extremely severe). Table 14-8, BPRS Form (6th ed, p 357), summarizes the scores.

1. Somatic concerns: 1
2. Anxiety: 3
3. Depression: 3
4. Suicidality: 1
5. Guilt: 3
6. Hostility: 1
7. Elevated mood: 1

8. Grandiosity: 1
9. Suspiciousness: 1
10. Hallucinations: 1
11. Unusual thought content: 1
12. Bizarre behavior: 1
13. Self-neglect: 1
14. Disorientation: 1
15. Conceptual disorganization: 1
16. Blunted affect: 1
17. Emotional withdrawal: 3
18. Motor retardation: 1
19. Tension: 3
20. Uncooperativeness: 1
21. Excitement: 1
22. Distractibility: 1
23. Motor hyperactivity: 1
24. Mannerisms and posturing : 1

Sum the total of the 24 BPRS symptom construct scores identified at maximal medical improvement: 34.

Find the BPRS impairment score in Table 14-9, Impairment Score of Brief Psychiatric Rating Scale (BPRS) (6th ed, p 357): 10% BPRS impairment score.

Step 2: Determine GAF score impairment at maximum medical improvement.

Mr Krupp currently experienced symptoms of major depression and some difficulty with his psychological, social, and occupational functioning, consistent with a GAF range of between 61 and 70. Using Table 14-10, Impairment Score of Global Assessment of Functioning Scale (GAF) (6th ed, p 358), this GAF range is consistent with a GAF impairment score of 5%.

Step 3: Determine the PIRS rating score.

The PIRS score is based on determining whether the patient experiences functional impairment, as assessed by the following tables in the *Guides* Sixth Edition:

- Table 14-11, Self-Care, Personal Hygiene, and Activities of Daily Living (p 358)
- Table 14-12, Role Functioning, Social and Recreational Activities (p 359)
- Table 14-13, Travel (p 359)
- Table 14-14, Interpersonal Relationships (p 359)
- Table 14-15, Concentration, Persistence, and Pace (p 359)
- Table 14-16, Resilience and Employability (p 360)

Determine the rating score for each table.

Table 14-11: Self-Care, Personal Hygiene, and Activities of Daily Living

Mr Krupp was able to provide self-care and maintain appropriate personal hygiene. He was able to carry out activities of daily living without any need for assistance from others. This behavior is consistent with a rating of no deficit. *Score = 1.*

Table 14-12: Role Functioning, Social and Recreational Activities

Mr Krupp continued to exhibit mild impairment in role functioning, particularly concerning social functioning. Although he occasionally went out to social or family events, he was much less likely to do so since the onset of depression. His wife confirmed that she had to prod him to attend family gatherings, something he once enjoyed. When he attended these events, he was more quiet and reserved than before the depression. They rarely entertained at home since he became depressed. *Score = 2.*

Table 14-13: Travel

Mr Krupp was able to drive his car and used it regularly in his work as a salesperson. He required no supervision to travel to new places. *Score = 1.*

Table 14-14: Interpersonal Relationships

Mr Krupp experienced mild impairment with interpersonal relationships. He and his wife reported strain and tension in their relationship since he became depressed. They tended to argue more about financial problems and his tendency to avoid dealing with problems. He had also reported the loss of some friends over the past 2 years. *Score = 2.*

Table 14-15: Concentration, Persistence, and Pace

Although Mr Krupp continued to express concerns about his ability to concentrate, he was able to manage the details of his sales job. *Score = 1.*

Table 14-16: Resilience and Employability

Mr Krupp continued to have trouble with work performance due to his symptoms of depression, as he was able to work only approximately 32 hours a week. His employer had reduced the number of customers he was responsible for managing. This was confirmed by a reduction in his base pay. *Score* = 2.

Arrange the scores: 1, 1, 1, 2, 2, 2

Select the middle two scores: 1, 2

Sum the middle two scores: 3

PIRS impairment score per Table 14-17, Impairment Score of Psychiatric Impairment Rating Scale (PIRS) (6th ed, p 360): 5% PIRS impairment score.

Step 4: List BPRS, GAF, and PIRS impairment scores.

BPRS impairment score: 10%

GAF impairment score: 5%

PIRS impairment score: 5%

Of the three impairment scores, the mental and behavioral disorder impairment rating is the middle value: 5%.

Impairment: 5% whole person impairment per the Sixth Edition.

Comment on Rating Process for Depression

Using the classification system outlined in Chapter 14, Mental and Behavioral Disorders (4th ed), it was determined that Mr Krupp experienced an overall class 2 impairment due to his symptoms of major depression. Because the Fifth Edition of the *Guides* does not direct the evaluator to provide an overall impairment rating, none was identified. Instead, the ratings of impairment were provided for the four domains: activities of daily living; social functioning; concentration, persistence, and pace; and adaptation.

This rating was conducted after it was determined by the evaluator that Mr Krupp had reached maximum medical improvement following a lengthy period of psychotherapy and several attempts to prescribe an antidepressant that adequately addressed his symptoms while limiting unpleasant side effects. Mr Krupp's psychiatrist also prescribed an antianxiety agent that Mr Krupp used to improve sleep when he felt particularly anxious. It is interesting to note that in the Fourth and Fifth Editions of the *Guides*, the evaluator could grant a 1% to 3% whole person impairment for the ongoing need for medication and its side effects, which could be used in this case if the long-term medication used to control Mr Krupp's depression caused side effects. There are specific instructions on this matter in Chapter 2 (4th ed, p 9; 5th ed, p 20).

Mr Krupp's symptoms of mild depression remained unchanged for 12 months following the first year of treatment. All three editions of the *Guides* point out the importance of conducting a whole person impairment rating once maximum medical improvement is attained and no additional changes in the patient's condition are expected in the next 12 months. However, it is important to note that maximum medical improvement as it relates to mental and behavioral disorders is a concept that often does not accurately reflect the course of a mental illness. The terms *remission* and *relapse* more accurately describe the course of a mental illness like bipolar disorder, recurrent major depressive disorder, and schizophrenia. The evaluator may want to note in the report the difference in the two perspectives—maximum medical improvement versus remission and relapse.

If one were to use the concept of maximum medical improvement in this evaluation, then the evaluator would point out that Mr Krupp was diagnosed with a single episode of major depression and that his symptoms improved and were stable for 12 months. If Mr Krupp had been evaluated a few months after the onset of his depressive episode, his impairment rating using any of the *Guides*—Fourth, Fifth, or Sixth Edition—would have been significantly higher and inaccurate, as he had not yet reached maximum medical improvement. For this case, the ratings were essentially the same, regardless of the method used to determine the impairment. The *Guides* Sixth Edition provided a numeric rating of 5% whole person impairment, which reflects a mild impairment level.

SUMMARY

Diagnosis	Major depressive disorder, single episode, currently mild
Fourth Edition References	Chapter 14 (4th ed, pp 291-302), Table (4th ed, p 301)

Fourth Edition Summary	Mental impairment in each of the four areas of functional limitation is rated on the five-category scale, which ranges from no impairment to extreme impairment.
Fourth Edition Impairment	Activities of daily living: Class 1, no impairment Social functioning: Class 2, mild impairment Concentration, persistence, and pace: Class 2, mild impairment Adaptation: Class 2, mild impairment Overall impairment: Class 2, mild impairment
Fifth Edition References	Chapter 14 (5th ed, pp 357-370), Table 14-1 (5th ed, p 363)
Fifth Edition Summary	Mental impairment in each of the four areas of functional limitation is rated on the five-category scale, which ranges from no impairment to extreme impairment.
Fifth Edition Impairment	Activities of daily living: Class 1, no impairment Social functioning: Class 2, mild impairment Concentration, persistence, and pace: Class 2, mild impairment Adaptation: Class 2, mild impairment Note: No overall impairment was provided, per directions of *Guides* Fifth Edition.
Sixth Edition References	Chapter 14 (6th ed, pp 347-382), Table 14-5 (6th ed, p 352), Tables 14-8 and 14-9 (6th ed, p 357), Tables 14-10 and 14-11 (6th ed, p 358), Tables 14-12 through 14-15 (6th ed, p 359), Tables 14-16 and 14-17(6th ed, p 360)
Sixth Edition Summary	The BPRS, GAF, and PIRS impairment scores are established. Then, the whole person impairment for mental and behavioral disorders is rated by determining the median (middle) impairment score of these three measures.
Sixth Edition Impairment	5% whole person impairment

CASE 14-2

Posttraumatic Stress Disorder Claim

Subject: Ms Jane, a 50-year-old woman.

History: Ms Jane was referred by a worker's compensation case manager, for an impairment evaluation subsequent to a diagnosis of posttraumatic stress disorder. The worker's compensation context of the referral was attributed to a history of the claimant having been a victim of an armed robbery and having witnessed the shooting of a coworker while working at a convenience store. The evaluator responded to the referral by explaining that such a claim probably would not be eligible for impairment rating due to the lack of objective evidence (*Guides* 6th ed, p 20, Table 2-1, item 9), the lack of relevance of the concept of permanent impairment for mental illness, and the obstacles to credibly claiming work-relatedness for claims of posttraumatic stress disorder. The case manager responded that all of this was understood and could be emphasized in the evaluator's final report, then explained that a judge had specified that she would not approve of any potential settlement for the worker's compensation claim until the requested impairment evaluation had been conducted. The judge reportedly had already stated that she understands that the concepts of permanent impairment and work-relatedness do not apply to mental illness, but she still wanted to have an impairment evaluation to assist her with her consideration of a proposed settlement. The evaluator subsequently agreed to move forward in an effort to facilitate the claimant's withdrawal from the worker's compensation system and to thereby spare the claimant from continued exposure to the reliably detrimental health effects of involvement in that system.

Basic Evaluation: The *Guides* Sixth Edition discussion of mental illness (Chapter 14, Mental and Behavioral Disorders, pp 347-382) creates an evaluation protocol that is far more demanding than that of either the Fourth or Fifth Edition. Subsequently, this basic evaluation section is based on the steps required in the Sixth Edition, because those steps also satisfy the basic evaluation demands of the Fourth and Fifth Editions. This case is presented in a step-by-step fashion that simplifies the protocol that is called for by Chapter 14 of the 6th Edition.

1. Ensure that the evaluator has a relevant professional history.

Consistent with Section 14.1a, Initial Considerations (6th ed, p 348), the evaluator in this example is a clinical psychologist.

2. Establish an independent basis for the evaluation.
   Consistent with Section 14.3a, Physician Alliance (6th ed, p 351), and with professional standards for mental health care, the evaluator insisted on this evaluation taking place on an independent basis. This meant that he had never provided treatment for the patient, that he committed to never providing any treatment for the patient at any time in the future, and that he committed to never establishing any type of relationship with the patient.

3. Conduct an evaluation of sufficient comprehensiveness to credibly determine whether mental illness is present.
   As explained in Section 14.2, Psychiatric/Psychological Evaluation (6th ed, pp 349-351), the evaluation process included thorough diagnostic interviewing based on the American Psychiatric Association's *Diagnostic and Statistical Manual of Mental Disorders,* Fourth Edition, Text Revision (DSM-IV-TR).[2] The process also included a review of records from the patient's entire life, collateral interviewing, objective psychological testing, and utilization of relevant forensic evaluation guidelines. The process revealed abnormalities consistent with several mental illnesses.

4. If mental illness is present, then continue the evaluation process until a diagnostic formulation can be credibly established.
   Section 14.1b, Diagnosis (6th ed, p 348), stipulates that a definitive diagnosis is necessary, based on DSM-IV-TR. The findings from the evaluation protocol were consistent with three mental illnesses: posttraumatic stress disorder, chronic; major depressive disorder, recurrent, mild; and obsessive-compulsive personality disorder.

5. Additional permanence considerations.
   Section 14.4, Maximum Medical Improvement (6th ed, pp 353-355), offers several considerations in regard to issues of permanence. In addition to the generic lack of relevance that the concept of permanent impairment has for mental illness, this case also involved a less than adequate treatment history. For example, the evaluation findings indicated that the treatment of choice for posttraumatic stress disorder, prolonged exposure, had never been included in the patient's treatment plan. Additionally, the patient's treatment plan had never focused on her personality disorder. Subsequently, the evaluator's final report specified that there were multiple obstacles to claiming that the patient had reached maximum medical improvement and to claiming that any impairment was of a permanent nature.

Discussion of Impairment Associated With the Posttraumatic Stress Disorder Claim

Fourth Edition Rating

Impairment rating was based on Chapter 14, Mental and Behavioral Disorders (4th ed, pp 291-302). The Fourth Edition specifies the lack of credibility for any effort to assign impairment percentages to mental illness, and subsequently forbids the utilization of percentage ratings (4th ed, p 300). The Fourth Edition calls for four ratings of current functioning, divided into separate categories.

The Fourth Edition rating process in this case produced an impairment assessment dominated by the personality disorder. Ratings in the four required categories (unnumbered table, 4th ed, page 301) were: activities of daily living, class 2 (compatible with most useful functioning); social functioning, class 2; concentration, persistence, and pace, class 2; and deterioration or decompensation in work or work-like settings, class 3 (compatible with some, but not all, useful functioning).

The case example from the Fourth Edition's mental illness chapter (p 302) indicates that the four ratings for subcategories of current functioning are to be summarized in a single "overall" rating. For this case, the overall rating would be class 2 (compatible with most useful functioning).

The final report from the evaluator would emphasize the prominent role of the personality disorder in these ratings and the subsequent clear lack of work-relatedness for the associated impairment (in addition to the generic obstacles to credibly claiming work-relatedness for mental illness). The evaluator's report would also emphasize the generic lack of relevance that the concept of permanent impairment has for claims of mental illness as well as the additional obstacles to claiming permanence that were unique to this case (eg, the patient's treatment plan had never focused on the personality disorder and had never included the treatment of choice for posttraumatic stress disorder).

Fifth Edition Rating

Impairment rating was based on Chapter 14, Mental and Behavioral Disorders (5th ed, pp 357-372). The Fifth Edition specifies the lack of credibility for any effort to assign impairment percentages to mental illness and subsequently forbids the utilization of percentage ratings (5th ed, p 361). The Fifth Edition calls for four ratings of current functioning, divided into separate categories.

The Fifth Edition rating process in this case produced an impairment assessment dominated by the personality disorder. Ratings in the four required categories (Table 14-1, 5th ed, p 363) were: activities of daily living, class 2 (compatible with most useful functioning); social functioning, class 2; concentration, persistence, and pace, class 2; and deterioration or decompensation in work or work-like settings, class 3 (compatible with some, but not all, useful functioning).

The final report from the evaluator would emphasize the prominent role of the personality disorder in these ratings, and the subsequent clear lack of work-relatedness for the associated impairment (in addition to the generic obstacles to credibly claiming work-relatedness for mental illness). The evaluator's report would also emphasize the generic lack of relevance that the concept of permanent impairment has for claims of mental illness, as well as the additional obstacles to claiming permanence that were unique to this case (eg, the patient's treatment plan had never focused on the personality disorder and had never included the treatment of choice for posttraumatic stress disorder).

Sixth Edition Rating

Chapter 14, Mental and Behavioral Disorders (6th ed, pp 347-382), is used to determine an impairment rating for psychiatric disorders. The step-by-step process that was initiated in the basic evaluation section continues:

6. Determine whether Chapter 14 can be used for impairment evaluation. Consistent with Section 14.1c, Diagnostic Categories (6th ed, pp 348-349), the patient had not been (and would not be) evaluated through any other chapter from the *Guides*. The lack of evaluation through any other *Guides* chapter is one requirement for making the patient eligible for a Chapter 14 evaluation.

7. Determine whether any diagnosed mental illness is eligible for an impairment rating.
   As explained in Section 14.1c, Diagnostic Categories (6th ed, pp 348-349), only mood disorders, anxiety disorders, and psychotic disorders are eligible for impairment ratings. Two of the diagnoses identified earlier (major depressive disorder and posttraumatic stress disorder) are included in these categories.

   The patient was not attempting to attribute her claims of mental illness to pain, the evaluation findings were not indicative of substance abuse, and the evaluation findings did not indicate any history of brain injury (if any of these issues are applicable, Chapter 14 considers the presentation of mental illness to be unratable; 6th ed, p 349).

8. When a patient is claiming work-relatedness, the evaluation process must include a focus on the nature of any pre-existing mental illness.
   As explained in Section 14.5d, Further Considerations (6th ed, pp 355-356), the evaluator must attempt to determine whether a ratable pre-existing mental illness applies to the patient. The evaluation findings indicated a preexisting history of major depressive disorder, recurrent (with severity ranging from severe to remission at various points in life).

9. Determine whether any psychological factors are present that must be excluded from the impairment assessment.
   As explained in Section 14.5d, Further Considerations (6th ed, pp 355-356), any impairment that is due to personality disorders or borderline (or lower) intelligence must be separated from the impairment assessment. In this case, any impairment associated with obsessive-compulsive personality disorder would have to be separated from the impairment ratings.

   The 7 Adult Intelligence Scale, Third Edition,[7] was administered to comply with the Chapter 14 requirement that intelligence must be assessed (so that any impairment attributable to borderline, or lower, intelligence can be excluded from the assessment of impairment). The resulting full-scale intelligence quotient was higher than the borderline range, thereby indicating that intelligence did not need to be considered in the impairment assessment process.

10. Continue the evaluation process until a credible determination can be made regarding whether the patient has additional forms of impairment that are not associated with mental illness and that must be excluded from the assessment.
    As explained in Section 14.5d, Further Considerations (6th ed, p 355), the impairment assessment must exclude any compromise of activities of daily living that could be attributed to financial limitations, lack of transportation, or general medical impairment. The evaluation failed to reveal any of these issues.

11. Continue the evaluation process until enough information is available to allow the evaluator to credibly complete the required ratings scales, for both current functioning and (if there was a preexisting ratable mental illness) preexisting functioning.
    As explained in Section 14.6, Method of Impairment Rating (6th ed, pp 356-360), the evaluator must extend the evaluation process beyond the usual diagnostic focus to include a specific focus on every aspect of the three ratings scales that are required by Chapter 14. This process included a focus on current functioning and a separate focus on pre-existing functioning (based on both interviewing and record review, with the consideration of preexisting functioning placing an emphasis on evidence from records rather than the patient's report).

12. Complete the rating scales for current functioning, but with an attempt to exclude impairment that was associated with factors that cannot be rated.
    As explained in Section 14.5, Concepts for Impairment Ratings (6th ed, pp 355-356), and Section 14.6, Method of Impairment Rating (6th ed, pp 356-360), three ratings scales must be completed by the evaluator, and the evaluator must attempt to exclude any impairment or compromise in activities of daily living associated with personality disorder, low intelligence, lack of money, lack of transportation, or general medical conditions. For this case, impairment from the personality disorder was to be excluded from the process of completing the rating scales (the evaluator emphasized in his documentation that there was not a scientifically credible way to do this, but it was being attempted nonetheless, simply because of the *Guides* requirement).

12 a. Determine the current Brief Psychiatric Rating Scale impairment score. The *Guides* Sixth Edition involves the use of the Brief Psychiatric Rating Scale (BPRS).[5] In accordance with the direction provided in Appendix 14.8, Appendix: Brief Psychiatric Rating Scale (Expanded Version) (6th ed, pp 369-381), the BPRS was scored through utilization of the Ventura reference's guidelines, in addition to the guidance that was available in the *Guides* itself.

1. Somatic concerns: 1 (Note: Significant somatic concern was clearly present, but the evaluation findings were consistent with such impairment being attributable to the personality disorder, and such impairment was subsequently excluded from the rating process.)
2. Anxiety: 4 (Note: Current functioning was actually more consistent with a rating of 5, but evaluation findings were clearly consistent with at least a portion being attributable to the personality disorder.)
3. Depression: 3 (Note: Current functioning was actually more consistent with a rating of 4, but evaluation findings were clearly consistent with at least a portion being attributable to the personality disorder.)
4. Suicidality: 1
5. Guilt: 1 (Note: Current functioning was actually more consistent with a rating of 3, but evaluation findings were consistent with the guilt being completely attributable to the personality disorder.)
6. Hostility: 1 (Note: Current functioning was actually more consistent with a rating of 3, but evaluation findings were consistent with the hostility being completely attributable to the personality disorder.)

7. Elevated mood: 1
8. Grandiosity: 1
9. Suspiciousness: 1 (Note: Current functioning was actually more consistent with a rating of 3, but evaluation findings were consistent with the suspiciousness being completely attributable to the personality disorder.)
10. Hallucinations: 4
11. Unusual thought content: 2
12. Bizarre behavior: 1
13. Self-neglect: 1
14. Disorientation: 1 (Note: Current functioning was actually more consistent with a rating of 2, but this mild confusion seemed to be attributable to the personality disorder.)
15. Conceptual disorganization: 1 (Note: Current functioning was actually more consistent with a rating of 2, but the tendency to ramble seemed to be attributable to the personality disorder.)
16. Blunted affect: 1
17. Emotional withdrawal: 1 (Note: Current functioning was actually more consistent with a rating of 3, but the social shortcomings seemed to be attributable to the personality disorder.)
18. Motor retardation: 1
19. Tension: 2 (Note: Current functioning was actually more consistent with a rating of 3, but the relevant behavior seemed to be at least partially attributable to the personality disorder.)
20. Uncooperativeness: 1
21. Excitement: 2
22. Distractibility: 1 (Note: Current functioning was actually more consistent with a rating of 3, but the lack of focus seemed to be attributable to the personality disorder.)
23. Motor hyperactivity: 1 (Note: Current functioning was actually more consistent with a rating of 2, but this talkativeness seemed to be attributable to the personality disorder.)
24. Mannerisms and posturing: 1

Sum the 24 BPRS ratings: 35

Find the current BPRS impairment score in Table 14-9, Impairment Score of Brief Psychiatric Rating Scale (BPRS) (6th ed, p 357): 10% BPRS impairment score.

12 b. Determine the current Global Assessment of Functioning Scale impairment score.
The *Guides* Sixth Edition involves the use of the Global Assessment of Functioning Scale (GAF).[5] The patient's current level of functioning seemed to be consistent with a GAF range of between 61 and 70, regardless of whether personality disorder issues were factored out of the assessment. Using Table 14-10, Impairment Score of Global Assessment of Functioning Scale (GAF) (6th ed, p 358), the range is consistent with a current GAF impairment score of 5%.

12 c. Determine the current Psychiatric Impairment Rating Scale impairment score.
The *Guides* Sixth Edition involves the use of the Psychiatric Impairment Rating Scale (PIRS).[5]

- Table 14-11, Self-Care, Personal Hygiene, and Activities of Daily Living (p 358). *Score = 1.*
- Table 14-12, Role Functioning, Social and Recreational Activities (p 359). *Score = 1.*
- Table 14-13, Travel (p 359). *Score = 1.*
- Table 14-14, Interpersonal Relationships (p 359). *Score = 1.* (Note: Current functioning is actually more consistent with a rating of 2, but the social difficulties were clearly due to the personality disorder).
- Table 14-15, Concentration, Persistence, and Pace (p 359). *Score = 1.* (Note: Formal testing was not utilized because the evaluation findings were consistent with a complete lack of impairment for this issue.)
- Table 14-16, Resilience and Employability (p 360). *Score = 1.*

Arrange the scores: 1, 1, 1, 1, 1, 1

Select the middle two scores: 1, 1

Sum the middle two scores: 2

PIRS impairment score per Table 14-17, Impairment Score of Psychiatric Impairment Rating Scale (PIRS) (6th ed, p 360): 0% PIRS impairment score.

13. Create the current impairment rating.
    In accordance with Section 14.6d (6th ed, p 357), the three current impairment scores were listed, and the median was chosen as the impairment rating. In this example, the three scores are:

    Current BPRS impairment score: 10%

    Current GAF impairment score: 5%

    Current PIRS impairment score: 0%

    The 5% score for the GAF is the median of this group (the score that is in the middle, quantitatively). Therefore, the current impairment rating is: 5% whole person impairment.

14. Create a prerobbery impairment rating.
    In accordance with Section 14.5d, Further Considerations (6th ed, pp 355-356), the evaluator must calculate a preexisting impairment rating when work-relatedness is being claimed and preexisting ratable mental illness has been identified. The circumstances of this referral called for consideration of new impairment that might be associated in time with the workplace robbery. Given the preexisting mental illness, a separate impairment rating was created, which focused on preexisting functioning.

    The examiner specified in his final report that an emphasis was being placed on evidence from records, rather than the patient's reports, because of the tradition of scientific findings that such pre-event versus post-event reports are unreliable when they are obtained from a claimant.

    In accordance with the dictates of the *Guides*, the rating process attempted to exclude impairment that was due to the personality disorder (6th ed, p 355). The evaluator emphasized in his documentation that there was not a scientifically credible way to do this, but it was being attempted nonetheless, simply because of the *Guides* requirement. The evaluator also noted in his final report that this requirement had the potential to create misleading results, because the preexisting personality disorder would have led to future distress/impairment (by definition), and because the preexisting major depressive disorder, recurrent, probably would have produced future impairment, regardless of whether a workplace robbery/shooting had occurred.

    The evaluator also specified in his final report that an attempt was being made to base this prerobbery impairment rating on the average prerobbery functioning of the patient. Due to the natural variability of impairment that would be attributable to her preexisting mental illness, it did not seem appropriate to base the prerobbery impairment on any single point in time. The evaluator specified that this was a highly speculative process, but such speculation had been made necessary by the requirements of the *Guides*.

14 a. Determine the pre-robbery BPRS impairment score.
In accordance with Appendix 14.8, Appendix: Brief Psychiatric Rating Scale (Expanded Version) (6th ed, pp 369-381), the BPRS was scored through utilization of the Ventura reference's guidelines, in addition to the guidance that was available in the *Guides* itself.

1. Somatic Concerns: 1 (Note: Significant somatic concern was clearly present prior to the robbery, but the evaluation findings were consistent with such impairment being attributable to the personality disorder, and such impairment was subsequently excluded from the rating process.)
2. Anxiety: 1 (Note: Prerobbery functioning was actually more consistent with a rating of 2, but evaluation findings were clearly consistent with at least a portion being attributable to the personality disorder.)
3. Depression: 5 (Note: Prerobbery functioning was actually more consistent with a rating of 6, but evaluation findings were clearly consistent with at least a portion being attributable to the personality disorder.)
4. Suicidality: 5 (Note: Prerobbery functioning was actually more consistent with a rating of 6, but evaluation findings were clearly consistent with at least a portion being attributable to the personality disorder.)
5. Guilt: 5 (Note: Prerobbery functioning was actually more consistent with a rating of 6, but evaluation findings were clearly consistent with at least a portion being attributable to the personality disorder.)
6. Hostility: 5 (Note: Prerobbery functioning was actually more consistent with a rating of 6, but evaluation findings were clearly consistent with at least a portion being attributable to the personality disorder.)
7. Elevated mood: 1
8. Grandiosity: 1
9. Suspiciousness: 1 (Note: Prerobbery functioning was actually more consistent with a rating of 3, but evaluation findings were consistent with the suspiciousness being completely attributable to the personality disorder.)

10. Hallucinations: 1 (Note: Prerobbery functioning was actually more consistent with a rating of 2, but evaluation findings were consistent with the personality disorder being the cause of such problems.)
11. Unusual thought content: 1 (Note: Prerobbery functioning was actually more consistent with a rating of 2, but evaluation findings were consistent with the personality disorder being the cause of such problems.)
12. Bizarre behavior: 1 (Note: Prerobbery functioning was at times consistent with a rating of 3, but evaluation findings were consistent with the personality disorder being the cause of such problems.)
13. Self-neglect: 4
14. Disorientation: 3
15. Conceptual disorganization: 2
16. Blunted affect: 3
17. Emotional withdrawal: 4
18. Motor retardation: 3
19. Tension: 3
20. Uncooperativeness: 4
21. Excitement: 1
22. Distractibility: 1 (Note: Prerobbery functioning was sometimes consistent with a rating of 6, but the lack of focus seemed to be attributable to the personality disorder.)
23. Motor hyperactivity: 3
24. Mannerisms and posturing: 1

Sum the total of the 24 BPRS ratings: 60

Find the prerobbery BPRS impairment score in Table 14-9 (6th ed, p 357): 30% BPRS impairment score.

14 b. Determine the pre-robbery GAF impairment score.
Prerobbery GAF scores had been documented in the patient's records and ranged as low as 10. The evaluator speculated that the average GAF score prior to the robbery would have been 45. Using Table 14-10, Impairment Score of Global Assessment of Functioning (GAF)

(6th ed, p 358), that GAF rating would be consistent with a pre-robbery GAF impairment score of 15%.

14 c. Determine the prerobbery PIRS impairment score according to the Sixth Edition.

- Table 14-11, Self-Care, Personal Hygiene, and ADLs (p 358). *Score = 2.*
- Table 14-12, Role Functioning, Social and Recreational Activities (p 359). *Score = 2.*
- Table 14-13, Travel (p 359) *Score = 1.*
- Table 14-14, Interpersonal Relationships (p 359). *Score = 2.* (Note: This average rating would have been higher if the *Guides* allowed impairment associated with personality disorders to be considered.)
- Table 14-15, Concentration, Persistence, and Pace (p 359). *Score = 2.* (Note: This average rating would have been higher if the *Guides* allowed impairment associated with personality disorders to be considered.)
- Table 14-16, Resilience and Employability (p 360). *Score = 1.*

Arrange the scores: 1, 1, 2, 2, 2, 2

Select the middle two scores: 2, 2

Sum the middle two scores: 4

Prerobbery PIRS impairment score (Table 14-17; 6th ed, p 360): 10%

14 d. Create the prerobbery impairment rating.
In accordance with Section 14.6d (6th ed, p 357), the three pre-existing impairment scores were listed, and the median was chosen as the impairment rating. In this example, the three scores are:

Prerobbery BPRS impairment score: 30%

Prerobbery GAF impairment score: 15%

Prerobbery PIRS impairment score: 10%

The 15% whole person impairment for the GAF is the median of this group (the score that is in the middle, quantitatively).

Therefore, the prerobbery impairment rating is: 15% whole person impairment.

15. Create the new impairment rating.
    In keeping with the requirements of Section 2.5c, Apportionment (6th ed, p 25), as well as Section 14.5d, Further Considerations (6th ed, pp 355-356), the prerobbery impairment rating was subtracted from the current impairment rating, so that the resulting math was:

    [Current impairment rating of 5% whole person impairment] minus [prerobbery impairment rating of 15% whole person impairment] equals [new impairment rating of negative 10% whole person impairment.]

    Because the concept of a negative impairment rating does not make sense, the evaluator's final report simply stated "No new impairment associated in time with the robbery/shooting."

    Section 14.5d, Further Considerations (6th ed, pp 355-356), specifies (without explanation) that an assessment of whether a claimant can work "must be made during the evaluation." In this case, the patient was working full-time at the time of the evaluation. Nonetheless, because of the requirement of the *Guides*, the evaluator's final report specified that the rate of unemployment is not elevated among individuals with this patient's *new* diagnosis of posttraumatic stress disorder. The report further emphasized that, for the sake of the patient's health, she needed to continue working.

Comment Associated With the Posttraumatic Stress Disorder Claim

This direct comparison of the Fourth, Fifth, and Sixth Edition systems for evaluating impairment associated with mental illness reveals the monumental nature of the changes that have been introduced in the Sixth Edition. Perhaps the most significant change is the Sixth Edition directive that impairment due to a personality disorder is to be excluded from the process (as opposed to the Fourth and Fifth Editions specifying that such impairment was to be included). Additionally, the Sixth Edition calls for claims of work-relatedness to be responded to with the creation of a *new* impairment rating, whereas neither the Fourth nor the Fifth Edition had such a provision. Further, while the Fourth and Fifth Editions correctly point out the lack of credibility for impairment percentages, the Sixth Edition actually calls for the creation of such percentages. Finally, although all forms of mental illness are eligible for impairment evaluation through utilization of the Fourth or Fifth Editions, only three categories of mental illness are eligible under the Sixth Edition.

None of the editions have offered any resolution of the fundamental incompatibilities between the basic principles and purposes of the *Guides* and the nature of mental illness (eg, the lack of relevance that the concept of permanent impairment has for mental illness, the lack of objective support for claims of impairment due to mental illness, and the obstacles to claiming work-relatedness for any form of mental illness).

The Sixth Edition is remarkable in that it calls for evaluators to engage in a variety of highly speculative endeavors (eg, evaluating preexisting impairment; separating out impairment that is due to a personality disorder, low intelligence, general medical conditions). Evaluators should subsequently be extremely cautious in their report writing, emphasizing that such issues are being addressed only because of the *Guides* requirement to do so and emphasizing the highly speculative nature of associated conclusions.

This case illustrates the significance of the change from evaluating impairment associated with personality disorders under the Fourth and Fifth Editions to excluding such impairment under the Sixth Edition. In this case, due to the pervasive nature of impairment from a personality disorder, the impairment assessment under the Fourth and Fifth Editions was dominated by personality disorder considerations. In contrast, personality disorder considerations were completely excluded from the impairment assessment under the Sixth Edition, despite their dominant role in the manifestation of any impairment.

This case also illustrates the importance of a thorough mental illness evaluation (eg, in order to avoid an inordinate focus on a referral diagnosis), the prominent role that personality disorders play in impairment from mental illness, and the naturally nonlinear variability of impairment associated with mental illness.

SUMMARY

Diagnosis	Obsessive-compulsive personality disorder; major depressive disorder, recurrent, currently mild; posttraumatic stress disorder, chronic
Fourth Edition References	Chapter 14 (4th ed, pp 291-302), Table (4th ed, p 301)
Fourth Edition Summary	Mental impairment in each of the four areas of functional limitation is rated on the five-

category scale that ranges from no impairment to extreme impairment. The ratings are summarized in a single final rating.

Fourth Edition Impairment Class 2, mild impairment (compatible with most useful functioning)

Fifth Edition References Chapter 14 (5th ed, pp 357-370), Table 14-1 (5th ed, p 363)

Fifth Edition Summary Mental impairment in each of the four areas of functional limitation is rated on the five-category scale that ranges from no impairment to extreme impairment. Unlike in the Fourth Edition, there is no single final rating.

Fifth Edition Impairment Activities of daily living: Class 2 (compatible with most useful functioning)

Social functioning: Class 2

Concentration, persistence, and pace: Class 2

Deterioration or decompensation in work or work-like settings: Class 3 (compatible with some, but not all, useful functioning)

Sixth Edition References Chapter 14 (6th ed, pp 347-382), Table 14-9 (6th ed, p 357), Tables 14-10 and 14-11 (6th ed, p 358), and Tables 14-12 though Table 14-15 (6th ed, p 359), Tables 14-16 and 14-17 (6th ed, p 360)

Sixth Edition Summary Rating limited to mood disorders, anxiety disorders, and psychotic disorders. Impairment that is due to personality disorders and borderline (or lower) intelligence must be excluded from the rating. The BPRS, GAF, and PIRS impairment scores are established. Then, impairment is rated by determining the median (middle) impairment score of these three measures. Claims of new impairment can be addressed by creating two sets of impairment ratings, one for current functioning and the other for preexisting functioning, and subtracting the preexisting rating from the current rating (so that any new impairment can be specified).

Sixth Edition Impairment Current impairment rating is 5%. Pre-incident impairment rating is 15%. Conclusion: There is no new impairment.

References:

1. Folstein MF, Folstein S, McHugh PR. Mini-Mental State: a practical method for grading the cognitive state of patients for the clinician. *J Psychiatr Res*. 1975;12-189.
2. American Psychiatric Association. *Diagnostic and Statistical Manual of Mental Disorders, Fourth Edition – Text Revision*. Washington, DC: American Psychiatric Association; 2000.
3. Derogatis LR. *SCL-90-R: Administration, Scoring and Procedures Manual – II*. 2nd ed. Minneapolis, MN: National Computer Center; 1994.
4. Regents of the University of Minnesota. *MMPI-2™ (Minnesota Multiphasic Personality Inventory-2)™ ; Manual for Administration, Scoring and Interpretation*, revised ed. Minneapolis, MN: University of Minnesota Press; 2001.
5. Overall JE, Gorham DR. Brief Psychiatric Rating Scale. *Psycho Rep*. 1962;10:799-812.
6. Overall JE, Gorham DR. Brief Psychiatric Rating Scale: Recent developments in ascertainment and scaling. *Psychopharmocol Bull*. 1988;24:97-99.
7. Wechler D. *Wechsler Adult Intelligence Scale*. 3rd ed. San Antonio, TX: Pearson; 1997.

Chapter 15

The Upper Extremities

CASE 15-1

Impingement Syndrome

Subject: Mr Adams, a 42-year-old man.

History: The patient is a house painter who developed progressively worsening right shoulder pain during a particularly busy summer 2 years previously. His work involved repetitive and sometimes prolonged painting with his right hand at or above shoulder level. He denied any preexisting injury or illness involving the right shoulder.

Mr Adams consulted an orthopedic surgeon. Examination demonstrated a loss of 40° of abduction and flexion, tenderness just inferior to anterior and lateral acromion, positive impingement signs (both Neer and Hawkins), and minimal weakness on resisted abduction and external rotation. Radiographs of the right shoulder showed a hooked acromion. The physician prescribed an anti-inflammatory drug, instructed Mr Adams in stretching exercises of the posterior capsule, and recommended that Mr Adams avoid painting. The anti-inflammatories provided partial, temporary pain relief when taken. Mr Adams was unsure whether the stretching exercises helped but admitted he did not perform them as regularly as advised. He was unable to comply with the recommended activity restriction without discontinuing employment.

Because of persistent symptoms, a local anesthetic-corticosteroid injection was given into the subacromial space. The injection resulted in complete pain relief lasting for several hours, followed by partial pain relief for a period of 8 weeks, and then a return of symptoms. Physical therapy was prescribed and included stretching and strengthening exercises. After 6 weeks, Mr Adams noted minimal benefit.

Failure of the nonoperative treatment prompted an open anterior acromioplasty and resection of subacromial bursa. At surgery, the rotator cuff was noted to be mildly inflamed but not torn. Mr Adams completed 4 weeks of physical therapy and then returned to work painting.

Current Symptoms: At the time of an independent medical examination 1 year postoperatively, Mr Adams reported considerable improvement from surgery, with some residual pain with activities above shoulder level. He had no problems with his other shoulder. He noted that the discomfort was mild, less frequent, and nondisabling.

Functional Assessment: The *Quick*DASH score was 18.

Physical Examination: Examination showed a 5-cm longitudinal scar, normal sensation apart from hypesthesia overlying the scar, and normal reflexes. Right shoulder flexion strength was slightly diminished (4+/5); otherwise, strength was normal. There was no atrophy. Active shoulder motions on the right were abduction 140°, adduction 40°, extension 50°, flexion 130°, external rotation 70°, and internal rotation 80°. Minimal crepitus was evident during some of the active shoulder motions. Repeat measurements of shoulder motions on two subsequent trials were within 5°. Passively it was possible to obtain another 10° of abduction, flexion, and external rotation. Left shoulder motion was normal per *Guides* criteria, except for flexion of 160°.

Clinical Studies: Radiographs of the right shoulder showed a hooked acromion.

Discussion of Impingement Syndrome

Fourth Edition Rating

Permanent impairment evaluation was based on Section 3.1j, Shoulder (4th ed, pp 41-45). According to Figure 38, Upper Extremity Impairments Due to Lack of Flexion and Extension of Shoulder (4th ed, p 43), there was 3% upper extremity impairment for Mr Adams' right flexion deficit. Normal shoulder flexion is 180°, and he had 140° of active flexion on the right. Extension was normal. According to Figure 41, Upper Extremity Impairments Due to Lack of Abduction and Adduction of Shoulder (4th ed, p 44), there was 2% upper extremity impairment for the abduction deficit. Normal abduction is 170°, and he had 130° of abduction. Adduction was normal. Rotation measurements were normal according to Figure 44, Upper Extremity Impairments Due to Lack of Internal and External Rotation of Shoulder (4th ed, p 45). The impairment values were added, being at the same joint, resulting in 5% upper extremity impairment. This converted by Table 3, Relationship of Impairment of the Upper Extremity to Impairment of the Whole Person (4th ed, p 20), to 3% whole person impairment.

Impairment: 3% whole person impairment per the Fourth Edition.

Fifth Edition Rating

Permanent impairment evaluation was based on Section 16.4j, Shoulder Motion Impairment (5th ed, pp 474-480). On the basis of Figure 16-40, Pie Chart of Upper Extremity Motion Impairments Due to Lack of Flexion and Extension of Shoulder (5th ed, p 476), there was 3% upper extremity impairment for his right flexion deficit and 1% upper extremity impairment for his left shoulder flexion deficit. Normal shoulder flexion per Figure 16-40 is 180°, and on the right there was 140° of active flexion; however, Mr Adams' left shoulder represented "normal" for him, and his left shoulder flexion was 160°. Therefore, the impairment for his right flexion deficit was 2% of the upper extremity, that is, 3%−1%. Extension was normal. According to Figure 16-43, Pie Chart of Upper Extremity Motion Impairments Due to Lack of Abduction and Adduction of Shoulder (5th ed, p 477), there was 2% upper extremity impairment for the abduction deficit. Normal abduction is 170°, and Mr Adams had 130° of abduction on the right. Adduction was normal. Rotation measurements were normal according to Figure 16-46, Pie Chart of Upper Extremity Impairments Due to Lack of Internal and External Rotation of Shoulder (5th ed, p 479). The impairment values were added, being at the same joint, resulting in 4% upper extremity impairment. This converted by Table 16-3, Conversion of Impairment of the Upper Extremity to Impairment of the Whole Person (5th ed, p 439), to 2% whole person impairment.

Impairment: 2% whole person impairment per the Fifth Edition.

Sixth Edition Rating

The *Guides* approach to the evaluation of impairment due to impingement is usually based on Section 15.2, Diagnosis-Based Impairment (6th ed, pp 387-405). Table 15-5, Shoulder Regional Grid: Upper Extremity Impairments (6th ed, pp 401-405), specifies for the diagnosis impingement syndrome there is a class 1 rating for "residual loss, functional with normal motion" (with a default impairment of 3% upper extremity). There were deficits of motion, and thus the *Guides* allows for motion impairment to be considered as an alternative approach. To evaluate motion impairment, Section 15.7, Range of Motion Impairment (6th ed, pp 459-478), should be referenced along with Section 15.7g, Shoulder Motion (6th ed, pp 472-478). The left shoulder, which was uninjured and uninvolved, served as his normal. Per Table 15-34, Shoulder Range of Motion (6th ed, p 475), flexion on the right was 140°, which would result in a mild severity and 3% upper extremity permanent impairment, because this is in the range of 90° to 170°. However, the left shoulder had motion of 160° with the same resulting impairment; that is, there is no difference. Furthermore, the motion on the right was within 10% of his normal on the left. Thus, there was no impairment for flexion. His abduction was 140°, which also resulted in mild severity and an impairment of 3% upper extremity permanent impairment; his left was normal. His other motions were normal. Therefore, his motion impairment was 3% upper extremity permanent impairment, which is the same impairment obtained using the diagnosis-based impairment approach, hypothetically he had residual loss, functional, with normal motion. These two approaches cannot be combined, per Section 15.7 (6th ed, p 461). This converted by Table 15-11, Impairment Values Calculated From Upper Extremity Impairment (6th ed, p 420), to 2% whole person impairment.

Impairment: 2% whole person impairment per the Sixth Edition.

Comment on Impingement Syndrome

In the Sixth Edition, the primary rating method is diagnosis-based impairment; however, in this case, with motion deficits, the assessment was performed using range of motion; the end result by either approach was the same value. The processes of assessing impairment using the Fourth and Fifth Editions are similar; however, the Fifth Edition includes the explanation that the contralateral joint may serve as a baseline.

SUMMARY

Diagnosis	Impingement syndrome
Fourth Edition References	Section 3.1 (4th ed, pp 41-45), Figure 38 (4th ed, p 77), Figure 41 (4th ed, p 78), Figure 44 (4th ed, p 78)
Fourth Edition Summary	Active range of motion is measured in each of the six directions shoulders move. Impairment is rated by loss of motion.
Fourth Edition Impairment	5% upper extremity impairment, 3% whole person impairment

Fifth Edition References	Section 16.4j (5th ed, pp 474-480), Figure 16-40 (5th ed, p 476), Figure 16-43 (5th ed, p 477), Figure 16-46 (5th ed, p 479)
Fifth Edition Summary	Active range of motion is measured in each of the six directions shoulders move. Impairment is rated by loss of motion, compared to the contralateral shoulder.
Fifth Edition Impairment	4% upper extremity impairment, 2% whole person impairment
Sixth Edition References	Section 15.2 (6th ed, pp 387-405), Table 15-5 (6th ed, pp 401-405); Section 15.7 (6th ed, pp 459-478); Section 15.7g (6th ed, pp 472-478), Table 15-34 (6th ed, p 475), Table 15-11 (6th ed, p 420)
Sixth Edition Summary	History (including functional history and inventories), physical evaluation, and clinical studies. First, diagnosis-based impairment, class, and default value are determined. Second, assessment is made by an alternative approach, range of motion. The method that provides the higher value is used.
Sixth Edition Impairment	3% upper extremity impairment, 2% whole person impairment

CASE 15-2

Blunt Trauma to Forearm

Subject: Mr Ryan, a 23-year-old man.

History: Mr Ryan, a right-hand–dominant pipe fitter, injured his right forearm when it was caught between an I-beam and the bucket of a cherry picker. He suffered a crush injury with a laceration to the forearm. He was evaluated in the emergency department. The radiographs were negative for fracture. The laceration was sutured without complications. There was no tendon or nerve injury, but Mr Ryan's forearm was quite swollen. Examination did not reveal any neurologic or vascular compromise. He was given a tetanus shot and a prescription for pain medication and was released to follow up with his family physician. Two weeks later the sutures were removed. The wound had healed. In the first months after injury, Mr Ryan completed rehabilitative exercise under the supervision of a physical therapist.

Three years later, Mr Ryan was back working modified duty. He complained of weakness of the right hand and tiring easily. He stated that he used to work 2 to 4 hours of overtime each day but now could barely complete his 8-hour shift. Pain was not a major problem. There was no sign of symptom exaggeration.

Because of his persisting complaints of forearm discomfort and early fatigue, a bone scan was done and read as negative. An electromyogram/nerve conduction velocity study of the right upper extremity did not show any evidence of denervation or peripheral nerve entrapment.

Current Symptoms: His most significant complaint was that of weakness occurring with many activities of daily living; he was able to perform self-care activities with modification but unassisted.

Functional Assessment: The *Quick*DASH score was 41.

Physical Examination: Clinical examination of the right upper extremity showed the sensation to be intact to pinprick, light touch, and two-point discrimination. The range of motion was within normal limits from proximal to distal. The pulses were intact. There was a large palpable defect in the forearm flexor muscle. The defect was consistent with a muscle tear and/or necrosis of the muscle from the injury. The right forearm circumference was 2 cm smaller than the left, measured above (not at) the muscle defect. Muscle power testing was normal at the elbow but 4+/5 at the wrist for resisted flexion. The Tinel test, Phalen test, and testing for thoracic outlet syndrome were negative. The muscle stretch reflexes were 2+.

Grip strength measurements were valid in that (1) they were reproducible on several office visits, (2) strength measurements showed a bell-shaped curve pattern when tests were performed with the Jamar dynamometer in all five handle positions, and (3) strength did not increase on rapid exchange testing. Hand grip strength testing with the Jamar dynamometer showed right-hand weakness as follows:

Right: 8 kg, 10 kg, 9 kg = 27 kg total, average = 9 kg

Left: 36 kg, 38 kg, 38 kg = 112 kg total, average = 37 kg

Clinical Studies: Plain radiographs of the forearm were normal. MRI revealed findings consistent with a tear involving the flexor carpi radialis.

Discussion of Blunt Trauma to Forearm

Fourth Edition Rating

Permanent impairment evaluation was based on Section 3.1m, Impairment Due to Other Disorders of the Upper Extremity (4th ed, p 65), and Table 34, Upper Extremity Impairment for Loss of Strength (4th ed, p 65), which gives the percentage strength loss index and formula for calculating the same.

$$\frac{37\text{ kg} - 9\text{ kg}}{37\text{ kg}} = \frac{28}{37} = 76\%\text{ Strength Loss Index}$$

On the basis of Table 34, a 76% strength loss index resulted in a 30% upper extremity impairment rating or 18% whole person impairment rating.

Impairment: 18% whole person impairment per the Fourth Edition.

Fifth Edition Rating

Permanent impairment evaluation was based on Section 16.8, Strength Evaluation (5th ed, pp 507-511), and Table 16-34, Upper Extremity Joint Impairment Due to Loss of Grip or Pinch Strength (5th ed, p 509), which gives the percentage strength loss index and formula for calculating the same.

$$\frac{37\text{ kg} - 9\text{ kg}}{37\text{ kg}} = \frac{28}{37} = 76\% \text{ Strength Loss Index}$$

On the basis of Table 16-34, a 76% strength loss index resulted in a 30% upper extremity impairment rating and converted by Table 16-3, Conversion of Impairment of the Upper Extremity to Impairment of the Whole Person (5th ed, p 439), to an 18% whole person impairment rating.

Impairment: 18% whole person impairment per the Fifth Edition.

Sixth Edition Rating

There are two potential ratable diagnoses per Section 15.2, Diagnosis-Based Impairment (6th ed, pp 387-405), and Section 15.2c, Wrist (6th ed, p 390)—that of a "soft tissue" injury of "wrist contusion or crush injury with healed minor soft tissue or skin injury" (class 1, default impairment 2% upper extremity permanent impairment) and "muscle/tendon" injury of "wrist laceration or ruptured muscle/tendon" (residual loss, functional with normal motion, class 1, default impairment 5% upper extremity permanent impairment). Only one diagnosis is ratable; therefore the diagnosis with the higher impairment was selected.

According to Section 15.3a, Adjustment Grid: Functional History (6th ed, pp 406-407), and Table 15-7, Functional History Adjustment: Upper Extremities (6th ed, p 406), the patient was assigned grade modifier 2; the functional history was consistent with pain/symptoms with normal activity, and the *Quick*DASH score was in the range of 41 to 60. According to Section 15.3b, Adjustment Grid: Physical Examination (6th ed, p 407), and Table 15-8, Physical Examination Adjustment: Upper Extremities (6th ed, p 408), the patient was assigned grade modifier 2 based on an opinion of "moderate palpatory findings" and 2 cm of atrophy. According to Section 15.3c, Adjustment Grid: Clinical Studies (6th ed, pp 407-409), and Table 15-9, Clinical Studies Adjustment: Upper Extremities (6th ed, pp 410-411), the patient was assigned grade modifier 1; the clinical studies confirmed the diagnosis, mild pathology. In summary, the adjustments were: functional history grade modifier 2, physical examination 2, and clinical studies grade modifier 1. The net adjustment compared to diagnosis class 1 was +2, grade E, 7% upper extremity impairment.

Class 1—Default for Diagnosis = 5% UEI			
CDX	GMFH	GMPE	GMCS
1	2	2	1
Net adjustment (GMFH − CDX) 2 − 1 = 1 + (GMPE − CDX) 2 − 1 = 1 + (GMCS − CDX) 1 − 1 = 0 Net adjustment = 2			

Result is class 1 adjustment 2, which results in class 1, grade E = 7% upper extremity impairment

Based on Table 15-11, Impairment Values Calculated From Upper Extremity Impairment (6th ed, p 420), this converted to 4% whole person impairment.

Impairment: 4% whole person impairment per the Sixth Edition.

Comment on Blunt Trauma to Forearm

This was a case of blunt trauma to the forearm without a neurologic deficit. However, Mr Ryan had loss of grip strength that was due to soft tissue trauma. There was no sign of symptom exaggeration in the history or physical examination. There were objective findings (muscle defect and atrophy) that correlated with Mr Ryan's symptoms of weakness and muscle fatigue and supported an impairment. The impairment was based solely on loss of grip strength without peripheral nerve injury. No other section of the *Guides* was applicable; therefore, loss of strength was used. The issue of dominant versus nondominant hand is not an issue because the *Guides* treats them equally.

Apparent loss of strength can be nonphysiologic (due to behavioral or motivational factors). Impairment should not be assessed by loss of strength unless the loss is clearly physiologic and reproducible. Adequate time should have elapsed and rehabilitative (strengthening) exercises performed in order to permit maximum medical improvement before impairment is assessed.

The Fourth and Fifth Editions stress that rating for strength loss is applicable in a rare case. Section 16.8a, Principles (5th ed, p 508), states:

> In a rare case, if the examiner believes that the individual's loss of strength represents an impairing factor that has not been considered adequately by other methods in the *Guides*, the loss of strength may be rated separately.

An example of this situation would be loss of strength due to a severe muscle tear that healed leaving a palpable muscle defect.

The Fifth Edition also provides a new procedure for rating manual muscle strength for the shoulder and elbow in Section 16.8c, Manual Muscle Testing (5th ed, p 509); however, in this case, only the wrist flexors were involved. Mr Ryan did not have any difficulties that would prohibit rating on the basis of strength loss. Section 16.8a, Principles (5th ed, p 508), states, "Decreased strength cannot be rated in the presence of decreased motion, painful conditions, deformities, or absence of parts (eg, thumb amputation) that prevent effective application of maximal force in the region being evaluated."

Despite these restrictions, grip strength was often used to inappropriately rate impairment. In the Sixth Edition, strength loss is not used as a basis for rating impairment.

SUMMARY

Diagnosis	Blunt trauma to forearm
Fourth Edition References	Section 3.1m (4th ed, p 64), Table 34 (4th ed, p 65)
Fourth Edition Summary	History and upper extremity evaluation including range of motion and neurologic assessment (sensation and strength testing). Any other objective findings that could be used for the impairment rating are determined.
Fourth Edition Impairment	30% upper extremity impairment, 18% whole person impairment
Fifth Edition References	Section 16.8 (5th ed, p 507), Table 34 (5th ed, p 509)
Fifth Edition Summary	History and upper extremity evaluation including range of motion and neurologic assessment (sensation and strength testing). Any other objective findings that could be used for the impairment rating or factors that would exclude rating for strength loss are determined.

Fifth Edition Impairment	30% upper extremity impairment, 18% whole person impairment
Sixth Edition References	Section 15.2 (6th ed, pp 387-405); Section 15.2c (6th ed, p 390); Section 15.3a (6th ed, pp 406-407); Section 15.3b (6th ed, p 407); Section 15.3c (6th ed, pp 407-409), Table 15-7 (6th ed, p 406), Table 15-8 (6th ed, p 408), Table 15-9 (6th ed, pp 410-411), Table 15-11 (6th ed, p 420)
Sixth Edition Summary	History (including functional history and inventories), physical evaluation, and clinical studies. First, diagnosis-based impairment, class, and default value are determined. Second, impairment is adjusted based on nonkey factors.
Sixth Edition Impairment	7% upper extremity impairment, 4% whole person impairment

CASE 15-3

Wrist Injury

Subject: Ms Haynes, a 55-year-old woman.

History: Ms Haynes was a clerical worker in a government organization, who worked full-time at a desk job with occasional work at a counter taking inquiries. Her desk work largely included computer data entry and some lifting of heavy files. She was right-hand dominant.

Ms Haynes had a fall at work, landing on her outstretched right hand, sustaining a Colles fracture of the wrist with marked angulation of the bony fragments. She did not sustain any other injury. She had immediate medical attention at the local hospital, where she had a reduction of the fracture under anesthesia and application of a simple plaster splint, which was kept on for 6 weeks. When the splint was removed, she still had pain and swelling with radiologic evidence of delayed union of the fracture of the distal radius. After a further 6-week period of immobilization in plaster, there appeared to be some fracture callus formation, and the bones were in satisfactory position. No further treatment was carried out. Review appointments were set, but Ms Haynes did not attend them, having had enough of doctors.

During the ensuing 2 to 3 years, she noted that pain accompanied most of her activities involving the right wrist, and she started to complain of increasing pain, crunching, and stiffness in the wrist. Approximately 4 years after injury, Ms Haynes agreed to be evaluated by an orthopedic surgeon because the pain was constant, and she was having difficulties carrying out her activities of daily living as well as her work. Radiographs showed marked degenerative changes in the wrist joint. She underwent a surgical wrist fusion, which resulted in considerable reduction in her pain levels. She was quite pleased with the result.

Current Symptoms: Ms Haynes reported mild discomfort with routine and self-care activities; however, lacking motion of the wrist, she had to modify use of her right hand.

Functional Assessment: The *Quick*DASH score was 45.

Physical Examination: Surgically fused right wrist. The wrist was ankylosed at 10° of flexion and 5° of radial deviation. There was no evidence of sensory loss in the hand, and manual muscle testing was considered to be normal. Left wrist motion was normal. All other ranges of movement for the fingers, thumb, and elbow (including pronation and supination) were normal when compared with the left (unaffected) side. There was no abnormality of the peripheral vascular system in the upper limbs and no other identified impairment associated with the right hand, wrist, or arm.

Clinical Studies: At impairment evaluation 1 year later, radiographs showed solid fusion of the right wrist.

Discussion of Wrist Injury

Fourth Edition Rating

Permanent impairment evaluation was based on Section 3.1h, Abnormal Motion of Wrist (4th ed, p 35). According to Figure 26, Upper Extremity Impairment Due to Lack of Flexion and Extension of Wrist Joint (4th ed, p 36), Ms Haynes had a 21% upper extremity impairment due to the ankylosis of the right wrist in 10° of flexion. According to Figure 29, Upper Extremity Impairments Due to Abnormal Radial and Ulnar Deviation of Wrist Joint (4th ed, p 38), the ankylosis of the right wrist in 5° of radial deviation gave a 12% impairment of the upper extremity. Because the relative value of each wrist functional unit had been taken into consideration in the impairment charts, impairment values derived from the relevant abnormal ranges of motion (or ankylosis) were added to determine the impairment of the upper extremity. Thus, the impairment of the right upper extremity was 21% + 12% = 33%.

No other impairments were identified (ie, amputation, sensory loss, motor loss, vascular abnormality). The condition was considered, at nearly 12 months after surgery, to have reached maximum medical improvement, and the impairment in the right wrist was considered permanent. From Table 3, Relationship of Impairment of the Upper Extremity to Impairment of the Whole Person (4th ed, p 20), the upper extremity impairment of 33% converted to 20% whole person impairment.

Impairment: 20% whole person impairment per the Fourth Edition.

Fifth Edition Rating

Permanent impairment evaluation was based on Section 16.4, Evaluating Abnormal Motion (5th ed, p 450), with specific reference to Section 16.4g, Wrist Motion Impairment (5th ed, p 466). According to Figure 16-28, Pie Chart of Upper Extremity Impairments Due to Lack of Flexion and

Extension of Wrist Joint (5th ed, p 467), Ms Haynes had a 21% upper extremity impairment due to the ankylosis of the right wrist in 10° of flexion. According to Figure 16-31, Pie Chart of Upper Extremity Impairments Due to Abnormal Radial and Ulnar Deviation of Wrist Joint (5th ed, p 469), the ankylosis of the right wrist in 5° of radial deviation gave a 12% impairment of the upper extremity. Because the relative value of each wrist functional unit was taken into consideration in the impairment charts, impairment values derived from the relevant abnormal ranges of motion (or ankylosis) were added to determine the impairment of the upper extremity. Thus, the impairment of the right upper extremity was 21% + 12% = 33%.

No other impairments were identified (ie, amputation, sensory loss, motor loss, vascular abnormality). The condition was considered, at nearly 12 months after surgery, to have reached maximum medical improvement, and the impairment in the right wrist was considered permanent. From Table 16-3, Conversion of the Impairment of the Upper Extremity to Impairment of the Whole Person (5th ed, p 439), the upper extremity impairment of 33% converted to 20% whole person impairment.

Impairment: 20% whole person impairment per the Fifth Edition.

Sixth Edition Rating

Impairments for arthrodesis in functional position are based on Section 15.2, Diagnosis-Based Impairment (6th ed, pp 387-405). Table 15-3, Wrist Regional Grid: Upper Extremity Impairments (6th ed, pp 395-397), under the category "Ligament/Bone/Joint" specifies for the diagnosis "wrist arthrodesis (fusion)" there is a class 3 rating for "wrist arthrodesis in functional position (10° extension to 10° flexion, radial 5° to ulnar 10°)" with a default impairment of 30% upper extremity impairment. According to Section 15.3a, Adjustment Grid: Functional History (6th ed, pp 406-407), and Table 15-7, Functional History Adjustment: Upper Extremities (6th ed, p 406), the patient was assigned grade modifier 2; the functional history was consistent with "pain/symptoms with normal activity; +/− medications to control symptoms; able to perform self-care activities independently," and the *Quick*DASH score was in the range of 41 to 60. Section 15.3b, Adjustment Grid: Physical Examination (6th ed, p 407), was not applicable, because it was used for placement, nor are Section 15.3c, Adjustment Grid: Clinical Studies (6th ed, pp 407-409), and Table 15-9, Clinical Studies Adjustment: Upper Extremities (6th ed, pp 410-411), because they reflect the diagnosis. A single adjustment factor was grade modifier 2, one less than the class 3 assignment. Therefore, the final grade is B, one place to the left of the default, which resulted in 28% upper extremity impairment.

Based on Table 15-11, Impairment Values Calculated From Upper Extremity Impairment (6th ed, p 420), this converted to 17% whole person impairment.

Impairment: 17% whole person impairment per the Sixth Edition.

Comment on Wrist Injury

This was a relatively straightforward case by all three editions. In the Sixth Edition, the primary rating method was diagnosis-based impairment, which served as the basis for the final rating. However, in the Fourth and Fifth Editions, the rating was based on range of motion deficits. There were no other ratable findings.

Per the Fourth and Fifth Editions, a wrist fusion results in at least 30% upper extremity impairment or 18% whole person impairment, because the minimum impairment for ankylosis of wrist flexion and extension is 21% upper extremity impairment, and the minimum impairment for ankylosis of radial and ulnar deviation is 9% upper extremity impairment.

With the Sixth Edition, the default impairment is 30% upper extremity impairment; the impairment rating was modified slightly, based on consideration of other factors, primarily the functional history. Physical examination findings were used for placement and therefore did not result in modification. If there had been nonoptimal positioning, the assessment would have been per Section 15.7, Range of Motion Impairment.

SUMMARY

Diagnosis	Ankylosis of right wrist
Fourth Edition References	Section 3.1h (4th ed, p 35), Table 3 (4th ed, p 20), Figure 26 (4th ed, p 36), Figure 29 (4th ed, p 38)

Fourth Edition Summary	History, upper extremity examination, specifically including measurement of ranges of motion (particularly wrist motion, eg, flexion, extension, ulnar and radial deviation) and neurologic assessment. Other ratable impairments in the right upper limb, including secondary effects of the initial injury and/or surgery (eg, motion deficits of other joints and neurologic damage) are considered.
Fourth Edition Impairment	33% upper extremity impairment, 20% whole person impairment
Fifth Edition References	Section 16.4g (5th ed, p 466), Figure 16-28 (5th ed, p 467), Figure 16-31 (5th ed, p 469)
Fifth Edition Summary	History, upper extremity examination specifically including measurement of ranges of motion (particularly wrist motion, eg, flexion, extension, ulnar and radial deviation) and neurologic assessment. Other ratable impairments in the right upper limb, including secondary effects of the initial injury and/or surgery (eg, motion deficits of other joints and neurologic damage) are considered.
Fifth Edition Impairment	33% upper extremity impairment, 20% whole person impairment
Sixth Edition References	Section 15.2 (6th ed, pp 387-405); Section 15.3a-c (6th ed, pp 406-409), Table 15-3 (6th ed, pp 395-397), Table 15-7 (6th ed, p 406), Table 15-9 (6th ed, pp 410-411), Table 15-11 (6th ed, p 420)
Sixth Edition Summary	History (including functional history and inventories), physical evaluation, and clinical studies. First, diagnosis-based impairment, class, and default value are determined. Second, impairment is adjusted based on nonkey factors.
Sixth Edition Impairment	28% upper extremity impairment, 17% whole person impairment

CASE 15-4

Complex Regional Pain Syndrome

Subject: Ms Parker, a 26-year-old woman.

History: Ms Parker, a right-handed woman, sustained a fracture of the tuft of the distal phalanx of the right little finger, which was treated with a splint. Three weeks later she complained of constant, severe burning pain of her entire right hand and forearm, with associated swelling, red discoloration, sensitivity to touch, and decreased grip strength. Examination of the right hand and forearm revealed edema, erythema, dyshidrosis, and reduced passive range of motion of the distal interphalangeal (DIP), proximal interphalangeal (PIP), and metacarpophalangeal (MP) joints of the little and ring fingers. Diagnostic testing included a three-phase bone scan, which demonstrated hypervascularity of the right fingers, hand, and forearm on the early images followed by diffusely increased uptake in a periarticular distribution on the delayed images. A diagnosis of reflex sympathetic dystrophy (RSD)/complex regional pain syndrome (CRPS) I was made and confirmed by a pain medicine specialist, and treatment including nonsteroidal anti-inflammatory medication and physical therapy was initiated. A comprehensive medical and psychological evaluation did not reveal alternative explanations. Over the subsequent 2 years, the patient had significant improvement.

Current Symptoms: Ms Parker reported resolution of her right forearm and hand pain, swelling, discoloration, and hypersensitivity but reported persistent stiffness of her ring finger, diminished grip strength, and difficulty with tasks requiring digital dexterity. She was able to use her right upper extremity for self-care, holding objects, and daily activities, including her occupational duties as a material handler.

Functional Assessment: The *Quick*DASH score was 30.

Physical Examination: No edema, erythema, or dyshidrosis in the right upper extremity. Active range of motion measurements in the limb were normal with the exception of the three joints of the right little finger. The MP joint had extension to 0° and flexion to 80°, the PIP joint had extension to 0° and flexion to 80°, and the DIP joint had extension to −10° (10° extension lag) and flexion to 50°. There was no discrepancy between active and passive motions of the three joints. The Minnesota Manual Dexterity

Test was scored at the 73rd percentile for the right hand (normal). The Purdue Pegboard Test for fingertip dexterity was scored at the 45th percentile, consistent with mildly diminished fingertip dexterity. Bilateral grip-strength assessment using a Jamar dynamometer showed a bell-shaped curve, good correlation between static-exchange and rapid-exchange grip, and a coefficient of variation on repeated trials of 10%. The position 2 maximum grip strength was 10 pounds greater for the left hand than for the right.

Clinical Studies: A three-phase bone scan demonstrated hypervascularity of the right fingers, hand, and forearm on the early images, followed by diffusely increased uptake in a periarticular distribution on the delayed images.

Discussion of Complex Regional Pain Syndrome

Fourth Edition Rating

The *Guides* Fourth Edition approach to the evaluation of upper extremity impairment due to RSD/CRPS I is described in Section 3.1k, Impairment of the Upper Extremity Due to Peripheral Nerve Disorders (4th ed, p 46). First, the impairment is rated due to loss of motion of each joint involved. Second, the pain or sensory deficit of the injured peripheral nerve is rated. Third, the motor deficit of the injured peripheral nerve is rated. Fourth, the impairment percentages for the loss of motion, pain or sensory deficits, and motor deficits are rated.

By definition, RSD/CRPS I does not involve a peripheral nerve injury, and Ms Parker had none. Consequently, Ms Parker's impairment was based on loss of motion of MP, PIP, and DIP joints of the right little finger and was rated per Section 3.1g, Fingers (4th ed, p 30), specifically Figures 18 to 23 (4th ed, pp 32-34) and Tables 1 to 3 (4th ed, pp 18-20). According to these criteria, Ms Parker had the following impairments of the right little finger due to extension/flexion of the three joints: MP 5/6, PIP 0/12, and DIP 2/10. Adding gave the total impairment for motion loss at each joint: 11, 12, and 12, respectively. The impairments for motion loss at each joint were combined to obtain the total right little finger impairment of 31%. This equated to 3% impairment of the right hand, which was, in turn, converted to 3% right upper extremity and, ultimately, 2% whole person impairment. This is illustrated in the Upper Extremity Impairment Evaluation Record (4th ed, p 16), as shown here on page 220.

Impairment: 2% whole person impairment per the Fourth Edition.

Fifth Edition Rating

The *Guides* Fifth Edition provides two mutually exclusive methods for rating upper extremity impairment due to RSD/CRPS I.

Chapter 13, The Central and Peripheral Nervous System, Section 13.8, Criteria for Rating Impairments Related to Chronic Pain (5th ed, p 343), uses Table 13-22, Criteria for Rating Impairment Related to Chronic Pain in One Upper Extremity (5th ed, p 343), which is based on a functional approach. Ms Parker's condition met the criteria for class 1, namely "Individual can use the involved extremity for self-care, daily activities, and holding, but is limited in digital dexterity." Because the RSD/CRPS I involved her dominant extremity, she had 1% to 9% whole person impairment.

In Chapter 16, The Upper Extremities, Section 16.5e, Complex Regional Pain Syndromes (CRPS), Reflex Sympathetic Dystrophy (CRPS I), and Causalgia (CRPS II) (5th ed, pp 495-497), uses an anatomic approach. First, the loss of motion of each involved joint is rated. Second, the pain is rated. Third, motor deficits or loss of power are not rated. Fourth, the upper extremity impairments due to loss of motion and pain are combined, then the upper extremity rating is converted to whole person impairment. Because Ms Parker had no residual pain, her impairment was based on loss of motion of the right little finger MP, PIP, and DIP joints and was rated using Section 16.4e, Finger Motion Impairment (5th ed, pp 461-465), specifically Figures 16-20 through 16-25 (5th ed, pp 461-464) and Tables 16-1, 16-2, and 16-3 (5th ed, pp 438-439).

According to these criteria, Ms Parker had the following impairments of the right little finger due to extension/flexion of the three joints: MP 5/6, PIP 0/12, and DIP 2/10. Adding gave the total impairment for motion loss at each joint: 11, 12, and 12, respectively. The impairments for motion loss at each joint were combined to obtain the total right little finger impairment of 31%. This equated to 3% impairment of the right hand, which was, in turn, converted to 3% right upper extremity and, ultimately, 2% whole person impairment. This is illustrated in Figure 16-1a, Upper Extremity Impairment Evaluation Record (5th ed, p 436).

In summary, the Fifth Edition functional approach yields a range of whole person impairment from 1% to 9%; the Fifth Edition anatomic approach yields a 2% whole person impairment. In Ms Parker's case, the anatomic approach yielded the impairment value that best reflected the severity of her condition. This is illustrated in the Upper Extremity Impairment Evaluation Record (5th ed, p 436), as shown here on page 221.

Impairment: 2% whole person impairment per the Fifth Edition.

Sixth Edition Rating

The method for rating CRPS of the upper extremity is presented in Section 15.5, Complex Regional Pain Syndrome Impairment (6th ed, p 450). "The diagnosis has been present for at least 1 year, the diagnosis has been verified by more than 1 physician, and comprehensive differential diagnosis process has clearly ruled out all other differential diagnoses" (6th ed, p 452). Ms Parker's clinical documentation indicated that she initially met the criteria for CRPS outlined in Table 15-24, Diagnostic Criteria for Complex Regional Pain Syndrome (6th ed, p 453); however, at the time of the impairment evaluation she no longer met those criteria. Ms Parker's CRPS was successfully treated. In terms of symptoms criteria specified in Table 15-24, at the time of the evaluation she had symptoms in the motor/tropic category and therefore did not meet the standard of at least one symptom in three of four categories. In terms of signs, at the time of the impairment evaluation she displayed only decreased motion; therefore she did not meet the standard of at least one sign in two or more of the categories, which must be "observed and documented at the time of the impairment evaluation." Therefore, although there was a history of CRPS, at the time of the impairment evaluation CRPS would no longer be considered a ratable diagnosis. It was also noted that at maximum medical improvement she had only two objective diagnostic criteria points per Table 15-25, Objective Diagnostic Criteria Points for Complex Regional Pain Syndrome (6th ed, p 453).

As noted in Table 2-1 (6th ed, p 20), "If the *Guides* provides more than one method to rate a particular impairment or condition, the method producing the higher rating must be used." Consequently, Ms Parker's impairment should be rated for the motion loss in the digits, based on Table 15-31, Finger Range of Motion (6th ed, p 470), or should utilize the diagnosis-based impairments from Table 15-2, Digit Regional Grid: Digit Impairments (6th ed, p 391). The diagnosis-based impairment in this case is limited to a rating range of 2% to 6% digit impairment for a distal phalanx fracture, based on class 1 assignment for "residual symptoms, consistent objective findings and/or functional loss, with normal motion." The range of motion loss is likely to be greater in this case and applicable based on the (*) noted under this diagnosis that range of motion loss can be rated separately and independently. In such a case, the range of motion impairment should be calculated first and, if greater, used in place of any diagnosis-based impairment rating that is less in value. The diagnosis-based impairment rating and range of motion ratings cannot be combined.

Under Table 15-31, Ms Parker had the following digit impairments of the right little finger due to extension/flexion of the three joints: MP 7/6, PIP 0/21, and DIP 2/10.

Adding gave the total impairment for motion loss at each joint: MP 13, PIP 21, and DIP 12. The impairments for motion loss at each joint were combined to obtain the total right little finger impairment of 39% digit impairment. Based on Table 15-12, Impairment Values Calculated From Digit Impairment (6th ed, p 421), 39% digit impairment equated to 4% impairment of the right hand, which was, in turn, converted to 4% right upper extremity and, ultimately, 2% whole person impairment. As stated previously, the range of motion methodology rating stands alone and cannot be combined with other ratings for this body part/injury. Grip loss is no longer a ratable factor in the Sixth Edition.

Impairment: 2% whole person impairment per the Sixth Edition.

Comment on Complex Regional Pain Syndrome

Fourth Edition Rating

Since the publication of the *Guides*, Fourth Edition, a consensus statement has been published by the International Association for the Study of Pain, proposing a redefinition of RSD. This led to the description of CRPS and replacement of the terms *reflex sympathetic dystrophy* and *causalgia* with CRPS types I and II, respectively. The most important difference between CRPS and earlier views of RSD is that sympathetic dysfunction is not assumed to be the basic pathophysiologic mechanism; consequently, regional sympathetic blockade has no role in the diagnosis of CRPS.

The criteria recommended by the *Guides*, Fourth Edition, for estimating impairment due to RSD are difficult to use and may not be adequate, because two of the three recommended criteria are based on objective findings resulting from peripheral nerve injury, which is absent in RSD/CRPS I. Consequently, an alternative approach used by some examiners to assess impairment due to RSD/CRPS I is to use Chapter 4, The Nervous System, Section 4.3, The Spinal Cord, wherein "the magnitude of the impairment would be estimated according to the effects on daily activities. . . ." (4th ed, p 147). In Section 4.3, the criteria for evaluating extremity impairment are found in Section 4.3a, Station and Gait (4th ed, pp 147-148), and in Section 4.3b, Use of Upper Extremities (4th ed, p 148). Table 14 (4th ed, p 148) provides the criteria for one impaired upper extremity. This scheme has advantages. First, it is consistent with the *Guides* concept of impairment; specifically, "impairments are defined as conditions that interfere with an individual's activities of daily living" (4th ed, p 1). Second, this approach is consistent with other schemes for assessing impairment due to RSD/CRPS I. For example, the State of Minnesota Permanent Partial Disability Schedule[1] bases extremity impairment due to RSD on mild, moderate, or severe incapacity to perform specified activities of daily living.

Ms Parker's presentation was consistent with the first criterion described in Table 14, namely, "patient can use the involved extremity for self-care, daily activities, and holding but has difficulty with digital dexterity." The impairing condition involved her preferred extremity. Consequently, per the criteria in Table 14, her whole person impairment was 1% to 9%. Ms Parker's whole person impairment based on loss of range of motion, namely 2%, fell within this range, illustrating the comparability of these two different approaches. In assessing impairment due to RSD/CRPS I, both of these approaches should be considered. A person's actual impairment rating is then left to the evaluating physician's discretion, keeping in mind the aforementioned definition of impairment as a condition that interferes with activities of daily living.

Grip and pinch strength measurements are not used to rate RSD/CRPS I. The *Guides*, Fourth Edition, states that, "because strength measurements are functional tests influenced by subjective factors that are difficult to control, and the *Guides* for the most part is based on anatomic impairment, the *Guides* does not assign a large role to such measurements" (4th ed, p 64).

Although pain is an absolute requirement for an RSD/CRPS I diagnosis, impairment due to RSD/CRPS I is not assessed with the *Guides*, Chapter 15, Pain. Chapter 15 describes the *Guide*s approach to assessing impairment due to chronic pain syndrome, which may be preceded by other conditions, including RSD/CRPS I. The impairment rating for RSD/CRPS I already takes into account the associated pain, and a person with this condition does not receive any additional impairment estimate from Chapter 15.

Fifth Edition Rating

The *Guides* Fifth Edition methods for rating upper extremity impairment due to causalgia, RSD, and CRPS differ from the approach in previous editions. The Fifth Edition methods for rating upper extremity impairment due to these conditions are found in two chapters: Chapter 13, The Central and Peripheral Nervous System, and Chapter 16, The Upper Extremities.

Methods for evaluating impairment due to causalgia, RSD, and CRPS can be described as having anatomic or functional bases. The history and a detailed physical examination determine the anatomic impairment. The anatomic approach for evaluating impairment due to these conditions is appealing because it bases impairment on objective findings a physician can identify during a physical examination using standard clinical techniques. The functional evaluation measures the individual's performance of activities of daily living or a specific task within a set time frame. The functional approach for evaluating impairment is appealing because it is consistent with the *Guides* concept of impairment, namely, "Impairment percentages . . .

are . . . estimates that reflect the severity of the medical condition and the degree to which the impairment decreases an individual's ability to perform common activities of daily living" (5th ed, p 4). The *Guides* Fifth Edition describes two methods for rating these conditions, one based on functional, and the other based on anatomic, aspects of impairment.

Chapter 13 considers causalgia and RSD in Section 13.8, Criteria for Rating Impairments Related to Chronic Pain (5th ed, p 343). The term *chronic pain* as used here has a specific connotation, namely, "Chronic pain in this section covers the diagnoses of causalgia, posttraumatic neuralgia, and reflex sympathetic dystrophy." In contradistinction to Chapters 16 and 17 and the glossary, "The new term *complex regional pain syndrome*, type I and type II, is not used here. . . ." A brief description of causalgia and RSD emphasizes the essential feature that distinguishes these conditions, namely, causalgia ". . . develops in a distal extremity following trauma to a peripheral nerve," whereas RSD "occurs without known nerve lesions." The importance of correct diagnosis is stressed: "To rate these conditions, diagnosis is key and is based on clinical criteria." The discussion of diagnosis describes symptoms, examination findings, and ancillary studies, but does not indicate how the diagnosis is established by means of the various criteria.

Chapter 13 utilizes a functional approach for assessing impairment due to these conditions, using Table 13-22, Criteria for Rating Impairment Related to Chronic Pain in One Upper Extremity (5th ed, p 343), and Table 13-15, Criteria for Rating Impairments Due to Station and Gait Disorders (5th ed, p 336). When using these tables, the evaluator should be aware that, unlike those of Chapter 16, impairment ratings in this chapter are adjusted for hand dominance. Second, the maximum whole person impairment due to lower extremity causalgia or RSD (60%) exceeds the maximum whole person amputation value (40%).

Explaining their choice to use a functional approach, the authors state, "It is difficult to examine individuals who are experiencing these symptoms; therefore, once the criteria for the diagnosis have been met, the impact on ADL is determined." No guidance is provided on how to determine the impact on activities of daily living. The unstated assumption is that a person's capacity to perform activities of daily living can be determined and agreed upon by the various parties involved. However, those parties (6th ed; patients, attorneys, insurers, employers, and others) often draw their own conclusions from perspectives sometimes influenced by their vested interests. For example, the criteria in Table 13-22 yield impairments of the whole person from 1% to 60% for circumstances ranging from limited digital dexterity to complete incapacity to use the involved upper extremity for self-care or daily activities. But how is capacity determined? Is it self-report, that is, what the individual says? Is it what the doctor opines? What about the expected divergent opinions? As the disability epidemic due to nonspecific low back pain has shown, there are no easy answers to these questions.

Example 13-45 describes RSD after carpal tunnel release surgery. A 40% whole person impairment is provided for the RSD diagnosis (apparently based on class 4, with the use of Table 13-22), but there is no analysis of, or comment on, any impairment related to the carpal tunnel syndrome or to pain. Because the use of Section 13.8 rates the overall functional consequences of any and all problems in the upper extremity, it would seem illogical to separately rate any coexisting problems in the upper extremity and then combine the impairments. Any functional deficit due to the other condition(s) already would have been accounted for in the rating for RSD, and combining other impairments would result in duplicative rating.

Chapter 16 considers CRPS in Section 16.5e, Complex Regional Pain Syndromes (CRPS), Reflex Sympathetic Dystrophy (CRPS I), and Causalgia (CRPS II) (5th ed, p 495). The authors begin with a discussion of recent changes in the understanding of these conditions, which resulted in revision of terminology, namely, replacement of *RSD* with *CRPS I* and *causalgia* with *CRPS II.* It is emphasized that sympathetic dysfunction is no longer assumed to be the underlying basis for the symptoms and signs of CRPS and, hence, "contrary to previous suggestions, regional sympathetic blockade has no role in the diagnosis of CRPS." Diagnostic criteria for CRPS are listed in Table 16-16, Objective Diagnostic Criteria for CRPS (RSD and Causalgia) (5th ed, p 496). Unlike in Chapter 13, a method for arriving at a diagnosis on the basis of the criteria is provided, namely, "at least eight [of 11] of these findings must be present concurrently for a diagnosis of CRPS." It is stressed that the criteria listed in Table 16-16 are signs, not symptoms; and "signs are objective evidence of disease perceptible to the examiner, as opposed to symptoms, which are subjective sensations of the individual."

Chapter 16 uses an anatomic approach for assessing impairment due to these conditions. The method is a variation of the Fifth Edition's scheme for rating upper extremity peripheral nerve disorders. Because CRPS I (RSD) occurs without a known nerve lesion, whereas CRPS II (causalgia) follows trauma to a peripheral nerve, the rating methods for these conditions differ.

In the evaluation of CRPS I (RSD):

1. The loss of motion of each joint involved is rated by means of Section 16.4.
2. The pain is rated with Section 16.5b, Table 16-10a. The percent value selected represents the upper extremity impairment. A nerve value

multiplier is not used because in CRPS I (RSD) there is no peripheral nerve injury.

3. Motor deficits or loss of power are not rated because in CRPS I (RSD) there is no peripheral nerve injury.
4. The upper extremity impairments due to loss of motion and pain are combined, then the upper extremity impairment is converted to a whole person impairment.

In the evaluation of CRPS II (causalgia):

1. The loss of motion of each joint involved is rated by means of Section 16.4.
2. Sensory deficits or pain are rated with Section 16.5b, Table 16-10a. The percent value selected is used with a nerve value multiplier for the injured peripheral nerve involved.
3. Motor and loss of power deficits due to the injured peripheral nerve involved are rated by means of Section 16.5b, Table 16-11a.
4. The upper extremity impairments due to loss of motion, sensory deficits or pain, and motor and loss of power deficits are combined, then the upper extremity impairment is converted to a whole person impairment.

In the rating of these conditions by means of Section 16.5e, (1) no additional impairment is assigned for decreased pinch or grip strength; (2) the impairment rating method described for sensory deficits due to lesions of digital nerves is not applied; and (3) in contrast to Chapter 13, impairment ratings are not adjusted for hand dominance.

Chapter 18 describes a qualitative method for evaluating permanent impairment due to chronic pain, explanation of which is beyond the scope of this review. Chronic pain is used differently in Chapters 13 and 18. In Chapter 13, chronic pain encompasses three diagnoses: causalgia, post-traumatic neuralgia, and RSD. In Chapter 18 (5th ed, p 566), chronic pain refers to "an evolving process in which injury may produce one pathogenic mechanism, which in turn produces others, so that the cause(s) of pain change over time."

Chapter 18 does not provide a method for assessing impairment due to causalgia, RSD, or CRPS per se, but CRPS type I (RSD) is referenced in Table 18-1, Illustrative List of Well-Established Pain Syndromes Without Significant, Identifiable Organ Dysfunction to Explain the Pain (5th ed, p 571), and CRPS type II (causalgia) is referenced in Table 18-2, Illustrative

List of Associated Pain Syndromes (5th ed, p 571). Although the conditions are referenced, these are not rating tables.

Example 18-2 describes a clinical scenario essentially identical to that in Example 13-45, namely, RSD after carpal tunnel release surgery with a poor outcome. In Example 13-45, a 40% whole person impairment was provided for the RSD diagnosis. In the case illustrated in Example 18-2, the authors estimated 22% whole person impairment based on decreased range of motion of the involved joints, but no additional impairment was provided for the chronic pain associated with the RSD or for the carpal tunnel syndrome. Interestingly, although in Chapter 18 permanent impairment due to chronic pain is based on a functional approach, Example 18-2 uses an anatomic basis (ie, decreased range of motion) to determine impairment.

In rating upper extremity impairment due to these conditions, the Fifth Edition methods are not internally consistent. Consequently, the evaluator can use the functional approach described in Chapter 13, the anatomic approach described in Chapter 16, or both methods, and then choose the impairment value that best reflects the severity of the condition.

Sixth Edition Rating

The method for rating CRPS of the upper extremity is presented in Section 15.5 (6th ed, p 450) of Chapter 15: The Upper Extremities.

First, it is determined whether a diagnosis of CRPS has been confirmed as defined in Table 15-24 (6th ed, p 453), has been present for at least 1 year and has been confirmed by at least two physicians and whether other conditions that could better explain the presentation have been eliminated. As illustrated in this case, the criteria in Table 15-24 must be met at the time of the impairment assessment; ratings are not made for a history of a resolved diagnosis.

Second, the number of objective diagnostic points is determined using Table 15-25 (6th ed, p 453).

Third, the functional history adjustment modification (6th ed, Table 15-7, p 406), the physical examination adjustment modification (6th ed, Table 15-8, p 408), and the clinical studies adjustment modification (6th ed, Table 15-9, p 410) are determined.

Fourth, the average of the functional history, physical examination, and clinical studies grade modifiers are calculated, then the average is used to determine the class of impairment using Table 15-26 (p 454). If the objective diagnostic criteria points do not support that class number, the highest class supported by those points is selected. For example, if a person has grade modifiers that result in assignment to class 1, but the objective diagnostic criteria points are less than four, then the impairment would be based on class 0.

Fifth, because the adjustment factors are used to determine the class of impairment, they cannot be used to determine the grade within the class. It is left to the evaluator to use clinical judgment to determine the grade within the class.

If the diagnosis is CRPS II, then the severity of the disorder is determined from Table 15-26; however, the actual impairment is obtained from Table 15-21, Peripheral Nerve Impairment: Upper Extremity Impairments (6th ed, p 436), referencing the specific nerve involved and the severity of the CRPS II.

Finally, the rating for CRPS is a "stand alone" approach. If impairment is assigned for CRPS, no additional impairment is assigned for pain from Chapter 3, nor is the CRPS impairment combined with any other approach for the same extremity from Chapter 15.

SUMMARY

Diagnosis	Upper extremity reflex sympathetic dystrophy/complex regional pain syndrome I
Fourth Edition References	Section 3.1k (4th ed, pp 46-57); Section 4.3 (4th ed, pp 147-150), Table 1 (4th ed, p 18), Table 2 (4th ed, p 19), Table 3 (4th ed, p 20), Table 14 (4th ed, p 148)
Fourth Edition Summary	History, upper extremity evaluation (including assessment of range of motion) and neurologic examination. Objective evidence of RSD/CRPS I on physical examination, radiographs, and/or a bone scan is verified. First, impairment due to loss of range of motion of each joint involved is determined. Second, impairment based on the criteria for one impaired upper extremity found in Table 14 (4th ed, p 148) of Section 4.3, The Spinal Cord, is determined. Finally, the actual impairment is that which most accurately reflects the degree to which the RSD/CRPS I interferes with the person's activities of daily living.

Fourth Edition Impairment 3% upper extremity impairment, 2% whole person impairment

Fifth Edition References Section 13.8 (5th ed, pp 343-344), Section 16.5e (5th ed, pp 495-497)

Fifth Edition Summary First, impairment based on the functional criteria by means of Table 13-22 (5th ed, p 343) is determined. Second, the impairment based on the anatomic approach in Section 16.5e (5th ed, pp 495-497) is determined. Finally, the actual impairment is that which most accurately reflects the degree to which the RSD/CRPS I interferes with the person's activities of daily living.

Fifth Edition Impairment 3% upper extremity impairment, 2% whole person impairment

Sixth Edition References Section 15.5 (6th ed, pp 450-454), Table 15-2 (6th ed, p 391), Table 15-7 (6th ed, p 406), Table 15-8 (6th ed, p 408), Table 15-9 (6th ed, p 410), Table 15-12 (6th ed, p 421), Table 15-25 (6th ed, p 453), Table 15-26 (6th ed, p 454), Table 15-31 (6th ed, p 470)

Sixth Edition Summary First, it is determined whether the CRPS diagnosis is credible and reliable by satisfying the four criteria outlined on page 451. If met, then the number of objective diagnostic points from Table 15-25 is determined. These points are used to determine severity and class from Table 15-26. The adjustment factor grade modifiers are then averaged to assist in the determination of the proper class rating from Table 15-26. If the diagnostic points do not match the grade modifier average, the diagnostic point class is used. The specific value chosen from within the class rating is then based on physician judgment. If the class points match with the grade modifier average, based on the adjustment factors, the rating can be chosen from within the class range. The CRPS rating is a stand-alone approach. If CRPS is not definable or ratable in the upper extremity, then other factors such as the diagnosis-based

	impairment rating methodology or range of motion methodology can be applied. The range of motion rating is a stand-alone approach.
Sixth Edition Impairment	4% upper extremity impairment, 2% whole person impairment

Reference

1. State of Minnesota, Department of Labor and Industry. *Permanent Partial Disability Schedule*. Effective July 1, 1993.

Upper Extremity Impairment Evaluation Record**–**Part 1 (Hand)** Side ☑R ☐L

Name Ms. Parker Age 26 Sex ☐M ☑F Dominant hand ☑R ☐L Date

Occupation Diagnosis RSD/CRPS I

			Abnormal motion Record motion, ankylosis, and impairment %				Amputation Mark level & impairment %	Sensory loss Mark type, level, & impairment %	Other disorders List type & impairment %	Hand impairment% • Combine digit IMP% *Convert to hand IMP%	
			Flexion	Extension	Ankylosis	IMP%					
Thumb	IP	Angle°									
		IMP%									
	MP	Angle°									
		IMP%									
			Motion		Ankylosis	IMP%	R L	R L			
	CMC	Radial abduction Angle°								Abnormal motion [1]	
		Radial abduction IMP%								Amputation [2]	
		Adduction CMS								Sensory loss [3]	
		Adduction IMP%								Other disorders [4]	
		Opposition CMS								Digit impairment % • Combine 1, 2, 3, 4	
		Opposition IMP%									
Add impairment % CMC + MP + IP =						[1]	[2] IMP % =	[3] IMP % =	[4] IMP % =	Hand impairment % *Convert above	

			Flexion	Extension	Ankylosis	IMP%	Amputation	Sensory loss	Other disorders	Hand impairment%	
Index	DIP	Angle°								Abnormal motion [1]	
		IMP%								Amputation [2]	
	PIP	Angle°								Sensory loss [3]	
		IMP%								Other disorders [4]	
	MP	Angle°								Digit impairment % • Combine 1, 2, 3, 4	
		IMP%									
• Combine impairment % MP + PIP + DIP =						[1]	[2] IMP % =	[3] IMP % =	[4] IMP % =	Hand impairment % *Convert above	
Middle	DIP	Angle°								Abnormal motion [1]	
		IMP%								Amputation [2]	
	PIP	Angle°								Sensory loss [3]	
		IMP%								Other disorders [4]	
	MP	Angle°								Digit impairment % • Combine 1, 2, 3, 4	
		IMP%									
• Combine impairment % MP + PIP + DIP =						[1]	[2] IMP % =	[3] IMP % =	[4] IMP % =	Hand impairment % *Convert above	
Ring	DIP	Angle°								Abnormal motion [1]	
		IMP%								Amputation [2]	
	PIP	Angle°								Sensory loss [3]	
		IMP%								Other disorders [4]	
	MP	Angle°								Digit impairment % • Combine 1, 2, 3, 4	
		IMP%									
• Combine impairment % MP + PIP + DIP =						[1]	[2] IMP % =	[3] IMP % =	[4] IMP % =	Hand impairment % *Convert above	
Little	DIP	Angle°	50	−10		12				Abnormal motion [1]	31
		IMP%	10	2						Amputation [2]	—
	PIP	Angle°	80	0		12				Sensory loss [3]	—
		IMP%	12	0						Other disorders [4]	—
	MP	Angle°	80	0		11				Digit impairment % • Combine 1, 2, 3, 4	31
		IMP%	6	5							
• Combine impairment % MP + PIP + DIP = 31						[1]	[2] IMP % =	[3] IMP % =	[4] IMP % =	Hand impairment % *Convert above	3

Total hand impairment (Add hand impairment % for thumb + index + middle + ring + little finger) = 3 %
Upper extremity impairment (†Convert total hand impairment % to upper extremity impairment %) = 3 %; enter on Part 2, Line II
If hand region impairment is only impairment, convert upper extremity impairment to whole-person impairment:‡ = 2 %

• Combined Values Chart; (p. 322-324) *Use Table 1 (Digits to hand p. 18); †Use Table 2 (Hand to upper extremity p. 19) ‡Use Table 3 (p. 20)

** Courtesy of G. de Groot Swanson, MD

Upper Extremity Impairment Evaluation Record–Part 1 (Hand) Side ☒R ☐L

Name Ms. Parker Age 26 Sex ☐M ☒F Dominant hand ☒R ☐L Date ______

Occupation ______ Diagnosis CRPS CASE 15-4

			Abnormal Motion: Record motion or ankylosis angles and digit impairment %				Amputation: Mark level & impairment %	Sensory Loss: Mark type, level, & impairment %	Other Disorders: List type & impairment %	Hand Impairment%: •Combine digit imp % ★Convert to hand imp %	
			Flexion	Extension	Ankylosis	Imp %					
Thumb	IP	Angle°									
		Imp %									
	MP	Angle°									
		Imp %					[2]				
				Motion	Ankylosis	Imp %					
	CMC	Radial abduction Angle°								Abnormal motion [1]	
		Radial abduction Imp %								Amputation [2]	
		Adduction Cm								Sensory loss [3]	
		Adduction Imp %								Other disorders [4]	
		Opposition Cm					‡UE IMP % = [5]			Total digit imp % •Combine 1, 2, 3, 4	
		Opposition Imp %									
Add digit impairment % CMC + MP + IP =						[1]	Digit IMP % = [2]	Digit IMP % = [3]	Digit IMP % = [4]	Hand impairment % ★Convert above	

			Flexion	Extension	Ankylosis	Imp %					
Index	DIP	Angle°								Abnormal motion [1]	
		Imp %								Amputation [2]	
	PIP	Angle°								Sensory loss [3]	
		Imp %								Other disorders [4]	
	MP	Angle°								Total digit imp % •Combine 1, 2, 3, 4	
		Imp %									
•Combine digit impairment % MP, PIP, DIP =						[1]	Digit IMP % = [2]	Digit IMP % = [3]	Digit IMP % = [4]	Hand impairment % ★Convert above	
Middle	DIP	Angle°								Abnormal motion [1]	
		Imp %								Amputation [2]	
	PIP	Angle°								Sensory loss [3]	
		Imp %								Other disorders [4]	
	MP	Angle°								Total digit imp % •Combine 1, 2, 3, 4	
		Imp %									
•Combine digit impairment % MP, PIP, DIP =						[1]	Digit IMP % = [2]	Digit IMP % = [3]	Digit IMP % = [4]	Hand impairment % ★Convert above	
Ring	DIP	Angle°								Abnormal motion [1]	
		Imp %								Amputation [2]	
	PIP	Angle°								Sensory loss [3]	
		Imp %								Other disorders [4]	
	MP	Angle°								Total digit imp % •Combine 1, 2, 3, 4	
		Imp %									
•Combine digit impairment % MP, PIP, DIP =						[1]	Digit IMP % = [2]	Digit IMP % = [3]	Digit IMP % = [4]	Hand impairment % ★Convert above	
Little	DIP	Angle°	50	-10		12				Abnormal motion [1]	31
		Imp %	10	2						Amputation [2]	—
	PIP	Angle°	80	0		12				Sensory loss [3]	—
		Imp %	12	0						Other disorders [4]	—
	MP	Angle°	80	0		11				Total digit imp % •Combine 1, 2, 3, 4	31
		Imp %	6	5							
•Combine digit impairment % MP, PIP, DIP = 31						[1]	Digit IMP % = [2]	Digit IMP % = [3]	Digit IMP % = [4]	Hand impairment % ★Convert above	3

Total hand impairment: Add hand impairment % for thumb + index + middle + ring + little finger =	3 %
Convert total hand impairment to upper extremity impairment† (if thumb metacarpal intact, enter on Part 2, line II) =	3 %
‡Add thumb ray upper extremity amputation imp [5] ____% + hand upper extremity imp ____% =	%
If hand region impairment is only impairment, convert upper extremity impairment to whole person impairment§ =	2 %

• Combined Values Chart (p. 604). ★Use Table 16-1 (digits to hand). †Use Table 16-2 (hand to upper extremity). §Use Table 16-3.
Courtesy of G. de Groot Swanson, MD, Grand Rapids, Michigan.

CASE 15-5

Peripheral Nerve Injury

Subject: Ms Eckard, a 38-year-old woman.

History: Ms Eckard slipped on a step 2 years earlier. She landed on her right arm and sustained a closed right humerus fracture. In addition to severe pain, she was immediately aware of difficulty extending her right wrist and fingers. There was also some numbness over the dorsal aspect of her right hand. She was treated with a hanging arm cast, and her fracture healed uneventfully and in anatomic position.

Current Symptoms: Approximately 1 year after the injury, Ms Eckard continued to have some weakness of elbow, wrist, and finger extension with numbness along the dorsal aspect of her right hand. She was no longer improving on serial physical examinations.

Functional Assessment: The *Quick*DASH score was 4.5.

Physical Examination: Mild tenderness at the fracture site. Shoulder range of motion was normal. Ms Eckard had some limitation of function in the right radial nerve. There was grade 4 weakness (ability to perform a full range of active movement against gravity with some resistance) in the right triceps and the right wrist and finger extensors. Mild resistance by the examiner prevented Ms Eckard from moving her elbow, wrist, and fingers through their full range of motion. Sensory examination showed evidence of decreased sensory perception (diminished light touch with equivocal difficulties with two-point discrimination), without pain, along the dorsal aspect of the right arm and hand. Median and ulnar nerve function was normal. Ms Eckard indicated that the decreased sensory perception was annoying, but she could not think of any activity with which it interfered. Her main complaints were weakness of straightening her elbow and wrist and weakness of grip (because of loss of the wrist extensors stabilizing the wrist for power grip).

Clinical Studies: Electromyograms and nerve conduction studies confirmed radial nerve injury, with some, but incomplete, improvement on serial studies.

Discussion of Peripheral Nerve Injury

Fourth Edition Rating

This individual sustained a partial radial nerve injury. Impairment was rated according to Section 3.1k, Impairment of the Upper Extremity Due to Peripheral Nerve Disorders (4th ed, p 46). The degree of sensory impairment was determined by means of Table 11, Determining Impairment of the Upper Extremity Due to Pain or Sensory Deficit Resulting From Peripheral Nerve Disorders (4th ed, p 48). Ms Eckard had a grade 2 sensory deficit, that is, decreased sensibility with or without abnormal sensation or pain, which is forgotten during activity, which represents a 1% to 25% sensory deficit multiplier. In this case, the examiner chose a 25% multiplier, because the sensory deficit was significant but was forgotten with activity. Table 15, Maximum Upper Extremity Impairments Due to Unilateral Sensory or Motor Deficits or Combined Deficits of the Major Peripheral Nerves (4th ed, p 54), specifies that for the radial nerve there may be as much as a 5% sensory impairment of the upper extremity. Multiplying the severity of the sensory deficit, 25%, by the maximum potential loss, 5%, yielded 1.25%, or, with rounding, a 1% upper extremity impairment for loss of sensation.

A similar method of analysis was used for the motor impairment. With the use of Table 12, Determining Impairment of the Upper Extremity Due to Loss of Power and Motor Deficits Resulting From Peripheral Nerve Disorders Based on Individual Muscle Rating (4th ed, p 49), Ms Eckard had a grade 4 loss of power that was a 1% to 25% motor deficit multiplier. In this case, because the weakness was severe enough that very little resistance could be added before the individual failed to move the wrist and fingers through their full range of motion, the examiner chose the 25% severity multiplier. Table 15 (4th ed, p 54) shows that injury to the radial nerve (upper arm with loss of triceps) can potentially be as much as 42% upper extremity impairment. Multiplying the severity of the motor deficit, 25%, by the maximum potential loss, 42%, yielded 10.5%, or, with rounding, an 11% upper extremity impairment for her motor deficit. Combining the 1% sensory impairment with the 11% motor impairment by means of the Combined Values Chart (4th ed, p 322) resulted in 12% upper extremity impairment for this partial radial nerve palsy. According to Table 3 (4th ed, p 20), this was equivalent to a 7% whole person impairment.

Impairment: 7% whole person impairment per the Fourth Edition.

Fifth Edition Rating

This individual sustained a partial radial nerve injury. Impairment was rated according to Section 16.5, Impairment of the Upper Extremities Due to

Peripheral Nerve Disorders (5th ed, pp 480-491). The degree of sensory impairment was determined by means of Table 16-10, Determining Impairment of the Upper Extremity Due to Sensory Deficits or Pain Resulting From Peripheral Nerve Disorders, Part a (5th ed, p 482). Ms Eckard had a grade 4 sensory deficit, that is, distorted superficial tactile sensibility (diminished light touch) with or without minimal abnormal sensations or pain that is forgotten during activity, which represents a 1% to 25% sensory deficit multiplier. In this case, the examiner chose a 25% multiplier, because the sensory deficit was significant (eg, diminished light touch) but was forgotten with activity. Table 16-15, Maximum Upper Extremity Impairment Due to Unilateral Sensory or Motor Deficits or Combined 100% Deficits of the Major Peripheral Nerves (5th ed, p 492), specifies that for the radial nerve there may be as much as a 5% sensory impairment of the upper extremity. Multiplying the severity of the sensory deficit, 25%, by the maximum potential loss, 5%, yielded 1.25%, or, with rounding, a 1% upper extremity impairment for loss of sensation.

A similar method of analysis was used for the motor impairment. According to Table 16-11, Determining Impairment of the Upper Extremity Due to Motor and Loss of Power Deficits Resulting From Peripheral Nerve Disorders Based on Individual Muscle Rating, Part a (5th ed, p 484), Ms Eckard had a grade 4 loss of power that was a 1% to 25% motor deficit multiplier. In this case, because the weakness was severe enough that very little resistance could be added before the individual failed to move the wrist and fingers through their full range of motion, the examiner chose the 25% severity multiplier. Table 16-15 (5th ed, p 492) shows that injury to the radial nerve (upper arm with loss of triceps) can potentially be as much as 42% upper extremity impairment. Multiplying the severity of the sensory deficit, 25%, by the maximum potential loss, 42%, yielded 10.5%, or, with rounding, an 11% upper extremity impairment for her motor deficit. Combining the 1% sensory impairment with the 11% motor impairment by means of the Combined Values Chart (5th ed, p 604) resulted in 12% upper extremity impairment for this partial radial nerve palsy. According to Table 16-3, Conversion of Impairment of the Upper Extremity to Impairment of the Whole Person (5th ed, p 439), this was equivalent to a 7% whole person impairment.

Impairment: 7% whole person impairment per the Fifth Edition.

Sixth Edition Rating

Permanent impairment evaluation was based on Section 15.4, Peripheral Nerve Impairment (6th ed, pp 419-450). The injured nerve was the radial nerve (upper arm with loss of triceps). The degree of sensory and motor impairment was determined by means of Table 15-14, Sensory and Motor

Severity (6th ed, p 425). Ms Eckard had a mild sensory and motor deficit, that is, distorted superficial tactile sensibility (diminished light touch) and weakness severe enough that very little resistance could be added before she failed to move the wrist and fingers through their full range of motion. According to Table 15-21, Peripheral Nerve Impairment: Upper Extremity Impairments (6th ed, p 441), injury to the radial nerve (upper arm with loss of triceps) with mild sensory deficit is a class 1 impairment with a default 1% upper extremity impairment. Referencing the same table for the mild motor deficit, there was a class 1 impairment with a default 6% upper extremity impairment. According to Table 15-7, Functional History Adjustment: Upper Extremities (6th ed, p 406), and her *Quick*DASH score of 4.5, there was a grade modifier 0. According to Table 15-9, Clinical Studies Adjustment: Upper Extremities (6th ed, p 410), there was a grade modifier 1. The net adjustment is −1, resulting in grade B, which resulted in 0% upper extremity impairment for sensory deficit and 3% upper extremity impairment for motor deficit. These values were combined to result in 3% upper extremity impairment, which converted to 2% whole person impairment.

Impairment: 2% whole person impairment per the Sixth Edition.

Comment on Peripheral Nerve Injury

One should allow a minimum of 1 year before determining a permanent partial impairment rating relative to a peripheral nerve injury. Severely injured nerves may regenerate at a rate of an inch a month, so some nerve injuries in the proximal arm may require 2 or even 3 years for maximum improvement. Most of the improvement will occur in the first year, and by 1 year after injury, Ms Eckard seemed to have stopped improving, both by physical examination and by electrodiagnostic studies. In order to accurately calculate impairment ratings in reference to peripheral nerve injuries, one must possess an accurate knowledge of neuroanatomy and the ability to do a peripheral neurologic examination.

The Sixth Edition bases peripheral nerve impairment on the nerve involved and the associated severity of sensory and motor deficits. This is similar to prior editions; however, the methodology used to calculate the impairment values is different. The Fifth Edition uses Tables 16-10 (5th ed, p 482) and 16-11 (5th ed, p 484) to determine assignment of a grade and percentage for motor and sensory deficits. These values are then multiplied times the maximum value for motor and sensory function of the injured nerve as defined in Table 16-15 (5th ed, p 492). The impairment values for both motor and sensory are then combined.

In contrast, the Sixth Edition requires only grading of the deficits as referenced in Table 15-14 (6th ed, p 425). The defined severity is placed in the appropriate class for the appropriate nerve in Table 15-21 (6th ed, pp 436-444). The default impairment value for both motor and sensory deficits are assigned and adjusted based on nonkey factors. After adjustment, the motor and sensory values are combined.

SUMMARY

Diagnosis	Radial nerve palsy, partial
Fourth Edition References	Section 3.1k (4th ed, p 46), Table 11 (4th ed, p 48), Table 12 (4th ed, p 49), Table 15 (4th ed, p 54)
Fourth Edition Summary	History, upper extremity examination, peripheral neurologic examination, electrophysiologic studies, as appropriate. Peripheral neurologic involvement and the severity of any sensory and/or motor deficits are defined.
Fourth Edition Impairment	12% upper extremity impairment, 7% whole person impairment
Fifth Edition References	Section 16.5 (5th ed, pp 480-491), Table 16-10, Part a (5th ed, p 482), Table 16-11, Part a (5th ed, p 484), Table 16-15 (5th ed, p 492)
Fifth Edition Summary	History, upper extremity examination, peripheral neurologic examination, electrophysiologic studies, as appropriate. Peripheral neurologic involvement and the severity of any sensory and/or motor deficits are defined.
Fifth Edition Impairment	12% upper extremity impairment, 7% whole person impairment
Sixth Edition References	Section 15.4 (6th ed, pp 419-450), Table 15-14 (6th ed, p 425), Table 15-21 (6th ed, pp 436-444), Table 15-7 (6th ed, p 406)

Sixth Edition Summary	History (including functional history and inventories), physical evaluation, and clinical studies. First, the nerve involved is determined. Second, sensory and motor deficits are graded. Third, the grade is applied to determine the default value. Adjustment modifiers for nonkey factors are applied, adjusting impairment values for each motor and sensory deficit. Finally, motor and sensory upper extremity impairment values are combined.
Sixth Edition Impairment	3% upper extremity impairment, 2% whole person impairment

CASE 15-6

Rotator Cuff Repair

Subject: Ms Redi, a 55-year-old woman.

History: Ms Redi had chronic pain in her right shoulder for a number of months. While on the job 6 months previously, she reached forward to lift a 25-pound piece of equipment and experienced sudden onset of pain in her right shoulder, which was worse than any pain she had experienced in the past. She reported this to her supervisor and was referred to a family practitioner who examined the shoulder and prescribed anti-inflammatory medications and Codman exercises. One week later, her condition was unimproved, and she was referred to an orthopedic surgeon.

On examination, Ms Redi was unable to actively abduct against resistance and had a positive impingement sign. Subsequent magnetic resonance imaging showed a complete tear of the rotator cuff, for which she underwent operative repair. It appeared to be a fresh tear, and the dictated operative report indicated that the repair was anatomic. After a period of immobilization, Ms Redi was started on range of motion and strengthening exercises through active physical therapy for approximately 3 months. At about 6 months, she was back to work and doing quite well but did have some limitation of motion of the right shoulder.

At 6 months Ms Redi was determined to be at maximal medical improvement because her motion and function had stopped improving on serial examinations.

Current Symptoms: The patient complained of mild discomfort in her right shoulder and difficulties with overhead activities.

Functional Assessment: The *Quick*DASH score was 25.

Physical Examination: Active motion of the right shoulder as measured with a goniometer was flexion 150°, extension 40°, abduction 140°, adduction 50°, internal rotation 60°, and external rotation 50°. Left shoulder motion was normal. Strength was within normal limits, except for minimal weakness of right shoulder abduction (4+/5). There was no evidence of atrophy, and the neurologic status was otherwise within normal limits.

Pulses were normally palpable. There was no evidence of loss of strength or sensation in the extremity below the elbow.

Clinical Studies: Preoperative magnetic resonance imaging revealed a complete tear of the rotator cuff.

Discussion of Rotator Cuff Repair

Fourth Edition Rating

This individual was rated by means of the range of motion system as described in the *Guides*, Abnormal Motion of Shoulder (4th ed, pp 41-45). This method measures the six motions of the shoulder: flexion, extension, abduction, adduction, and internal and external rotation. By means of the pie charts on pages 43 to 45 in the Fourth Edition, the rater determines the impairment for each motion. The impairment values are then added "because the relative value of each shoulder function has been taken into consideration in the impairment charts" (4th ed, p 45).

According to Figure 38, Upper Extremity Impairments Due to Lack of Flexion and Extension (4th ed, p 43), having only 150° of flexion is a 2% upper extremity impairment, and 40° of extension is a 1% impairment. According to Figure 41, Upper Extremity Impairments Due to Lack of Abduction and Adduction of Shoulder (4th ed, p 44), having only 140° of abduction is a 2% impairment, and 50° of adduction is a 0% impairment. According to Figure 44, Upper Extremity Impairments Due to Lack of Internal and External Rotation of Shoulder (4th ed, p 45), having only 50° of external rotation is a 1% impairment, and 60° of internal rotation is a 2% upper extremity impairment. These impairments were added to yield a final rating of 8% upper extremity impairment. Using Table 3, Relationship of Impairment of the Upper Extremity to Impairment of the Whole Person (4th ed, p 20), the 8% upper extremity impairment was converted to a 5% whole person impairment rating.

Impairment: 5% whole person impairment per the Fourth Edition.

Fifth Edition Rating

This individual was rated by means of the range of motion system as described in the *Guides*, Section 16.4i, Shoulder Motion Impairment (5th ed, p 474). This method measures the six motions of the shoulder: flexion, extension, abduction, adduction, and internal and external rotation. By means of the pie charts on pages 476 to 479 in the Fifth Edition, the rater determines the impairment for each motion. The impairment values are then added.

According to Figure 16-40, Pie Chart of Upper Extremity Motion Impairments Due to Lack of Flexion and Extension of Shoulder (5th ed, p 476), having only 150° of flexion is a 2% upper extremity impairment, and 40° of extension is a 1% impairment. According to Figure 16-43, Pie Chart of Upper Extremity Motion Impairments Due to Lack of Abduction and Adduction of Shoulder (5th ed, p 477), having only 140° of abduction is a 2% impairment, and 50° of adduction is a 0% impairment. According to Figure 16-46, Pie Chart of Upper Extremity Impairments Due to Lack of Internal and External Rotation of Shoulder (5th ed, p 479), having only 50° of external rotation is a 1% impairment, and 60° of internal rotation is a 2% upper extremity impairment. These impairments were added to yield a final rating of 8% upper extremity impairment. Using Table 16-3, Conversion of Impairment of the Upper Extremity to Impairment of the Whole Person (5th ed, p 439), the 8% upper extremity impairment was converted to a 5% whole person impairment rating.

Impairment: 5% whole person impairment per the Fifth Edition.

Sixth Edition Rating

This individual could have been rated by two possible methods: Section 15.2, Diagnosis-Based Impairment (6th ed, p 387), or Section 15.7g, Shoulder Motion (6th ed, p 472). Diagnosis-based impairment involves the use of Table 15-5, Shoulder Regional Grid: Upper Extremity Impairments (6th ed, pp 401-405). Range of motion impairment involves the use of Table 15-34, Shoulder Range of Motion (6th ed, p 475). Both methods were reviewed; however, this individual was rated by means of the range of motion method because that resulted in a higher rating. This method measures the six motions of the shoulder: flexion, extension, abduction, adduction, and internal and external rotation. By using Table 15-34, Shoulder Range of Motion (6th ed, p 475), the rater determines the impairment for each motion of the joint. These impairment values are then added.

According to Table 15-34, Shoulder Range of Motion (6th ed, p 475), for 150° of flexion there is a 3% upper extremity impairment, for 40° of extension there is a 1% upper extremity impairment. For 140° of abduction there is a 3% upper extremity impairment, and for 50° of adduction there is a 0% upper extremity impairment. For 60° of internal rotation there is a 2% upper extremity impairment, and for 50° of external rotation there is a 2% upper extremity impairment. These impairments were added for a total of 11% upper extremity impairment.

Referencing Table 15-35, Range of Motion Grade Modifiers (6th ed, p 477), based on motion deficits of less than 12% upper extremity impairment for the shoulder, the grade modifier is 1. Referencing Table 15-7, Functional History Adjustment: Upper Extremities (6th ed, p 406), the modifier is 1. Because the patient's range of motion and functional history adjustments were equal, no modification of her impairment was required, per Table 15-36, Functional History Grade Adjustment: Range of Motion (6th ed, p 477). Therefore, the final rating was 11% upper extremity impairment. Using Table 15-11, Impairment Values Calculated From Upper Extremity Impairment (6th ed, p 420), 11% upper extremity impairment was converted to 7% whole person impairment.

Impairment: 7% whole person impairment per the Sixth Edition.

Comment on Rotator Cuff Repair

This case was best rated via range of motion, whether assessed by the Fourth, Fifth, or Sixth Editions. With the Sixth Edition, most impairments are rated using the diagnosis-based impairment approach. However, in this case, the range of motion approach resulted in greater impairment, and, therefore, this approach was used. In the Sixth Edition, range of motion impairment values are provided in a table, rather than a pie chart. The Fifth Edition provides more direction on how to measure motion, but the values for motion deficits remain the same as in the Fourth Edition. Motion measurements falling between those shown in a pie chart may be adjusted or interpolated.

New to the Fifth Edition are instructions permitting apportionment of diminished joint motion. "If a contralateral 'normal' joint has a less than average mobility, the impairment value(s) corresponding to the uninvolved joint can serve as a baseline and are subtracted from the calculated impairment for the involved joint" (5th ed, p 453). In this case, however, the uninvolved shoulder had normal motion. These same directives are present in the Sixth Edition.

A process for rating weakness of the shoulder was provided in the Fifth Edition. Strength deficits for the shoulder are obtained from clinical assessment and based on ranges derived from unit of motion values. The ratings are presented in Table 16-35, Impairment of the Upper Extremity Due to Strength Deficit From Musculoskeletal Disorders Based on Manual Muscle Testing of Individual Units of Motion of the Shoulder and Elbow (5th ed, p 510). As in the Fourth Edition, loss of strength is rated only "in a rare case, if the examiner believes [it] . . . represents an impairing factor . . . not . . . considered adequately by other methods in the *Guides*. . . ." (5th ed, p 508). A rating for weakness could be combined with other impairments but only if due to an unrelated cause. The Fifth Edition states that strength loss "cannot be rated in the presence of decreased motion, painful conditions, deformities, or absence of parts" (5th ed, p 508). It would not be appropriate to combine impairment for strength loss in this case, because this is not a rare case, and there was decreased motion. Strength loss is not rated with the Sixth Edition.

SUMMARY

Diagnosis	Rotator cuff tear
Fourth Edition References	Section 3.1j (4th ed, p 41); Section 3.1m (4th ed, p 63), Figures 38, 41, and 44 (4th ed, pp 43-45)
Fourth Edition Summary	Range of motion of the six shoulder motions is measured and compared to pie charts.
Fourth Edition Impairment	8% upper extremity impairment, 5% whole person impairment
Fifth Edition References	Section 16.4i (5th ed, pp 474-479), Figure 16-40 (5th ed, p 476), Figure 16-43 (5th ed, p 477), Figure 16-46 (5th ed, p 479)
Fifth Edition Summary	Range of motion of the six shoulder motions is measured and compared to pie charts. Rating is made for strength loss in the rare case and only if motion is normal and the condition is not painful.
Fifth Edition Impairment	8% upper extremity impairment, 5% whole person impairment
Sixth Edition References	Section 15.7g (6th ed, pp 472-478), Table 15-34 (6th ed, p 475)
Sixth Edition Summary	Determination is made whether the rating should be made by diagnosis-based impairments or by range of motion. Range of motion of the six shoulder motions is measured and compared to the table.
Sixth Edition Impairment	11% upper extremity impairment, 7% whole person impairment

CASE 15-7

Lacerated Extensor Tendon

Subject: Ms Brown, a 29-year-old woman.

History: Ms Brown, who is right-handed, lacerated the dorsum of her left hand with a box-cutting knife at work. She was taken immediately to a local emergency department, where she was treated by a qualified hand surgeon. He operated the same day and repaired the extensor tendons to her index finger. A well-trained hand therapist supervised her rehabilitation. Despite medically necessary and reasonable treatment, Ms Brown developed adherence of the tendons at the site of repair. The surgeon recommended a tenolysis 4 months after injury, but Ms Brown preferred not to have further surgery.

Current Symptoms: The patient reported difficulties with movement of her fingers; however, this did not result in any significant difficulties with her activities of daily living.

Functional Assessment: The *Quick*DASH score was 21.

Physical Examination: Examination 6 months after injury showed a well-healed, supple, nontender scar on the dorsum of the hand. There was full passive range of motion in all the joints of the index finger. When Ms Brown tried to extend all her fingers at the same time, she could extend all the joints of her index finger to 0° extension. Her left index finger metacarpophalangeal (MP) joint did not hyperextend; it was limited to 0°. Her right index finger was able to hyperextend to 20°. With her MP joints at 0°, when she flexed her interphalangeal (IP) joints, active PIP joint flexion in her left index finger was 100°, and her active DIP joint flexion was 70°. When Ms Brown attempted to flex all of her fingers at the same time, the MP joint flexed 50°, the PIP joint flexed 60°, and the DIP joint flexed 30°. The remainder of her hand examination was normal.

Clinical Studies: None

Discussion of Lacerated Extensor Tendon

Fourth Edition Rating

Ms Brown's permanent impairment evaluation was based on Section 3.1g, Fingers (4th ed, pp 30-34). First, the flexion and extension impairments of each joint were added. Second, the joint impairments were combined, thereby estimating impairment of the entire finger. Third, the finger impairment was expressed in terms of the hand, upper extremity, and whole person. This process is summarized in the Upper Extremity Impairment Evaluation Record (4th ed, p 16), as shown here on page 242.

Figure 18, Neutral Position and Flexion of Finger DIP Joint (4th ed, p 32); Figure 20, Neutral Position and Flexion of Finger PIP Joint (4th ed, p 33); and Figure 22, Finger Impairments Due to Abnormal Position at the MP Joint (4th ed, p 34), show the examiner how to have the patient actively move the hand to the postures in which the maximal degree of motion is measured. When flexion of the DIP joint is measured, the PIP joint is flexed, as illustrated in Figure 18, although the text provides different advice, stating "distal joints are evaluated with the proximal joints in the neutral (straight line position)" (4th ed, p 31). Flexion of the MP joint is measured with the DIP and PIP joints flexed.

Ms Brown's impairment rating was based on loss of range of motion of her index finger MP, PIP, and DIP joints according to Figure 19, Finger Impairments Due to Abnormal Motion at the DIP Joint (4th ed, p 32); Figure 21, Finger Impairments Due to Abnormal Motion at PIP Joint (4th ed, p 33); and Figure 23, Finger Impairments Due to Abnormal Motion at the MP Joint (4th ed, p 34). The motion measurements in this case were all performed as described by the *Guides* and thus could be used to estimate the patient's impairment.

Ms Brown's active extension at the DIP joint and PIP joint was 0°, which is normal, and there was no impairment. Her MP joint extension was limited to 0°, but the MP joint of her right index finger hyperextended 20°. Thus, for loss of extension at the MP joint, Ms Brown's digit impairment was 5%, according to Figure 23.

Flexion of Ms Brown's DIP and PIP joints was within normal limits when measured as shown in Figures 18 and 20 (70° at the DIP joint and 100° at the PIP joint). Thus, she did not have impairment for loss of flexion at these joints according to Figures 19 and 21. When she attempted to make a fist, placing her hand in the position that Figure 22 demonstrates for measuring MP flexion, she could flex the index MP joint only to 50° because the excursion or motion of the extensor tendon was limited by scarring of the tendon to the wound. According to Figure 23, having only 50° of MP joint flexion equated with 22% impairment of the digit.

Because the losses of MP joint extension and flexion were in the same joint, the 5% for loss of extension and the 22% for loss of flexion were added to result in 27% impairment of the index finger. Using Table 1, Relationship of Impairment of the Digits to Impairment of the Hand (4th ed, p 18), the 27% finger impairment was converted to 5% hand impairment. Using Table 2, Relationship of Impairment of the Hand to Impairment of the Upper Extremity (4th ed, p 19), the 5% hand impairment was converted to 5% upper extremity impairment. Using Table 3, Relationship of Impairment of the Upper Extremity to Impairment of the Whole Person (4th ed, p 20), the 5% upper extremity impairment was converted to 3% whole person impairment.

Impairment: 3% whole person impairment per the Fourth Edition.

Fifth Edition Rating

Ms Brown's permanent impairment evaluation was based on Section 16.4e, Finger Motion Impairment (5th ed, pp 461-466). First, the flexion and extension impairments of each joint were added. Second, the joint impairments were combined, thereby estimating impairment of the entire finger. Third, the finger impairment was expressed in terms of the hand, upper extremity, and whole person. This process is summarized in the Upper Extremity Impairment Evaluation Record (5th ed, p 436), as shown here on page 243.

The Fifth Edition presents two methods for measuring motion of the digital joints: (1) measurement of individual joints with proximal joints stabilized in extension and (2) measurement of the total active range of motion of the digit while all three joints are flexed simultaneously (5th ed, p 451). The technique that best reflects the existing impairment was selected.

The examiner needs to compare the impairment ratings from each of these two methods. The method used in the Third and Fourth Editions works well when joint pathology limits motion (eg, a PIP joint fracture or dislocation). The Fifth Edition adds a second method option, the total active range of motion method (TAM), because in situations of adhesions involving tendons, the traditional method of measuring limitation of motion underestimates the effect of the limited motion on activities of daily living.

The first method, the traditional method, is unchanged from the Third and Fourth Editions. Figure 16-20, Neutral Position and Flexion of Finger DIP

Joint (5th ed, p 461); Figure 16-22, Neutral Position and Flexion of Finger PIP Joint (5th ed, p 463); and Figure 16-24, Neutral Position and Flexion of Finger MP Joint (5th ed, p 464), show the examiner how to have the patient actively move the hand to the postures in which the maximal degree of motion is measured. When flexion of the DIP joint is measured, the PIP joint is flexed, as illustrated in Figure 16-20. Flexion of the MP joint is measured with the DIP and PIP joints flexed.

Ms Brown's impairment rating was based on loss of range of motion of her index finger MP, PIP, and DIP joints, by means of Figure 16-21, Finger Impairments Due to Abnormal Motion at the DIP Joint (5th ed, p 461); Figure 16-23, Finger Impairments Due to Abnormal Motion at PIP Joint (5th ed, p 463); and Figure 16-25, Finger Impairments Due to Abnormal Motion at the MP Joint (5th ed, p 464). These motion measurements were all performed as described by the *Guides,* and thus can be used to estimate the patient's impairment.

Ms Brown's active extension at the DIP joint and PIP joint was 0°, which is normal, and there was no impairment. Her MP joint extension was limited to 0°, but the right index finger MP joint hyperextended 20°. Thus, for loss of extension at the MP joint, Ms Brown's digit impairment was 5%, according to Figure 16-25.

Flexion of Ms Brown's DIP and PIP joints was within normal limits when measured as shown in Figures 16-21 and 16-23 (70° at the DIP joint and 100° at the PIP joint). Thus, she did not have impairment for loss of flexion at these joints, according to Figures 16-21 and 16-23. When she attempted to make a fist, placing her hand in the position that Figure 16-24 demonstrates for measuring MP flexion, she could flex the index MP joint only to 50° because the excursion or motion of the extensor tendon was limited by scarring of the tendon to the wound. According to Figure 16-25, having only 50° of MP flexion equates to 22% impairment of the digit.

Because the losses of MP joint extension and flexion were in the same joint, the 5% for loss of extension and the 22% for loss of flexion were added to result in 27% impairment of the index finger. Using Table 16-1, Conversion of Impairment of the Digits to Impairment of the Hand (5th ed, p 438), the 27% finger impairment was converted to 5% hand impairment. Using Table 16-2, Conversion of Impairment of the Hand to Impairment of the Upper Extremity (5th ed, p 439), the 5% hand impairment was converted to 5% upper extremity impairment. Using Table 16-3, Relationship of Impairment of the Upper Extremity to Impairment of the Whole Person (5th ed, p 439), the 5% upper extremity impairment was converted to 3% whole person impairment.

The second option is the TAM method. This process is further explained in Section 16.4a, Clinical Measurements of Motion (5th ed, p 451):

> Digital joints are measured with the wrist held in neutral position and the forearm pronated. To measure the ROM [range of motion] of individual joints, the proximal joint(s) are stabilized in extension, and only the joint being measured is flexed. Note that if all three joints are flexed simultaneously, as in making a fist, active flexion of the metacarpophalangeal joint will be decreased. In some cases of decreased finger motion due to limited excursion of the activating musculotendinous unit or blockage of motion by the antagonistic musculotendinous unit, the measurement of individual joints, as described earlier, can be normal or near normal. In these situations, the total active range of motion (TAM) of the digit is measured. Flexion of each joint is measured while all three joints are held in a position of maximum active flexion, or the finger is flexed as a whole unit; similarly, extension of each joint is measured while all three joints are held in maximum extension. The methods used to derive motion impairment of a digit using individual joint measurements and the total active range of motion of a digit are different, as explained on p. 465, Combining Abnormal Motion at More Than One Finger Joint. The joint measurement technique that best reflects the existing impairment is selected.

Ms Brown had limited excursion of her surgically repaired extensor tendon. This is the exact clinical situation for which the new method (TAM) was added to the *Guides*. When the patient placed her index finger in full simultaneous extension, all three joints came to 0°, but the MP joint did not hyperextend like her normal contralateral index finger MP joint. When she placed her index finger in full simultaneous flexion of all three joints, her MP joint flexed 50°, her PIP joint flexed 60°, and her DIP joint flexed 30°. This limitation of motion limited her ability to use the index finger with her thumb for pinch grip and delicate tasks.

Thus, in the TAM method, her MP joint had a range of motion of 0° (no hyperextension) to 50° of flexion. Figure 16-25, Finger Impairment Due to Abnormal Motion at the MP Joint (5th ed, p 464), indicates that 0° of extension is a 5% impairment of the finger, and 50° of flexion is a 22% impairment of the finger. Because both were impairments of the same joint, they were added. Ms Brown's index finger MP joint impairment was 27%.

In the TAM method, Ms Brown's PIP joint had a range of motion of 0° to 60° of flexion. Figure 16-23, Finger Impairment Due to Abnormal Motion at the PIP Joint (5th ed, p 463), indicates that 0° of extension is a 0% impairment of the finger, and 60° of flexion is a 24% impairment of the finger. Because both were impairments of the same joint, they were added. Her index finger PIP joint impairment was 24%.

In the TAM method, Ms Brown's DIP joint had a range of motion of 0° to 30° of flexion. Figure 16-21, Finger Impairment Due to Abnormal Motion at the DIP Joint (5th ed, p 461), indicates that 0° of extension is a 0% impairment of the finger, and 30° of flexion is a 21% impairment of the finger. Because both were impairments of the same joint, they were added. The patient's index finger DIP joint impairment was 21%.

The total impairment of Ms Brown's index finger was determined by combining the 27% impairment of the MP joint, the 24% impairment of the PIP joint, and the 21% impairment of the DIP joint. The Fifth Edition directions state, "If three or more values are to be combined, the two lowest values are first selected and their combined value is found. The combined value and the third value are then combined to give the total value. This procedure can be repeated indefinitely. . . ." (5th ed, p 438).

The order in which Ms Brown's impairments should be combined is 21%, 24%, and finally 27%. Thus, her combined index finger impairment was 56%.

Using Table 16-1, Conversion of Impairment of the Digits to Impairment of the Hand (5th ed, p 438), the 56% index finger impairment was converted to 11% hand impairment. Using Table 16-2, Conversion of Impairment of the Hand to Impairment of the Upper Extremity (5th ed, p 439), the 11% hand impairment was converted to 10% upper extremity impairment. Using Table 16-3, Relationship of Impairment of the Upper Extremity to Impairment of the Whole Person (5th ed, p 439), the 10% upper extremity impairment was converted to 6% whole person impairment.

Comparing the two rating methods, the 6% whole person rating from the TAM method was felt to better reflect the difficulties in activities of daily living that Ms Brown experienced because it reflected measurements of motion in the finger when the finger was being used for grip and pinch. Thus, her rating was 6% whole person impairment.

Impairment: 6% whole person impairment per the Fifth Edition.

Sixth Edition Rating

The *Guides* approach to the evaluation of impairment due to a lacerated extensor tendon can be based on the diagnosis-based impairment International Classification of Functioning, Disability and Health (ICF) methodology described in Section 15.2, Diagnosis-Based Impairment (6th ed, p 387), and more specifically, for tendon injuries to the digits, within Table 15-2, Digit Regional Grid: Digit Impairments (6th ed, p 391). In this case, however, there was motion loss associated with the injury to the lacerated extensor tendon. As such, the *Guides* provides an alternative methodology based on Section 15.7, Range of Motion Impairment (6th ed, p 459), and Section 15.7d, Finger Motion (6th ed, p 468). The alternative method was used in this case, as the range of motion method provided a greater impairment rating.

Table 15-31, Finger Range of Motion (6th ed, p 470) was used to evaluate impairment based on the range of motion measurements recorded previously. For the DIP joint, flexion of 70° and extension of 0° resulted in a 0% digit impairment. For the PIP joint, flexion of 100° and extension of 0° also resulted in a 0% digit impairment per Table 15-31. For the MP joint, flexion of 50° resulted in a 19% digit impairment, and 0° for extension resulted in a 7% digit impairment. These values of the MP joint were added for a total of 26% digit impairment.

Based on the resultant motion deficit from earlier in comparison with Table 15-35, Range of Motion Grade Modifiers (6th ed, p 477), for the digit, the patient was assigned a grade modifier 2, 20% to 39% digit impairment.

Adjustments for functional history are discussed on page 473 of the *Guides,* which states:

> Adjustments for functional history may be made if: (1) range of motion impairment is the only approach used to rate the extremity, (2) there are reliable findings of motion impairment, (3) the evaluator determines that the resulting impairment does not adequately reflect functional loss, and (4) functional reports are determined to be reliable. The adjustment is a percentage add-on to total range of motion impairment; this add-on is based on the relative difference between the Range of Motion impairment class and the functional history grade modifier.

According to Section 15.3a, Adjustment Grid: Functional History (6th ed, p 406), and Table 15-7, Functional History Adjustment: Upper Extremities (6th ed, p 406), the patient was assigned grade modifier 1; the functional history was consistent with "pain/symptoms with strenuous activity," and the *Quick*DASH score was in the range of 21 to 40.

The functional history net modifier, per Table 15-36, Functional History Grade Adjustment: Range of Motion (6th ed, p 477), was equal to or less than the range of motion modifier of 2. Therefore, there was no change to the impairment rating provided under the range of motion method of 26% digit impairment.

Based on Table 15-12, Impairment Values Calculated From Digit Impairment (6th ed, p 421), for the index finger this rating was converted to 3% whole person impairment.

Impairment: 3% whole person impairment per the Sixth Edition.

Comment on Lacerated Extensor Tendon

Ms Brown sustained a laceration of the dorsum of her left hand that was complicated by limited excursion of her index finger extensor tendon because of scarring. Although Ms Brown retained the capacity to actively flex each joint separately, she was unable to fully flex them simultaneously. Similarly, in active maximal simultaneous extension, she had an extension lag at the MP joint (MP joints should be hyperextensible). Although measurement of extension (perhaps hyperextension in the case of the MP joint) is uncomplicated, different techniques may be used to assess finger joint flexion.

The Sixth Edition provides two separate methodologies to rate this case. The diagnosis-based impairment ICF methodology is likely to be applicable only if the motion loss is minor or there is none at all. Otherwise, the range of motion loss methodology is similar in calculation as determined in the Fourth and Fifth Editions, although there are only tables of values and no pie charts to interpolate.

SUMMARY

Diagnosis	Lacerated extensor tendon, index finger
Fourth Edition References	Section 3.1g (4th ed, pp 30-35); Section 3.1m (4th ed, pp 63-64), Table 1 (4th ed, p 18), Table 2 (4th ed, p 19), Table 3 (4th ed, p 20), Figure 19 (4th ed, p 32), Figure 21 (4th ed, p 33), Figure 23 (4th ed, p 34)
Fourth Edition Summary	History, upper extremity evaluation (including assessment of finger range of motion). First, flexion and extension impairments of each joint are added. Second, the joint impairments are combined. Third, finger impairment is expressed in terms of the hand, upper extremity, and whole person.

Fourth Edition Impairment 5% upper extremity impairment, 3% whole person impairment

Fifth Edition References Section 16.4a (5th ed, pp 450-451); Section 16.4e (5th ed, pp 461-466), Table 16-1 (5th ed, p 438), Table 16-2 (5th ed, p 439), Table 16-3 (5th ed, p 439), Figure 16-20 (5th ed, p 461), Figure 16-21 (5th ed, p 461), Figure 16-23 (5th ed, p 463), Figure 16-24 (5th ed, p 464), Figure 16-25 (5th ed, p 464)

Fifth Edition Summary History, upper extremity evaluation (including assessment of finger range of motion). First, flexion and extension impairments of each joint are added. Second, joint impairments are combined. Third, the finger impairment is expressed in terms of the hand, upper extremity, and whole person. Whether the total active range of motion method is appropriate is considered; if it is, the impairment is calculated by means of the measurements taken with the joints in full, simultaneous extension and in full, simultaneous flexion.

Fifth Edition Impairment 10% upper extremity impairment, 6% whole person impairment

Sixth Edition References Section 15.3a (6th ed, pp 406-407); Section 15.7 (6th ed, pp 459-478); Section 15.7d (6th ed, pp 468-469), Table 15-7 (6th ed, p 406), Table 15-12 (6th ed, p 421), Table 15-31 (6th ed, p 470), Table 15-35 (6th ed, p 477), Table 15-36 (6th ed, p 477)

Sixth Edition Summary History (including functional history and inventories) and physical evaluation. Impairment is based on range of motion by adding joint impairments for the digit. Then the range of motion modifier is compared against the functional history modifier to determine if an additional percentage of impairment should be included. Then digit impairment is converted to whole person impairment.

Sixth Edition Impairment 26% digit impairment, 5% hand and upper extremity impairment, 3% whole person impairment

Upper Extremity Impairment Evaluation Record**–**Part 1 (Hand)** Side ☐ R ☒ L

Name Ms. Brown Age 29 Sex ☐ M ☒ F Dominant hand ☒ R ☐ L Date

Occupation Diagnosis Lacerated Extensor Tendon

			Abnormal motion				Amputation	Sensory loss	Other disorders	Hand impairment%	
			Record motion, ankylosis, and impairment %				Mark level & impairment %	Mark type, level, & impairment %	List type & impairment %	• Combine digit IMP% *Convert to hand IMP%	
			Flexion	Extension	Ankylosis	IMP%					
Thumb	IP	Angle°					R L	R L			
		IMP%									
	MP	Angle°									
		IMP%									
			Motion		Ankylosis	IMP%					
	CMC	Radial abduction Angle°								Abnormal motion [1]	
		Radial abduction IMP%								Amputation [2]	
		Adduction CMS								Sensory loss [3]	
		Adduction IMP%								Other disorders [4]	
		Opposition CMS								Digit impairment % • Combine 1, 2, 3, 4	
		Opposition IMP%									
Add impairment % CMC + MP + IP =						[1]	[2] IMP % =	[3] IMP % =	[4] IMP % =	Hand impairment % *Convert above	

			Flexion	Extension	Ankylosis	IMP%					
Index	DIP	Angle°	70	0						Abnormal motion [1]	27
		IMP%	0	0		0				Amputation [2]	—
	PIP	Angle°	100	0						Sensory loss [3]	—
		IMP%	0	0		0				Other disorders [4]	—
	MP	Angle°	50	0						Digit impairment % • Combine 1, 2, 3, 4	27
		IMP%	22	5		27					
• Combine impairment % MP + PIP + DIP = 27						[1]	[2] IMP % =	[3] IMP % =	[4] IMP % =	Hand impairment % *Convert above	5
Middle	DIP	Angle°								Abnormal motion [1]	
		IMP%								Amputation [2]	
	PIP	Angle°								Sensory loss [3]	
		IMP%								Other disorders [4]	
	MP	Angle°								Digit impairment % • Combine 1, 2, 3, 4	
		IMP%									
• Combine impairment % MP + PIP + DIP =						[1]	[2] IMP % =	[3] IMP % =	[4] IMP % =	Hand impairment % *Convert above	
Ring	DIP	Angle°								Abnormal motion [1]	
		IMP%								Amputation [2]	
	PIP	Angle°								Sensory loss [3]	
		IMP%								Other disorders [4]	
	MP	Angle°								Digit impairment % • Combine 1, 2, 3, 4	
		IMP%									
• Combine impairment % MP + PIP + DIP =						[1]	[2] IMP % =	[3] IMP % =	[4] IMP % =	Hand impairment % *Convert above	
Little	DIP	Angle°								Abnormal motion [1]	
		IMP%								Amputation [2]	
	PIP	Angle°								Sensory loss [3]	
		IMP%								Other disorders [4]	
	MP	Angle°								Digit impairment % • Combine 1, 2, 3, 4	
		IMP%									
• Combine impairment % MP + PIP + DIP =						[1]	[2] IMP % =	[3] IMP % =	[4] IMP % =	Hand impairment % *Convert above	

Total hand impairment (Add hand impairment % for thumb + index + middle + ring + little finger) = 5 %
Upper extremity impairment (†Convert total hand impairment % to upper extremity impairment %) = 5 %; enter on Part 2, Line II
If hand region impairment is only impairment, convert upper extremity impairment to whole-person impairment:‡ = 3 %

• Combined Values Chart; (p. 322-324) *Use Table 1 (Digits to hand p. 18); †Use Table 2 (Hand to upper extremity p. 19) ‡Use Table 3 (p. 20)

** Courtesy of G. de Groot Swanson, MD

Upper Extremity Impairment Evaluation Record–Part 1 (Hand) Side ☐R ☒L

Name *Ms Brown* Age *29* Sex ☐M ☒F Dominant hand ☐R ☒L Date ____

Occupation ____ Diagnosis *Lacerated Extensor Tendon* *CASE 15-7*

			Abnormal Motion				**Amputation**	**Sensory Loss**	**Other Disorders**	**Hand Impairment%**	
			Record motion or ankylosis angles and digit impairment %				Mark level & impairment %	Mark type, level, & impairment %	List type & impairment %	•Combine digit imp % *Convert to hand imp %	
			Flexion	Extension	Ankylosis	Imp %					
Thumb	IP	Angle°					[2]				
		Imp %									
	MP	Angle°									
		Imp %									
				Motion	Ankylosis	Imp %					
	CMC	Radial abduction	Angle°							Abnormal motion [1]	
			Imp %							Amputation [2]	
		Adduction	Cm							Sensory loss [3]	
			Imp %							Other disorders [4]	
		Opposition	Cm				‡UE IMP % = [5]			Total digit imp % •Combine 1, 2, 3, 4	
			Imp %								
Add digit impairment % CMC + MP + IP =						[1]	Digit IMP % = [2]	Digit IMP % = [3]	Digit IMP % = [4]	Hand impairment % *Convert above	

			Flexion	Extension	Ankylosis	Imp %					
Index	DIP	Angle°	*70*	*0*		*0*				Abnormal motion [1]	*27*
		Imp %	*0*	*0*						Amputation [2]	*—*
	PIP	Angle°	*100*	*0*		*0*				Sensory loss [3]	*—*
		Imp %	*0*	*0*						Other disorders [4]	*—*
	MP	Angle°	*50*	*0*		*27*				Total digit imp % •Combine 1, 2, 3, 4	*27*
		Imp %	*22*	*5*							
•Combine digit impairment % MP, PIP, DIP = *27*						[1]	Digit IMP % = [2]	Digit IMP % = [3]	Digit IMP % = [4]	Hand impairment % *Convert above	*5*
Middle	DIP	Angle°								Abnormal motion [1]	
		Imp %								Amputation [2]	
	PIP	Angle°								Sensory loss [3]	
		Imp %								Other disorders [4]	
	MP	Angle°								Total digit imp % •Combine 1, 2, 3, 4	
		Imp %									
•Combine digit impairment % MP, PIP, DIP =						[1]	Digit IMP % = [2]	Digit IMP % = [3]	Digit IMP % = [4]	Hand impairment % *Convert above	
Ring	DIP	Angle°								Abnormal motion [1]	
		Imp %								Amputation [2]	
	PIP	Angle°								Sensory loss [3]	
		Imp %								Other disorders [4]	
	MP	Angle°								Total digit imp % •Combine 1, 2, 3, 4	
		Imp %									
•Combine digit impairment % MP, PIP, DIP =						[1]	Digit IMP % = [2]	Digit IMP % = [3]	Digit IMP % = [4]	Hand impairment % *Convert above	
Little	DIP	Angle°								Abnormal motion [1]	
		Imp %								Amputation [2]	
	PIP	Angle°								Sensory loss [3]	
		Imp %								Other disorders [4]	
	MP	Angle°								Total digit imp % •Combine 1, 2, 3, 4	
		Imp %									
•Combine digit impairment % MP, PIP, DIP =						[1]	Digit IMP % = [2]	Digit IMP % = [3]	Digit IMP % = [4]	Hand impairment % *Convert above	

Total hand impairment: Add hand impairment % for thumb + index + middle + ring + little finger =	*5*	%
Convert total hand impairment to upper extremity impairment† (if thumb metacarpal intact, enter on Part 2, line II) =	*5*	%
‡Add thumb ray upper extremity amputation imp [5] ___% + hand upper extremity imp ___% =		%
If hand region impairment is only impairment, convert upper extremity impairment to whole person impairment§ =	*3*	%

• Combined Values Chart (p. 604). *Use Table 16-1 (digits to hand). †Use Table 16-2 (hand to upper extremity). §Use Table 16-3.
Courtesy of G. de Groot Swanson, MD, Grand Rapids, Michigan.

Chapter 15

CASE 15-8

Wrist Arthroplasty

Subject: Ms Engels, a 46-year-old woman.

History: Ms Engels, who is right-handed, complained of pain, weakness, and deformity of her left wrist of 5 years' duration. She had no problem with her wrist until 5 years earlier, when she slipped and fell on an icy spot in the parking lot of her employer, sustaining a comminuted fracture of her left distal radius. She was treated initially with closed reduction and an external fixator. After healing of the fracture, she had persistent deformity, weakness, and pain in her wrist. Two years after her injury, Ms Engels underwent a prosthetic arthroplasty of an extent that would be considered total for her wrist (distal radius to proximal carpal row). She had good relief of pain initially, but some ulnar deviation deformity was evident immediately after surgery. During the next 3 years, she noted increasing pain in her wrist.

Current Symptoms: She reported that although the pain had been troublesome only with activity, she now had pain even at rest. She was able to perform activities of daily living, however with difficulties.

Functional Assessment: The *Quick*DASH score was 52.

Physical Examination: Examination showed scars on the radial side of the second metacarpal and the midshaft of the radius, where the external fixator had been anchored. There was also a dorsal longitudinal scar centered over the wrist joint. At rest, the wrist assumed a position of flexion and ulnar deviation. Ms Engels lacked 20° of being able to bring her wrist up to neutral; that is, she had an extension lag. She flexed to 40°. She lacked 20° of being able to bring her wrist from the ulnar deviated position to neutral radial-ulnar deviation, and she could ulnar deviate to 40°. She could pronate 40° and supinate 20°. There was full range of motion in the elbow and fingers. Her neurologic examination was normal, and there was no significant atrophy.

Clinical Studies: None available for review.

Discussion of Wrist Arthroplasty

Fourth Edition Rating

The *Guides* approach to the evaluation of impairment due to wrist arthroplasty is described in Section 3.1m, Impairment Due to Other Disorders of the Upper Extremity (4th ed, pp 58-65). First, the impairment due to arthroplasty is determined. Second, the impairment due to abnormal motion is determined. Third, the impairment due to arthroplasty is combined with the impairment due to abnormal motion.

According to Table 27, Impairment of the Upper Extremity After Arthroplasty of Specific Bones or Joints (4th ed, p 61), Ms Engels had a 30% upper extremity impairment due to wrist implant arthroplasty.

According to Figure 26, Extremity Impairment Due to Lack of Flexion and Extension of Wrist Joint (4th ed, p 36), with flexion of 40° and a 20° extension lag, there was a 3% upper extremity impairment for the flexion deficit and an 18% upper extremity impairment for the extension deficit, which added to a 21% upper extremity impairment. According to Figure 29, Upper Extremity Impairments Due to Abnormal Radial and Ulnar Deviations of Wrist Joint (4th ed, p 38), with her 20° lack of being able to bring her wrist to neutral radial-ulnar deviation, there was a 12% upper extremity impairment. Ulnar deviation was normal. These values for wrist motion deficit together yielded a 33% upper extremity impairment due to range of motion deficits. This range of motion impairment was combined with the 30% upper extremity impairment due to her arthroplasty by means of the Combined Values Chart (4th ed, p 322), resulting in 53% upper extremity impairment.

Ms Engels also had 6% upper extremity impairment due to abnormal elbow motion, per Figure 35, Upper Extremity Impairments Due to Lack of Pronation and Supination (4th ed, p 41). Pronation limited to 40° resulted in a 3% upper extremity impairment, and supination limited to 20° also resulted in a 3% upper extremity impairment.

Combining the wrist 53% upper extremity impairment with the elbow 6% upper extremity impairment resulted in a 56% upper extremity impairment. With the use of Table 3, Relationship of Impairment of the Upper Extremity to Impairment of the Whole Person (4th ed, p 20), this converted to 34% whole person impairment. This process is illustrated in Figure 1, Upper Extremity Impairment Evaluation Record (4th ed, p 17).

Impairment: 34% whole person impairment per the Fourth Edition.

Fifth Edition Rating

The *Guides* approach to the evaluation of impairment due to wrist arthroplasty is described in Section 16.7, Impairment Due to Other Disorders of the Upper Extremity (5th ed, pp 498-507), and, more specifically, Section 16.7, Arthroplasty (5th ed, p 505). First, the impairment due to arthroplasty is determined. Second, the impairment due to abnormal motion is determined. Third, the impairment due to arthroplasty is combined with the impairment due to abnormal motion.

According to Table 16-27, Impairment of the Upper Extremity After Arthroplasty of Specific Bones or Joints (5th ed, p 506), Ms Engels had a 24% upper extremity impairment due to total wrist implant arthroplasty.

According to Figure 16-28, Pie Chart of Upper Extremity Motion Impairments Due to Lack of Flexion and Extension of Wrist Joint (5th ed, p 467), with flexion of 40° and a 20° extension lag, there was a 3% upper extremity impairment for the flexion deficit and an 18% upper extremity impairment for the extension deficit, which added to a 21% upper extremity impairment. According to Figure 16-31, Pie Chart of Upper Extremity Motion Impairments Due to Abnormal Radial and Ulnar Deviations of Wrist Joint (5th ed, p 469), with her 20° lack of being able to bring her wrist to neutral radial-ulnar deviation, there was a 12% upper extremity impairment. Ulnar deviation was normal. These values for wrist motion deficit were added to yield a 33% upper extremity impairment due to range of motion deficits. This range of motion impairment was combined with the 24% upper extremity impairment due to arthroplasty by means of the Combined Values Chart (5th ed, p 604), resulting in 49% upper extremity impairment.

Ms Engels also had 6% upper extremity impairment due to abnormal elbow motion, per Figure 16-37, Pie Chart of Upper Extremity Motion Impairments Due to Lack of Pronation and Supination (5th ed, p 474). Pronation limited to 40° resulted in a 3% upper extremity impairment, and supination limited to 20° also resulted in a 3% upper extremity impairment.

Combining the wrist 49% upper extremity impairment with the elbow 6% upper extremity impairment resulted in 52% upper extremity impairment. By means of Table 16-3, Conversion of Impairment of the Upper Extremity to Impairment of the Whole Person (5th ed, p 439), this converted to 31% whole person impairment. This process is illustrated in Figure 16-1b, Upper Extremity Impairment Evaluation Record (5th ed, p 437).

Impairment: 31% whole person impairment per the Fifth Edition.

Sixth Edition Rating

Table 15-3, Wrist Regional Grid: Upper Extremity Impairments (6th ed, p 397), specifies that for wrist arthrodesis, "if nonoptimal positioning, assess per Section 15.7, Range of Motion Impairment." "Range of Motion ratings cannot be combined with other approaches, with the exception of amputation" (6th ed, p 387). Section 15.7, Range of Motion Impairment, also explains, "This section is to be used as a ***stand-alone*** rating when other grids refer you to this section or when no other diagnosis-based sections of this chapter are applicable for impairment rating of a condition" (6th ed, p 461).

According to Section 15.7e, Wrist Motion Impairment (6th ed, pp 469-471), and Table 15-32, Wrist Range of Motion (6th ed, p 473), with flexion of 40° and a 20° extension lag, there was a 3% upper extremity impairment for the flexion deficit and a 9% upper extremity impairment for the extension deficit, which added to a 12% upper extremity impairment. With her 20° lack of being able to bring her wrist to neutral radial-ulnar deviation, there was an 18% upper extremity impairment. Ulnar deviation was normal. These values for wrist motion deficit added yielded 30% upper extremity impairment due to range of motion deficits.

According to Section 15.7f, Forearm/Elbow Motion (6th ed, p 471), and Table 15-33, Elbow/Forearm Range of Motion (6th ed, p 474), for pronation limited to 40° there was a 3% upper extremity impairment, and supination limited to 20° resulted in a 2% upper extremity impairment, a total of 5% upper extremity impairment.

Combining the wrist 30% upper extremity impairment with the elbow 5% upper extremity impairment resulted in 34% upper extremity impairment.

Per Table 15-35, Range of Motion Grade Modifiers (6th ed, p 477), a finding in the range of 24% to 42% upper extremity impairment was consistent with grade modifier 3. According to Section 15.3a, Adjustment Grid: Functional History (6th ed, p 406), and Table 15-7, Functional History Adjustment: Upper Extremities (6th ed, p 406), the patient was assigned grade modifier 2. Although the patient reported significant problems with pain, she did not require assistance to perform self-care activities, and her *Quick*DASH score was in the range of 41 to 60. Because her functional history grade modifier was not higher than the range of motion impairment grade modifier, no further adjustments were required.

By means of Table 15-11, Impairment Values Calculated From Upper Extremity Impairment (6th ed, p 420), 34% upper extremity impairment converted to 20% whole person impairment.

Impairment: 20% whole person impairment per the Sixth Edition.

Comment on Wrist Arthroplasty

Prosthetic (implant) arthroplasty of the wrist is not indicated in a healthy person who will put the usual stresses of ordinary daily activities on the wrist. Failure of the prosthesis, which occurred in this individual, is to be expected. The patient may need an arthrodesis (fusion) of her wrist. With the Fourth and Fifth Editions, if she had a successful arthrodesis in neutral position, her impairment would be 30% of the upper extremity, the default impairment per the Sixth Edition for a wrist arthrodesis in functional position. If it is probable that she will have an arthrodesis, she would not be considered at maximum medical improvement.

The Fifth Edition contains a paragraph of instructions not contained in earlier editions of the *Guides*. "A severe symptomatic failure of an implant arthroplasty procedure (eg, symptomatic breakage or subluxation of the device) is given 100% of the joint value as listed in Table 16-18" (5th ed, p 505). Ms Engels clearly, by examination, had a subluxed wrist. No mention was made of the radiographic status of her wrist, but, assuming that radiographs confirmed a subluxed wrist prosthesis, she would be eligible for a rating of 60% upper extremity impairment, as that is the value of the wrist as listed in Table 16-18, Maximum Impairment Values for the Digits, Hand, Wrist, Elbow, and Shoulder Due to Disorders of Specific Joints or Units. The Sixth Edition does not provide in Table 15-3 (6th ed, pp 395-397) a rating for failure of an implant arthroplasty.

In the Sixth Edition, Section 15.2, Diagnosis-Based Impairment (6th ed, pp 387-405), is the primary approach to assessing impairment in most cases. If the patient's wrist (total) arthroplasty resulted in normal motion, she would have a class 2 impairment with a default of 24% upper extremity impairment, with a maximum of 25% upper extremity impairment.

SUMMARY

Diagnosis	Wrist arthroplasty
Fourth Edition References	Section 3.1m (4th ed, pp 58-65); Section 3.1h (4th ed, pp 35-38); Section 3.1i (4th ed, pp 38-41), Table 3 (4th ed, p 20), Table 27 (4th ed, p 61), Figure 26 (4th ed, p 36), Figure 29 (4th ed, p 38), Figure 35 (4th ed, p 41)

Fourth Edition Summary History, upper extremity evaluation (including assessment of range of motion), and neurologic assessment (including sensation and strength testing). Arthroplasty may be carried out with or without implant. First, impairment due to arthroplasty (resection or implant) is determined. Second, impairment due to abnormal motion is determined. Third, impairment due to arthroplasty is combined with impairment due to abnormal motion.

Fourth Edition Impairment 56% upper extremity impairment, 34% whole person impairment

Fifth Edition References Section 16.7 (5th ed, p 505), Table 16-3 (5th ed, p 439), Table 16-27 (5th ed, p 506), Figure 16-28 (5th ed, p 467), Figure 16-31 (5th ed, p 469), Figure 16-37 (5th ed, p 474)

Fifth Edition Summary History, upper extremity evaluation (including assessment of range of motion), and neurologic assessment (including sensation and strength testing). Arthroplasty may be carried out with or without implant. First, impairment due to arthroplasty (resection or implant) is determined. Second, impairment due to abnormal motion is determined. Third, impairment due to arthroplasty is combined with impairment due to abnormal motion.

Fifth Edition Impairment 52% upper extremity impairment, 31% whole person impairment

Sixth Edition References Section 15.7e (6th ed, pp 469-471); Section 15.7f (6th ed, p 471), Table 15-32 (6th ed, p 473), Table 15-7 (6th ed, p 406), Table 15-11 (6th ed, p 420), Table 15-33 (6th ed, p 474)

Sixth Edition Summary History (including functional history and inventories), physical evaluation, and clinical studies. First, whether diagnosis-based impairment is not applicable is determined. Impairment rating is made due to abnormal motion.

Sixth Edition Impairment 34% upper extremity impairment, 20% whole person impairment

CASE 15-9

Carpal Instability

Subject: Mr Whitley, a 45-year-old man.

History: Mr Whitley, a right-handed factory worker, had onset of pain in his right wrist 8 months previously while he was lifting a part that weighed about 25 pounds, experiencing a sharp pain and a popping in his right wrist. He consulted the company occupational health clinic, where a diagnosis of sprain was made. He was treated with a splint, anti-inflammatory medications, and limited duty. When his condition failed to respond to these conservative measures, he was referred to an orthopedic surgeon. The surgeon found some diffuse tenderness of the wrist, but no swelling or limitation of motion. Plain radiographs, an arthrogram of the wrist, and a bone scan were done. The plain radiographs and bone scan were interpreted by the radiologist as within normal limits. The arthrogram showed torn radioscaphoid and radiolunate ligaments. Mr Whitley declined surgical intervention and last saw a physician 1 year prior to the evaluation.

Current Symptoms: Mr Whitley complained of continued weakness and pain in his wrist. During power grip and heavy lifting activities, if his wrist moved, he felt a painful clicking in the wrist. He was working regularly but had limitations on lifting.

Functional Assessment: The *Quick*DASH score was 21.

Physical Examination: No swelling of the wrist. There was full active range of motion, with some complaints of discomfort on the extremes of motion. There was poorly localized tenderness dorsally about midway between the radial and ulnar styloid processes. There were no reproducible grip strength deficits.

Clinical Studies: Radiographs show that the radioscaphoid angle was 50° and the radiolunate angle was 5° palmar. The scapholunate angle was 45°. The carpal height ratio was 0.52 (4% deviation from average normal of 0.54). There was no carpal translation and no evidence of arthritis.

Discussion of Carpal Instability

Fourth Edition Rating

Permanent impairment evaluation was based on Section 3.1m, Impairment Due to Other Disorders of the Upper Extremity (4th ed, p 58), specifically Table 26, Upper Extremity Impairment Due to Carpal Instability Patterns (4th ed, p 61), and the accompanying text. First, carpal instability patterns resulting from lunate or scaphoid abnormalities are classified as mild, moderate, or severe on the basis of the severity of the radiographic findings. Second, only one category of severity of carpal instability impairment should be selected on the basis of the greatest severity of the radiographic findings. Third, these radiographic criteria are used only when all other wrist factors are normal except after carpal bone resection or implant arthroplasty, when the carpal instability impairment is combined with the arthroplasty impairment.

Mr Whitley's impairment rating was based on a clinical diagnosis of carpal instability. He had a believable history of a wrist ligament strain, with typical symptoms of weakness and a painful clicking in the wrist.

The radiographic findings listed under Mild Instability in Table 26 were all normal findings, because dynamic instability is what this table is rating as mild. In static instability, the wrist ligament injury allows the carpal bones to malrotate into positions of fixed deformity that show on static (motionless) radiographs. In dynamic instability, the injury is less severe, so the malrotation of the carpal bones does not occur when the wrist is at rest in a neutral position (like that used for routine radiographs). In dynamic instability, the carpal bone malrotation occurs during wrist motion, producing the painful click. This can be confirmed on cineradiography, but that test is not routinely available.

Mr Whitley's impairment rating was based on his radiographic findings with the use of Table 26. Specifically, Mr Whitley's radioscaphoid angle of 50° was consistent with mild impairment, and his radiolunate angle of 5° was consistent with mild impairment. Consequently, he had a mild upper extremity impairment due to carpal instability, which was 6% of his upper extremity, which equated to a 4% whole person impairment, according to Table 3, Relationship of Impairment of the Upper Extremity to Impairment of the Whole Person (4th ed, p 20).

Impairment: 4% whole person impairment per the Fourth Edition.

Fifth Edition Rating

Permanent impairment evaluation was based on Section 16.7, Impairment of the Upper Extremities Due to Other Disorders (5th ed, p 498), specifically, the discussion of carpal instability (5th ed, p 502), and Table 16-25, Upper Extremity Impairment Due to Carpal Instability Patterns (5th ed, p 503). First, carpal instability patterns are classified as mild, moderate, or severe on the basis of the severity of the radiographic findings. Second, only one category of severity of carpal instability impairment should be selected on the basis of the greatest severity of the radiographic findings. Third, these radiographic criteria may be combined only with limited wrist motion. Pain and decreased strength were not rated separately.

Mr Whitley's impairment might be based on radiographic findings by means of Table 16-25. Radiographs showed that the radiolunate angle was 5° palmar, and the scapholunate angle was 45°, neither of which is abnormal according to Table 16-25. Mr Whitley had no range of motion deficits and no reproducible strength deficits. Thus, he had no ratable impairment on the basis of static radiographs.

The text (5th ed, p 502) states:

> A mild carpal instability exists also when a ligament tear has been diagnosed by arthrogram, arthroscopy, or MRI, even though the static roentgenographic findings may be normal. Certain individuals may have wrist pain and loss of strength related to a dynamic or nondissociative carpal instability that cannot be measured by changes of angles on static roentgenograms. Symptoms of nondissociative wrist instability are painful clicking and clunking with activities of daily living.

Mr Whitley's symptoms were typical, and his arthrogram showed torn ligaments to objectively validate the clinical diagnosis. Thus, he was rated as having mild instability, in keeping with the text directions. According to Table 16-25 (5th ed, p 503), this resulted in an 8% impairment of the upper extremity. This was the same as a 5% whole person impairment, by means of Table 16-3, Conversion of Impairment of the Upper Extremity to Impairment of the Whole Person (5th ed, p 439).

Impairment: 5% whole person impairment per the Fifth Edition.

Sixth Edition Rating

The *Guides* approach to the evaluation of impairment due to carpal instability is based on Section 15.2, Diagnosis-Based Impairment (6th ed, pp 387-404).

In Table 15-3, Wrist Regional Grid: Upper Extremity Impairments, section on Ligament/Bone/Joint (p 396), for the diagnosis "Wrist sprain/h/o dislocation including carpal instability" there is a class 1 rating for mild instability (with a default impairment of 8%). Table 15-9, Clinical Studies Adjustment: Upper Extremities (6th ed, pp 410-411), documents the radiographic findings consistent with wrist instability similar to the findings used in the Fifth Edition of the *Guides*. For this case, the radiographic findings did not support the clinical finding of wrist instability. However, this case illustrates a condition of dynamic instability as supported by Mr Whitley's symptoms, which were typical, and his arthrogram showed torn ligaments, to objectively validate the clinical diagnosis. Thus, he was rated as having mild instability.

According to Section 15.3a, Adjustment Grid: Functional History (6th ed, p 406), and Table 15-7, Functional History Adjustment: Upper Extremities (6th ed, p 406), the patient was assigned grade modifier 1, the functional history was consistent with pain/symptoms with strenuous activity, and the score of 21 was in the range of 21 to 40 for *Quick*DASH. According to Section 15.3b, Adjustment Grid: Physical Examination (6th ed, p 407), and Table 15-8, Physical Examination Adjustment: Upper Extremities (6th ed, p 408), the patient was assigned grade modifier 1; the physical examination revealed "clicking or clunking by history but not reproducible on physical examination." The modifier for clinical studies was not applicable, as it was inclusive in the diagnosis. In summary, the adjustments were functional history grade modifier 1 and physical examination 1. The net adjustment compared to diagnosis class 1 is 0.

Class 1—Default for Diagnosis = 8% Upper Extremity Impairment			
CDX	GMFH	GMPE	GMCS
1	1	1	N/A
Net adjustment (GMFH − CDX) 1 − 1 = 0 + (GMPE − CDX) + 1 − 1 = 0 + (GMCS − CDX) + x− y = N/A Net adjustment = 0			

There was no adjustment made.

Based on Table 15-11, Impairment Values Calculated From Upper Extremity Impairment (6th ed, p 420), 8% upper extremity impairment converted to 5% whole person impairment.

Impairment: 5% whole person impairment per the Sixth Edition.

Comment on Carpal Instability

In the Fourth and Fifth Editions, this case was rated on the basis of Other Disorders; in the Sixth Edition, it was rated on the basis of diagnosis-based impairment.

According to the work of Linscheid et al,[1] the normal scapholunate angle is between 30° and 60°; less than 30° indicates a volar instability pattern, and more than 60° indicates a dorsal instability pattern. In Mr Whitley's case, the scapholunate angle was 45° (radioscaphoid angle of 50° minus radiolunate angle of 5°) and, by these criteria, was normal. A radiolunate angle of less than 10° is also normal by these criteria. According to the research of Youm et al,[2] the normal carpal height ratio is 0.54 ± 0.03 (about 6%).

The section on carpal instability was revised in the Fifth Edition. It was recognized that the previous impairment values were the lower limits of normal to permit rating dynamic instability; however, to minimize confusion, in the Fifth Edition the table to rate impairment contains criteria for mild instabilities that are abnormal. Dynamic instability is dealt with by the text, stating that it should also be rated as mild.

The minimums needed to define a mild impairment for the Fourth and Fifth Editions, per Table 26 (4th ed, p 61) and Table 16-25 (5th ed, p 503), are illustrated in the following table:

	Fourth Edition-Mild	Fifth Edition-Mild
Roentgenographic Findings	(6%)	(8%)
Radioscaphoid angle	45°-59°	Not listed
Radiolunate angle	<10°	11°-20°
Carpal height collapse	<5%	Not listed
Carpal translation	Mild	Not listed
Arthritic changes	Mild	Not listed
Scapholunate angle	Not listed	61°-70°
Scapholunate gap	Not listed	>3 mm
Triquetrolunate stepoff	Not listed	>1 mm
Ulnar translation	Not listed	Mild

In the Fifth Edition, the scapholunate angle is used for base measurement. Figure 16-51, Techniques for Measuring the Scaphoid (S), Lunate Axis (L), and Long Axis of the Radius (R) and Corresponding Angles (5th ed, p 503), illustrates how to measure the scapholunate and radiolunate angles. The impairment values in the Fifth Edition are higher than in the Fourth; for example, mild is 8% upper extremity impairment (vs 6%), moderate is 16% (vs 12%), and severe is 24% (vs 18%).

In the Sixth Edition, the diagnosis-based impairment approach is used. The classification is based on criteria for carpal instability provided in the Adjustment Grid: Clinical Studies; therefore, there is no further adjustment for clinical studies. The parameters provided for classification in this grid are the same as used in the Fifth Edition.

SUMMARY

Diagnosis	Carpal instability
Fourth Edition References	Section 3.1m (4th ed, pp 58-65), Table 26 (4th ed, p 61)
Fourth Edition Summary	History, upper extremity evaluation, radiographs of wrist. First, carpal instability patterns are classified as mild, moderate, or severe on the basis of the severity of the radiographic findings. Second, only one category of severity of carpal instability impairment should be selected. Third, to avoid duplicate impairment ratings, these radiographic criteria are used only when all other wrist factors are normal except after carpal bone resection or implant arthroplasty.
Fourth Edition Impairment	6% upper extremity impairment, 4% whole person impairment
Fifth Edition References	Section 16.7 (5th ed, pp 498-507), Table 16-25 (5th ed, p 503)
Fifth Edition Summary	History, upper extremity evaluation, radiographs of wrist. First, carpal instability patterns are classified as mild, moderate, or severe on the basis of the severity of the radiographic findings. Second, only one category of severity of carpal instability impairment should be selected. Third, these radiographic criteria may be combined only with limited wrist motion. Pain and decreased strength are not rated separately.

Fifth Edition Impairment	8% upper extremity impairment, 5% whole person impairment
Sixth Edition References	Section 15.2 (6th ed, pp 387-404), Table 15-3 (6th ed, p 396); Section 15.3a, (6th ed, p 406), Table 15-7 (6th ed, p 406); Section 15.3b (6th ed, p 407), Table 15-8 (6th ed, p 408), Table 15-9 (6th ed, pp 410-411); Table 15-11 (6th ed, p 420)
Sixth Edition Summary	History (including functional history and inventories), physical evaluation, and clinical studies. First, diagnosis-based impairment, class, and default value are determined. Second, impairment is adjusted based on non-key factors. In this case, no adjustment was made, as modifiers were equal to the diagnosis-based impairment class.
Sixth Edition Impairment	8% upper extremity impairment, 5% whole person impairment

References

1. Linscheid RL, Dobyns JH, Bebout JW. Traumatic instability of the wrist: diagnosis, classification and pathomechanics. *J Bone Joint Surg Am.* 1972;54A:1612-1632.
2. Youm Y, McMurthy RY, Flatt AE, Gillespie TE. Kinematics of the wrist, I: an experimental study of radial-ulnar deviation and flexion-extension. *J Bone Joint Surg Am.* 1978;60A:423-431.

CASE 15-10

Arthritic Thumb

Subject: Mr Jaeger, a 58-year-old man.

History: Mr Jaeger, a right-handed man, described pain and stiffness of his right thumb of 20 years' duration. He had worked for the same construction company for more than 30 years. Twenty years previously, he had sustained a Bennett fracture of the base of the right thumb, which was treated by closed reduction and percutaneous K-wire fixation. Mr Jaeger had been able to resume light work 2 months after injury and his usual work 3 months after injury. He did generally well for many years, although he did have some pain in the base of his thumb after a hard day's work.

Current Symptoms: Mr Jaeger reported that in recent years, the pain had become more frequent and intense, and in the past few months, the pain was so severe that he was unable to work on several occasions for 1 or 2 days at a time.

Functional Assessment: The *Quick*DASH score was 41.

Physical Examination: Prominence of the base of the right thumb. Abduction was limited to 20° at the carpometacarpal (CMC) joint. To compensate for this limited abduction at the CMC joint, Mr Jaeger developed hyperextension at the MP joint. The MP joint flexed 30° and hyperextended 40°. At rest, the MP joint was hyperextended 20°. There was considerable crepitus in the CMC joint on circumduction of the thumb. On maximum opposition effort, there was 4 cm between the flexor crease of the IP joint of the thumb and the distal palmar crease over the third MP joint. On maximum adduction effort, there was 3 cm between the flexor crease of the thumb IP joint and the distal palmar crease over the MP joint of the little finger. The remainder of the hand examination was normal.

Discussion of Arthritic Thumb

Fourth Edition Rating

Permanent impairment evaluation was based on Section 3.1f, Thumb (4th ed, pp 24-30). First, thumb motion impairments of flexion and extension, adduction, radial abduction, and opposition were determined. Second, these values were added to determine abnormal thumb impairment. Because the relative value of each thumb functional unit had been taken into consideration in the impairment values of the entire thumb, impairments of thumb motions were added, whereas those of the fingers were combined.

According to Figure 13, Thumb Impairments Due to Abnormal Motion at the MP Joint (4th ed, p 27), there was a 3% thumb impairment due to abnormal flexion motion of 30° at the MP joint. According to Table 5, Thumb Impairment Values Due to Lack of Adduction and to Ankylosis (4th ed, p 28), there was a 3% thumb impairment due to the 3-cm lack of adduction. According to Table 6, Thumb Impairments Due to Lack of Radial Abduction and to Ankylosis (4th ed, p 28), there was a 7% thumb impairment due to lack of radial abduction, that is, limited to 20°. According to Table 7, Thumb Impairments Due to Lack of Opposition and to Ankylosis (4th ed, p 29), there was a 9% thumb impairment due to the measured opposition of 4 cm. Adding these impairments yielded a total thumb impairment of 22%, which equated to a 9% impairment of the hand (Table 1, Relationship of Impairment of the Digits to Impairment of the Hand; 4th ed, p 19), which equated to an 8% impairment of the upper extremity (Table 2, Relationship of Impairment of the Hand to Impairment of the Upper Extremity; 4th ed, p 19), which equated to a 5% whole person impairment (Table 3, Relationship of Impairment of the Upper Extremity to Impairment of the Whole Person; 4th ed, p 20). This rating process is summarized in the Upper Extremity Impairment Evaluation Record (4th ed, p 16), as shown here on page 264.

Impairment: 5% whole person impairment per the Fourth Edition.

Fifth Edition Rating

Permanent impairment evaluation was based on Section 16.4d, Thumb Ray Motion Impairment (5th ed, pp 454-460). First, thumb motion impairments of flexion and extension, adduction, radial abduction, and opposition were determined. Second, these values were added to determine abnormal thumb impairment. Because the relative value of each thumb functional unit had been taken into consideration in the impairment values of the entire thumb, impairments of thumb motions were added while those of the fingers were combined.

According to Figure 16-15, Pie Chart of Thumb Impairments Due to Abnormal Motion at the MP Joint (5th ed, p 457), there was a 3% thumb impairment due to abnormal flexion motion of 30° at the MP joint. According to Table 16-8a, Thumb Impairment Values Due to Lack of Radial Abduction and to Ankylosis (5th ed, p 459), there was a 9% thumb impairment due to lack of radial abduction, that is, limited to 20°.

According to Table 16-8b, Thumb Impairment Values Due to Lack of Adduction and to Ankylosis (5th ed, p 459), there was a 3% thumb impairment due to the 3-cm lack of adduction. According to Table 16-9, Thumb Impairments Due to Lack of Opposition and to Ankylosis (5th ed, p 460), there was a 9% thumb impairment due to the measured opposition of 4 cm. Adding these impairments yielded a total thumb impairment of 24%, which equated to a 10% impairment of the hand (Table 16-1, Relationship of Impairment of the Digits to Impairment of the Hand; 5th ed, p 438), which equated to a 9% impairment of the upper extremity (Table 16-2, Relationship of Impairment of the Hand to Impairment of the Upper Extremity; 5th ed, p 439), which equated to a 5% whole person impairment (Table 16-3, Relationship of Impairment of the Upper Extremity to Impairment of the Whole Person; 5th ed, p 439). This rating process is summarized in the Upper Extremity Impairment Evaluation Record (5th ed, p 436), as shown here on page 265.

Impairment: 5% whole person impairment per the Fifth Edition.

Sixth Edition Rating

The *Guides* approach to the evaluation of impairment due to thumb pain is typically based on Chapter 15, specifically, Section 15.2, Diagnosis-Based Impairment (6th ed, pp 387-404), Table 15-2 Digit Regional Grid: Upper Extremity Impairments (6th ed, p 397), listed under Ligament/Bone/Joint, specifically, posttraumatic degenerative joint disease. The default rating for Table 15-2 is class 1, grade C, which is 6% for the digit, and the maximum is 8% digit impairment. The alternative method can be impairment due to motion deficits rated via range of motion, Section 15.7c, Thumb Motion (6th ed, pp 465-468), and Table 15-30, Thumb Range of Motion (6th ed, p 468).

Range of motion being both an alternative and a grade modifier, motion must be assessed using Table 15-30, Thumb Range of Motion (6th ed, p 468). Abnormal MP flexion motion of 30° resulted in a 4% digit impairment; CMC joint adduction of 3 cm resulted in a 4% digit impairment; lack of radial abduction, that is, limited to 20°, resulted in a 10% digit impairment; and opposition of 4 cm resulted in a 9% digit impairment. These were added, resulting in a 27% digit impairment. Per Table 15-35, Range of Motion Grade Modifiers (6th ed, p 477), this was a grade modifier 2 because the motion impairment was in the range of 20% to 39% digit impairment. In Section 15.3a, Adjustment Grid: Functional History (6th ed, pp 406-407), and Table 15-7, Functional History Adjustment: Upper Extremities (6th ed, p 406), the patient was assigned a grade modifier 2; the functional history was consistent with the observation that "he did have some pain in the base of his thumb after a hard day's work" for many years, but in the past few months "the pain was so severe that he was unable to work on several occasions for 1 or 2 days at a time." His *Quick*DASH score was 41, which was also consistent with grade modifier 2. Because his functional history grade modifier was equivalent to the range of motion grade modifier, no adjustment of the digit impairment was required.

By the range of motion method, the patient's impairment was 27% of the digit, significantly greater than the maximum of 8% of the digit impairment if diagnosis-based impairment were used. Therefore 27% of the digit was used, and this equated per Table 15-12, Impairment Values Calculated From Digit Impairment (6th ed, 421), to a 10% upper extremity permanent impairment and a 6% whole person impairment.

Impairment: 6% whole person impairment per the Sixth Edition.

Comment on Arthritic Thumb

The initial injury was a Bennett fracture, which is a fracture dislocation, intra-articular fracture, at the base of the CMC joint of the thumb. It involves an oblique intra-articular metacarpal fracture (known as the *palmar beak fragment*), which remains attached to the palmar beak ligament. It is the most frequent of all thumb fractures and was described in 1882 by Dr Edward Bennett. The patient developed posttraumatic degenerative disease with associated motion deficits.

In assessing thumb impairment due to lack of adduction, differences between linear measurements of thumb adduction in centimeters and percentages of lost range of motion must be noted. In assessing impairment due to lack of opposition, hand size can be important. For example, a normal, small hand may not be able to oppose to 8 cm.

Table 19, Impairment From Joint Crepitation (4th ed, p 59), did not apply in this case because the impairment from abnormal motion took precedence. The *Guides* states that "the evaluator must take care to avoid duplication of impairments when other findings, such as synovial hypertrophy, carpal collapse with arthritic changes, or limited motion are present. Those findings might indicate a greater severity of the same pathologic process and take precedence over evaluation of joint crepitation, which should not be rated in that instance" (4th ed, p 58). The Fifth Edition does not rate impairment on the basis of joint crepitation.

In the Fifth Edition, Table 16-8a, Thumb Impairment Values Due to Lack of Radial Abduction and to Ankylosis (5th ed, p 459), includes rating for lack of radial adduction (thumb "stuck out in the hitchhiking position" and unable to return to its anatomic position next to the index metacarpal). This did not appear in the Fourth Edition in Table 6, Thumb Impairments Due to Lack of Radial Abduction and to Ankylosis (4th ed, p 28).

In the Fifth Edition, the maximum impairment for lack of radial abduction, that is, 10% thumb impairment, is obtained with 15° of measured radial abduction, and in the Fourth Edition this occurs with 0° of measured radial abduction. The Fifth Edition correctly points out that 15° is the minimum value for radial abduction "due to anatomic considerations" (the thumb and index metacarpals touch proximally but are separated distally by soft tissue) (5th ed, p 458).

In both the Fourth and Fifth Editions, pinch strength would not be combined with motion deficits. The Fifth Edition states that "decreased strength cannot be rated in the presence of decreased motion, painful conditions, deformities, or absence of parts (eg, thumb amputation) that prevent effective application of maximal force in the region being evaluated" (5th ed, p 508). Either the decreased motion or the pain would prevent meaningful strength testing.

In the Sixth Edition, the preferred methodology is diagnosis-based impairments. The CMC joint was involved, therefore the region used is Digits/Hand. Table 15-2, Digit Regional Grid: Digit Impairments (6th ed, p 393), specifies that "posttraumatic degenerative joint disease" with "residual pain and/or functional loss with normal range of motion" is a class 1 impairment with a 6% digit impairment. For the thumb, per Table 15-12 (6th ed, p 421), this resulted in a 1% whole person impairment; this is a lesser impairment than one based on motion deficits; therefore the rating was based on motion impairment. If there were not findings of posttraumatic degenerative disease, it is probable that the impairment would be based on the patient's fracture. Per Table 15-2 (6th ed, p 393), a fracture of the "thumb metacarpal, intra-articular" with "residual symptoms, consistent objective findings and/or functional loss, with no motion" there was a class 1 impairment with a default 10% digit impairment, which converted per Table 15-12 (6th ed, p 421) to a 3% upper extremity impairment and a 2% whole person impairment.

SUMMARY

Diagnosis	Traumatic arthropathy of the thumb
Fourth Edition References	Section 3.1f (4th ed, pp 24-30); Section 3.1m (4th ed, pp 58-59), Figure 13 (4th ed, p 27), Figure 14 (4th ed, p 28), Figure 16 (4th ed, p 29), Table 5 (4th ed, p 28), Table 6 (4th ed, p 28), Table 7 (4th ed, p 29)
Fourth Edition Summary	History, upper extremity evaluation (including range of motion). First, thumb motion impairments of flexion and extension, adduction, radial abduction, and opposition are measured and recorded. Second, these values are added to determine abnormal thumb motion impairment. Note, impairment of thumb motions are added, whereas those of the fingers are combined.
Fourth Edition Impairment	8% upper extremity impairment, 5% whole person impairment
Fifth Edition References	Section 16.4d (5th ed, pp 24-30), Figure 16-15 (5th ed, p 457), Table 16-8a (5th ed, p 459), Table 16-8b (5th ed, p 459), Table 16-9 (5th ed, p 460), Table 16-1 (5th ed, p 438), Table 16-2 (5th ed, p 439), Table 16-3 (5th ed, p 439)
Fifth Edition Summary	History, upper extremity evaluation (including range of motion). First, thumb motion impairments of flexion and extension, adduction, radial abduction, and opposition are measured and recorded. Second, these values are added to determine abnormal thumb motion impairment. Note, impairment of thumb motions are added, whereas those of the fingers are combined.
Fifth Edition Impairment	9% upper extremity impairment, 5% whole person impairment

Sixth Edition References	Section 15.7c (6th ed, pp 465-468), Table 15-30 (6th ed, p 468); Section 15.2 (6th ed, pp 387-404); Section 15.3a (6th ed, pp 406-407), Table 15-7 (6th ed, p 406); Table 15-12 (6th ed, p 421)
Sixth Edition Summary	History (including functional history and inventories), physical evaluation, and clinical studies. First, diagnosis-based impairment, class, and potential values are determined. Second, range of motion impairment is determined. Determining range of motion impairment was greater, and this was used to define impairment.
Sixth Edition Impairment	10% upper extremity impairment, 6% whole person impairment

Upper Extremity Impairment Evaluation Record–**Part 1 (Hand)**

Side ☑R ☐L

Name Mr. Jaeger Age 58 Sex ☑M ☐F Dominant hand ☑R ☐L Date

Occupation Diagnosis Arthritic Thumb

			Abnormal motion				**Amputation**	**Sensory loss**	**Other disorders**	**Hand impairment%**	
			Record motion, ankylosis, and impairment %				Mark level & impairment %	Mark type, level, & impairment %	List type & impairment %	• Combine digit IMP% *Convert to hand IMP%	
			Flexion	Extension	Ankylosis	IMP%					
Thumb	IP	Angle°									
		IMP%									
	MP	Angle°	30	+40		3					
		IMP%	3	0							
				Motion	Ankylosis	IMP%					
	CMC	Radial abduction: Angle°		20		7				Abnormal motion [1]	22
		Radial abduction: IMP%		7						Amputation [2]	—
		Adduction: CMS		3		3				Sensory loss [3]	—
		Adduction: IMP%		3						Other disorders [4]	—
		Opposition: CMS		4		9	R L	R L		Digit impairment % • Combine 1, 2, 3, 4	22
		Opposition: IMP%		9							
Add impairment % CMC + MP + IP = 22 [1]							IMP % = [2]	IMP % = [3]	IMP % = [4]	**Hand impairment % *Convert above**	9

			Flexion	Extension	Ankylosis	IMP%					
Index	DIP	Angle°								Abnormal motion [1]	
		IMP%								Amputation [2]	
	PIP	Angle°								Sensory loss [3]	
		IMP%								Other disorders [4]	
	MP	Angle°								Digit impairment % • Combine 1, 2, 3, 4	
		IMP%									
• Combine impairment % MP + PIP + DIP = [1]							IMP % = [2]	IMP % = [3]	IMP % = [4]	**Hand impairment % *Convert above**	
Middle	DIP	Angle°								Abnormal motion [1]	
		IMP%								Amputation [2]	
	PIP	Angle°								Sensory loss [3]	
		IMP%								Other disorders [4]	
	MP	Angle°								Digit impairment % • Combine 1, 2, 3, 4	
		IMP%									
• Combine impairment % MP + PIP + DIP = [1]							IMP % = [2]	IMP % = [3]	IMP % = [4]	**Hand impairment % *Convert above**	
Ring	DIP	Angle°								Abnormal motion [1]	
		IMP%								Amputation [2]	
	PIP	Angle°								Sensory loss [3]	
		IMP%								Other disorders [4]	
	MP	Angle°								Digit impairment % • Combine 1, 2, 3, 4	
		IMP%									
• Combine impairment % MP + PIP + DIP = [1]							IMP % = [2]	IMP % = [3]	IMP % = [4]	**Hand impairment % *Convert above**	
Little	DIP	Angle°								Abnormal motion [1]	
		IMP%								Amputation [2]	
	PIP	Angle°								Sensory loss [3]	
		IMP%								Other disorders [4]	
	MP	Angle°								Digit impairment % • Combine 1, 2, 3, 4	
		IMP%									
• Combine impairment % MP + PIP + DIP = [1]							IMP % = [2]	IMP % = [3]	IMP % = [4]	**Hand impairment % *Convert above**	

Total hand impairment (Add hand impairment % for thumb + index + middle + ring + little finger) =	9 %
Upper extremity impairment (†Convert total hand impairment % to upper extremity impairment %) =	8 %; enter on Part 2, Line II
If hand region impairment is only impairment, convert upper extremity impairment to whole-person impairment:‡ =	5 %

• Combined Values Chart; (p. 322-324) *Use Table 1 (Digits to hand p. 18); †Use Table 2 (Hand to upper extremity p. 19) ‡Use Table 3 (p. 20)

** Courtesy of G. de Groot Swanson, MD

Upper Extremity Impairment Evaluation Record–Part 1 (Hand) Side ☒R ☐L

Name *Mr. Jaeger* Age *58* Sex ☒M ☐F Dominant hand ☒R ☐L Date ______

Occupation ______ Diagnosis *Arthritic Thumb* *CASE 15-10*

			Abnormal Motion				Amputation	Sensory Loss	Other Disorders	Hand Impairment%	
			Record motion or ankylosis angles and digit impairment %				Mark level & impairment %	Mark type, level, & impairment %	List type & impairment %	•Combine digit imp % *Convert to hand imp %	
			Flexion	Extension	Ankylosis	Imp %					
Thumb	IP	Angle°									
		Imp %									
	MP	Angle°	*30*	*+40*		*3*					
		Imp %	*3*	*0*			[2]				
				Motion	Ankylosis	Imp %					
	CMC	Radial abduction Angle°		*20*		*7*				Abnormal motion [1]	*22*
		Radial abduction Imp %		*7*						Amputation [2]	*—*
		Adduction Cm		*3*		*3*				Sensory loss [3]	*—*
		Adduction Imp %		*3*						Other disorders [4]	*—*
		Opposition Cm		*4*		*9*	‡UE IMP % = [5]			Total digit imp % •Combine 1, 2, 3, 4	*22*
		Opposition Imp %		*9*							
Add digit impairment % CMC + MP + IP = *22*						[1]	**Digit IMP % =** [2]	**Digit IMP % =** [3]	**Digit IMP % =** [4]	**Hand impairment % *Convert above**	*9*
			Flexion	Extension	Ankylosis	Imp %					
Index	DIP	Angle°								Abnormal motion [1]	
		Imp %								Amputation [2]	
	PIP	Angle°								Sensory loss [3]	
		Imp %								Other disorders [4]	
	MP	Angle°								Total digit imp % •Combine 1, 2, 3, 4	
		Imp %									
•Combine digit impairment % MP, PIP, DIP =						[1]	**Digit IMP % =** [2]	**Digit IMP % =** [3]	**Digit IMP % =** [4]	**Hand impairment % *Convert above**	
Middle	DIP	Angle°								Abnormal motion [1]	
		Imp %								Amputation [2]	
	PIP	Angle°								Sensory loss [3]	
		Imp %								Other disorders [4]	
	MP	Angle°								Total digit imp % •Combine 1, 2, 3, 4	
		Imp %									
•Combine digit impairment % MP, PIP, DIP =						[1]	**Digit IMP % =** [2]	**Digit IMP % =** [3]	**Digit IMP % =** [4]	**Hand impairment % *Convert above**	
Ring	DIP	Angle°								Abnormal motion [1]	
		Imp %								Amputation [2]	
	PIP	Angle°								Sensory loss [3]	
		Imp %								Other disorders [4]	
	MP	Angle°								Total digit imp % •Combine 1, 2, 3, 4	
		Imp %									
•Combine digit impairment % MP, PIP, DIP =						[1]	**Digit IMP % =** [2]	**Digit IMP % =** [3]	**Digit IMP % =** [4]	**Hand impairment % *Convert above**	
Little	DIP	Angle°								Abnormal motion [1]	
		Imp %								Amputation [2]	
	PIP	Angle°								Sensory loss [3]	
		Imp %								Other disorders [4]	
	MP	Angle°								Total digit imp % •Combine 1, 2, 3, 4	
		Imp %									
•Combine digit impairment % MP, PIP, DIP =						[1]	**Digit IMP % =** [2]	**Digit IMP % =** [3]	**Digit IMP % =** [4]	**Hand impairment % *Convert above**	

Total hand impairment: Add hand impairment % for thumb + index + middle + ring + little finger =	*9*	%
Convert total hand impairment to upper extremity impairment† (if thumb metacarpal intact, enter on Part 2, line II) =	*8*	%
‡Add thumb ray upper extremity amputation imp [5] ___% + hand upper extremity imp ___% =		%
If hand region impairment is only impairment, convert upper extremity impairment to whole person impairment§ =	*5*	%

• Combined Values Chart (p. 604). *Use Table 16-1 (digits to hand). †Use Table 16-2 (hand to upper extremity). §Use Table 16-3.
Courtesy of G. de Groot Swanson, MD, Grand Rapids, Michigan.

CASE 15-11

Elusive Cumulative Trauma Disorder

Subject: Ms Ryan, a 42-year-old woman.

History: Ms Ryan was employed as a certified nursing assistant at a medium-sized hospital. Her position involved frequent assistance to patients in basic care activities, thus requiring heavy lifting. She presented with a 2-month complaint of soreness in the left wrist area. She claimed that the pain had started when she was transferring a patient. Although she had no focal numbness, she complained of general numbness from the elbow distally, without neurologic distribution. She had vague and diffuse soreness in the forearm and wrist, mainly on the palmar and dorsal aspects. She claimed the forearm and hands were swollen. Notes from the previous physician who had treated her for 2 months and referred her indicated that she had had identical complaints 6 months prior to this episode in the right upper extremity. Her right upper extremity was investigated with electrodiagnostic studies, multiple examinations and treatments, and radiographs, but no definitive diagnosis could be made. She was presently working full-time, without restrictions.

Treatment began with nonsteroidal anti-inflammatory agents and physical therapy for several weeks, followed by a trial of paroxetine with amitriptyline. There was no reported improvement, and Ms Ryan continued to complain of wrist pain with activity. A bone scan was normal. After 6 weeks of therapy and further trial of other pain medications, she similarly had no reported improvement. Four weeks later, Ms Ryan was determined to be at maximal medical improvement.

Current Symptoms: Ms Ryan complained of pain with any use of her hand. She was able to perform activities of daily living independently; however, she reported significant difficulties with many activities of daily living.

Functional Assessment: The *Quick*DASH score was 75.

Physical Examination: No visible swelling, although Ms Ryan insisted that there was swelling. There was normal range of motion of the wrist in flexion, extension, and radial and ulnar deviation. Examination of other joints of the upper extremities was normal. Her wrist had no localized tenderness, nor subluxation or click with manual subluxation stress testing to suggest carpal instability. Manual muscle strength testing showed poor effort so that accurate assessment of strength was invalid. All upper extremity reflexes were brisk and symmetric. Ms Ryan had full range of motion of the cervical spine in flexion, extension, side bending, and rotation. Sensory examination with two-point discrimination was normal in all digits of the hand. Pinprick examination of the remainder of the upper extremity was normal. The Finkelstein maneuver was questionable, as were provocative tests for tendinitis of the proximal forearm. Mild tenderness was reported on palpation diffusely over the dorsal and radial forearm. Circulation was judged as normal on the basis of color, warmth, radial and ulnar artery pulses, and the absence of edema.

Clinical Studies: Radiographs were normal. Motor and sensory nerve conduction studies were normal for the median, radial, and ulnar nerves.

Discussion of Elusive Cumulative Trauma Disorder

Fourth Edition Rating

In terms of cumulative trauma disorder, the *Guides* specifically states in Section 3.1a, Evaluation (4th ed, pp 15-19):

> A patient with wrist or hand pain or other symptoms may not have evidence of a permanent impairment. Alteration of the patient's daily activities or work-related tasks may reduce the symptoms. Such an individual should not be considered to be permanently impaired under *Guides* criteria. [4th ed, p 19]

There were no findings that resulted in ratable impairment; that is, motion measurements were normal, there was no evidence of neurologic involvement, and there was no other ratable impairment.

Although this case was frustrating for the physician, it reflects a frequent situation in which no definitive diagnosis can be made. The individual may or may not have a history of compensation claims and makes little or no improvement with basic treatment for soft-tissue complaints. Some evaluators would place such ill-defined presentations into the broad rubric of "cumulative trauma disorder." This diagnosis remains controversial. There were two difficult issues in this case. First, can we perform impairment rating for an individual in whom no objective pathology can be determined?

Second, were there other reasons for the individual's enduring complaints aside from "tissue pathology," such as psychological problems or secondary gain? Without underlying objectively defined impairment, the impairment rating is 0%.

Impairment: 0% whole person impairment per the Fourth Edition.

Fifth Edition Rating

Section 16.7d, Tendinitis (5th ed, p 507), states, "Several syndromes involving the upper extremity are variously attributed to tendinitis, fasciitis, or epicondylitis. . . . Although these conditions may be persistent for some time, they are not given a permanent impairment rating unless there is some other factor that must be considered." It would not be appropriate to rate by strength loss, because the *Guides* states, "Decreased strength cannot be rated in the presence of decreased motion, painful conditions . . ." (5th ed, p 508). Ms Ryan's complaint of pain clearly prevents rating on the basis of strength testing. Therefore, there is no ratable impairment by Chapter 16, The Upper Extremities.

An individual with tendinitis may possibly have ratable impairment by Chapter 18, Pain, if the individual is credible and the diagnosed condition has a well-defined pathophysiologic basis. In this case, however, the pain complaints were diffuse, beyond a specific anatomic distribution, and there was no documentation of limitation in the performance of activities of daily living. In addition, the instructions give a three-question test to determine whether use of the pain chapter is appropriate. If the answer to any of the three questions is "No," the chapter is not to be used. The third question is, "Is the condition one that is widely accepted by physicians as having a well-defined pathophysiologic basis?" In cumulative trauma disorders like Ms Ryan's, there is no objectively definable pathophysiology, and the source of her pain is speculative.

Impairment: 0% whole person impairment per the Fifth Edition.

Sixth Edition Rating

The *Guides* approach to the evaluation of impairment due to wrist pain is based on Section 15.2, Diagnosis-Based Impairment (6th ed, pp 387-404), and Section 15.2c, Wrist (6th ed, p 390).

In Table 15-3, Wrist Regional Grid, section on Muscle/Tendon (6th ed, p 395), for the diagnosis wrist sprain/strain there is a class 1 rating for

"History of painful injury, residual symptoms without consistent objective findings," with a default impairment of 1% upper extremity.

According to Section 15.3a, Adjustment Grid: Functional History (6th ed, pp 406-407), and Table 15-7, Functional History Adjustment: Upper Extremities (6th ed, p 406), the patient was assigned grade modifier 3; the functional history was consistent with "pain with any use of her hand" and the *Quick*DASH score was in the range of 61 to 80. In Section 15.3b, Adjustment Grid: Physical Examination (6th ed, p 407), and Table 15-8, Physical Examination Adjustment: Upper Extremities (6th ed, p 408), the patient was assigned grade modifier 0; the physical examination revealed normal range of motion of the wrist, no localized tenderness or carpal instability, and normal reflexes and sensory examination. Mild tenderness was reported on palpation diffusely over the dorsal and radial forearm; however, this was neither focal nor anatomical. Circulation was judged as normal. According to Section 15.3c, Adjustment Grid: Clinical Studies (6th ed, pp 407-409), and Table 15-9, Clinical Studies Adjustment: Upper Extremities (6th ed, p 410), the patient was assigned grade modifier 0; the clinical studies revealed normal radiographs and normal nerve conduction. The functional history grade modifier differed by two or more from the physical examination and clinical studies adjustment factors; therefore, it was excluded. In summary, the adjustments were: functional history grade modifier, n/a; physical examination, 0; and clinical studies grade modifier, 0. The net adjustment compared to diagnosis class 1 is −2, grade A, 0%.

Class 1—Default for Diagnosis = 1% Upper Extremity Impairment			
CDX	GMFH	GMPE	GMCS
1	3	0	0
Net adjustment			
(GMFH − CDX) 3 − 1 = 2 (invalid)			
+ (GMPE − CDX) + 0 − 1 = −1			
+ (GMCS − CDX) + 0 − 1 = −1			
Net adjustment = −2			

Result is class 1 adjustment −2, which results in class 1, grade A = 0% upper extremity impairment

Based on Table 15-11, Impairment Values Calculated From Upper Extremity Impairment (6th ed, p 420), this converted to 0% whole person impairment.

Impairment: 0% whole person impairment per the Sixth Edition.

Comment on Elusive Cumulative Trauma Disorder

In many cases, the basis of impairment rating is to evaluate pain in the context of an underlying objectively defined impairment. The Social Security Administration and the US Department of Veterans Affairs view pain as significant only when it is associated with mental impairment. The Fourth Edition states, "In general, the impairment percents shown in the chapters that consider the various organ systems make allowance for the pain that may accompany the impairing conditions" (4th ed, p 9). It also notes, "Pain is a subjective perception. Usually no exact relationships exist among the degree of pain, extent of physical change, and extent of impairment" (4th ed, p 309).

The Fifth Edition states in Section 2.5e, Pain, "The impairment ratings in the body organ system chapters make allowance for any accompanying pain" (5th ed, p 20). Chapter 18, Pain, provides a mechanism for rating cases, providing up to a 3% whole person impairment in selected cases.

In the Sixth Edition it is possible to have ratable impairment for certain soft tissue and muscle tendon injuries without objective findings; however, the default impairment value is 1% upper extremity impairment, and this impairment can be provided only once in a lifetime. If other chapters were used for rating, then impairment cannot be based on Chapter 3, Pain-Related Impairment.

SUMMARY

Diagnosis	Cumulative trauma disorder without objectively defined impairment
Fourth Edition References	Section 3.1a (4th ed, p 19), Chapter 15
Fourth Edition Summary	Upper extremity pain complaints without a definable cause on repeat examination/evaluation. Pain in itself is not an entity that can be rated without underlying impairment.
Fourth Edition Impairment	0% upper extremity impairment, 0% whole person impairment
Fifth Edition References	Section 16.7d (5th ed, p 507), Chapter 18

Fifth Edition Summary Upper extremity pain complaints without a definable cause on repeat examination/evaluation. Pain itself may be ratable in selected cases as explained in Chapter 18.

Fifth Edition Impairment 0% upper extremity impairment, 0% whole person impairment

Sixth Edition References Section 15.2 (6th ed, pp 387-404); Section 15.3a (6th ed, pp 406-407); Section 15.3b (6th ed, p 407); Section 15.3c (6th ed, pp 407-409), Table 15-3 (6th ed, p 395), Table 15-7 (6th ed, p 406), Table 15-8 (6th ed, p 408), Table 15-9 (6th ed, p 410), Table 15-11 (6th ed, p 420)

Sixth Edition Summary History (including functional history and inventories), physical evaluation, and clinical studies. First, diagnosis-based impairment, class, and default value are determined. Second, impairment rating is adjusted based on nonkey factors.

Sixth Edition Impairment 0% upper extremity impairment, 0% whole person impairment

---

CASE 15-12

Severe Degenerative Arthritis of Wrist

Subject: Mr Cashion, a 44-year-old man.

History: Mr Cashion was a manual laborer who fell over a set of pallets on the job and injured his left wrist. He was seen in the emergency department. He had a decreased range of motion in flexion, extension, and radial deviation. Radiographs showed no sign of fracture, but there were signs of degenerative arthritis. A questionable radiodense line across the left scaphoid, compatible with an old injury, was also seen. Complete loss of joint space between the scaphoid and lunate was present.

Mr Cashion was placed in a splint, without improvement. Because of persistent discomfort with conservative treatment and advanced scapholunate collapse with degenerative arthritis, intercarpal fusion with scaphoid excision was performed. Mr Cashion was placed in a cast for immobilization, and extensive physical therapy was arranged. He was released without restrictions to his previous job of heavy manual labor and truck driving 2 years later.

Current Symptoms: Mr Cashion reported mild discomfort at times, was able to perform all activities of daily living, which included shoeing his own horses for the upcoming hunting season.

Functional Assessment: The *Quick*DASH score was 11.

Physical Examination: Physical examination demonstrated a left-hand–dominant individual. He had a well-healed surgical scar over the medial radial aspect of his left wrist. The left wrist demonstrated palmar flexion of 10°, extension of 0°, radial deviation of 10°, and ulnar deviation of 0°. There was no crepitation, grinding, or instability. He had no muscle wasting or atrophy. Right hand grip strength was 24 kg, and left hand grip strength was 23 kg. Sensation was intact.

Clinical Studies: Radiographs revealed a solid fusion.

Discussion of Severe Degenerative Arthritis of Wrist

Fourth Edition Rating

According to Figure 26, Upper Extremity Impairments Due to Lack of Flexion and Extension of Wrist Joint (4th ed, p 36), Mr Cashion had an 8% impairment for flexion of 10° and an 11% impairment for extension of 0°. On the basis of Figure 29, Upper Extremity Impairments Due to Abnormal Radial and Ulnar Deviation of Wrist Joint (4th ed, p 38), there was a 2% impairment for radial deviation of 10° and a 5% impairment for ulnar deviation of 0°. Because the relative value of each wrist function unit has to be taken into consideration in the impairment charts, the impairment of flexion and extension and of radial and ulnar deviation were added to determine the impairment of the upper extremity. There was a 26% impairment of the left upper extremity for range of motion deficits.

Section 3.1m, Impairment Due to Other Disorders of the Upper Extremity, was applicable, because Mr Cashion underwent a resection arthroplasty. According to Table 27, Impairment of the Upper Extremity After Arthroplasty of Specific Bones or Joints (4th ed, p 61), there was a 12% impairment of the upper extremity (carpal bones). The combined value of 26% (for the range of motion deficits) and 12% (for the resection arthroplasty) was 35% upper extremity impairment. According to Table 3, Relationship of Impairment of the Upper Extremity to Impairment of the Whole Person (4th ed, p 20), this was equivalent to 21% whole person impairment.

Impairment: 21% whole person impairment per the Fourth Edition.

Fifth Edition Rating

The *Guides* approach to the evaluation of impairment due to wrist arthroplasty is described in Section 16.7b, Arthroplasty (5th ed, p 505). The impairment due to arthroplasty was combined with the impairment due to abnormal motion.

According to Table 16-27, Impairment of the Upper Extremity After Arthroplasty of Specific Bones or Joints (5th ed, p 506), Mr Cashion had a 10% upper extremity impairment due to the carpal bone resection arthroplasty (carpal bone [isolated]).

According to Figure 16-28, Pie Chart of Upper Extremity Motion Impairments Due to Lack of Flexion and Extension of Wrist Joint (5th ed, p 467), Mr Cashion had an 8% impairment for flexion of 10° and an 11%

impairment for extension of 0°. According to Figure 16-31, Pie Chart of Upper Extremity Motion Impairments Due to Abnormal Radial and Ulnar Deviations of Wrist Joint (5th ed, p 469), there was a 2% impairment for radial deviation of 10° and a 5% impairment for ulnar deviation of 0°. Because the relative value of each wrist function unit has to be taken into consideration in the impairment charts, the impairment of flexion and extension and of radial and ulnar deviation were added to determine the impairment of the upper extremity. There was a 26% impairment of the left upper extremity for range of motion deficits.

The combined value of 10% upper extremity impairment for the resection arthroplasty and 26% for the range of motion deficits, according to the Combined Values Chart (5th ed, p 604), was 33% upper extremity impairment. By means of Table 16-3, Conversion of Impairment of the Upper Extremity to Impairment of the Whole Person (5th ed, p 439), this converted to 20% whole person impairment.

Impairment: 20% whole person impairment per the Fifth Edition.

Sixth Edition Rating

The *Guides* approach to the evaluation of impairment due to wrist arthritis is based on Chapter 15, The Upper Extremities, specifically, Section 15.2c, Wrist (6th ed, p 390). This gentleman had a scaphoid excision arthroplasty. Table 15-3, Wrist Regional Grid: Upper Extremity Impairments (6th ed, p 397), under Ligament/Bone/Joint, has a class 1 category for "ulnar head isolated, proximal carpectomy, or carpal bone arthroplasty." This grade C default rating is 10% upper extremity, but the category notes with an asterisk that "if motion loss is present, this impairment may alternatively be assessed using Section 15-7, Range of Motion Impairment (6th ed, p 459). A range of motion impairment stands alone and is not combined with diagnosis impairment." Section 15.7e, Wrist Motion Impairment (6th ed, p 469), on page 471 states "If range of motion is used as a stand alone approach, the total impairment for all planes of motion must be calculated. All values for the joint are added and the impairment is converted to whole person using Table 15-11." According to Table 15-32, Wrist Range of Motion (6th ed, p 473), for flexion of 10° there was a 9% upper extremity impairment, for extension of 10° there was a 9% upper extremity impairment, for radial deviation of 10° there was a 2% upper extremity impairment, and for ulnar deviation of 0° there was a 4% upper extremity impairment. These values were added for a total of 24% upper extremity impairment. Per Table 15-35, Range of Motion Grade Modifiers (6th ed, p 477), there was a grade modifier 3. Per Table 15-7, Functional History Adjustment: Upper Extremities (6th ed, p 406), Mr Cashion's functional complaints supported a grade modifier 1, and his *Quick*DASH score a grade modifier 0. There was no need for adjustment of the final range of motion impairment because his functional history grade modifier was less.

The 24% upper extremity impairment converted to a whole person impairment using Table 15-11, Impairment Values Calculated From Upper Extremity Impairment (6th ed, p 420), to equal 14% whole person impairment.

Impairment: 14% whole person impairment per the Sixth Edition.

Comment on Severe Degenerative Arthritis of Wrist

In the Fourth and Fifth Editions, Section 3.lm, Impairment Due to Other Disorders of the Upper Extremity (4th ed, p 58), or Section 16.7, Impairment of the Upper Extremities Due to Other Disorders (5th ed, p 498), is used only when the other criteria have not adequately encompassed the extent of the impairment. This section is used primarily for bone and joint disorders, the presence of resection or implant arthroplasty, musculotendinous disorders, and loss of strength. The Fourth Edition advises that, "the evaluator must take care to avoid duplication of impairments when other findings such as synovial hypertrophy, carpal collapse with arthritic changes, or limited motion are present" (4th ed, p 58). The Fifth Edition states that "some of the conditions described in this section can be concurrent with each other and with decreased motion because they share overlapping pathomechanics. The evaluator must have good understanding of pathomechanics of deformities and apply proper judgment to avoid duplication of impairment ratings (5th ed, p 499).

Many of the tables in this section determine severity for a condition that relates to a percentage of joint impairment. This percentage is multiplied by the impairment values for specific joints as provided in the Fourth Edition in Table 18, Impairment Values for Digits, Hand, Upper Extremity, and the Whole Person for Disorders of Specific Joints (4th ed, p 58), and in the Fifth Edition in Table 16-18, Maximum Impairment Values for the Digits, Hand, Wrist, Elbow, and Shoulder Due to Disorders of Specific Joints or Units (5th ed, p 499). However, the values in Table 27, Impairment of the Upper Extremity After Arthroplasty of Specific Bones or Joints (4th ed, p 61), or Table 16-27, Impairment of the Upper Extremity After Arthroplasty of Specific Bones or Joints (5th ed, p 506), present directly the specific arthroplasty impairment percentages.

In this case, the individual did not have an implant arthroplasty but had a resection arthroplasty. The scaphoid was removed in its entirety, and the individual underwent an intercarpal fusion, involving the proximal carpal row. The Fourth Edition specifies that simple resection arthroplasty is given 40% impairment of the joint value, and implant arthroplasty is given 50% of the joint value; that is, lower values are given for a resection arthroplasty than for an implant arthroplasty. In the Fifth Edition, resection and implant ratings are usually reversed compared to the Fourth Edition, so that implants now obtain a lower rating, whereas resection rates are higher. This change reflects the advancements that have occurred in upper extremity replacement prosthesis design and surgical technique over the last decade.

In the Sixth Edition, in Chapter 2, Table 2-1, Fundamental Principles of the *Guides* (6th ed, p 20), item 12 states "If the *Guides* provides more than one method to rate a particular impairment or condition, the method producing the higher rating must be used." In this case, although a diagnosis-based impairment was possible, it would have yielded at most a 12% upper extremity impairment value (default rating of 10% upper extremity impairment for class 1, grade C, Table 15-3, p 397). In this case, the range of motion method yielded a higher value and was the appropriate choice.

SUMMARY

Diagnosis	Degenerative arthritis of the left wrist after resection arthroplasty
Fourth Edition References	Section 3.1m (4th ed, pp 58-65); Section 3.1h (4th ed, pp 35-38); Section 3.1i (4th ed, pp 38-41), Table 3 (4th ed, p 20), Table 27 (4th ed, p 61), Figure 26 (4th ed, p 36), Figure 29 (4th ed, p 38)
Fourth Edition Summary	History, upper extremity evaluation (including assessment of range of motion) and neurologic assessment (including sensation and strength testing). Arthroplasty may be carried out with or without implant. First, impairment due to arthroplasty (resection or implant) is determined. Second, impairment due to abnormal motion is determined. Third, impairment due to arthroplasty is combined with impairment due to abnormal motion.
Fourth Edition Impairment	35% upper extremity impairment, 21% whole person impairment

Fifth Edition References	Section 16.7 (5th ed, pp 498-507); Section 16.7 (5th ed, p 505), Table 16-27 (5th ed, p 506), Figure 16-28 (5th ed, p 467), Figure 16-31 (5th ed, p 469), Figure 16-37 (5th ed, p 474), Table 16-3 (5th ed, p 439)
Fifth Edition Summary	History, upper extremity evaluation (including assessment of range of motion), and neurologic assessment (including sensation and strength testing). Arthroplasty may be carried out with or without implant. First, impairment due to arthroplasty (resection or implant) is determined. Second, impairment due to abnormal motion is determined. Third, impairment due to arthroplasty is combined with impairment due to abnormal motion.
Fifth Edition Impairment	33% upper extremity impairment, 20% whole person impairment
Sixth Edition References	Section 15.2c (6th ed, p 390); Section 15.7 (6th ed, pp 459-478); Section 15.7e (6th ed, pp 469-471), Table 15-3 (6th ed, p 397), Table 15-7 (6th ed, p 406), Table 15-11 (6th ed, p 420), Table 15-32 (6th ed, p 473), Table 15-35 (6th ed, p 477)
Sixth Edition Summary	History (including functional history and inventories, physical evaluation, and clinical studies). In this case the range of motion method was more accurate, as it led to a higher impairment rating, which was appropriate, given the clinical situation.
Sixth Edition Impairment	24% upper extremity impairment, 14% whole person impairment

CASE 15-13

Carpal Instability

Subject: Mr Jones, a 35-year-old man.

History: Mr Jones, a maintenance worker in a local factory, accidentally stepped on a metal part that had dropped to the floor. He fell and landed on his outstretched, nondominant, left wrist and experienced immediate pain. He left work early and went to the local hospital emergency department, where radiographs of the wrist were taken and were reported as "negative for fracture." Mr Jones' left wrist pain continued. One week after his injury, he went to the local convenient care clinic, still complaining of left wrist pain. Radiographs there were also "negative for fracture." Mr Jones' pain persisted.

Three months after injury, Mr Jones still experienced left wrist pain that made it difficult for him to use tools. He went to an orthopedic surgeon. Physical examination showed less motion in the left wrist than in the right wrist, but enough motion to call "normal." Radiographs in the orthopedist's office showed no fractures but evidence of carpal instability. On the anterior to posterior view, a 5-mm gap between the scaphoid and the lunate was revealed. In addition, on the lateral view, the angle between the axis of the scaphoid and the axis of the radius was 68° (radioscaphoid angle).

Current Symptoms: When seen for permanent impairment evaluation 1 year after injury, Mr Jones continued to complain of left wrist pain with activity. This limited his ability to use the left hand for power grip. Because he was right-hand dominant, he used most tools in his right hand, but he said he was unable to use the left hand for "extra power." Mr Jones used to play the guitar but stopped because of pain when he used the left hand to finger chords. He also no longer played in the church softball league, as swinging the baseball bat provoked his pain.

Functional Assessment: The *Quick*DASH score was 41.

Physical Examination: The left wrist appeared normal, with no redness, warmth, swelling, ecchymosis, or deformity. There was no atrophy in the hand intrinsics, forearm, or arm. Range of motion was as follows:

	Left Wrist	Right Wrist
Extension	65°	80°
Flexion	65°	90°
Radial deviation	25°	35°
Ulnar deviation	35°	45°

Grip testing with the Jamar dynamometer produced a bell-shaped curve and reproducible maximal strength. Maximal grip was 40 kg on the left and 50 kg on the right. There was no crepitus in the wrist.

On neurologic examination, Mr Jones had normal sensation, including sharp-dull recognition and two-point discrimination. On manual muscle testing, no weakness was demonstrable, but power grip and use of the wrist flexors and extensors against resistance provoked Mr Jones' complaint of wrist pain.

Clinical Studies: One year after the injury, radiographs on the anteroposterior view revealed the gap between the scaphoid and the lunate to be 7 mm. On the lateral view, the radioscaphoid angle on the symptomatic left wrist was 68°, whereas the radioscaphoid angle on the asymptomatic right wrist was 48°. On both of these lateral radiographs, similar positioning was used so that the axis of the third metacarpal was parallel to the axis of the radius, and the films were judged appropriate to use to measure the radioscaphoid angle.

Discussion of Carpal Instability

Fourth Edition Rating

Impairment rating for carpal instability is discussed under Section 3.1m, Impairment Due to Other Disorders of the Upper Extremity (4th ed, p 61). Table 26, Upper Extremity Impairment Due to Carpal Instability Patterns (4th ed, p 61), is used to rate carpal instability or, in this case, scapholunate instability. The directions are a little unclear, and additional information was provided in *The Guides Newsletter*, March/April 1998, "Instability of the Wrist" (pp 1-3).

The range of motion of the left, symptomatic, wrist fell within the range considered normal by the *Guides*. Figure 26 (4th ed, p 36) and Figure 29 (4th ed, p 36) indicated that the left wrist range of motion was normal, and there was no impairment rating then for loss of range of motion, even though the left wrist had less motion than the right wrist. This was a joint injury, and there was no neurologic deficit. There was no atrophy. Thus, none of the other sections of the *Guides* were appropriate for rating this impairment.

Page 61 indicates that the carpal instability section should be used to rate impairment "only when all other risk factors are normal." Table 26 lists the upper extremity impairment percentages for mild, moderate, or severe carpal instability patterns.

The lateral radiograph is used to estimate impairment in scapholunate dissociation or instability. The radioscaphoid angle needs to be measured on a true or properly positioned lateral view, which was done in this case. According to Table 26, a radioscaphoid angle of 68° is a moderate-severity instability pattern. This would be a 12% upper extremity impairment rating.

Table 3 (4th ed, p 20) converts a 12% upper extremity impairment to a 7% whole person impairment rating.

Impairment: 7% whole person impairment per the Fourth Edition.

Fifth Edition Rating

Permanent impairment evaluation was based on Section 16.7, Impairment of the Upper Extremities Due to Other Disorders (5th ed, pp 498-507), specifically the discussion for carpal instability (5th ed, pp 502-503), and Table 16-25, Upper Extremity Impairment Due to Carpal Instability Patterns (5th ed, p 503). Carpal instability patterns are classified as mild, moderate, or severe, on the basis of the severity of the radiographic findings, and the category reflecting the greatest severity is selected. Radiographic criteria may be combined only with limited wrist motion. Pain and decreased strength are not rated separately.

The gap between the scaphoid and the lunate was 7 mm, and this met the definition of a moderate instability (16% upper extremity impairment) according to Table 16-25. In the Fourth Edition, Table 26, Upper Extremity Impairment Due to Carpal Instability Patterns, lists the radioscaphoid angle as a criterion for instability. This angle increases with either volar intercalated segment instability or dorsal intercalated segment instability. The Fifth Edition Table 16-25, Upper Extremity Impairment Due to Carpal Instability Patterns, does not list the radioscaphoid angle as a criterion. If the scapholunate angle and/or radiolunate angle had been given at the time of rating, the examiner would also compare that/those angle(s) to the criteria in Table 16-25. "Only one category of severity of carpal instability impairment is selected, based on the greatest severity of the roentgenographic findings" (5th ed, pp 502-503).

Figure 16-26 (5th ed, p 467) and Figure 16-31 (5th ed, p 469) would indicate that the left wrist range of motion was normal; however, the uninvolved joint had flexibility beyond normal. The Fifth Edition states, "If an involved joint has 'normal' motion according to the values specified in the *Guides* and the contralateral uninvolved joint has greater than average motion, there is a relative loss of motion. However, a loss of motion in a zone beyond the normal values does not as a rule represent a loss of function or impairment. In rare cases, based on the examiner's clinical judgment, an impairment not to exceed 2% of the maximum regional impairment value of a unit of motion could be given. The rationale for this decision must be explained in the report" (5th ed, p 454). In this case, the examiner felt that this did represent additional impairment and provided Mr Jones with the benefit of the doubt. The wrist functional unit represents 60% of the upper extremity function (5th ed, p 466); therefore, 2% of the maximum regional impairment value for the wrist represents 1% upper extremity impairment.

The 16% upper extremity impairment due to carpal instability was combined with the 1% upper extremity impairment due to relative wrist motion deficits by means of the Combined Values Chart (5th ed, p 604), resulting in a 17% upper extremity impairment. Table 16-3 (5th ed, p 639) converts 17% upper extremity impairment to a 10% whole person impairment rating.

Impairment: 10% whole person impairment per the Fifth Edition.

Sixth Edition Rating

The *Guides* approach to the evaluation of impairment due to carpal instability is based on Section 15.2, Diagnosis-Based Impairment (6th ed, pp 387-390).

In Table 15-3, Wrist Regional Grid: Upper Extremity Impairments, Section on Ligament/Bone/Joint (p 396), for the diagnosis wrist sprain h/o dislocation including carpal instability, there is a class 2 rating for moderate instability (with a default impairment of 16%).

According to Section 15.3a, Adjustment Grid: Functional History (6th ed, p 405), and Table 15-7, Functional History Adjustment: Upper Extremities (6th ed, p 406), the patient was assigned grade modifier 2, and the functional history was consistent with a *Quick*DASH score of 41. According to Section 15.3b, Adjustment Grid: Physical Examination (6th ed, p 407), and Table 15-8, Physical Examination Adjustment: Upper Extremities

(6th ed, p 408), the patient was assigned grade modifier 1; the physical examination revealed mild range of motion deficit of the injured wrist compared to the uninjured opposite side. The modifier for clinical studies was not applicable as it was inclusive in the diagnosis. In summary, the adjustments were: functional history grade modifier 2 and physical examination 1. The net adjustment compared to diagnosis class 2 was −1.

Class 1—Default for Diagnosis = 8% Upper Extremity Impairment			
CDX	GMFH	GMPE	GMCS
2	2	1	N/A
Net adjustment			
(GMFH − CDX) 2 − 2 = 0			
+ (GMPE − CDX) + 1 − 2 = −1			
+ (GMCS − CDX) + x − y = N/A			
Net adjustment = −1			

The result was class 2 adjustment −1, which resulted in class 2, grade B = 15% upper extremity impairment.

Based on Table 15-11, Impairment Values Calculated From Upper Extremity Impairment (6th ed, p 420), this converted to a 9% whole person impairment.

Impairment: 9% whole person impairment per the Sixth Edition.

Comment on Carpal Instability

The section on carpal instability was totally revised in the Fifth Edition, including changes in methodology, criteria, and impairment values. The impairment was moderate according to both the Fourth and Fifth Editions; however, the value for moderate was now 16% upper extremity impairment compared with 12% upper extremity impairment in the Fourth Edition. Furthermore, provisions are made in "rare cases" for providing a rating of 2% of the joint value when the involved joint has normal motion, according to *Guides* Fifth Edition criteria, but the contralateral uninvolved joint has motion beyond normal. It was noted that this was 2% of the joint value, not 2% upper extremity impairment.

In the Fourth Edition, the criteria in Table 26 for mild instability are actually normal values. Milder forms of instability do not have fixed deformities that can be seen on standard roentgenograms. The instability in these cases can be detected by cineradiography and can be strongly suspected by physical examination. The Fourth Edition recognizes this, stating, "Certain patients may have wrist pain and loss of strength related to a dynamic or nondissociative carpal instability that cannot be measured by changes of angles on roentgenograms. The examiner should assess the severity of this type of instability and estimate the resulting upper extremity impairment as mild (6%), moderate (12%), or severe (18%)" (4th ed, p 61).

In the Fifth Edition, the criteria in Table 16-25 were revised, and the previous criteria for mild instability became abnormal values. The text continued to recognize that mild instability can occur without fixed deformity being seen on static roentgenograms. Between the publication of the Fourth and Fifth Editions, advances in imaging and in arthroscopy have occurred. Thus, the Fifth Edition states, "A mild carpal instability exists also when a ligament tear has been diagnosed by arthrogram, arthroscopy, or MRI, even though the static roentgenographic findings may be normal. Certain individuals may have wrist pain and loss of strength related to a dynamic or nondissociative carpal instability that cannot be measured by changes of angles on static roentgenograms" (5th ed, p 502).

An interesting aside is that, if the grip strength section were used in our example, we would have a similar impairment rating in the Fourth Edition and a lower rating than that obtained from the Fifth Edition. With 50 kg of grip strength on the normal, right side, if grip strength on the injured left side fell anywhere between 35 kg and 45 kg, the percent strength loss index described in the Fourth Edition (Table 34, p 65) or Fifth Edition (Table 16-34, p 509) would be between 10% and 30%. Accordingly, this would yield a 10% upper extremity impairment rating. Strength loss ratings cannot be combined with ratings for carpal instability.

In the Sixth Edition, most ratings are performed on the basis of diagnosis-based impairments, and therefore Table 15-3 (6th ed, p 396) is applicable using the diagnosis of wrist sprain/h/o dislocation including carpal instability. The classification of instability is based on the same radiographic criteria described in the Sixth Edition. Strength loss is not used as a determinate of impairment nor as an adjustment factor. The impairment from the diagnosis-based impairment may not be combined with range of motion.

SUMMARY

Diagnosis	Carpal instability
Fourth Edition References	Section 3.1m (4th ed, pp 58-65), Table 26 (4th ed, p 61)
Fourth Edition Summary	History, upper extremity evaluation, radiographs of wrist. First, carpal instability patterns are classified as mild, moderate, or severe, according to severity of radiographic findings. Second, only one category of severity of carpal instability impairment should be selected. Third, to avoid duplicate impairment ratings, these radiographic criteria are used only when all other wrist factors are normal, except after carpal bone resection or implant arthroplasty.
Fourth Edition Impairment	12% upper extremity impairment, 7% whole person impairment
Fifth Edition References	Section 16.7 (5th ed, pp 498-507), Table 16-25 (5th ed, p 503)
Fifth Edition Summary	History, upper extremity evaluation, radiographs of wrist. First, carpal instability patterns are classified as mild, moderate, or severe, according to severity of radiographic findings. Second, only one category of severity of carpal instability impairment should be selected. Third, these radiographic criteria may be combined only with limited wrist motion. Pain and decreased strength are not rated separately.
Fifth Edition Impairment	17% upper extremity impairment, 10% whole person impairment
Sixth Edition References	Section 15.2 (6th ed, pp 387-405); Section 15.3a, (6th ed, p 406); Section 15.3b (6th ed, p 407), Table 15-3 (6th ed, p 396), Table 15-7 (6th ed, p 406), Table 15-8 (6th ed, p 408), Table 15-11 (6th ed, p 420)

Sixth Edition Summary	History, upper extremity evaluation, radiographs of wrist. First, carpal instability patterns are classified as mild, moderate, or severe, according to severity of radiographic findings. Second, only one category of severity of carpal instability impairment should be selected. Third, these radiographic criteria may be combined only with limited wrist motion. Pain and decreased strength are not rated separately.
Sixth Edition Impairment	15% upper extremity impairment, 9% whole person impairment

CASE 15-14

Nerve Injury

Subject: Mr Richmond, a 30-year-old man.

History: Mr Richmond was a forest ranger who, while hiking through his work territory, fell on some slippery rocks. His left elbow hit rocks that were covered with wild animal excrement, and he sustained a "nasty laceration" on the medial side of the elbow. Medical care was delayed, because Mr Richmond had to hike out of the wilderness to reach medical care.

When evaluated 20 hours after injury, Mr Richmond had a 6-inch-long laceration on the medial aspect of his elbow. The laceration, which was contaminated with foreign material, was explored in the operating room. The ulnar nerve was exposed, but there was no visible damage to it. Mr Richmond was treated in the early phase of his hospitalization with a first-generation cephalosporin antibiotic.

Mr Richmond developed a wound infection with culture documentation of both *Pseudomonas* and anaerobes. He underwent two more operative debridements, followed ultimately by a delayed primary closure of the wound. During the phase of active infection, he began to manifest symptoms of ulnar nerve dysfunction. His ulnar nerve function decreased progressively over the first 3 weeks. When seen 1 year later, Mr Richmond was back at work as a forest ranger.

He was evaluated for permanent impairment 2 years post injury. One month prior, Mr Richmond had seen his family physician, who felt that he had the typical physical findings of total lack of function in the ulnar nerve from a lesion at or about the elbow. Despite considerable difficulty with the limb, Mr Richmond refused further surgical intervention on the elbow and preferred to live with it "as is."

Current Symptoms: Mr Richmond complained of pain and numbness involving the medial side of the left forearm and radiating into the left little finger and the ulnar half of the ring finger. He also complained that the hand was weak and clumsy.

The pain he described was a burning dysesthesia sensation that made it hard to use the arm for activity. Because he was stoic, he did use the arm for most activity despite his symptoms. He did not use the arm for repetitious, heavy work. This was primarily because of pain but also, to a degree, because of weakness.

Functional Assessment: The *Quick*DASH score was 42.

Physical Examination: Healed 6-inch scar on the medial aspect of the left elbow. The fingers, thumb, wrist, elbow, and shoulder all had normal range of motion, although the hand spontaneously postured in a clawed finger position. There was atrophy in the hypothenar eminence as well as in the interosseous muscles (visible on the dorsum of the hand between the metacarpals). There was also skin atrophy involving the little finger with a decreased fingerprint pattern. When Mr Richmond physically exerted himself and perspired, there was no sweating of the little finger.

On sensory examination, Mr Richmond had normal 4-mm, two-point recognition ability on the thumb, index, middle, and radial half of the ring finger. Two-point recognition on the ulnar half of the ring finger and on the little finger was greater than 20 mm. He had absent sharp/dull discrimination on the ulnar half of the ring finger and entire little finger.

On manual muscle testing, there was no muscle function in the flexor carpi ulnaris, flexor digitorum profundus to the little finger, adductor pollicis, or the muscles of the hypothenar eminence.

Clinical Studies: Radiographs taken at the time of injury and 1 year later both demonstrated no fractures or bony pathology. There was no post-traumatic arthritis in the elbow. Electrodiagnostic studies had not been performed.

Discussion of Nerve Entrapment

Fourth Edition Rating

Peripheral nerve impairment was rated by means of Chapter 3, Section 3.1k, Impairment of the Upper Extremity Due to Peripheral Nerve Disorders (4th ed, p 46). The nerve that was injured was identified in Table 15, Maximum Upper Extremity Impairments Due to Unilateral Sensory or Motor Deficits or Combined Deficits of the Major Peripheral Nerves (4th ed, p 54). This table lists the maximum percentage of upper extremity impairment that could be assigned in the case where the peripheral nerve in question was totally destroyed and had no function.

If the nerve injury is partial, the maximum value for sensory deficit or pain (from Table 15) is multiplied by a severity multiplier from Table 11, Determining Impairment of the Upper Extremity Due to Pain or Sensory Deficits Resulting From Peripheral Nerve Disorders (4th ed, p 48).

Similarly, the maximum impairment due to motor deficit (Table 15) is multiplied by a severity multiplier found in Table 12, Determining Impairment of the Upper Extremity Due to Loss of Power and Motor Deficits Resulting From Peripheral Nerve Disorders Based on Individual Muscle Rating (4th ed, p 49). The impairment due to sensory deficit or pain is then combined with the impairment due to motor deficit by means of the Combined Values Chart (4th ed, p 322).

Because no motor function and no sensory function were demonstrable in the ulnar nerve, the third column of Table 15, impairment "due to combined motor and sensory deficits," was utilized to derive a 50% upper extremity impairment rating. Alternatively, Table 16 could be consulted. A severe ulnar nerve entrapment at the elbow according to that table is a 50% upper extremity impairment.

Thus, the correct impairment rating was 50% impairment of the left upper extremity. According to Table 3, Relationship of Impairment of the Upper Extremity to Impairment of the Whole Person (4th ed, p 20), a 50% upper extremity impairment converted to 30% whole person impairment.

Impairment: 30% whole person impairment per the Fourth Edition.

Fifth Edition Rating

Section 16.5, Impairment of the Upper Extremities Due to Peripheral Nerve Disorders (5th ed, p 480) was used to define impairment. Mr Richmond could be considered as having an Entrapment/Compression Neuropathy (5th ed, p 491). He did have an "objectively verifiable diagnosis" on the basis of "positive clinical findings and loss of function" (5th ed, p 493). The nerve that was injured was identified in Table 16-15, Maximum Upper Extremity Impairment Due to Unilateral Sensory or Motor Deficits or to Combined 100% Deficits of the Major Peripheral Nerves (5th ed, p 492). This table lists the maximum percentage of upper extremity impairment that could be assigned in the case in which the peripheral nerve in question was totally destroyed and had no function.

If the nerve injury is partial, the maximum value for sensory deficit or pain (from Table 16-15) is multiplied by a severity multiplier from Table 16-10, Determining Impairment of the Upper Extremity Due to Sensory Deficits or

Pain Resulting From Peripheral Nerve Disorders (5th ed, p 482). Similarly, the maximum impairment due to motor deficit (Table 16-15) is multiplied by a severity multiplier found in Table 16-11, Determining Impairment of the Upper Extremity Due to Motor and Loss-of-Power Deficits Resulting From Peripheral Nerve Disorders Based on Individual Muscle Rating (5th ed, p 484). The impairment due to sensory deficit or pain is then combined with the impairment due to motor deficit by means of the Combined Values Chart (5th ed, p 604).

Mr Richmond had no function whatsoever in his ulnar nerve distal to the elbow. Table 16-15 indicates that the maximum percentage upper extremity impairment due to sensory deficit or pain for an ulnar nerve (above midforearm) is 7%. The maximum impairment due to motor deficit is 46%. By means of the Combined Values Chart (5th ed, p 604), these would combine to 50%. Thus, Table 16-15 lists the maximum impairment due to combined motor and sensory deficit of the ulnar nerve (above midforearm) as 50%.

Because no motor function and no sensory function were demonstrable in the ulnar nerve, the third column of Table 16-15, impairment "due to combined motor and sensory deficits," was utilized to derive a 50% upper extremity impairment rating.

According to Table 16-3, Conversion of Impairment of the Upper Extremity to Impairment of the Whole Person (5th ed, p 439), 50% upper extremity impairment converted to 30% whole person impairment.

Impairment: 30% whole person impairment per the Fifth Edition.

Sixth Edition Rating

Section 15.4e, Peripheral Nerve and Brachial Plexus Impairment (6th ed, p 429), was used. The beginning of this section explains that "impairment from traumatic injury to peripheral nerves is defined by the specific nerves involved, and the associated severity of sensory and motor deficits. This section is *not* used for nerve entrapments since nerve entrapments are not isolated traumatic events; nerve entrapments are rated in Section 15.4f" (6th ed, p 429).

According to Table 15-21, Peripheral Nerve Impairment: Upper Extremity Impairments (6th ed, p 443), for involvement of the ulnar nerve above the midforearm for "very severe sensory deficit" there is class 1 impairment with a default of 6% upper extremity impairment and for "very severe motor deficit" there is class 3 impairment with a default of 40% upper extremity impairment.

According to Section 15.3a, Adjustment Grid: Functional History (6th ed, p 406), and Table 15-7, Functional History Adjustment: Upper Extremities (6th ed, p 406), the patient was assigned grade modifier 2; he did not require assistance to perform self-care activities, and his *Quick*DASH score was in the range of 41 to 60. No applicable clinical studies (ie, electrodiagnostic studies) were available to serve as a basis for adjustment.

Based on functional history grade modifier 2, the patient's class 1, very severe sensory deficit was increased by one position to the right from default value C of 6% upper extremity impairment to grade D, 7% upper extremity impairment (GMFH value 2 – CDX value 1 = net adjustment value 1), and his class 3, very severe motor deficit was decreased by one position (GMFH value 2 – CDX value 1 to the left from default value C of 40% upper extremity impairment to grade B, 36% upper extremity impairment. The sensory 7% upper extremity impairment and the motor 36% upper extremity impairment were combined using Appendix A, Combined Values Chart (6th ed, p 604), resulting in a 40% upper extremity impairment.

According to Table 15-11, Impairment Values Calculated From Upper Extremity Impairment (6th ed, p 420), this converted to 24% whole person impairment.

Impairment: 24% whole person impairment per the Sixth Edition.

Comment on Nerve Entrapment

The impairment was the result of specific, isolated traumatic injury; it was not reflective of the typical compression neuropathy, such as a cubital tunnel syndrome. It is very unusual to see total loss of peripheral nerve function. If Mr Richmond had lesser degrees of ulnar nerve injury, his impairment rating would be less. For example, he might still have had burning dysesthesia that made it hard to use the arm for most activity. On physical examination, two-point discrimination might have been 12 mm on the little finger and ulnar half of the ring finger. On manual muscle testing, he may have had the ability to move the involved joints completely through a range of motion against gravity but basically with no additional strength ("barely antigravity"). This weakness would still be in the muscles served by the ulnar nerve distal to the elbow.

In this circumstance, if rated by the Fourth or Fifth Editions, Mr Richmond's maximum impairments due to sensory deficits or pain and due to motor deficit (4th ed, Table 11, p 54; 5th ed, Table 16-15, p 492) would be graded by the multipliers of sensory deficit or pain (4th ed, Table 11, p 48; 5th ed,

Table 16-10, p 482) and for muscle rating (4th ed, Table 12, p 49; 5th ed, Table 16-11, p 484). For sensory deficits, the multiplication would yield the following percentages:

Severity Multiplier	Upper Extremity Impairment Percentage
1%-25%	0.07%-1.75%
26%-60%	1.82%-4.2%
61%-80%	4.3%-5.6%
81%-100%	5.7%-7.0%

If, on the basis of this example, we placed Mr Richmond's pain and sensory deficit in grade 4, we could assign an impairment percentage between 4.3% and 5.6%. For this alternative scenario, we will choose 5% upper extremity impairment.

Using the severity multipliers to multiply by the maximum value of 46% would yield a table somewhat similar to the table we described for sensory deficit.

Severity Multiplier	Upper Extremity Impairment Due to Motor Deficit
1%-25%	0.5%-11.5%
26%-50%	12%-23%
51%-75%	23.5%-34.5%
76%-99%	35%-45.5%
100%	46%

In this example, because motor function was antigravity but with no added resistance, we would use a multiplier from grade 3. If we chose a 50% severity multiplier, this would yield an upper extremity impairment of 23%.

Thus, in this example, if we combine the 5% deficit due to loss of sensation and pain with a 23% impairment due to motor deficit, this would yield a 27% impairment of the upper extremity.

In the Sixth Edition, it is not necessary to multiply a sensory or motor deficit against the maximum value assigned; rather the ranges are incorporated in Table 15-21, Peripheral Nerve Impairment: Upper Extremity Impairments (6th ed, pp 436-444). Deficits are graded using Table 15-14, Sensory and Motor Severity (6th ed, p 425). Defining severity is based on classifications of deficits from the Fourth and Fifth Editions as illustrated in the following table:

Sixth Edition Severity	Sixth Edition Deficit	Fifth Edition Sensory Grade	Fifth Edition Motor Grade	Fourth Edition Sensory Grade	Fourth Edition Motor Grade
0	Normal	5	5	1	5
1	Mild	4	4	2	4
2	Moderate	3	3	3	3
3	Severe	2	2	4	2
4	Very severe or complete loss	0-1	0-1	5	0-1

The following table illustrates the relationship between sensory impairment values in Table 15-21, Peripheral Nerve Impairment: Upper Extremity Impairments (6th ed, pp 436-444), and previously defined severity grades:

Severity Multiplier	Fourth and Fifth Editions Upper Extremity Impairment Percentage	Sixth Edition Severity	Sixth Edition Upper Extremity Impairment Values
0	0%	Normal	0
1%-25%	0.07%-1.75%	Mild	0 0 1 1 2
26%-60%	1.82%-4.2%	Moderate	2 2 3 4 4
61%-80%	4.3%-5.6%	Severe	4 5 5 5 6
81%-100%	5.7%-7.0%	Very severe	6 6 6 7 7

The following illustrates the relationship for motor deficits:

Severity Multiplier	Upper Extremity Impairment Due to Motor Deficit	Sixth Edition Severity	Sixth Edition Impairment Values
0%	0%	Normal	0
1%-25%	0.5%-11.5%	Mild	0 3 6 9 12
26%-50%	12%-23%	Moderate	14 15 17 20 23
51%-75%	23.5%-34.5%	Severe	26 26 29 32 35
76%-99%	35%-45.5%	Very severe	33 36 40 43 46

The values provided in Table 15-21 were based on prior approaches; however, adjustments to the defined ranges for each class were necessary. For example, a severe motor deficit is assigned to class 3, and that class can reflect only values of 26% to 49% upper extremity impairment by definition. Therefore, the values of 24% and 25% upper extremity impairment, which could be seen in prior editions, are not available.

SUMMARY

Diagnosis	Entrapment neuropathy, ulnar nerve at the elbow
Fourth Edition References	Section 3.1k (4th ed, pp 46-57), Table 11 (4th ed, p 48), Table 12 (4th ed, p 49), Table 15 (4th ed, p 54), Table 16 (4th ed, p 57)
Fourth Edition Summary	Severity of sensory loss and pain are documented. Severity of muscle weakness is documented. Physical examination showed evidence of serious ulnar nerve injury. Impairment could be rated by means of either Tables 11, 12, and 15 (preferred method) or, alternatively, Table 16.
Fourth Edition Impairment	50% upper extremity impairment, 30% whole person impairment
Fifth Edition References	Section 16.5d (5th ed, pp 491-495), Table 16-15 (5th ed, p 492), Table 16-10 (5th ed, p 482), Table 16-11 (5th ed, p 484), Table 16-3 (5th ed, p 439)
Fifth Edition Summary	Severity of sensory loss and pain are documented. Severity of muscle weakness is documented. Physical examination showed evidence of serious ulnar nerve injury. Impairment was rated by grading the sensory and motor losses and multiplying this by the maximum loss for the ulnar nerve.
Fifth Edition Impairment	50% upper extremity impairment, 30% whole person impairment
Sixth Edition References	Section 15.3a (6th ed, p 406); Section 15.4e (6th ed, p 429), Table 15-7 (6th ed, p 406), Table 15-21 (6th ed, p 443)

Sixth Edition Summary	Severity of sensory loss and pain are documented. Severity of muscle weakness is documented. Physical examination showed evidence of serious ulnar nerve injury. Impairment was rated by grading the sensory and motor deficits and identifying the associated impairment for the severity of the deficits of the ulnar nerve.
Sixth Edition Impairment	40% upper extremity impairment, 24% whole person impairment

CASE 15-15

Joint Instability

Subject: Mr Juarez, a 75-year-old man.

History: Mr Juarez was a car mechanic who injured his right middle finger in a car fan when his wrench fell, and he tried to catch it. He underwent surgery. The medical records confirmed that Mr Juarez had had a severe, crush type of laceration injury to the PIP joint of the right middle finger with loss of tissue.

Current Symptoms: At examination 16 months later, the patient stated that he still could not bend the finger as well as before the injury. He stated that the finger "wiggled in the first joint," but he did not wish any further surgery. He was able to perform all activities of daily living.

Functional Assessment: The *Quick*DASH score was 25.

Physical Examination: Well-healed scars of the right middle finger. The PIP joint flexed to 60° and extended to −10° (10° extension lag). Other than this flexion contracture, there was no fixed deformity. The joint had excessive passive mediolateral motion when compared to the other joints of the hand. There was ulnar deviation of 26° of ligamentous stress testing. The rest of the examination was normal. The diagnosis was "history of crush laceration injury to the right middle finger with residual loss of range of motion and excessive mediolateral motion of the PIP joint."

Clinical Studies: None available for review.

Discussion of Joint Instability of the PIP Joint

Fourth Edition Rating

The permanent impairment was determined through the use of Section 3.1g, Fingers (4th ed, pp 30-34), and Section 3.1m, Impairment Due to Other Disorders of the Upper Extremity (4th ed, pp 58-65), of Chapter 3.

The range of motion loss of the finger PIP joint was calculated by means of Figure 21, Finger Impairments Due to Abnormal Motion at PIP Joint (4th ed, p 33). Flexion of 60° equaled a 24% digit impairment, and extension of −10° (10° extension lag) equaled a 3% digit impairment. Because these impairments were in the same joint, they were added to give a 27% digit impairment due to loss of range of motion.

Under Section 3.1m, Impairment Due to Other Disorders of the Upper Extremity, the Joint Instability section on page 60 was used to determine an impairment due to joint instability. This case example shows the PIP joint of the right middle finger to have "passive ulnar deviation of 26°." According to Table 24, Impairment From Joint Mediolateral Instability (4th ed, p 60), this falls under the severe category, that is, greater than 20°, giving a 60% joint impairment. The relative value of the PIP joint in relation to the middle finger is given in Table 18, Impairment Values for Digits, Hand, Upper Extremity, and the Whole Person for Disorders of Specific Joints (4th ed, p 58), and it was found to be 80%. The value of the joint (80%) was then multiplied by the impairment to that joint on the basis of the clinical examination (60%) to give a 48% digit impairment due to the joint instability.

The Joint Instability section states that "if other impairments of the same joint are present they are combined . . ." (4th ed, p 60). Thus, in this case, it would not be a duplication to give an impairment for both the loss of range of motion and the joint instability. By means of the Combined Values Chart on page 322, the 48% digit impairment due to the joint instability was combined with the 27% digit impairment due to loss of range of motion to give a 62% total digit impairment. The 62% middle finger digit impairment converted to a 12% hand impairment on the basis of Table 1, Relationship of Impairment of the Digits to Impairment of the Hand (4th ed, p 18). The 12% hand impairment converted to an 11% upper extremity impairment on the basis of Table 2, Relationship of Impairment of the Hand to Impairment of the Upper Extremity (4th ed, p 19). The 11% upper extremity impairment converted to a 7% whole person impairment on the basis of Table 3, Relationship of Impairment of the Upper Extremity to Impairment of the Whole Person (4th ed, p 20). This rating process is summarized in the Upper Extremity Evaluation Record, as shown here on page 302.

Impairment: 7% whole person impairment per the Fourth Edition.

Fifth Edition Rating

The permanent impairment was determined through the use of Section 16.4e, Finger Motion Impairment (5th ed, p 461), and Section 16.7a, Bone and Joint Deformities (5th ed, p 499).

Range of motion loss of the finger PIP joint was calculated by means of Figure 16-23, Finger Impairments Due to Abnormal Motion at PIP Joint

(5th ed, p 463). Flexion of 60° equaled a 24% digit impairment, and an extension lag of 10° equaled a 3% digit impairment. Because these impairments were in the same joint, they were added to give a 27% digit impairment due to loss of range of motion.

Under Section 16.7a, Bone and Joint Deformities (5th ed, p 499), the subsection Joint Passive Mediolateral Instability on pages 501 to 502 was used to determine an impairment due to joint instability. This case example shows the PIP joint of the right middle finger to have "passive ulnar deviation of 26°." According to Table 16-23, Joint Impairment Due to Excessive Passive Mediolateral Instability (5th ed, p 502), this falls under the severe category, that is, >20°, giving a 60% joint impairment. The relative value of the PIP joint in relation to the middle finger per Table 16-18, Maximum Impairment Values for the Digits, Hand, Wrist, Elbow, and Shoulder Due to Disorders of Specific Joints or Units (5th ed, p 499), was 30%. The value of the joint (30%) was then multiplied by the impairment to that joint, based on the clinical examination (60%) to give an 18% digit impairment due to the joint instability.

The Fifth Edition advises, "If the same joint presents other findings, the rules outlined on page 499 must be followed to avoid duplication of impairment" (5th ed, p 501). The instructions on page 499 state:

> Limited motion impairment is rated according to Section 16.4 and can be appropriately combined with impairments due to "other disorders" listed in this section, except with those due to joint swelling from synovial hypertrophy, persistent joint subluxation or dislocation, and musculotendinous disorders (Section 16.7c). Joint instability impairment values can be combined with other appropriate impairment values, including decreased motion, but not with arthroplasty.

Thus, it would not be a duplication to give an impairment for both the loss of range of motion and the joint instability. By means of the Combined Values Chart (5th ed, p 604), the 18% digit impairment due to the joint instability was combined with the 27% digit impairment due to loss of range of motion to give a 40% total digit impairment. The 40% middle finger digit impairment converted to an 8% hand impairment per Table 16-1, Conversion of Impairment of the Digits to Impairment of the Hand (5th ed, p 438); this converted to 7% upper extremity impairment per Table 16-2, Conversion of Impairment of the Hand to Impairment of the Upper Extremity (5th ed, p 439), and to a 4% whole person impairment per Table 16-3, Conversion of Impairment of the Upper Extremity to Impairment of the Whole Person (5th ed, p 439). This rating process is summarized in the Upper Extremity Impairment Evaluation Record, as shown here on page 303.

Impairment: 4% whole person impairment per the Fifth Edition.

Sixth Edition Rating

The *Guides* approach to the evaluation of impairment due to digit instability is based on Section 15.2, Diagnosis-Based Impairment (6th ed, p 387).

In Table 15-2, Digit Regional Grid (6th ed, p 393), for the diagnosis of joint dislocation or sprain with specific reference to a finger PIP joint with >20° instability, there is a class 2 impairment with a default impairment of 25% of the digit. The table notes with an asterisk that, "if motion loss is present, this impairment may alternatively be assessed using Section 15.7, Range of Motion Impairment. A range of motion impairment stands alone and is not combined with diagnosis impairment" (6th ed, p 394).

According to Section 15.7d, Finger Motion (6th ed, p 468), and Table 15-31, Finger Range of Motion (6th ed, p 470), PIP flexion of 60° equals a 21% digit impairment, and extension lag of 10° equals a 3% digit impairment. (Note that in the first printing of the Sixth Edition there was a typographical error; for PIP extension, a mild severity is −10° = 3% digit impairment, and a moderate severity is −20° to −50° lag = 14% digit impairment.) These were added, resulting in a 24% digit impairment; this value was less than that obtained from the diagnosis-based impairment. Per Table 15-35, Range of Motion Grade Modifiers (6th ed, p 477), a 20% to 39% digit impairment is grade modifier 2.

In Section 15.3a, Adjustment Grid: Functional History (6th ed, pp 406-407), and Table 15-7, Functional History Adjustment: Upper Extremities (6th ed, pp 406-407), the patient was assigned grade modifier 1 based both on his reported symptoms and his *Quick*DASH score, which was in the range of 21 to 40.

The physical examination findings of instability cannot be used for adjustment; however, the separate findings of motion can be used. These were consistent with grade modifier 2.

No clinical studies were applicable for grade modification.

In summary, the adjustments were functional history grade modifier 1 and physical examination 2. Clinical studies were not applicable. The net adjustment compared to diagnosis class 2, grade B, 23% digit impairment.

Class 2—Default for Diagnosis = 25% digit impairment			
CDX	GMFH	GMPE	GMCS
2	1	2	N/A
Net adjustment (GMFH − CDX) 1 − 2 = −1 + (GMPE − CDX) + 2 − 2 = 0 + (GMCS − CDX) + n/a Net adjustment = −1			

Result is class 2 adjustment −1, which results in class 2, grade B = 23% digit impairment.

Based on Table 15-12, Impairment Values Calculated From Digit Impairment (6th ed, p 421), 23% digit impairment for the middle finger resulted in 4% hand, 4% upper extremity, and 2% whole person impairment.

Impairment: 2% whole person impairment per the Sixth Edition.

Comment on Joint Instability of the PIP Joint

This case illustrates the necessary steps to determine an impairment as a result of a joint instability. It also illustrates significant differences with the Sixth Edition.

With the Fourth and Fifth Editions, it is important to look at each part of the Impairment Due to Other Disorders of the Upper Extremity section (4th ed, Section 3.1m; 5th ed, Section 16.7) to determine what deformities may be combined with other types of impairment and what deformities may not be combined with other types of impairment. This case demonstrates a common technique in which a physician has to use one type of table to determine the degree of an impairment to a specific area on the basis of clinical judgment, the findings and measurements from the physical examination, and pertinent diagnostic studies. After this first type of table is used, the final impairment to that area is found by multiplying by the value of the area or region from another table.

In the Sixth Edition, impairment is based on the diagnosis-based impairment or range of motion but not on both.

SUMMARY

Diagnosis	Joint instability of the PIP joint of the middle finger. Range of motion loss in the same joint
Fourth Edition References	Section 3.1g (4th ed, p 30); Section 3.1m (4th ed, p 58), Table 1 (4th ed, p 18), Table 2 (4th ed, p 19), Table 3 (4th ed, p 20), Table 18 (4th ed, p 58), Table 24 (4th ed, p 60), Figure 20 (4th ed, p 33), Figure 21 (4th ed, p 33)
Fourth Edition Summary	History, range of motion measurements of the PIP joint. Clinical degree of joint instability is assessed. Range of motion loss of the PIP joint is calculated, and impairment is determined. Joint instability is rated, and impairment is determined. Instability due to motion deficits and instability are combined.
Fourth Edition Impairment	11% upper extremity impairment, 7% whole person impairment
Fifth Edition References	Section 16.4e (5th ed, p 461); Section 16.7a (5th ed, p 499), Table 16-1 (5th ed, p 438), Table 16-2 (5th ed, p 439), Table 16-3 (5th ed, p 439), Table 16-23 (5th ed, p 502), Table 16-18 (5th ed, p 499), Figure 16-23 (5th ed, p 463)
Fifth Edition Summary	History, range of motion measurements of the PIP joint. Assess clinical degree of joint instability. Calculate range of motion loss of the PIP joint and determine impairment. Rate joint instability and determine impairment. Combine instability due to motion deficits and instability.
Fifth Edition Impairment	7% upper extremity impairment, 4% whole person impairment
Sixth Edition References	Section 15.2 (6th ed, p 387); Section 15.3a (6th ed, p 406); Section 15.7d (6th ed, p 468), Table 15-2 (6th ed, p 393), Table 15-7 (6th ed, p 406), Table 15-12 (6th ed, p 421), Table 15-31 (6th ed, p 470), Table 15-35 (6th ed, p 477)

Sixth Edition Summary	History, range of motion measurements of the PIP joint. Assess clinical degree of joint instability. Calculate diagnosis-based impairment and range of motion loss of the PIP joint, noting both cannot be rated. Adjust diagnosis-based impairment based on nonkey factors.
Sixth Edition Impairment	4% upper extremity impairment, 2% whole person impairment

Upper Extremity Impairment Evaluation Record–**Part 1 (Hand)** Side ☑R ☐L

Name MR. JUAREZ Age 75 Sex ☑M ☐F Dominant hand ☑R ☐L Date

Occupation Diagnosis Joint Instability CASE 15-15

			Abnormal motion: Record motion, ankylosis, and impairment %				Amputation: Mark level & impairment %	Sensory loss: Mark type, level, & impairment %	Other disorders: List type & impairment %	Hand impairment%: • Combine digit IMP% *Convert to hand IMP%	
			Flexion	Extension	Ankylosis	IMP%					
Thumb	IP	Angle°									
		IMP%									
	MP	Angle°									
		IMP%									
				Motion	Ankylosis	IMP%	R L	R L			
	CMC	Radial abduction	Angle°							Abnormal motion [1]	
			IMP%							Amputation [2]	
		Adduction	CMS							Sensory loss [3]	
			IMP%							Other disorders [4]	
		Opposition	CMS							Digit impairment % • Combine 1, 2, 3, 4	
			IMP%								
Add impairment % CMC + MP + IP =						[1]	IMP % = [2]	IMP % = [3]	IMP % = [4]	Hand impairment % *Convert above	
			Flexion	Extension	Ankylosis	IMP%					
Index	DIP	Angle°								Abnormal motion [1]	
		IMP%								Amputation [2]	
	PIP	Angle°								Sensory loss [3]	
		IMP%								Other disorders [4]	
	MP	Angle°								Digit impairment % • Combine 1, 2, 3, 4	
		IMP%									
• Combine impairment % MP + PIP + DIP =						[1]	IMP % = [2]	IMP % = [3]	IMP % = [4]	Hand impairment % *Convert above	
Middle	DIP	Angle°							Table 24 Instability Severe 60% × Table 18 80%	Abnormal motion [1]	27
		IMP%								Amputation [2]	—
	PIP	Angle°	60	-10		27				Sensory loss [3]	—
		IMP%	24	3						Other disorders [4]	48
	MP	Angle°								Digit impairment % • Combine 1, 2, 3, 4	62
		IMP%									
• Combine impairment % MP + PIP + DIP = 27						[1]	IMP % = [2]	IMP % = [3]	IMP % = 48 [4]	Hand impairment % *Convert above	12
Ring	DIP	Angle°								Abnormal motion [1]	
		IMP%								Amputation [2]	
	PIP	Angle°								Sensory loss [3]	
		IMP%								Other disorders [4]	
	MP	Angle°								Digit impairment % • Combine 1, 2, 3, 4	
		IMP%									
• Combine impairment % MP + PIP + DIP =						[1]	IMP % = [2]	IMP % = [3]	IMP % = [4]	Hand impairment % *Convert above	
Little	DIP	Angle°								Abnormal motion [1]	
		IMP%								Amputation [2]	
	PIP	Angle°								Sensory loss [3]	
		IMP%								Other disorders [4]	
	MP	Angle°								Digit impairment % • Combine 1, 2, 3, 4	
		IMP%									
• Combine impairment % MP + PIP + DIP =						[1]	IMP % = [2]	IMP % = [3]	IMP % = [4]	Hand impairment % *Convert above	

Total hand impairment (Add hand impairment % for thumb + index + middle + ring + little finger) = 12 %
Upper extremity impairment (†Convert total hand impairment % to upper extremity impairment %) = 11 %; enter on Part 2, Line II
If hand region impairment is only impairment, convert upper extremity impairment to whole-person impairment:‡ = 7 %

• Combined Values Chart; (p. 322-324) *Use Table 1 (Digits to hand p. 18); †Use Table 2 (Hand to upper extremity p. 19) ‡Use Table 3 (p. 20)

** Courtesy of G. de Groot Swanson, MD

Upper Extremity Impairment Evaluation Record–**Part 1 (Hand)** Side ☒R ☐L

Name *Mr. Juarez* Age *75* Sex ☒M ☐F Dominant hand ☒R ☐L Date

Occupation *Car Mechanic* Diagnosis *Joint Instability* *CASE 15-15*

				Abnormal Motion				Amputation	Sensory Loss	Other Disorders	Hand Impairment%	
				Record motion or ankylosis angles and digit impairment %				Mark level & impairment %	Mark type, level, & impairment %	List type & impairment %	•Combine digit imp % *Convert to hand imp %	
				Flexion	Extension	Ankylosis	Imp %					
Thumb	IP	Angle°										
		Imp %										
	MP	Angle°										
		Imp %						[2]				
					Motion	Ankylosis	Imp %					
	CMC	Radial abduction	Angle°								Abnormal motion [1]	
			Imp %								Amputation [2]	
		Adduction	Cm								Sensory loss [3]	
			Imp %								Other disorders [4]	
		Opposition	Cm					‡UE			Total digit imp % •Combine 1, 2, 3, 4	
			Imp %					IMP % = [5]				
Add digit impairment % CMC + MP + IP =							[1]	Digit IMP % = [2]	Digit IMP % = [3]	Digit IMP % = [4]	Hand impairment % *Convert above	
				Flexion	Extension	Ankylosis	Imp %					
Index	DIP	Angle°									Abnormal motion [1]	
		Imp %									Amputation [2]	
	PIP	Angle°									Sensory loss [3]	
		Imp %									Other disorders [4]	
	MP	Angle°									Total digit imp % •Combine 1, 2, 3, 4	
		Imp %										
•Combine digit impairment % MP, PIP, DIP =							[1]	Digit IMP % = [2]	Digit IMP % = [3]	Digit IMP % = [4]	Hand impairment % *Convert above	
Middle	DIP	Angle°								*Table 16-23*	Abnormal motion [1]	*27*
		Imp %									Amputation [2]	*–*
	PIP	Angle°		*60*	*-10*		*27*			*Saved 60 %*	Sensory loss [3]	*–*
		Imp %		*24*	*3*						Other disorders [4]	*18*
	MP	Angle°								*Table 16-18 30%*	Total digit imp % •Combine 1, 2, 3, 4	*40*
		Imp %										
•Combine digit impairment % MP, PIP, DIP = *27*							[1]	Digit IMP % = [2]	Digit IMP % = [3]	Digit IMP % = *18* [4]	Hand impairment % *Convert above	*8*
Ring	DIP	Angle°									Abnormal motion [1]	
		Imp %									Amputation [2]	
	PIP	Angle°									Sensory loss [3]	
		Imp %									Other disorders [4]	
	MP	Angle°									Total digit imp % •Combine 1, 2, 3, 4	
		Imp %										
•Combine digit impairment % MP, PIP, DIP =							[1]	Digit IMP % = [2]	Digit IMP % = [3]	Digit IMP % = [4]	Hand impairment % *Convert above	
Little	DIP	Angle°									Abnormal motion [1]	
		Imp %									Amputation [2]	
	PIP	Angle°									Sensory loss [3]	
		Imp %									Other disorders [4]	
	MP	Angle°									Total digit imp % •Combine 1, 2, 3, 4	
		Imp %										
•Combine digit impairment % MP, PIP, DIP =							[1]	Digit IMP % = [2]	Digit IMP % = [3]	Digit IMP % = [4]	Hand impairment % *Convert above	

Total hand impairment: Add hand impairment % for thumb + index + middle + ring + little finger =	*8*	%
Convert total hand impairment to upper extremity impairment† (if thumb metacarpal intact, enter on Part 2, line II) =	*7*	%
‡Add thumb ray upper extremity amputation imp [5] ____% + hand upper extremity imp ____% =		%
If hand region impairment is only impairment, convert upper extremity impairment to whole person impairment§ =	*4*	%

• Combined Values Chart (p. 604). *Use Table 16-1 (digits to hand). †Use Table 16-2 (hand to upper extremity). §Use Table 16-3.
Courtesy of G. de Groot Swanson, MD, Grand Rapids, Michigan.

CASE 15-16

Arthritic Shoulder

Subject: Mr Payne, a 57-year-old man.

History: Mr Payne fell while performing on in-line skates during an intermission at a music show. Although he was wearing head, knee, and elbow protection, he injured his left shoulder and required medical evaluation at the local university hospital. At the current examination, 14 months after injury, Mr Payne stated that his shoulder region had had "tremendous bruising and swelling" from the fall, which had been present when he was evaluated at the university hospital. Mr Payne stated that the physicians did not find any fractures, even though extensive diagnostic studies were performed, and he was in "terrible pain." He stated that he had been discharged from the emergency department with an arm sling, pain medication, and a prescription for physical therapy. He was asked to return for follow-up at an orthopedic clinic in a few days.

Mr Payne stated that he had gone to see a "bone doctor" whom his family physician recommended the next day, and that the new physician had told him he had sustained a "fracture of the shoulder bone." He was treated conservatively by his new physician with analgesics, arm sling, and physical therapy.

Current Symptoms: Mr Payne stated that he gradually improved without surgery, but he complained of aching and stiffness of the left shoulder, which improved after exercise and use of the shoulder. He also had "grinding and crackling" in the joint. He was able to perform all of his activities of daily living. At the time of evaluation, 14 months after the fall, Mr Payne was back touring with the music group and performing on skates. He did not wish to have any surgery or any further tests.

Functional Assessment: The *Quick*DASH score was 27.

Physical Examination: Normal right shoulder with full range of motion. The left shoulder did not have any swelling or tender areas. There was flexion of 150° and extension of 50°. There was abduction to 140°, and adduction to 30°. Internal rotation was 40° and external rotation was 70°. There was crepitation during active and passive range of motion.

Clinical Studies: The medical records reflected that there was a "possible hairline fracture of the humerus of the left shoulder" on magnetic resonance imaging, which had been performed during his evaluation at the university hospital. Radiographic studies performed approximately 4 months before the current examination showed significant changes "compatible with traumatic arthritis" of the glenohumeral joint of the left shoulder.

Discussion of Arthritic Shoulder

Fourth Edition Rating

The permanent impairment was determined using Section 3.1j, Shoulder (4th ed, p 41), and Section 3.1m, Impairment Due to Other Disorders of the Upper Extremity (4th ed, p 58).

Because there was a range of motion loss of the shoulder, this was first calculated by means of Section 3.1j. After the range of motion measurements for the shoulder were found, as demonstrated in the *Guides,* Figure 36, Shoulder Extension and Flexion (4th ed, p 42); Figure 39, Shoulder Abduction and Adduction (4th ed, p 43); and Figure 42, Shoulder External Rotation and Internal Rotation (4th ed, p 44), the upper extremity impairment was calculated by means of the pie charts for the shoulder motions. According to the pie chart in Figure 38, Upper Extremity Impairments Due to Lack of Flexion and Extension of Shoulder (4th ed, p 43), the flexion of 150° equaled a 2% upper extremity impairment, and extension of 50° equaled 0%. Figure 41, Upper Extremity Impairments Due to Lack of Abduction and Adduction of Shoulder (4th ed, p 44), was used in a similar manner for abduction and adduction. Abduction of 140° gave a 2% impairment, and adduction of 30° gave a 1% impairment. On the basis of Figure 44, Upper Extremity Impairments Due to Lack of Internal and External Rotation of Shoulder (4th ed, p 45), the internal rotation of 40° gave a 3% impairment, and the external rotation of 70° gave a 0% impairment. Because these impairments were in the same joint, they were added to give an 8% upper extremity impairment due to loss of range of motion.

Section 3.1m, Impairment Due to Other Disorders of the Upper Extremity, Joint Crepitation With Motion, part of Bone and Joint Deformities (4th ed, p 58), was used to determine an impairment due to joint crepitation. This case showed crepitation with active and passive motion. On the basis of Table 19, Impairment From Joint Crepitation (4th ed, p 59), this fell under the severe category, giving a 30% joint impairment. The value of the glenohumeral joint in relation to the upper extremity is given in Table 18,

Impairment Values for Digits, Hand, Upper Extremity, and the Whole Person for Disorders of Specific Joints (4th ed, p 58), and it was found to be 60%. The value of the joint (60%) was then multiplied by the impairment to that joint based on the clinical examination (30%) to give an 18% upper extremity impairment.

Because it would be a duplication to give an impairment for both the loss of range of motion and the crepitation, the highest impairment value, the 18% upper extremity impairment due to the crepitation, was used. This converted to an 11% whole person impairment on the basis of Table 3, Relationship of Impairment of the Upper Extremity to Impairment of the Whole Person (4th ed, p 20).

Impairment: 11% whole person impairment per the Fourth Edition.

Fifth Edition Rating

The permanent impairment was determined by means of Section 16.4i, Shoulder Motion Impairment (5th ed, p 474). After range of motion measurements for the shoulder were determined, as demonstrated in the *Guides* in Figure 16-38, Shoulder Flexion and Extension (5th ed, p 475); Figure 16-41, Shoulder Abduction and Adduction (5th ed, p 477); and Figure 16-44, Shoulder External Rotation and Internal Rotation (5th ed, p 478), the upper extremity impairment was calculated by means of the pie charts for the shoulder motions. According to Figure 16-40, Pie Chart of Upper Extremity Motion Impairments Due to Lack of Flexion and Extension of Shoulder (5th ed, p 476), the flexion of 150° equaled a 2% upper extremity impairment, and extension of 50° equaled 0%. Figure 16-43, Pie Chart of Upper Extremity Motion Impairments Due to Lack of Abduction and Adduction of Shoulder (5th ed, p 477), was used in a similar manner for abduction and adduction. Abduction of 140° gave a 2% impairment, and adduction of 30° gave a 1% impairment. On the basis of Figure 16-46, Pie Chart of Upper Extremity Impairments Due to Lack of Internal and External Rotation of Shoulder (5th ed, p 479), the internal rotation of 40° gave a 3% impairment, and the external rotation of 70° gave a 0% impairment. Because these impairments were in the same joint, they were added to give an 8% upper extremity impairment due to loss of range of motion. This converted to a 5% whole person impairment on the basis of Table 16-3, Conversion of Impairment of the Upper Extremity to Impairment of the Whole Person (5th ed, p 439).

Impairment: 5% whole person impairment per the Fifth Edition.

Sixth Edition Rating

In Table 15-5, Shoulder Regional Grid (6th ed, p 405), for the diagnosis of posttraumatic degenerative joint disease with documented specific injury, mild asymmetric arthritic changes noted on imaging, there is a class 1 impairment with a default impairment of 5% upper extremity impairment. The table notes with an asterisk that "if motion loss is present, this impairment may alternatively be assessed using Section 15.7, Range of Motion Impairment. A range of motion impairment stands alone and is not combined with diagnosis impairment" (6th ed, p 405).

According to Section 15.7g, Shoulder Motion (6th ed, p 472), and Table 15-34, Shoulder Range of Motion (6th ed, p 475), flexion of 150° equaled a 3% upper extremity impairment, extension of 50° equaled no impairment, abduction to 140° equaled a 3% upper extremity impairment, adduction to 30° equaled a 1% upper extremity impairment, internal rotation of 40° equaled a 4% upper extremity impairment, and external rotation of 70° equaled no ratable impairment. These were added, resulting in an 11% upper extremity impairment.

Per Table 15-35, Range of Motion Grade Modifiers (6th ed, p 477), this was consistent with grade modifier 1.

In Section 15.3a, Adjustment Grid: Functional History (6th ed, p 406), and Table 15-7, Functional History Adjustment: Upper Extremities (6th ed, p 406), the patient was assigned grade modifier 1, based both on his reported symptoms and his *Quick*DASH score, which was in the range of 21 to 40.

The range of motion impairment was greater than the diagnosis-based impairment; therefore, range of motion was used to define the impairment. No further adjustment to the motion impairment was required because the functional history was also grade modifier 1.

Based on Table 15-11, Impairment Values Calculated From Upper Extremity Impairment (6th ed, p 420), 11% upper extremity impairment converted to 7% whole person impairment.

Impairment: 7% whole person impairment per the Sixth Edition.

Comment on Arthritic Shoulder

The Sixth Edition approach to the evaluation of impairment due to posttraumatic degenerative joint disease is based on Section 15.2, Diagnosis-Based Impairment (6th ed, pp 387-405); however, when range of motion results in greater impairment, it is used as an alternative.

Crepitation was referenced in the Fourth Edition but was not used in subsequent editions. In all editions it is important to differentiate what can and cannot be combined. If this case were rated by the Fourth Edition, it would be important to avoid duplicating the rating by combining both the impairment for motion deficits and the impairment for crepitation.

SUMMARY

Diagnosis	Arthritis of the shoulder joint with range of motion loss in the same joint
Fourth Edition References	Section 3.1j (4th ed, p 41); Section 3.1m (4th ed, p 58), Table 3 (4th ed, p 20), Table 18 (4th ed, p 58), Table 19 (4th ed, p 59), Figure 38 (4th ed, p 43), Figure 41 (4th ed, p 44), Figure 44 (4th ed, p 45)
Fourth Edition Summary	History, range of motion measurements of the shoulder joint. Clinical degree of crepitation is assessed. Range of motion loss of the shoulder is calculated, and impairment is determined. Crepitation is rated, and impairment is determined. The more significant, final impairment in the same joint is determined.
Fourth Edition Impairment	18% upper extremity impairment, 11% whole person impairment
Fifth Edition References	Section 16.4i (5th ed, p 474), Figure 16-40 (5th ed, p 476), Figure 16-43 (5th ed, p 477), Figure 16-46 (5th ed, p 479)
Fifth Edition Summary	History, range of motion measurements of the shoulder joint. Range of motion loss of the shoulder is calculated, and impairment is determined.
Fifth Edition Impairment	8% upper extremity impairment, 5% whole person impairment
Sixth Edition References	Section 15.2 (6th ed, pp 387-405); Section 15.3a (6th ed, p 406); Section 15.7g (6th ed, pp 472-478), Table 15-5 (6th ed, p 405), Table 15-7 (6th ed, p 406), Table 15-11 (6th ed, p 420), Table 15-34 (6th ed, p 475), Table 15-35 (6th ed, p 477)

Sixth Edition Summary	History (including functional history and inventories), physical evaluation, and clinical studies. Diagnosis-based impairment and range of motion impairment are determined. The greater impairment is selected.
Sixth Edition Impairment	11% upper extremity impairment, 7% whole person impairment

CASE 15-17

Saw Injury to the Hand

Subject: Mr Joshua, a 25-year-old man.

History: Mr Joshua, a right-handed construction worker, approximately 18 months before being seen for a final evaluation, was injured when his left hand was cut by a table saw. He was taken to the local university hospital, where he underwent surgery to repair the injuries. The operative records showed that he had revision and closure of an amputation of the distal part of the left thumb. The index finger required repair of the radial digital nerve, open reduction and internal fixation of the proximal phalanx, and repair of the profundus and superficialis flexor tendons. The middle finger required repair of the radial digital nerve, open reduction and internal fixation of the proximal and distal phalanges, and repair of the profundus and superficialis tendons.

Current Symptoms: Although Mr Joshua returned to work, he complained of difficulty grasping objects due to loss of a great deal of function of the thumb because of the partial amputation. He also had stiffness, which varied as to time of day and the weather, in the joints of the index and middle fingers. He stated he was able to feel most objects fairly well but occasionally discovered that he had burned the index finger on the side next to the thumb after cooking or handling hot objects.

Functional Assessment: The *Quick*DASH score was 26. Mr Joshua's in-office examination findings and complaints were consistent with difficulties to the injured hand with grasping and lifting. Activities of daily living with self-care were done independently without limitations. Some sensory function deficits in the digits limited hand protective function slightly.

Physical Examination: Physical examination showed that the left thumb had been amputated just proximal to the IP joint. The index finger had a well-healed scar between the PIP and MP joints with two-point discrimination of 12 mm distal to the scar on the radial side. The two-point discrimination proximal to the scar on the radial side and on the entire ulnar side was 4 mm. Flexion of the DIP joint was 60°, and extension was −20° (20° extension lag). The PIP joint had flexion to 50° and extension to −20°. The MP joint flexed to 60° and extended to 0°.

The middle finger had well-healed scars with two-point discrimination of 4 mm on the ulnar side and on the radial side, except the two-point discrimination became 11 mm on the radial side distal to a scar just proximal to the DIP joint. The middle finger DIP joint flexed to 30° and extended to 0°. The PIP joint flexed to 40° and extended to −10°. The MP joint flexed to 70° and extended to 0°. The ring and little fingers did not have any abnormalities.

Medical evaluation confirmed the loss of function to the left hand due to the saw injury. The diagnoses were as follows:

1. Amputation of the distal part of the left thumb
2. Sensory loss of the radial digital nerve of the left index finger
3. Sensory loss of the radial digital nerve of the left middle finger
4. Status post open reduction and internal fixation proximal phalanx, left index finger
5. Status post repair of the profundus and superficialis flexor tendons, left index finger
6. Status post open reduction and internal fixation proximal and distal phalanx, left middle finger
7. Status post repair of the profundus and superficialis flexor tendons, left middle finger
8. Range of motion loss of the DIP, PIP, and MP joints of the left index finger
9. Range of motion loss of the DIP, PIP, and MP joints of the left middle finger

Clinical Studies: Radiographs confirmed that the left thumb had been amputated just proximal to the IP joint.

Discussion of Saw Injury to the Hand

Fourth Edition Rating

Impairment was based on Section 3.1, The Hand and Upper Extremity (4th ed, pp 15-74). The result of the injury in terms of the loss of function of the hand or upper extremity was measured to determine the final whole person impairment rating. Impairment rating was based on deficits due to amputation, loss of range of motion, nerve injuries, vascular disorders, musculotendinous disorders, and bone and joint disorders. Through the use of the measurements obtained by the physical examination, a series of calculations can be made by means of the tables and figures in Chapter 3 to determine the final whole person impairment.

The permanent impairment was determined through the use of Section 3.1f, Thumb (4th ed, pp 24-30), and Section 3.1g, Fingers (4th ed, pp 30-35). The impairment evaluation process is summarized in Figure 1, Upper Extremity Impairment Evaluation Record (4th ed, p 16). The use of this form is highly recommended for hand impairment cases. It should accompany the written report.

Thumb Impairment

The thumb impairment is calculated by means of Figure 7, Impairment of Thumb Due to Amputation at Various Levels (4th ed, p 24). On Figure 7, a line is drawn across the thumb, representing the level of amputation, to the line on the graph. The percentage of impairment of the thumb is obtained from the top scale of Figure 7. In this case, the amputation was proximal to the IP joint, with a value found in the top scale of 60% impairment of the thumb.

Index Finger Impairment

Impairment of the index finger was based on the combined impairments due to the digital nerve injury and motion deficits.

The index finger had a 12-mm, two-point discrimination on the radial side. This is a partial sensory loss, because the two-point discrimination was between 15 and 7 mm (4th ed, p 21). It is also a longitudinal (one digital nerve) loss, as opposed to a transverse (both digital nerves) loss. When a longitudinal loss is determined, a two-step process is performed. First, the relative value for the percentage of the nerve that has been damaged is determined on the basis of Figure 17, Finger Impairment Due to Amputation at Various Levels (4th ed, p 30), by means of the top scale. In this case, the nerve was damaged, with abnormal and decreased sensation starting at the scar on the radial side between the PIP and MP joints. By drawing a line from the finger figure of Figure 17 across to the line on the graph, then intersecting with the top scale, a value of 90% was found. This amputation impairment percentage equaled the percentage of digit length. Second, because the injury was to the index finger, Table 9, Longitudinal Sensory Loss Impairments of Index, Middle, and Ring Fingers (4th ed, p 31), was used. Ninety percent of the digit length with a partial loss of the radial digital nerve corresponds to 14% digit impairment.

The index finger also had loss of range of motion of the DIP, PIP, and MP joints. According to Figure 19, Finger Impairments Due to Abnormal

Motion at the DIP Joint (4th ed, p 32), the flexion of 60° gave a 5% digit impairment, and the extension of −20° gave a 4% digit impairment. These impairments were added, because they were in the same joint, to give a 9% digit impairment due to the loss of range of motion in the DIP joint. The range of motion impairment of the digit due to the loss of motion of the PIP joint was determined by means of Figure 21, Finger Impairments Due to Abnormal Motion at the PIP Joint (4th ed, p 33). The index PIP joint flexed to 50°, giving 30% digit impairment. The extension of the PIP joint of −20° degrees gave a 7% digit impairment. These impairments were added, because they were in the same joint, to give a 37% digit impairment. The range of motion impairment of the digit due to the loss of motion of the MP joint was determined by means of Figure 23, Finger Impairments Due to Abnormal Motion at the MP Joint (4th ed, p 34). The MP joint flexion of 60° gave a 17% digit impairment, and extension to 0° gave a 5% impairment. These impairments were added, because they were in the same joint, to give a 22% digit impairment. In the fingers, the impairment values to the digit from each separate joint were combined by means of the Combined Values Chart (4th ed, pp 322-324). The 37% digit impairment (the largest) due to the loss of range of motion in the PIP joint was combined with the 22% digit impairment (the second largest) due to the loss of range of motion in the MP joint, to give 51%. The 51% was combined with the 9% impairment due to the loss of range of motion of the DIP joint to give total digit impairment due to loss of range of motion of 55%.

Because the sensory loss impairment and the range of motion loss impairment were different types of impairments, these impairments were combined. The 55% digit impairment due to loss of range of motion was combined with the 14% digit impairment due to the sensory loss, to give a 61% total impairment to the index finger digit.

Middle Finger Impairment

Impairment of the middle finger was based on the combined impairments due to the digital nerve injury and motion deficits.

The middle finger had 11 mm of two-point discrimination on the radial side. This was similar to the index finger impairment in that it was a partial sensory loss, based on the discussion of sensory quality on page 21 of the Fourth Edition. It was also a longitudinal (one digital nerve) loss, as opposed to a transverse (both digital nerves) loss. As was done for the index finger, a two-step process was performed. First, the relative value for the percentage of the nerve that had been damaged was determined according to Figure 17, with the use of the top scale. In this case, the nerve was damaged, with abnormal and decreased sensation starting at the scar on the radial side just proximal to the DIP joint. By drawing a line from the finger figure of Figure 17 across to the graph and looking at the top scale, a value of 50% was found. Second, because the injury was to the middle finger, Table 9 was used. Table 9 shows that the 50% value for the relative digit length of the damaged nerve corresponds to an 8% digit impairment due to the radial digital nerve partial sensory loss.

Using the same process as for the index finger, according to Figure 19 (4th ed, p 32), for the middle finger the flexion of 30° gave a 21% digit impairment, and the extension of 0° gave a 0% digit impairment. These impairments were added, because they were in the same joint, to give 21% digit impairment due to the loss of range of motion in the DIP joint. The middle PIP joint flexed to 40°, giving a 36% digit impairment based on Figure 21 (4th ed, p 33). The extension of the PIP joint of −10° gave a 3% digit impairment. These impairments were added, because they were in the same joint, to give a 39% digit impairment. The range of motion impairment of the digit due to the loss of motion of the MP joint was determined by means of Figure 23 (4th ed, p 34). The MP joint flexion of 70° gave an 11% digit impairment, and extension to 0° gave a 5% impairment. These impairments were added, because they were in the same joint, to give a 16% digit impairment. In a similar manner as was done for the index finger, the impairments of the separate joints were combined by means of the Combined Values Chart. The 39% digit impairment (the largest) due to the loss of range of motion in the PIP joint was combined with the 21% digit impairment (the second largest) due to the loss of range of motion in the DIP joint, to give 52%. The 52% was combined with the 16% impairment due to the loss of range of motion of the MP joint to give total digit impairment due to loss of range of motion of 60%.

Because the sensory loss impairment and the range of motion loss impairment were different types of impairments, they were combined. The 60% digit impairment due to loss of range of motion was combined with the 8% digit impairment due to the sensory loss, to give a 63% total impairment to the middle finger digit.

Hand Impairment

Because two or more digits of the hand were involved, the final impairment was determined by the procedure outlined on page 35. According to Table 1, Relationship of Impairment of the Digits to Impairment of the Hand (4th ed, p 18), the 60% impairment of the thumb equaled a 24% hand impairment. The 61% index finger impairment equaled a 12% hand impairment, and the 63% middle finger impairment equaled a 13% hand impairment. These hand impairments were added to give a 49% total hand impairment.

Table 2, Relationship of Impairment of the Hand to Impairment of the Upper Extremity (4th ed, p 19), was used to convert the 49% hand impairment to a 44% upper extremity impairment. Table 3, Relationship of Impairment of the Upper Extremity to Impairment of the Whole Person (4th ed, p 20), was used to convert the 44% upper extremity impairment to a 26% whole person impairment. There is no deduction in Chapter 3 for an injury to the "nonpreferred" hand.

Impairment: 26% whole person impairment per the Fourth Edition.

Fifth Edition Rating

Impairment was based on Chapter 16, The Upper Extremities (5th ed, pp 433-521). Impairment is based on deficits due to amputations, loss of range of motion, nerve injuries, vascular disorders, musculotendinous disorders, bone and joint disorders, arthroplasty, and/or strength loss, as appropriate.

The permanent impairment was determined through the use of Section 16.2, Amputations (5th ed, pp 441-445); Section 16.3, Sensory Impairments Due to Digital Nerve Lesion (5th ed, pp 445-450); and Section 16.4e, Finger Motion Impairment (5th ed, pp 461-466). The impairment evaluation process is summarized in Figure 16-1a, Upper Extremity Impairment Evaluation Record (5th ed, p 436). The use of this form is highly recommended for hand impairment cases. It should accompany the written report.

Thumb Impairment

As instructed in Section 16.2, Amputations (5th ed, pp 441-445), the thumb impairment was calculated by means of Figure 16-4, Digit Impairment Percent for Thumb Amputation at Various Levels (5th ed, p 443). A line was drawn across the figure of the thumb, representing the level of amputation, to the line on the graph. The percentage of impairment of the thumb was obtained from the top scale of Figure 16-4. In this case, the amputation was proximal to the IP joint, with a value found in the top scale of 60% impairment of the thumb.

Index Finger Impairment

Impairment of the index finger was based on the combined impairments due to the digital nerve injury and motion deficits. The sensory impairment of the digital injury to the index finger was assessed by means of Section 16.3, Sensory Impairments Due to Digital Nerve Lesion (5th ed, pp 445-450). The index finger had a 12-mm two-point discrimination on the radial side. This was a partial sensory loss, per Table 16-4, Sensory Quality Impairment Classification (5th ed, p 447), because the two-point discrimination was between 15 mm and 7 mm. It was also a longitudinal (one digital nerve) loss, as opposed to a transverse (both digital nerves) loss.

When a longitudinal loss is determined, a two-step process is performed. First, the relative value for the percentage of the nerve that has been damaged is determined according to Figure 16-7, Digit Impairment Due to Finger Amputation at Various Levels (5th ed, p 447), with the use of the top scale. In this case, the nerve was damaged, with abnormal and decreased sensation starting at the scar on the radial side between the PIP and MP joints. By drawing a line from the finger figure of Figure 16-7 across to the line on the graph, then intersecting with the top scale, a value of 90% was found. This amputation impairment percentage equaled the percent of digit length. Second, because the injury was to the index finger, Table 16-7, Digit Impairment for Transverse and Longitudinal Sensory Losses in Index, Middle, and Ring Fingers Based on the Percentage of Digit Length Involved (5th ed, p 448), was used. Ninety percent of the digit length with a partial loss of the radial digital nerve corresponded to a 14% digit impairment.

Section 16.4e, Finger Motion Impairment (5th ed, pp 461-466), was used to assess digital motion impairment. The index finger had loss of range of motion of the DIP, PIP, and MP joints. According to Figure 16-21, Finger Impairments Due to Abnormal Motion at the DIP Joint (5th ed, p 461), the flexion of 60° gave a 5% digit impairment, and the extension lag of −20° gave a 4% digit impairment. These impairments were added, because they were in the same joint, to give a 9% digit impairment due to the loss of range of motion in the DIP joint.

The range of motion impairment of the digit due to the loss of motion of the PIP joint was determined by means of Figure 16-23, Finger Impairments Due to Abnormal Motion at the PIP Joint (5th ed, p 463). The index PIP joint flexed to 50°, giving a 30% digit impairment. The extension lag of the PIP joint of −20° gave a 7% digit impairment. These impairments were added, because they were in the same joint, to give a 37% digit impairment.

The range of motion impairment of the digit due to the loss of motion of the MP joint was determined by means of Figure 16-25, Finger Impairments Due to Abnormal Motion at the MP Joint (5th ed, p 464). The MP flexion of 60° gave a 17% digit impairment, and extension to 0° gave a 5% impairment. These impairments were added, because they were in the same joint, to give a 22% digit impairment.

In the fingers, the impairment values to the digit from each separate joint were combined using the Combined Values Chart (5th ed, p 604). The 9% impairment due to the loss of range of motion of the DIP joint (the smallest) was combined with the 22% digit impairment (the second largest) due to the loss of range of motion in the MP joint to give 29%. The 37% digit impairment (the largest) due to the loss of range of motion in the PIP joint was combined with the 29% digit impairment, to give 55%.

Because the sensory loss impairment and the range of motion loss impairment were different types of impairments, they were combined. The 55% digit impairment due to loss of range of motion was combined with the 14% digit impairment due to the sensory loss, to give a 61% total impairment to the index finger digit.

Middle Finger Impairment
Impairment of the middle finger was based on the combined impairments due to the digital nerve injury and motion deficits.

The middle finger had 11 mm of two-point discrimination on the radial side. This was similar to the impairment of the index finger in that it was a partial loss. It was also a longitudinal (one digital nerve) loss, as opposed to a transverse (both digital nerves) loss. As was done for the index finger, a two-step process was performed. First, the relative value for the percentage of the nerve that had been damaged was determined on the basis of Figure 16-7, with the top scale. The nerve was damaged, with abnormal and decreased sensation starting at the scar on the radial side just proximal to the DIP joint. By drawing a line from the finger figure of Figure 16-7 across to the graph and looking at the top scale, a value of 50% was found. Second, because the injury was to the middle finger, Table 16-7 was used. Table 16-7 shows that, in this case, the 50% value for the relative digit length for a partial radial digital nerve impairment corresponded to 8% digit impairment due to the radial digital nerve partial sensory loss.

Using the same process as for the index finger, according to Figure 16-21, Finger Impairments Due to Abnormal Motion at the DIP Joint (5th ed, p 461), for the middle finger the flexion of 30° gave a 21% digit impairment, and the extension of 0° gave a 0% digit impairment. These impairments were added, because they were in the same joint, to give a 21% digit impairment due to the loss of range of motion in the DIP joint.

The middle PIP joint flexed to 40°, giving a 36% digit impairment based on Figure 16-23, Finger Impairments Due to Abnormal Motion at the PIP Joint (5th ed, p 463). The extension lag of the PIP joint of −10° gave a 3% digit impairment. These impairments were added, because they were in the same joint, to give a 39% digit impairment.

The range of motion impairment of the digit due to the loss of motion of the MP joint was determined by means of Figure 16-25, Finger Impairments Due to Abnormal Motion at the MP Joint (5th ed, p 464). The MP joint flexion of 70° gave an 11% digit impairment, and extension to 0° gave a 5% impairment. These impairments were added, because they were in the same joint, to give a 16% digit impairment.

In a similar manner as was done for the index finger, the impairments of the separate joints were combined by means of the Combined Values Chart (5th ed, p 604). "If three or more values are to be combined, the two lowest values are first selected and their combined value found. The combined value and the third value are then combined to give the total value. This procedure can be repeated indefinitely, with the value in each case being a combination of all the previous values" (5th ed, p 438). The 16% impairment (smallest) due to the loss of range of motion of the MP joint was combined with the 21% digit impairment (the second largest) due to the loss of range of motion in the DIP joint, to give 34%. The 39% digit impairment (the largest) due to the loss of range of motion in the PIP joint was combined with the 34%, to give 60%. The 60% was combined with the 16% impairment due to the loss of range of motion of the MP joint to give a total digit impairment due to loss of range of motion of 66%.

Because the sensory loss impairment and the range of motion loss impairment were different types of impairments, they were combined. The 66% digit impairment due to loss of range of motion was combined with the 8% digit impairment due to the sensory loss, to give a 69% total impairment to the middle finger digit.

Hand Impairment

Because two or more digits of the hand were involved, the final impairment was determined by the procedure outlined on pages 465 to 466 of the Fifth Edition. With the use of Table 16-1, Conversion of Impairment of the Digits to Impairment of the Hand (5th ed, p 438), the 60% impairment of the thumb equaled a 24% hand impairment. The 61% index finger impairment equaled a 12% hand impairment, and the 69% middle finger impairment equaled a 14% hand impairment. These hand impairments were added to give a 50% total hand impairment.

Table 16-2, Conversion of Impairment of the Hand to Impairment of the Upper Extremity (5th ed, p 439), was used to convert the 50% hand impairment to a 45% upper extremity impairment. Table 16-3, Conversion of Impairment of the Upper Extremity to Impairment of the Whole Person (5th ed, p 439), was used to convert the 45% upper extremity impairment to a 27% whole person impairment. There is no deduction in Chapter 16 for an injury to the nonpreferred hand.

Impairment: 27% whole person impairment per the Fifth Edition.

Sixth Edition Rating

The Sixth Edition approach to the evaluation of impairment is due to:

1. Amputation of the distal part of the left thumb
2. Sensory loss of the radial digital nerve of the left index finger
3. Sensory loss of the radial digital nerve of the left middle finger
4. Status post open reduction and internal fixation proximal phalanx, left index finger
5. Status post repair of the profundus and superficialis flexor tendons, left index finger
6. Status post open reduction and internal fixation proximal and distal phalanx, left middle finger
7. Status post repair of the profundus and superficialis flexor tendons, left middle finger
8. Range of motion loss of the DIP, PIP, and MP joints of the left index finger
9. Range of motion loss of the DIP, PIP, and MP joints of the left middle finger

Rating was based on Section 15.2, Diagnosis-Based Impairment (6th ed, p 387); Section 15.2b, Thumb/Finger/Hand (6th ed, p 390); Section 15.4c, Digital Nerve Impairment (6th ed, p 425); Section 15.6a, Thumb Amputation Impairment (6th ed, p 454), Figure 15-11, Thumb Amputation Digit Impairments (6th ed, p 458); Section 15.6e, Final Amputation Rating (6th ed, p 459), Table 15-29, Amputation Impairment Regional Grid (6th ed, p 461); and Section 15.7d, Finger Range of Motion (6th ed, p 467), Table 15-31, Finger Range of Motion (6th ed, p 470).

Thumb Amputation

In the Sixth Edition, there are two distinct methods to consider for rating amputations of the digits. For the thumb, the most specific method to use, if the data are available, is Figure 15-11, Digit Impairment Percents for Thumb Amputation at Various Levels (6th ed, p 458), to calculate the exact impairment rating based on the exact location of the amputation. This methodology is explained in the *Guides* Sixth Edition in Section 15.6e, Final Impairment Rating (6th ed, p 459). "If an amputation is only to a digit and the resulting impairment is to be expressed at the digit level, the processes described above will allow a more precise calculation of digit impairment." In this case, there were injuries involving more than the single digit, and there were other impairment values to be considered, therefore, the other methodology that is associated with the diagnosis-based impairment utilizes the general location of the amputation injury based on which joint is most closely involved. Specifically for this case, Table 15-29, Amputation Impairment (6th ed, p 460), provides rating upper extremity values for amputations at the thumb IP, MP, half metacarpal, or CMC joint.

If one were to utilize the data involved in this case in comparison with the exact digital impairments based on Figure 15-11, this case would rate a 60% thumb digit impairment or 22% upper extremity impairment based on conversion using Table 15-11 (6th ed, p 420).

For this case, however, the proper method is the diagnosis-based method as outlined in the regional grid Table 15-29 (6th ed, p 460). Based on the diagnosis and clinical studies noted with a "thumb amputation proximal to the IP joint," there was a class 2 rating (with a default impairment of 18% upper extremity impairment).

In Section 15.3, Adjustment Grid: Functional History (6th ed, p 405), and Table 15-7, Functional History Adjustment: Upper Extremities (6th ed, p 406), the patient was assigned grade modifier 1 for the involved partially amputated thumb; the functional history was consistent with clinical symptoms and a *Quick*DASH score of 26. Section 15.3b, Adjustment Grid: Physical Examination (6th ed, p 407), and Table 15-8, Physical Examination Adjustment: Upper Extremities (6th ed, p 408), and Section 15.3c, Adjustment Grid: Clinical Studies (6th ed, p 407), and Table 15-9, Clinical Studies Adjustment: Upper Extremities (6th ed, p 410), are not applicable. In summary, the adjustments were: functional history grade modifier 1, physical examination N/A, and clinical studies grade N/A. The net adjustment for the thumb amputation class 2 was −1, grade B, or 18% upper extremity impairment.

Calculation: Thumb Amputation Impairment

Thumb Amputation Impairment Class 1—Default for Diagnosis = 18% Upper Extremity Impairment			
CDX	GMFH	GMPE	GMCS
2	1	N/A	N/A
Net adjustment (GMFH − CDX) 1 − 2 = −1 + (GMPE − CDX) + N/A + (GMCS − CDX) + N/A Net adjustment = −1			

Result is class 2 adjustment −1, which results in class 2, grade B = 18% upper extremity impairment.

Final impairment value for the thumb amputation was 18% upper extremity impairment. No motion deficits or neurological deficits were noted for the thumb, which can be combined if applicable in cases of amputation injuries.

Thumb impairment: 18% upper extremity impairment per the Sixth Edition. Because additional impairments to the other digits in the involved hand must be added at the hand level, the upper extremity impairment value of 18% can be converted to a 20% hand impairment using Table 15-11 (6th ed, p 420).

Left Index and Middle Fingers ICF Diagnosis-Based Impairment Ratings
This case involved digital nerve injuries to the index and middle fingers as well as motion impairments from traumatic injuries resulting from surgical repair of tendon lacerations and phalanx fractures. In addition to the primary methodology of the diagnosis-based impairment method, the *Guides* Sixth Edition provides alternative approaches to performing impairment ratings for such injuries based on the range of motion and peripheral nerve deficits. If done separately, however, the range of motion or peripheral nerve deficits cannot be combined as stated in Section 15.2 (6th ed, p 387) and in the footnote to Table 15-2 (6th ed, p 405). For educational purposes, all methods will be calculated in this case. The primary diagnosis-based impairment method, however, is expected to be used in most instances. In addition, as will be explained, digital nerve injuries were done separately and combined with the diagnosis-based impairment methodology as outlined in Section 15.4c, Digital Nerve Impairment (6th ed, p 425).

The *Guides* approach to the evaluation of impairment due to multiple injuries to the hand/digits is to determine the most applicable diagnosis for the case and its resultant impairment. Per Section 15.2a, Diagnosis-Based

Impairment Class Assignment: Regional Grids (6th ed, p 389), "If more than 1 diagnosis can be used, the one that provides the most clinically accurate impairment rating should be used; this will generally be the more specific diagnosis." In this case, the injuries included a proximal phalanx fracture of the left index finger and proximal and distal phalanx fractures of the left middle finger requiring surgical pinning. The other significant diagnosis was flexor tendon injuries to the profundus and superficialis of the left index and middle fingers. Based on Table 15-2 (6th ed, p 405), the flexor tendon injury diagnosis or the proximal phalanx fracture can be used. Both are class 1 conditions (with a default rating of 6% digit impairment). The flexor tendon category rating is asterisked. As explained earlier, the footnote to Table 15-2 documents that a rating of the flexor tendons with motion loss can be done separately based on range of motion impairments as outlined in Section 15.7d, Finger Motion (6th ed, p 468), and Table 15-31, Finger Range of Motion (6th ed, p 470). The range of motion impairments, however, stand alone without combination of any other rating.

Assuming the use of the ICF diagnosis-based impairment methodology, the class 1 rating for the fracture or the flexor tendon injuries would then need to be adjusted for nonkey factors. In Section 15.3, Adjustment Grid: Functional History (p 405), and Table 15-7, Functional History Adjustment: Upper Extremities (p 406), the patient was assigned grade modifier 1 for the involved index and middle finger limitations; the functional history was consistent with clinical symptoms and a *Quick*DASH score of 26. Section 15.3b, Adjustment Grid: Physical Examination (p 407), and Table 15-8, Physical Examination Adjustment: Upper Extremities (p 408), and Section 15.3c, Adjustment Grid: Clinical Studies (p 407), and Table 15-9, Clinical Studies Adjustment: Upper Extremities (p 410), are not applicable. In summary, the adjustments were: functional history grade modifier 1, physical examination N/A, and clinical studies grade N/A. The net adjustment for the left index and middle finger injuries, which were both class 1, is 0, grade C, 6% digit impairment.

The final diagnosis-based impairment rating would be a 6% digit impairment for the left index finger and a 6% digit impairment for the left middle finger.

Left Index and Middle Fingers Digital Nerve Ratings

Combined with the diagnosis-based rating would be the digital nerve injury rating based on Section 15.4c (p 425). The index finger had a 12-mm two-point discrimination on the radial side. This was a partial sensory loss, per Table 15-15, Sensory Quality Impairment Classification (6th ed, p 426), because the two-point discrimination was between 15 mm and 7 mm. It was also a longitudinal (one digital nerve) loss, as opposed to a transverse (both digital nerves) loss. When a longitudinal loss is determined, a two-step process is performed. First, the relative value for the percentage of the nerve that has been damaged is determined according to Figure 15-5, Digit Impairment Due to Finger Amputation at Various Lengths (top scale) or Total Transverse Sensory Loss (bottom scale) (6th ed, p 426), with the use of the top scale. In this case, the nerve was damaged, with abnormal and decreased sensation starting at the scar on the radial side between the PIP and MP joints. By drawing a line from the finger figure of Figure 15-5 across to the line on the graph, then intersecting with the top scale, a value of 90% was found. This amputation impairment percentage equaled the percent of digit length. Second, because the injury was to the index finger, Table 15-17, Digit Impairment for Transverse and Longitudinal Sensory Losses in Index, Middle, and Ring Fingers Based on the Percentage of Digit Length Involved (6th ed, p 427), was used. Ninety percent of the digit length with a partial loss of the radial digital nerve corresponded to a 14% digit impairment for the left index finger.

The middle finger had 11 mm of two-point discrimination on the radial side. This is similar to the impairment of the index finger in that it was a partial loss. It was also a longitudinal (one digital nerve) loss, as opposed to a transverse (both digital nerves) loss. As was done for the index finger, a two-step process was performed. First, the relative value for the percentage of the nerve that was damaged was determined on the basis of Figure 15-5 (6th ed, p 426), with the top scale. In this case, the nerve was damaged, with abnormal and decreased sensation starting at the scar on the radial side just proximal to the DIP joint. By drawing a line from the finger figure of Figure 15-5 across to the graph and looking at the top scale, a value of 50% was found. Table 15-17, Digit Impairment for Transverse and Longitudinal Sensory Losses in Index, Middle, and Ring Fingers Based on Percent of Digital Length Involved (6th ed, p 427), shows that, in this case, the 50% value for the relative digit length for a partial radial digital nerve impairment corresponded to an 8% digit impairment due to the radial digital nerve partial sensory loss of the middle finger.

Final Combined Diagnosis-Based Impairment and Digital Nerve Impairments
Based on the diagnosis-based impairment methodology, the final impairment values for the left index finger would be: 6% digit impairment for the diagnosis-based impairment combined with a 14% digit impairment for the digital nerve injury. This equated to a 19% digit impairment. Per Table 15-12, Impairment Values Calculated From Digit Impairment (6th ed, p 421), this converted to a 4% hand impairment.

Based on the diagnosis-based impairment methodology, the final impairment values for the left middle finger would be: 6% digit impairment for the diagnosis-based impairment combined with 8% digit impairment for the digital nerve injury. This equated to a 14% digit impairment. Per Table 15-12 (6th ed, p 421), this converted to a 3% hand impairment.

The final thumb amputation rating was 20% impairment of the hand.

These individual hand impairments (derived from digit impairments, ie, 4% hand impairment for left index finger, 3% hand impairment for left middle finger, and 20% hand impairment for left thumb) were added, resulting in a 27% hand impairment, which equated to a 24% upper extremity impairment or 14% whole person impairment.

Alternate Range of Motion Impairment Rating for the Left Index and Middle Fingers

Based on Section 15.7, Range of Motion Impairment (6th ed, pp 459-478), this rating methodology stands alone and cannot be combined with any other rating methodology. Therefore, peripheral nerve impairments as calculated earlier involving the digital nerves cannot be combined with the range of motion impairment ratings. If the range of motion rating is greater, or if there is no specific diagnosis-based impairment diagnosis for which to classify the injury, the range of motion methodology may be the more applicable method.

The index finger had loss of range of motion of the DIP, PIP, and MP joints. According to Table 15-31, Finger Range of Motion (6th ed, p 470), the DIP flexion of 60° gave a grade modifier 1 rating with a 10% digit impairment. The extension of −20° also gave a grade modifier 1 rating with a 2% digit impairment. Adding these two impairments equated to a 12% digit impairment for loss of range of motion in the DIP joint. The range of motion impairment of the digit due to the loss of motion of the PIP joint was determined by means of Table 15-31 as well. The index PIP joint flexed to 50°, giving a grade modifier 1 rating with a 21% digit impairment. The extension of the PIP joint of −20° gave a grade modifier 1 rating with a 14% digit impairment. These impairments were added, because they were in the same joint, to give a 35% digit impairment. The range of motion impairment of the digit due to the loss of motion of the MP joint was also determined by means of Table 15-31. The MP joint flexion of 60° gave a grade modifier 1 rating of 19% digit impairment, and extension to 0° gave a grade modifier 1 rating of a 7% digit impairment. These impairments were added, because they were in the same joint, to give a 26% digit impairment. The joint ratings for the left index finger for range of motion impairment were then combined with 12%, 14%, and 35% digit impairments, resulting in a 51% digit impairment for the index finger.

Similar calculations also using Table 15-31 were made for the left middle finger. The middle PIP joint flexed to 40°, giving a grade modifier 2 rating of 42% digit impairment. The extension lag of the PIP joint of −10° gave a grade modifier 2 rating of a 14% digit impairment. These impairments were added, because they were in the same joint, to give a 56% digit impairment. The impairment for MP joint flexion of 70° gave a grade modifier 1 rating of 19% digit impairment, and extension to 0° gave a grade modifier 1 rating of 7% digit impairment. These impairments were added, because they were in the same joint, to give a 26% digit impairment. The DIP joint flexion of 30° gave a grade modifier 2 rating of 25% digit impairment, and the 0° extension gave a grade modifier 0 of 0% digit impairment. These impairments were added, because they were in the same joint, to give a 25% digit impairment. The final range of motion joint impairments for the middle finger resulted in combined values of 56%, 26%, and 25% digit impairments, resulting in a 75% digit impairment.

Referencing Table 15-7, Functional History Adjustment: Upper Extremities (6th ed, p 406), the patient's symptoms and *Quick*DASH score were consistent with a grade modifier 1, a lower grade modifier than that derived from the digit impairment per Table 15-35 (6th ed, p 477). Therefore, no adjustment was required.

It is inappropriate to combine the digital nerve impairment with the range of motion impairment. The final rating for range of motion impairment cannot combine digital nerve impairment. The left index finger motion impairment of 51% digit impairment, per Table 15-12 (6th ed, p 422), can be converted to a 10% impairment of the hand. The left middle finger motion impairment of 75% digit impairment, per Table 15-12 (6th ed, p 422), converts to a 15% impairment of the hand.

These individual hand impairments (derived from digit impairments, ie, 10% hand impairment for left index finger, 15% hand impairment for left middle finger, and 20% hand impairment for left thumb amputation), were added, resulting in a 45% hand impairment, which equated per Table 15-11 (6th ed, p 420) to a 41% upper extremity impairment or 25% whole person impairment. Using range of motion instead of diagnosis-based impairment resulted in a greater impairment and therefore was used for the final rating.

Comment on Saw Injury to the Hand

This case shows the different steps that have to be performed in order to transform a complex injury to the hand involving multiple digits to a final whole person impairment. Although at first it can be overwhelming to consider trying to evaluate such a complex injury that has an amputation, nerve damage, and range of motion losses in multiple digits, so long as the appropriate steps are taken and the correct tables used, a final determination of the whole person impairment can be made.

This case also demonstrates the steps necessary to determine different types of impairment in the same digit as well as to calculate impairments for range of motion losses in different joints of the same finger. Range of motion impairments in the same joint of a finger were added. Range of motion impairments in different joints of a finger were combined. The exception to this rule in the hand is the thumb. Range of motion impairments in different joints of the thumb were added.

As is demonstrated in this case, whether in the thumb or the fingers, different types of impairments in the thumb or the same finger, such as loss of sensation or range of motion, were combined. The process used in this case is unchanged from the Fourth to Fifth Editions.

Specific for the Sixth Edition, this case offers a new methodology to rate these complex injuries, that being the diagnosis-based impairment methodology. An alternative approach is also provided for motion deficits of the involved digits. In this case, the rating was greater with this alternative method than with the range of motion methodology.

SUMMARY

Diagnosis	Saw injury to multiple digits of the left hand
Fourth Edition References	Section 3.1f (4th ed, pp 24-30); Section 3.1g (4th ed, pp 30-35), Figure 1 (4th ed, p 16), Table 1 (4th ed, p 18), Table 2 (4th ed, p 19), Table 3 (4th ed, p 20), Figure 7 (4th ed, p 24), Table 4 (4th ed, p 25), Figure 17 (4th ed, p 30), Table 8 (4th ed, p 31), Table 9 (4th ed, p 31), Figure 19 (4th ed p 32), Figure 21 (4th ed, p 33), and Figure 23 (4th ed, p 34)
Fourth Edition Summary	History and physical examination documenting and basing impairment on amputation level of the thumb, digital sensory deficits, and range of motion deficits of DIP, PIP, and MP joints.

Fourth Edition Impairment	44% upper extremity impairment, 26% whole person impairment
Fifth Edition References	Section 16.2 (5th ed, pp 441-445); Section 16.3 (5th ed, pp 445-450); Section 16.4e (5th ed, pp 461-466), Figure 16-1a (5th ed, p 436), Table 16-1 (5th ed, p 438), Table 16-2 (5th ed, p 439), Table 16-3 (5th ed, p 439), Figure 16-4 (5th ed, p 443), Table 16-4 (5th ed, p 447), Figure 16-7 (5th ed, p 447), Table 16-7 (5th ed, p 448), Figure 16-21 (5th ed, p 461), Figure 16-23 (5th ed, p 463), Figure 16-25 (5th ed, p 464)
Fifth Edition Summary	History and physical examination documenting and basing impairment on amputation level of the thumb, digital sensory deficits, and range of motion deficits of DIP, PIP, and MP joints.
Fifth Edition Impairment	45% upper extremity impairment, 27% whole person impairment
Sixth Edition References	Section 15.2 (6th ed, pp 387-405); Section 15.2b (6th ed, p 390); Section 15.4c (6th ed, p 425); Section 15.6a (6th ed, p 454), Figure 15-11 (6th ed, p 458); Section 15.6e (6th ed, p 459), Table 15-29 (6th ed, p 460); Section 15.7d (6th ed, p 468), Table 15-31 (6th ed, p 470)
Sixth Edition Summary	History (including functional history and inventories), physical evaluation, and clinical studies are all used for this rating. Due to the motion deficits related to the digit injuries, alternative approaches can be considered for rating the index and middle fingers. The final rating would be the combined values for the index and middle fingers and the thumb amputation rating.
Sixth Edition Impairment	42% upper extremity impairment, 25% whole person impairment

CASE 15-18

Arthroplasty of the Metacarpophalangeal Joint

Subject: Mr Barnes, a 28-year-old man.

History: Mr Barnes was a right-handed National Basketball Association basketball star who, approximately 16 months before evaluation, caught his left ring finger in the net of the basket while slam-dunking the basketball. When his finger caught in the net, he was jerked backward and twisted, hanging briefly by his ring finger before it finally was released. He suffered a severe fracture of the proximal phalanx of the ring finger and the fourth metacarpal, involving the MP joint. Review of the medical records confirmed that Mr Barnes was treated by surgery initially with an open reduction and internal fixation of the fractures. This was followed by three other surgical procedures. After failure to obtain any functional range of motion in the MP joint, a resection arthroplasty of the MP joint was performed approximately 6 months before the current evaluation.

Current Symptoms: Mr Barnes returned to basketball but complained of loss of function in the left ring finger. He was unable to grip a ball as well as before the accident because of stiffness of the joints. He complained of periodically having an aching feeling in all the finger joints.

Functional Assessment: The *Quick*DASH score was 27.

Physical Examination: The thumb and index, middle, and little fingers appeared normal. Well-healed surgical scars were present on the ring finger. The MP joint region of the ring finger had loss of its normal shape with flattening of the area. The resected joint region was palpable with minimal tenderness. Range of motion of the DIP joint of the ring finger showed flexion of 50° and extension of 0°. Range of motion of the PIP joint showed flexion of 80° and extension of 0°. Range of motion of the MP joint showed flexion of 70° and extension of 0°.

Clinical Studies: None available for review.

Discussion of Arthroplasty of the MP Joint

Fourth Edition Rating

The permanent impairment was calculated through the use of Section 3.1g, Fingers (4th ed, pp 30-35), and Section 3.1m, Impairment Due to Other Disorders of the Upper Extremity (4th ed, pp 58-65). The process of assessing impairment is summarized in Section 3.1o, Summary of Steps for Evaluating Impairments of the Upper Extremity (4th ed, p 66).

The ring finger had loss of range of motion of the DIP, PIP, and MP joints. According to Figure 19, Finger Impairments Due to Abnormal Motion at the DIP Joint (4th ed, p 32), the flexion of 50° gave a 10% digit impairment, and the extension of 0° gave a 0% digit impairment. These impairments were added, because they were in the same joint, to give a 10% digit impairment due to the loss of range of motion in the DIP joint.

The range of motion impairment of the digit due to the loss of motion of the PIP joint was determined by means of the pie chart for the PIP joint in Figure 21, Finger Impairments Due to Abnormal Motion at PIP Joint (4th ed, p 33). The ring finger PIP joint flexed to 80°, giving a 12% digit impairment. The extension of the PIP joint of 0° gave a 0% digit impairment. These impairments were added, because they were in the same joint, to give a 12% digit impairment.

The range of motion impairment of the digit due to the loss of motion of the MP joint was determined by means of Figure 23, Finger Impairments Due to Abnormal Motion at the MP Joint (4th ed, p 34). The MP joint flexion of 70° gave an 11% digit impairment, and extension to 0° gave a 5% impairment. These impairments were added, because they were in the same joint, to give a 16% digit impairment due to the loss of range of motion.

Impairments for range of motion deficit for the three different joints were combined by means of the Combined Values Chart (4th ed, pp 322-324). The combined value of the digit impairment for the DIP joint (10%), the PIP joint (12%), and the MP joint (16%) yielded a 33% digit impairment.

The MP joint also had an impairment due to the resection arthroplasty. This was calculated by means of Section 3.1m, Impairments Due to Other Disorders of the Upper Extremity. This section is a mixed section in that it has different disorders outlined and various tables that are used for both the hand and upper extremity. Care has to be taken as to the specific types of impairment values given under each heading and table. Some tables and sections are in digit impairment, some are in upper extremity, and others are in joint. Some types of these deformities may be combined with other impairments involving the same joint, such as loss of range of motion, whereas others may not be combined.

The MP joint had loss of range of motion as well as a resection arthroplasty of the joint. According to Table 27, Impairment of the Upper Extremity After Arthroplasty of Specific Bones or Joints (4th ed, p 61), resection arthroplasty gave a 40% impairment of the value of the joint. The value of the MP joint relative to the ring finger is found in Table 18, Impairment Values for Digits, Hand, Upper Extremity, and Whole Person for Disorders of Specific Joints (4th ed, p 58), and it was 100% of the unit (ie, digit). This 100% was multiplied by 40% for a 40% digit impairment due to the resection arthroplasty.

The 33% digit impairment for motion was combined with the 40% digit impairment due to the resection arthroplasty, that is, other disorder, yielding a 60% digit impairment. With the use of Table 1, Relationship of Impairment of the Digits to Impairment of the Hand (4th ed, p 18), the 60% impairment of the ring finger equaled a 6% hand impairment, because the ring finger was involved. The 6% hand impairment, according to Table 2, Relationship of Impairment of the Hand to Impairment of the Upper Extremity (4th ed, p 19), converted to a 5% upper extremity impairment. Table 3, Relationship of Impairment of the Upper Extremity to Impairment of the Whole Person (4th ed, p 20), was then used to convert the 5% upper extremity impairment to a 3% whole person impairment. There is no deduction in Chapter 3 for an injury to the nondominant hand.

Impairment: 3% whole person impairment per the Fourth Edition

Fifth Edition Rating

The permanent impairment was calculated through the use of Section 16.4e, Finger Motion Impairment (5th ed, pp 461-466), and Section 16.7, Impairment of the Upper Extremity Due to Other Disorders (5th ed, pp 498-507). Hand impairment assessments were reported with the use of Figure 16-1a, Upper Extremity Impairment Evaluation Record (5th ed, p 436).

The ring finger had loss of range of motion of the DIP, PIP, and MP joints. According to Figure 16-21, Finger Impairments Due to Abnormal Motion at the DIP Joint (5th ed, p 461), the flexion of 50° gave a 10% digit impairment, and the extension of 0° gave a 0% digit impairment. These impairments were added, because they were in the same joint, to give a 10% digit impairment due to the loss of range of motion in the DIP joint.

The range of motion impairment of the digit due to the loss of motion of the PIP joint was determined with Figure 16-23, Finger Impairments Due to

Abnormal Motion at PIP Joint (5th ed, p 463). The ring finger PIP joint flexed to 80°, giving a 12% digit impairment. The extension of the PIP joint of 0° gave a 0% digit impairment. These impairments were added, because they were in the same joint, to give a 12% digit impairment.

The range of motion impairment of the digit due to the loss of motion of the MP joint was determined by means of Figure 16-25, Finger Impairments Due to Abnormal Motion at the MP Joint (5th ed, p 464). The MP joint flexion of 70° gave an 11% digit impairment, and extension to 0° gave a 5% impairment. These impairments were added, because they were in the same joint, to give a 16% digit impairment due to the loss of range of motion.

Impairments for range of motion deficit for the three different joints were combined by means of the Combined Values Chart (5th ed, pp 604-606). The combined value of the digit impairment for the DIP joint (10%), the PIP joint (12%), and the MP joint (16%) yielded a 33% digit impairment. This 33% digit impairment of the ring finger converted by Table 16-1, Conversion of Impairment of the Digits to Impairment of the Hand (5th ed, p 438), to a 3% hand impairment, which converted to a 3% upper extremity impairment by Table 16-2, Conversion of Impairment of the Hand to Impairment of the Upper Extremity (5th ed, p 439).

The MP joint also had an impairment due to the resection arthroplasty. This was calculated by means of Section 16.7, Impairment of the Upper Extremity Due to Other Disorders, and more specifically Section 16.7b, Arthroplasty (5th ed, p 505). This section is a mixed section in that it has different disorders outlined and various tables that are used for both the hand and upper extremity. Care has to be taken as to the specific types of impairment values given under each heading and table. Some tables and sections are in digit impairment, some tables are in upper extremity, and others are in joint. Some types of these deformities may be combined with other impairments involving the same joint, such as loss of range of motion, whereas others may not be combined.

The MP joint had loss of range of motion as well as a resection arthroplasty of the joint. According to Table 16-27, Impairment of the Upper Extremity After Arthroplasty of Specific Bones or Joints (5th ed, p 506), resection arthroplasty gave a 2% upper extremity impairment.

The 3% upper extremity impairment for motion deficits was combined with the 2% upper extremity impairment for the resection arthroplasty by means of the Combined Values Chart (5th ed, p 604), resulting in a 5% whole person impairment. Table 16-3, Conversion of Impairment of the Upper Extremity to Impairment of the Whole Person (5th ed, p 439), was then used to convert the 5% upper extremity impairment to a 3% whole person impairment. There is no deduction in Chapter 3 for an injury to the non-dominant hand.

Impairment: 3% whole person impairment per the Fifth Edition.

Sixth Edition Rating

The permanent impairment was calculated through the use of Section 15.2, Diagnosis-Based Impairment (6th ed, pp 387-405), for the resection arthroplasty of the MP joint and Section 15.7d, Finger Motion (6th ed, p 468), for the motion deficits of the DIP and PIP joints. Section 15.7, Range of Motion Impairment, explains, “This section is to be used as a stand-alone rating when other grids refer you to this section or when no other diagnosis-based sections of this chapter are applicable for impairment rating of a condition.” Although it is not possible to combine impairment for both resection of the MP joint and range of motion deficits for that same joint, the motion deficits of the other joints should be rated.

Table 15-3, Digit Regional Grid: Upper Extremity Impairments (6th ed, p 394), specifies that for arthroplasty of the finger MP joint there is class 2 impairment for “residual symptoms, consistent objective findings and/or functional loss, with normal motion” with a default impairment of 20% digit impairment. An asterisk indicates that “if motion loss is present, this impairment may alternatively be assessed using Section 15.7, Range of Motion Impairment” (6th ed, p 394).

The ring finger had loss of range of motion of the DIP, PIP, and MP joints. According to Table 15-31, Finger Range of Motion (6th ed, p 470), the DIP flexion of 50° gave a 10% digit impairment, and the extension of 0° gave a 0% digit impairment. These impairments were added, because they were in the same joint, to give a 10% digit impairment due to the loss of range of motion in the DIP joint. The ring finger PIP joint flexed to 80°, giving a 21% digit impairment. The extension of the PIP joint of 0° gave a 0% digit impairment. These impairments were added, because they were in the same joint, to give a 21% digit impairment.

It is noted that MP joint flexion of 70° gave a 19% digit impairment, and extension to 0° gave a 7% digit impairment. These impairments were added, because they were in the same joint, to give a 26% digit impairment due to the loss of range of motion. The motion deficits of the MP joint were greater than the impairment due to resection arthroplasty.

Impairments for range of motion deficit for the three different joints were combined using Appendix A, Combined Values Chart (6th ed, p 604). The largest values were combined first; 26% combined with 21% resulted in 42%, and this combined with 10% resulted in a 48% digit impairment.

By means of Table 15-12 (6th ed, p 422), a 48% digit impairment was equivalent to a 5% hand impairment, 4% upper extremity impairment, and 3% whole person impairment.

Impairment: 3% whole person impairment per the Sixth Edition.

Comment on Arthroplasty of the MP Joint

This case shows the calculation of a whole person impairment after a resection arthroplasty has been performed on a finger joint. There was an impairment due to a loss of range of motion and an impairment due to arthroplasty in the same joint.

In the Fourth Edition, implant arthroplasties were considered more impairing to the joint (representing a 50% joint impairment) than resection arthroplasties (40% joint impairment); however, in the Fifth Edition, implant arthroplasties are considered less impairing. The Fifth Edition does not state percentage of joint impairments; rather, it expresses all impairments as upper extremity. Therefore, this is somewhat problematic in hand cases where digit impairment components are combined at the digit level, but the values in Table 16-27 (5th ed, p 506) are expressed as upper extremity. In jurisdictions that require impairments expressed at the smallest body part applicable (eg, a digit impairment would be expressed as digit), it is necessary to convert backward from the upper extremity impairment to the digit impairment by means of Table 16-2 (5th ed, p 439) and Table 16-1 (5th ed, p 438).

In the Sixth Edition it is not appropriate to combine for the same structure both a diagnosis-based impairment and a motion impairment.

SUMMARY

Diagnosis	Arthroplasty of the MP joint with range of motion loss in the same joint
Fourth Edition References	Section 3.1g (4th ed, p 30); Section 3.1m (4th ed, p 58), Table 1 (4th ed, p 18), Table 2 (4th ed, p 19), Table 3 (4th ed, p 20), Figure 19 (4th ed, p 32), Figure 21 (4th ed, p 33), Figure 23 (4th ed, p 34), Table 18 (4th ed, p 58), Table 27 (4th ed, p 61)
Fourth Edition Summary	History, range of motion measurements of the DIP, PIP, and MP joints of the digits of the hand. Impairment secondary to the resection arthroplasty is assessed. Range of motion loss of the DIP, PIP, and MP joints of the ring finger is assessed. Ability to rate resection arthroplasty and range of motion impairment in the same joint is verified.
Fourth Edition Impairment	5% upper extremity impairment, 3% whole person impairment
Fifth Edition References	Section 16.4e (5th ed, p 461); Section 16.7 (5th ed, p 498), Table 16-1 (5th ed, p 438), Table 16-2 (5th ed, p 439), Table 16-3 (5th ed, p 439), Table 16-27 (5th ed, p 506), Figure 16-21 (5th ed, p 461), Figure 16-23 (5th ed, p 463), Figure 16-25 (5th ed, p 464)
Fifth Edition Summary	History, range of motion measurements of the DIP, PIP, and MP joints of the digits of the hand. Impairment secondary to the resection arthroplasty is assessed. Range of motion loss of the DIP, PIP, and MP joints of the ring finger is assessed. Ability to rate resection arthroplasty and range of motion impairment in the same joint is verified.
Fifth Edition Impairment	5% upper extremity impairment, 3% whole person impairment
Sixth Edition References	Section 15.2 (6th ed, pp 387-405); Section 15.7d (6th ed, p 468), Table 15-3, Digit (6th ed, p 394), Table 15-31 (6th ed, p 470), Table 15-12 (6th ed, p 422)

Sixth Edition Summary	History, range of motion measurements of the DIP, PIP, and MP joints of the digits of the hand. Impairment secondary to the diagnosis-based impairment for resection arthroplasty is assessed. Range of motion impairment of the DIP, PIP, and MP joints of the ring finger is assessed. In this case motion impairment for the MP joint exceeds the diagnosis-based impairment.
Sixth Edition Impairment	5% upper extremity impairment, 3% whole person impairment

CASE 15-19

Injuries to Multiple Nerves in the Upper Extremities

Subject: Dr Henderson, a 47-year-old man.

History: Dr Henderson, a semiretired general surgeon, was working part-time in the clinic of the County Refuse Department. He inserted his right arm into a receptacle containing broken glass, resulting in lacerations of the antecubital fossa and distal third of the posterolateral aspect of the arm. Dr Henderson was taken immediately to the emergency department of his hospital, where a former colleague attempted to reanastomose the radial nerve just above the elbow and a severed nerve in the forearm. Dr Henderson noticed immediately that he was unable to extend his wrist, extend his fingers, or pinch with his thumb and index finger. He was not aware of any numbness in the forearm.

Current Symptoms: Dr Henderson described an inability to use his right hand, wrist, or elbow with any dexterity or force. He was specifically unable to grip or grasp anything with his right hand. Numbness and decreased sensation were also noted in the dorsum of the hand, thumb, index, middle, and ring fingers. Activities of daily living were significantly impacted.

Functional Assessment: The *Quick*DASH score was 53. The interoffice examination findings and complaints were consistent with difficulties to the injured hand, wrist, and forearm with grasping and lifting. Activities of daily living with self-care were done independently without limitations. Some sensory function deficits in the digits limited hand protective function.

Physical Examination: An independent examination performed 1 year after injury revealed a complete right wrist drop, mild apparent weakness of abduction and adduction of the fingers, and marked weakness (3/5) of the flexors of the distal phalanges of the thumb and index finger. Mild weakness of supination and pronation of the forearm was noted. There was hypesthesia and hypalgesia of the dorsum of the hand and of the dorsal proximal two-thirds of the thumb, index finger, middle finger, and ring finger (radial half). Specifically, there was abnormal monofilament testing but normal two-point discrimination. The little finger and ulnar half of the ring finger had preserved sensation.

Clinical Studies: An electromyogram performed 5 months after injury showed 4+ fibrillation potentials and absent voluntary motor units in the wrist extensors and supinator, finger extensors, thumb extensors, and long abductor. The flexor digitorum profundus I and II and the flexor pollicis longus had 2+ fibrillations, large motor units mixed with some small polyphasics, and a reduced interference pattern. The dorsal interossei, lumbricales, and adductor pollicis were normal. On the nerve conduction study, no responses could be obtained in the radial motor and sensory nerves below the elbow. The median and ulnar motor and sensory nerve conduction studies were normal.

Discussion of Injuries to Multiple Nerves in the Upper Extremities

The clinical and electrodiagnostic findings were consistent with a complete injury to the radial nerve just above the elbow and to the anterior interosseous branch of the median nerve in the forearm. The radial nerve at this level supplies sensation only to the dorsum of the hand and fingers as described and innervates all of the extensor muscles and supinator of the forearm and the abductor pollicis longus. The anterior interosseous nerve supplies the deep flexors of the thumb, index finger, and middle finger and the pronator quadratus but has no sensory function. The dorsal interossei appeared to be weak clinically because of the inability to abduct the fingers against moderate resistance with the wrist flexed.

Fourth Edition Rating

Permanent impairment evaluation was based on Section 3.1k, Impairment of the Upper Extremity Due to Peripheral Nerve Disorders (4th ed, p 46). Table 15, Maximum Upper Extremity Impairments Due to Unilateral Sensory or Motor Deficits or Combined Deficits of the Major Peripheral Nerves (4th ed, p 54), specifies the maximum percentage upper extremity impairment due to sensory deficit/pain, motor deficit, and combined motor and sensory deficits for each of the peripheral nerves.

The upper extremity motor impairment due to multiple peripheral nerve injuries may be calculated according to the following schema:

Muscles Involved (With Innervation)	Motor Function Grade Table 12 (4th ed, p 49)	Percent Motor Deficit Table 12 (4th ed, p 49)	Maximum % Upper Extremity Motor Impairment per Nerve, Tables 10 and 15 (4th ed, pp 47-54)	Upper Extremity Motor Impairment for Each Nerve (% Motor Deficit x Maximum Upper Extremity Impairment)
Extensor carpi ulnaris, extensor carpi radialis, extensor digitorum communis, extensor indicis proprius, abductor pollicis longus, supinator (radial nerve, elbow, triceps sparing)	0/5	100%	35%	35%
Flexor digitorum profundus II and III, flexor pollicis longus (median, anterior interosseous branch)	3/5	40%	15%	6%

The upper extremity sensory impairment due to multiple peripheral nerve injuries may be calculated according to the following schema:

Sensory Nerves Involved	Percent Sensory Deficit, Table 11 (4th ed, p 48)	Maximum % Upper Extremity Sensory Impairment per Nerve, Tables 10 and 15 (4th ed, pp 47-54)	Upper Extremity Impairment for Each Nerve (% Motor Deficit x Maximum Upper Extremity Impairment)
Radial (below elbow)	25%	5%	1%
Median (anterior interosseous branch)	0%	0%	0%

The combined motor and sensory impairment of the upper extremity due to the radial nerve deficit was 36% (35% combined with 1%). The combined motor and sensory impairment of the upper extremity due to the interosseous nerve deficit was 6% (6% combined with 0%). The combined impairment of the upper extremity due to the radial and anterior interosseous nerve impairments was 40% (36% combined with 6%). According to Table 3, Relationship of Impairment of the Upper Extremity to Impairment of the Whole Person (4th ed, p 20), this was equivalent to a 24% whole person impairment.

Impairment: 24% whole person impairment per the Fourth Edition.

Fifth Edition Rating

Permanent impairment evaluation was based on Section 16.5, Impairment of the Upper Extremity Due to Peripheral Nerve Disorders (5th ed, p 480). Table 16-15, Maximum Upper Extremity Impairments Due to Unilateral Sensory or Motor Deficits or Combined 100% Deficits of the Major Peripheral Nerves (5th ed, p 492), specifies the maximum percentage upper extremity impairment due to sensory deficit/pain, motor deficit, and combined motor and sensory deficits for each of the peripheral nerves.

The upper extremity motor impairment due to multiple peripheral nerve injuries may be calculated according to the following schema:

Muscles Involved (With Innervation)	Motor Function Grade, Table 16-11 (5th ed, p 484)	Percent Motor Deficit, Table 16-11 (5th ed, p 484)	Maximum % Upper Extremity Motor Impairment per Nerve, Table 16-15 (5th ed, p 492)	Upper Extremity Motor Impairment for Each Nerve (% Motor Deficit x Maximum Upper Extremity Impairment)
Extensor carpi ulnaris, extensor carpi radialis, extensor digitorum communis, extensor indicis proprius, abductor pollicis longus, supinator (radial nerve, elbow, triceps sparing)	0/5	100%	35%	35%
Flexor digitorum profundus II and III, flexor pollicis longus (median, anterior interosseous branch)	3/5	40%	15%	6%

The upper extremity sensory impairment due to multiple peripheral nerve injuries may be calculated according to the following schema:

Sensory Nerves Involved	Percent Sensory Deficit, Table 16-10 (5th ed, p 482)	Maximum % Upper Extremity Sensory Impairment per Nerve, Table 16-15 (5th ed, p 492)	Upper Extremity Impairment for Each Nerve (% Motor Deficit x Maximum Upper Extremity Impairment)
Radial (below elbow)	25%	5%	1%
Median (anterior interosseous branch)	0%	0%	0%

The combined motor and sensory impairment of the upper extremity due to the radial nerve deficit was 36% (35% combined with 1%). The combined motor and sensory impairment of the upper extremity due to the interosseous nerve deficit was 6% (6% combined with 0%). The combined impairment of the upper extremity due to the radial and anterior interosseous nerve impairments was 40% (36% combined with 6%). According to Table 16-3, Conversion of Impairment of the Upper Extremity to Impairment of the Whole Person (5th ed, p 439), this was equivalent to a 24% whole person impairment.

Impairment: 24% whole person impairment per the Fifth Edition.

Sixth Edition Rating

The *Guides* approach to the evaluation of impairment due to multiple peripheral nerve injuries is based on Section 15.4, Peripheral Nerve Impairment (6th ed, p 419), and Section 15.4e, Peripheral Nerve and Brachial Plexus Impairment (6th ed, p 429). Table 15-21, Peripheral Nerve Impairment (6th ed, p 436), is used to rate conditions of peripheral nerve injury involving diagnoses such as motor and sensory deficits of the radial nerve below the elbow triceps sparing and motor deficits of the anterior interosseous nerve.

Based on the complete motor deficits noted from Table 15-14, Motor and Sensory Severity (6th ed, p 425), there was a complete loss severity 4 for the radial nerve motor loss and moderate severity 2 for the anterior interosseous nerve motor loss, plus mild severity 1 for sensory loss of the radial nerve. Table 15-21 criteria would place this impairment at a class 1 rating for the anterior interosseous nerve motor loss (with a default rating of 6% upper extremity impairment), class 3 rating for the radial nerve motor loss (with a default rating of 31% upper extremity impairment), and class 1 rating for the radial nerve sensory loss (with a default rating of 1% upper extremity impairment).

According to Section 15.3, Adjustment Grid: Functional History (6th ed, p 405), and Table 15-7, Functional History Adjustment: Upper Extremities (6th ed, p 406), the patient was assigned grade modifier 2 for both the radial and anterior interosseous nerves; the functional history was consistent with clinical symptoms and a *Quick*DASH score of 53. Section 15.3b, Adjustment Grid: Physical Examination (6th ed, p 407), and Table 15-8, Physical Examination Adjustment: Upper Extremities (6th ed, p 408), were not applicable because the class rating utilized the examination findings. According to Section 15.3c, Adjustment Grid: Clinical Studies (6th ed, p 407), and Table 15-9, Clinical Studies Adjustment: Upper Extremities

(6th ed, p 410), the patient was assigned grade modifier 4 for the radial nerve motor deficit, a grade modifier 2 for the anterior interosseous nerve motor deficit, and a grade modifier 4 for the sensory deficit of the radial nerve. In summary, the adjustments were: functional history grade modifier 2 for all three components, including the motor impairments of the radial and anterior interosseous nerves and the sensory impairment for the radial nerve, physical examination N/A, and clinical studies grade modifier 4 for the radial motor and sensory impairments and grade modifier 2 for the anterior interosseous nerve.

The net adjustment for the radial nerve below the elbow (triceps sparing) motor class 3 was +2, grade C, 35% upper extremity impairment.

The net adjustment for the radial nerve below the elbow (triceps sparing) sensory class 1 was +4, grade E, 1% upper extremity impairment.

The net adjustment for the anterior interosseous nerve motor class 1 was +2, grade E, 8% upper extremity impairment.

Example calculation: Anterior Interosseous Nerve Motor Impairment

Motor Impairment Anterior Interosseous Nerve
Class 1—Default for Diagnosis = 6% Upper Extremity Impairment
Moderate Motor Deficit

CDX	GMFH	GMPE	GMCS
1	2	N/A	2

Net adjustment

(GMFH − CDX) 2 − 1 = 1
+ (GMPE − CDX) + N/A
+ (GMCS − CDX) + 2 − 1 = 1

Net adjustment = +2

Result is class 1 adjustment +2, which results in class 1, grade E = 8% upper extremity impairment.

Final impairment values for this case include:

Radial nerve motor = 35% upper extremity impairment.

Radial nerve sensory = 1% upper extremity impairment.

Anterior interosseous nerve motor = 8% upper extremity impairment.

The combined value was 41% upper extremity impairment.

Based on Table 15-11, Impairment Values Calculated from Upper Extremity Impairment (6th ed, p 420), this converted to a 25% whole person impairment.

Impairment: 25% whole person impairment per the Sixth Edition.

Comment on Injuries to Multiple Nerves in the Upper Extremities

Anatomic localization should be as precise as possible and may be aided by the electrodiagnostic findings. The grading of the motor and sensory deficits is clinical, although electromyography and nerve conduction studies are useful in confirming that specific muscles and sensory nerves are involved. In this case, there was apparent clinical weakness of the interossei (due to wrist flexion) but no actual denervation or motor unit loss in these ulnar innervated muscles. Therefore, the interossei were not included in the combined motor impairment rating.

The electromyogram may also help in determining whether further clinical improvement can be expected. In the example, small polyphasic potentials were seen in the muscles innervated by the anterior interosseous nerve. These potentials (nascent potentials) were evidence of early nerve regeneration and suggested that some improvement in strength may be seen later on, making the evaluation of permanent impairment in these muscles difficult.

The process of rating impairment in this case was the same in the Fifth Edition as it was in the Fourth Edition. There were, however, changes in definitions in the grading for sensory deficits.

The process of rating impairment in this case is similar in the Sixth Edition based on the concept that the degree of severity for each involved nerve be considered for its sensory/motor deficits. However, the calculations are no longer done by exact calculations; rather the diagnosis-based impairment method is used to calculate the final rating by identifying the particular class of impairment values for the specific sensory or motor deficits for each nerve involved and utilizing adjustment factors of functional history, examination findings, and clinical studies to determine the true value within the range. In addition, Figure 15-2, the upper extremity impairment evaluation record, should be completed in all upper extremity cases.

SUMMARY

Diagnosis	Radial nerve injury, anterior interosseous nerve injury
Fourth Edition References	Section 31.k (4th ed, pp 46-57), Table 11 (4th ed, p 48), Table 12 (4th ed, p 49), Table 15 (4th ed, p 54)
Fourth Edition Summary	History, detailed neurologic examination, electromyogram, and nerve conduction study. Involvement of peripheral nerves is confirmed by means of appropriate electrodiagnostic studies. Motor and sensory deficits in each nerve are specified and graded. Nerve deficits are combined to determine upper extremity impairment.
Fourth Edition Impairment	40% upper extremity impairment, 24% whole person impairment
Fifth Edition References	Section 16.5 (5th ed, p 480), Table 16-10 (5th ed, p 482), Table 16-11 (5th ed, p 484), Table 16-15 (5th ed, p 492)
Fifth Edition Summary	History, detailed neurologic examination, electromyogram, and nerve conduction study. Involvement of peripheral nerves is confirmed by means of appropriate electrodiagnostic studies. Motor and sensory deficits in each nerve are specified and graded. Nerve deficits are combined to determine upper extremity impairment.
Fifth Edition Impairment	40% upper extremity impairment, 24% whole person impairment
Sixth Edition References	Section 15.4 (6th ed, p 419); Section 15-3 (6th ed, p 405); Section 15.3a (6th ed, p 406); Section 15.3b (6th ed, p 407); Section 15.3c (6th ed, p 407), Table 15-7 (6th ed, p 406), Table 15-8 (6th ed, p 408), Table 15-9 (6th ed, p 410), Table 15-11 (6th ed, p 420), Table 15-14 (6th ed, p 425), Table 15-21 (6th ed, p 436)

Sixth Edition Summary	History (including functional history and inventories), physical evaluation, and clinical studies are all included in the ICF methodology outlined in Chapter 15, The Upper Extremities. First, the correct nerve involved is identified, the impairment is classified within the Diagnosis-Based Impairment table based on class and default value. Second, the impairment rating is adjusted based on nonkey factors.
Sixth Edition Impairment	41% upper extremity impairment, 25% whole person impairment

CASE 15-20

Brachial Plexus Injury

Subject: Mr Miller, a 55-year-old man.

History: Mr Miller, a construction worker, fell 3.6 m (12 feet) from a scaffold onto a concrete sidewalk. He incurred a posterior dislocation of the right humeral head. Initially he complained of moderate pain in the shoulder area and inner aspect of the upper arm, but the pain dissipated in approximately 2 months. Since the time of the injury, however, he noted persistent numbness and weakness in his right arm. There was no history of underlying medical disease other than hypertension, nor was there a known family history of neurologic disease.

Current Symptoms: After 3 years from his date of injury, the patient continued to complain of weakness in his right forearm, particularly in the hand. He was unable to write with his right hand. The ulnar side of his right hand felt numb, including the entire fourth and fifth fingers. He also experienced numbness and dysesthesias along the medial side of the forearm to the elbow. He had minimal complaints of pain in his right arm.

Functional Assessment: The *Quick*DASH score was 59. The interoffice examination findings and complaints were consistent with difficulties to the injured shoulder, arm, and hand. Activities of daily living with self-care were done independently without limitations. Significant weakness in the right hand caused problems with gripping and grasping along with dexterity issues. Some diminished sensation also limited dexterity and tactile function.

Physical Examination: Strength testing showed profound weakness in the flexor carpi ulnaris, the ulnar half of the flexor digitorum profundus, opponens pollicis, flexor pollicis longus, extensor indicis proprius, interossei, adductor pollicis, and abductor digiti quinti. The strength was 2/5, that is, active movement with gravity eliminated, and approached 1/5, that is, slight contraction and no movement. Strength was otherwise normal throughout the upper extremities. The deep tendon reflexes were normal throughout the upper and lower extremities except for a decreased right finger flexor reflex. The plantar responses (Babinski sign) were flexor bilaterally. The sensory examination showed diminished temperature, touch, and pain appreciation in the following distribution: fourth (radial and ulnar sides) and fifth fingers, the ulnar side of the palm and dorsum of the hand, and the medial aspect of the forearm. A right lid ptosis and pupillary miosis were also noted.

These clinical findings were most consistent with an injury to the lower trunk of the right brachial plexus, although additional partial avulsion injuries of the C8 and/or T1 nerve roots could not be ruled out.

Clinical Studies: Magnetic resonance imaging performed approximately 1 year after the injury of the brachial plexus and cervical spine was negative other than showing mild degenerative changes at C5-6 and C6-7, including disk space narrowing and minimal neuroforaminal encroachment by spurring at both levels.

An electromyogram and nerve conduction study of the right upper extremity performed 3 years after the injury showed denervation with an estimated 50% loss of motor units in a C8-T1 distribution in the right upper extremity. No denervation was found in the cervical paraspinal musculature. The nerve conduction study showed normal motor nerve conduction velocities in the median and ulnar nerves with markedly decreased amplitudes of the compound motor action potentials in both nerves. The ulnar nerve sensory amplitude was markedly decreased, whereas the median nerve and radial nerve sensory amplitudes were normal and symmetric on the right and left sides.

Discussion of Brachial Plexus Injury

Fourth Edition Rating

Permanent impairment evaluation was based on Section 3.1k, Impairment of the Upper Extremity Due to Peripheral Nerve Disorders (4th ed, pp 46-57). Table 14, Maximum Upper Extremity Impairments Due to Unilateral Sensory Loss or Motor Deficits of Brachial Plexus, or to Combined Deficits (4th ed, p 52), specifies that the maximum percentage upper extremity impairment for the lower trunk of the brachial plexus is 20% due to sensory deficit or pain and 70% due to motor deficit, with a maximum upper extremity impairment due to combined motor and sensory deficits of 76%. The brachial plexus anatomy is shown in Figure 47 (4th ed, p 53).

With the use of Table 11 (4th ed, p 48), sensory grading was judged to be grade 3, that is, decreased sensibility with or without abnormal sensation or pain, which interferes with activity, which corresponded to a 26% to 60% sensory deficit. The sensory deficit appeared to be closer to grade 4;

therefore, the examiner chose to assign a 55% sensory deficit. According to Table 12 (4th ed, p 49), motor grading was 2/5, which corresponded to a 51% to 75% deficit. Because it approached grade 1/5, a 75% motor deficit was selected.

On the basis of Table 14, the upper extremity motor impairment may be calculated according to the following schema:

Involved Muscles in the Right Upper Extremity	Motor Function Grade, Table 12 (4th ed, p 49)	Percent Motor Deficit, Table 12 (4th ed, p 49)	Maximum % Upper Extremity Motor Impairment, Lower Trunk, Table 14 (4th ed, p 52)	Upper Extremity Impairment (% Motor Deficit x Maximum Upper Extremity Impairment)
Flexor carpi ulnaris, adductor pollicis flexor digitorum profundus IV and V, interossei, lumbricales IV and V, abductor digiti quinti, abductor pollicis brevis, opponens pollicis, flexor pollicis longus, extensor indicis proprius	2/5	75%	70%	53%

The motor impairment of the upper extremity was 53%.

On the basis of Table 14, the upper extremity sensory impairment may be calculated according to the following schema:

Sensory Loss in the Right Upper Extremity	Percent Sensory Deficit, Table 11 (4th ed, p 48)	Maximum % Upper Extremity Sensory Impairment, Lower Trunk, Table 14 (4th ed, p 52)	Upper Extremity Impairment (% Sensory Deficit x Maximum Upper Extremity Impairment)
Ulnar aspect of hand, medial aspect of forearm	55%	20%	11%

The sensory impairment of the upper extremity was 11%.

The combined impairment of the upper extremity by means of the Combined Values Chart (4th ed, p 322) was 58% (53% motor impairment combined with 11% sensory impairment).

Impairment: 35% whole person impairment per the Fourth Edition.

Fifth Edition Rating

Permanent impairment evaluation was based on Section 16.5, Impairment of the Upper Extremity Due to Peripheral Nerve Disorders (5th ed, pp 480-497), with specific reference to Brachial Plexus in Section 16.5c, Regional Impairment Determination (5th ed, pp 488-491). Table 16-14, Maximum Upper Extremity Impairments Due to Unilateral Sensory Loss or Motor Deficits of Brachial Plexus, or to Combined Deficits (5th ed, p 490), specifies that the maximum percentage upper extremity impairment for the lower trunk of the brachial plexus is 20% due to sensory deficit or pain and 70% due to motor deficit, with a maximum upper extremity impairment due to combined motor and sensory deficits of 76%. The brachial plexus anatomy is shown in Figure 16-50 (5th ed, p 490).

With the use of Table 16-10, Determining Impairment of the Upper Extremity Due to Sensory Deficits or Pain Resulting From Peripheral Nerve Disorders (5th ed, p 482), sensory grading was judged to be grade 3, that is, distorted superficial tactile sensibility (diminished light touch and two-point discrimination), with some abnormal sensations or slight pain, that interferes with some activities. The sensory deficit appeared to be closer to grade 2; therefore, the examiner chose to assign a 55% sensory deficit. According to Table 16-11, Determining Impairment of the Upper Extremity Due to Motor and Loss-of-Power Deficits Resulting From Peripheral Nerve Disorders Based on Individual Muscle Testing (5th ed, p 484), motor grading was 2/5, which corresponded to a 51% to 75% deficit. Because it approached a grade 1/5, a 75% motor deficit was selected.

On the basis of Table 16-14, the upper extremity motor impairment may be calculated according to the following schema:

Involved Muscles in the Right Upper Extremity	Motor Function Grade, Table 16-11 (5th ed, p 484)	Percent Motor Deficit, Table 16-11 (5th ed, p 484)	Maximum % Upper Extremity Motor Impairment, Lower Trunk, Table 16-14 (5th ed, p 490)	Upper Extremity Impairment (% Motor Deficit x Maximum Upper Extremity Impairment)
Flexor carpi ulnaris, adductor pollicis flexor digitorum profundus IV and V, interossei, lumbricales IV and V, abductor digiti quinti, abductor pollicis brevis, opponens pollicis, flexor pollicis longus, extensor indicis proprius	2/5	75%	70%	53%

The motor impairment of the upper extremity was 53%.

On the basis of Table 16-14, the upper extremity sensory impairment may be calculated according to the following schema:

Sensory Loss in the Right Upper Extremity	Percent Sensory Deficit, Table 16-10 (5th ed, p 482)	Maximum % Upper Extremity Sensory Impairment, Lower Trunk, Table 16-14 (5th ed, p 490)	Upper Extremity Impairment (% Sensory Deficit x Maximum Upper Extremity Impairment)
Ulnar aspect of hand, medial aspect of forearm	55%	20%	11%

The sensory impairment of the upper extremity was 11%.

The combined impairment of the upper extremity by means of the Combined Values Chart (5th ed, pp 604-606) was 58% (53% motor impairment combined with 11% sensory impairment).

Impairment: 35% whole person impairment per the Fifth Edition.

Sixth Edition Rating

The *Guides* approach to the evaluation of impairment due to multiple peripheral nerve injuries is based on Section 15.4, Peripheral Nerve Impairment (6th ed, p 419), and Section 15.4e, Peripheral Nerve and Brachial Plexus Impairment (6th ed, p 429). Table 15-20, Brachial Plexus Impairment (6th ed, p 434), is used to rate conditions of peripheral nerve injury involving the brachial plexus lower trunk (C8-T1, Dejerine-Klumpke), with adjustments made for functional history, physical examination, and clinical studies findings.

Based on the complete motor deficits noted from Table 15-14, Motor and Sensory Severity (6th ed, p 425), there was a sensory loss most consistent with a moderate severity 2 for the lower trunk innervated region based on "distorted superficial tactile sensibility with abnormal sensation." A severe or level 3 severity rating was assigned for the more significant 2/5 motor function grade identified on physical examination.

Table 15-20 criteria would place the sensory deficits at a class 1 impairment rating for the lower trunk lesion (with a default rating of 9% upper extremity impairment), and a class 3 impairment rating for the motor deficits of the lower trunk lesion (with a default rating of 44% upper extremity impairment).

According to Section 15.3, Adjustment Grid: Functional History (6th ed, p 405), and Table 15-7, Functional History Adjustment: Upper Extremities (6th ed, p 406), the patient was assigned grade modifier 2 for the involved lower trunk nerves; the functional history was consistent with clinical symptoms and a *Quick*DASH score of 59. Section 15.3b, Adjustment Grid: Physical Examination (6th ed, p 407), and Table 15-8, Physical Examination Adjustment: Upper Extremities (6th ed, p 408), were not applicable because the class rating utilized the examination findings. According to Section 15.3c, Adjustment Grid: Clinical Studies (6th ed, p 407), and Table 15-9, Clinical Studies Adjustment: Upper Extremities (6th ed, p 410), the patient was assigned grade modifier 2 for the lower trunk electromyogram and nerve conduction study testing. In summary, the adjustments were: functional history grade modifier 2, physical examination N/A, and clinical studies grade modifier 2. The net adjustment for the motor class 3 was −2, grade A, 36% upper extremity impairment. The net adjustment for the sensory class 1 was +2, grade E, 12% upper extremity impairment.

Calculation: Brachial Plexus Lower Trunk Motor Impairment

Motor Impairment – Brachial Plexus Lower Trunk (C8 T1)
Class 1—Default for Diagnosis = 14% Upper Extremity Impairment
Severe Motor Deficit

CDX	GMFH	GMPE	GMCS
3	2	N/A	2

Net adjustment

(GMFH − CDX) 2 − 3 = −1
+ (GMPE − CDX) + N/A
+ (GMCS − CDX) + 2 − 3 = −1

Net adjustment = −2

Result is class 3 adjustment −2, which results in class 3, grade A = 36% upper extremity impairment.

Calculation: Brachial Plexus Lower Trunk Sensory Impairment

Sensory Impairment – Brachial Plexus Lower Trunk (C8 T1) Class 1—Default for Diagnosis = 9% Upper Extremity Impairment Moderate Motor Deficit			
CDX	GMFH	GMPE	GMCS
1	2	N/A	2
Net adjustment (GMFH – CDX) 2 – 1 = 1 + (GMPE – CDX) + N/A + (GMCS – CDX) + 2 – 1 = 1 Net adjustment = +2			

Result is class 1 adjustment +2, which results in class 1, grade E = 12% upper extremity impairment.

Final impairment values for this case include:

Brachial Plexus Lower Trunk motor = 36% upper extremity impairment.

Brachial Plexus Lower Trunk sensory = 12% upper extremity impairment.

The combined value was 44% upper extremity impairment. Based on Table 15-11, Impairment Values Calculated From Upper Extremity Impairment (6th ed, p 420), this converted to a 26% whole person impairment.

Impairment: 26% whole person impairment per the Sixth Edition.

Comment on Brachial Plexus Injury

Blunt trauma from falls, industrial accidents, and roadway accidents is the most common cause of brachial plexus injury. Upper trunk injuries occur more commonly than do injuries to the lower trunk, and isolated middle trunk injuries are least common.[1] This case illustrates the impairment rating process for an isolated lower trunk injury without root avulsion. The sensory and motor distribution of the lower trunk (C8 and T1 root contributions to the median, ulnar, and radial motor nerves and the medial antebrachial cutaneous nerve) was limited and well defined, making the impairment evaluation process somewhat less ambiguous than in an upper trunk lesion. The lower trunk lesion also illustrates the particular usefulness of the electromyogram and nerve conduction study in distinguishing plexus versus pure cervical root lesions. Ulnar and medial antebrachial cutaneous sensory potentials are absent or diminished in plexus lesions but not in isolated root lesions, because the sensory ganglia are distal to the neuroforamina.

The process of rating impairment in this case is the same in the Fifth Edition as it was in the Fourth Edition. There are, however, changes in definitions in the grading for sensory deficits.

In the Sixth Edition, the diagnosis-based impairment method is used to calculate the impairment rating by identifying the particular class of impairment values for the specific sensory or motor deficits for the brachial plexus root involved and utilizing adjustment factors of functional history, examination findings, and clinical studies to determine the true value within the range.

SUMMARY

Diagnosis	Brachial plexus injury, lower trunk
Fourth Edition References	Section 31.k (4th ed, pp 46-57), Table 10 (4th ed, p 47), Table 11 (4th ed, p 48), Table 12 (4th ed, p 49), Table 14 (4th ed, p 52), Figure 47 (4th ed, p 53)
Fourth Edition Summary	History, detailed neurologic examination, electromyogram and nerve conduction study, magnetic resonance imaging of plexus and cervical spine. Lesion is localized to brachial plexus (trunk or division or both) versus cervical nerve roots by means of clinical examination, electrodiagnostic testing, and imaging studies. Motor and sensory deficits are specified and graded clinically.
Fourth Edition Impairment	58% upper extremity impairment, 35% whole person impairment
Fifth Edition References	Section 16.5 (5th ed, pp 480-497), Table 16-10 (5th ed, p 482), Table 16-11 (5th ed, p 484), Table 16-14 (5th ed, p 490)

Fifth Edition Summary History, detailed neurologic examination, electromyogram and nerve conduction study, magnetic resonance imaging of plexus and cervical spine. Lesion is localized to brachial plexus (trunk or division or both) versus cervical nerve roots by means of clinical examination, electrodiagnostic testing, and imaging studies. Motor and sensory deficits are specified and graded clinically.

Fifth Edition Impairment 58% upper extremity impairment, 35% whole person impairment

Sixth Edition References Section 15.4 (6th ed, p 419); Section 15.4e (6th ed, p 429), Table 15-20, (6th ed, p 434), Table 15-14 (6th ed, p 425); Section 15.3 (6th ed, p 405), Table 15-7 (6th ed, p 406); Section 15.3b (6th ed, p 407); Table 15-8 (6th ed, p 408); Section 15.3c (6th ed, p 407), Table 15-9 (6th ed, p 410), Table 15-11 (6th ed, p 420)

Sixth Edition Summary The diagnosis supported by history, physical evaluation, and clinical studies establishes the class of impairment based on Table 15-20 (6th ed, p 434). After determining the diagnosis-based impairment class and associated default value, the same functional history, physical examination, and clinical studies are used to adjust impairments based on nonkey factors.

Sixth Edition Impairment 44% upper extremity impairment, 26% whole person impairment

---

Reference

1. Evans, RW. *Neurology and Trauma*. Philadelphia, PA: WB Saunders Co; 1996.

CASE 15-21

Carpal Tunnel Syndrome

Subject: Ms Jones, a 45-year-old woman.

History: Ms Jones worked on an assembly line, and her work involved repetitively packing boxes. She had the insidious onset of numbness and tingling in her right, dominant hand, with the sensation of her hand falling asleep at night. She saw her primary care physician, who treated her with a hand splint. Her problems persisted, and 1 month later, nerve conduction studies revealed findings consistent with a sensory conduction delay. She underwent a carpal tunnel release. After 10 months her symptoms stabilized and had been stable for the previous 4 months. Although Ms Jones was overweight and also had risk factors of age and gender, her carpal tunnel syndrome was determined administratively to be work related.

Current Symptoms: Complaints of occasional sensations of tingling; however, was able to perform all activities of daily living.

Functional Assessment: The *Quick*DASH score was 20.

Physical Examination: Well-healed scar. Sensory examination revealed normal monofilament testing (at 1.65 g of force) and normal two-point discrimination (5 mm) in all digits. Focal muscle testing was normal, without atrophy.

Clinical Studies: Preoperative electrodiagnostic studies revealed mild sensory conduction delays of the right median nerve; motor studies were normal.

Discussion of Nerve Entrapment

Fourth Edition Rating

In section 3.1k, Impairment of the Upper Extremity Due to Peripheral Nerve Disorders (4th ed, p 46-57), subsection Entrapment Neuropathy, the *Guides* states that "impairment of the hand and upper extremity secondary to entrapment neuropathy may be derived by measuring the sensory and motor deficits. An alternative method is provided in Table 16 (4th ed, p 57) [eg, Upper Extremity Impairment Due to Entrapment Neuropathy]. The evaluator should not use both methods. Impairment of the upper extremity secondary to an entrapment neuropathy is estimated according to the severity of involvement of each major nerve at each entrapment site" (4th ed, p 56). Table 16, however, does not provide definitions for the terms for the degree of severity, and therefore is not the preferred approach.

The most precise approach to assessing impairment is done by grading the severity using Table 11, Determining Impairment of the Upper Extremity Due to Pain or Sensory Deficit (4th ed, p 48), and Table 12, Determining Impairment of the Upper Extremity Due to Loss of Power and Motor Deficits (4th ed, p 49). Objective decreased sensibility is required to have a sensory deficit; for example, pain alone is not ratable. These deficits are then multiplied by the values for the median nerve (below midforearm) provided in Table 15, Maximum Upper Extremity Impairments Due to Unilateral Sensory or Motor Deficits or Combined Deficits of the Major Peripheral Nerves (4th ed, p 54). For example, if the entire median nerve is involved, there is a 38% upper extremity impairment due to sensory deficit or pain and 10% due to motor deficit. In this case, there was no objective evidence of ongoing sensory or motor deficits on clinical examination. Therefore, according to the *Guides* Fourth Edition, there is no ratable impairment.

Impairment: 0% whole person impairment per the Fourth Edition.

Fifth Edition Rating

Carpal tunnel syndrome impairment assessment is discussed in Section 16.5d, Entrapment/Compression Neuropathy (5th ed, pp 491-495), and specifically on page 495. The *Guides* notes that "only individuals with an *objectively verifiable diagnosis* should qualify for a permanent impairment rating. The diagnosis is made not only on believable symptoms but, more important, on the presence of *positive clinical findings and loss of function.* The diagnosis should be documented by electromyography as well as sensory and motor nerve conduction studies" (5th ed, p 493). "The sensory deficits or pain, and/or the motor deficits and loss of power, are evaluated according to the impairment determinations method described in Section 16.5b. In compression neuropathies, additional impairment values are not given for decreased grip strength. In the absence of CRPS, additional impairment values are not given for decreased motion" (5th ed, p 494).

The Fifth Edition states on page 495 that:

> if, after an *optimal recovery time* following surgical decompression, an individual continues to complain of pain, paresthesias, and/or difficulties in performing certain activities, three possible scenarios can be present:

1. Positive clinical findings of median nerve dysfunction and electrical conduction delay(s): the impairment due to residual CTS is rated according to the sensory and/or motor deficits as described earlier.
2. Normal sensibility and opposition strength with abnormal sensory and/or motor latencies or abnormal EMG testing of the thenar muscles: a residual CTS is still present, and an impairment rating not to exceed 5% of the upper extremity may be justified.
3. Normal sensibility (two-point discrimination and Semmes-Weinstein monofilament testing), opposition strength, and nerve conduction studies: there is no objective basis for an impairment rating.)

In this case, when the patient reached maximum medical improvement there were no objective, anatomical findings consistent with ongoing median nerve involvement. In the past, however, the diagnosis of carpel tunnel syndrome was confirmed by electrophysiological studies. Therefore, scenario two exists, and according to the *Guides,* "an impairment rating not to exceed 5% of the upper extremity may be justified." Based on mild symptoms, a 2% upper extremity impairment was assigned, which, per Table 16-3 (5th ed, p 439), converted to a 1% whole person impairment.

Impairment: 1% whole person impairment per the Fifth Edition.

Sixth Edition Rating

The diagnosis of carpal tunnel syndrome was confirmed electrodiagnostically (with an appropriate preoperative evaluation), and the patient was at maximum medical improvement. Rating was performed as described in Section 15.4f, Entrapment Neuropathy (6th ed, p 432), and Table 15-23, Entrapment/Compression Neuropathy (6th ed, p 449). Test findings were grade modifier 1 (conduction delay), history was grade modifier 0 or 1 (mild intermittent symptoms), and physical findings were grade modifier 0 or 1 (normal). The grade modifiers therefore could range from a total of 1 (1 + 0 + 0) to 3 (1 + 1 + 1), and thus averaged between 0.33 and 1. Providing her with the benefit of the doubt, she was assigned grade modifier 1. Her *Quick*DASH score was in the normal range at 0, therefore the lowest impairment for grade modifier 1 was assigned, that is, 1% upper extremity impairment, which is equivalent to a 1% hand impairment or 1% whole person impairment.

Impairment: 1% whole person impairment per the Sixth Edition.

Comment on Nerve Entrapment

Carpal tunnel syndrome is the most common peripheral nerve entrapment. Compression of the median nerve at the wrist may cause symptoms such as pain, weakness, numbness, and/or paresthesias of the hand and digits as well as causing functional limitations. Important issues include:

1. To what degree hand-digit symptoms are due to carpal tunnel syndrome or some other condition
2. If symptoms are due to carpel tunnel syndrome, the other factors that may contribute to median nerve entrapment in the specific case
3. Impairment rating by the *Guides* for any residual physical and/or electrodiagnostic findings

The approaches to rating this illness are quite different among the three editions.

SUMMARY

Diagnosis	Carpal tunnel syndrome
Fourth Edition References	Section 3.1k (4th ed, p 46), Table 11 (4th ed, p 48), Table 12 (4th ed, p 49), Table 15 (4th ed, p 54), Table 16 (4th ed, p 57)
Fourth Edition Summary	Severity of sensory loss and pain are documented. Severity of muscle weakness is documented. Impairment can be rated by means of either Tables 11, 12, and 15 (preferred method) or, alternatively, Table 16.
Fourth Edition Impairment	0% upper extremity impairment, 0% whole person impairment
Fifth Edition References	Section 16.5d (5th ed, p 491)
Fifth Edition Summary	Severity of sensory loss and pain are documented. Severity of muscle weakness is documented. Appropriate scenario for rating as described on page 495 is identified.

Fifth Edition Impairment	2% upper extremity impairment, 1% whole person impairment
Sixth Edition References	Section 15.4f (6th ed, p 433), Table 15-23 (6th ed, p 449)
Sixth Edition Summary	Test findings are assessed. History is clarified and sensory and motor findings are determined. Average grade modifier is defined. *Quick*DASH score is assessed, and impairment is selected.
Sixth Edition Impairment	1% upper extremity impairment, 1% whole person impairment

Chapter 16

The Lower Extremities

CASE 16-1

Total Knee Replacement

Subject: Mr Jerome, a 50-year-old man.

History: Mr Jerome sustained a series of right-knee injuries during his career as a football player. His first injury occurred on the football field at age 19; it involved a twisting mechanism and resulted in a complex tear of the medial meniscus. It was treated with an open total medial meniscectomy. Mr Jerome recovered, completed the remainder of his college career, and went on to play professional football. However, during his second year in the pros, he was struck in the posterolateral knee, resulting in complete tears of the medial collateral and anterior cruciate ligaments. The medial collateral ligament was repaired and the anterior cruciate ligament reconstructed. After 1 year of rehabilitation (during which the previously solid repair and reconstruction stretched slightly), Mr Jerome resumed playing but never achieved his former level of proficiency. During that and the subsequent season, he experienced three episodes of his knee "giving way" when he was cutting or pivoting, the last resulting in a flap tear of the lateral meniscus. He was treated with an arthroscopic partial lateral meniscectomy. Mr Jerome missed the remaining 6 weeks of that season, could not pass the physical examination at the start of the next, and retired from the game.

Twenty-five years later, Mr Jerome experienced almost circumferential pain in his right knee while weightbearing, particularly when ascending or descending stairs. He also complained of pain and stiffness upon awakening in the morning and after any prolonged immobilization. Mr Jerome also reported at that time that the knee gave way perhaps twice a month, for instance, when stepping off a curb or rounding a corner. These episodes were typically associated with swelling and increased pain lasting several days. These symptoms prompted orthopedic evaluation 2 years prior to the impairment evaluation.

Examination at that time showed mild diffuse edema with a small effusion, 2-cm-greater circumference of the right knee, 2+ Lachman and anterior drawer signs, 3+ laxity on valgus stress, and a positive pivot shift. Patellofemoral crepitus was also noted with positive inhibition; the examination was otherwise unremarkable. X rays showed moderately severe tricompartmental degenerative arthritis. Therefore, approximately 2 years before the impairment evaluation, Mr Jerome underwent total knee replacement, with significant improvement in the pain and instability.

Current Symptoms: At the current examination, he had discomfort only when ascending or descending stairs, and then only occasionally. While the right knee still felt looser and weaker than the left, Mr Jerome denied any episodes of the knee giving way since the surgery.

Functional Assessment: The American Academy of Orthopaedic Surgeons (AAOS) Lower Limb Outcome Scale score was 94.

Physical Examination: Examination showed an active range of motion (with gravity eliminated) of 5° extension to 95° flexion, 8 mm of anterior-posterior motion on drawer testing, and 7° of medial-lateral angulation on valgus-varus ligamentous instability testing. Mr Jerome had an extension lag of 10° (maximal extension was to 5° of flexion; extension lag is the difference between passive extension and active extension), but passively it was possible to extend the knee to 5°. Standing alignment was 4° valgus. Mr Jerome's continued well-developed right quadriceps and hamstrings were equal in strength to their counterparts on the left. Sensory testing showed hypesthesia overlying 6-cm medial, 3-cm anteromedial, and 20-cm anterior surgical scars, as well as lateral to the distal half of the latter scar, corresponding to the distribution of the infrapatellar branch of the saphenous nerve. His gait was mildly antalgic, with a shortened stance phase.

Clinical Studies: X-ray films prior to the knee replacement showed moderately severe tricompartmental degenerative arthritis.

Discussion of Total Knee Replacement

Fourth Edition Rating

Impairment evaluation is based on Section 3.2i, Diagnosis-Based Estimates (4th ed, pp 84-88). According to Table 66, Rating Knee Replacement

Results (4th ed, p 66), the quality of the surgical result is scored on a point system, which Table 64, Impairment Estimates for Certain Lower Extremity Impairment (4th ed, pp 85-86), converts into an impairment percentage. Points are added for three categories, with points deducted for complications in three different categories.

Mr Jerome's occasional pain noted on "stairs only" warrants 40 points. The total of 100° of motion (5° of extension to 95° of flexion), at 1 point for each 5°, yields another 20 points. Anterior-posterior motion (instability) of 8 mm and 7° of medial-lateral angulation (instability) warrant ratings of 5 and 10 points, respectively. Adding the points in categories a, b, and c yields a total of 75. There is no flexion contracture, as the knee passively extends to 5° of extension. The 10° extension lag warrants a deduction of 10 points. The valgus alignment of 4° results in no point deduction. Totaling categories d, e, and f results in a deduction of 10 points. The point total for Mr Jerome's knee replacement is 75 − 10 = 65.

According to Table 64, this constitutes a fair result, equivalent to 50% impairment of the lower extremity or 20% whole person impairment.

Impairment: 20% whole person impairment per the Fourth Edition.

Fifth Edition Rating

Impairment evaluation is based on Section 17.2j, Diagnosis-Based Estimates (5th ed, pp 545-549). According to Table 17-35, Rating Knee Replacement Results (5th ed, p 549), the quality of the surgical result is scored on a point system, which Table 17-33, Impairment Estimates for Certain Lower Extremity Impairments (5th ed, pp 546-547), converts into an impairment percentage. Points are added for three categories, with points deducted for complications in three different categories.

Mr Jerome's occasional pain noted on "stairs only" warrants 40 points. The total of 100° of motion (5° of extension to 95° of flexion), at 1 point for each 5°, yields another 20 points. Anterior-posterior motion or instability of 8 mm and 7° of medial-lateral angulation (instability) warrant ratings of 5 and 10 points, respectively. Adding the points in categories a, b, and c yields a total of 75. There is no flexion contracture, as the knee passively extends to 5° of extension. The 10° extension lag warrants a deduction of 10 points. The valgus alignment of 4° results in no point deduction, however. Totaling categories d, e, and f results in a deduction of 10 points. The point total for Mr Jerome's knee replacement is 75 − 10 = 65.

According to Table 17-33, this constitutes a fair result, equivalent to 50% impairment of the lower extremity or 20% whole person impairment.

Impairment: 20% whole person impairment per the Fifth Edition.

Sixth Edition Rating

The *Guides* approach to the evaluation of impairment due to total knee replacement is based on Section 16.2, Diagnosis-Based Impairment (6th ed, p 497).

In Table 16-3, Knee Regional Grid—Lower Extremity Impairments (6th ed, p 511), in the section on Osteotomy/Knee Replacement for the diagnosis "Total Knee Replacement," there is a class 3 rating for "fair result" (with a default impairment of 37% lower extremity impairment). The *Guides* does not provide quantitative parameters for determination of "fair result"; however, the physical examination findings are consistent with "fair position, mild instability and/or mild motion deficit."

In Section 16.3a, Adjustment Grid: Functional History (6th ed, p 516), and Table 16-6, Functional History Adjustment: Lower Extremities (6th ed, p 516), the patient is assigned grade modifier 1; the functional history is consistent with "antalgic limp with asymmetric shortened stance, corrects with footwear modifications and/or orthotics." Section 16.3b, Adjustment Grid: Physical Examination (6th ed, p 517), Table 16-7, Physical Examination Adjustment: Lower Extremities (6th ed, p 517), would not be applicable since physical examination findings were used to define "fair result" and class placement. Section 16.3c, Adjustment Grid: Clinical Studies (6th ed, p 518), and Table 16-8, Clinical Studies Adjustment: Lower Extremities (6th ed, p 519), are also not applicable since the X-ray films were preoperative. In summary, the adjustments are as follows: functional history grade modifier (GMFH) 1, physical examination (GMPE) not applicable, and clinical studies (GMCS) not applicable. Net adjustment compared to diagnosis class (CDX) 3 is −2, grade A, 31% lower extremity impairment.

Class 3—Default for Diagnosis = 37% lower extremity impairment			
CDX	GMFH	GMPE	GMCS
3	1	n/a	n/a
Net adjustment			
(GMFH − CDX) 1 − 3 = −2			
+ (GMPE − CDX) + n/a			
+ (GMCS − CDX) + n/a			
Net adjustment = −2			

Result is class 3 adjustment −2, which results in class 3, grade A = 31% lower extremity impairment.

According to Table 16-10, Impairment Values Calculated From Lower Extremity Impairment (6th ed, p 530), 31% lower extremity impairment converts to 12% whole person impairment.

Impairment: 12% whole person impairment per the Sixth Edition.

Comment on Total Knee Replacement

The Fourth and Fifth Editions used a point system to rate the results of total knee replacement. The rating system is minimally modified from a published rating system devised by the Knee Society.[1] In the Fourth and Fifth Editions, Table 64 (4th ed, p 85) or Table 17-33 (5th ed, pp 546-547), Impairment Estimates for Certain Lower Extremity Impairments, classifies the results of knee replacement as good, fair, or poor on the basis of a 0- to 100-point rating system. Percentages for whole person impairment (and for lower extremity impairment) for good, fair, and poor results are listed as 15% (37%), 20% (50%), and 30% (75%) of the whole person (lower extremity). The point system is described in Table 66 (4th ed, p 88) or Table 17-35 (5th ed, p 549), Rating Knee Replacement Results. Points to describe the individual's pain status, range of motion, and stability are assigned and added together. A perfect result would yield a score of 100 points when these three factors are considered.

Deductions from the score are then computed for flexion contracture, extension lag, and alignment problems (if present). The final point score is thus the sum of the points from categories a, b, and c, minus the sum of points in categories d, e, and f. The point score is used to classify a result as good, fair, or poor in the Fourth Edition with Table 64 or the Fifth Edition with Table 17-33.

Category a awards points on the basis of the physician's assessment of the individual's pain. In assessing operative results for medical research, the person's perception of pain would be the only factor considered. In impairment rating, however, the physician's assessment of the patient's pain is what is rated in category a.

Category b awards points for range of motion. If a 125° arc of motion is present, the individual would have a maximal score of 25 points (one point per 5°). If the knee only moves a total of 50° (for example, from 10° to 60° of flexion), the result would earn 10 points in this category.

Category c is the clinical estimation of stability. This estimation is done by a physician. Anterior-posterior stability indicates the amount of anterior drawer sign and/or posterior drawer sign present when the knee is examined at 90° of flexion. The movement or displacement of the tibia relative to the femur is rated in millimeters of motion that occur. The "mediolateral" stability is measured in degrees of angulation between the femur and the tibia with the goniometer on the anterior aspect of the leg while the physician stresses the medial collateral ligament complex by valgus stress and then the lateral collateral ligament complex by varus stress.

Category d describes deductions for flexion contracture. A flexion contracture is the failure of the knee to come to the fully extended or 0° position in its passive range of motion.

Category e describes extension lag that is different from flexion contracture. Extension lag describes the difference in range-of-motion testing between the individual's active extension and passive extension. For example, if on passive range-of-motion examination the examiner is able to move the individual's knee from 10° of flexion to 100° of flexion, then a 10° flexion contracture is present. If the person is only able to actively extend his or her knee to 30°, then a 20° extension lag is present (the difference between 30° and 10°). If the person's active extension lag is identical to the passive flexion contracture, no points are deducted for extension lag, as the flexion contracture category adequately considers the impairment.

Category f describes the clinical alignment of the leg (valgus or knock-kneed, as opposed to varus or bow-legged). Alignment is assessed by placing the goniometer on the anterior aspect of the knee, aligning the top arm of the goniometer with the femur and the bottom arm of the goniometer with the tibia. This is not measuring the "Q angle" for patellar alignment, but rather measuring the alignment of the tibia relative to the femur. For alignment problems between 5° and 15° of either varus or valgus, 3 points are deducted for each degree of malalignment. This would be a potential total of 33 points deducted for having a knee with a 15° alignment angle. If the malalignment is worse than 15°, 20 additional points are deducted in addition to the 33 points derived from the "3 points per degree" calculation.

By considering the six separate categories, a point score can be obtained that permits a permanent impairment percentage to be derived in the Fourth Edition from Table 64 or the Fifth Edition from Table 17-33.

In the Sixth Edition, the rating is based on the Diagnosis-Based Impairment approach. Descriptions are provided for good, fair, and poor results; however, quantitative criteria are not provided. The default impairment values are 25% lower extremity impairment for good result, 37% lower extremity impairment for fair result, and 67% lower extremity permanent impairment for poor result; previous values were a corresponding 37%, 50%, and 75% lower extremity impairment. The values were decreased on the basis of improved outcomes with newer technologies used for total knee replacement.

SUMMARY

Diagnosis	Total knee replacement
Fourth Edition References	Section 3.2i (4th ed, pp 84-88), Table 64 (4th ed, pp 85-86), Table 66 (4th ed, p 88)
Fourth Edition Summary	Measure range of motion, stability, flexion contracture, extension lag, and alignment. Assess pain. Determine impairment on the basis of pain and physical examination—not radiographic criteria.
Fourth Edition Impairment	50% lower extremity impairment, 20% whole person impairment
Fifth Edition References	Section 17.2j (5th ed, pp 545-549), Table 17-33 (5th ed, pp 546-547), Table 17-35 (5th ed, p 549)
Fifth Edition Summary	Measure range of motion, stability, flexion contracture, extension lag, and alignment. Assess pain. Determine impairment on the basis of pain and physical examination—not radiographic criteria.
Fifth Edition Impairment	50% lower extremity impairment, 20% whole person impairment
Sixth Edition References	Section 16.2 (6th ed, p 497), Table 16-3 (6th ed, p 511), Table 16-6 (6th ed, p 516), Table 16-7 (6th ed, p 517), Table 16-8 (6th ed, p 519), Table 16-10 (6th ed, p 530)
Sixth Edition Summary	Measure range of motion, stability, flexion contracture, extension lag, and alignment. Assess pain. Determine result on the basis of pain and physical examination. Base impairment on Diagnosis-Based Impairment.
Sixth Edition Impairment	31% lower extremity impairment, 12% whole person impairment

CASE 16-2

Below-Knee Amputation

Subject: Mr Franklin, a 34-year-old man.

History: Mr Franklin was a forklift operator who drove off a loading platform. His right leg was crushed under the forklift, resulting in extensive bony and soft-tissue destruction. Multiple surgical procedures were done to salvage the limb, but all were unsuccessful. Mr Franklin underwent a right below-knee amputation (BKA) 28 days after the initial injury. He developed a postoperative stump infection and suture site skin slough. These ultimately healed and closed well with intravenous antibiotics, whirlpool, and local wound care.

Mr Franklin spent 4 weeks on a rehabilitation unit, participating in stump wrapping techniques, dynamic stump exercises, and gait training activities with a temporary prosthesis. A permanent below-knee prosthesis was fabricated 12 weeks after the BKA when the residual limb swelling had subsided. The residual limb measured only 2.5 inches from the medial tibial plateau to the fleshy end. This necessitated a prosthesis with a suprapatellar strap in order to hold the prosthesis onto his limb.

Current Symptoms: Mr Franklin used a straight cane routinely for gait stability and had mild complaints of pain with flat surfaces, increased to moderate going up or down stairs. He had no pain at night. He complained of "stiffness" of his knee, not being able to fully bend or extend his remaining stump. He was independent with donning and doffing the prosthesis as well as in self-care skills.

Functional Assessment: The AAOS Lower Limb Outcomes Questionnaire score was 71 (standardized mean).

Physical Examination: Examination of the right lower extremity 2 years after the amputation showed the sensation, skin, and circulation to be intact. The range of knee motion was restricted from 10° to 100°. The muscle power was normal (5/5) in knee flexion and extension. The suture site was well healed without evidence of neuroma or phantom limb pain. Evaluation of the right hip and nonaffected left lower extremity were normal.

Clinical Studies: None available.

Discussion of Below-Knee Amputation

Fourth Edition Rating

Impairment evaluation is based on Section 3.2h, Amputations, Table 63, Impairment Estimates for Amputations (4th ed, p 83), and Table 41, Knee Impairment (4th ed, p 78). According to Table 63, a BKA with a residual limb less than 3 inches long qualifies for a 32% whole person impairment rating.

Furthermore, Table 41 lists the 10° knee flexion contracture as a moderate 8% whole person impairment. Limited flexion to 100° is listed as a mild impairment with a 4% whole person impairment rating. The highest category of rating is used, giving 8% whole person impairment.

Combining the impairment for the amputation (32% of the whole person) with the motion impairment (8% of the whole person) by means of the Combined Values Chart (4th ed, pp 322-324) results in a 37% whole person impairment.

Impairment: 37% whole person impairment per the Fourth Edition.

Fifth Edition Rating

Impairment evaluation is based on Section 17.2i, Amputations; Table 17-32, Impairment Estimates for Amputations (5th ed, p 545); Section 17.2f, Range of Motion (5th ed, pp 533-538); and Table 17-10, Knee Impairment (5th ed, p 537). According to Table 17-32, a BKA with a residual limb less than 3 inches long qualifies for a 32% whole person impairment or 80% lower extremity rating.

Furthermore, Table 17-10 lists the 10° knee flexion contracture as a moderate impairment of 8% of the whole person or 20% of the lower extremity. Limited flexion to 100° is listed as a mild impairment with a 4% whole person or 10% lower extremity impairment rating. Section 17.2f advises, "Range-of-motion restrictions in multiple directions do increase the impairment. Add range-of-motion impairments for a single joint to determine the total joint range-of-motion impairments." Therefore, the impairment from loss of motion and ankylosis is 12% of the whole person or 30% of the lower extremity.

Table 17-2, Guide to the Appropriate Combination of Evaluation Methods (5th ed, p 526), indicates that ratings for amputations may be combined with ratings for loss of range of motion or ankylosis.

Section 17.2a, Converting From Lower Extremity to Whole Person Impairment (5th ed, pp 527-528), contains directions for combining multiple lower extremity impairments. In this case, the knee and the BKA are in the same "region" of the lower extremity. "If there are multiple impairments within a region, . . . combine these regional, lower extremity impairments . . . and convert . . . to a whole person impairment" (5th ed, p 528).

Combining the impairment for the amputation (80% lower extremity) with the motion impairment (30% lower extremity) by means of the Combined Values Chart (5th ed, p 604) results in an 86% lower extremity impairment. Table 17-3, Whole Person Impairment Values Calculated From Lower Extremity Impairment (5th ed, p 527), converts the 86% lower extremity impairment to a 34% whole person impairment. This rating process is summarized in Figure 17-10 (5th ed, p 561), as shown here on page 371.

Impairment: 34% whole person impairment per the Fifth Edition.

Sixth Edition Rating

Impairment evaluation is based on Section 16.6, Amputation Impairment (6th ed, pp 542-543). Per Table 16-16, Amputation Impairment (6th ed, p 542), for an amputation "below knee, < 3 inches" there is a default impairment of 80% lower extremity impairment. According to Table 16-6, Functional History Adjustment—Lower Extremities (6th ed, p 516), and Mr Franklin's use of a single gait aid (cane), there is grade modifier 2 (moderate problem).

Any motion deficits of the knee are assessed per Section 16.7, Range-of-Motion Impairment (6th ed, pp 543-551), and per Table 16-23, Knee Motion Impairments (6th ed, p 549); flexion of 100° results in a 10% lower extremity impairment (mild severity), and flexion contracture of 10° results in a 20% lower extremity impairment (moderate severity). These impairments are added, resulting in 30% lower extremity impairment. According to Table 16-25, Range of Motion ICF Classification (6th ed, p 550), this is consistent with class 3 (severe). The range-of-motion impairment (30% lower extremity) is combined with the amputation impairment (80% lower extremity), resulting in 86% lower extremity impairment. Per Table 16-10, Impairment Values Calculated From Lower Extremity Impairment (6th ed, p 530), this converts to 34% whole person impairment.

Impairment: 34% whole person impairment per the Sixth Edition.

Comment on Below-Knee Amputation

The Sixth Edition bases amputation impairment on the level of the amputation with default values equivalent to the Fourth and Fifth Editions. The values may be modified to higher values if supported by functional history, proximal physical examination findings, and the results of clinical studies.

The amputation impairment may also be combined with proximal motion deficits, as has occurred in this case.

Earlier editions had a similar approach in defining the impairment on the level of the amputation combined with other impairments, such as proximal motion deficits; however, there were no adjustment factors.

Regarding motion deficits, specific directions were provided in the Fifth Edition advising that multiple deficits of motion of the same joint are to be added. This same directive is provided in the Sixth Edition.

In the Fourth and Fifth Editions, no additional impairment rating was given for the routine use of a cane; however, in the Sixth Edition this can serve as a basis for defining the functional history modifier. In the Fourth and Fifth Editions gait derangement is a stand-alone impairment not combined with any other impairment evaluation method, and, whenever possible, the evaluator should use a more specific method. In this particular case, the below-knee amputation with restricted knee range of motion is the specific condition determining the impairment, not the gait derangement with use of a cane.

SUMMARY

Diagnosis	Below-knee amputation
Fourth Edition References	Section 3.2h (4th ed, p 83), Table 63 (4th ed, p 83), Table 41 (4th ed, p 78)
Fourth Edition Summary	Length of residual limb, restricted motion, and, as applicable, impairment for proximal conditions.
Fourth Edition Impairment	37% whole person impairment
Fifth Edition References	Section 17.2i (5th ed, p 545), Section 17.2f (5th ed, pp 533-538), Table 17-32 (5th ed, p 545), Table 17-10 (5th ed, p 537)
Fifth Edition Summary	Length of residual limb, restricted motion, and, as applicable, impairment for proximal conditions.
Fifth Edition Impairment	86% lower extremity impairment, 34% whole person impairment

Sixth Edition References	Section 16.6 (6th ed, pp 542-543), Table 16-16 (6th ed, p 542), Table 16-6 (6th ed, p 516), Section 16.7 (6th ed, pp 543-551), Table 16-23 (6th ed, p 549), Table 16-10 (6th ed, p 530)
Sixth Edition Summary	History (including functional history and inventories), physical evaluation, and clinical studies. First, determine amputation impairment, class, and default value. Second, determine range of motion impairment and combine.
Sixth Edition Impairment	86% lower extremity impairment, 34% whole person impairment

Lower Extremity Impairment Evaluation Record and Worksheet

Name Mr. Franklin Age 34 Sex M Side ☒R ☐L Date

Diagnosis Below-the-knee Amputation CASE 16-2

Region	Abnormal Motion	Regional Impairments	Table #	Percent	Amputation Location	Amputation Percent	Final Impairment Utilized: Methodology	Percent
Pelvis		DBE DJD Skin Leg Length Amp	17-33 17-31 17-36 17-4 17-32	% % % % %			DBE DJD Skin Leg Length Amputation	% % % % %
Hip	Tables 17-9 and 17-15 to 17-19 Flexion / Extension / Ankylosis / Impairment % Angle / Impairment Abduction / Adduction / Ankylosis / Impairment % Angle / Impairment Internal Rot / External Rot / Ankylosis / Impairment % Angle / Impairment Add impairment % ROM or use largest ankylosis = %	DBE DJD Skin Leg Length Weakness Amp	17-33/34 17-31 17-36 17-4 17-8 17-32	% % % % % %			DBE DJD Skin Leg Length Weakness ROM Amputation	% % % % % % %
Thigh	(Consider related pathology at hip and knee)	Atrophy DJD Skin Leg Length Amp	17-6 17-31 17-36 17-4 17-32	% % % % %			Atrophy DJD Skin Leg Length Amputation	% % % % %
Knee	Tables 17-10 and 17-20 to 17-23 Flexion / Extension / Ankylosis / Impairment % Angle: 100 / -10 Impairment: 10% LE / 20% LE Add impairment % ROM or use largest ankylosis = 30 LE %	DBE DJD Skin Weakness Amp	17-33/35 17-31 17-36 17-8 17-32	% % % % 80 % LE	BKA <3″		DBE DJD Skin Weakness Amputation + ROM >86	% % % % % LE
Calf	(Consider related pathology at knee and ankle)	Atrophy DBE Skin Leg Length Amp	17-6 17-33 17-36 17-4 17-32	% % % % %			Atrophy DBE Skin Leg Length Amputation	% % % % %
Ankle/ Foot	Tables 17-11 to 17-13 and 17-24 to 17-28 Dorsiflex / Plantarflex / Ankylosis / Impairment % Angle / Impairment Inversion / Eversion / Ankylosis / Impairment % Angle / Impairment Add impairment % ROM or use largest ankylosis = %	DBE DJD Skin Weakness Amp	17-29/33 17-31 17-36 17-8/9 17-32	% % % % %			DBE DJD Skin Weakness ROM Amputation	% % % % % %
Toe	Tables 17-14 and 17-30 Great Toe: MP Dorsiflex / IP Plantarflex / Ankylosis / Impairment % Angle / Impairment Lesser Toes: MP Dorsiflex / Ankylosis / Impairment % Angle / Impairment Add impairment % ROM or use largest ankylosis = %	DBE DJD Skin Weakness Amp	17-33 17-31 17-36 17-8/14 17-32	% % % % %			DBE DJD Skin Weakness ROM Amputation	% % % % % %

Peripheral Nervous System Impairment

		Grade %	Nerve %	Total %	Nerve	Maximum Motor %	Maximum Sensory %	Maximum Dysesthesia %
Motor Grade (Table 16-14)		×	=					
Sensory Grade (Table 16-15)		×	=					
Dysesthesia Grade		×	=			Combine all neurologic components %		

Peripheral Vascular System Impairment (Table 17-38)

Grade ______ Total vascular system impairment %

Gait Derangement (This is a *stand-alone* impairment and may *not* be combined) (Table 17-5) 20 % WP

Final Combined Impairment (An explanation should be provided if more than one methodology is used, justifying the rationale for each methodology used) 86% LE, 34 % WP

DBE = diagnosis-based estimates; DJD = degenerative joint disease (arthritis).

CASE 16-3

Osteomyelitis Secondary to Frostbite

Subject: Mr Adams, a 53-year-old man.

History: Mr Adams sustained a frostbite injury to his left second, third, fourth, and fifth toes while working outside in frigid December weather. He presented to the local hospital emergency department with pain, redness, and swelling of the left foot and toes. Conservative treatment was begun. Mr Adams returned 24 hours later with crusting and scabbing at the tips of toes 2 through 5. He admitted to increased alcohol consumption during the previous several days and also gave a history of borderline adult-onset diabetes, controlled with diet, and smoking one pack of cigarettes per day. During the ensuing weeks, Mr Adams presented with increased swelling, pain, and discomfort in the toes, and finally ulceration and seepage, from which culture yielded *Staphylococcus aureus*. The problem progressed to amputation of toes 2, 3, and 4 at the metatarsophalangeal joint. Pathologic evaluation was consistent with osteomyelitis.

Current Symptoms: He complained of mild discomfort and some difficulties with gait; however, he was able to ambulate without assistance.

Physical Examination: On examination, Mr Adams had clean amputation sites of the left second, third, and fourth toes. There were no ulcerations on the plantar surface of the foot. His great toe metatarsophalangeal extension was 35°, and interphalangeal flexion was 25°. The fifth toe metatarsophalangeal extension was 12°. The ankle and midtarsal aspect of the foot had normal range of motion. He had intact nail growth on the first and fifth toes and had hair present on his foot. Vascular examination showed intact arterial supply to the feet. His gait was normal, and there was no evidence of any neurologic difficulties.

Clinical Studies: None available.

Discussion of Osteomyelitis Secondary to Frostbite

Fourth Edition Rating

Section 3.2h, Amputations, and Table 63, Impairment Estimates for Amputations (4th ed, p 83), are used to assess Mr Adams' impairment. On the basis of the amputation of the three middle toes, numbers 2, 3, and 4, there is 1%

whole person impairment for each toe, for a total whole person impairment of 3%. According to Table 45, Toe Impairments (4th ed, p 78), he had no impairment for any range-of-motion deficits. His great toe metatarsal joint extended to 35° and the interphalangeal joint flexed to 25°, which is a 0% impairment. His fifth toe metatarsophalangeal joint extended to 12°, which is also 0% impairment. No other methods are applicable in this case for assessing impairment.

Impairment: 3% whole person impairment per the Fourth Edition.

Fifth Edition Rating

Section 17.2i, Amputations, and Table 17-32, Impairment Estimates for Amputations (5th ed, p 545), are used to assess Mr Adams' impairment. On the basis of the amputation of the three middle toes, numbers 2, 3, and 4, there is 1% whole person impairment for each toe, for a total whole person impairment of 3%. According to Table 17-14, Toe Impairments (5th ed, p 537), he had no impairment for any range-of-motion deficits. His great toe metatarsal joint extended to 35° and the interphalangeal joint flexed to 25°, which is a 0% impairment. His fifth toe metatarsophalangeal joint extended to 12°, which is also 0% impairment. No other methods are applicable in this case for assessing impairment.

Impairment: 3% whole person impairment per the Fifth Edition.

Sixth Edition Rating

Impairment evaluation is based on Section 16.6, Amputation Impairment (6th ed, pp 542-543). Per Table 16-16, Amputation Impairment (6th ed, p 542), for an amputation of toes 2, 3, and 4 at the metatarsophalangeal joint there is a default impairment of 2% lower extremity permanent impairment for each toe. According to Table 16-6, Functional History Adjustment—Lower Extremities (6th ed, p 516), the patient is placed on a grade modifier 0 (no problem), as no gait derangement is documented on physical examination. This warrants adjustment of the default impairments by −1 to result in 2% lower extremity impairment for each toe, resulting in 6% lower extremity impairment, which is converted to 2% whole person impairment.

According to Table 16-18, Lesser Toe Impairments (6th ed, p 549), and Table 16-19, Greater Toe Impairments (6th ed, p 549), Mr Adams had no impairment for any range-of-motion deficits. His great toe metatarsal joint extended to 35° and the interphalangeal joint flexed to 25°, which is a 0% impairment. His fifth toe metatarsophalangeal joint extended to 12°, which is also 0% impairment. No other methods are applicable in this case for assessing impairment.

Impairment: 2% whole person impairment per the Sixth Edition.

Comment on Osteomyelitis Secondary to Frostbite

In describing his condition, Mr Adams did present with the classic description of frostbite: he was in his fourth to fifth decade of age with a history of recent alcohol abuse, exposure to cold, and the wearing of inappropriate footwear in extreme cold. He was also using nicotine products at the time. He had a previous diagnosis of adult-onset diabetes mellitus; however, his diabetes was not long-standing. While his underlying diabetes may have contributed to the severity of his frostbite injury and subsequent amputations, he does not qualify for a diagnosis of amputation secondary to diabetes. The development of frostbite secondary to cold exposure is the cause of his injury.

SUMMARY

Diagnosis	Frostbite injury to foot, resulting in amputation of toes 2, 3, and 4
Fourth Edition References	Fourth Edition References Section 3.2h (4th ed, p 83), Table 63 (4th ed, p 83), Table 45 (4th ed, p 78)
Fourth Edition Summary	History, lower extremity examination, including gait, amputation level, range of motion, and any neurologic involvement. Assess lower extremity to define applicable models for assessing impairment, eg, amputation level and any applicable motion deficits.
Fourth Edition Impairment	3% whole person impairment
Fifth Edition References	Section 17.2i (5th ed, p 545), Table 17-32 (5th ed, p 545), Table 17-14 (5th ed, p 537)
Fifth Edition Summary	History, lower extremity examination, including gait, amputation level, range of motion, and any neurologic involvement. Assess lower extremity to define applicable models for assessing impairment, eg, amputation level and any applicable motion deficits.
Fifth Edition Impairment	3% whole person impairment
Sixth Edition References	Section 16.6 (6th ed, pp 542-543), Table 16-16 (6th ed, p 542), Table 16-6 (6th ed, p 516), Table 16-18 and Table 16-19 (6th ed, p 549)

Sixth Edition Summary History (including functional history and inventories), physical evaluation, and clinical studies. First, determine amputation impairment, class, and default value. Second, determine range-of-motion Impairment and combine. *In this case there was no ratable range of motion loss.*

Sixth Edition Impairment 6% lower extremity impairment, 2% whole person impairment

---

CASE 16-4

Total Hip Replacement

Subject: Mr Rubin, a 69-year-old man.

History: Mr Rubin slipped on some oil on the floor at work and sustained a femoral neck fracture of the right hip. His fracture was pinned, but he subsequently developed avascular necrosis of the hip with loss of joint space. Conservative management was attempted, including anti-inflammatories, exercises, and an occasional corticosteroid injection into the hip. All of these provided temporary relief, but his pain kept him awake at night, significantly limiting his activities and requiring codeine for pain relief.

Mr Rubin underwent total hip arthroplasty. Six months after surgery, his surgeon felt he had reached maximal medical improvement, in that the surgeon had not seen improvement in either motion or function for the past 2 months, and it was unlikely that Mr Rubin would make any further significant improvement.

Current Symptoms: Mr Rubin reported continued slight pain in the groin on long walks, and indicated that he could walk about 6 blocks before having to stop. He could climb stairs evenly by using the railing but could not ascend stairs without some assistance. He could put on his socks and shoes without difficulty. His sitting activities were unlimited, and he could use public transportation.

Functional Assessment: The AAOS Lower Limb Questionnaire raw score was 17 of 35. His interoffice examination findings and complaints are consistent with mild difficulties, with no limp on ambulation, pain with long walks and going up stairs, and no use of supportive devices.

Physical Examination: At examination, Mr Rubin walked with a normal gait and did not use any supports or assistive devices. No instability or subluxation was noted. Range-of-motion testing revealed no flexion contracture. His range of motion included flexion of 80°, abduction of 15°, adduction of 15°, external rotation of 30°, and internal rotation of 15°. His pelvis was level, and there was no evidence of leg length discrepancy.

Clinical Studies: Postsurgical radiographs documented a well-positioned prosthesis.

Discussion of Total Hip Replacement

Fourth Edition Rating

This patient's condition is evaluated by Section 3.2i, Diagnosis-Based Estimates (4th ed, pp 84-88), with the use of Table 65, Rating Hip Replacement Results (4th ed, p 87), and Table 64, Impairment Estimates for Certain Lower Extremity Impairments (4th ed, p 85). The scoring mechanism presented in Table 65 is a score sheet known as the Harris Hip Score, used to evaluate outcomes of total hip arthroplasty. The individual is given a number of points based on pain, function, activities, deformity, and range of motion. After evaluating the individual and scoring him or her on the basis of these five criteria, the rater then refers to Table 64. A total of 85 to 100 points on the Harris Hip Score is equal to a good result and results in an impairment rating of 37% of the lower extremity or 15% of the whole person. A score of 50 to 84 points is a fair result, a 50% impairment of the lower extremity or 20% of the whole person. Less than 50 points is a poor result and is equal to 75% impairment of the lower extremity or 30% of the whole person.

The history and examination described permit assessment of a total point score by means of Table 65.

Criterion	Description	No. of Points
a. Pain	Slight (with long walks)	40
b. Function	Limp—None	11
	Supportive device—None	11
	Distance walked—Six blocks	8
c. Activities	Stair climbing—Using railing	2
	Putting on shoes and socks—With ease	4
	Sitting—Any chair, 1 hour	4
	Public transportation—Able to use	1
d. Deformity	Fixed adduction—not applicable (n/a)	1
	Fixed internal rotation—n/a	1
	Fixed external rotation—n/a	1
	Fixed contracture—n/a	1
	Leg length discrepancy—n/a	1
e. Range of motion	Flexion—80°	0
	Abduction—15°	0
	Adduction—15°	0
	External rotation—30°	0
	Internal rotation—10°	0
Total	Points from the above are added to yield a total	86

Mr Rubin has a total score of 86, which is consistent with a good result; therefore, he is given a rating of 37% of the lower extremity or 15% of the whole person.

Impairment: 15% whole person impairment per the Fourth Edition.

Fifth Edition Rating

Mr Rubin's condition is evaluated by Section 17.2j, Diagnosis-Based Estimates (5th ed, pp 545-549), with the use of Table 17-34, Rating Hip Replacement Results (5th ed, p 548), and Table 17-33, Impairment Estimates for Certain Lower Extremity Impairments (5th ed, pp 546-547). The scoring mechanism presented in Table 17-34 is a score sheet known as the Harris Hip Score, used to evaluate outcomes of total hip arthroplasty. The individual is given a number of points based on pain, function, activities, deformity, and range of motion. After evaluating the individual and scoring him or her on the basis of these five criteria, the rater then refers to Table 17-33. A total of 85 to 100 points on the Harris Hip Score is equal to a good result and results in an impairment rating of 37% of the lower extremity or 15% of the whole person. A score of 50 to 84 points is a fair result, a 50% impairment of the lower extremity or 20% of the whole person. Less than 50 points is a poor result and is equal to 75% impairment of the lower extremity or 30% of the whole person.

The history and examination described permit assessment of a total point score with the use of Table 17-34. Table 17-34 is identical to Table 65, Rating Hip Replacement Results (4th ed, p 87), and the results of the scoring are as presented above in the Fourth Edition rating. Mr Rubin has a total score of 86, which is consistent with a good result; therefore, he is given a rating of 37% of the lower extremity or 15% of the whole person.

Impairment: 15% whole person impairment per the Fifth Edition.

Sixth Edition Rating

The *Guides* approach to the evaluation of impairment due to total hip replacement is based on Section 16.2, Diagnosis-Based Impairment (6th ed, p 497), and Section 16.2d, Hip (6th ed, p 500).

In Table 16-4, Hip Regional Grid—Lower Extremity Impairments (6th ed, 512), in the section on Ligament/Bone/Joint (6th ed, p 516), for the diagnosis "total hip replacement" there is a class 2 rating for good result (with a default impairment of 25%).

In Section 16.3a, Adjustment Grid: Functional History (6th ed, p 516), and Table 16-6, Functional History Adjustment: Lower Extremities (6th ed, p 516), the patient is assigned grade modifier 1; the functional history is consistent with mild difficulties with no limp on ambulation, pain with long walks and going up stairs, and no use of supportive devices. The AAOS Lower Limb Instrument score is consistent with a mild deficit. Section 16.3b, Adjustment Grid: Physical Examination (6th ed, p 517), and Table 16-7, Physical Examination Adjustment: Lower Extremities (6th ed, p 517), are not applicable since they were used in determining a good result. Section 16.3c, Adjustment Grid: Clinical Studies (6th ed, p 518), and Table 16-8, Clinical Studies Adjustment: Lower Extremities (6th ed, p 519), are also not applicable, since radiographic studies were performed prior to the replacement. In summary, the adjustments are as follows: functional history grade modifier 1, physical examination n/a, and clinical studies grade modifier n/a. Net adjustment compared to diagnosis class 2 is −1, grade B, 23% lower extremity impairment.

Class 2—Default for Diagnosis = 25% lower extremity impairment			
CDX	GMFH	GMPE	GMCS
2	1	n/a	n/a
Net adjustment (GMFH − CDX) 1 − 2 = −1 + (GMPE − CDX) n/a + (GMCS − CDX) n/a			
Net adjustment = −1			

Result is class 2 adjustment –1, which results in class 2, grade B = 23% lower extremity impairment.

According to Table 16-10, Impairment Values Calculated From Lower Extremity Impairment (6th ed, p 530), 23% lower extremity impairment converts to 9% whole person impairment.

Impairment: 9% whole person impairment per the Sixth Edition.

Comment on Total Hip Replacement

After total hip arthroplasty, individuals are rated on the basis of their functional outcome as derived from the Harris Hip Score. The resulting score categorizes the individual as having a good, fair, or poor result. The process is the same in the Fourth and Fifth Editions. Knee evaluation is very similar, using a rating scale and then classifying the result. The impairment values are the same for the hip and knee in each of the categories, eg, there will be at least a 15% whole person impairment (if there is a "good" result), with a maximum of 30% whole person impairment (if there is a "poor" result). The approach to rating arthroplasties in the upper extremity is different, since this is based on a combined impairment for the arthroplasty and for motion deficits. In the lower extremity, hip and knee range of motion is included in the factors evaluated to give the "point score" to determine the rating of the hip or knee replacement.

The Sixth Edition uses the Diagnosis-Based Impairment as the primary approach. Similar to the prior editions, hip arthroplasty cannot be combined with motion impairment, although functional and examination deficits are included per the design of Table 16-4, Hip Regional Grid: Lower Extremity Impairments (6th ed, p 513). In general, physical examination findings will be excluded from the impairment calculation because they are used for placement in an impairment class on the regional grids (eg, good, fair, or poor result). The preoperative diagnosis is not rated, since the impairment rating is calculated after the joint replacement. Impairment ratings, in general, will be lower than with previous editions for hip arthroplasties, reflecting improved outcomes with newer technologies.

SUMMARY

Diagnosis	Total hip arthroplasty
Fourth Edition References	Section 3.2i (4th ed, pp 84-88), Table 65 (4th ed, p 87), Table 64 (4th ed, p 85)
Fourth Edition Summary	History and lower extremity evaluation are performed to provide required data to score hip replacement results.
Fourth Edition Impairment	37% lower extremity impairment, 15% whole person impairment
Fifth Edition References	Section 17.2j (5th ed, pp 545-549), Table 17-34 (5th ed, p 548), Table 17-33 (5th ed, pp 546-547)
Fifth Edition Summary	History and lower extremity evaluation are performed to provide required data to score hip replacement results.
Fifth Edition Impairment	37% lower extremity impairment, 15% whole person impairment

Sixth Edition References	Section 16.2 (6th ed, p 497), Section 16.2d (6th ed, p 500), Table 16-4 (6th ed, 512), Section 16.3a (6th ed, p 516), Table 16-6 (6th ed, p 516), Table 16-10 (6th ed, p 530)
Sixth Edition Summary	History (including functional history and inventories), physical evaluation, and clinical studies. First, determine diagnosis-based impairment, class, and default value. Second, adjust impairment on basis of nonkey factors.
Sixth Edition Impairment	21% lower extremity impairment, 9% whole person impairment

CASE 16-5

Total Hip Replacement With Catastrophic Result

Subject: Ms Costello, a 30-year-old woman.

History: Ms Costello developed Legg-Calve-Perthes disease of the right femoral head at 10 years of age. Progressive hip pain had been treated conservatively until she underwent right total hip arthroplasty at the age of 12 years (in 1980). During the procedure, a metal bolt from the overhead operating room light fixture inadvertently dropped into the surgically exposed hip wound. She developed a persistent postoperative low-grade fever, and then, when she fell 5 weeks later, the trochanteric wires disrupted, with proximal migration of the trochanter. Months later, during surgery to revise the prosthesis, open culture and biopsy yielded *Staphylococcus epidermidis*. She was treated with multiple antibiotics.

During the next several months, intolerable right hip pain developed. A Girdlestone procedure was performed in early 1981 (removal of the prosthetic femoral head and prosthetic acetabulum). *Staphylococcus epidermidis* again was cultured. Ms Costello was treated with antibiotics and prolonged traction. Radiographs, gallium scan, and erythrocyte sedimentation rate suggested persistent infection.

Ms Costello was readmitted to the hospital in July 1982 for extensive debridement. Massive scarring, chronic infection, and a dollar-size acetabular defect were found at surgery. Postoperatively, she developed an acute abdomen when a section of intestine and the right ovary herniated through the defect. The herniated small bowel and right ovary were resected. A further debridement of the right hip was required and was allowed to heal secondarily. Antibiotics were continued.

She became independent in all activities of daily living and performed right leg flexion and abduction against gravity. However, she had chronic diarrhea because of a short bowel syndrome. She was treated with cholestyramine (Questran) and loperamide (Imodium). By March 1984 she was ambulating with full weight-bearing without crutches, despite a 4-cm leg length discrepancy.

After tests ruled out persistent infection, she was readmitted for total hip arthroplasty in April 1984 (her second total hip arthroplasty and fifth operation). She received a noncemented total arthroplasty followed by extensive physical therapy and was discharged.

Current Symptoms: Ms Costello continued to have chronic burning and stabbing pain, which she rated as 6 out of 10. She used hydrocodone every 4 hours and acetaminophen as needed. Her leg would occasionally "collapse" during ambulation, although she did not fall. Intermittent hip subluxation was confirmed radiographically (on supine vs standing films).

Ms Costello could sit in any chair for an hour, but not longer. She could not climb stairs because of weakness in her hip extensors and knee extensors. She could ride in a car or taxi, but she could not use the bus or subway, as stair climbing was required to enter those types of public transportation. She could don and doff her own shoes and socks with some difficulty because of her reduced hip and knee flexion.

She discontinued her cholestyramine and loperamide on her own accord, and persisted in having up to 15 bowel movements per day. She had irregular menstrual periods. She was employed as a practicing psychologist.

Functional Assessment: The AAOS Lower Limb Questionnaire raw score was 31 of 35. Physical examination findings and complaints were consistent with severe difficulties with sitting, ambulation on flat ground or stairs, problems with public transportation, difficulties with putting on socks and shoes, and use of two supportive crutches routinely.

Physical Examination: On physical examination 5 years after her last surgery, Ms Costello was obviously overweight but refused to be weighed (height, 5 ft 3 in; estimated weight, 240 lb). There was hypertrophic scarring of the right lateral thigh and buttock consequent to several hip surgeries. She had a 4-cm leg length discrepancy.

Ms Costello ambulated always using two overly long crutches and used axillary weight-bearing to substitute for partial right lower extremity weight-bearing. In her right stance phase she had a stiff knee with a relative loss of the knee component of gait. She leaned to the right with each right step in a compensated Trendelenburg gait pattern.

Musculoskeletal examination further showed the following findings:

- Intermittent hip subluxation with a palpable click
- Four-centimeter leg length discrepancy (right leg short)
- Abnormal right lower extremity range of motion

Right Hip		Right Knee	
Flexion	0°-90°	Flexion	110°
Extension	0°-10°	Extension	0° (no extension lag)
Abduction	0°-45°		
Adduction	0°-20°		
External rotation	0°-65°		
Internal rotation	0°-70°		

Neurologic examination showed the following findings:

- Hypesthesia over the right anterior and lateral thigh
- Weakness on right lower extremity manual muscle testing

Hip extensor	3/5
Hip flexor	2/5
Adductor	4/5
Hip abductor	2/5
Hip external rotator	3/5
Knee extensor	3/5
Knee flexor	3/5
Ankle dorsiflexor	5/5
Peroneal	4/5
Extensor hallucis longus	5/5

Electrodiagnostic evaluation (electromyography and nerve conduction studies) of the right lower extremity, including gluteal muscles, was normal.

Clinical Studies: Postoperative radiographs documented 4-cm leg length discrepancy (right leg short) and subluxing total hip prosthesis. Electrodiagnostic studies of the bilateral lower extremities were found to be normal.

Discussion of Total Hip Replacement With Catastrophic Result

The following medical problems are noted.

- Gait abnormality: Ms Costello reported that she was able to walk short distances up to several blocks with two crutches
- Right lateral femoral cutaneous nerve cutaneous neuropathy
- Diffuse right-leg weakness
- Chronic pain, currently on maintenance opioids
- Right-hip arthroplasty with altered range of motion (decreased flexion) and intermittent subluxation (instability)
- Chronic diarrhea secondary to small-bowel resection
- Loss of right ovary

Fourth Edition Rating

Impairment is based on the combined impairment from Chapter 3 (The Musculoskeletal System), Chapter 10 (The Digestive System), and Chapter 11 (The Urinary and Reproductive System).

Musculoskeletal System Impairment

There are anatomic, diagnostic, and functional methods of assessing lower extremity impairment, as outlined in Section 3.2, The Lower Extremity (4th ed, pp 75-93). Page 75 explains that, "in general, only one evaluation should be used to evaluate a specific impairment . . . in some instances, a combination of two or three methods may be required."

The usual way of rating a total hip replacement is to use Table 65, Rating Hip Replacement Results (4th ed, p 87), to determine a "point score," and then to consult Table 64, Impairment Estimates for Certain Lower Extremity Impairments (4th ed, p 85), to convert the point score to an impairment percentage, depending on whether the point score characterizes the result as good, fair, or poor. Leg length discrepancy and range of motion are part of the hip replacement scoring system, so they should not be used to rate impairment with Table 35, Impairment for Limb Length Discrepancy (4th ed, p 73), and Table 40, Hip Motion Impairments (4th ed, p 78). Muscle atrophy and weakness affect function, so those factors are considered in the "function" and "activities" sections of Table 65; thus, Tables 37 to 39 should not be used.

On the basis of Table 65, Ms Costello's hip replacement is scored as follows:

a. Pain	Marked	10
b. Function	Limp—Severe Supportive device—Two crutches Distance walked—Three blocks	0 0 5
c. Activities	Stair climbing—Unable Putting on shoes and socks—With difficulty Sitting—Any chair, 1 hour Public transportation—Unable to use	0 2 4 0
d. Deformity	Fixed adduction—n/a Fixed internal rotation—n/a Fixed external rotation—n/a Fixed contracture—n/a Leg length discrepancy—4 cm	1 1 1 1 0
e. Range of Motion	Flexion—90° Abduction—45° Adduction—20° External rotation—65° Internal rotation—70°	0 1 1 1 1
Total	Points from the above are added to yield a total	29

The totaled points are then used in Table 64 (4th ed, p 85). A score of less than 50 points is considered a poor result and equates to a whole person impairment of 30%.

According to Table 68, Impairments From Nerve Deficits (4th ed, p 89), the right lateral femoral cutaneous neuropathy can be rated as a 1% whole person impairment. This is probably a surgical complication that is not reflected in the hip replacement rating system, so this additional 1% whole person impairment can be combined with the 30% impairment for the total hip scoring system to yield a final rating of 31%.

Ms Costello also has a gait disturbance that could be rated with Section 3.2b, Gait Derangement (4th ed, p 76). Since she requires the constant use of two crutches for reasons medically consistent with pathologic findings (instability of the prosthetic hip and muscle weakness), Table 36, Lower Limb Impairment From Gait Derangement (4th ed, p 76), would classify her impairment as moderate in severity, with a 40% whole person impairment rating. The lower extremity impairments shown in this table should stand alone and should not be combined. Whenever possible, the evaluator should use the more specific methods of those other parts in estimating impairment. Therefore, Ms Costello's musculoskeletal impairment rating is the 31% whole person impairment derived from the use of Tables 65, 64, and 68.

Digestive System Impairment

For her digestive system impairment, Ms Costello was clearly able to maintain adequate weight. She had clearly delineated gastrointestinal pathology, having had a bowel resection and a shortened bowel. When she was using her medications, her bowel movements were reasonably well controlled, although she chose not to use medications. In Chapter 10, The Digestive System, according to Table 2, Classes of Impairment of the Upper Digestive Tract (4th ed, p 239), she would qualify as class 2: 10% to 25% whole person impairment. She was rated as having 10% whole person impairment.

Reproductive System Impairment

For the loss of the right ovary, the *Guides* provides several case vignettes in Chapter 11, The Urinary and Reproductive Systems, in the section entitled Criteria for Evaluating Permanent Impairment of the Fallopian Tubes and Ovaries (4th ed, p 262). Ms Costello required no ongoing treatment for this condition. She would be rated as class I at 5% whole person impairment as a premenopausal woman with only one ovary.

Combined Impairment

Ms Costello's whole person impairments of 31% (musculoskeletal), 10% (digestive), and 5% (reproductive) are combined by means of the Combined Values Chart (4th ed, p 322), resulting in a 41% whole person impairment.

Impairment: 41% whole person impairment per the Fourth Edition.

Fifth Edition Rating

Impairment is based on the combined impairment from Chapter 17 (The Lower Extremities), Chapter 6 (The Digestive System), and Chapter 7 (The Urinary and Reproductive Systems).

Musculoskeletal System Impairment

There are anatomic, diagnostic, and functional methods of assessing lower extremity impairment, as outlined in Section 17.2, Methods of Assessment (5th ed, pp 525-560). Page 527 explains that, "Typically, one method will adequately characterize the impairment and its impact on the ability to perform ADL. In some cases, however, more than one method needs to be used to accurately assess all features of the impairment" (5th ed, p 527).

Section 17.2j, Diagnosis-Based Estimates (5th ed, pp 545-550), is used to rate hip replacements. Table 17-34, Rating Hip Replacement Results (5th ed, p 548), determines a "point score," and Table 17-33, Impairment Estimates for Certain Lower Extremity Impairments (5th ed, p 546), converts the point score to an impairment percentage, depending on whether the point score characterizes the result as good, fair, or poor. Leg length discrepancy and range of motion are part of the hip replacement scoring system, so they should not be used to rate impairment with Table 17-4, Impairment Due to Limb Length Discrepancy (5th ed, p 528), or Table 17-9, Hip Motion Impairments (5th ed, p 537). Muscle atrophy and weakness affect function, so those factors are considered in the "function" and "activities" sections of Table 17-34; thus, Tables 17-6 to 17-8 should not be used.

On the basis of Table 17-34, Ms Costello's hip replacement is scored as follows:

a. Pain	Marked	10
b. Function	Limp—Severe Supportive device—Two crutches Distance walked—Three blocks	0 0 5
c. Activities	Stair climbing—Unable Putting on shoes and socks—With difficulty Sitting—Any chair, 1 hour Public transportation—Unable to use	0 2 4 0
d. Deformity	Fixed adduction—n/a Fixed internal rotation—n/a Fixed external rotation—n/a Fixed contracture—n/a Leg length discrepancy—4 cm	1 1 1 1 0
e. Range of Motion	Flexion—90° Abduction—45° Adduction—20° External rotation—65° Internal rotation—70°	0 1 1 1 1
Total	Points from the above are added to yield a total	29

The totaled points are then used in Table 17-33, Impairment Estimates for Certain Lower Extremity Impairments (5th ed, p 546). A score of less than 50 points is considered a poor result and equates to a whole person impairment of 30%.

With Table 17-37, Impairments From Nerve Deficits (5th ed, p 552), the right lateral femoral cutaneous neuropathy can be rated as a 1% whole person impairment. This is probably a surgical complication that is not reflected in the hip replacement rating system, so this additional 1% whole person impairment can be combined with the 30% impairment for the total hip scoring system to yield a final rating of 31%.

Ms Costello also has a gait disturbance that could be rated with Section 17.2c, Gait Derangement (5th ed, pp 529-531). Since she requires the constant use of two crutches for reasons medically consistent with pathologic findings (instability of the prosthetic hip and muscle weakness), Table 17-5, Lower Limb Impairment Due to Gait Derangement (5th ed, p 529), would classify her impairment as moderate in severity, with a 40% whole person impairment rating. The lower extremity impairments shown in this table should stand alone and should not be combined. Whenever possible, the evaluator should use the more specific methods of those other parts in estimating impairment. Therefore, Ms Costello's musculoskeletal impairment rating is the 31% whole person impairment based on the rating of her hip replacement (30%) and her femoral cutaneous neuropathy (1%).

Digestive System Impairment

For her digestive system impairment, Ms Costello was clearly able to maintain adequate weight. She had clearly delineated gastrointestinal pathology, having had a bowel resection and a shortened bowel. When she was using her medications, her bowel movements were reasonably well controlled, although she chose not to use the medications. In Chapter 6, The Digestive System, Section 6.2, Upper Digestive Tract (5th ed, pp 120-127), according to Table 6-3, Criteria for Rating Permanent Impairment Due to Upper Digestive Tract Disease (5th ed, p 121), she would qualify as class 2: 10% to 22% whole person impairment. She was rated at the lower range as having 10% whole person impairment.

Reproductive System Impairment

The loss of Ms Costello's right ovary is rated in Chapter 7, The Urinary and Reproductive Systems, with the use of Section 7.8f, Fallopian Tubes and Ovaries (5th ed, pp 167-169). According to Table 7-11, Criteria for Rating Permanent Impairment of the Fallopian Tubes and Ovaries (5th ed, p 167), she receives a rating of class 1 at 5% whole person impairment. This is based on not requiring continuous treatment and having only one functioning ovary in the premenopausal period.

Combined Impairment

Ms Costello's whole person impairments of 31% (lower extremity), 10% (digestive), and 5% (reproductive) are combined by means of the Combined Values Chart (5th ed, p 604), resulting in a 41% whole person impairment.

Impairment: 41% whole person impairment per the Fifth Edition.

Sixth Edition Rating

Impairment is based on the combined impairment from Chapter 16 (The Lower Extremities), Chapter 6 (The Digestive System), and Chapter 7 (The Urinary and Reproductive Systems).

Musculoskeletal System Impairment

The *Guides* approach to the evaluation of impairment due to total hip replacement is based on Section 16.2, Diagnosis-Based Impairment (6th ed, p 497), and Section 16.2d, Hip (6th ed, p 500). In Table 16-4, Hip Regional Grid—Lower Extremity Impairments, in the section on Osteotomy/Joint Replacement (6th ed, p 515), for the diagnosis "total hip replacement" there is a class 4 rating for "poor result" (with a default impairment of 67%). Poor result is defined as "poor position, moderate to severe instability, and/or moderate to severe motion deficit."

In Section 16.3a, Adjustment Grid: Functional History (6th ed, p 516), and Table 16-6, Functional History Adjustment: Lower Extremities (6th ed, p 516), the patient is assigned initially grade modifier 3; the functional history is consistent with severe difficulties with sitting, ambulation on flat ground or stairs, problems with public transportation, difficulties with putting on socks and shoes, and use of two supportive crutches routinely. With the diagnostic class rating being a class 4 impairment, 1 is added to each of the nonkey factors, resulting in a functional history adjustment of grade modifier 4. Section 16.3b, Adjustment Grid: Physical Examination (6th ed, p 517), and Table 16-7, Physical Examination Adjustment: Lower Extremities (6th ed, p 517), are not applied since these were used for class placement. Section 16.3c, Adjustment Grid: Clinical Studies (6th ed, p 518), and Table 16-8, Clinical Studies Adjustment: Lower Extremities (6th ed, p 520), are not applicable since the preoperative radiographic findings are resolved. In summary, the adjustments are as follows: functional history grade modifier 4, physical examination n/a, and clinical studies grade modifier n/a. Net adjustment compared to diagnosis class 4 is 0, grade C, 67% lower extremity impairment.

Hip Arthroplasty Impairment Class 2—Default for Diagnosis = 67% lower extremity impairment			
CDX	GMFH	GMPE	GMCS
4	4	n/a	n/a
Net adjustment (GMFH – CDX) 3 – 4 = –1 +1 for Grade 4 = 0 + (GMPE – CDX) n/a + (GMCS – CDX) n/a Net adjustment = 0			

Result is class 2 adjustment 0, which results in class 4, grade C = 67% lower extremity impairment.

According to Table 16-10, Impairment Values Calculated From Lower Extremity Impairment (6th ed, p 531), this converts to 27% whole person impairment for the hip arthroplasty.

The *Guides* approach to the evaluation of impairment due to peripheral nerve impairment is based on Section 16.4, Peripheral Nerve Impairment (6th ed, p 531). For right lateral femoral cutaneous neuropathy, using Table 16-12, Peripheral Nerve Impairment Regional Grid—Lower Extremity Impairments, in the section on Sensory Nerves (6th ed, p 534), in this case there is a class 1 rating for mild problems (with a default impairment of 3% lower extremity impairment). Using the appropriate adjustment grids, in Section 16.3a, Adjustment Grid: Functional History (6th ed, p 516), and Table 16-6, Functional History Adjustment: Lower Extremities (6th ed, p 516), the patient is assigned grade modifier 1; the functional history is consistent with sensory deficit only in the appropriate distribution. Section 16.3b, Adjustment Grid: Physical Examination (6th ed, p 517), is not applicable since the neurologic findings were used to define the impairment ranges. In Section 16.3c, Adjustment Grid: Clinical Studies (6th ed, p 518), and Table 16-8, Clinical Studies Adjustment: Lower Extremities (6th ed, p 519), the patient is assigned grade modifier 0; the clinical studies revealed "normal electrodiagnostic studies." In summary, the adjustments are as follows: functional history grade modifier 1, physical examination n/a, and clinical studies grade modifier 0. Net adjustment compared to diagnosis class 1 is −1, grade B, 2% lower extremity impairment.

This is probably a surgical complication that is not reflected in the hip replacement rating system, so this additional 2% lower extremity impairment can be combined with the 67% lower extremity impairment for the

Peripheral Nerve Impairment Class 1—Default for Diagnosis = 3% lower extremity impairment			
CDX	GMFH	GMPE	GMCS
1	1	n/a	0
Net adjustment (GMFH – CDX) 1 – 1= 0 + (GMPE – CDX) + n/a + (GMCS – CDX) + 0 – 1 = –1 Net adjustment = –1			

Result is class 1 adjustment –1, which results in class 1, grade B = 2% lower extremity impairment.

total hip scoring system to yield a final rating of 68% lower extremity impairment.

Lower Extremity Impairment: According to Table 16-10, Impairment Values Calculated From Lower Extremity Impairment (6th ed, p 531), the 68% lower extremity impairment converts to 27% whole person impairment per the Sixth Edition.

Digestive System Impairment

For her digestive system impairment, Ms Costello was clearly able to maintain adequate weight. She had clearly delineated gastrointestinal pathology, having had a bowel resection and a shortened bowel. When she was using her medications, her bowel movements were reasonably well controlled, although she chose not to use the medications.

The *Guides* approach to the evaluation of impairment due to small-bowel resection is based on Section 6.2, Upper Digestive Tract (6th ed, p 106), and Table 6-4, Criteria for Rating Permanent Impairment Due to Upper Digestive Tract Disease (6th ed, p 107). The key factor is history, which is most consistent with "frequent minimal or occasional mild symptoms or signs of upper digestive tract disease *and* continuous treatment is not required." This results in a class 1 rating (with a default impairment of 5% whole person impairment). In Section 6.1, Principles of Assessment (6th ed, p 102), the methodology of rating within the specific classes of impairments is explained. Nonkey factors include physical findings (ie, weight); she is overweight, and this could be interpreted as class 0 or class 1 ("maintains weight at desirable level, higher classes reflect weight loss). The other nonkey factor is objective test results. On the basis of her surgery it would be reasonable to interpret this as "moderate documented anatomic or functional loss" resulting in class 2. In this case, as explained in Section 6.1, the impairment value should move the grade up one level to 7% whole person impairment.

Reproductive System Impairment

The loss of Ms Costello's right ovary is rated in Chapter 7, The Urinary and Reproductive Systems, with the use of Section 7.8e, Fallopian Tubes and Ovaries (6th ed, p 153). According to Table 7-12, Criteria for Rating Permanent Impairment Due to Fallopian Tube and Ovarian Disease (6th ed, p 154), she receives a rating of class 1 (with a default impairment of 3% whole person impairment). In Section 7.1, Principles of Assessment (6th ed, p 130), the methodology of rating within the specific classes of impairments is explained. Identification of nonkey factors within a specific class would require identification of the key factor. In this case the key factor as identified is the objective finding of only one functioning ovary in the premenopausal period. The nonkey factor including irregular menstrual periods not requiring continuous treatment should keep the rating at 3% whole person impairment. This is assuming that the irregularity of menstrual periods is directly related to the ovarian loss and not some other cause.

Combined Impairment

Ms Costello's whole person impairments of 27% (lower extremity), 7% (digestive), and 3% (reproductive) are combined by means of the Combined Values Chart (6th ed, p 604), resulting in 34% whole person impairment.

Impairment: 34% whole person impairment per the Sixth Edition.

Comment on Hip Replacement With Catastrophic Result

This case represents an extremely complicated application of the AMA *Guides*, yet it clearly indicates that systematic application of the *Guides* provides a reproducible method of arriving at an impairment rating.

SUMMARY

Diagnosis	Legg-Calve-Perthes disease treated with total hip arthroplasty, complicated by deep wound infection, partial small-bowel resection, and right oophorectomy
Fourth Edition References	Section 3.2 (4th ed, pp 75-93), Section 10.4 (4th ed, pp 239-241), Section 11.6c (4th ed,

pp 261-262), Table 64 (4th ed, p 85), Table 65 (4th ed, p 87), Table 68 (4th ed, p 89), Table 2 (4th ed, p 239)

Fourth Edition Summary Detailed musculoskeletal system evaluation required, as well as evaluation of other involved systems, eg, short bowel syndrome and loss of an ovary. Analyze impact of the underlying medical conditions. For the lower extremity disorder, consider alternative methods for assessment and rate the results of the total hip replacement.

Fourth Edition Impairment 76% lower extremity impairment, 41% whole person impairment

Fifth Edition References Section 17.2 (5th ed, pp 525-560), Section 17.2j (5th ed, pp 545-550), Table 17-34 (5th ed, p 548), Table 17-33 (5th ed, p 546), Table 17-37 (5th ed, p 552); Section 6.2 (5th ed, pp 120-127), Table 6-3 (5th ed, p 121), Section 7.8f (5th ed, pp 167-169), Table 7-11 (5th ed, p 167)

Fifth Edition Summary Detailed musculoskeletal system evaluation required, as well as evaluation of other involved systems, eg, short bowel syndrome and loss of an ovary. Analyze impact of the underlying medical conditions. For the lower extremity disorder, consider alternative methods for assessment and rate the results of the total hip replacement.

Fifth Edition Impairment 76% lower extremity impairment, 41% whole person impairment

Sixth Edition References Section 16.2 (6th ed, p 497), Section 16.2d, Hip (6th ed, p 500), Table 16-4 (6th ed, p 515), Table 16-10 (6th ed, p 531), Section 16.3a (6th ed, p 516), Table 16-6 (6th ed, p 516), Section 16.3b (6th ed, p 517), Table 16-7 (6th ed, p 517), Section 16.3c (6th ed, p 518), Table 16-8 (6th ed, p 520), Section 16.4 (6th ed, p 531), Table 16-12 (6th ed, p 534), Section 6.1 (6th ed, p 102), Section 6.2 (6th ed, p 106), Table 6-4 (6th ed, p 107), Section 7.1 (6th ed, p 130), Section 7.8e (6th ed, p 153), Table 7-12 (6th ed, p 154)

Sixth Edition Summary	A detailed history (including functional history and inventories), physical evaluation, and clinical studies involving the several organ systems including the musculoskeletal, gastrointestinal, and reproductive systems. After determining the proper class for each organ system on basis of the diagnosis or key factor involved, nonkey factors are used to adjust impairment.
Sixth Edition Impairment	67% lower extremity impairment, 34% whole person impairment

---

Reference

Gore RM, Hendrix RW, Hartz WH, Stulberg D. Transacetabular herniation of small bowel and right adnexa: unusual complication of hip arthroplasty. *JAMA*. 1983;250: 2349-2350.

CASE 16-6

Patellar Injury

Subject: Mr Morrison, a 28-year-old man.

History: Mr Morrison, a factory assembly line worker, stepped on a part that had fallen to the floor, falling and striking his anterior knee (patella) on the concrete floor. He had immediate pain, swelling, and ecchymosis over the patella. He left work before the end of his shift and went to the local hospital emergency department. X-ray films of his knee were normal, and Mr Morrison was told that he had bruised his leg. For the first 3 weeks after his injury, Mr Morrison's knee pain improved, but then it steadily worsened.

Mr Morrison was treated with nonsteroidal anti-inflammatories, two courses of physical therapy (including exercises as well as passive modalities), and several knee braces and pads. None of the treatments was successful. Follow-up X-ray films, including an axial patellar "sunrise" view, were normal. A magnetic resonance image showed only "chondromalacia patella." Mr Morrison would not consent to any surgical procedure.

Current Symptoms: Mr Morrison continued to complain of anterior knee pain. His pain was provoked by activity and relieved to a degree by rest. He reported that climbing either stairs or ladders "really hurt." Lifting and carrying heavy boxes at work and running also provoked his pain. By the end of each workday, Mr Morrison had begun limping, and his supervisor was aware of this consistent limp. Sitting with the knee at 90° or more of flexion for more than an hour caused enough pain that he had to stand and walk for a while. Mr Morrison had knee pain that awakened him during sleep about four times a week.

Because of the pain, Mr Morrison voluntarily transferred to a lower-paying job in the factory where he could alternate between standing and sitting, and where he did not have to lift and carry heavier objects.

Functional Assessment: The AAOS Lower Limb Questionnaire standardized mean score was 70. Mr Morrison's interoffice examination findings and complaints were consistent with mild difficulties with no limp on ambulation, pain with activities including lifting of heavy weights and climbing stairs or ladders, and no use of supportive devices.

Physical Examination: On physical examination 1 year after his injury, Mr Morrison did not limp. He was not using a cane or brace. His knees had no redness, warmth, swelling, effusion, or deformity. Measurements of his involved calf and thigh were 0.5 cm smaller than the contralateral side measurements. Ligamentous and meniscal stress tests were normal and painless. His knee range of motion was 0° to 135°. Manual muscle testing showed normal strength in his extremity.

Mr Morrison's knees had normal alignment (8° of valgus, with a Q angle of 12°). Patellar tracking was normal (no tendency to subluxations). When the examiner attempted to passively sublux the patella, it did not result in excessive patellar mobility and did not provoke pain. The injured knee had patellofemoral crepitus that was consistently palpable. The contralateral knee did not have crepitus. He had consistent pain with patellofemoral compression.

Clinical Studies: Current X-ray films of the knee were normal, including an axial (sunrise) view of the patella, which showed a 5-mm patellofemoral cartilage interval. A magnetic resonance image showed only "chondromalacia patella."

Discussion of Patellar Injury

Mr Morrison's history, examination results, and magnetic resonance image all suggest that his pain may be radiating from the patellofemoral joint. Patellofemoral pain is usually localized to the anterior knee. This type of pain is made worse by activities that increase the pressure on the patellofemoral joint, like walking, running, climbing stairs or ladders, and sitting with the knee flexed for extended periods. Many times patellofemoral pain is severe enough at night to awaken the individual.

Fourth Edition Rating

Impairment evaluation is based on Section 3.2g, Arthritis (4th ed, pp 82-83). The other sections of the *Guides* that discuss lower extremity impairment do not apply to this case. Section 3.2b, Gait Derangement (Table 36, 4th ed, p 76), is not applicable. There is minimal atrophy, consistent with the history. According to Table 37, Impairments From Leg Muscle Atrophy (4th ed, p 77), 0.5 cm of atrophy is not an impairment. There is no muscle weakness, in reference to Table 39, Impairments From Lower Extremity Muscle Weakness (4th ed, p 77). Range of motion is normal, according to Table 41, Knee Impairment (4th ed, p 78). In Table 64, Impairment Estimates for Certain Lower Extremity Impairments (4th ed, p 85), no listed diagnosis is applicable. Mr Morrison has patellar pain but not patellar subluxations or dislocations.

Section 3.2g, Arthritis (4th ed, pp 82-83), rates arthritis primarily on the joint "cartilage interval," as measured on roentgenograms (4th ed, plain X-ray films). Mr Morrison has normal knee X-ray films, including a normal 5-mm cartilage interval for the patellofemoral joint. According to Table 62, Arthritis Impairments Based on Roentgenographically Determined Cartilage Intervals (4th ed, p 83), there is no impairment unless the patellofemoral cartilage interval is 2 mm or less. However, there is a footnote to Table 62 that reads, "In a patient with a history of direct trauma, a complaint of patellofemoral pain, and crepitation on physical examination, but without joint space narrowing on roentgenograms, a 2% whole person or 5% lower extremity impairment is given." This would be the only basis for an impairment rating in Mr Morrison's case.

Impairment: 2% whole person impairment per the Fourth Edition.

Fifth Edition Rating

Impairment evaluation is based on Section 17.2h, Arthritis (5th ed, pp 544-545). The other sections of the *Guides* that discuss lower extremity impairment do not apply to this case. Section 17.2c, Gait Derangement (Table 17-5, 5th ed, p 529), is not applicable. There is minimal atrophy, consistent with the history. According to Table 17-6, Impairments From Leg Muscle Atrophy (5th ed, p 530), 0.5 cm of atrophy is not an impairment. There is no muscle weakness, in reference to Table 17-8, Impairments From Lower Extremity Muscle Weakness (5th ed, p 532). Range of motion is normal, according to Table 17-10, Knee Impairment (5th ed, p 537). In Table 17-33, Impairment Estimates for Certain Lower Extremity Impairments (5th ed, pp 546-547), no listed diagnosis is applicable. Mr Morrison has patellar pain but not patellar subluxations or dislocations.

Section 17.2h, Arthritis (5th ed, pp 544-545), rates arthritis primarily on the joint "cartilage interval," as measured on roentgenograms (4th ed, plain X-ray films). Mr Morrison has normal knee X-ray films, including a normal 5-mm cartilage interval for the patellofemoral joint. According to Table 17-31, Arthritis Impairments Based on Roentgenographically Determined Cartilage Intervals (5th ed, p 544), there is no impairment unless the patellofemoral cartilage interval is 2 mm or less. However, a small footnote to Table 17-31 reads, "In a patient with a history of direct trauma, a complaint of patellofemoral pain, and crepitation on physical examination, but without joint space narrowing on roentgenograms, a 2% whole person or 5% lower extremity impairment is given." This would be the only basis for an impairment rating in Mr Morrison's case.

Impairment: 2% whole person impairment per the Fifth Edition.

Sixth Edition Rating

The *Guides* approach to the evaluation of impairment due to patellofemoral syndrome or chondromalacia patella is based on Section 16.2, Diagnosis-Based Impairment (6th ed, p 497), and Section 16.2c, Knee (6th ed, p 500).

In Table 16-3, Knee Regional Grid: Lower Extremity Impairments (6th ed, p 509), there is no specific rating for chondromalacia patella with no evidence of arthritis or joint space narrowing on radiographs. However, in the section titled Soft Tissue for a diagnosis of contusion, there is a class 1 rating for mild problems (with a default impairment of 1% lower extremity impairment).

In Section 16.3a, Adjustment Grid: Functional History (6th ed, p 516), and Table 16-6, Functional History Adjustment: Lower Extremities (6th ed, p 516), the patient is assigned grade modifier 1; the functional history is consistent with pain with activities including lifting of heavy weights and climbing stairs or ladders, and no use of supportive devices. In Section 16.3b, Adjustment Grid: Physical Examination (6th ed, p 517), and Table 16-7, Physical Examination Adjustment: Lower Extremities (6th ed, p 517), the patient is assigned grade modifier 1; the physical examination revealed "good knee motion, crepitance of the patello-femoral joint and no limb length discrepancy." In Section 16.3c, Adjustment Grid: Clinical Studies (6th ed, p 518), and Table 16-8, Clinical Studies Adjustment: Lower Extremities (6th ed, p 519), the patient is assigned grade modifier 1; the clinical studies revealed chondromalacia of the patella. In summary, the adjustments are as follows: functional history grade modifier 1, physical examination 1, and clinical studies grade modifier 1. Net adjustment compared to diagnosis class 1 is 0, grade C, 1% lower extremity impairment.

Class 2—Default for Diagnosis = 1% lower extremity impairment			
CDX	GMFH	GMPE	GMCS
1	1	1	1
Net adjustment (GMFH – CDX) 1 – 1 = 0 + (GMPE – CDX) + 1 – 1 = 0 + (GMCS – CDX) + 1 – 1 = 0 Net adjustment = 0			

Result is class 1 adjustment 0, which results in class 1, grade C = 1% lower extremity impairment.

According to Table 16-10, Impairment Values Calculated From Lower Extremity Impairment (6th ed, p 530), this converts to 1% whole person impairment.

Impairment: 1% whole person impairment per the Sixth Edition.

Comment on Patellar Injury

Anatomic, diagnostic, and functional assessments are aspects of the International Classification of Functioning, Disability and Health (ICF) model in evaluating permanent impairment of the lower extremity. In general, the diagnosis-based impairment method is the only evaluation method used to evaluate a specific impairment.

SUMMARY

Diagnosis	Posttraumatic patellofemoral pain, or chondromalacia patella
Fourth Edition References	Section 3.2g (4th ed, pp 82-83), Table 62 (4th ed, p 83), footnote
Fourth Edition Summary	History of direct (6th ed, patellar) trauma and patellofemoral pain; physical examination documentation of crepitation; no other ratable impairment; patellar injury, patellar pain by history and examination; no subluxations or dislocations.
Fourth Edition Impairment	5% lower extremity impairment, 2% whole person impairment
Fifth Edition References	Section 17.2h (5th ed, pp 544-545), Table 17-31 (5th ed, p 544), footnote
Fifth Edition Summary	History of direct (6th ed, patellar) trauma and patellofemoral pain; physical examination documentation of crepitation; no other ratable impairment; patellar injury, patellar pain by history and examination; no subluxations or dislocations.

Fifth Edition Impairment	5% lower extremity impairment, 2% whole person impairment
Sixth Edition References	Section 16.2 (6th ed, p 497), Section 16.2c, (6th ed, p 500), Table 16-3, (6th ed, p 509), Section 16.3a (6th ed, p 516), Table 16-6 (6th ed, p 516), Section 16.3b (6th ed, p 517), Table 16-7 (6th ed, p 517), Section 16.3c (6th ed, p 518), Table 16-8 (6th ed, p 519), Table 16-10 (6th ed, p 530)
Sixth Edition Summary	History (including functional history and inventories), physical evaluation, and clinical studies. First, determine diagnosis-based impairment, class, and default value. Second, adjust impairment on basis of nonkey factors.
Sixth Edition Impairment	1% lower extremity impairment, 1% whole person impairment

CASE 16-7

Knee Injury

Subject: Ms Carlton, a 36-year-old woman.

History: Ms Carlton, a delivery service employee, tripped over a package at work, twisting her left knee. Initial evaluation showed a positive McMurray sign. Conservative measures failed, symptoms of locking and catching of the knee persisted, and magnetic resonance imaging confirmed a large tear of the medial meniscus. Six weeks after the injury, she underwent arthroscopy. A total resection of the medial meniscus was performed, followed by a vigorous rehabilitation program.

Impairment evaluation was performed 6 months after surgery. Ms Carlton was determined to be at maximal medical improvement.

Current Symptoms: At maximal medical improvement, she complained of mild morning stiffness in her knee with aching after prolonged standing. She denied any problems with swelling, locking, or buckling since her surgery.

Functional Assessment: The AAOS Lower Limb Questionnaire standardized mean score was 70. Physical examination findings and complaints were consistent with mild difficulties with prolonged standing and morning stiffness; however, there was no pain with going up or down stairs or ladders, and no use of supportive devices.

Physical Examination: Physical examination showed the following relevant findings: gait was normal, left thigh circumference (measured 10 cm above the patella with the knee fully extended and the muscles relaxed) was 0.5 cm smaller than the right, quadriceps and hamstrings were of normal strength, and range of motion was from 2° of flexion to 140° of flexion.

Clinical Studies: X-ray films of the knee showed a medial joint space of 4.0 mm.

Discussion of Knee Injury

Fourth Edition Rating

Impairment is based on Section 3.2, The Lower Extremity (4th ed, pp 75-94). The applicable methods to be considered in this case are leg muscle atrophy, range-of-motion deficits, arthritis, and diagnosis. The left thigh is 0.5 cm smaller than the right. According to Table 37, Impairments From Leg Muscle Atrophy (4th ed, p 77), in Section 3.2c, Muscle Atrophy, there is no associated impairment for less than 1-cm difference in circumference. In reference to Table 41, Knee Impairments (4th ed, p 78), in Section 3.2e, Range of Motion, Ms Carlton's range of motion is normal; therefore, there is no impairment for motion deficits. Section 3.2g, Arthritis, defines impairment on the basis of roentgenographically determined cartilage intervals. According to Table 62, Arthritis Impairments Based on Roentgenographically Determined Cartilage Intervals (4th ed, p 83), a joint space of 4 mm is considered normal; therefore, there is no impairment for arthritis. With the diagnosis of total medial meniscectomy and with reference to Section 3.2i, Diagnosis-Based Estimates, Table 64, Impairment Estimates for Certain Lower Extremity Impairments (4th ed, p 85), she has a 3% whole person impairment. The only ratable method is the diagnosis-based estimate of 3% whole person impairment.

Impairment: 3% whole person impairment per the Fourth Edition.

Fifth Edition Rating

Impairment is based on Section 17.2, Methods of Assessment (5th ed, pp 525-554). The applicable methods to be considered in this case are leg muscle atrophy, range-of-motion deficits, arthritis, and diagnosis. The left thigh is 0.5 cm smaller than the right. According to Table 27-6, Impairment Due to Unilateral Leg Muscle Atrophy (5th ed, p 530), in Section 17.2d, Muscle Atrophy (Unilateral) (5th ed, pp 530-531), there is no associated impairment for less than 1 cm difference in circumference. With reference to Table 17-10, Knee Impairment (5th ed, p 537), in Section 17.2f, Range of Motion (5th ed, pp 533-538), her range of motion is normal; therefore, there is no impairment for motion deficits. Section 17.2h, Arthritis (5th ed, pp 544-545), defines impairment on the basis of roentgenographically determined cartilage intervals. According to Table 17-31, Arthritis Impairments Based on Roentgenographically Determined Cartilage Intervals (5th ed, p 544), a joint space of 4 mm is considered normal; therefore, there is no impairment for arthritis. With the diagnosis of total medial meniscectomy and according to Section 17.2j, Diagnosis-Based Estimates (5th ed, pp 545-549), and specifically Table 17-33, Impairment Estimates for Certain Lower Extremity Impairments (5th ed, p 546), she has a 3% whole person impairment. The only ratable method is the diagnosis-based estimate of 3% whole person impairment.

Impairment: 3% whole person impairment per the Fifth Edition.

Sixth Edition Rating

The *Guides* approach to the evaluation of impairment due to medial meniscus tear with total medial meniscectomy is based on Section 16.2, Diagnosis-Based Impairment (6th ed, p 497), and Section 16.2c, Knee (6th ed, p 500).

In Table 16-3, Knee Regional Grid: Lower Extremity Impairments (6th ed, p 509), in the section on Ligament/Bone/Joint, for the diagnosis "total medial or lateral meniscectomy," there is a class 1 rating for mild problems (with a default impairment of 7% lower extremity impairment).

In Section 16.3a, Adjustment Grid: Functional History (6th ed, p 517), and Table 16-6, Functional History Adjustment: Lower Extremities (6th ed, p 516), the patient is assigned grade modifier 1; the functional history is consistent with no limp on ambulation, mild difficulties with prolonged standing, no pain with lifting of heavy weights and climbing stairs or ladders, and no use of supportive devices. In Section 16.3b, Adjustment Grid: Physical Examination (6th ed, p 517), and Table 16-7, Physical Examination Adjustment: Lower Extremities (6th ed, p 517), the patient is assigned grade modifier 0; the physical examination revealed "no knee motion loss, no instability, atrophy or limb length discrepancy." In Section 16.3c, Adjustment Grid: Clinical Studies (6th ed, p 518), and Table 16-8, Clinical Studies Adjustment: Lower Extremities (6th ed, p 519), the patient is assigned grade modifier 1; the clinical studies revealed "large tear of the medial meniscus," which confirms the diagnosis and is in the category of "mild pathology." In summary, the adjustments are as follows: functional history grade modifier 1, physical examination 1, and clinical studies grade modifier 1. Net adjustment compared to diagnosis class 1 is −1, grade B, 6% lower extremity impairment.

Class 2—Default for Diagnosis = 7% lower extremity impairment			
CDX	GMFH	GMPE	GMCS
1	1	0	1
Net adjustment (GMFH – CDX) 1 – 1 = 0 + (GMPE – CDX) + 0 – 1 = –1 + (GMCS – CDX) + 1 – 1 = 0 Net adjustment = −1			

Result is class 1 adjustment –1, which results in class 1, grade B = 6% lower extremity impairment.

According to Table 16-10, Impairment Values Calculated From Lower Extremity Impairment (6th ed, p 530), this converts to 2% whole person impairment.

Impairment: 2% whole person impairment per the Sixth Edition.

Comment on Knee Injury

Anatomic, diagnostic, and functional assessments are aspects of the ICF model in evaluating permanent impairment of the lower extremity. In most cases, the diagnosis-based impairment method is the only evaluation method used to evaluate a specific impairment.

SUMMARY

Diagnosis	Total medial meniscectomy
Fourth Edition References	Section 3.2 (4th ed, pp 75-93), Table 37 (4th ed, p 77), Table 41 (4th ed, p 78), Table 62 (4th ed, p 83), Table 64 (4th ed, pp 85-86)
Fourth Edition Summary	Assess, as applicable, gait, muscle strength/atrophy, range of motion, flexion contracture, extension lag, alignment, and stability. Determine impairment on the basis of anatomic, diagnostic, and functional methods.
Fourth Edition Impairment	3% whole person impairment
Fifth Edition References	Section 17.2 (5th ed, pp 525-554), Section 17.2j (5th ed, pp 545-549), Table 27-6 (5th ed, p 530), Table 17-10 (5th ed, p 537), Table 17-31 (5th ed, p 544), Table 17-33 (5th ed, p 546)
Fifth Edition Summary	Assess, as applicable, gait, muscle strength/atrophy, range of motion, flexion contracture, extension lag, alignment, and stability. Determine impairment on the basis of anatomic, diagnostic, and functional methods.
Fifth Edition Impairment	3% whole person impairment

Sixth Edition References	Section 16.2 (6th ed, p 497), Section 16.2c (6th ed, p 500), Table 16-3, (6th ed, p 509), Section 16.3a (6th ed, p 516), Table 16-6 (6th ed, p 516), Section 16.3b (6th ed, p 517), Table 16-7 (6th ed, p 517), Section 16.3c (6th ed, p 518), Table 16-8 (6th ed, p 519), Table 16-10 (6th ed, p 530)
Sixth Edition Summary	History (including functional history and inventories), physical evaluation, and clinical studies. First, determine diagnosis-based impairment, class, and default value. Second, adjust impairment on basis of nonkey factors.
Sixth Edition Impairment	6% lower extremity impairment, 2% whole person impairment

CASE 16-8

Talus Fracture

Subject: Ms Weitz, a 34-year-old woman.

History: Ms Weitz, a garden and nursery worker, mistakenly stepped off the back of a truck while carrying a 50-lb bag of grass seed. She sustained a displaced fracture to the neck of the talus noted on plain radiographs and magnetic resonance images. An open reduction and internal fixation of the talus was undertaken. Unfortunately, she did not do well. Fourteen months later, a second procedure was required to remove hardware and debride areas of avascular necrosis of the talar dome.

Current Symptoms: Eighteen months after this procedure, Ms Weitz continued to have moderate ankle pain. She declined any further treatment. At present, she has morning stiffness with pain on prolonged ambulation and going up and down stairs. She does not use any supportive devices.

Functional Assessment: The AAOS Lower Limb Questionnaire raw score was 17 of 35. Her interoffice examination findings and complaints were consistent with moderate difficulties with prolonged standing, morning stiffness, and pain going up or down stairs.

Physical Examination: Physical examination showed the following relevant findings: gait was mildly antalgic, there was mild tenderness over the tibiotalar junction, no calf atrophy was noted, and strength appeared normal. Ankle and subtalar range of motion showed 20° of flexion, 10° of extension, 20° of inversion, and 5° of eversion.

Clinical Studies: X-ray films demonstrated avascular necrosis with partial dome collapse and a 2-mm tibiotalar joint space.

Discussion of Talus Fracture

Fourth Edition Rating

Impairment is based on Section 3.2, The Lower Extremity (4th ed, pp 75-93). Options for calculation include Sections 3.2b, Gait Derangement (4th ed, pp 75-76); 3.2e, Range of Motion (4th ed, pp 77-78); 3.2g, Arthritis (4th ed, pp 82-83); and 3.2i, Diagnosis-Based Estimates (4th ed, pp 84-88). For each of these options, the corresponding impairment is calculated.

For gait, with the use of Table 36, Lower Limb Impairment From Gait Disturbance (4th ed, p 76), Ms Weitz best fits the category of mild severity, ie, "Antalgic limp with shortened stance phase and documented moderate to advanced arthritic changes of hip, knee, or ankle," which corresponds to a 7% whole person impairment.

According to Table 42, Ankle Motion Impairment Estimates (4th ed, p 78), there is a mild impairment, by both flexion and extension measurements, corresponding to 3% whole person impairment. According to Table 43, Hindfoot Impairment Estimates (4th ed, p 78), 20° of inversion and 5° of eversion are consistent with a mild impairment (1% of the whole person). The range-of-motion impairments for the ankle and hindfoot are combined by means of the Combined Values Chart (4th ed, pp 322-324), resulting in a 4% whole person impairment.

The 2-mm narrowing of the cartilage interval of the tibiotalar joint results in a 6% whole person impairment according to Table 62, Arthritis Impairments Based on Roentgenographically Determined Cartilage Intervals (4th ed, p 83).

According to Table 64, Impairment Estimates for Certain Lower Extremity Impairments (4th ed, p 86), an avascular necrosis of the talus with collapse corresponds to a 6% whole person impairment.

The *Guides* advises that, "in general, only one evaluation method should be used to evaluate a specific impairment. In some instances, however, . . . a combination of two or three methods may be required" (4th ed, p 75). Rating on the basis of gait derangement alone should rarely be used; "whenever possible the evaluator should use the more specific methods of those other parts in estimating impairments" (4th ed, p 75).

Fractures, however, in and about joints with degenerative changes should be rated either by means of the diagnosis-based estimates method and combining of the rating for arthritic degeneration or by means of the range-of-motion section. It is recommended that the section providing the greater impairment estimate be used (4th ed, p 84). In this case, the rating would be based on the combined impairment due to arthritis and the diagnosis-based estimate (6% and 6%, ie, 12% of the whole person), rather than the lower rating due to range-of-motion deficits (4%).

Impairment: 12% whole person impairment per the Fourth Edition.

Fifth Edition Rating

Impairment was based on Section 17.2, Methods of Assessment (5th ed, pp 525-554). There are anatomic, diagnostic, and functional methods of assessing lower extremity impairment. Page 527 explains that, "Typically, one method will adequately characterize the impairment and its impact on the ability to perform ADL. In some cases, however, more than one method needs to be used to accurately assess all features of the impairment" (5th ed, p 527). The options for calculation include Section 17.2, Gait Derangement (5th ed, p 529); Section 17.2f, Range of Motion (5th ed, pp 533-538); Section 17.2h, Arthritis (5th ed, pp 544-545); and Section 17.2j, Diagnosis-Based Estimates (5th ed, pp 545-549). For each of these options, the corresponding impairment is calculated. In terms of combining impairments, the Fifth Edition states:

> Some individuals may have several impairments involving different parts of the same lower extremity; others may have several impairments of the same lower extremity part. If there are several impairments involving different regions of lower extremity (eg, the thigh and the foot), evaluate each impairment separately, convert these regional impairments to whole person impairments, and combine the whole person impairment rating using the Combined Values Chart (6th ed, p 604). If there are multiple impairments within a region (eg, the toes and the ankle), combine these regional, lower extremity impairments of the foot and convert the combined foot impairment to a whole person impairment. Similarly, when using several methods in the same region, combine the regional impairments before converting to a whole person impairment rating.

For gait, with the use of Table 17-5, Lower Limb Impairment From Gait Disturbance (5th ed, p 529), Ms Weitz best fits the category of mild severity, ie, "Antalgic limp with shortened stance phase and documented moderate to advanced arthritic changes of hip, knee, or ankle," which corresponds to a 7% whole person impairment. Rating on the basis of gait derangement would be excluded, since, as indicated in the instructions for Section 17.2c (5th ed, p 529), gait derangement is a stand-alone impairment not combined with any other impairment evaluation method, and, whenever possible, the evaluator should use a more specific method.

According to Table 17-11, Ankle Motion Impairment Estimates (5th ed, p 537), there is a mild impairment, by both the 20° flexion and 10° extension measurements, each corresponding to 3% whole person, 7% lower extremity, or 10% foot impairment. The Fifth Edition states, "range-of-motion restrictions in multiple directions do increase the impairment. Add range-of-motion impairments for a single joint to determine the total joint range-of-motion impairments" (5th ed, p 533). Therefore, this represents 6% whole person, 14% lower extremity, or 20% foot impairment.

According to Table 17-12, Hindfoot Impairment Estimates (5th ed, p 537), 20° of inversion and 5° of eversion each is consistent with a mild impairment, eg, 1% whole person, 2% lower extremity, or 3% foot impairment; therefore, there is a total of 2% whole person, 4% lower extremity, or 6% foot impairment. Combining the impairments at the foot level, ie, 20% foot impairment for ankle deficits and 6% foot impairment for hindfoot involvement, according to the Combined Values Chart (5th ed, p 604), results in 25% foot impairment.

The 2-mm narrowing of the cartilage interval of the tibiotalar (ankle) joint results in a 6% whole person, 15% lower extremity, or 21% foot impairment according to Table 17-31, Arthritis Impairments Based on Roentgenographically Determined Cartilage Intervals (5th ed, p 544).

According to Table 17-33, Impairment Estimates for Certain Lower Extremity Impairments (5th ed, p 547), an avascular necrosis of the talus with collapse corresponds to a 6% whole person, 15% lower extremity, or 21% foot impairment.

Section 17.2j, Diagnosis-Based Estimates (5th ed, pp 545-549), advises, "fractures in and about joints with degenerative changes should be rated either by using this section and combining the rating with that for arthritis (Table 17-31 and Combined Values Chart, p 604) or by using the loss of range-of-motion method. It is recommended that the method providing the greater of the two impairment estimates be used" (5th ed, p 549). Since there are multiple impairments within a region, we combine these regional, lower extremity impairments of the foot and then convert the combined foot impairment to a whole person impairment. In this case, the rating based on the combined impairment due to arthritis (21% foot) and the diagnosis-based estimate (21% foot) results in 38% foot impairment, per the Combined Values Chart (5th ed, p 604). This is greater than the 25% foot impairment due to motion deficits. "To calculate the lower extremity impairment from a specific part impairment (eg, foot), multiply by 0.7. To calculate whole person impairment from a lower extremity impairment, multiply by 0.4" (5th ed, p 527). Therefore, the 38% combined foot impairment is equivalent to a 27% lower extremity impairment, and this is equivalent to an 11% whole person impairment.

Impairment: 11% whole person impairment per the Fifth Edition.

Sixth Edition Rating

The *Guides* approach to the evaluation of impairment due to ankle fracture of the talus is based on Section 16.2, Diagnosis-Based Impairment (6th ed, p 497), and Section 16.2b, Foot and Ankle (6th ed, p 500).

In Table 16-2, Foot and Ankle Regional Grid: Lower Extremity Impairments (6th ed, p 503), in the section on Fracture/Dislocation, for the diagnosis "Talus Fracture," there is a class 2 rating for moderate problems (with a default impairment of 22% lower extremity impairment). This rating is used because of the avascular necrosis and talar body collapse.

In Section 16.3a, Adjustment Grid: Functional History (6th ed, p 516), and Table 16-6, Functional History Adjustment: Lower Extremities (6th ed, p 516), the patient is assigned grade modifier 1; the functional history is consistent with no limp on ambulation, pain with prolonged standing and climbing stairs or ladders, but no use of supportive devices. In Section 16.3b, Adjustment Grid: Physical Examination (6th ed, p 517), and Table 16-7, Physical Examination Adjustment: Lower Extremities (6th ed, p 517), the patient is assigned grade modifier 2; the physical examination revealed "moderate ankle motion loss, no instability, atrophy or limb length discrepancy." In Section 16.3c, Adjustment Grid: Clinical Studies (6th ed, p 518), and Table 16-8, Clinical Studies Adjustment: Lower Extremities (6th ed, p 519), the patient is assigned grade modifier 3; the clinical studies revealed "avascular necrosis with moderate posttraumatic arthrosis." In summary, the adjustments are as follows: functional history grade modifier 1, physical examination 2, and clinical studies grade modifier 3. Net adjustment compared to diagnosis class 1 is 0, grade C, 22% lower extremity impairment.

Class 2—Default for Diagnosis = 22% lower extremity impairment			
CDX	GMFH	GMPE	GMCS
2	1	2	3
Net adjustment (GMFH – CDX) 1 – 2 = –1 + (GMPE – CDX) + 2 – 2 = 0 + (GMCS – CDX) + 3 – 2 = 1 Net adjustment = 0			

Result is class 1 adjustment 0, which results in class 1, grade C = 22% lower extremity impairment.

According to Table 16-10, Impairment Values Calculated From Lower Extremity Impairment (6th ed, p 530) this converts to 9% whole person impairment.

Impairment: 9% whole person impairment per the Sixth Edition.

Comment on Talus Fracture

Before assessing impairment, it is necessary to determine whether the individual is at maximal medical improvement. In this case, it is likely that Ms Weitz would have had a progressive increase in arthritis of the tibiotalar joint and would later require fusion. If this were done in optimal, neutral position without flexion, extension, varus, or valgus, her rating would be 4% whole person impairment (4th ed, p 80; 5th ed, p 541). In this case, the impairment would drop from 11% of the whole person to 4% of the whole person, and this is logical, since the surgery should improve her condition. However, because she declined any further treatment, the evaluator judged that she was at maximal medical improvement.

It is important to determine which method(s) to use in assessing lower extremity impairment. The process of rating range-of-motion deficits is based on a classification of mild, moderate, or severe. The Fourth Edition text did not provide direction on how to approach multiple motion deficits within a joint, but the example given (4th ed, pp 77-78) indicates that the examiner is to select a category to characterize the joint impairment. In the Fifth Edition, the impairments present in each direction of joint motion are added. The impairment in this case was slightly lower than in the Fourth Edition due to combining values at the foot level, as specifically directed, rather than at the whole person level. As larger values are combined, their combined value decreases, since less remains of the unimpaired component. As noted in the Combined Values Chart (5th ed, p 604), "the values are derived from the formula $A + B (1 - A)$ = combined value of A and B, where A and B are the decimal equivalent of the impairment ratings" (5th ed, p 604). The combining of any two numbers of 7% or less results in the same value as if they were added, since the remaining unimpaired component is large. For example, the combined value of 7% and 7% expressed mathematically is $0.07 + 0.07 (1 - 0.07) = 0.07 + 0.07 (0.93) = 0.07 + 0.0651 = 0.1351 = 0.14 = 14\%$.

Regarding the Sixth Edition, anatomic, diagnostic, and functional assessments are aspects of the ICF model in evaluating impairment of the lower extremity. In most cases, the diagnosis-based impairment method is the only evaluation method used to evaluate a specific impairment.

SUMMARY

Diagnosis Talus fracture, complicated by avascular necrosis of the talar dome

Fourth Edition References	Section 3.2 (4th ed, pp 75-93), Table 36 (4th ed, p 76), Table 42 (4th ed, p 78), Table 43 (4th ed, p 78), Table 62 (4th ed, p 83), Table 64 (4th ed, pp 85-86)
Fourth Edition Summary	Assess gait, muscle strength/atrophy, range of motion, ankylosis, and any other ratable disorders. Evaluate X-ray films and define diagnoses. Determine impairment on the basis of anatomic, diagnostic, and functional methods.
Fourth Edition Impairment	12% whole person impairment
Fifth Edition References	Section 17.2 (5th ed, pp 525-554), Section 17.2f (5th ed, pp 533-538), Section 17.2h (5th ed, pp 544-545), Section 17.2j (5th ed, pp 545-549), Table 17-5 (5th ed, p 529), Table 17-11 (5th ed, p 537), Table 17-12 (5th ed, p 537), Table 17-31 (5th ed, p 544), Table 17-33 (5th ed, p 547)
Fifth Edition Summary	Assess gait, muscle strength/atrophy, range of motion, ankylosis, and any other ratable disorders. Evaluate X-ray films and define diagnoses. Determine impairment on the basis of anatomic, diagnostic, and functional methods.
Fifth Edition Impairment	27% lower extremity impairment, 11% whole person impairment
Sixth Edition References	Section 16.2 (6th ed, p 497), Section 16.2b (6th ed, p 500), Table 16-2 (6th ed, p 503), Section 16.3a (6th ed, p 516), Table 16-6 (6th ed, p 516), Section 16.3b (6th ed, p 517), Table 16-7 (6th ed, p 517), Section 16.3c (6th ed, p 518), Table 16-8 (6th ed, p 519), Table 16-10 (6th ed, p 530)
Sixth Edition Summary	History (including functional history and inventories), physical evaluation, and clinical studies. First, determine diagnosis-based impairment, class, and default value. Second, adjust impairment on basis of nonkey factors.
Sixth Edition Impairment	22% lower extremity impairment, 9% whole person impairment

CASE 16-9

Femoral Neck Fracture

Subject: Ms Walker, a 61-year-old woman.

History: Ms Walker fell at work, sustaining a right femoral neck fracture. Neurovascular function remained intact. Near-anatomic reduction and rigid internal fixation were obtained at surgery, and the fracture healed uneventfully.

Current Symptoms: At maximal medical improvement, she complained of mild morning stiffness in her hip and mild aching after prolonged standing or squatting, as well as going up and down stairs. Putting on socks and shoes was occasionally difficult because of hip stiffness. She denied any need for any supportive devices.

Functional Assessment: The AAOS Lower Limb Questionnaire raw score was 15 of 35. Her interoffice examination findings and complaints were consistent with mild difficulties with prolonged standing along with going up or down stairs, but no use of supportive devices.

Physical Examination: After appropriate rehabilitation, examination was unremarkable apart from diminished hip motions. Measurements were as follows: flexion, 95°; extension, 5°; internal rotation, 10°; external rotation, 12°; abduction, 12°; and adduction, 10°.

Clinical Studies: Postsurgical radiographs document a healed fracture in near anatomic positioning with internal fixation.

Discussion of Femoral Neck Fracture

Fourth Edition Rating

Impairment was based on Section 3.2, The Lower Extremity (4th ed, pp 75-94). Section 3.2i, Diagnosis-Based Estimates, states, "Fractures in and about joints with degenerative changes should be rated either by using this section and combining (Combined Values Chart, p 322) the rating for arthritic degeneration or by using the range-of-motion section. It is recommended that the section providing the greater impairment estimate be used" (4th ed, p 84). In this case, we are not told of any arthritic changes in the hip, and Table 64, Impairment Estimates for Certain Lower Extremity

Impairments, states, "Femoral neck fracture, healed in good position, evaluate according to examination findings" (4th ed, p 85). Thus, there is no "diagnosis rating" for the fracture, and we are not told of any degenerative changes in the hip, so this section is not applicable.

The only ratable impairment in this case is diminished range of motion, evaluated per Section 3.2e, Range of Motion (4th ed, pp 77-78). Table 40, Hip Motion Impairments (4th ed, p 78), provides ratings for these deficits. In the lower extremity, when there is diminished joint motion in more than one direction, only the most severe deficit is rated. This is not directly mentioned in the text but is illustrated by the example given in the range-of-motion section (4th ed, pp 77-78). Unlike for upper extremity joints, the examiner does not add the ratings for each motion deficit.

In this example, given the absence of any flexion contracture, there is no impairment of extension. The flexion, internal rotation, and adduction measurements all fall into the mild column. The measurements for abduction and external rotation both lie in the moderate column. A moderate hip motion deficit warrants a rating of 4% whole person impairment.

Impairment: 4% whole person impairment per the Fourth Edition.

Fifth Edition Rating

Impairment was based on Section 17.2, Methods of Assessment (5th ed, pp 525-554). Section 17.2i, Diagnosis-Based Estimates, states, "Fractures in and about joints with degenerative changes should be rated either by using this section and combining the rating with that for arthritis (Table 17-31 and Combined Values Chart, p 604) or by using the loss of range-of-motion method. It is recommended that the method providing the greater of the two impairment estimates be used" (5th ed, p 549).

In this case, we are not told of any arthritic changes in the hip, and Table 17-33, Impairment Estimates for Certain Lower Extremity Impairments, states, "Femoral neck fracture, healed in good position, evaluate according to examination findings" (5th ed, p 546). Thus, there is no "diagnosis rating" for the fracture, and we are not told of any degenerative changes in the hip, so this section is not applicable.

The only ratable impairment in this case is diminished range of motion, eg, per Section 17.2f, Range of Motion (5th ed, pp 533-538). Table 17-9, Hip Motion Impairment (5th ed, p 537), provides ratings for these deficits. Figures 17-1, 17-2, and 17-3 (5th ed, pp 534-535) illustrate how these measurements are obtained. The Fifth Edition states, "range-of-motion restrictions in multiple directions do increase the impairment. Add range-of-motion impairments for a single joint to determine the total joint range-of-motion impairment" (5th ed, p 533). The corresponding categories and impairments for the motion deficits are as follows:

Motion	Measurement	Class	Lower Extremity Impairment	Whole Person Impairment
Flexion	195°	Mild	5%	2%
Extension	5°	Normal	0%	0%
Internal rotation	10°	Mild	5%	2%
External rotation	12°	Moderate	10%	4%
Abduction	12°	Moderate	10%	4%
Adduction	10°	Mild	5%	2%
Total (addition)			35%	14%

The added impairment for the hip is 14% whole person impairment. This rating process is summarized in Figure 17-10 (5th ed, p 561), as shown here on page 419.

Impairment: 14% whole person impairment per the Fifth Edition.

Sixth Edition Rating

The *Guides* approach to the evaluation of impairment due to femoral neck fracture is based on Section 16.2, Diagnosis-Based Impairment (6th ed, p 497), and Section 16.2d, Hip (6th ed, p 500). An alternative approach is by range of motion, as explained in Section 16.7, Range-of-Motion Impairment (6th ed, p 543), and the use of Table 16-24, Hip Motion Impairments—Lower Extremity Impairment (6th ed, p 549).

In that hip motion is to be considered as an alternative methodology and that the severity of the motion deficit needs to be determined, first the range of motion impairment must be determined according to Table 16-24, Hip Motion Impairments—Lower Extremity Impairment (6th ed, p 549). For flexion of 95° there is 5% lower extremity impairment, for extension of 5° there is 0%, for internal rotation of 10° there is 5%, for external rotation of 12° there is 10%, for abduction of 12° there is 10%, and for adduction 10° there is 5% lower extremity impairment; these are added, resulting in 35% lower extremity impairment. Per Table 16-25, Range of Motion ICF Classification (6th ed, p 550), this is class 3, severe.

In Table 16-4, Hip Regional Grid: Lower Extremity Impairments (6th ed, p 514), in the section on Ligament/Bone/Joint, for the diagnosis femoral neck fracture there is a class 3 rating for "femoral neck, intertrochanteric, or subtrochanteric fracture with severe motion deficits and/or malalignment (malunion)," with a default impairment of 30% lower extremity impairment.

In Section 16.3a, Adjustment Grid: Functional History (6th ed, p 516), and Table 16-6, Functional History Adjustment: Lower Extremities (6th ed, p 516), the patient is assigned grade modifier 1; the functional history is consistent with mild difficulties with no limp on ambulation, pain with long walks and going up stairs, and no use of supportive devices. In terms of Section 16.3b, Adjustment Grid: Physical Examination (6th ed, p 517), and Table 16-7, Physical Examination Adjustment: Lower Extremities (6th ed, p 517), this adjustment is not applicable since physical findings were used for class placement in the class. In Section 16.3c, Adjustment Grid: Clinical Studies (6th ed, p 518), and Table 16-8, Clinical Studies Adjustment: Lower Extremities (6th ed, p 519), the patient is assigned grade modifier 1; the clinical studies revealed "healing of femoral neck fracture with near anatomic positioning on radiographs." In summary, the adjustments are as follows: functional history grade modifier 1, physical examination n/a, and clinical studies grade modifier 1. Net adjustment compared to diagnosis class 1 is −4, grade A, 26% lower extremity impairment.

Class 3—Default for Diagnosis = 30% lower extremity impairment			
CDX	GMFH	GMPE	GMCS
3	1	n/a	1
Net adjustment (GMFH – CDX) 1 – 3 = –2 + (GMPE – CDX) + n/a + (GMCS – CDX) + 1 – 3 = –2 Net adjustment = –4			

Result is class 3 adjustment –2, which results in class 3, grade A = 26% lower extremity impairment.

Thus, the range of motion impairment is 35% lower extremity impairment and the diagnosis-based impairment is 26% lower extremity impairment. "Range of motion will, in some cases, serve as an alternative approach to rating impairment. It is not combined with the diagnosis-based impairment, and stands alone as an impairment rating." The approach resulting in higher impairment is selected; the final impairment is based on range of motion at 35% lower extremity impairment. According to Table 16-10, Impairment

Values Calculated From Lower Extremity Impairment (6th ed, p 530), this converts to 14% whole person impairment.

Impairment: 14% whole person impairment per the Sixth Edition.

Comment on Femoral Neck Fracture

According to each of the editions, the final impairment was based on range of motion. With the Sixth Edition most ratings are by diagnosis-based impairment; however, if range of motion results in higher impairment, it may be used.

The Fifth Edition used motion deficit impairment, while the Fourth Edition text did not provide direction on how to approach multiple motion deficits within a joint, but the example given in the range-of-motion section did, and it indicated that the direction of motion restriction that qualifies for the largest impairment is selected to represent the impairment of the joint. Thus, the lower extremity range-of-motion ratings were done differently from range-of-motion ratings in the upper extremity. In the Fifth Edition, the various motion impairments are added (just as they are in the upper extremity).

SUMMARY

Diagnosis	Femoral neck fracture
Fourth Edition References	Section 3.2e (4th ed, pp 77-78), Table 40 (4th ed, p 78)
Fourth Edition Summary	Assess, as applicable, gait, muscle strength/atrophy, range of motion, arthritis, and diagnosis-based estimates. Determine impairment on the basis of anatomic, diagnostic, and functional methods.
Fourth Edition Impairment	4% whole person impairment
Fifth Edition References	Section 17.2f (5th ed, pp 533-538), Table 17-9 (5th ed, p 537)
Fifth Edition Summary	Assess, as applicable, gait, muscle strength/atrophy, range of motion, arthritis, and diagnosis-based estimates. Determine

	impairment on the basis of anatomic, diagnostic, and functional methods.
Fifth Edition Impairment	14% whole person impairment
Sixth Edition References	Section 16.2 (6th ed, p 497), Section 16.2d (6th ed, p 500), Section 16.3a (6th ed, p 516), Section 16.3b (6th ed, p 517), Section 16.3c (6th ed, p 518), Section 16.7 (6th ed, p 543), Table 16-4 (6th ed, p 514), Table 16-6 (6th ed, p 516), Table 16-7 (6th ed, p 517), Table 16-8 (6th ed, p 519), Table 16-24 (6th ed, p 549)
Sixth Edition Summary	History (including functional history and inventories), physical evaluation, and clinical studies. First, determine diagnosis-based impairment, class, and default value. Second, adjust impairment on basis of nonkey factors. The range-of-motion loss does not rate separately as in the Fifth Edition; rather, it is used as an adjustment factor.
Sixth Edition Impairment	14% whole person impairment

Lower Extremity Impairment Evaluation Record and Worksheet

Name Ms. Walker Age 61 Sex F Side ☒R ☐L Date

Diagnosis Femoral Neck Fracture CASE 16-9

Potential Impairments | **Final Impairment Utilized**

Region	Abnormal Motion	Regional Impairments	Table #	Percent	Amputation Location	Amputation Percent	Methodology	Percent
Pelvis		DBE DJD Skin Leg Length Amp	17-33 17-31 17-36 17-4 17-32	% % % % %			DBE DJD Skin Leg Length Amputation	% % % % %
Hip	Tables 17-9 and 17-15 to 17-19 Flexion: Angle 95, Impairment 2; Extension: Angle 5, Impairment 0; Ankylosis: —; Impairment % 2 Abduction: Angle 12, Impairment 4; Adduction: Angle 10, Impairment 2; Ankylosis: —; Impairment % 6 Internal Rot: Angle 10, Impairment 2; External Rot: Angle 12, Impairment 4; Ankylosis: —; Impairment % 6 Add impairment % ROM or use largest ankylosis = 14 %	DBE DJD Skin Leg Length Weakness Amp	17-33/34 17-31 17-36 17-4 17-8 17-32	% % % % % %			DBE DJD Skin Leg Length Weakness ROM Amputation	% % % % % 14 % %
Thigh	(Consider related pathology at hip and knee)	Atrophy DJD Skin Leg Length Amp	17-6 17-31 17-36 17-4 17-32	% % % % %			Atrophy DJD Skin Leg Length Amputation	% % % % %
Knee	Tables 17-10 and 17-20 to 17-23 Flexion / Extension / Ankylosis / Impairment % Angle Impairment Add impairment % ROM or use largest ankylosis = ___ %	DBE DJD Skin Weakness Amp	17-33/35 17-31 17-36 17-8 17-32	% % % % %			DBE DJD Skin Weakness Amputation	% % % % %
Calf	(Consider related pathology at knee and ankle)	Atrophy DBE Skin Leg Length Amp	17-6 17-33 17-36 17-4 17-32	% % % % %			Atrophy DBE Skin Leg Length Amputation	% % % % %
Ankle/ Foot	Tables 17-11 to 17-13 and 17-24 to 17-28 Dorsiflex / Plantarflex / Ankylosis / Impairment % Angle Impairment Inversion / Eversion / Ankylosis / Impairment % Angle Impairment Add impairment % ROM or use largest ankylosis = ___ %	DBE DJD Skin Weakness Amp	17-29/33 17-31 17-36 17-8/9 17-32	% % % % %			DBE DJD Skin Weakness ROM Amputation	% % % % % %
Toe	Tables 17-14 and 17-30 Great Toe: MP Dorsiflex / IP Plantarflex / Ankylosis / Impairment % Angle Impairment Lesser Toes: MP Dorsiflex / Ankylosis / Impairment % Angle Impairment Add impairment % ROM or use largest ankylosis = ___ %	DBE DJD Skin Weakness Amp	17-33 17-31 17-36 17-8/14 17-32	% % % % %			DBE DJD Skin Weakness ROM Amputation	% % % % % %

Peripheral Nervous System Impairment	Grade %	Nerve %	Total %	Nerve	Maximum Motor %	Maximum Sensory %	Maximum Dysesthesia %
Motor Grade (Table 16-14)	___	× ___	= ___	___			
Sensory Grade (Table 16-15)	___	× ___	= ___	___			
Dysesthesia Grade	___	× ___	= ___	___	Combine all neurologic components %		

Peripheral Vascular System Impairment (Table 17-38)

Grade ___ Total vascular system impairment %

Gait Derangement (This is a *stand-alone* impairment and may *not* be combined) (Table 17-5) %

Final Combined Impairment (An explanation should be provided if more than one methodology is used, justifying the rationale for each methodology used) 14 %

DBE = diagnosis-based estimates; DJD = degenerative joint disease (arthritis).

CASE 16-10

Internal Knee Derangement

Subject: Mr Wilson, a 45-year-old man.

History: Mr Wilson slipped on a wet stair at work, injuring his left knee. Imaging evaluation showed a medial meniscus tear and ruptured anterior cruciate ligament (ACL). Partial medial meniscectomy and reconstruction of the ACL were performed, followed by an appropriate rehabilitation program.

Current Symptoms: At maximal medical improvement, he complained of mild stiffness in his knee with prolonged running. He denied any problems with swelling, locking, or buckling since his surgery.

Functional Assessment: The AAOS Lower Limb Questionnaire raw score was 10 of 35. Mr Wilson's interoffice examination findings and complaints were consistent with mildly antalgic gait and mild difficulties with prolonged running. There was no pain with going up or down stairs or ladders, and no use of supportive devices.

Physical Examination: One year after surgery, examination showed well-healed surgical scars and a mildly antalgic gait. Left thigh circumference was 1.5 cm smaller than that of the normal right, with knee motion of −5° (5° extension lag) to 120°, and mild laxity of the ACL. His right-knee range of motion was 0° to 140°. His examination was otherwise normal.

Clinical Studies: Weight-bearing anteroposterior X-ray films of the knees showed a 3-mm cartilage interval in the medial joint space bilaterally.

Discussion of Internal Knee Derangement

Fourth Edition Rating

Impairment is based on Section 3.2, The Lower Extremity (4th ed, pp 75-94). Potential rating methods include the following:

Condition	Degree	Section	Table	Page	Rating (% Whole Person)
Gait derangement	Mild	3.2b	36	76	7%
Atrophy	Mild	3.2c	37	77	1%-2%
Loss of motion (flexion contracture)	Mild	3.2e	41	78	4%
Arthritis	3 mm	3.2g	62	83	3%
Anterior cruciate ligament laxity	Mild	3.2i	64	85	3%
Medial meniscectomy	Partial	3.2i	64	85	1%

It would be inappropriate to use each of these methods in the final impairment calculation. Gait derangement, for example, is a stand-alone rating that is not combined with any other. Although it "may serve as a general guide for estimating many lower extremity impairments," whenever possible, the evaluator should use a more specific rating method (4th ed, p 75).

Given the presence of a normal right thigh for comparison and absence of any swelling or varicosity that would invalidate the circumference measurement of the left thigh, one might base a rating on the 1.5-cm atrophy. The *Guides* provides support for such an approach even though no weakness was noted. "Manual muscle testing gives an incomplete picture: even when results of muscle strength tests are normal, the injured extremity may fatigue more rapidly than usual. Evaluating the impairment in terms of atrophy gives an impairment estimate that more closely matches the patient's capabilities when results of manual muscle testing are normal" (4th ed, p 76). However, knee trauma or disease commonly results in thigh, primarily quadriceps, atrophy, and most examiners would consider it more appropriate to rate the primary rather than secondary condition. Furthermore, there are other, more specific methods for rating impairment in this case (see below), suggesting muscle atrophy is not the best means.

Range of motion is the next rating option. The loss of 5° of extension, which constitutes an impairment, and the diminished flexion, which does not, may be due to arthritis. However, given the mild severity of the medial compartment narrowing, the absence of diminished motion in the contralateral knee despite identical narrowing therein, and the fact that loss of extension and/or flexion frequently complicates ACL reconstruction, the motion deficits are more probably attributable to the surgery. According to the *Guides*, "The evaluating physician must determine whether diagnostic or examination criteria best describe the impairment of a specific patient" (4th ed, p 84). Since the decreased motion is probably secondary to the ligamentous reconstruction, it would be more appropriate to rate the primary condition, the ACL tear.

Although the partial medial meniscectomy and residual laxity of the ACL may have caused accelerated wear of the medial and, to a lesser extent, other compartments of the left knee, resulting in some posttraumatic arthritis, the symmetric narrowing of the medial joint space indicates it is more probably degenerative in etiology, ie, preexisting and unrelated to the individual's occupational injury. This suggests that Table 62, Arthritis Impairments Based on Roentgenographically Determined Cartilage Intervals (4th ed, p 83), is not the best choice for rating residuals of this trauma.

The two remaining rating options both employ diagnosis-based estimates. Because Table 64, Impairment Estimates for Certain Lower Extremity Impairments (4th ed, pp 85-86), lists both primary conditions in this case, it provides the most specific, and probably best, method for estimating impairment. Since the lax ACL and partially excised meniscus represent two separate structures, and an examiner would still be using "only one approach for each anatomic part" (4th ed, p 84), it is appropriate to rate both and then combine the estimates. The whole person impairment ratings would be 3% due to the mild ACL laxity combined with 1% due to the partial medial meniscectomy, for a total of 4%.

Interestingly, had one chosen instead to use findings on physical examination, specifically the diminished range of motion, the whole person rating would have been identical, 4%.

Impairment: 4% whole person impairment per the Fourth Edition.

Fifth Edition Rating

Impairment is based on Section 17.2, Methods of Assessment (5th ed, pp 525-554). Potential rating methods include the following:

Condition	Degree	Section	Table	Page	Rating (% Whole Person)
Gait derangement	Mild	17.2c	17-5	529	7%
Atrophy	Mild	17.2d	17-6	530	1%-2%
Loss of motion (flexion contracture)	Mild	17.2f	17-9	537	4%
Arthritis	3 mm	17.2h	17-31	544	3%
Anterior cruciate ligament laxity	Mild	17.2j	17-33	546	3%
Medial meniscectomy	Partial	17.2j	17-33	546	1%

It would be inappropriate to use each of these methods in the final impairment calculation. Gait derangement, for example, is a stand-alone rating that is not combined with any other. "Typically, whenever possible, the evaluator should use a more specific method" (5th ed, p 528).

Given the presence of a normal right thigh for comparison and absence of any swelling or varicosity that would invalidate the circumference measurement of the left thigh, one might base a rating on the 1.5-cm atrophy. Examination failed to show clinically any weakness. Knee trauma or disease commonly results in thigh, primarily quadriceps, atrophy, and most examiners would consider it more appropriate to rate the primary rather than secondary condition. Furthermore, there are other, more specific methods for rating impairment in this case (see below), suggesting muscle atrophy is not the best means.

Range of motion is the next rating option. The loss of 5° of extension, which constitutes an impairment, and the diminished flexion, which does not, may be due to arthritis. However, given the mild severity of the medial compartment narrowing, the absence of diminished motion in the contralateral knee despite identical narrowing therein, and the fact that loss of extension and/or flexion frequently complicates ACL reconstruction, the motion deficits are more probably attributable to the surgery. According to the *Guides*, "Selecting the optimal approach or combining several methods requires judgment and experience" (5th ed, p 527). Since the decreased motion is probably secondary to the ligamentous reconstruction, it would be more appropriate to rate the primary condition, the ACL tear. Furthermore, Table 17-2, Guide to the Appropriate Combination of Evaluation Methods (5th ed, p 526), states that range of motion and ankylosis are not to be combined with diagnosis-based estimates.

Although the partial medial meniscectomy and residual laxity of the ACL may have caused accelerated wear of the medial and, to a lesser extent, other compartments of the left knee, resulting in some posttraumatic arthritis, the symmetric narrowing of the medial joint space indicates it is more probably degenerative in etiology, ie, preexisting and unrelated to the individual's occupational injury. This suggests that Table 17-31, Arthritis Impairments Based on Roentgenographically Determined Cartilage Intervals (5th ed, p 544), is not the best choice for rating residuals of this trauma.

The two remaining rating options both employ diagnosis-based estimates from Section 17.2j, Diagnosis-Based Estimates (5th ed, p 545). Because Table 17-33, Impairment Estimates for Certain Lower Extremity Impairments (5th ed, p 546), lists both primary conditions in this case, it provides the most specific, and probably best, method for estimating impairment. Since the lax ACL and partially excised meniscus represent two separate structures, it is appropriate to rate both and then combine the estimates. The examiner would still be following the guidance, "typically, one method will adequately characterize the impairment and its impact on the ability to perform ADL. In some cases, however, more than one method needs to be used to accurately assess all features of the impairment" (5th ed, p 527). The whole person impairment ratings would be 3% whole person impairment due to the mild ACL laxity combined with 1% whole person impairment due to the partial medial meniscectomy, for a total of 4% whole person impairment. This rating process is summarized in Figure 17-10 (5th ed, p 561), as shown here on page 428.

Interestingly, had one chosen instead to use findings on physical examination, specifically the diminished range of motion, the whole person rating would have been identical, 4%.

Impairment: 4% whole person impairment per the Fifth Edition.

Sixth Edition Rating

The *Guides* approach to the evaluation of impairment due to ACL and medial meniscus tear with ACL reconstruction and partial medial meniscectomy is based on Section 16.2, Diagnosis-Based Impairment (6th ed, p 497), and Section 16.2c, Knee (6th ed, p 500).

In Table 16-3, Knee Regional Grid: Lower Extremity Impairments (6th ed, p 510), in the section on Ligament/Bone/Joint, for the diagnosis "ACL reconstruction" there is a class 1 rating for mild problems (with a default impairment of 10% lower extremity impairment). Recall that, at this step, the most applicable diagnosis was the ACL reconstruction and not the partial medial meniscectomy.

In Section 16.3a, Adjustment Grid: Functional History (6th ed, p 516), and Table 16-6, Functional History Adjustment: Lower Extremities (6th ed, p 516), the patient is assigned grade modifier 1; the functional history is consistent with a mildly antalgic gait, mild difficulties with prolonged running, no described pain with lifting of heavy weights and climbing stairs or ladders, and no use of supportive devices. In Section 16.3b, Adjustment Grid: Physical Examination (6th ed, p 517), and Table 16-7, Physical Examination Adjustment: Lower Extremities (6th ed, p 517), the patient is assigned grade modifier 1; the physical examination revealed "mild instability and motion loss, 1.5 cm of calf atrophy, no deformity or limb length discrepancy." In Section 16.3c, Adjustment Grid: Clinical Studies (6th ed, p 518), and Table 16-8, Clinical Studies Adjustment: Lower Extremities (6th ed, p 519), the patient is assigned grade modifier 2; the clinical studies revealed a "torn medial meniscus and ruptured ACL." In summary, the adjustments are as follows: functional history grade modifier 1, physical examination 1, and clinical studies grade modifier 2. Net adjustment compared to diagnosis class 1 is +1, grade D, 12% lower extremity impairment.

Class 2—Default for Diagnosis = 10% lower extremity impairment			
CDX	GMFH	GMPE	GMCS
1	1	1	2
Net adjustment (GMFH – CDX) 1 – 1 = 0 + (GMPE – CDX) + 1 – 1 = 0 + (GMCS – CDX) + 2 – 1 = 1 Net adjustment = 1			

Result is class 1 adjustment 1, which results in class 1, grade D = 12% lower extremity impairment.

According to Table 16-10, Impairment Values Calculated From Lower Extremity Impairment (6th ed, p 530), this converts to 5% whole person impairment.

Impairment: 5% whole person impairment per the Sixth Edition.

Comment on Internal Knee Derangement

Although, as indicated above, an examiner must determine whether examination or diagnostic criteria best describe the impairment, the Fourth Edition, in Section 3.1, Impairment Due to Other Disorders of Extremity (4th ed, pp 58-65), states if "the estimate for the anatomic impairment does not sufficiently reflect the severity of the patient's condition, the examiner may increase the impairment percent, explaining the reason for the increase in writing" (4th ed, p 64). Some evaluators have used this as a basis for adjusting impairment ratings other than those due to upper extremity injury. This statement does not appear in the Fifth Edition. Another individual having undergone the same surgical procedures might be left with mild laxity of the ACL but no flexion contracture. Despite the better outcome, he or she would have the same 4% rating. If the examiner concluded that the injured worker's 5° extension deficit represented an impairment not adequately reflected in the aforementioned rating, the 4% from the diagnosis-based estimates could be combined with the 4% due to the flexion contracture, yielding a total whole person impairment of 8%. Although contrary to instructions in the *Guides*, one might further rationalize this approach by noting that it yields a result similar to that obtained if the rating had been based on gait derangement. Alternatively, a rating more than 4% but less than 8% might be chosen, since both conditions affect the same joint from the same pathophysiologic mechanisms.

The Sixth Edition diagnosis-based impairment methodology requires that the evaluator choose a single diagnosis for rating a case. The *Guides* state on page 499 (6th ed), "Selecting the optimal diagnosis require judgment and experience. If more than 1 diagnosis can be used, the 1 that provides the most clinically accurate impairment rating should be used; this will generally be the more specific diagnosis. Typically, 1 diagnosis will adequately characterize the impairment and its impact on ADL's." In this case, the ACL injury with reconstruction and residual laxity was the most appropriate diagnosis.

SUMMARY

Diagnosis	Internal knee derangement: partial medial meniscectomy and anterior cruciate laxity
Fourth Edition References	Table 36 (4th ed, p 76), Table 37 (4th ed, p 77), Table 41 (4th ed, p 78), Table 62 (4th ed, p 83), Table 64 (4th ed, p 78)
Fourth Edition Summary	Assess, as applicable, gait, muscle strength/atrophy, range of motion, arthritis, and diagnosis-based estimates. Determine impairment on the basis of anatomic, diagnostic, and functional methods.
Fourth Edition Impairment	4% whole person impairment
Fifth Edition References	Section 17.2 (5th ed, pp 525-554), Section 17.2j (5th ed, p 545), Table 17-5 (5th ed, p 529), Table 15-6 (5th ed, p 530), Table 17-9 (5th ed, p 537), Table 17-31 (5th ed, p 544), Table 17-33 (5th ed, p 546)
Fifth Edition Summary	Assess, as applicable, gait, muscle strength/atrophy, range of motion, arthritis, and diagnosis-based estimates. Determine impairment on the basis of anatomic, diagnostic, and functional methods.

Fifth Edition Impairment 4% whole person impairment

Sixth Edition References Section 16.2 (6th ed, p 497), Section 16.2c (6th ed, p 500), Section 16.3a (6th ed, p 516), Section 16.3b (6th ed, p 517), Section 16.3c (6th ed, p 518), Table 16-3 (6th ed, p 510), Table 16-6 (6th ed, p 516), Table 16-7 (6th ed, p 517), Table 16-8, (6th ed, p 519)

Sixth Edition Summary History (including functional history and inventories), physical evaluation, and clinical studies. First, determine diagnosis-based impairment, class, and default value. Second, adjust impairment on basis of nonkey factors. Determining the most applicable diagnosis to use requires judgment and experience.

Sixth Edition Impairment 12% lower extremity impairment, 5% whole person impairment

Lower Extremity Impairment Evaluation Record and Worksheet

Name Mr. Wilson Age 45 Sex M Side ☐R ☒L Date

Diagnosis Internal Knee Derangement CASE 16-10

Region	Abnormal Motion	Regional Impairments	Table #	Percent	Amputation Location	Amputation Percent	Final Impairment Utilized: Methodology	Percent
Pelvis		DBE DJD Skin Leg Length Amp	17-33 17-31 17-36 17-4 17-32	% % % % %			DBE DJD Skin Leg Length Amputation	% % % % %
Hip	Tables 17-9 and 17-15 to 17-19 Flexion / Extension / Ankylosis / Impairment % Angle Impairment Abduction / Adduction / Ankylosis / Impairment % Angle Impairment Internal Rot / External Rot / Ankylosis / Impairment % Angle Impairment Add impairment % ROM or use largest ankylosis = %	DBE DJD Skin Leg Length Weakness Amp	17-33/34 17-31 17-36 17-4 17-8 17-32	% % % % % %			DBE DJD Skin Leg Length Weakness ROM Amputation	% % % % % % %
Thigh	(Consider related pathology at hip and knee)	Atrophy DJD Skin Leg Length Amp	17-6 17-31 17-36 17-4 17-32	1-2 % % % % %			Atrophy DJD Skin Leg Length Amputation	% % % % %
Knee	Tables 17-10 and 17-20 to 17-23 Flexion / Extension / Ankylosis / Impairment % Angle Impairment: 120 / −5 Add impairment % ROM or use largest ankylosis = %	DBE DJD Skin Weakness Amp	17-33/35 17-31 17-36 17-8 17-32	4 % 3 % % % %			DBE ~~DJD~~ Skin Weakness Amputation	4 % % % % %
Calf	(Consider related pathology at knee and ankle)	Atrophy DBE Skin Leg Length Amp	17-6 17-33 17-36 17-4 17-32	% % % % %			Atrophy DBE Skin Leg Length Amputation	% % % % %
Ankle/ Foot	Tables 17-11 to 17-13 and 17-24 to 17-28 Dorsiflex / Plantarflex / Ankylosis / Impairment % Angle Impairment Inversion / Eversion / Ankylosis / Impairment % Angle Impairment Add impairment % ROM or use largest ankylosis = %	DBE DJD Skin Weakness Amp	17-29/33 17-31 17-36 17-8/9 17-32	% % % % %			DBE DJD Skin Weakness ROM Amputation	% % % % % %
Toe	Tables 17-14 and 17-30 Great Toe: MP Dorsiflex / IP Plantarflex / Ankylosis / Impairment % Angle Impairment Lesser Toes: MP Dorsiflex / Ankylosis / Impairment % Angle Impairment Add impairment % ROM or use largest ankylosis = %	DBE DJD Skin Weakness Amp	17-33 17-31 17-36 17-8/14 17-32	% % % % %			DBE DJD Skin Weakness ROM Amputation	% % % % % %

Peripheral Nervous System Impairment	Grade %	Nerve %	Total %	Nerve	Maximum Motor %	Maximum Sensory %	Maximum Dysesthesia %
Motor Grade (Table 16-14)		×	=				
Sensory Grade (Table 16-15)		×	=				
Dysesthesia Grade		×	=		Combine all neurologic components %		

Peripheral Vascular System Impairment (Table 17-38)

Grade ______ Total vascular system impairment %

Gait Derangement (This is a *stand-alone* impairment and may *not* be combined) (Table 17-5) 7 %

Final Combined Impairment (An explanation should be provided if more than one methodology is used, justifying the rationale for each methodology used) 4 %

DBE = diagnosis-based estimates; DJD = degenerative joint disease (arthritis).

CASE 16-11

Ankle Injury

Subject: Ms Smith, a 40-year-old woman.

History: Ms Smith slipped and inverted her right ankle. Examination showed diminished ankle motions, swelling and tenderness over the lateral ankle, and instability of lateral collateral ligaments. Despite immobilization for 6 weeks, followed by extensive physical therapy, the laxity persisted. Imaging studies confirmed ligament disruption. Reconstruction of the lateral collateral ligaments was recommended but was declined by Ms Smith.

Current Symptoms: Ms Smith had a mild limp on walking along with moderate pain and swelling to the ankle with prolonged ambulation. No supportive device or orthosis was being used.

Functional Assessment: The AAOS Lower Limb Questionnaire raw score was 15 of 35. Her interoffice examination findings and complaints were consistent with moderate difficulties with ambulation including a mild limp, but no use of orthotics.

Physical Examination: Examination performed a year later showed an antalgic gait with shortened stance phase but not requiring a walking aid, 1.0-cm smaller circumference of the right leg (calf) than the normal left, 15° dorsiflexion and 20° plantar flexion of the right ankle, 12° eversion and 15° inversion of the ipsilateral hindfoot, positive anterior drawer test, and instability on inversion.

Clinical Studies: Cartilage interval on a weight-bearing mortise radiograph of the right ankle was 4 mm. Varus stress X-ray films of both ankles showed 5-mm greater laxity on the right (measured from the lateral margin of the talus to the tibial plafond on the anteroposterior view).

Discussion of Ankle Injury

Fourth Edition Rating

Impairment is based on Section 3.2, The Lower Extremity (4th ed, pp 75-94). Potential rating methods include the following:

Condition	Degree	Section	Table	Page	Rating (% Whole Person)
Gait derangement	Mild	3.2b	36	76	7%
Atrophy	Mild	3.2c	37b	77	1%
Ankle motions	Mild	3.2e	42	78	3%
Hindfoot motions	Mild	3.2g	43	78	1%
Diagnosis—ankle ligamentous instability	Moderate	3.2i	64	86	4%

It would be incorrect to utilize each of these methods in the final impairment estimate.

Gait derangement is rated by means of Table 36, Lower Limb Impairment From Gait Derangement (4th ed, p 76). This is a stand-alone impairment not combined with any other. Although it may be used as a guide for rating many lower limb impairments, the evaluator should use a more specific method whenever possible (4th ed, p 75).

Given a normal contralateral leg for comparison, the 1.0-cm atrophy of the right leg presents another possible rating method, according to Table 37, Impairments From Leg Muscle Atrophy (4th ed, p 77). Being one of the few truly objective findings, limb circumference measurements are generally more valuable than other components of a musculoskeletal examination. However, other rating methods, more specific for this injury and its residuals, are available.

The range-of-motion deficits offer a third methodologic option for rating. Although potentially due to pain or suboptimal effort, some motion loss is expected given the third-degree sprain and subsequent prolonged immobilization. According to Table 42, Ankle Motion Impairment Estimates (4th ed, p 78), there is a 3% whole person, 7% lower extremity, or 10% foot impairment due to loss of plantar flexion. According to Table 43, Hindfoot Impairment Estimates, there is a 1% whole person, 2% lower extremity, or 3% foot impairment due to the limited inversion. Eversion was normal. These values are combined by means of the Combined Values Chart (4th ed, pp 322-324) for a total of 4% whole person, 9% lower extremity, or 13% foot impairment.

The last option, an estimate based on the diagnosis, ligamentous instability, is clearly the most specific and perhaps the best choice. According to Table 64, Impairment Estimates for Certain Lower Extremity Impairments

(4th ed, p 86), Ms Smith is considered to have a moderate ligamentous instability of her ankle, since varus stress X-ray films of both ankles showed 5-mm greater laxity on the right. Interestingly, the diagnostic and functional (range-of-motion) methods provide identical results, tending to substantiate 4% whole person impairment as the correct rating.

Impairment: 4% whole person impairment per the Fourth Edition.

Fifth Edition Rating

Impairment is based on Section 17.2, Methods of Assessment (5th ed, pp 525-554). Potential rating methods include the following:

Condition	Degree	Section	Table	Page	Rating (% Whole Person)
Gait derangement	Mild	17.2c	17-5	529	7%
Atrophy	Mild	17.2d	17-6	530	1%
Ankle motions	Mild	17.2f	17-11	537	3%
Hindfoot motions	Mild	17.2f	17-12	537	1%
Diagnosis—ankle ligamentous instability	Moderate	17.2j	17-33	547	4%

It would be incorrect to utilize each of these methods in the final impairment estimate. Gait derangement is rated by means of Table 17-5, Lower Limb Impairment Due to Gait Derangement (5th ed, p 529). This is a stand-alone impairment not combined with any other. Although it may be used as a guide for rating many lower limb impairments, the evaluator should use a more specific method whenever possible (5th ed, p 529).

Given a normal contralateral leg for comparison, the 1.0-cm atrophy of the right leg presents another possible rating method, according to Table 17-6, Impairments From Leg Muscle Atrophy (5th ed, p 530). Being one of the few truly objective findings, limb circumference measurements are generally more valuable than other components of a musculoskeletal examination. However, other rating methods, more specific for this injury and its residuals, are available.

The range-of-motion deficits offer a third methodologic option for rating. Although potentially due to pain or suboptimal effort, some motion loss is expected given the third-degree sprain and subsequent prolonged immobilization. According to Table 17-11, Ankle Motion Impairment

Estimates (5th ed, p 537), there is 3% whole person, 7% lower extremity, or 10% foot impairment due to loss of plantar flexion. Extension (dorsiflexion) was normal. According to Table 17-12, Hindfoot Impairment Estimates (5th ed, p 537), there is a 1% whole person, 2% lower extremity, or 3% foot impairment due to the limited inversion. These values are combined by means of the Combined Values Chart (5th ed, pp 602-604) for a total of 4% whole person, 9% lower extremity, or 13% foot impairment.

The last option, an estimate based on the diagnosis, ligamentous instability, is clearly the most specific and perhaps the best choice. According to Table 17-33, Impairment Estimates for Certain Lower Extremity Impairments (5th ed, p 547), Ms Smith is considered to have a moderate ligamentous instability of her ankle, since varus stress X-ray films of both ankles revealed 5-mm greater laxity on the right. This results in a 4% whole person, 10% lower extremity, or 14% foot impairment. This rating process is summarized in Figure 17-10 (5th ed, p 561), as shown here on page 436.

Interestingly, the diagnostic and functional (range-of-motion) methods provide identical results, tending to substantiate 4% whole person impairment as the correct rating.

Impairment: 4% whole person impairment per the Fifth Edition.

Sixth Edition Rating

The *Guides* approach to the evaluation of impairment due to ankle sprain with ligament disruption is based on Section 16.2, Diagnosis-Based Impairment (6th ed, p 497), and Section 16.2b, Foot and Ankle (6th ed, p 500).

In Table 16-2, Foot and Ankle Regional Grid: Lower Extremity Impairments (6th ed, p 502), in the section on Ligament, for the diagnosis "ankle sprain," due to the moderate ligament laxity there is a class 1 rating for mild problems (with a default impairment of 10% lower extremity impairment).

In Section 16.3a, Adjustment Grid: Functional History (6th ed, p 516), and Table 16-6, Functional History Adjustment: Lower Extremities (6th ed, p 516), the patient is assigned grade modifier 1; the functional history is consistent with mild limp on ambulation and pain with prolonged ambulation, but no use of supportive devices. In Section 16.3b, Adjustment Grid: Physical Examination (6th ed, p 517), and Table 16-7, Physical Examination Adjustment: Lower Extremities (6th ed, p 517), the patient is assigned grade modifier 2 with moderate ligament laxity, decreased motion, and atrophy. Section 16.3c, Adjustment Grid: Clinical Studies (6th ed, p 518), and Table 16-8, Clinical Studies Adjustment: Lower Extremities (6th ed, p 519), were not applicable since the clinical studies result of "5 mm of ligament laxity" was used to place the patient into a class rating. In summary, the adjustments are as follows: functional history grade modifier 1, physical examination grade modifier 2, and clinical studies grade modifier not applicable. Net adjustment compared to diagnosis class 1 is +1, grade D, 12% lower extremity impairment.

Class 2—Default for Diagnosis = 10% lower extremity impairment			
CDX	GMFH	GMPE	GMCS
1	1	2	n/a

Net adjustment

(GMFH – CDX) 1 – 1 = 0

+ (GMPE – CDX) + 2 – 1 = 1

+ (GMCS – CDX) + n/a

Net adjustment = 1

Result is class 1 adjustment +1, which results in class 1, grade D = 12% lower extremity impairment.

According to Table 16-10, Impairment Values Calculated From Lower Extremity Impairment (6th ed, p 530), this converts to 5% whole person impairment.

Impairment: 5% whole person impairment per the Sixth Edition.

Comment on Ankle Injury

Since the *Guides* Fifth Edition instructs examiners to use only one rating approach for each anatomic part, the diagnosis-based and functional ratings should not be combined. Table 17-2, Guide to the Appropriate Combination of Evaluation Methods (5th ed, p 526), in the Fifth Edition defines which methods may be combined. Had this example involved a bony rather than a ligamentous injury, specifically an intra- or juxta-articular fracture with posttraumatic arthritis, the appropriate diagnosis-based rating would be combined with that for arthritis, or the range-of-motion method would be used. The *Guides* Fifth Edition recommends use of whichever method provides the greater estimate.

The ligamentous laxity and associated impairment probably would have been diminished, if not eliminated, after reconstruction of lateral collateral ligaments. While there may have been no improvement in ankle or hindfoot motion after such operative intervention, one might be inclined to disallow or decrease the impairment rating in this case given the claimant's refusal of potentially curative treatment (failure to mitigate damages, in legal parlance). However, the view of the *Guides* contributors is that if a patient declines therapy for a permanent impairment, that decision should neither decrease nor increase the estimated percentage (4th ed, p 9; 5th ed, p 20).

Per the Sixth Edition, the diagnosis-based impairment does not usually allow for combination with any other methods. In this case, the ligament laxity noted on examination and imaging findings document objective findings useful in the correct placement of the patient into her specific impairment rating class.

SUMMARY

Diagnosis	Ankle injury
Fourth Edition References	Section 3.2 (4th ed, pp 75-93), Table 36 (4th ed, p 76), Table 37b (4th ed, p 77), Table 42 (4th ed, p 78), Table 43 (4th ed, p 78), Table 64 (4th ed, p 86)
Fourth Edition Summary	Assess, as applicable, gait, muscle strength/atrophy, range of motion, arthritis, and diagnosis-based estimates. Determine impairment on the basis of anatomic, diagnostic, and functional methods.
Fourth Edition Impairment	9% lower extremity impairment, 4% whole person impairment
Fifth Edition References	Section 17.2 (5th ed, pp 525-554), Section 17.2j (5th ed, p 545), Table 17-5 (5th ed, p 529), Table 15-6 (5th ed, p 530), Table 17-11 (5th ed, p 537), Table 17-12 (5th ed, p 537), Table 17-31 (5th ed, p 544), Table 17-33 (5th ed, p 546)
Fifth Edition Summary	Assess, as applicable, gait, muscle strength/atrophy, range of motion, arthritis, and diagnosis-based estimates. Determine impairment on the basis of anatomic, diagnostic, and functional methods.

Fifth Edition Impairment	10% lower extremity impairment, 4% whole person impairment
Sixth Edition References	Section 16.2 (6th ed, p 497), Section 16.2b (6th ed, p 500), Section 16.3a (6th ed, p 516), Section 16.3b (6th ed, p 517), Section 16.3c (6th ed, p 518), Table 16-2 (6th ed, p 502), Table 16-6 (6th ed, p 516), Table 16-7 (6th ed, p 517), Table 16-8 (6th ed, p 519), Table 16-10 (6th ed, p 530)
Sixth Edition Summary	History (including functional history and inventories), physical evaluation, and clinical studies. First, determine diagnosis-based impairment, class, and default value. Second, adjust impairment on basis of nonkey factors.
Sixth Edition Impairment	12% lower extremity impairment, 5% whole person impairment

Lower Extremity Impairment Evaluation Record and Worksheet

Name Ms. Smith Age 40 Sex F Side ☒R ☐L Date

Diagnosis Ankle Injury CASE 16-11

Potential Impairments							Final Impairment Utilized	
Region	Abnormal Motion	Regional Impairments	Table #	Percent	Amputation Location	Amputation Percent	Methodology	Percent
Pelvis		DBE DJD Skin Leg Length Amp	17-33 17-31 17-36 17-4 17-32	% % % % %			DBE DJD Skin Leg Length Amputation	% % % % %
Hip	Tables 17-9 and 17-15 to 17-19 (see below)	DBE DJD Skin Leg Length Weakness Amp	17-33/34 17-31 17-36 17-4 17-8 17-32	% % % % % %			DBE DJD Skin Leg Length Weakness ROM Amputation	% % % % % % %
Thigh	(Consider related pathology at hip and knee)	Atrophy DJD Skin Leg Length Amp	17-6 17-31 17-36 17-4 17-32	% % % % %			Atrophy DJD Skin Leg Length Amputation	% % % % %
Knee	Tables 17-10 and 17-20 to 17-23 (see below)	DBE DJD Skin Weakness Amp	17-33/35 17-31 17-36 17-8 17-32	% % % % %			DBE DJD Skin Weakness Amputation	% % % % %
Calf	(Consider related pathology at knee and ankle) 1cm	Atrophy DBE Skin Leg Length Amp	17-6 17-33 17-36 17-4 17-32	1 % % % % %			Atrophy DBE Skin Leg Length Amputation	% % % % %
Ankle/ Foot	Tables 17-11 to 17-13 and 17-24 to 17-28 (see below)	DBE DJD Skin Weakness Amp	17-29/33 17-31 17-36 17-8/9 17-32	4 % % % % %			DBE DJD Skin Weakness ROM Amputation	4 % % % % % %
Toe	Tables 17-14 and 17-30 (see below)	DBE DJD Skin Weakness Amp	17-33 17-31 17-36 17-8/14 17-32	% % % % %			DBE DJD Skin Weakness ROM Amputation	% % % % % %

Hip — Tables 17-9 and 17-15 to 17-19

	Flexion	Extension	Ankylosis	Impairment %
Angle Impairment				
	Abduction	Adduction	Ankylosis	Impairment %
Angle Impairment				
	Internal Rot	External Rot	Ankylosis	Impairment %
Angle Impairment				

Add impairment % ROM or use largest ankylosis = %

Knee — Tables 17-10 and 17-20 to 17-23

	Flexion	Extension	Ankylosis	Impairment %
Angle Impairment				

Add impairment % ROM or use largest ankylosis = %

Ankle/Foot — Tables 17-11 to 17-13 and 17-24 to 17-28

	Dorsiflex	Plantarflex	Ankylosis	Impairment %
Angle	15	20		
Impairment	0	3		3
	Inversion	Eversion	Ankylosis	Impairment %
Angle	15	12		
Impairment	1	0		1

Add impairment % ROM or use largest ankylosis = 4 %

Toe — Tables 17-14 and 17-30

Great Toe	MP Dorsiflex	IP Plantarflex	Ankylosis	Impairment %
Angle Impairment				
Lesser Toes	MP Dorsiflex		Ankylosis	Impairment %
Angle Impairment				

Add impairment % ROM or use largest ankylosis = %

Peripheral Nervous System Impairment		Grade %	Nerve %	Total %	Nerve	Maximum Motor %	Maximum Sensory %	Maximum Dysesthesia %
Motor Grade (Table 16-14)			×	=				
Sensory Grade (Table 16-15)			×	=				
Dysesthesia Grade			×	=		Combine all neurologic components %		

Peripheral Vascular System Impairment (Table 17-38)

Grade ______ Total vascular system impairment %

Gait Derangement (This is a *stand-alone* impairment and may *not* be combined) (Table 17-5) 7 %

Final Combined Impairment (An explanation should be provided if more than one methodology is used, justifying the rationale for each methodology used) 4 %

DBE = diagnosis-based estimates; DJD = degenerative joint disease (arthritis).

CASE 16-12

Osteomyelitis Secondary to Trauma

Subject: Mr Smith, a 48-year-old man.

History: Mr Smith, an appliance deliveryman with diabetes, had a refrigerator fall on his left forefoot, resulting in widely displaced fractures of metatarsal shafts 2 through 5. He underwent open reduction and internal fixation thereof, and the fractures healed in anatomic alignment. However, despite preoperative and postoperative antibiotics, Mr Smith developed chronic osteomyelitis. Because of continued drainage requiring dressing changes and inability to wear his work shoes over the dressings, he was limited to sedentary work.

Current Symptoms: Mr Smith had no significant pain but mild swelling daily associated with chronic drainage. There were no problems with ambulation. Daily dressing changes were required, but he had no current need for braces or assistive devices.

Functional Assessment: The AAOS Lower Limb Questionnaire raw score was 10 of 35. Mr Smith's interoffice examination findings and complaints were consistent with minimal difficulties with ambulation due to dressing requirements. No limp or need for braces or orthotics was found.

Physical Examination: Examination 2 years after injury showed healed surgical scars but draining sinuses on the dorsum of the left foot. The range of motion was normal, as was the rest of the examination, with the exception of mild peripheral neuropathy bilaterally.

Clinical Studies:

Discussion of Osteomyelitis Secondary to Trauma

Fourth Edition Rating

Impairment is based on Section 3.2, The Lower Extremity (4th ed, pp 75-94). Section 3.2j, Skin Loss (4th ed, p 88), and Table 67, Impairments for Skin Loss (4th ed, p 88), provide the best means for rating residuals of this occupational injury and the resulting surgery. Chronic osteomyelitis of the foot with active drainage, "requiring periodic redressing and limiting time using footwear," warrants a rating of 10% whole person impairment.

Impairment: 10% whole person impairment per the Fourth Edition.

Fifth Edition Rating

Impairment is based on Section 17.2, Methods of Assessment (5th ed, pp 525-554). Section 17.2k, Skin Loss (5th ed, p 550), and Table 17-36, Impairments for Skin Loss (5th ed, p 550), provide the best means for rating residuals of this occupational injury and the resulting surgery. Chronic osteomyelitis of the foot with active drainage, "requiring periodic redressing and limiting time using footwear," warrants a rating of 10% whole person impairment.

Impairment: 10% whole person impairment per the Fifth Edition.

Sixth Edition Rating

The *Guides* approach to the evaluation of impairment due to chronic wound drainage is described in Section 8.1, Principles of Assessment (6th ed, p 160), and Table 8-2, Criteria for Rating Permanent Impairment Due to Skin Disorders (6th ed, p 166). Due to the chronic draining skin wound, by functional history criteria assigned with mild interference of activities of daily living, there is a class 2 rating for moderate problems (with a default impairment of 19% whole person impairment).

Functional history is not applicable since the history is used to assess the initial rating class. According to criteria assigned in Table 8-2, Criteria for Rating Permanent Impairment Due to Skin Disorders (6th ed, p 166), and Table 8-3, Skin Impairment Evaluation Summary (6th ed, p 178), for physical examination adjustment the patient is assigned grade modifier 1 with less than 10% of the body surface area involved. Using the same Tables 8-2 and 8-3, for clinical studies adjustment, a grade modifier was not applicable. In summary, the adjustments are as follows: functional history grade modifier not applicable, physical examination grade modifier 1, and clinical studies grade modifier not applicable. Net adjustment compared to diagnosis class 1 is −1, grade B, 15% whole person impairment.

Impairment: 15% whole person impairment per the Sixth Edition.

Comment on Osteomyelitis Secondary to Trauma

Impairment Estimates for Certain Lower Extremity Impairments (Table 64, 4th ed, pp 85-87; Table 17-33, 5th ed, pp 546-547; Table 16-2, 6th ed, p 501) provides diagnosis-based estimates for metatarsal fractures, but only those that are malaligned, or with other examination findings or metatarsalgia. The Sixth Edition criteria for skin disorders due to chronic draining sinuses from osteomyelitis are most applicable.

SUMMARY

Diagnosis	Osteomyelitis
Fourth Edition References	Section 3.2 (4th ed, pp 75-93), Section 3.2j (4th ed, p 88), Table 67 (4th ed, p 88)
Fourth Edition Summary	History, lower extremity examination, with impairment based on skin loss.
Fourth Edition Impairment	10% whole person impairment
Fifth Edition References	Section 17.2 (5th ed, pp 525-554), Section 17.2k (5th ed, p 550), Table 17-36 (5th ed, p 550)
Fifth Edition Summary	History, lower extremity examination, with impairment based on skin loss.
Fifth Edition Impairment	10% whole person impairment
Sixth Edition References	Section 8.1 (6th ed, p 160), Table 8-2 (6th ed, p 166), Table 8-3, (6th ed, p 178)
Sixth Edition Summary	History (including functional history) documents criteria for class placement; physical evaluation and clinical studies are then used to adjust for the correct rating value within the class. Functional history is not used to adjust within the class since it is used to initially establish the correct class.
Sixth Edition Impairment	15% whole person impairment

Chapter 17

The Spine and Pelvis

CASE 17-1

Catastrophic Injury

Subject: Mr Costner, a 34-year-old man.

History: Mr Costner, a construction worker, lost his balance and fell into an elevator shaft, striking portions of scaffolding before landing on a dirt surface two stories below. He was airlifted to a trauma center where he was examined. He was found to have a right parietal scalp laceration, four-part fracture of the proximal right humerus, fractures of posterolateral right fifth, sixth, and seventh ribs, and a burst fracture of the L2 vertebral body, with two large retropulsed fracture fragments on computed tomographic scan, and near-total paraplegia. After repair of the scalp laceration in the emergency department, Mr Costner underwent decompression of the spinal canal, with an instrumented lumbar fusion from T12 to L3. After an unsuccessful attempt at open reduction and internal fixation of the four-part fracture of the proximal humerus, with intraoperative notation of damage to the articular surface of the scapula (glenoid), a total shoulder arthroplasty was performed.

Current Symptoms: The scalp laceration and rib fractures healed without residuals, and extensive rehabilitation resulted in improvement in right shoulder motions and strength. Bowel and bladder control were absent, and the patient had no lower extremity neurologic function below L2. Mr Costner used a wheelchair for "ambulation" full-time, and because of the shoulder injury and subsequent stiffness and weakness after shoulder replacement, he required assistance with transfers to and from the bed, toilet, car, etc. He was unable to stand without help.

Functional Assessment: Pain Disability Questionnaire (PDQ) score was 110. Upper extremity functional assessment was consistent with "requires assistance to perform self-care activities" and a *Quick*DASH score of 80.

Physical Examination: Independent medical examination 2 years after injury showed a healed right parietal scar and nontender right chest wall with normal respiratory function. Pulmonary function testing was within normal limits. In addition to the surgical scar, examination of the right shoulder demonstrated slightly limited motion, consistent with shoulder arthroplasty, with abduction of 120°, adduction of 20°, extension of 30°, flexion of 140°, external rotation of 60°, and internal rotation of 50°. The right arm and forearm were 1.5 and 1 cm smaller than their counterparts on the left. Sensation was intact in the right upper extremity, but grade 4/5 weakness was noted upon all resisted motions of that shoulder. Neurologic function was absent below the L2 level, including absent bowel and bladder control.

Clinical Studies: Postoperative studies document a solid instrumented lumbar fusion from T12 to L3 and a well-positioned right shoulder total joint replacement.

Discussion of Catastrophic Injury

Fourth Edition Rating

Impairment evaluation for the right shoulder is based on Section 3.1m, Impairment Due to Other Disorders of the Upper Extremity (4th ed, p 58). According to Table 27, Impairment of the Upper Extremity After Arthroplasty of Specific Bones or Joints (4th ed, p 61), the total shoulder arthroplasty results in 30% upper extremity impairment.

The instructions for arthroplasty begin on page 61 and continue on page 62 of the *Guides*. According to page 62, "In the presence of decreased motion, motion impairments are derived separately and combined with arthroplasty impairments." According to Figure 38, Upper Extremity Impairments Due to Lack of Flexion and Extension of Shoulder (4th ed, p 43), shoulder flexion of 140° is a 3% upper extremity impairment, and extension of 30° is a 1% upper extremity impairment.

According to Figure 41, Upper Extremity Impairments Due to Lack of Abduction and Adduction of Shoulder (4th ed, p 44), shoulder abduction of 120° is a 3% upper extremity impairment and adduction of 20° is a 1% upper extremity impairment. According to Figure 44, Upper Extremity Impairments Due to Lack of Internal and External Rotation of Shoulder (4th ed, p 45), internal rotation of 50° is a 2% upper extremity impairment and external rotation of 60° is a 0% upper extremity impairment. The impairment percentages for loss of shoulder motion in each of these six directions are then added (3% + 1% + 3% + 1% + 2% + 0% = 10% upper extremity impairment).

The final impairment rating for the shoulder is then 30% upper extremity impairment (arthroplasty) combined with 10% upper extremity impairment (motion), which yields a rating of 37% upper extremity impairment. According to Table 3, Relationship of Impairment of the Upper Extremity to Impairment of the Whole Person (4th ed, p 20), 37% upper extremity impairment is equivalent to a 22% whole person impairment.

Impairment for the L2 burst fracture and resulting paraplegia is based on Section 3.3f, Specific Procedures and Directions (4th ed, p 101). The paraplegia warrants a rating of diagnosis-related estimate (DRE) lumbosacral category VIII, equivalent to 75% whole person impairment, as specified in Table 72, DRE Lumbosacral Spine Impairment Categories (4th ed, p 110).

Combining the 75% whole person impairment for paraplegia with the 22% whole person impairment rating for the shoulder injury results in 81% whole person impairment.

Impairment: 81% whole person impairment per the Fourth Edition.

Fifth Edition Rating

There are three conditions to rate for permanent impairment: total shoulder replacement, with restricted motion, and paraplegia below L2. Treatment of the L2 burst fracture with a fusion is combined with the rating of the spinal cord injury, as discussed below.

Impairment evaluation for the right shoulder is based on Section 16.7b, Arthroplasty. According to Table 16-27, Impairment of the Upper Extremity After Arthroplasty of Specific Bones or Joints (5th ed, p 506), the total shoulder arthroplasty is a 24% upper extremity impairment. The instructions for arthroplasty state, “In the presence of decreased motion, motion impairments are derived separately (Section 16.4) and combined with the arthroplasty impairment (Combined Values Chart, p 604)” (5th ed, p 505).

According to Figure 16-40, Pie Chart of Upper Extremity Impairments Due to Lack of Flexion and Extension of Shoulder (5th ed, p 476), shoulder flexion of 140° is a 3% upper extremity impairment and extension of 30° is a 1% upper extremity impairment. According to Figure 16-43, Pie Chart of Upper Extremity Impairments Due to Lack of Abduction and Adduction of

Shoulder (5th ed, p 477), shoulder abduction of 120° is a 3% upper extremity impairment and adduction of 20° is a 1% upper extremity impairment. According to Figure 16-46, Pie Chart of Upper Extremity Impairments Due to Lack of Internal and External Rotation of Shoulder (5th ed, p 479), internal rotation of 50° is a 2% upper extremity impairment and external rotation of 60° is a 0% upper extremity impairment. The impairment percentages for loss of shoulder motion in each of these six directions are then added (3% + 1% + 3% + 1% + 2% + 0% = 10%).

The final impairment rating for the shoulder is then 24% upper extremity impairment (arthroplasty) combined with 10% upper extremity impairment (motion), which yields a rating of 32% upper extremity impairment. According to Table 16-3, Conversion of Impairment of the Upper Extremity to Impairment of the Whole Person (5th ed, p 439), the 32% upper extremity impairment is equivalent to a 19% whole person impairment.

Paraplegia is rated by means of Section 15.7, Rating Corticospinal Tract Damage (5th ed, pp 395-398). In the Fifth Edition, quadriplegia and paraplegia are rated by the system contained in the Nervous System chapter, which information is reprinted in the Spine chapter. Mr Costner has several findings that qualify for impairment rating.

Table 15-6, Rating Corticospinal Tract Impairment, Part c, Criteria for Rating Impairments Due to Station and Gait Disorders (5th ed, p 396), would rate his inability to stand as a class 4 impairment, which has a range of 40% to 60% whole person impairment. An individual with a high thoracic paraplegia would easily qualify for the 60% whole person impairment rating. Having more neurologic function (down to L2) would suggest that Mr Costner should be rated at the lower end of this scale, as 45% whole person impairment.

The directions state, "Once a class has been selected, the exact value is obtained by combining the value with the corresponding additional impairment from DRE categories II through V for cervical and lumbar impairment and DRE categories II through IV for thoracic impairment" (5th ed, p 396). While this additional step is not performed if spinal cord pathology is rated by means of the Nervous System chapter, and while this seems like "double rating" the motor consequences of this injury, the directions state that this is to be performed. Mr Costner was treated with a surgical fusion, which would place him in at least DRE category IV, which is 20% to 23% whole person impairment. From that range, a rating of 20% whole person impairment could be selected.

Other factors that must be considered in impairment rating are Mr Costner's urinary incontinence, fecal incontinence, and loss of sexual functioning. The Fifth Edition states, "If there is additional bowel or bladder dysfunction, combine the upper extremity or lower extremity loss with impairments in bladder, anorectal, and/or neurologic sexual impairment as warranted" (5th ed, p 396).

Table 15-6, Rating Corticospinal Tract Impairment, Part d, Criteria for Rating Neurologic Impairment of the Bladder (5th ed, p 397), indicates that Mr Costner's areflexic bladder is a class 4 impairment, which is anywhere from a 40% to a 60% whole person impairment. No guidance is given as to which person with no bladder function deserves a 40% whole person impairment rating and which person with no bladder function deserves a 60% whole person impairment rating. Since Mr Costner does not have complications from his neurogenic bladder, a 50% whole person impairment might be appropriate.

Table 15-6, Rating Corticospinal Tract Impairment, Part e, Criteria for Rating Neurologic Anorectal Impairment (5th ed, p 397), indicates that Mr Costner's fecal incontinence with no control is a class 3 impairment, which is anywhere from a 40% to a 50% whole person impairment. Again, no directions are given to help the examiner choose from the stated range of impairments. A middle of the range value of 45% whole person impairment might be chosen.

Table 15-6, Rating Corticospinal Tract Impairment, Part f, Criteria for Rating Neurologic Sexual Impairment, indicates that Mr Costner's complete lack of sexual function is a class 3 impairment, which is 20% whole person impairment. In the Nervous System chapter and in the Urinary and Reproductive System chapter, the ratings for loss of male sexual functioning are adjusted for the age of the individual. The Spine chapter does not contain this instruction.

Thus, the rating for paraplegia would be derived by combining the ratings for lower extremity neurologic loss (45% whole person impairment), additional "category II-V loss" (20% whole person impairment), urinary incontinence (50% whole person impairment), fecal incontinence (45% whole person impairment), and neurologic sexual dysfunction (20% whole person impairment). The Spine chapter does not have instruction on how to combine multiple impairments, but the Upper Extremity chapter does: "If three or more values are to be combined, the two lowest values are first selected and their combined value is found. The combined value and the third value are then combined to give the total value. This procedure is repeated indefinitely, with the value obtained in each case being a combination of all the previous values" (5th ed, p 438).

If this principle is followed, the order in which to combine Mr Costner's spinal impairments would be 20%, 20%, 45%, 45%, and finally 50%. These combine to 91% whole person impairment.

The shoulder and the spine injury impairments need to be "combined." According to the Combined Values Chart (5th ed, p 605), the 91% whole person impairment for paraplegia and the 19% whole person impairment for the shoulder fracture result in a final 93% whole person impairment.

Unlike earlier editions, the Fifth Edition permits some thoughtful variation in how ratings are to be combined or added.

> A scientific formula has not been established to indicate the best way to combine multiple impairments. Given the diversity of impairments and great variability inherent in combining multiple impairments, it is difficult to establish a formula that accounts for all situations. A combination of some impairments could decrease overall functioning more than suggested by just adding the impairment ratings for the separate impairments (eg, blindness and inability to use both hands). When other impairments are combined, a less than additive approach may be more appropriate. . . . Other options are to combine (add, subtract, or multiply) multiple impairments based upon the extent to which they affect an individual's ability to perform activities of daily living." [5th ed, p 10]

While Mr Costner's rating is already high (93% whole person impairment), a good argument could be made that this is one of the uncommon situations in which the impairment is greater than suggested by combining impairments. Unlike others with L2-level paraplegia, but with normal upper extremities, Mr Costner's total shoulder replacement and resultant weakness and stiffness prevent him from doing unassisted transfers. Thus, his shoulder problem, although adequately rated for impairment on the basis of its effect on his upper extremity function, is also affecting his lower extremity status or ability to move about in his environment. Adjusting his impairment somewhat higher than 93% whole person impairment might be appropriate.

Impairment: 93% whole person impairment per the Fifth Edition.

Sixth Edition Rating

Upper Extremity Rating

The *Guides* approach to the evaluation of impairment due to total shoulder arthroplasty is based on Section 15.2, Diagnosis-Based Impairment (6th ed, p 387), and Section 15.2e, Shoulder (6th ed, p 390).

In Table 15-5, Shoulder Regional Grid: Upper Extremity Impairments (6th ed, p 401), for the diagnosis "total shoulder arthroplasty" there is a class 2 rating for "implant with normal motion" (with a default impairment of 24% upper extremity impairment).

In Section 15.3a, Adjustment Grid: Functional History (6th ed, p 406), and Table 15-6, Adjustment Grid: Summary (6th ed, p 406), the patient is assigned grade modifier 3; the functional history is consistent with "requires assistance to perform self-care activities." In Section 15.3b, Adjustment Grid: Physical Examination (6th ed, p 407), and Table 15-8, Physical Examination Adjustment: Upper Extremities (6th ed, p 408), the patient is assigned grade modifier 1; the physical examination revealed a range of motion (ROM) of "mild (10-19%) decrease from normal or uninjured opposite side." Muscle atrophy was also grade modifier 1. According to Section 15.3c, Adjustment Grid: Clinical Studies (6th ed, p 407), and Table 15-9, Clinical Studies Adjustment: Upper Extremities (6th ed, p 410), the patient is assigned grade modifier 2; "clinical studies confirm diagnosis, moderate pathology." In summary, the adjustments are as follows: functional history grade modifier (GMFH) 3, physical examination (GMPE) 1, and clinical studies grade modifier (GMCS) 2. The net adjustment compared to diagnosis class (CDX) 2 is 0, grade C, 24% upper extremity impairment.

Class 2—Default for Diagnosis = 24% upper extremity impairment			
CDX	GMFH	GMPE	GMCS
2	3	1	2
Net adjustment			
(GMFH − CDX) 3 − 2 = 1			
+ (GMPE − CDX) + 1 − 2 = −1			
+ (GMCS − CDX) + 2 − 2 = 0			
Net adjustment = 0			

Result is class 2 adjustment 0, which results in class 2, grade C = 24% upper extremity impairment.

According to Table 15-11, Impairment Values Calculated From Upper Extremity Impairment (6th ed, p 420), this converts to 14% whole person impairment.

Corticospinal Tract Spinal Rating

Impairment due to corticospinal tract injury is based on Section 13.4, Criteria for Rating Impairment Due to Spinal Cord Dysfunction and Movement Disorders (6th ed, p 333), and Section 13.4a, Spinal Cord Disorders (6th ed, p 333). Section 13.6, Criteria for Rating Impairments of Station, Gait, and Movement Disorders (6th ed, p 336), and Table 13-12,

Criteria for Rating Impairments Due to Station and Gait Disorders (6th ed, p 336), are used to determine an impairment rating in the range of 36% to 50% whole person impairment (Class 4). An impairment rating of 50% whole person impairment is assigned in this case, given the significance of the functional deficits.

Additional impairments are calculated for absence of bowel and bladder control. According to Section 13.7, Criteria for Rating Neurogenic Bowel, Bladder, and Sexual Dysfunction (6th ed, p 336), Table 13-13, Criteria for Rating the Neurogenic Bowel (6th ed, p 337), and Table 13-14, Criteria for Rating the Neurogenic Bladder (6th ed, p 337), are used to determine impairment ratings for incontinence related to Central Nervous System injury. An impairment rating in the range of 21% to 50% whole person impairment for total bowel incontinence and 21% to 30% whole person impairment for total bladder incontinence may be ascribed to each of these conditions. In this example, absent more detail, an impairment of 30% whole person impairment is assigned to each.

Using the Combined Values Chart (6th ed, p 604) to combine impairments of 50%, 30%, and 30%, a whole person impairment of 76% is related to central nervous system injury.

Lumbar Spine Rating

The *Guides* approach to the evaluation of impairment due to fracture of the lumbar spine is based on Section 17.2, Diagnosis-Based Impairment (6th ed, p 560), and Section 17.2c, Lumbar Spine (6th ed, p 566).

In Table 17-4, Lumbar Spine Regional Grid: Spine Impairments (6th ed, pp 570-574), for the diagnosis "fractures/dislocations of the spine" there is a class 3 rating for "single or multiple level fractures . . . with or without bony retropulsion into the canal" (with a default impairment of 19% whole person impairment).

In Section 17.3a, Adjustment Grid: Functional History (6th ed, p 569), and Table 17-6, Functional History Adjustment: Spine (6th ed, p 575), the patient is assigned grade modifier 3; the functional history is consistent with "severe disability" on the basis of a PDQ score of 110. Section 17.3b, Adjustment Grid: Physical Examination (6th ed, p 572), and Table 17-7, Physical Examination Adjustment: Spine (6th ed, p 576), would be used if physical findings had not already been addressed on the basis of the neurologic injury. Therefore, this modifier is not included in the net adjustment calculation. Similarly, X-ray films and other imaging studies were used to make the diagnosis of a fracture, and that modifier is also excluded from the calculation. In summary, the adjustments are as follows:

functional history grade modifier 3; physical examination and clinical studies are excluded from the calculation (not applicable [n/a]). The net adjustment compared to diagnosis class 3 is 0, grade C, 19% whole person impairment.

Class 3—Default for Diagnosis = 19% whole person impairment			
CDX	GMFH	GMPE	GMCS
3	3	n/a	n/a
Net adjustment			
(GMFH − CDX) 3 − 3 = 0			
+ (GMPE − CDX) + n/a			
+ (GMCS − CDX) + n/a			
Net adjustment = 0			

Result is class 3 adjustment 0, which results in class 3, grade C = 19% whole person impairment.

The patient has a 19% whole person impairment for the spinal fracture at L2.

Summary of Combined Ratings
Section 2.2c, The Combined Values Chart (6th ed, p 22), explains that "multiple impairments are successively combined by first combining the largest number with the next largest remaining number, and then further combining it with the next largest number, and then further repeating the process until all given impairment numbers are combined" (6th ed, p 23). Combining the values for all the impairments, with 76% whole person impairment related to corticospinal tract injury, 19% whole person impairment for spinal fracture at L2, and 14% whole person impairment for the shoulder arthroplasty, the patient has 84% whole person impairment.

Impairment: 84% whole person impairment per the Sixth Edition.

Comment on Catastrophic Injury

Mr Costner's paraplegia is his most serious impairment. According to the Fourth Edition, since he was injured, the injury model is to be used. Paraplegia without neurologic function below L2 is category VIII by the criteria on page 102 of the Fourth Edition.

The Fifth Edition uses a different method to rate the injuries to the corticospinal tract. The system that has been in the Nervous System chapter is now used; thus, ratings will be somewhat higher.

The upper extremity impairment is all due to a shoulder injury. Both the arthroplasty and the ROM are rated and the ratings are combined. The atrophy and weakness are expected after shoulder replacement and are not rated separately.

The ratings for loss of shoulder motion are identical in the Fourth and Fifth Editions. The ratings for arthroplasty differ. The Fourth Edition gave higher ratings for joint replacement, and the somewhat lower ratings in the Fifth Edition may reflect improvements in the prostheses that have occurred during the last decade.

The Sixth Edition ratings for the lumbar spine injury require the examiner to choose the most applicable diagnosis along with the neurologic rating from Chapter 13 resulting from the corticospinal tract involvement. In this case, the burst fracture with fracture fragment displacement is the most applicable class diagnosis from Table 17-4, Lumbar Spine Regional Grid: Spine Impairments (6th ed, p 571). In situations such as this, the most specific diagnosis that resulted in the condition at maximal medical improvement (MMI) should prevail. Since the burst fracture is the primary diagnosis and includes the discussion in the table that any value should be combined with the cauda equina ratings, then this diagnostic class is the most specific.

The final combined whole person impairment value is less with the Sixth Edition than prior editions. In the Sixth Edition, adjustments were made to the maximum impairment values associated with spinal cord dysfunction, and with the shoulder the rating is based on arthroplasty alone (this cannot be combined with motion deficit).

SUMMARY

Diagnosis	L2 fracture with paraplegia; proximal humerus fracture/total shoulder replacement
Fourth Edition References	Section 3.1j (4th ed, p 41), Section 3.1m (4th ed, p 61), Section 3.3g (4th ed, p 101), Table 3 (4th ed, p 20), Table 70 (4th ed, p 108), Figures 38, 41, 44 (4th ed, p 43)
Fourth Edition Summary	Degree of spinal neurologic deficit, presence of shoulder prosthesis (replacement), shoulder ROM.
Fourth Edition Impairment	81% whole person impairment

Fifth Edition References	Section 15.7 (5th ed, p 395), Section 16.4i (5th ed, p 474), Section 16.7b (5th ed, p 505), Table 15-3 (5th ed, p 384), Table 15-6 (5th ed, p 396), Table 16-27 (5th ed, p 506), Figure 16-40 (5th ed, p 476), Figure 16-43 (5th ed, p 477), Figure 16-46 (5th ed, p 479)
Fifth Edition Summary	Degree of spinal neurologic deficit, presence of shoulder prosthesis (replacement), shoulder ROM
Fifth Edition Impairment	93% whole person impairment
Sixth Edition References	Section 13.4 (6th ed, p 333), Section 13.4a (6th ed, p 333), Section 13.6 (6th ed, p 336), Section 13.7 (6th ed, p 336), Section 15.2 (6th ed, p 387), Section 15.2e (6th ed, p 390), Section 15.3a (6th ed, p 406), Section 15.3b (6th ed, p 407), Section 17.3b (6th ed, p 572), Section 15.3c (6th ed, p 407), Section 17.2 (6th ed, p 560), Section 17.2c (6th ed, p 566), Section 17.3a (6th ed, p 569), Table 13-12 (6th ed, p 336), Table 13-13 (6th ed, p 337), Table 13-14 (6th ed, p 337), Table 15-5 (6th ed, p 401), Table 15-6 (6th ed, p 406), Table 15-8 (6th ed, p 408), Table 15-9 (6th ed, p 410), Table 15-11 (6th ed, p 420), Table 17-4 (6th ed, p 570), Table 17-6 (6th ed, p 575), Table 17-7 (6th ed, p 576)
Sixth Edition Summary	History (including functional history and inventories), physical evaluation, and clinical studies. First, determine diagnosis-based impairment (DBI), class, and default value. In cases of multiple injuries, each diagnosis is rated. Second, adjust impairment on basis of nonkey factors where appropriate.
Sixth Edition Impairment	84% whole person impairment

CASE 17-2

Cervical Sprain/Strain

Subject: Ms Welch, a 55-year-old woman.

History: Ms Welch had sustained injury when she stopped her 1995 Ford Escort on a freeway 2 years earlier. She was restrained by shoulder and lap belts on a high-backed bucket seat. A sport utility vehicle hit her car from the rear at an estimated 40 miles per hour. The initial collision pushed the Escort forward 8 feet into the back of the car that had stopped ahead of it. The Escort sustained $9,000 in damage, primarily to its rear end.

Ms Welch was unaware of the impending collision, and, with the impact, she reported that she was thrown backward, then forward. She did not lose consciousness. She had posterior neck pain at the accident scene and was transported to a hospital emergency department with full spinal immobilization. Examination there was unremarkable apart from cervical paraspinal tenderness and limited motion of the cervical spine. Cervical X-ray films revealed diminished lordosis and preexisting mild narrowing of the C5-6 disk space, with small anterior marginal osteophytes at this level. She was discharged with a cervical collar and a prescription for analgesics. That evening Ms Welch noted onset of occipital headaches and increased posterior neck pain. Her pain worsened the following morning. The pain radiated from her neck into her upper back and down the lateral left upper extremity into the thumb and index finger, with accompanying tingling of these digits and the radial part of the hand.

She sought chiropractic treatment, and during the next 5 months she underwent numerous adjustments at gradually diminishing frequency. The chiropractor also referred her to a massage therapist, who rendered weekly massages during this time. Both the spinal manipulations and the massages typically resulted in partial pain relief lasting for 2 to 3 days.

Her symptoms persisted, and 6 months after her injury she went to see an orthopedic surgeon, who made a diagnosis of cervical sprain/strain injury, which was attributed to soft-tissue injuries. A 4-week course of physical therapy was recommended along with over-the-counter nonsteroidal anti-inflammatory medication on an as-needed basis.

Ms Welch did well for several weeks after therapy and then experienced a recurrence of her symptoms, including posterior neck pain, occipital headaches, and radiation of pain into the left upper extremity. She sought a neurosurgical opinion at that time. No abnormal neurologic findings were noted on physical examination. The examining neurosurgeon recommended a course of home traction and regular use of a nonsteroidal anti-inflammatory medication. She noted some improvement of her symptoms with traction but found that if she did not use the traction on an almost daily basis, her pain continued.

Current Symptoms: Ms Welch complained of intermittent, but daily, occipital headaches and posterior neck pain. About twice a week the pain radiated down the lateral left upper extremity into the thumb and index finger. The pain was accompanied by tingling in the radial hand, thumb, and index finger. She also complained of limited cervical motion, noted primarily when attempting to check her blind spot while driving. Despite her pain, she had only modest interference with activities of daily living (ADLs).

Functional Assessment: The PDQ score was 80.

Physical Examination: On examination, Ms Welch maintained a forward head posture. Cervical ROM was evaluated and motions were as follows: flexion, 30°; extension, 40°; lateral flexion, 15° to left and 30° to right; and rotation, 40° to left and 60° to right. There was mild tenderness and increased resting muscular tension throughout the cervical paraspinal muscles. Arm circumferences were equal, while circumference of the dominant right forearm was 1 cm larger than that of the left. Neurologic examination was normal. The Spurling foraminal compression test on the left caused posterior neck pain only.

Clinical Studies: Plain films of the cervical spine were taken in the emergency department and were interpreted as remarkable for diminished lordosis and preexisting mild narrowing of the C5-6 disk space, with small anterior marginal osteophytes at this level. Magnetic resonance imaging was never performed, as Ms Welch was quite clear in expressing that she was not interested in surgical treatment.

Discussion of Cervical Sprain/Strain

Fourth Edition Rating

Impairment evaluation was based on Section 3.3h, Cervicothoracic Spine Impairment (4th ed, p 103). Pain extending from the cervical spine to the thumb and index finger, with numbness in the thumb and index finger, is symptomatic of a C6 nerve root syndrome. Table 71, DRE Impairment Category Differentiators (4th ed, p 109), states under the discussion of "guarding" that "Radicular complaints that follow anatomic pathways but cannot be verified by neurological findings belong with this differentiator." According to Table 73, DRE Cervicothoracic Spine Impairment Categories (4th ed, p 110), Ms Welch has a DRE impairment category II, ie, "Minor impairment: clinical signs of neck injury are present without radiculopathy or loss of motion segment integrity." This corresponds to a 5% whole person impairment.

Impairment: 5% whole person impairment per the Fourth Edition.

Fifth Edition Rating

The diagnosis-related estimates (DRE) method must be used to assess impairment in this case, since the impairment is due to an injury and none of the six clinical scenarios that require the use of the ROM method is present (5th ed, p 379). The Fifth Edition states in Section 15.2, Determining the Appropriate Method for Assessment (5th ed, p 379), "The DRE method is the principal methodology used to evaluate an individual who has had a distinct injury" (5th ed, p 379). Section 15.3, Diagnosis-Related Estimates Method (5th ed, pp 381-384), explains the process used to obtain the rating:

> To use the DRE method, obtain an individual's history, examine the individual, review the results of appropriate diagnostic studies, and place the individual in the appropriate category. . . . almost all individuals will fall into one of the first three DRE categories. Altered motion segment integrity (ie, increased motion or loss of motion) qualifies the individual for category IV or V.
>
> In most cases, using the definitions provided in Box 15-1, the physician can assign an individual to DRE category I, II, or III. An individual in category I has only subjective findings. In category II, the individual has objective findings but no radiculopathy or alteration of structural integrity, while in category III, radiculopathy with objective verification must be present. Since an individual is evaluated after having reached maximal medical improvement (MMI), a previous history of objective findings may not define the current, ratable condition but is important in determining the course and whether MMI has been reached. The impairment rating is based on the condition once MMI is reached, not on prior symptoms or signs.

Box 15-1, Definition of Clinical Findings Used to Place an Individual in a DRE Category (5th ed, p 382), specifies the clinical findings used in a DRE model classification. The rating of a cervical (neck) injury is performed according to Section 15.6, DRE: Cervical Spine (5th ed, p 393), and with Table 15-5, Criteria for Rating Impairment Due to Cervical Disorders

(5th ed, p 392). This case was critically reviewed to determine the findings documented when at MMI.

Ms Welch's examination revealed increased resting muscular tension throughout cervical paraspinal muscles; this could be interpreted as muscle spasm or guarding. In Box 15-1, the following definitions are provided for these findings:

> Muscle spasm is a sudden, involuntary contraction of a muscle or group of muscles. Paravertebral muscle spasm is common after acute spinal injury but is rare in chronic back pain. It is occasionally visible as a contracted paraspinal muscle but is more often diagnosed by palpation (a hard muscle). To differentiate true muscle spasm from voluntary muscle contraction, the individual should not be able to relax the contractions. The spasm should be present standing as well as in the supine position and frequently causes a scoliosis. The physician can sometimes differentiate spasm from voluntary contraction by asking the individual to place all his or her weight first on one foot and then the other while the physician gently palpates the paraspinous muscles. With this maneuver, the individual normally relaxes the paraspinal muscles on the weight-bearing side. If the examiner witnesses this relaxation, it usually means that true muscle spasm is not present.
>
> Guarding is a contraction of muscle to minimize motion or agitation of the injured or diseased tissue. It is not true muscle spasm because the contraction can be relaxed. In the lumbar spine, the contraction frequently results in loss of the normal lumbar lordosis, and it may be associated with reproducible loss of spinal motion.

Ms Welch also had asymmetric motion of her spine, which is defined as follows:

> Asymmetric motion of the spine in one of the three principal planes is sometimes caused by muscle spasm or guarding. That is, if an individual attempts to flex the spine, he or she is unable to do so moving symmetrically; rather, the head or trunk leans to one side. To qualify as true asymmetric motion, the finding must be reproducible and consistent and the examiner must be convinced that the individual is cooperative and giving full effort.

Although Ms Welch had no objective evidence of radiculopathy, she did have nonverifiable radicular pain, defined as follows:

> Nonverifiable pain is pain that is in the distribution of a nerve root but has no identifiable origin; ie, there are no objective physical, imaging, or electromyographic findings. For dermatomal distributions, see Figures 15-1 and 15-2.

There was no alteration of motion segment integrity, nor any cord involvement.

In summary, on the basis of these findings (guarding, asymmetric loss of motion, and nonverifiable radicular complaints), Ms Welch meets the criteria for DRE cervical category II in Table 15-5 (5th ed, p 392):

> Clinical history and examination findings are compatible with a specific injury; findings may include muscle guarding or spasm observed at the time of the examination by a physician, asymmetric loss of range of motion or nonverifiable radicular complaints, defined as complaints of radicular pain without objective findings; no alteration of the structural integrity.

Any one of these three findings (guarding, asymmetric loss of motion, or nonverifiable radicular complaints) would be sufficient to classify her impairment in DRE category II. This corresponds with a rating of 5% to 8% whole person impairment. The *Guides* states, "if residual symptoms or objective findings impact the ability to perform ADLs, despite treatment, the higher percentage in each range should be assigned." On the basis of the reported modest interference with ADLs, Ms Welch is assigned 6% whole person impairment.

Impairment: 6% whole person impairment per the Fifth Edition.

Sixth Edition Rating

The *Guides* approach to the evaluation of impairment due to chronic neck pain or sprain/strain type injury of the cervical spine is based on Section 17.2, Diagnosis-Based Impairment (6th ed, p 560), and Section 17.2a, Cervical Spine (6th ed, p 563).

In Table 17-2, Cervical Spine Regional Grid: Spine Impairments (6th ed, p 564), for the diagnosis "non-specific chronic, or chronic recurrent neck pain," there is a class 1 rating for "documented history of sprain/strain type injury with continued complaints of axial and/or nonverifiable radicular complaints; similar findings documented in previous examination as and present at the time of evaluation" (with a default impairment of 2% whole person impairment).

In Section 17.3a, Adjustment Grid: Functional History (6th ed, p 569), and Table 17-6, Functional History Adjustment: Spine (6th ed, p 575), the patient is assigned grade modifier 2; the functional history is consistent with "pain; symptoms with normal activity" and the PDQ score is in the range of 71 to 100. In Section 17.3b, Adjustment Grid: Physical Examination (6th ed, p 572), and Table 17-7, Physical Examination Adjustment: Spine

(6th ed, p 576), the patient is assigned grade modifier 0; the physical examination revealed no ratable findings, ie, there were observations of limited ROM, neurologic examination was normal, and Spurling foraminal compression test caused only posterior neck pain, without reproduction of radicular symptoms. In Section 17.3c, Adjustment Grid: Clinical Studies (6th ed, p 577), and Table 17-9, Clinical Studies Adjustment: Spine (6th ed, p 581), the patient is assigned grade modifier 0; the clinical studies revealed "diminished lordosis and pre-existing mild narrowing of the C5-6 disk space, with small anterior marginal osteophytes at this level." The Functional History differed by 2 grades from the other adjustment factors; therefore, it is assumed to be unreliable and is excluded. In summary, the adjustments are as follows: functional history grade modifier n/a, physical examination 0, and clinical studies grade modifier 0. Net adjustment compared to diagnosis class 1 is −2, grade A, 1% whole person impairment.

Class—Default for Diagnosis = 2% whole person impairment			
CDX	GMFH	GMPE	GMCS
n/a	n/a	0	0

Net adjustment

(GMFH − CDX) n/a

\+ (GMPE − CDX) + 0 − 1 = −1

\+ (GMCS − CDX) + 0 − 1 = −1

Net adjustment = −2

Result is class 1 adjustment −2, which results in class 1, grade A = 1% whole person impairment.

Impairment: 1% whole person impairment per the Sixth Edition.

Comment on Cervical Sprain/Strain

A physical examination is a critical component of the spinal impairment evaluation. In both the Fourth and Fifth Editions, there are two examination methods—the DRE method and the ROM method. Evaluators prefer the DRE method, which they use in the vast majority of the cases involving an injury. The Fifth Edition states in Section 15.2, "The DRE method is the principal methodology used to evaluate an individual who has had a distinct injury" (5th ed, p 372). In the Fifth Edition, there are differences in how the methods are selected and how the DRE method is defined.[1] The elements of physical examination are described in Section 15.1a, Interpretation of Symptoms and Signs (5th ed, pp 374-378). In the Sixth Edition, only the diagnosis-based impairment (DBI) method is used. "Range of motion is no longer used to define impairment; current evidence does not support range of motion as a reliable diagnostic factor or as a basis for measuring functional status" (6th ed, p 558).

In the Fourth Edition, seven differentiators are presented in Table 71, DRE Impairment Category Differentiators (4th ed, p 109). These differentiators are guarding, loss of reflexes, decreased circumference (atrophy), electrodiagnostic evidence, loss of motion segment integrity, loss of bowel or bladder control, and bladder studies. Each of these is associated with a specific definition previously explored in the *Guides Newsletter*.[2]

In the Fourth Edition, the rating was based solely on the results of the injury. A major change in the Fifth Edition is that evaluators now take into account the treatment results. As a result, the DRE rating is based on objective findings at the time of the evaluation. The objective findings are muscle spasm; muscle guarding; asymmetric spinal motion (6th ed; previously called *dysmetria*); nonverifiable radicular pain; reflexes; neurologic changes such as weakness or loss of sensation, atrophy, radiculopathy, and electrodiagnostic changes; alteration of motion segment integrity; cauda equina–like syndrome; and urodynamic tests.[3] Imaging studies may also help the evaluator categorize an individual. Box 15-1, Definition of Clinical Findings Used to Place an Individual in a DRE Category (5th ed, p 382), specifies the clinical findings used in a DRE method classification.

Ms Welch's lateral left upper extremity pain and the paresthesias involving radial left hand, thumb, and index finger, but the normal neurologic examination including sensation, motor function, and reflexes, meet criteria for category II, "nonverifiable radicular complaints." However, there are not "significant signs of radiculopathy" required for category III.

In the Sixth Edition, like the Fifth Edition, the rating requires that the patient's condition be at MMI, and treatment results are, therefore, taken into account. However, in the Sixth Edition, only the DBI method is used to calculate impairment in the spine. After a diagnosis has been made, the appropriate class within that diagnosis is selected. Ms Welch has a history of "sprain/strain type injury" of the cervical spine, with continued complaints of axial neck pain and "nonverifiable radicular complaints." These findings were "documented in previous examinations (chiropractor, orthopedic surgeon and neurosurgeon) and remained present at the time of evaluation" (6th ed, p 563, General Considerations). These findings are consistent with impairment class 1 in Table 17-2, Cervical Spine Regional Grid: Spine Impairments (6th ed, p 564). The functional history grade modifier is determined by considering both factors in Table 17-6, Functional History Adjustment: Spine (6th ed, p 575) and choosing the higher of reliable grade modifier values. In this example, both activity and PDQ results are grade modifier 2. Table 17-7, Physical Examination Adjustment: Spine (6th ed, p 576), is consulted to determine the grade modifier for that adjustment. Although ROM is routinely part of a physical examination, it is no longer used as part of the impairment calculation in the spine. The cervical foraminal compression test was considered negative, because there was no reproduction of radicular pain, consistent with grade modifier 0. All other grade modifiers in this adjustment are also 0 because the neurologic examination was negative. The clinical studies grade modifier (Table 17-9, Clinical Studies Adjustment: Spine, 6th ed, p 581) is also 0 because imaging findings showed only "normal age-related changes." After the necessary calculations for the net adjustment formula are performed, Ms Welch is found to have a net adjustment of −1. This moves the value of the impairment 1 place to the left of the default value of 2% to a 1% impairment of the cervical spine, equivalent to a 1% whole person impairment.

SUMMARY

Diagnosis	Cervical sprain/strain
Fourth Edition References	Section 3.3h (4th ed, p 103), Table 71 (4th ed, p 109)
Fourth Edition Summary	Determine whether injury occurred; assess clinical history, symptoms, and interference with ADLs; physical examination determines presence or absence of differentiators; select appropriate category, based on historical findings.
Fourth Edition Impairment	5% whole person impairment
Fifth Edition References	Section 15.2 (5th ed, p 379), Section 15.3 (5th ed, p 381), Section 15.6 (5th ed, p 393), Box 15-1 (5th ed, 382), Table 15-5 (5th ed, p 392)
Fifth Edition Summary	Determine whether injury occurred; assess clinical history, symptoms, and interference with ADLs; physical examination determines presence or absence of specific clinical findings; select appropriate category, based on current findings.
Fifth Edition Impairment	6% whole person impairment

Sixth Edition References	Section 17.2 (6th ed, p 560), Table 17-2 (6th ed, p 564), Table 17-6 (6th ed, p 575), Table 17-7 (6th ed, p 576), Table 17-9 (6th ed, p 581)
Sixth Edition Summary	Determine whether injury occurred and whether condition is at MMI. Assess clinical history (including functional history, functional assessment tool results (6th ed, PDQ or other), physical examination, and clinical studies and identify appropriate grade modifiers for each adjustment. Determine DBI, class, and default value. Adjust impairment rating on basis of nonkey factors by using the net adjustment calculation and grade modifier values.
Sixth Edition Impairment	1% whole person impairment

References

1. Haralson RH. Spinal impairment evaluation: fifth edition changes. *Guides Newsletter*. January-February 2001.
2. Haralson RH. Objectifying the low back exam. *Guides Newsletter*. January-February 1997.
3. Haralson RH. Objectifying the spinal impairment examination—fifth edition approaches. *Guides Newsletter*. September-October 2001.

CASE 17-3

Traumatic Low Back Pain

Subject: Mr Williams, a 27-year-old man.

History: Mr Williams was a machine operator who slipped from a ladder. He fell 24 feet, striking his lower back on the frame of a metal saw. He experienced sudden and severe low back pain and right posterolateral thigh pain. He was seen at the Industrial Work Injury Clinic. X-ray films were read as showing no fracture. There was no neurologic deficit on examination. The diagnosis was lumbar contusion and strain/sprain. He was released home for 3 days of bed rest followed by physical therapy three times per week for 8 weeks. There was no long-term benefit. Methylprednisolone in a tapering dose was tried, without benefit. Transcutaneous electrical nerve stimulation gave only brief relief. Mr Williams continued to suffer from persistent low back pain and right posterior thigh pain that interfered with his mobility. Flexion-extension X-ray films were interpreted as showing "instability"; Mr Williams underwent an instrumented spinal fusion of the L4-5 level (one-level fusion). He wore a plastic body jacket for 12 weeks. The surgery reduced his back pain tremendously and alleviated his right posterolateral thigh pain. Follow-up X-ray films demonstrated the bony fusion to be solid.

Current Symptoms: Mr Williams described a deep nagging pain that worsened with spinal bending and twisting, especially forward flexion and extension. The pain was relieved if he lay supine in bed or sat in his reclining chair. Mr Williams had some residual low back pain, but significantly less than before surgery. His posterolateral thigh pain also persisted in what appeared to be an L5 nerve root distribution on the right. He reported marked interference with many ADLs.

Functional Assessment: Mr Williams reported that he had symptoms with less than normal activity. The PDQ score was 120.

Physical Examination: Physical examination showed muscle guarding and restricted lumbosacral spine ROM. Sensation and motor function were intact. Reflexes were normal. Straight-leg-raising at 60° of elevation of either leg resulted in complaints of mid-lumbar pain but no radicular pain. Neurologic examination was within normal limits in the lower extremities.

Clinical Studies: A preoperative lumbar MRI showed a bulging disk at L5-S1. No herniations were seen. Preoperative lateral lumbar spine X-ray films in flexion and extension revealed 7 mm of translation (loss of motion segment integrity) at L4-5. Postoperative lateral lumbar spine X rays in flexion and extension revealed no translation and a healed interbody fusion at L4-5. Anteroposterior X-ray films of the lumbar spine showed satisfactory lateral fusion masses and well-positioned internal fixation.

Discussion of Traumatic Low Back Pain

Fourth Edition Rating

Impairment evaluation was based on Section 3.3d, Evaluating Impairments: The Injury or Diagnosis-Related Estimates Model (4th ed, p 99), and Figure 62, Loss of Motion Segment Integrity: Translation (4th ed, p 98). The differentiator that places the individual in the highest category should be used. The criteria for loss of motion segment integrity on page 98 state:

> The loss of integrity is defined as an anteroposterior motion or slipping of one vertebra over another greater than 3.5 mm for a cervical vertebra or greater than 5 mm for a vertebra in the thoracic or lumbar spine (Fig. 62 . . .); or a difference in the angular motion of two adjacent motion segments greater than 11° in response to flexion and extension (Fig. 63 . . .).

This definition is also provided in Table 71, DRE Impairment Category Differentiators (4th ed, p 109). Mr Williams' flexion-extension X-ray films show 7 mm of translation at L4-5, which exceeds the criteria for DRE lumbosacral category IV, ie, "at least 5 mm of translation of one vertebra on another . . ." (4th ed, p 102). Thus, a rating of "injury model, category IV, 20% whole person impairment" is appropriate, as specified in Table 72, DRE Lumbosacral Spine Impairment Categories (4th ed, p 110).

In the Fourth Edition, the examiner is to rate the severity of the injury, not the condition of the individual at MMI. The treatment (including surgery) is not considered in the rating. Thus, the documented instability, and not the subsequent fusion, is the basis for the rating.

Mr Williams did not have radiculopathy. If, in addition to loss of motion segment integrity, he had also had differentiators for true radiculopathy, a category V rating would have been appropriate.

Impairment: 20% whole person impairment per the Fourth Edition.

Fifth Edition Rating

The DRE method must be used to assess impairment in this case, since the impairment is due to an injury. The Fifth Edition states in Section 15.2,

Determining the Appropriate Method for Assessment (5th ed, p 379), "The DRE method is the principal methodology used to evaluate an individual who has had a distinct injury" (5th ed, p 379). Section 15.3, Diagnosis-Related Estimates Method (5th ed, p 381), explains the process used to obtain the rating:

> To use the DRE method, obtain an individual's history, examine the individual, review the results of appropriate diagnostic studies, and place the individual in the appropriate category. . . . Altered motion segment integrity (ie, increased motion or loss of motion) qualifies the individual for category IV or V. . . . The impairment rating is based on the condition once MMI is reached, not on prior symptoms or signs [5th ed, p 383].

Box 15-1, Definition of Clinical Findings Used to Place an Individual in a DRE Category (5th ed, p 382), specifies the clinical findings used in a DRE model classification. The rating of a lumbar (low back) injury is performed according to Section 15.4, DRE: Lumbar Spine (5th ed, p 384), and using Table 15-3, Criteria for Rating Impairment Due to Lumbar Disorders (5th ed, p 384). Mr Williams has alteration of motion segment integrity, defined as follows:

> Motion segment alteration can be either loss of motion segment integrity (increased translational or angular motion) or decreased motion secondary to developmental fusion, fracture healing, healed infection, or surgical arthrodesis. An attempt at arthrodesis may not necessarily result in a solid fusion but may significantly limit motion at a motion segment. Motion of the individual spine segments cannot be determined by a physical examination but is evaluated with flexion and extension roentgenograms The loss of motion segment integrity is defined in Section 15.lb [5th ed, p 383].

The specifics of determining motion segment integrity are discussed in Section 15.1b, Description of Clinical Studies (5th ed, p 378). Mr Williams' flexion-extension X-ray films, before his surgery, showed 7 mm of translation at L4-5. One of the definitions of lumbar spine loss of motion segment integrity is "anteroposterior motion of one vertebra over another that is . . . greater than 4.5 mm in the lumbar spine." A DRE lumbar category IV rating is defined in Table 15-3 (5th ed, p 383) as follows:

> Loss of motion segment integrity defined from flexion and extension radiographs as at least 4.5 mm of translation of one vertebra on another or angular motion greater than 15° at L1-2, L2-3, and L3-4, greater than 20° at L4-5, and greater than 25° at L5-S1 (Figure 15-3); may have complete or near complete loss of motion of a motion segment due to developmental fusion, or successful or unsuccessful attempt at surgical arthrodesis.

While true "instability" was documented in this case, in the Fifth Edition, spinal impairment is to be rated on the basis of the individual's condition at MMI, which now includes the effects of treatment. Since Mr Williams has had a spinal fusion, he is rated as category IV, on the basis of surgical arthrodesis (fusion) having created "loss of motion segment integrity."

Mr Williams' surgery was a one-level fusion (L4-5). If his surgery had been a two-level fusion (from L4 to the sacrum), he would then have to have been rated by the ROM method. The instructions in Section 15.2 (5th ed, p 379) specify six situations in which the ROM method is to be used. In that list, the third scenario is "where there is alteration of motion segment integrity (eg, fusions) at multiple levels in the same spinal region."

In the Fifth Edition, each of the DRE categories now has a range of potential impairments from which the examiner is to choose an appropriate percentage. Category IV has a range from 20% to 23% whole person impairment. The *Guides* states, "If residual symptoms or objective findings impact the ability to perform ADLs, despite treatment, the higher percentage in each range should be assigned." On the basis of the reported marked interference of ADLs, Mr Williams is assigned a 23% whole person impairment.

Impairment: 23% whole person impairment per the Fifth Edition.

Sixth Edition Rating

The *Guides* approach to the evaluation of impairment due to motion segment lesions is based on Section 17.2, Diagnosis-Based Impairment (6th ed, p 560), and Section 17.2c, Lumbar Spine (6th ed, p 566).

In Table 17-4, Lumbar Spine Regional Grid: Spine Impairments (6th ed, p 570), in the section on Motion Segment Lesions for the diagnosis "intervertebral disc herniation and/or AOMSI," there is a class 1 rating for documented alteration of motion segment integrity (AOMSI) at a single level with documented nonverifiable radicular complaints at clinically appropriate levels (with a default impairment of 7% whole person impairment). In this case, the examiner could also use, as an alternative, the diagnosis "degenerative spondylolisthesis, with or without spinal stenosis" for which there is a similar class 1 rating and a default impairment of 7% whole person impairment.

A detailed discussion of AOMSI, emphasizing the importance of technical considerations and interpretation of radiographic studies and specific criteria for AOMSI in each region, is presented in Section 17.3c, Adjustment Grid: Clinical Studies (6th ed, pp 577-580). The region-specific criteria for AOMSI described in this section must be met before a diagnosis of AOMSI is used for placement in the DBI grid (for cervical, thoracic, or lumbar spine.) Alteration of motion segment integrity also includes surgical intervention with use of motion preservation devices including dynamic stabilization and disk arthroplasty, reflecting changes in "fusion technology" including motion preservation over the last several years.

In Section 17.3a, Adjustment Grid: Functional History (6th ed, p 569), and Table 17-6, Functional History Adjustment: Spine (6th ed, p 575), the patient is assigned grade modifier 3. The functional history is consistent with "pain; symptoms with less than normal activity," and the PDQ score is in the range of 101 to 130. In Section 17.3b, Adjustment Grid: Physical Examination (6th ed, p 572), and Table 17-7, Physical Examination Adjustment: Spine (6th ed, p 576), the patient is assigned grade modifier 0; the physical examination revealed that "neurologic examination was within normal limits." In Section 17.3c, Adjustment Grid: Clinical Studies (6th ed, p 577), and Table 17-9, Clinical Studies Adjustment: Spine (6th ed, p 581), no grade modifier is necessary, because imaging studies were used to make the diagnosis. Functional history cannot be used as an adjustment since "if the grade for Functional History differs by two or more grades from that described by Physical Examination or Clinical Studies, the Functional History should be assumed to be unreliable." When any adjustment or grade modifier is necessary as part of the class determination, it may not be used again in the impairment calculation. In summary, the adjustments are as follows: functional history grade modifier not applicable, physical examination 0, and clinical studies grade modifier not applicable. Net adjustment compared to diagnosis class is −1, grade B, 6% whole person impairment. This result is the same, whether the diagnosis is "intervertebral disk herniation and/or AOMSI" or "degenerative spondylolisthesis with or without spinal stenosis."

Class 1—Default for Diagnosis = 7% whole person impairment			
CDX	GMFH	GMPE	GMCS
1	n/a	0	n/a
Net adjustment (GMFH − CDX) n/a + (GMPE − CDX) + 0 − 1 = −1 + (GMCS − CDX) + n/a Net adjustment = −1			

Result is class 1 adjustment 1, which results in class 1, grade D = 8% whole person impairment.

Impairment: 6% whole person impairment per the Sixth Edition.

Comment on Traumatic Low Back Pain

Mr Williams' case is quite uncommon. Major trauma in young individuals usually causes spinal fractures and rarely causes loss of motion segment integrity. Degenerative spondylolisthesis is more common in women; however, loss of motion integrity can occur as a postoperative complication as well. Most individuals do not need flexion-extension X-ray films of the lumbar spine before impairment rating. If there is clinical concern for instability, for instance, concern about spondylolisthesis, pseudoarthrosis after fusion, or decompensation of the level above or below a fusion, flexion-extension X-ray films may be appropriate. Spinal fusion for back pain without demonstrated loss of motion segment integrity remains controversial.

Since treatment is now considered in the Fifth and Sixth Editions, there needed to be some method to take into account those individuals who undergo arthrodesis or implant of motion-preserving devices for treatment of motion segment pathology. The Fifth Edition authors elected to include in the definition of AOMSI those patients who have had successful or even unsuccessful attempts at surgical arthrodesis of the spine and those who developed loss of all or nearly all motion in a motion segment due to developmental arthrodesis, secondary to trauma or infection. The Sixth Edition includes newer technologies in the definition of AOMSI, recognizing recent clinical advances. These definitions, including the parameters for translation and angular motion, are the only definitions of loss of motion segment integrity in the *Guides*. The term *instability* was not used because the definition of that term is variable.

The question arises as to whether flexion and extension X-ray films must be taken in every examinee to rule out AOMSI. The answer, according to the *Guides*, is no. Alteration of motion segment integrity is nearly always suggested on routine X-ray films. It is extremely rare in the presence of normal lateral X-ray films. In fact, AOMSI, other than for arthrodesis or as a postoperative complication, is extraordinarily rare in the workers' compensation arena. It is nearly always developmental or degenerative, and, though it may be aggravated by injury, in the lumbar spine it is rarely caused by an injury. The exceptions are certain fractures of the pedicles that result from severe trauma or aggressive posterior decompression at the time of surgery, without fusion. If an individual demonstrates spondylolisthesis and there is a question as to whether it is developmental or secondary to a recent injury, review of previous X-ray films or bone scans may be helpful.[1]

In the Sixth Edition, the criteria for instability in AOMSI in each spinal region are clearly articulated. As in the Fifth Edition, AOMSI as a result of fusion or failed attempt at fusion is included. In addition, AOMSI includes the use of new techniques in addressing motion segment integrity, including disk arthroplasty and other surgical motion-preservation techniques. The diagnosis of AOMSI can be made only radiographically, and therefore, the clinical studies grade modifier should be excluded from the impairment calculation. Functional history is used as a modifier only when reliable; the difference of more than two grades from other factors results in assumption of its being unreliable. After the necessary calculations for the net adjustment formula are performed, Mr Williams is found to have a net adjustment of −1. This moves the value of the impairment one place to the left of the default value of 7% to a 6% impairment of the lumbar spine, which is a 6% whole person impairment.

SUMMARY

Diagnosis	Low back pain induced by trauma
Fourth Edition References	Section 3.3d (4th ed, p 99), Figure 62 (4th ed, p 98)
Fourth Edition Summary	Determine magnitude of injury; assess clinical history, symptoms, and interference with ADLs; physical examination; performance of flexion-extension X-ray films of the lumbar spine.
Fourth Edition Impairment	20% whole person impairment
Fifth Edition References	DRE: Lumbar Spine (5th ed, p 384), Box 15-1 (5th ed, p 382), Table 15-3 (5th ed, p 384)
Fifth Edition Summary	Determine magnitude of injury; assess clinical history, symptoms, and interference with ADLs; physical examination; performance of flexion-extension X-ray films of the lumbar spine.
Fifth Edition Impairment	23% whole person impairment
Sixth Edition References	Section 17.2 (6th ed, p 560), Section 17.3a (6th ed, p 569), Section 17.3b (6th ed, p 572), Section 17.3c (6th ed, p 577), Table 17-4 (6th ed, p 570), Table 17-6 (6th ed, p 575), Table 17-7 (6th ed, p 576), Table 17-9 (6th ed, p 581)
Sixth Edition Summary	History (including functional history and inventories), physical evaluation, and clinical studies. First, determine DBI, class, and default

	value. Second, adjust impairment on basis of nonkey factors. Where nonkey factors are used to determine class, they are not included in the impairment value calculation.
Sixth Edition Impairment	6% whole person impairment

Reference

1. Haralson RH, Brigham CR. Objectifying the spinal impairment examination—fifth edition approaches. *Guides Newsletter*. September-October 2001.

CASE 17-4

Neck Pain

Subject: Ms Smith, a 25-year-old woman.

History: Ms Smith, a primary school teacher, had been in excellent health with no medical history of illness, operations, or injuries of any significance. She was diligent in her exercise, being involved in regular swimming, aerobics, and walking. She had been driving home from work 12 months previously and was stopped at a traffic light. She was wearing her seat belt and heard the screech of brakes and then a crash in the rear of her car. The impact threw her body backward and then forward. Her car was pushed about 6 feet onto the road in front of her. Fortunately, she did not have any further impact with vehicles. She experienced soreness in her neck almost immediately after she had the accident but was preoccupied with the business of getting the other driver's details, speaking to the police, and then getting her car towed to a body shop.

By the time she got home, her neck was very painful and stiff, and her right arm was aching. She did not have pins and needles or loss of sensation in the arm. She went to see her family physician, who gave her a soft collar to wear, prescribed some anti-inflammatory medications, and suggested she have some physiotherapy. As she continued to have a sore and stiff neck, her physician decided to obtain plain cervical x-ray films. These were reported as normal, apart from some flattening of the normal lordosis, thought to be due to muscle spasm. Ms Smith continued with her medications and physiotherapy but felt that neither of these was particularly helpful in relieving her symptoms. After about 2 months, Ms Smith discontinued both medications and physiotherapy. She saw her family physician at 3 months after the accident, still complaining of stiffness and pain in the neck, particularly in the nape, but she did say that the ache in her right arm was by then almost gone. Her physician ordered an MRI of the neck, and this was reported as being entirely normal. He suggested that Ms Smith continue swimming and walking, but avoid aerobics. He said there was no more to be done and advised that she "would probably be better within about 6 to 12 months." He told her that she had a whiplash injury to the neck.

Current Symptoms: Twelve months after the accident, Ms Smith presented as a straightforward historian. She noted that, during the past 9 months, there had been some improvement in her condition. She felt stiffness in the neck only occasionally, when she was tired, or after a hard day's work at school, but she found that this resolved with rest. She had no symptoms that suggested cervical nerve root irritation or cervical radiculopathy. She did not manifest much pain behavior.

Functional Assessment: The PDQ score was 10.

Physical Examination: Ms Smith appeared to have a good range of movement of the neck, and this was also noted when she removed her upper clothing for the examination. At formal examination, the ROM in the neck was normal, without evidence of spasm or muscle guarding. The rest of the physical examination was normal, without any clinical evidence of neurologic abnormality in the upper limbs (6th ed; power, sensation, and reflexes all normal). There was no muscular atrophy in the arms.

Clinical Studies: An MRI of the cervical spine was interpreted as normal.

Discussion of Neck Pain

Fourth Edition Rating

Impairment evaluation was based on the DRE or injury model. Ms Smith had an identifiable injury to the cervical region with no evidence of preexisting or comorbid conditions to account for her symptoms. Her injury is identified by means of Table 70, Spine Impairment Categories (4th ed, p 108), with reference to Section 3.3h, Cervicothoracic Spine Impairment (4th ed, p 103), where cervicothoracic spine impairment (DRE categories) is discussed.

Ms Smith has no significant clinical findings, no muscle guarding, no neurologic impairment, no significant radiographic abnormality, and, thus, no indication of impairment related to her injury or illness. There are no structural inclusions, as specified in Table 71, DRE Impairment Category Differentiators (4th ed, p 109). Ms Smith complains only of intermittent symptoms that are transient. These criteria place her in the DRE cervicothoracic category I: complaints or symptoms, with the impairment being 0% whole person impairment. Table 70, Spine Impairment Categories (4th ed, p 108), and Table 73, DRE Cervicothoracic Spine Impairment Categories (4th ed, p 110), may be used to assist in categorizing the impairment.

Impairment: 0% whole person impairment per the Fourth Edition.

Fifth Edition Rating

The DRE method must be used to assess impairment in this case, since the impairment is due to an injury, and none of the six clinical situations is present that would require the use of the ROM method (5th ed, p 379). The

Fifth Edition states in Section 15.2, Determining the Appropriate Method for Assessment (5th ed, p 379), "The DRE method is the principal methodology used to evaluate an individual who has had a distinct injury" (5th ed, p 379). Section 15.3, Diagnosis-Related Estimates Method (5th ed, p 381), explains the process used to obtain the rating:

> To use the DRE method, obtain an individual's history, examine the individual, review the results of appropriate diagnostic studies, and place the individual in the appropriate category. . . . Almost all individuals will fall into one of the first three DRE categories. . . . In most cases, using the definitions provided in Box 15-1, the physician can assign an individual to DRE category I, II, or III. An individual in category I has only subjective findings. . . . The impairment rating is based on the condition once MMI is reached, not on prior symptoms or signs.

Box 15-1, Definition of Clinical Findings Used to Place an Individual in a DRE Category (5th ed, p 382), specifies the clinical findings used in a DRE model classification. The rating of a cervical (neck) injury is performed according to Section 15.6, DRE: Cervical Spine (5th ed, p 393), and with the use of Table 15-5, Criteria for Rating Impairment Due to Cervical Disorders (5th ed, p 392). Ms Smith had no significant clinical findings when she was at MMI. Therefore, she meets the definition of DRE cervical category I in Table 15-5 (5th ed, p 392): no significant clinical findings, no observed muscle guarding or spasm, no documentable neurologic impairment, no documented alteration in structural integrity, no other indication of impairment related to injury or illness, and no fractures. There is no ratable impairment.

Impairment: 0% whole person impairment per the Fifth Edition.

Sixth Edition Rating

Evaluation of impairment due to cervical (neck) injury is based on Section 17.2, Diagnosis-Based Impairment (6th ed, p 560), and Section 17.2a, Cervical Spine (6th ed, p 563). In Table 17-2, Cervical Spine Regional Grid: Spine Impairments (6th ed, p 564), for the diagnosis "non-specific chronic, or chronic recurrent neck pain," there is a class 0 rating for a documented history of injury, with resolution or continued complaints of neck pain with no objective findings (with a default impairment of 0% whole person impairment).

For class 0 DBI, no further considerations are necessary; the adjustments and determination of grade modifiers do not change the 0% impairment value associated with class 0 diagnoses. However, the nonkey factors, if evaluated, would be at most grade 1. In Section 17.3a, Adjustment Grid: Functional

History (6th ed, p 569), and Table 17-6, Functional History Adjustment: Spine (6th ed, p 575), the patient is assigned grade modifier 1; the functional history is consistent with "problem resolved" and the PDQ score is in the range of 0 to 10. In Section 17.3b, Adjustment Grid: Physical Examination (6th ed, p 572), and Table 17-7, Physical Examination Adjustment: Spine (6th ed, p 576), the patient is assigned grade modifier 0; the physical examination revealed no significant findings. In Section 17.3c, Adjustment Grid: Clinical Studies (6th ed, p 577), and Table 17-9, Clinical Studies Adjustment: Spine (6th ed, p 581), the patient is assigned grade modifier 0; the clinical studies showed that "structural diagnosis is within normal limits." In summary, net adjustment does not need to be calculated for class 0 impairment, which results in a 0% impairment of the cervical spine.

Impairment: 0% whole person impairment per the Sixth Edition.

Comment on Neck Pain

This is an example of an injury that was symptomatic and has clearly improved, with minor intermittent residual symptoms and no other clinical (objective) abnormality suggestive of a more serious impairment. This type of case is not unusual, since acceleration-deceleration injuries to the cervical spine are relatively common. The nature of the injury, the clinical progress of the case, the presence or absence of significant radiographic findings, and the presence or absence of abnormal physical examination findings (cervical spinal mobility, spasm and guarding, peripheral nervous system findings, central nervous system findings) all must be carefully assessed and documented. These clinical findings, including clinical studies (X-ray films, computed tomography, MRI) provide the criteria that allow the evaluating physician to be accurate and consistent in the impairment assessment.

In the Sixth Edition, as was the case in the Fifth Edition, the impairment rating is determined after MMI is reached and is not based on prior symptoms or signs. In this example, given the absence of significant clinical findings, neurologic impairment, muscle guarding, and radiographic abnormalities, there is little doubt as to the DBI class.

SUMMARY

Diagnosis	Recovered cervical musculoligamentous strain
Fourth Edition References	Section 3.3h (4th ed, p 103), Table 70 (4th ed, p 108), Table 71 (4th ed, p 109), Table 73 (4th ed, p 110)

Fourth Edition Summary	Determine whether injury occurred; assess clinical history, symptoms, and interference with ADLs; physical examination determines presence or absence of differentiators; appropriate category is selected. If no history or presence of differentiators or structural inclusions, assigned a category I rating.
Fourth Edition Impairment	0% whole person impairment
Fifth Edition References	Section 15.2 (5th ed, p 379), Section 15.3 (5th ed, p 381), Section 15.6 (5th ed, p 393), Box 15-1 (5th ed, p 382), Table 15-5 (5th ed, p 392)
Fifth Edition Summary	Determine whether injury occurred; assess clinical history, symptoms, and interference with ADLs; physical examination determines presence or absence of differentiators; appropriate category is selected. If significant clinical findings or structural inclusions absent when at MMI, assign a category I rating.
Fifth Edition Impairment	0% whole person impairment
Sixth Edition References	Section 17.2 (6th ed, p 560), Section 17.2a (6th ed, p 563), Section 17.3a (6th ed, p 569), Section 17.3b (6th ed, p 572), Table 17-2 (6th ed, p 564), Table 17-6 (6th ed, p 575), Table 17-7 (6th ed, p 576), Table 17-9 (6th ed, p 581)
Sixth Edition Summary	Determine whether injury occurred and whether condition is at MMI. Assess clinical history, including functional history, functional assessment tool results (6th ed, PDQ or other), physical examination, and clinical studies. If the condition has resolved or findings are inconsistent, on basis of the DBI method, the diagnosis is class 0. No adjustment calculations need to be performed, and the impairment rating is 0% whole person impairment.
Sixth Edition Impairment	0% whole person impairment

CASE 17-5

Recurrent Lumbar Radiculopathy

Subject: Mr Orange, a 53-year-old man.

History: Mr Orange experienced the onset of acute low back and right leg pain while lifting and twisting at work. Mr Orange described burning pain, diminished sensation, and "tingling" of his right lateral calf and the dorsum of his right foot, but he denied leg weakness or loss of bowel or bladder control. Mr Orange's relevant history included two lumbar injuries resulting in lumbar radiculopathy, each time caused by a herniated nucleus pulposus at L4-5, for which he underwent two lumbar microdiskectomies. After surgery for each of these two injuries with radiculopathy, Mr Orange returned to work without restrictions in his usual occupation as an over-the-road truck driver.

After this most recent onset of pain, a trial of conservative therapy failed, and Mr Orange underwent a third surgical procedure, which included decompressive laminectomy at L4-5, excision of herniated disk at L4-5 on the right, posterior lumbar interbody fusion at L4-5 with implantation of an interbody metal cage at L4-5, and posterolateral transverse process arthrodesis at L4-5 with a pedicle screw device.

Current Symptoms: One year after surgery, Mr Orange reported mild residual low back pain and diminished sensation of the dorsum of his right foot. Mr Orange was working full-time but at a different job because of new permanent restrictions prescribed by his treating surgeon.

Functional Assessment: The PDQ score was 65.

Physical Examination: On examination, Mr Orange exhibited diminished sensation over the dorsum of his right foot, but the remainder of his neurologic examination was normal. On straight-leg-raising testing, he developed right leg pain (below the knee) when the right leg was raised to 40°. Waddell signs were absent. There was no atrophy. Lumbar ROM was remarkable for limited flexion and mild limitation in other planes.

Clinical Studies: Preoperative lumbar spine MRI with contrast enhancement showed a recurrent herniated nucleus pulposus at L4-5, impinging on the right L5 nerve root. The diagnosis of recurrent lumbar radiculopathy was confirmed with electromyography, which showed multiple positive sharp waves and fibrillation potentials, indicative of acute nerve root compromise, in the anterior tibial and extensor hallucis longus muscles. Lumbar plain films with flexion and extension views disclosed grade I spondylolisthesis of L4 on L5, but no loss of motion segment integrity by the criteria set out in the Fifth and Sixth Editions of the *Guides*.

One year after surgery, when Mr Orange was considered at MMI, X-ray films of the lumbar spine showed a solid fusion at L4-5.

Discussion of Recurrent Lumbar Radiculopathy

Fourth Edition Rating

Impairment evaluation is based on Section 3.3, The Spine (4th ed, p 94). The *Guides*, Fourth Edition, describes two approaches for the assessment of spine impairment. One approach is called the *injury model*, also known as the *DRE model*. The injury model involves assigning a patient to one of eight categories, such as "minor injury," "radiculopathy," "loss of spine structure integrity," or "paraplegia," on the basis of objective clinical findings.

The other approach is the ROM model, which was recommended in previous *Guides* editions. In the *Guides*, Fourth Edition, the injury model must be used if the individual's condition is one of those listed in Table 70, Spine Impairment Categories (4th ed, p 108). The injury model, for example, is applicable to a person with a herniated lumbar disk and evidence of nerve root irritation. The ROM model is used in two circumstances, namely, if none of the eight categories of the injury model is applicable and if disagreement exists about the category of the injury model in which a person belongs. In either of these two circumstances, the ROM model is used to help determine into which of the eight injury model categories to place an individual; however, the rating still comes from the injury model, not from the ROM model.

Mr Orange's condition, radiculopathy, is one of those listed in Table 70 (4th ed, p 108). Consequently, Mr Orange's spine impairment must be based on the injury model, not the ROM model. The injury model is described in Sections 3.3a through 3.3i (4th ed, p 95).

Mr Orange's first injury, which resulted in radiculopathy for which he underwent his initial lumbar spine surgery, is consistent with DRE lumbosacral category III: radiculopathy, as described on page 102. The DRE lumbosacral category III yields a 10% whole person impairment. Consequently, Mr Orange retained a 10% whole person impairment as a consequence of his initial injury and radiculopathy. Mr Orange retains no additional whole person impairment as a consequence of his second and third injuries and radiculopathy.

Mr Orange's diagnostic evaluation documented grade I spondylolisthesis of L4 and L5, but no loss of motion segment integrity. Consequently, his current condition is not consistent with DRE lumbosacral category IV: loss of motion segment integrity, nor with DRE lumbosacral category V: radiculopathy and loss of motion segment integrity. Mr Orange will retain no additional whole person impairment due to loss of motion segment integrity.

Impairment: 10% whole person impairment per the Fourth Edition (apportioned as 10% for the first injury, 0% for the second injury, and 0% for the third injury).

Fifth Edition Rating

Impairment evaluation is based on Section 15.2, Determining the Appropriate Method for Assessment (5th ed, pp 379-381); Section 15.8, Range-of-Motion Method (5th ed, pp 398-404); Section 15.9, ROM: Lumbar Spine (5th ed, p 405); and Section 1.6, Causation, Apportionment Analysis, and Aggravation (5th ed, p 11).

The Fifth Edition contains specific instructions that the ROM method must be used in six specific situations. Mr Orange's recurrent radiculopathy is rated by means of the ROM method because he has "recurrent radiculopathy caused by a new (recurrent) disk herniation" (5th ed, p 380). The ROM method consists of three elements that need to be assessed: (1) the ROM of the impaired spine region, (2) accompanying diagnoses, and (3) any spinal nerve deficit.

Since the sum of Mr Orange's sacral (hip) flexion and sacral (hip) extension is within 15° of his straight-leg-raising test on his tighter side (right), his flexion and extension motion measurements are valid and thus ratable. Table 15-8, Impairment Due to Abnormal Motion of the Lumbar Region: Flexion and Extension (5th ed, p 407), is used to determine his impairment due to abnormal flexion and extension. Mr Orange's sacral (hip) flexion angle is 35° and his true lumbar spine flexion angle is 20°, which yield a 7% whole person impairment for loss of flexion. His lumbar extension is 10°, which yields a 5% whole person impairment. Consulting Table 15-9, Impairment Due to Abnormal Motion and Ankylosis of the Lumbar Region: Lateral Bending (5th ed, p 409), shows that his lateral bending of 25° each to the left and to the right is normal and thus does not qualify for an additional impairment. Because "impairments due to loss of motion in more than one plane in the same spinal region . . . are added" (5th ed, p 403), Mr Orange will retain a 12% whole person impairment due to abnormal motion.

According to Table 15-7, Criteria for Rating Whole Person Impairment Percent Due to Specific Spine Disorders to Be Used as Part of the ROM Method (5th ed, p 404), paragraph IIE, "surgically treated disk lesion with residual, medically documented pain and rigidity" qualifies for a 10% whole person impairment. According to paragraph IIG, the second operation justifies an additional 2% rating, and the third operation justifies an additional 1% whole person impairment. Thus, Mr Orange's rating for the diagnosis portion of the ROM method is 13% (10% + 2% + 1%).

While spondylolisthesis is present, Mr Orange had a disk operation and not a spondylolisthesis operation at the time of his first and second surgeries. In addition, his spine surgeon for his third (current) surgery opined in deposition that the fusion surgery was done for recurrent radiculopathy due to recurrent disk herniation and not due to the spondylolisthesis. Thus, paragraph IV, which includes "spondylolisthesis, operated on," is not utilized.

Since Mr Orange has no spinal nerve motor deficit (weakness), he retains no impairment for this element of the ROM method. His decreased sensation on the dorsum of the foot fits with an L5 dermatome sensory pattern, which is logical, since his surgeries have been to decompress the L5 nerve root.

Table 15-18, Unilateral Spinal Nerve Root Impairment Affecting the Lower Extremity (5th ed, p 424), indicates that the maximum potential value of the L5 nerve root for sensory deficit and pain is 5% lower extremity impairment.

Table 15-15, Determining Impairment Due to Sensory Loss (5th ed, p 424), lists the six possible grades for loss of sensation and pain. From grade 4, a "midrange" rating of 13% can be chosen as a sensory "severity multiplier." Multiplying the 5% potential value of the nerve root by the 13% severity multiplier yields a 0.65% lower extremity impairment for neurologic deficit. This can be rounded off to 1% lower extremity impairment. Multiplying this 1% by 0.4 (the value of the lower extremity) converts this to a 0.4% whole person impairment, which can be rounded off to 0%.

Mr Orange's 12% whole person impairment due to abnormal motion is combined with his 13% whole person impairment for the accompanying diagnosis, which yields a 23% whole person impairment.

Since Mr Orange had a prior condition (radiculopathy due to herniated disk at the same level), his current impairment must be apportioned between his current and prior conditions. In Mr Orange's circumstance, the *Guides* advises, "If the previous evaluation was based on the DRE method and the individual now is evaluated with the ROM method, and prior ROM measurements do not exist to calculate a ROM impairment rating, the previous

DRE percent can be subtracted from the ROM ratings" (5th ed, p 381). Mr Orange's impairment due to his recurrent radiculopathy is 23% of the whole person, and his impairment due to his radiculopathy after the first and second injuries is 10% of the whole person. Since 23 − 10 = 13, Mr Orange will retain a 13% whole person impairment as a consequence of his third episode of radiculopathy.

Impairment: 23% whole person impairment per the Fifth Edition (apportioned as 10% for the first injury, 0% for the second injury, and 13% for the third injury).

Sixth Edition Rating

The *Guides* approach to the evaluation of impairment due to single-level fusion for recurrent disk herniation with radiculopathy is based on Section 17.2, Diagnosis-Based Impairment (6th ed, p 560), and Section 17.2c, Lumbar Spine (6th ed, p 566).

In Table 17-4, Lumbar Spine Regional Grid: Spine Impairments (6th ed, p 570), in the section on Motion Segment Lesions, for the diagnosis "intervertebral disk herniation" there is a class 2 rating for intervertebral disk herniation and/or AOMSI at a single level with medically documented findings, with or without surgery and with documented radiculopathy at the clinically appropriate level, present at the time of examination (with a default impairment of 11% whole person impairment).

In Section 17.3a, Adjustment Grid: Functional History (6th ed, p 569), and Table 17-6, Functional History Adjustment: Spine (6th ed, p 575), the patient is assigned grade modifier 2; the functional history is consistent with "pain; symptoms with strenuous/vigorous activity" (grade modifier 1) and the PDQ score is in the range of 71 to 100 (grade modifier 2). In Section 17.3b, Adjustment Grid: Physical Examination (6th ed, p 572), and Table 17-7, Physical Examination Adjustment: Spine (6th ed, p 576), the patient is assigned grade modifier 2; the physical examination revealed "positive straight leg raising test, with reproducible radicular pain at 35°-70°." In Section 17.3c, Adjustment Grid: Clinical Studies (6th ed, p 577), and Table 17-9, Clinical Studies Adjustment: Spine (6th ed, p 581), the patient is assigned no grade modifier because imaging studies are necessary to make the diagnosis of a fusion. Although the preoperative symptoms were "recurrent lumbar radiculopathy" related to a recurrent disk herniation, at MMI, the diagnosis was AOMSI related to a fusion at that same level. In summary, the adjustments are as follows: functional history grade modifier 2, physical examination grade modifier 2, and clinical studies grade modifier not applicable. Net adjustment compared to diagnosis class 2 is 0, grade C, 12% whole person impairment.

Class 2—Default for Diagnosis = 12% whole person impairment			
CDX	GMFH	GMPE	GMCS
2	2	2	n/a
Net adjustment (GMFH − CDX) 2 − 2 = 0 + (GMPE − CDX) + 2 − 2 = 0 + (GMCS − CDX) + n/a Net adjustment = 0			

Result is class 2 adjustment 0, which results in class 2, grade C = 12% whole person impairment.

Therefore, his current impairment is 12% whole person impairment.

Assuming that Mr Orange reached MMI after his two previous surgeries and prior to the third injury, apportionment might be appropriate. According to the information that is available, Mr Orange underwent a laminectomy and disk excision for a disk herniation at L4-5. To apportion the injuries, the initial injury rating should be converted to a Sixth Edition impairment rating, and because there is insufficient historical and clinical information to accurately perform the adjustments (eg, no information regarding functional history, physical examination, or clinical studies), the default value for the diagnosis is used. Mr Orange's previous diagnosis was "intervertebral disk herniation or documented AOMSI at a single level . . . with medically documented findings; with or without surgery and with documented resolved radiculopathy at clinically appropriate level," which is a class 1 diagnosis under Motion Segment Lesions (Table 17-4), for which the default rating is 7%. His impairment rating for the second surgery was unchanged. The present impairment rating of 12% − 7% for the previous injury and impairment leaves an impairment of 5% whole person impairment attributable to the third injury.

Impairment: 12% whole person impairment per the Sixth Edition (apportioned as 7% for the first injury, 0% for the second injury, and 5% for the third injury).

Comment on Recurrent Lumbar Radiculopathy

The Fourth Edition does not specifically address the situation of rating a back injury by the injury model after there has been surgery. The philosophy of the Fourth Edition is that radiculopathy is not quantifiable and, once radiculopathy is present, it is permanent. Thus, there is no increase in the rating when recurrent radiculopathy occurs. While this may not seem fair, the philosophy of the Fourth Edition is that radiculopathy can be assigned to a person only once.

The revisions that were made in the Fifth and Sixth Edition criteria for rating permanent impairments of the spine will, in many cases, lead to different results than prior editions.

The Fifth Edition handles recurrent radiculopathy very differently than the Fourth. If Mr Orange had never had the first and second injuries and surgeries, his current (and, in this hypothetical case, first) injury would be rated by the injury model as loss of motion segment integrity, and thus category IV, 20% to 23% whole person impairment. Because he did have prior injury(ies) with radiculopathy, his new (third) injury with recurrent radiculopathy must be rated by the ROM method (5th ed, p 380). The directions on apportioning specifically instruct the examiner to subtract the prior injury rating (by using the injury model) from the current rating (by using the ROM method). Interestingly, Mr Orange's impairment by the ROM method (23%) is very similar to his hypothetical rating if a first injury with radiculopathy had been treated with a surgical fusion (20%-23%).

In the Sixth Edition, there is again a change from the previous method of rating impairment for radiculopathy. The absence or presence of sensory and motor findings associated with the radiculopathy will determine the impairment grade within a class. This method eliminates the ranges and percentages previously used to calculate the percentage impairment associated with radicular findings. The impairment values are different from those obtained with the Fifth Edition and are intended to more accurately reflect the outcome of treatment and impact on functional level.

In this case, the issue of apportionment is raised because Mr Orange has had previous injuries. If apportionment is necessary, the previous impairment rating should be recalculated by the method described in the Sixth Edition. In cases in which there is insufficient clinical information (lack of detail in the medical records) to permit determination of the grade modifiers for use in the net adjustment formula, the default value is used for the diagnosis-based class as the impairment value, and apportionment is assigned accordingly.

SUMMARY

Diagnosis	Lumbar radiculopathy
Fourth Edition References	Section 3.3 (4th ed, pp 94), *Guides* Newsletter (July/August 1997, pp 1-), *Guides* Newsletter

	(September/October 1997, p 1), Table 70 (4th ed, p 108), Table 75 (4th ed, p 113), Figure 62 (4th ed, p 98), Figure 63 (4th ed, p 98)
Fourth Edition Summary	History, musculoskeletal and neurologic evaluation. Verify the presence of radiculopathy, including loss of relevant reflexes, unilateral atrophy, and differentiators, including electrodiagnostic evidence. Determine whether any other ratable impairment is present, including loss of motion segment integrity. Impairment is then based on the injury model.
Fourth Edition Impairment	10% whole person impairment
Fifth Edition References	Section 15.2 (5th ed, p 379), Section 15.8 (5th ed, p 398), Section 15.9 (5th ed, p 405), Section 1.6 (5th ed, p 11), Table 15-7 (5th ed, p 404)
Fifth Edition Summary	Determine the appropriate method for assessment, then apply the specific method to the individual's circumstances.
Fifth Edition Impairment	23% whole person impairment
Sixth Edition References	Section 17.2 (6th ed, p 560), Section 17.2c (6th ed, p 566), Section 17.3a (6th ed, p 569), Section 17.3b (6th ed, p 572), Section 17.3c (6th ed, p 577), Table 17-4 (6th ed, p 570), Table 17-6 (6th ed, p 575), Table 17-7 (6th ed, p 576), Table 17-9 (6th ed, p 581)
Sixth Edition Summary	History (including functional history and inventories), physical evaluation, and clinical studies. First, determine DBI, class, and default value. Second, adjust impairment on basis of nonkey factors. If apportionment is necessary, rate the previous diagnosis by the 6th edition, using grade modifiers if they are available, or the default value for the appropriate class if there is insufficient information to determine grade modifiers.
Sixth Edition Impairment	12% whole person impairment

CASE 17-6

Lumbar Radiculopathy, Resolved

Subject: Ms Jensen, a 31-year-old woman.

History: Ms Jensen experienced the onset of acute low back and left leg pain while lifting and twisting at work. Ms Jensen's relevant history included no similar prior episodes. Examination before treatment showed diminished sensation of her left medial calf, diminished strength of her left anterior tibialis (grade 4/5), diminished sensation left lateral calf, and radicular pain on left straight-leg raising, producing leg pain below the knee at 30° of elevation of the left leg. Waddell signs were absent. She was prescribed a course of conservative management, which included modified work duty, nonsteroidal anti-inflammatory medication, physical therapy, and conditioning. Eight weeks after her injury, Ms Jensen returned, having completed her prescribed course of treatment, reporting mild residual back pain and left leg symptoms. She was released to return to work, full time, full duty, without accommodation or restriction.

Current Symptoms: Ms Jensen reported mild residual low back pain and diminished sensation of her medial left calf.

Functional Assessment: The PDQ score was 10.

Physical Examination: On examination, Ms Jensen exhibited no abnormal findings. She had a normal neurologic examination; straight leg raising was negative bilaterally.

Clinical Studies: Diagnostic evaluation included MRI of the lumbar spine, which showed a herniated nucleus pulposus at L4-5, impinging on the left L5 nerve root. The diagnosis of lumbar radiculopathy was confirmed with electromyography, which disclosed multiple positive sharp waves and fibrillation potentials, indicative of acute nerve root compromise. Lumbar plain films with flexion and extension views showed no loss of motion segment integrity and no spondylolisthesis.

Discussion of Lumbar Radiculopathy, Resolved

Fourth Edition Rating

Impairment evaluation is based on Section 3.3, The Spine (4th ed, p 94). The *Guides*, Fourth Edition, describes two approaches for the assessment of spine impairment. One approach is called the injury model, also known as the DRE model. The injury model involves assigning an individual to one of eight categories, such as "minor injury," "radiculopathy," "loss of motion segment integrity," or "paraplegia," on the basis of objective clinical findings. The other approach is the ROM model, which was recommended in previous *Guides* editions. In the Fourth Edition, the injury model must be used if the individual's condition is one of those listed in Table 70, Spine Impairment Categories for Cervicothoracic, Thoracolumbar, and Lumbosacral Regions (4th ed, p 108). The injury model, for example, is applicable to a person with a herniated lumbar disk and evidence of nerve root irritation.

The ROM model is used in two circumstances, namely, if none of the eight categories of the injury model is applicable or if disagreement exists about the category of the injury model in which an individual belongs. In either of these two circumstances, the ROM model is used to help determine into which of the eight injury model categories to place a person; however, the rating still comes from the injury model, not from the ROM model.

Ms Jensen's condition, radiculopathy, is one of those listed in Table 70 (4th ed, p 108). Consequently, Ms Jensen's spine impairment must be based on the injury model, not the ROM model. The injury model is described in Sections 3.3a through 3.3i (4th ed, p 95).

Ms Jensen's injury, which resulted in radiculopathy, is consistent with DRE lumbosacral category III: radiculopathy, as described on page 102 and listed in Table 72, DRE Lumbosacral Spine Impairment Categories (4th ed, p 110). The DRE lumbosacral category III yields a 10% whole person impairment. Consequently, Ms Jensen retained a 10% whole person impairment as a consequence of her injury and radiculopathy.

Impairment: 10% whole person impairment per the Fourth Edition.

Fifth Edition Rating

The DRE method must be used to assess impairment in this case, since the impairment is due to an injury, and since none of the six clinical situations that require the use of the ROM method is present (5th ed, p 379). The Fifth Edition states in Section 15.2, Determining the Appropriate Method for Assessment (5th ed, pp 379-381), "The DRE method is the principal methodology used to evaluate an individual who has had a distinct injury" (5th ed, p 379). Section 15.3, Diagnosis-Related Estimates Model (5th ed, p 381), explains the process used to obtain the rating:

> To use the DRE method, obtain an individual's history, examine the individual, review the results of appropriate diagnostic studies, and place the individual in the appropriate category. . . . almost all individuals will fall into one of the first three DRE categories. . . . The impairment rating is based on the condition once MMI is reached, not on prior symptoms or signs.

If the individual had a radiculopathy caused by a herniated disk or lateral spinal stenosis that responded to conservative treatment and currently has no radicular symptoms or signs, he or she is placed in category II, since at MMI there is no radiculopathy. Category III is for individuals with a symptomatic radiculopathy, after either medical or surgical treatment, or for individuals who have a history of previous radiculopathy caused by disk herniation or lateral spinal stenosis but have improved or become asymptomatic following surgery (5th ed, p 383).

Although the result of Ms Jensen's injury was lumbar radiculopathy, her radiculopathy resolved with conservative, nonsurgical treatment; that is, when Ms Jensen reached MMI, lumbar radiculopathy was no longer present. Her lumbar injury is rated according to Section 15.4, DRE: Lumbar Spine (5th ed, p 384), and with the use of Table 15-3, Criteria for Rating Impairment Due to Lumbar Disorders (5th ed, p 384). Ms Jensen's outcome is consistent with the DRE lumbar category II criterion, "individual had a clinically significant radiculopathy and has an imaging study that demonstrates a herniated disk at the level and on the side that would be expected based on the previous radiculopathy, but no longer has the radiculopathy following conservative treatment" (5th ed, p 384).

The DRE lumbar category II corresponds with a rating of 5% to 8% whole person impairment. Since Ms Jensen has had an excellent result without significant impact on her ability to perform ADLs, she is assigned a 5% whole person impairment.

Impairment: 5% whole person impairment per the Fifth Edition.

Sixth Edition Rating

The *Guides* approach to the evaluation of impairment due to lumbar radiculopathy is based on Section 17.2, Diagnosis-Based Impairment (6th ed, p 560), and Section 17.2c, Lumbar Spine (6th ed, p 566).

In Table 17-4, Lumbar Spine Regional Grid: Spine Impairments (6th ed, p 570), in the section on Motion Segment Lesions, for the diagnosis "intervertebral disk herniation or documented AOMSI at a single level or multiple levels with medically documented findings; with or without surgery and with documented resolved radiculopathy at clinically appropriate level," there is a class 1 rating (with a default impairment of 7% whole person impairment).

In Section 17.3a, Adjustment Grid: Functional History (6th ed, p 569), and Table 17-6, Functional History Adjustment: Spine (6th ed, p 575), the patient is assigned grade modifier 1; although the functional history is consistent with "problem resolved," the PDQ score is in the range of 0 to 70, which is consistent with grade modifier 1. When the adjustment grids are used, the grade modifier value used in the net adjustment calculation is the highest value for the factors in that grid. In Section 17.3b, Adjustment Grid: Physical Examination (6th ed, p 572), and Table 17-7, Physical Examination Adjustment: Spine (6th ed, p 576), the patient is assigned grade modifier 0; the physical examination revealed "normal neurologic examination." In Section 17.3c, Adjustment Grid: Clinical Studies (6th ed, p 577), and Table 17-9, Clinical Studies Adjustment: Spine (6th ed, p 581), the patient is assigned grade modifier 2; the clinical studies revealed "imaging studies consistent with clinical presentation." In summary, the adjustments are as follows: functional history grade modifier 1, physical examination 0, and clinical studies grade modifier 2. Net adjustment compared to diagnosis class 1 is 0, grade C, 7% whole person impairment.

Class 1—Default for Diagnosis = 7% whole person impairment			
CDX	GMFH	GMPE	GMCS
1	1	0	2
Net adjustment (GMFH − CDX) 1 − 1 = 0 + (GMPE − CDX) + 0 − 1 = −1 + (GMCS − CDX) + 2 − 1 = 1 Net adjustment = 0			

Result is class 1 adjustment 1, which results in class 1, grade C = 7% whole person impairment.

Impairment: 7% whole person impairment per the Sixth Edition.

Comment on Lumbar Radiculopathy, Resolved

In the Fourth Edition, Section 3.3 (4th ed, p 94), the injury model applies to individuals' traumatic injuries, assigning people to one of eight categories on the basis of objective clinical findings. The injury model predicates spine impairment upon the individual's injury-related condition or diagnosis, not upon the type of treatment a person receives, nor upon the outcome of a person's treatment. When spine impairment is assessed with the injury model, the impairment the individual will retain as a result of his or her injury is known once the diagnosis is determined on the basis of objective clinical findings. For example, when a diagnosis of lumbar radiculopathy is established according to objective clinical findings, the individual will retain a 10% whole person impairment on the basis of DRE lumbosacral category III: radiculopathy; neither the type of treatment nor the outcome influences the impairment.

As discussed in the *Guides*, Fourth Edition (6th ed, p 100), and in the *Guides* Newsletter (July/August 1997 and September/October 1997), with the injury model, surgery to treat an impairment does not modify the original impairment; that is, the injury model bases impairment on the result of the injury (for example, minor injury, radiculopathy, loss of motion segment integrity, paraplegia), not the treatment (for example, conservative treatment, surgery without fusion, fusion). The result of Ms Jensen's injury was radiculopathy. Hence, her impairment is based on radiculopathy. Ms Jensen's impairment is not based on her nonsurgical treatment, which resolved her painful symptoms.

In the Fifth Edition, with the DRE method, the rating is based on the findings when the individual is at MMI. This accounts for the difference between the percentage of impairment determined with the *Guides* Fourth Edition and that with the *Guides* Fifth Edition.

Although Ms Jensen required no permanent restrictions or accommodations to facilitate her safe return to the workplace, she retained a permanent impairment. This is not counterintuitive if one considers the critical distinction between impairment and disability. Impairment is the loss, loss of use, or derangement of any body part, system, or function. An evaluation or rating of impairment is a medical assessment, which consists of analyzing data accumulated in the course of an impairment evaluation and comparing them to data within the *Guides*. Disability is a decrease in, or the loss or absence of, a capacity of a person to meet personal, social, or occupational demands or to meet statutory or regulatory requirements. Disability may be caused by medical impairment or by nonmedical factors. Evaluation or rating of disability is a nonmedical assessment of the degree to which a person does or does not have the capacity to meet personal, social, occupational, or other demands or to meet statutory or regulatory requirements. Impairment and disability are not synonymous. A person can have a large impairment and little or no disability, or (conversely) a person can have a small impairment and substantial disability.

In the Sixth Edition, like the Fifth edition, the rating requires that the patient's condition be at MMI, and treatment results are taken into account. Although Ms Jensen has returned to her regular activities after treatment, without the need for permanent restrictions or accommodations, she has impairment by the definition provided in the *Guides*.

SUMMARY

Diagnosis	Lumbar radiculopathy, resolved
Fourth Edition References	Section 3.3 (4th ed, p 94), Table 70 (4th ed, p 108)
Fourth Edition Summary	History, musculoskeletal and neurologic evaluation. Verify the presence of radiculopathy, including loss of relevant reflexes, unilateral atrophy, and differentiators, including electro-diagnostic evidence. Determine whether any other ratable impairment is present, including loss of motion segment integrity. Impairment is then based on the injury model.
Fourth Edition Impairment	10% whole person impairment
Fifth Edition References	Section 15.2 (5th ed, p 379), Section 15.3 (5th ed, p 381), Section 15.4 (5th ed, p 384), Box 15-1 (5th ed, p 382), Table 15-3 (5th ed, p 384)
Fifth Edition Summary	History, musculoskeletal and neurologic evaluation. Verify the presence of radiculopathy, including physical examination findings and electrodiagnostic evidence. Determine whether any other ratable impairment is present, including loss of motion segment integrity.
Fifth Edition Impairment	5% whole person impairment
Sixth Edition References	Section 17.2 (6th ed, p 560), Section 17.2c (6th ed, p 566), Section 17.3a (6th ed, p 569), Section 17.3b (6th ed, p 572), Section 17.3c (6th ed, p 577), Table 17-4 (6th ed, p 570), Table 17-6 (6th ed, p 575), Table 17-7 (6th ed, p 576), Table 17-9 (6th ed, p 581)

Sixth Edition Summary	History (including functional history and inventories), physical evaluation, and clinical studies. First, determine DBI, class and default value. Second, adjust impairment on basis of nonkey factors, using the net adjustment calculation and grade modifier values.
Sixth Edition Impairment	7% whole person impairment

CASE 17-7

Back Pain and Lower Extremity Dysfunction

Subject: Mr Martin, a 54-year-old man.

History: Mr Martin experienced the onset of low back pain and bilateral lower extremity "numbness" while lifting at work. His relevant history included no similar prior episodes. He had no difficulty initiating urination, and he had no urinary or fecal incontinence.

Shortly after injury, physical examination showed muscle guarding and dysmetria of the spine. Neurologic examination demonstrated moderate weakness of his quadriceps femoris bilaterally; mild weakness of his gastrocnemius, extensor hallucis longus, and anterior tibialis muscles bilaterally; diminished sensation of his perineum, thighs, and proximal anterior calves bilaterally; absent patellar tendon and Achilles tendon reflexes; and normal anal sphincter tone. Ankle clonus was noted bilaterally as well. Waddell signs and nonorganic physical signs were absent. An MRI of the lumbar spine showed a large posterocentral herniated nucleus pulposus at L3-4 with a free disk fragment, resulting in multilevel nerve root compression. Surgical treatment included decompressive laminectomy at L3-4 with excision of the herniated disk material and free fragment.

Current Symptoms: One year after surgery, at MMI, Mr Martin reported mild residual low back pain, but no leg pain. He had considerable difficulty with stair climbing; he required use of his arms to ascend a 1-ft step with either leg (quadriceps weakness). He denied difficulty with bowel or bladder control.

Functional Assessment: The PDQ score was 100.

Physical Examination: Mr Martin reported diminished sensation over his left anterolateral thigh, anterior knee, and medial leg and foot. Right leg sensation was normal. Perineal sensation was normal. Patellar deep tendon reflexes were absent on the left and trace present on the right. Muscle strength of his quadriceps femoris, anterior tibial, and gastrocnemius was mildly diminished bilaterally (4/5), although clearly improved from his preoperative status. The remainder of his neurologic examination was normal. Straight leg raising was negative bilaterally, and Waddell signs were absent.

Clinical Studies: Preoperative studies included MRI of the lumbar spine, which showed a large posterocentral herniated nucleus pulposus at L3-4 with a free disk fragment, resulting in multilevel nerve root compression consistent with a cauda equina–like syndrome. Lumbar plain films were unremarkable for any structural changes.

Discussion of Back Pain and Lower Extremity Dysfunction

Fourth Edition Rating

Impairment evaluation is based on Section 3.3, The Spine (4th ed, p 94). The *Guides*, Fourth Edition, describes two approaches for the assessment of spine impairment. One approach is called the *injury model*, also known as the *DRE model*. The injury model involves assigning an individual to one of eight categories (such as "minor injury," "radiculopathy," "loss of spine structure integrity," or "paraplegia") on the basis of objective clinical findings. The other approach is the ROM model, which was used in previous *Guides* editions. In the *Guides*, Fourth Edition, the injury model, for example, is applicable to an individual with a herniated lumbar disk and evidence of nerve root irritation. The ROM model is used in two circumstances: one, if none of the eight categories of the injury model is applicable (for example, if no injury has occurred), and two, if disagreement exists about which category of the injury model a person belongs to. In the latter circumstance, the ROM model is used to determine which of the eight injury model categories applies to the individual; the rating still comes from the injury model, not from the ROM model.

Mr Martin's condition, a cauda equina syndrome without bowel or bladder impairment, is listed in Table 70, Spine Impairment Categories for Cervicothoracic, Thoracolumbar, and Lumbosacral Regions (4th ed, p 108). Since his condition was causally related to a work injury, the spine impairment should be based on the injury model, not the ROM model. The injury model is described in Sections 3.3a through 3.3i (4th ed, p 95). Mr Martin's injury is consistent with DRE lumbosacral category VI: Cauda Equina–Like Syndrome Without Bowel or Bladder Signs, as described on page 103 and listed in Table 72, DRE Lumbosacral Spine Impairment Categories (4th ed, p 116). The DRE lumbosacral category VI provides a 40% whole person impairment.

Impairment: 40% whole person impairment per the Fourth Edition.

Fifth Edition Rating

Mr Martin has cauda equina syndrome with bilateral leg weakness from injury to multiple nerve roots in each leg (L4, L5, and S1 roots by physical examination). He does not have any impairment of bladder, bowel, or sexual functioning.

The DRE method combined with a rating for corticospinal tract damage is used to assess impairment in this case. The Fifth Edition states in Section 15.2, Determining the Appropriate Method for Assessment (5th ed, pp 379-381), "The DRE method is the principal methodology used to evaluate an individual who has had a distinct injury" (5th ed, p 379).

Section 15.7, Rating Corticospinal Tract Damage, actually applies to lumbar nerve root injuries that result in cauda equina syndrome in addition to cervical and thoracic injuries that damage the corticospinal tract of the spinal cord. The recommended system is that from the nervous system chapter, which has been reprinted in the spine chapter, with one difference. The directions state:

> For impairments involving loss of use of the lower extremities, use the section in Table 15-6 pertaining to station and gait impairment. If there is additional bowel or bladder dysfunction, combine the upper extremity or lower extremity loss with impairments in bladder, anorectal, and/or neurologic sexual impairment as warranted.

Once a class has been selected, the exact value is obtained by combining the value with the corresponding additional impairment from DRE categories II through V for cervical and lumbar impairment and DRE categories II through IV for thoracic impairment. An exact value is determined on the basis of the degree of impairment of ADLs (5th ed, p 396).

According to Table 15-6, Rating Corticospinal Tract Impairment, Section c, Criteria for Rating Impairments Due to Station and Gait Disorders (5th ed, p 396), Mr Martin meets the definition of class 2, eg, "Rises to standing position, walks some distance with difficulty and without assistance, but is limited to level surfaces." This corresponds with a 10% to 19% whole person impairment. A midrange value of 15% was selected. There were no other applicable impairments from Table 15-6, as Mr Martin had no difficulty with upper extremity function; respiration; or bladder, bowel, and sexual function.

Box 15-1, Definitions of Clinical Findings Used to Place an Individual in a DRE Category (5th ed, p 382), specifies the clinical findings used in a DRE method classification. Lumbar (low back) injury is rated according to Section 15.4, DRE: Lumbar Spine (5th ed, pp 384-388), and by means of Table 15-3, Criteria for Rating Impairment Due to Lumbar Disorders (5th ed, p 384). Mr Martin had surgery for his radiculopathy; therefore, he meets the second definition of DRE lumbar category III in Table 15-3 (5th ed, p 384): history of a herniated disk at the level and on the side that would be expected from objective clinical findings, associated with radiculopathy, or individuals who had surgery for radiculopathy but are now asymptomatic.

Impairment: 26% whole person impairment per the Fifth Edition.

Sixth Edition Rating

The *Guides* approach to the evaluation of impairment due to back pain and lower extremity dysfunction is based on Section 17.2, Diagnosis-Based Impairment (6th ed, p 560), Section 17.2c, Lumbar Spine (6th ed, p 566), and Section 13.6, Criteria for Rating Impairments of Station, Gait, and Movement Disorders (6th ed, p 336).

Musculoskeletal Rating

In Table 17-4, Lumbar Spine Regional Grid: Spine Impairments (6th ed, p 570), for the diagnosis "intervertebral disk herniation AOMSI," there is a class 2 rating for "intervertebral disk herniation AOMSI at a single level with medically documented findings, with or without surgery and radiculopathy at the clinically appropriate level" (with a default impairment of 12% whole person impairment).

In Section 17.3a, Adjustment Grid: Functional History (6th ed, p 569), and Table 17-6, Functional History Adjustment: Spine (6th ed, p 575), the patient is assigned grade modifier 2; the functional history is consistent with "symptoms with normal activity" and the PDQ score is in the range of 71 to 100. In Section 17.3b, Adjustment Grid: Physical Examination (6th ed, p 572), and Table 17-7, Physical Examination Adjustment: Spine (6th ed, p 576), the patient is assigned grade modifier 2; the physical examination revealed "new and asymmetrical abnormality (reflexes) consistent with other radicular findings." In Section 17.3c, Adjustment Grid: Clinical Studies (6th ed, p 577), and Table 17-9, Clinical Studies Adjustment: Spine (6th ed, p 581), the patient is assigned grade modifier 2; the clinical studies revealed "CT/MRI/other imaging findings consistent with presentation." In summary, the adjustments are as follows: functional history grade modifier 2, physical examination 2, and clinical studies grade modifier 2. Net adjustment compared to diagnosis class 2 is 0, grade C, 12% whole person impairment.

Separate Neurologic Rating

Section 17.2c, Lumbar Spine (6th ed, p 566), states that "in all cases, if there is documented cauda equina syndrome or spinal cord injury . . . an

Class 2—Default for Diagnosis = 12% whole person impairment			
CDX	GMFH	GMPE	GMCS
2	2	2	2
Net adjustment (GMFH − CDX) 2 − 2 = 0 + (GMPE − CDX) + 2 − 2 = 0 + (GMCS − CDX) + 2 − 2 = 0 Net adjustment = 0			

Result is class 2 adjustment 0, which results in class 2, grade C = 12% whole person impairment.

additional impairment calculation is appropriate, using Chapter 13 (Central and Peripheral Nervous System)." Individual radiculopathies are not rated separately.

For the cauda equina–like syndrome, using Table 13-12, Criteria for Rating Impairments Due to Station and Gait Disorders (6th ed, p 336), there is a class 1 rating (range of impairment, 1%-10%) for "rises to standing position; walks but has difficulty with elevations, grades, stairs, deep chairs and/or long distances." Based on the clinical information provided, an impairment of 10% is appropriate.

Combined Impairment
12% whole person impairment related to the lumbar spine per the Sixth Edition and 10% whole person impairment related to station and gait disorders (Chapter 13, The Central and Peripheral Nervous System). These impairments are combined, according to the Combined Values Chart (6th ed, p 604), for a total 21% whole person impairment.

Impairment: 21% whole person impairment per the Sixth Edition.

Comment on Back Pain and Lower Extremity Dysfunction

In terms of the Fourth Edition, with the injury model, surgical treatment does not modify the original impairment. The injury model bases impairment on the result of the injury (for example, minor injury, radiculopathy, loss of motion segment integrity, etc), not the treatment (for example, conservative treatment, surgery without fusion, fusion, etc). The result of Mr Martin's injury was a cauda equina–like syndrome without bowel or bladder compromise, and his impairment is based on that syndrome.

Mr Martin's impairment is not based on his surgical treatment, which included decompressive lumbar laminectomy.

The Fifth Edition explains that in prior editions of the *Guides*, spinal cord injury was rated either through a combination of DRE categories or in the nervous system chapter. It was decided in this edition to evaluate spinal cord injuries on the basis of the criteria in the nervous system chapter (Chapter 13). These criteria are repeated in the section. For bilateral neurologic or corticospinal tract damage, consultation with a spinal cord injury specialist and review of Chapter 13, The Central and Peripheral Nervous System, are recommended (5th ed, p 396). Section 13.7, Criteria for Rating Spinal Cord and Related Impairments (5th ed, pp 340-342), provides a circular reference stating, "See Chapter 15, The Spine, for spine impairment rating by neurological level of involvement" (5th ed, p 340). Section 13.7 explains the process of rating impairment on the basis of the ability to perform ADLs and the results of neurologic examination and testing; however, it does not specifically discuss the process of combining impairment with a DRE category (the one difference between the nervous system chapter and the spine chapter).

Hypothetically, with the Fifth Edition, if Mr Martin had a multilevel or bilateral radiculopathy, the ROM method could be used to assess his impairment. Since the Fourth Edition rating of 40% seems to more accurately describe his "real-world" difficulties with ADLs than does the Fifth Edition rating of 26%, use of the ROM method might be considered. This impairment would be based on the combined impairment from Table 15-7, Criteria for Rating Whole Person Impairment Percent Due to Specific Spine Disorders to Be Used as Part of the ROM Method (5th ed, p 404), any ROM impairments, and neurologic impairments. Section 15.12, Nerve Root and/or Spinal Cord (5th ed, p 423), states:

> If there is bilateral spinal nerve impairment or spinal cord involvement, especially if in conjunction with head injury, consultation with a neurologist and/or neurosurgeon and review of the diagnostic criteria in the neurology chapter (Chapter 13) is advisable. The physician should decide whether evaluation by the spine or neurology chapter criteria is most appropriate.

In the Sixth Edition, there is no provision for rating individual radiculopathies, since radiculopathy is a clinical finding associated with many spine-related conditions. To address a cauda equina–like syndrome, Section 17.2, Diagnosis-Based Impairment (6th ed, p 560), the specific section for the lumbar region, states, "In all cases, if there is documented cauda equina syndrome or spinal cord injury with findings of neurogenic bowel or bladder, or neurogenic sexual dysfunction related to the spinal cord injury and other related findings, an additional impairment calculation is appropriate, using Chapter 13. The neurologic whole person impairment should be combined with the spine-related whole person impairment" (6th ed, p 566). Since cauda equina–like syndrome is the more accurate diagnosis in this case, Chapter 13 is consulted to address Mr Martin's station and gait abnormalities. Combining the lumbar spine impairment (whole person impairment) and the nervous system impairment results in a total of 21% whole person impairment for this condition.

SUMMARY

Diagnosis	Cauda equina–like syndrome without bowel or bladder signs
Fourth Edition References	Section 3.3 (4th ed, p 94), *Guides* Newsletter (July/August 1997, p 1), *Guides* Newsletter (September/October 1997, p 1)
Fourth Edition Summary	History, musculoskeletal and neurologic evaluation. Verify the presence of cauda equina–like syndrome without bowel or bladder signs.
Fourth Edition Impairment	40% whole person impairment
Fifth Edition References	Section 15.2 (5th ed, p 379), Section 15.3 (5th ed, p 381), Section 15.4 (5th ed, p 384), Section 15.7 (5th ed, p 395), Box 15-1 (5th ed, p 382), Table 15-3 (5th ed, p 384), Table 15-6 (5th ed, p 396)
Fifth Edition Summary	History, musculoskeletal and neurologic evaluation. If injury model is applicable, select appropriate "corticospinal tract category" and combine with appropriate category II through V rating from Table 15-3.
Fifth Edition Impairment	26% whole person impairment
Sixth Edition References	Section 13.6 (6th ed, p 336), Section 17.2 (6th ed, p 560), Section 17.2c (6th ed, p 566), Section 17.3a (6th ed, p 569), Section 17.3b (6th ed, p 572), Section 17.3c (6th ed, p 577), Table 13-12 (6th ed, p 336), Table 17-4 (6th ed,

	p 570), Table 17-6 (6th ed, p 575), Table 17-7 (6th ed, p 576), Table 17-9 (6th ed, p 581), Combined Values Chart (6th ed, p 604)
Sixth Edition Summary	History (including functional history and inventories), physical evaluation, and clinical studies. First, determine DBI, class, and default value. Second, adjust impairment on basis of nonkey factors. In this case, there is a second impairment calculation related to impairment secondary to cauda equina–like syndrome without bowel or bladder involvement. This impairment is combined with the spine-related impairment by the Combined Values Chart.
Sixth Edition Impairment	21% whole person impairment

CASE 17-8

Muscle Injury

Subject: Mr Thomas, a 34-year-old man.

History: Mr Thomas was a telecommunications technician working full time installing pay-television cables. The physical aspects of his job included driving a van, lifting a 55-lb, 16-ft ladder off the roof rack, carrying the ladder from the van to various sites, climbing onto roofs, crawling under floors in houses, and scaling the ladder to make cable connections with street cables strung between power poles. He described his work as quite heavy, particularly the repeated lifting and carrying of his ladder.

Mr Thomas reported pain in the back to the left of the midline that had begun 6 months earlier. He associated the onset of the pain with repeated carrying of a ladder at work. On the day that he developed symptoms, he was doing a lot of lifting and relocating of the ladder. He explained how he would carry the extension ladder over his right shoulder, tilting his body to the left to counterbalance it. On downloading the ladder he would usually twist and tilt to the left, placing the ladder down and then positioning it as necessary. His back pain did not diminish, and he saw his family physician, who diagnosed strained muscles and advised over-the-counter analgesics. He also went to a chiropractor for manipulations. The chiropractor diagnosed the disorder as muscular pain and did not offer ongoing treatment.

Mr Thomas continued with his normal duty and was plagued with continuing back pain. He became increasingly frustrated by the limitations imposed by his back symptoms. He became angry and eventually depressed by the persistence of his symptoms. His physician placed him on an antidepressant medication, which he used only sporadically because he did not like taking medications. He also avoided taking analgesic or anti-inflammatory medication for the same reason. He believed that if he avoided physical activity at home and in his leisure time he would be well enough to do his normal duties. He needed the money and could not afford to be out of work. Before his injury, he exercised regularly. Since the injury, he avoided any exercise and tended to rest at home. He had not had any formal rehabilitation and had not been instructed in self-managed exercises to increase his general muscle condition and fitness. Mr Thomas' employer sent him for a general assessment that included a request for an evaluation of the permanent impairment of his back.

His past medical history was unremarkable except for a fall that he had had 2 years earlier. He had fractured the scaphoid bone of his left hand after falling 6 ft from a ladder. He had recovered from his injury in about 8 weeks without any residual problems.

Current Symptoms: Mr Thomas' back pain was reported as severe, spreading up and down the thoracolumbar spine, to the left of the midline. There was no referred pain in the legs or elsewhere in his back.

Physical Examination: At examination, Mr Thomas was of slight build at 138 lb and 5 ft 8 in tall. Examination of the neck, thoracic spine, lumbar spine, and lower limbs failed to identify any objective signs of musculoskeletal or neurologic abnormality. He had tenderness in the erector spinae muscles on the left, especially at the level of the thoracolumbar junction. Active ranges of lumbar and thoracic spinal movements were normal throughout. Mr Thomas complained of pain that localized to the left of the midline in the erector spinae muscles when he tilted left and right, or when he extended his back. The thoracolumbar spine was not tender to percussion, and there were no signs of nerve root irritation or radiculopathy.

Clinical Studies: Lumbar spine X-ray films and a computed tomographic scan did not show any pathology.

Discussion of Muscle Injury

Although Mr Thomas has an impairment at the time of his evaluation, he does not have a permanent impairment because he has not yet reached MMI. Mr Thomas' impairment evaluation must be postponed until he has reached MMI.

Fourth Edition Rating

In the Fourth Edition, permanent impairment is defined as "impairment that has become static or well stabilized with or without medical treatment and is not likely to remit despite medical treatment" (4th ed, p 314).

Fifth Edition Rating

Section 2.4, When Are Impairment Ratings Performed? (5th ed, p 19), states, "an impairment should not be considered permanent until the clinical findings indicate that the medical condition is static and well stabilized, often termed the date of maximal medical improvement (MMI)." The Glossary defines permanent impairment as "an impairment that has reached maximal medical improvement" (5th ed, p 602). Maximal medical improvement is defined as "a condition or state that is well stabilized and unlikely to change substantially in the next year, with or without medical treatment. Over time, there may be some change; however, further recovery or deterioration is not anticipated" (5th ed, p 601).

Sixth Edition Rating

Section 2.5, Concepts Important to the Independent Medical Examiner (6th ed, p 25), and specifically Section 2.5e, Maximum Medical Improvement (6th ed, p 26), states, "Maximum Medical Improvement refers to a status where patients are as good as they are going to be from the medical and surgical treatment available to them." Maximum medical improvement "can also be conceptualized as a date from which further recovery or deterioration is not anticipated, although over time (beyond 12 months) there may be some expected change." In the example presented, Mr Martin had not yet participated in a rehabilitation program, which could be considered appropriate treatment prior to finding his condition stationary.

Comment on Muscle Injury

If Mr Thomas' condition remained static despite all reasonable therapeutic modalities and it was clearly established by the evaluating physician that the thoracolumbar muscular impairment was permanent, then the assessment would be done with the injury model or the DRE model. With the Fifth Edition, if he had no objective findings when he was at MMI, he would be assigned to DRE thoracic category I per Table 15-4, Criteria for Rating Impairment Due to Thoracic Spine Injury (5th ed, p 389), ie, "No significant clinical findings, no observed muscle guarding, no documentable neurologic impairment, no documented changes in structural integrity, and no other indication of impairment related to injury or illness; no fractures." This is associated with 0% whole person impairment.

Using the Sixth Edition, if Mr Thomas had no objective findings when he was at MMI, his condition would fall under class 0 in Table 17-3, Thoracic Spine Regional Grid (6th ed, p 567), and his impairment rating would be 0. In Section 17.2, Diagnosis-Based Impairment (6th ed, p 560), under the heading General Considerations (6th ed, p 563), this edition of the *Guides* addresses the category of patients who present with persistent pain and/or "nonverifiable" radicular complaints "that are documented repeatedly after an identifiable injury." If Mr Thomas' failed to improve with adequate rehabilitation, according to Table 17-3, Thoracic Spine Regional Grid (6th ed, p 567), he might have a class 1 impairment, range 0% to 3%, when he reached MMI.

SUMMARY

Diagnosis	Muscle injury, not at MMI
Fourth Edition References	Section 2.3 (4th ed, p 9), Glossary (4th ed, p 315), Section 3.3d-I (4th ed, p 99), Table 71 (4th ed, p 109), Table 74 (4th ed, p 111)
Fourth Edition Summary	History, musculoskeletal and neurologic evaluation. Determine whether at MMI. If not at MMI, unable to assign permanent impairment.
Fourth Edition Impairment	n/a
Fifth Edition References	Section 2.4 (5th ed, p 19), Glossary (5th ed, p 602), Section 15.2 (5th ed, p 379), Section 15.3 (5th ed, pp 381-384), Section 15.6 (5th ed, p 388), Box 15-1 (5th ed, p 382), Table 15-4 (5th ed, p 389)
Fifth Edition Summary	History, musculoskeletal and neurologic evaluation. Determine whether at MMI. If not at MMI, unable to assign permanent impairment.
Fifth Edition Impairment	n/a
Sixth Edition References	Section 2.5 (6th ed, p 25), Section 2.5e (6th ed, p 26), Section 17.2 (6th ed, p 560), Table 17-3 (6th ed, p 567)
Sixth Edition Summary	Determine whether there was an injury and whether the condition is at MMI. Obtain history (including functional history and inventories), physical evaluation, and clinical studies. If the condition is not at MMI, then impairment rating is not appropriate.
Sixth Edition Impairment	n/a

CASE 17-9

Cervical Spine Dislocation

Subject: Ms Stevens, a 23-year-old woman.

History: Ms Stevens, a right-hand–dominant woman, slipped and fell at work, striking the back of her head against a piece of furniture with subsequent hyperflexion of her neck. She had immediate onset of neck pain and an inability to move her arms or legs.

Her initial examination showed a dense quadriparesis, loss of sensation of her trunk and lower extremities, hypesthesia of her ring and small fingers bilaterally, and absent anal sphincter tone. She was incontinent of urine. Initial diagnostic studies included plain films of the neck that showed a 5-mm anterior subluxation of C6 on C7. A cervical MRI scan disclosed a posterocentral herniated nucleus pulposus at C6-7 compressing the spinal cord and the exiting C7 nerve roots bilaterally.

Ms Stevens was placed in cervical traction and the dislocation of C6 on C7 was brought into anatomic alignment. She underwent an anterior cervical diskectomy and interbody fusion at C6-7. Rehabilitation management produced some recovery of extremity function, but her neurogenic bladder persisted and was confirmed by cystometrogram.

Current Symptoms: Ms Stevens was paraparetic but able to ambulate short distances in bilateral above-knee orthoses. About half of her "ambulation" was by means of a wheelchair. She only had limited voluntary control of her rectal sphincter. She was incontinent of urine, requiring chronic catheterization. An indwelling Foley catheter was present. She had no sexual functioning.

Functional Assessment: The PDQ score was 135.

Physical Examination: Ms Stevens was evaluated 1 year after her injury. Her neck incision was well healed. She was not wearing any type of collar or neck brace. Her reflexes were hyperactive, with bilateral positive Babinski sign. On motor examination, she had good strength in the deltoids and biceps bilaterally. Her triceps muscles were weak, as were all her wrist and hand muscles, but with assistive devices on her hands she was able to feed herself and perform some self-care activities. She was weak in her lower extremities diffusely, but she showed no evidence of spasm. She had some rectal sphincter tone. On sensory testing, she had complete loss of two-point discrimination in the ring and little fingers of both hands. In the lower extremities she had complete loss of vibratory sensation at the iliac crest, at both knees, and at the ankles, and she had pinprick hypesthesia from the C7 level distally.

Clinical Studies: X-ray films of the cervical spine showed a solid fusion at the C6-7 level.

Discussion of Cervical Spine Dislocation

Fourth Edition Rating

Impairment evaluation is based on Section 3.3, The Spine (4th ed, p 94). The *Guides*, Fourth Edition, describes two approaches for the assessment of spine impairment. One approach is called the *injury model*, also known as the *DRE model*. The injury model involves assigning an individual to one of eight categories, such as "minor injury," "radiculopathy," "loss of spine structure integrity," or "paraplegia," on the basis of objective clinical findings. The other approach is the ROM model, which was used in previous *Guides* editions. The ROM model is used in two circumstances: one, if none of the eight categories of the injury model is applicable, and two, if disagreement exists about the category of the injury model that applies to the person. In the latter circumstance, the ROM model is used to help determine into which of the eight injury model categories to place a person. The impairment rating still comes from the injury model, not from the ROM model.

Ms Stevens' condition, vertebral body dislocation with spinal cord injury, is one of the examples listed in Table 70, Spine Impairment Categories for Cervicothoracic, Thoracolumbar, and Lumbosacral Regions (4th ed, p 108). Her spine impairment is based on the injury model, not the ROM model. The injury model is described in Sections 3.3a through 3.3i (4th ed, p 95).

Her injury, which resulted in a cauda equina syndrome with bladder compromise, is consistent with DRE cervicothoracic category VII: cauda equina syndrome with bowel or bladder compromise, ie, "the patient has severe lower extremity impairment as defined in cervicothoracic category VI, with permanent bowel or bladder involvement requiring an assistive device" (4th ed, p 105). The DRE cervicothoracic category VII yields a 60% whole person impairment. This rating would be combined with the most appropriate impairment estimate from cervicothoracic categories II, III, IV, or V by means of the Combined Values Chart (4th ed, p 322). Ms Stevens requires assistive devices on her hands to feed herself and perform some self-care activities. This condition is consistent with DRE cervicothoracic category V: severe upper extremity neurologic compromise, ie, "the patient has objectively demonstrated a significant upper extremity impairment requiring the use of upper extremity external functional or adaptive device(s). There may be total neurologic loss at single level or severe, multi-level neurologic loss" (4th ed, p 104). The DRE cervicothoracic category V yields a 35% whole person impairment. With the use of the Combined Values Chart, this equates to a 74% whole person impairment.

Impairment: 74% whole person impairment per the Fourth Edition.

Fifth Edition Rating

The DRE method combined with a rating for corticospinal tract damage is used to assess impairment in this case. The Fifth Edition states in Section 15.2, Determining the Appropriate Method for Assessment (5th ed, p 379), "The DRE method is the principal methodology used to evaluate an individual who has had a distinct injury" (5th ed, p 379). Section 15.3, Diagnosis-Related Estimates Model (5th ed, p 381), explains the process used to obtain the rating.

Box 15-1, Definition of Clinical Findings Used to Place an Individual in a DRE Category (5th ed, p 382), specifies the clinical findings used in a DRE method classification. A cervical (neck) injury is rated according to Section 15.6, DRE: Cervical Spine (5th ed, p 393), and with the use of Table 15-5, Criteria for Rating Impairment Due to Cervical Disorders (5th ed, p 392). Ms Stevens meets the definition of AOMSI, on the basis of her fusion and also her bilateral radiculopathy. The specifics of determining motion segment integrity are discussed in Section 15.1b, Description of Clinical Studies (5th ed, p 378). The presence of AOMSI results in a DRE cervical category IV rating. Table 15-5 (5th ed, p 392) defines this category as follows:

> Alteration of motion segment integrity *or bilateral or multilevel radiculopathy* [italics added]; alteration of motion segment integrity is defined from flexion and extension radiographs as at least 3.5 mm of translation of one vertebra on another, or angular motion of more than 11° greater than at each adjacent level (Figures 15-3a and 15-3b); alternatively, the individual may have loss of motion of a motion segment due to a developmental fusion or successful or unsuccessful attempt at surgical arthrodesis; radiculopathy as defined in cervical category III need not be present if there is alteration of motion segment integrity.

This corresponds with a rating of 25% to 28% whole person impairment. The *Guides* states, "if residual symptoms or objective findings impact the ability to perform ADLs, despite treatment, the higher percentage in each range should be assigned." On the basis of the reported interference with ADLs, Ms Stevens is assigned a 28% whole person impairment.

Section 15.7, Rating Corticospinal Tract Damage (5th ed, pp 395-398), explains that impairment is based on impairment for corticospinal involvement combined with impairment from a DRE category:

> Once a class has been selected, the exact value is obtained by combining the value with the corresponding additional impairment from DRE categories II through V for cervical and lumbar impairment and DRE categories II through IV for thoracic impairment. An exact value is determined based on the degree of impairment of ADL [5th ed, p 396].

Ms Stevens receives multiple ratings from Table 15-6, Rating Corticospinal Tract Impairment (5th ed, p 396). She has bilateral upper extremity impairment, ie, "with assistive devices on her hands she was able to feed herself and perform some self-care activities." According to Section b, Criteria for Rating Impairments of Two Upper Extremities, she meets the definition of a class 3 impairment, ie, "individual can use both upper extremities but has difficulty with self-care activities." This is associated with a range of impairment from 40% to 79% whole person impairment, and she is assigned a midrange impairment of 60% whole person impairment.

"She was paraparetic but able to ambulate short distances in bilateral above-knee orthoses. About half of her 'ambulation' was by means of a wheelchair." According to Section c, Criteria for Rating Impairments Due to Station and Gait Disorders, she meets the definition of a class 4 impairment, ie, "cannot stand without help, mechanical support, and/or an assistive device." This is associated with a range of impairment from 40% to 60% whole person impairment, and she is assigned a midrange impairment of 50% whole person impairment.

For her neurologic impairment of the bladder (ie, she "was incontinent of urine, requiring chronic catheterization. An indwelling Foley catheter was present"), according to Section d, Criteria for Rating Neurologic Impairment of the Bladder, she meets the definition of a class 4 impairment, ie, "individual has no reflex or voluntary control of bladder." This is associated with a range of impairment from 40% to 60% whole person impairment, and she is assigned an upper-range of 60% whole person impairment.

For her neurologic anorectal impairment (ie, "some rectal sphincter tone, but only limited voluntary control"), according to Section e, Criteria for Rating Neurologic Anorectal Impairment, she meets the definition of a class 1 impairment, ie, "individual has reflex regulation but only limited voluntary control." This is associated with a range of impairment from 1% to 19% whole person impairment, and she is assigned an upper-range rating of 19% whole person impairment.

Ms Stevens had no sexual functioning; therefore, according to Section f, Criteria for Rating Neurologic Sexual Impairment, she is in class 3 and has a 20% whole person impairment.

Her corticospinal impairment is the combined value, per the Combined Values Chart (5th ed, p 604), of these impairments of the whole person, ie, bilateral upper extremity (60%), station and gait (50%), bladder (60%), anorectal (19%), and sexual (20%). The spine chapter does not have instruction on how to combine multiple impairments, but the upper extremity chapter does: "If three or more values are to be combined, the two lowest values are first selected and their combined value is found. The combined value and the third value are then combined to give the total value. This procedure is repeated indefinitely, with the value obtained in each case being a combination of all the previous values" (5th ed, p 438).

If this principle is followed, the order in which to combine Ms Stevens' spinal impairments would be 19%, 20%, 50%, 60%, and finally 60%. This results in a 95% whole person impairment.

The 28% whole person impairment from the DRE method is combined with the 15% whole person impairment for corticospinal tract by means of the Combined Values Chart (5th ed, p 604), resulting in a 96% whole person impairment.

Impairment: 96% whole person impairment per the Fifth Edition.

Sixth Edition Rating

The impairment in this case is based on the combined spinal and neurologic impairment.

Spine Impairment

The *Guides* approach to the evaluation of impairment due to cervical spine dislocation is based on Section 17.2, Diagnosis-Based Impairment (6th ed, p 560), and Section 17.2a, Cervical Spine (6th ed, p 563).

In Table 17-2, Cervical Spine Regional Grid: Spine Impairments (6th ed, p 564), for the diagnosis "dislocation/fracture dislocation" there is a class 2 rating for single level dislocation with or without fracture. Healed, with or without surgical intervention, including fusion and may have documented radiculopathy at the clinically appropriate level present at the time of examination (with a default impairment of 11% whole person impairment). Additional impairment is calculated for the findings related to spinal cord injury (see below).

In Section 17.3a, Adjustment Grid: Functional History (6th ed, p 569), and Table 17-6, Functional History Adjustment: Spine (6th ed, p 575), the patient is assigned grade modifier 4; the functional history is consistent with "limited to sedentary activity" and the PDQ score is in the range of 131 to 150. In Section 17.3b, Adjustment Grid: Physical Examination (6th ed, p 572), and Table 17-7, Physical Examination Adjustment: Spine (6th ed, p 576), the patient is assigned grade modifier 4, since the physical examination revealed "absent two-point discrimination" in the ring and little fingers. In Section 17.3c, Adjustment Grid: Clinical Studies (6th ed, p 577), and Table 17-9, Clinical Studies Adjustment: Spine (6th ed, p 581), no grade modifier is assigned, since the diagnosis of dislocation requires an imaging study. If an adjustment is used in making the diagnosis, it may not be used again to calculate the impairment rating. In summary, the adjustments are as follows: functional history grade modifier 4, physical examination 4, and clinical studies grade modifier not applicable.

Therefore, in this case the net adjustment to diagnosis class 2 is 4, grade E, 14% whole person impairment.

Class 2—Default for Diagnosis = 11% whole person impairment			
CDX	GMFH	GMPE	GMCS
2	4	4	n/a
Net adjustment (GMFH − CDX) 4 − 2 = 2 + (GMPE − CDX) + 4 − 2 = 2 + (GMCS − CDX) n/a Net adjustment = 4			

Note: The maximum adjustment in any class is +2; which moves the grade from C to E.

Result is class 2 adjustment 4, which results in class 2, grade E = 14% whole person impairent.

Nervous System Impairment

Spinal injury impairment with residual neurologic impairments can be combined with the neurologic impairments calculated from Chapter 13, The Central and Peripheral Nervous System (6th ed, p 321). These impairments can include issues relating to station and gait, use of the upper extremities, respiration, urinary bladder function, anorectal function, sexual function, and pain. Ranges for impairments are provided by distinct classes of impairments based on impact to ADLs. The higher values within each range should be applied to any given case depending on the degree of impact to ADLs for that specific condition.

Section 13.5, Criteria for Rating Impairments of Upper Extremities Due to CNS Dysfunction (6th ed, p 335), states that when the spinal cord disorder affects both upper extremities, the ratings for dominant and nondominant impairment ratings should be combined. According to Table 13-11, Criteria for Rating Impairments of the Upper Extremities Due to CNS Dysfunction (6th ed, p 335), these findings fall into class 2, "individual can use the involved extremity for ADLs, can grasp and hold objects with difficulty, but has no digital dexterity." The maximum value for the nondominant upper extremity impairment is 15% whole person impairment, and for dominant upper extremity impairment, 20% whole person impairment. Section 13.6, Criteria for Rating Impairments of Station, Gait, and Movement Disorders (6th ed, p 336), indicates that impairment ratings for station and gait disorders are determined according to the effect on ambulation. According to Table 13-12, Criteria for Rating Impairments Due to Station and Gait Disorders (6th ed, p 336), since an assistive device was required 50% of the time, the finding was class 4, with a range of 36% to 50% whole person impairment, for a 40% whole person impairment. Neurogenic bowel and bladder are discussed in Section 13.7, Criteria for Rating Neurogenic Bowel, Bladder, and Sexual Dysfunction (6th ed, p 336). According to Table 13-13, Criteria for Rating the Neurogenic Bowel (6th ed, p 337), the available clinical information is consistent with class 3 and an impairment range of 11% to 20% whole person impairment, for an impairment rating of 11% whole person impairment. With respect to urinary incontinence, clinical findings were consistent with class 4, impairment range 21% to 30% whole person impairment according to Table 13-14, Criteria for Rating the Neurogenic Bladder (6th ed, p 337), for a rating of 25% whole person impairment.

Ms Stevens' corticospinal impairment is the combined value, per the Combined Values Chart, of these impairments of the whole person, ie, nondominant upper extremity (15% whole person impairment), dominant upper extremity (20% whole person impairment), station and gait (40% whole person impairment), neurogenic bowel (11% whole person impairment), and neurogenic bladder (25%) whole person impairment. The Sixth Edition follows the principle of combining the two highest values first, and then combining the third, and so on to reach the total combined value, as explained in Section 2.2c, The Combined Values Chart (6th ed, p 22). If this principle is followed, the order in which to combine Ms Stevens' spinal impairments would be 40%, 25%, 20%, 15%, and finally 11%. According to the Combined Values Chart (6th ed, p 604) this results in 72% whole person impairment.

Impairment: 14% spine-related whole person impairment per the Sixth Edition and 72% neurologic impairment. These values are combined for an impairment rating of 76% whole person impairment per the Sixth Edition.

Comment on Cervical Spine Dislocation

In the Fourth Edition, with the injury model, "surgery to treat an impairment does not modify the original impairment estimate, which remains the same in spite of any changes in signs or symptoms that may follow the surgery and whether the patient has a favorable or unfavorable response to treatment." In the Fourth Edition, the injury model bases impairment on the result of the injury (for example, minor injury, radiculopathy, loss of motion segment integrity, etc), not the treatment (for example, conservative treatment, surgery without fusion, fusion, etc). The result of Ms Stevens' injury was cauda equina syndrome with bladder compromise, and her impairment is based on this finding. It is not based on her surgical treatment, which included cervical fusion.

This case exemplifies significant changes with the Fifth Edition. Surgery to treat a disorder may modify an impairment, and the performance of a single-level fusion results in the minimum of a DRE category IV rating. Information is provided on when to use the ROM method vs the DRE method, with one of the directives being "when there is multilevel involvement in the same spinal region (eg, fractures at multiple levels, disk herniations, or stenosis with radiculopathy at multiple levels or bilaterally)" (5th ed, p 380). This statement is somewhat unclear as written; however, it is meant to refer to significant multiple-level involvement, such as multiple-level radiculopathy or bilateral radiculopathy. Table 15-5 (5th ed, p 393) defines DRE cervical category IV as AOMSI or bilateral or multiple radiculopathy.

The Fifth Edition explains that "in prior editions of the Guides, rating spinal cord injury was done either through a combination of DRE categories or in the nervous system chapter. It was decided in this edition to evaluate spinal cord injuries based on the criteria in the nervous system chapter

(Chapter 13)." Because of the multiple neurologic impairments present in Ms Stevens' case, her resulting impairment is substantially greater with the Fifth Edition than with the Fourth Edition.

In the Sixth Edition, spinal cord injuries resulting from a fracture/dislocation are rated by a combination of DBI and nervous system impairment.

SUMMARY

Diagnosis	Cervical fracture dislocation with residual radiculopathy and spinal cord injury
Fourth Edition References	Section 3.3 (4th ed, p 94), *Guides Newsletter* (July/August 1997), *Guides Newsletter* (September/October 1997), Table 70 (4th ed, p 108)
Fourth Edition Summary	History, musculoskeletal and neurologic evaluation, and bladder studies. Verify the presence of cauda equina syndrome with bladder compromise. Verify the presence of severe upper extremity neurologic compromise. Impairment is based on the injury model, noting that impairments from cervicothoracic categories VI through VIII should be combined with impairments from categories II, III, IV, and V.
Fourth Edition Impairment	74% whole person impairment
Fifth Edition References	Section 15.1b (5th ed, p 378), Section 15.2 (5th ed, p 379), Section 15.3 (5th ed, p 381), Section 15.6 (5th ed, p 393), Section 15.7 (5th ed, p 395), Box 15-1 (5th ed, p 382), Table 15-5 (5th ed, p 392), Table 15-6 (5th ed, p 396)
Fifth Edition Summary	History, musculoskeletal and neurologic evaluation. If injury model is applicable, select appropriate DRE category and combine with corticospinal impairment(s).
Fifth Edition Impairment	96% whole person impairment

Sixth Edition References Section 13.5 (6th ed, p 335), Section 13.6 (6th ed, p 336), Section 13.7 (6th ed, p 336), Section 17.2 (6th ed, p 560), Section 17.2a (6th ed, p 563), Section 17.3a (6th ed, p 569), Section 17.3b (6th ed, p 572), Section 17.3c (6th ed, p 577), Table 13-11 (6th ed, p 335), Table 13-12 (6th ed, p 336), Table 13-13 (6th ed, p 337), Table 13-14 (6th ed, p 337), Table 17-2 (6th ed, p 564), Table 17-6 (6th ed, p 575), Table 17-7 (6th ed, p 576), Table 17-9 (6th ed, p 581)

Sixth Edition Summary History (including functional history and inventories), physical evaluation, and clinical studies. First, determine DBI, class, and default value. Second, adjust impairment on basis of nonkey factors. In the case of spinal cord involvement or cauda equina syndrome, additional impairment is calculated to account for neurologic findings. This impairment is combined with the DBI rating for the spine by means of the Combined Values Chart.

Sixth Edition Impairment 76% whole person impairment

CASE 17-10

Lumbar Strain

Subject: Mr Samuels, a 34-year-old man.

History: Mr Samuels worked as a materials handler and denied any previous difficulty with his back. Six months earlier he had had the onset of pain in his back without leg pain when he twisted to the right to lift a 15-lb box of tools. The pain was sharp and stabbing. It was located in the region of the left sacroiliac joint. He denied any radiation of pain into his legs. At the time of his initial evaluation, he told the physician that on the day of injury he had been unable to stand upright. The physician documented that Mr Samuels had a list to the left.

On reexamination 1 week later, in the standing position, Mr Samuels had markedly limited motion of the back because of pain. There was true spasm, and both a forward list of 10° and a sciatic scoliosis were present. In the sitting position, patellar and knee tendon reflexes were normal and symmetric. Sensation was intact. Toe extensor and flexor strength were normal. Quadriceps and hamstring strength were normal. He had normal sensation to light touch and to pinprick throughout both lower extremities. Pulses were normally palpable. The supine straight-leg-raising test caused back pain bilaterally at about 80° to 90° and was aggravated by dorsiflexion of the foot but not by plantar flexion of the foot. Straight leg raising in the sitting position caused pain in the low back at about 80° bilaterally. He had difficulty getting off and on the examining table. His pain gradually resolved over a period of weeks with physical therapy and nonsteroidal anti-inflammatory medication.

Current Symptoms: When reexamined 6 months after injury, he no longer had pain. He was back at work in his original job without difficulty.

Functional Assessment: The PDQ score was 0.

Physical Examination: Examination of his low back and neurologic examination were completely normal.

Clinical Studies: None.

Discussion of Lumbar Strain

Fourth Edition Rating

Mr Samuels' evaluation should be performed with the use of the spine section of the musculoskeletal chapter of the AMA *Guides*. In this section, the instructions are to use the DRE model (injury model) unless the individual does not fit the conditions in Table 70, Spine Impairment Categories for Cervicothoracic, Thoracolumbar, and Lumbosacral Regions (4th ed, p 108). This means that basically all spine injuries can be evaluated by the injury model. The injury model rates the severity of the injury, not the end result. Therefore, the physician rating the impairment must review the medical records from the individual's initial care to look for the presence of objective signs of injury. Mr Samuels had true observable muscle spasm or guarding on examination on the day of injury, as well as when reexamined 1 week later, which is one of the differentiators of specific injury; therefore, DRE lumbosacral category II must be considered. Table 71, DRE Impairment Category Differentiators (4th ed, p 109), provides definitions for these differentiators. Since Mr Samuels had no evidence of radiculopathy, as evidenced by loss of reflex, numbness, or weakness in an anatomic distribution, the diagnosis of radiculopathy is not appropriate. Therefore, as specified in Table 72, DRE Lumbosacral Spine Impairment Categories (6th ed, p 110), he is assigned to lumbosacral DRE category II and a resultant 5% permanent impairment.

According to the instructions, if the individual has objective findings described by one or more of the differentiators, then he or she may be placed in category II if there are no signs of significant radiculopathy or loss of motion segment integrity. Categories I, II, and III make up by far the majority of evaluations in the lumbar spine.

Since both low back pain and acute muscle spasm are extremely common, and Mr Samuels had no documentation of spasm after a week and was subsequently asymptomatic, some examiners may not have based impairment on these acute findings, and rather would have assigned him to category I and a 0% whole person impairment.

Impairment: 5% whole person impairment per the Fourth Edition.

Fifth Edition Rating

The DRE method must be used to assess impairment in this case, since the impairment is due to an injury. The Fifth Edition states in Section 15.2, "The DRE method is the principal methodology used to evaluate an individual who has had a distinct injury" (5th ed, p 372).

Unlike the Fourth Edition, the Fifth Edition directions on page 383 state that spinal impairment is to be based on the individual's condition at MMI:

> To use the DRE method, obtain an individual's history, examine the individual, review the results of appropriate diagnostic studies, and place the individual in the appropriate category. . . . almost all individuals will fall into one of the first three DRE categories. . . . An individual in category I has only subjective findings. . . . Since an individual is evaluated after having reached MMI, a previous history of objective findings may not define the current, ratable condition but is important in determining the course and whether MMI has been reached. The impairment rating is based on the condition once MMI is reached, not on prior symptoms or signs.

Box 15-1, Definition of Clinical Findings Used to Place an Individual in a DRE Category (5th ed, p 382), specifies the clinical findings used in a DRE method classification. A lumbar (low back) injury is rated according to Section 15.4, DRE: Lumbar Spine (5th ed, pp 384-388), and with the use of Table 15-3, Criteria for Rating Impairment Due to Lumbar Spine Injury (5th ed, p 384). There were no significant clinical findings documented at the time of MMI. Therefore, Mr Samuels meets the definition of a DRE lumbar category I impairment:

> No significant clinical findings, no observed muscle guarding or spasm, no documentable neurologic impairment, no documented alteration in structural integrity, and no other indication of impairment related to injury or illness: no fractures.

There is no ratable impairment, ie, 0% whole person impairment.

Impairment: 0% whole person impairment per the Fifth Edition.

Sixth Edition Rating

The *Guides* approach to the evaluation of impairment due to lumbar strain is based on Section 17.2, Diagnosis-Based Impairment (6th ed, p 560), and Section 17.2c, Lumbar Spine (6th ed, p 566).

In Table 17-4, Lumbar Spine Regional Grid: Spine Impairments (6th ed, p 570), for the diagnosis "non-specific chronic or chronic, recurrent low back pain" there is a class 0 rating for "history of sprain/strain–type injury, now resolved," with an impairment value of 0% whole person impairment.

The nonkey factors of functional history, physical examination, and clinical studies do not play a role in calculating the impairment.

Impairment: 0% whole person impairment per the Sixth Edition.

Comment on Lumbar Strain

The DRE model is used to rate Mr Samuels' impairment, by both the Fourth and the Fifth Editions. It is not appropriate, in any recent edition of the *Guides*, to rate this individual by use of the ROM method.

With the Fourth Edition, if the physician is having difficulty placing the individual in one of the categories, or if two physicians disagree as to which category a person belongs in, then the instructions in the *Guides* are to refer to the ROM system as the "ultimate differentiator." This means that if the rater is having difficulty determining whether to assign a person to category I or category II, ie, the presence of guarding is uncertain, then the rater might do a ROM study. The rater would assign the individual to the category closest to the ROM percentage rating. In no instance does the final rating come directly from the ROM method. With the Fourth Edition, the ROM method is merely a way to assist the physician in categorizing the individual.

With the Fifth Edition, the impairment is no longer based on prior findings; rather, it is based on the condition once MMI is reached. Furthermore, no reference is made to the ROM method as a differentiator.

In the Sixth Edition, the impairment is based on the condition at MMI. If the symptoms related to the condition or the condition itself has resolved, then it corresponds with a class 0 rating. In class 0, no additional calculations are needed, since the adjustment factors will not change the final impairment value.

SUMMARY

Diagnosis	Low back strain
Fourth Edition References	Section 3.3 (4th ed, pp 94-102), Table 70 (4th ed, p 108), Table 71 (4th ed, p 109)
Fourth Edition Summary	Determine whether injury occurred, assess clinical history, symptoms, and interference with ADLs; physical examination determines presence or absence of differentiators; based on history, appropriate category is selected.
Fourth Edition Impairment	5% whole person impairment

Fifth Edition References Section 15.2 (5th ed, p 372), Section 15.4 (5th ed, pp 384-388), Box 15-1 (5th ed, p 382), Table 15-3 (5th ed, p 384)

Fifth Edition Summary Determine whether injury occurred, assess clinical history, symptoms, and interference with ADLs; physical examination determines presence or absence of differentiators; on basis of findings at the time of the examination, appropriate category is selected. If significant clinical findings or structural inclusions are absent when at MMI, assign a category I rating.

Fifth Edition Impairment 0% whole person impairment

Sixth Edition References Section 17.2 (6th ed, p 560), Section 17.2c (6th ed, p 566), Table 17-4 (6th ed, p 570)

Sixth Edition Summary History (including functional history and inventories), physical evaluation, and clinical studies. First, determine DBI, class, and default value. There is no need to adjust impairment on basis of nonkey factors if the class is 0.

Sixth Edition Impairment 0% whole person impairment

CASE 17-11

Severe Cervical Spine Injury

Subject: Mr Fields, a 34-year-old man.

History: Mr Fields was a crane operator at a local aluminum company. He operated the crane from a cage approximately 25 feet off the floor. At the end of a busy shift, he attempted to descend the ladder when he fell, landing head first with his neck in flexion. He had immediate onset of severe pain in his neck. He was placed on a spine board by paramedics and taken to the emergency department, where X-ray films disclosed a partial dislocation of C3 on C4 but no fractures. He was neurologically intact. He was placed in a halo vest, and after several days he was allowed to ambulate. He wore the halo vest for approximately 3 months and then began rehabilitation.

Six months after injury, although he remained neurologically intact, Mr Fields continued to have significant neck pain and right shoulder pain. Flexion and extension x-ray films showed a 4-mm translation of C3 on C4. He subsequently underwent an arthrodesis (fusion) of C3-4 with posterior wiring and bone grafting.

Current Symptoms: Mr Fields continued to have neck pain with activity, which he believed precluded his return to construction work. He also had pain and paresthesias on the top and posterior of his right shoulder apparently consistent with the C4 nerve root distribution. He had given up participation in his bowling league and in his church softball league.

Functional Assessment: The PDQ score was 90.

Physical Examination: Physical examination findings were remarkable for tenderness in the paraspinous muscles of the cervical spine. Range of motion was restricted by pain. Neurologic examination of strength and reflexes was normal, with symmetrical strength in the upper and lower extremities. Decreased sensation over the shoulder posteriorly on the right was noted in the C4 dermatome with otherwise normal sensation. No clinical findings of myelopathy were noted.

Clinical Studies: Preoperative flexion and extension X-ray films showed a 4-mm translation of C3 on C4. Postoperative X-ray films showed an intact cervical fusion.

Discussion of Severe Cervical Spine Injury

Fourth Edition Rating

Mr Fields has loss of motion segment integrity and, according to Table 70, Spine Impairment Categories (4th ed, p 108), qualifies for cervicothoracic DRE category IV. Loss of motion segment integrity is defined as at least a 3.5-mm translation of one vertebra on another on flexion-extension X-ray films, or a difference of the angular motion of two adjacent vertebrae of 11° or more. The description of identifying loss of motion segment integrity is on page 98 of the Fourth Edition of the *Guides*. Figure 62, Loss of Motion Segment Integrity: Translation (4th ed, p 98), and Figure 63, Loss of Motion Segment Integrity: Angular Motion (4th ed, p 98), illustrate how to superimpose the two pieces of X-ray film to perform these measurements.

Definitions for loss of motion segment integrity are also provided in Table 71, DRE Impairment Category Differentiators (4th ed, p 109). According to Table 73, DRE Cervicothoracic Spine Impairment Categories (4th ed, p 110), a DRE impairment category IV corresponds to a 25% whole person impairment.

To qualify for a category IV rating on the basis of loss of motion segment integrity, the individual must fit one of these two definitions. There are no other criteria. This is not "instability." Narrowing of the disk (including asymmetric narrowing) does not qualify as loss of motion segment integrity. The impairment rating is for the results of the injury, not for the treatment. Therefore, the fact that the individual had an arthrodesis, and may or may not have residual symptoms, does not affect the rating. If there were neurologic symptoms, then the findings may qualify the patient for a higher rating described in categories V through VIII (4th ed, pp 104-105). If the person has long tract signs in addition to the loss of motion segment integrity, then this may require that the 25% from category IV be combined with the percentage impairment for category VI, VII, or VIII as appropriate (see cervicothoracic category descriptions, 4th ed, p 105).

Impairment: 25% whole person impairment per the Fourth Edition.

Fifth Edition Rating

The Fifth Edition states in Section 15.2, Determining the Appropriate Method for Assessment (5th ed, pp 379-381), "The DRE method is the principal methodology used to evaluate an individual who has had a distinct injury" (5th ed, p 379). The DRE method must be used to assess impairment in this case, since the impairment is due to an injury and since none of the criteria enumerated in Section 15.2 (5th ed, p 379) for using the ROM method are present. Section 15.3, Diagnosis-Related Estimates Method (5th ed, p 381), explains the process used to obtain the rating:

> To use the DRE method, obtain an individual's history, examine the individual, review the results of appropriate diagnostic studies, and place the individual in the appropriate category. . . . Altered motion segment integrity (ie, increased motion or loss of motion) qualifies the individual for category IV or V. . . . The impairment rating is based on the condition once MMI is reached, not on prior symptoms or signs.

Box 15-1, Definition of Clinical Findings Used to Place an Individual in a DRE Category (5th ed, p 382), specifies the clinical findings used in a DRE method classification. A cervical (neck) injury is rated according to Section 15.6, DRE: Cervical Spine (5th ed, pp 393-395), and by means of Table 15-5, Criteria for Rating Impairment Due to Cervical Disorders (5th ed, p 392). Mr Fields meets the definition of AOMSI on the basis of both his 4-mm translation of C3 on C4 and the performance of an arthrodesis (fusion) of C3 on C4. However, the patient would not have been at MMI until after the fusion, and ratings in the Fifth Edition are determined with consideration of treatment.

The specifics of determining motion segment integrity are discussed in Section 15.1b, Description of Clinical Studies (5th ed, pp 378-379). In the cervical spine, alteration of motion integrity can be "either loss of motion segment integrity (increased translation or angular motion) or decreased motion resulting mainly from developmental changes, fusion, fracture healing, healed infection or surgical arthrodesis."

The presence of AOMSI results in a DRE cervical category IV rating. Table 15-5 (5th ed, p 392) defines this category as follows:

> Alteration of motion segment integrity or bilateral or multilevel radiculopathy; alteration of motion segment integrity is defined from flexion and extension radiographs as at least 3.5 mm of translation of one vertebra on another, or angular motion of more than 11° greater than at each adjacent level (Figures 15-3a and 15-3b); alternatively, the individual may have loss of motion of a motion segment due to a developmental fusion or successful or unsuccessful attempt at surgical arthrodesis; radiculopathy as defined in cervical category III need not be present if there is alteration of motion segment integrity.

This corresponds with a rating of 25% to 28% whole person impairment. The *Guides* states, "if residual symptoms or objective findings impact the ability to perform ADL, despite treatment, the higher percentage in each range should be assigned." On the basis of the reported interference with ADLs, Mr Fields is assigned a 28% whole person impairment.

Impairment: 28% whole person impairment per the Fifth Edition.

Sixth Edition Rating

The *Guides* approach to the evaluation of impairment due to severe cervical spine injury is based on Section 17.2, Diagnosis-Based Impairment (6th ed, p 560), and Section 17.2a, Cervical Spine (6th ed, p 563).

In Table 17-2, Cervical Spine Regional Grid: Spine Impairments (6th ed, p 566), for the diagnosis "dislocations/fracture-dislocations" there is a class 2 rating for "single level dislocation with or without fracture; Healed, with or without surgical intervention, including fusion may have documented radiculopathy at the clinically appropriate level present at the time of examination" (with a default impairment of 11% cervical spine impairment).

In Section 17.3a, Adjustment Grid: Functional History (6th ed, p 569), and Table 17-6, Functional History Adjustment: Spine (6th ed, p 575), the patient is assigned grade modifier 2; the functional history is consistent with "pain; symptoms with normal activity" and the PDQ score is in the range of 71 to 100. In Section 17.3b, Adjustment Grid: Physical Examination (6th ed, p 572), and Table 17-7, Physical Examination Adjustment: Spine (6th ed, p 576), the patient is assigned grade modifier 2; the physical examination revealed "diminished light touch (with some abnormal sensations or slight pain) in a clinically appropriate distribution that interferes with some activities." Clinical studies adjustment for the spine using radiographic findings is not appropriate in this case, since the imaging study findings were essential to making the class diagnosis. In summary, the adjustments are as follows: functional history grade modifier 2, physical examination 2, and clinical studies grade modifier excluded. Net adjustment compared to diagnosis class 2 is 0, grade C, 11% whole person impairment.

Class 2—Default for Diagnosis = 11% whole person impairment			
CDX	GMFH	GMPE	GMCS
2	2	2	n/a
Net adjustment (GMFH − CDX) 2 − 2 = 0 + (GMPE − CDX) + 2 − 2 = 0 + (GMCS − CDX) n/a			
Net adjustment = 0			

Result is class 2 adjustment 0, which results in class 2, grade C = 11% whole person impairment.

Impairment: 11% whole person impairment per the Sixth Edition.

Comment on Severe Cervical Spine Injury

The usual method for evaluating spinal injuries is the DRE method (injury model).

With the Fourth Edition, it is improper to use the ROM model for the final rating. The ROM model is used only if necessary to assist the evaluator in placing the individual in the proper DRE category. The final rating is never taken from the ROM model. For instance, it might be difficult to measure the translation on flexion-extension X-ray films to within the degree of accuracy required to differentiate between 3.4 and 3.6 mm. Yet, in the absence of radiculopathy, this would mean the difference in a rating of 5% (category II) and 25% (category IV). In this case, the evaluator may use the ROM model as the "ultimate differentiator." If the ROM model is used, it must be used in its entirety, which means that the impairment for loss of motion is combined with impairment for diagnosis from Table 75 (4th ed, p 113) and the impairment for neurologic deficit, if any is present. This rating from the ROM method is then used to categorize the individual in the DRE model. That is, if the ROM method yielded a rating above 25%, the individual would be placed in DRE category IV and given a rating of 25%. If the ROM method yielded a rating of less than 5%, then the individual would be placed in DRE category II and given a rating of 5%. If the ROM method yielded a rating between 5% and 25%, the evaluator should choose the DRE category closest to the ROM rating. Thus, if the ROM method yielded a rating between 6% and 12%, DRE category II (5%) would be chosen to represent the impairment. If the ROM method yielded a rating between 13% and 24%, category IV (25%) would be chosen as the impairment rating.

With the Fifth Edition, the ROM method is not used as a differentiator; rather, there are specific circumstances when the ROM method is used, as discussed in Section 15.2, Determining the Appropriate Method for Assessment. The definition of AOMSI has changed to include the performance of arthrodesis, eg, surgical fusions. The definitions of loss of motion segment integrity involve different techniques of measurement with the use of flexion and extension radiographs, which should permit more accurate measurement of potential instability.

In the Sixth Edition, a diagnosis of either "dislocation/fracture-dislocation" or "intervertebral disk herniation and/or AOMSI" because of the postinjury fusion would be reasonable, although the descriptor for dislocation includes surgical treatment, making it a better choice. Either diagnosis would result in a class 2 impairment with a default value C of 11% whole person impairment. Grade modifiers based on adjustment factors would be the same, and the final impairment rating would be 11% regardless of the diagnosis used.

SUMMARY

Diagnosis	Loss of motion segment integrity, cervical spine
Fourth Edition References	Section 3.3h (4th ed, pp 103-105), Table 70 (4th ed, p 108), Table 71 (4th ed, p 109), Table 73 (4th ed, p 110), Figures 62 and 63 (4th ed, p 98)
Fourth Edition Summary	History, careful physical examination to rule out neurologic findings, evaluation of flexion-extension X-ray films. Verify that the individual does or does not meet the definition of loss of motion segment integrity.
Fourth Edition Impairment	25% whole person impairment
Fifth Edition References	Section 15.1b (5th ed, p 378), Section 15.2 (5th ed, p 379), Section 15.3 (5th ed, p 381), Section 15.6 (5th ed, p 393), Box 15-1 (5th ed, p 382), Table 15-5 (5th ed, p 392)
Fifth Edition Summary	History, careful physical examination to rule out neurologic findings, evaluation of flexion-extension X-ray films. Verify that the individual does or does not meet the definition of loss of motion segment integrity.
Fifth Edition Impairment	28% whole person impairment
Sixth Edition References	Section 17.2 (6th ed, p 560), Section 17.2a (6th ed, p 563), Section 17.3a (6th ed, p 569), Section 17.3b (6th ed, p 572), Table 17-2 (6th ed, p 566), Table 17-6 (6th ed, p 575), Table 17-7 (6th ed, p 576)
Sixth Edition Summary	History (including functional history and inventories), physical evaluation, and clinical studies. First, determine DBI, class, and default value. Second, adjust impairment on basis of nonkey factors. In this case, a diagnosis of dislocation/fracture dislocation includes imaging findings, and the clinical studies adjustment is excluded from the impairment calculation.
Sixth Edition Impairment	11% whole person impairment

CASE 17-12

Thoracic Compression Fracture

Subject: Mr Bateman, a 55-year-old man.

History: Mr Bateman worked as a heavy equipment repair technician. He had a history of occasional low back pain that routinely resolved with over-the-counter medication. He fell from a piece of equipment and sustained an injury to the midportion of his back. He was taken to the emergency department for evaluation. Plain X-ray films of the thoracic spine were remarkable for compression fractures of 40% at T10 and 10% at T11. He had no neurologic findings.

The patient was referred to an orthopedic surgeon for further evaluation. The orthopedic surgeon recommended that he undergo a vertebroplasty to address the pain and deformity of the vertebral bodies. This procedure was done several days after the injury, and Mr Bateman experienced dramatic relief of his symptoms.

Current Symptoms: When reexamined 6 months after injury, he no longer had pain. He had returned to work in his original job without difficulty.

Functional Assessment: The PDQ score was 20.

Physical Examination: Examination of his thoracic spine was remarkable for some mild tenderness over the spinous processes of T10 and T11. A mild kyphotic deformity was noted. Range of motion of the thoracic spine was obtained in accordance with the methods described in the Fifth Edition. Flexion of the thoracic spine was measured at 50°, and extension was limited to neutral. Rotation was full and symmetrical bilaterally. Neurologic examination was completely normal.

Clinical Studies: Postoperative imaging studies showed the compression fractures after treatment, with methylmethacrylate in the vertebral body.

Discussion of Compression Fractures

Fourth Edition Rating

The injury model, as outlined in the Fourth Edition, is always used for the final rating of spinal impairment. It is inappropriate in this case to use the

ROM model to determine the final impairment rating. The injury model is a significant change from the ROM model that was utilized in earlier editions of the *Guides*. The ROM is not used as a primary method of rating; rather, it is used as a differentiator when it is unclear in which category a patient should be placed.

In this case, there are two ratable conditions including the 40% and the 10% compression fractures. The Fourth Edition does not provide specific direction on what to do when there is more than one ratable condition. For the purpose of education, both ratings will be calculated and combined here, although the recommendation would be for the clinician to determine what impairment is most appropriate and applicable for any given case. In some cases, the rating may be best left to assign the more severe impairment only.

The injury model is explained in Section 3.3d, Evaluating Impairments: The Injury or Diagnosis-related Estimates Model (4th ed, pp 99-100). This case was analyzed and compared to the criteria in Table 70, Spine Impairment Categories for Cervicothoracic, Thoracolumbar, and Lumbosacral Regions (4th ed, p 109). On the basis of the 40% compression fracture, the classification is DRE impairment category III, "vertebral body compression fracture 25%-50%." This corresponds with a 15% whole person impairment.

Similarly, on the basis of the criteria outlined in Table 70, a 10% compression fracture would be rated as a DRE impairment category II with 5% whole person impairment. The final values can be combined according to the Combined Values Chart for a total of 19% whole person impairment.

Impairment: 19% whole person impairment per the Fourth Edition.

Fifth Edition Rating

In the Fifth Edition, Section 15.8, Range-of-Motion Method (5th ed, p 380), states that the ROM method should be used when there is "multilevel involvement in the same spinal region (eg, fracture at multiple levels, disk herniations, or stenosis . . .)." In this case, the patient has two fractures in the thoracic region, and therefore, the ROM method is appropriate.

Unlike the Fourth Edition, the Fifth Edition directions on page 383 state that spinal impairment is to be based on the individual's condition at MMI:

> Since an individual is evaluated after having reached MMI, a previous history of objective findings may not define the current, ratable condition but is important in determining the course and whether MMI has been reached. The impairment rating is based on the condition once MMI is reached, not on prior symptoms or signs.

The ROM method requires that ROM of the thoracic spine be measured, and the methods of measurement are described in detail in Section 15.8b, Principles of Inclinometry and Spine Motion Measurement (5th ed, p 400). In addition, the diagnosis must be identified by means of Table 15-7, Criteria for Rating Whole Person Impairment Percent Due to Specific Spine Disorders to be Used as Part of the Range of Motion Method (5th ed, p 404).

Range of motion of the thoracic spine was documented with no impairment (ie, 0% whole person impairment) attributable to loss of motion. Neurologic examination is normal with 0% whole person impairment as well. According to Table 15-7, Criteria for Rating Whole Person Impairment Percent Due to Specific Spine Disorders to be Used as Part of the Range of Motion Method, a thoracic compression fracture (one vertebral body) of 40% rates to 3% whole person impairment, and the note states that compression fractures of several vertebrae are combined with the Combined Values Chart. The second compression fracture of 10% warrants a 2% impairment. Combining these values gives a whole person impairment of 5% for the injuries.

Impairment: 5% whole person impairment per the Fifth Edition.

Sixth Edition Rating

The *Guides* approach to the evaluation of impairment due to thoracic compression fractures is based on Section 17.2, Diagnosis-Based Impairment (6th ed, p 560), and Section 17.2b, Thoracic Spine (6th ed, p 563).

In Table 17-3, Thoracic Spine Regional Grid: Spine Impairments (6th ed, p 567), for the diagnosis “compression fractures of 1 or more vertebral bodies” there is a class 2 rating for “single or multiple level fractures with 25%-50% compression of any vertebral body . . . healed with or without surgery,” with a default impairment value of 9%.

The nonkey factor of functional history is grade modifier 1, based on a PDQ score of 10 and Table 17-6, Functional History Adjustment: Spine (6th ed, p 575), and the grade modifier for physical examination is 0. Clinical studies do not play a role in calculating the impairment, because the class of impairment was based on the extent of the compression fracture on imaging studies. This default rating is for class 2 grade C impairment, with a 9% whole person impairment rating.

Class 2—Default for Diagnosis = 9% whole person impairment			
CDX	GMFH	GMPE	GMCS
2	1	0	n/a
Net adjustment (GMFH − CDX) 1 − 2 = −1 + (GMPE − CDX) + 0 − 2 = −2 + (GMCS − CDX) + n/a Net adjustment = −3			

Result is class 2 adjustment −3, which results in class 2, grade A = 7% whole person impairment.

After adjustment with the functional history and examination findings, the grade value was reduced by −3. The final rating is class 2, grade A, with 7% whole person impairment.

In a case where the net adjustment is −2 or less, the rating can go at most two places to the left of the default value and will be grade A within the class.

Impairment: 7% whole person impairment per the Sixth Edition.

Comment on Thoracic Spine Fractures

Interestingly, the Fourth, Fifth, and Sixth Edition rating methodologies are all different. The injury model is used for Fourth Edition with a combined value provided in this case for both compression fractures. The ROM model is used by the Fifth Edition on the basis of findings of multiple fractures within the same spinal region. Impairments are combined for multiple levels of fracture along with motion and neurologic deficits. In the Sixth Edition, the impairment is based on the diagnosis of the most severe compression fracture within the Thoracic Spine Regional Grid. Adjustments based on functional history, examination findings, and clinical studies can be used to calculate the final impairment rating. In the case of spinal fractures, however, the clinical studies were excluded from the impairment calculation because the imaging studies are used to determine the diagnosis-based class rating.

SUMMARY

Diagnosis	Thoracic compression fractures
Fourth Edition References	Section 3.3d (4th ed, p 99), Table 70 (4th ed, p 109)
Fourth Edition Summary	Rate by the injury model on the basis of the clinical history, symptoms, and examination findings. Multiple impairments can be combined if appropriate.
Fourth Edition Impairment	19% whole person impairment
Fifth Edition References	Section 15.8 (5th ed, p 398), Section 15.8b (5th ed, p 400), Table 15-7 (5th ed, p 404)
Fifth Edition Summary	Determine whether injury occurred, assess clinical history, symptoms, and interference with ADLs; physical examination determines presence or absence of differentiators; based on findings at the time of the examination, appropriate category is selected.
Fifth Edition Impairment	5% whole person impairment
Sixth Edition References	Section 17.2 (6th ed, p 560), Section 17.2b (6th ed, p 563), Table 17-3 (6th ed, p 567), Table 17-6 (6th ed, p 575)
Sixth Edition Summary	History (including functional history and inventories), physical evaluation, and clinical studies. First, determine DBI, class, and default value. Then adjust the value within the class, on basis of nonkey factors and the net adjustment value that has been calculated.
Sixth Edition Impairment	7% whole person impairment

Index

B

C

D

E

F

Index

G

Index

H

I

K

L

M

N

O

P

Q

R

S

Index

T

U

V

W

Keep current on impairment evaluation trends

The Guides Newsletter

Expert advice, practical information, and current trends on impairment evaluation

January/February 2008

In upcoming issues

Upper Extremities: Sixth Edition

Lower Extremities: Sixth Edition

International Classification of Function, Disability and Health

Functional Inventories

Sixth Edition Case Exercises

Sixth Edition: the New Standard

by Christopher R. Brigham, MD, MMS, Robert D. Rondinelli, MD, PhD, Elizabeth Genovese, MD, MBA, Craig Uejo, MD, MPH and Marjorie Eskay-Auerbach, MD, JD

The Sixth Edition[1], published in December 2007, introduces new approaches to rating impairment. An innovative methodology is used to enhance the relevancy of impairment ratings, improve internal consistency, promote greater precision and simplify the rating process. The approach is based on a modification of the conceptual framework of the International Classification of Functioning, Disability, and Health (ICF),[2] although the fundamental principles underlying the *Guides* remain unchanged. To appreciate the impact of the Sixth Edition, it is useful to understand the history and structure of the *Guides*, previous criticisms, and these new approaches.

Use of the Guides

The approach to impairment evaluation has evolved over the past fifty years since the *Guides* started in 1958 with publication by the American Medical Association (AMA) of the article, "A Guide to the Evaluation of Permanent Impairment of the Extremities and Back"[3]. In 1971 a compendium of 13 guides became the First Edition.[4] The Second Edition[5] was published thirteen years later in 1984, and the Third Edition[6] was published in 1988. The Third Edition was the first to use the Swanson methodology[7] which assigned discreet impairment ratings to specific range of motion (ROM) deficits of the upper extremities. It was replaced two years later by the Third Edition, Revised[8], which is still used by the State of Colorado for workers compensation cases.

The Fourth Edition[9], published in 1993, provided many refinements, including the Diagnosis-Related Estimates (DRE) or "injury" model for evaluation of spinal injuries, alternative approaches to assessing lower extremity impairment, and a pain chapter. The DRE model was unique in allowing for assignment of an impairment rating based solely on the diagnosis, even if maximum medical improvement (MMI) had not yet been reached. The Fourth Edition is still used for assessing workers' compensation cases in Alabama, Arkansas, Connecticut, Kansas, Maine, Maryland, Mississippi, South Dakota, Texas, and West Virginia.

The Fifth Edition[10], published in 2000, was nearly twice the size of its predecessor. It provided more detailed directives in all chapters, and modified the approaches used for spinal impairment evaluation by providing guidance on the choice of the rating method and the impairment ranges for DRE categories. Prior to the availability of the Sixth Edition twenty-six states made use of the Fifth Edition, including Alaska, Arizona, California, Delaware, Georgia, Hawaii, Idaho, Indiana, Iowa, Kentucky, Louisiana, Massachusetts, Montana, Nevada, New Hampshire, New Mexico, North

AMA AMERICAN MEDICAL ASSOCIATION

The Guides Newsletter

Ease the transition from the *Guides Fifth* to the *Guides Sixth* with *The Guides Newsletter*. Stay up to date on the latest evaluations from experienced practitioners in medicine, law and policy. With this resource you have convenient access to nationally recognized experts who offer the practical, real-life facts you need to make difficult decisions with confidence.

One-year subscription—six issues

Order #: NG034096
Price: $200 **AMA member price: $150**

Please visit us at ***www.amabookstore.com***
or call **(800) 621-8335** for more information.